The Impact of War and Extraordinary Situations on
Law in the Context of Agression against Ukraine

Lyra Jakulevičienė / Patrick R. Hugg /
Dmytro Luchenko (eds.)

The Impact of War and Extraordinary Situations on Law in the Context of Agression against Ukraine

PETER LANG

Berlin - Bruxelles - Chennai - Lausanne - New York - Oxford

Library of Congress Cataloging-in-Publication
A record in the CIP catalog has been requested for this book.
of the Library of Congress.

Bibliographic information published by the Deutsche Nationalbibliothek
The Deutsche Nationalbibliothek collects this publication in the Deutsche Nationalbibliografie; detailed bibliographic data are available on the Internet at .Nationalbibliografie; detailed bibliographic data are available on the Internet at http://dnb.d-nb.de.

Copy-editor: MB "Kopis"

Approved by Mykolas Romeris University Law School Council on 5 June 2024 by resolution No. 1T-13 (1.12 E-20401).

ISBN 978-3-631-92350-4 (Print)
E-ISBN 978-3-631-92813-4 (E-PDF)
E-ISBN 978-3-631-92814-1 (E-PUB)
DOI.10.3726/b22448

Lyra Jakulevičienė / Patrick R. Hugg / Dmytro Luchenko (Eds.), 2024
Published by Peter Lang GmbH, Berlin, Deutschland
info@peterlang.com - www.peterlang.com

Mykolas Romeris University

Reviewers:

Prof. dr. Jesús Verdú Baeza (University of Cádiz)

Prof. dr. Iman Prihandono (Universitas Airlangga)

Prof. dr. Teresa Gardocka (SWPS University of Social Sciences and Humanities)

Prof. dr. Kristian Bankov (New Bulgarian University)

Prof. dr. Edita Gruodytė (Vytautas Magnus University)

Prof. dr. Toma Birmontienė (Mykolas Romeris University)

Assoc. Prof. dr. iur. Jānis Pleps (University of Latvia)

Assoc. Prof. dr. Pavlo Romaniuk (Yaroslav Mudryi National Law University)

Assoc. Prof. dr. Jolanta Apolewicz (Mykolas Romeris University)

Dr. Filip Cyuńczyk (SWPS University of Social Sciences and Humanities)

Dr. Dovilė Pūraitė-Andrikienė (Law Institute of the Lithuanian Center for Social Sciences)

Dr. Agnė Limantė (Law Institute of the Lithuanian Center for Social Sciences)

Authors

Patrick R. Hugg | Loyola University New Orleans
Foreword

Mindaugas Verbickas | MRU
Chapter 1 Section 1.1

Asta Benetytė | MRU
Chapter 1 Section 1.2.

Juozas Valčiukas | MRU
Chapter 1 Section 1.3.

Jolita Miliuvienė | MRU
Chapter 1 Section 1.4.

Inga Motuzienė | MRU
Chapter 2 Section 2.1.

Justinas Žilinskas | MRU
Chapter 2 Section 2.2.

Dovilė Sagatienė | MRU
Chapter 2 Section 2.3.

Saulius Katuoka | MRU
Chapter 2 Section 2.4.

Olesia Gorbun | MRU
Chapter 2 Section 2.4.

Rima Ažubalytė | MRU
Chapter 3 Chapter 3.1.

Paulo Pereira | MRU
Chapter 3 Section 3.2.

Rūta Slidžiauskaitė-Maskoliūnė | MRU
Chapter 3 Section 3.2.

Simona Dementavičienė | MRU
Chapter 3 Section 3.3.

Laura Matjošaitytė | MRU
Chapter 3 Section 3.4.

Ieva Deviatnikovaitė | MRU
Chapter 3 Section 3.5.

Yuliya Vashchenko | Comenius University in Bratislava
Chapter 3 Section 3.5.

Radmyla Hrevtsova | Taras Shevchenko National University of Kyiv
Chapter 3 Section 3.6.

Olena Uvarova | Yaroslav Mudryi National Law University
Chapter 3 Section 3.7.

Olha Bodnar-Petrovska | MRU
Chapter 3 Section 3.8.

Andrzej Jackiewicz | University of Bialystok
Chapter 3 Section 3.9.

Anna Rytel-Warzocha | University of Gdańsk
Chapter 3 Chapter 3.9.

Contents

Foreword

This impressive new book, *The Impact of War and Extraordinary Situations on Law in the Context of Aggression Against Ukraine*, represents a significant contribution to the examination and understanding of Russia's military invasion of Ukraine in 2022, a deeply destructive event in history and legal science. I am honoured to offer this Foreword to it. Having researched, written about, and taught international law extensively, I am confident that readers will find this book engaging as well as instructive regarding the legal and moral dimensions of the ensuing war.

An initial perusal of the many topics examined in this book illustrates the breadth of its coverage, while thoughtful reading reveals its depth. This compilation of scholarly analysis is a must-read for academics and lay observers alike in the fields of international and domestic law, as well as within the sweeping overlay of human rights. Likewise, this book's list of authors includes specialists whose expertise is well illustrated within its pages.

The varied contributing authors examine Russia's aggression against Ukraine in the context of armed conflicts and emergencies in three parts: (1) the role of values, identity, and human rights; (2) challenges for international law, including battlefield and genocide issues; and (3) challenges in specific fields of law, such as criminal prosecutions, constitutional requirements, elections in wartime, human rights in healthcare, and cyber defence. This scholarly book traverses the broad legal landscape.

Russia's notorious military invasion of Ukraine in February 2022 – boldly announced beforehand on television by Russian President Vladimir Putin – shocked the world. The first Russian missiles began exploding in Ukrainian territory minutes after Putin spoke (The Kyiv Independent 2022), while troops and tanks attacked from Russia, Crimea, and Belarus (Netherlands Times 2022). The continent of Europe had not experienced such a broad attack on national sovereignty since World War II. Predictably, news media broadcasted the subsequent events in vivid detail, magnified by the personal video and audio messages sent around the world by legions of Ukrainian eye-witnesses (Aljazeera 2022a; Sangal *et al.* 2022). The war was on. So were the satellites.

Within seven days, the International Criminal Court (hereafter – the ICC) prosecutor had announced the opening of an official war crimes investigation (Corder 2022). The United Nations (hereafter – the UN), the European Union (hereafter – the EU), the Council of Europe, the Organization for Security and Co-operation in Europe (hereafter – OSCE), the North Atlantic Treaty Organisation (hereafter – NATO), the Group of Seven (hereafter – G7), and numerous Western democracies condemned the invasion, alleging numerous war crimes in violation of international law (BBC 2022; Aljazeera 2022c). Many Western countries simultaneously launched an extensive array of economic sanctions on Russia and set in motion the delivery of military weapons to Ukraine (Diehn 2022). Six days after the invasion, the UN General Assembly (hereafter – UNGA) adopted a Resolution condemning the invasion and calling on Russia to withdraw (UN News 2022). UN Secretary-General António Guterres amplified these calls: 'The message of the General Assembly is loud and clear: End hostilities in Ukraine now. Silence the guns now. Open the door to dialogue and diplomacy now' (UN News 2022). He based his statement on the foundational doctrine of the post-World War II international order, the totemic Article 2 of the UN Charter:

> Day after day, I have been clear that such unilateral measures conflict directly with the United Nations Charter. The Charter [Article 2] is clear: 'All members shall refrain in their international relations from the threat or use of force against the territorial integrity or political independence of any state, or in any other manner inconsistent with the Purposes of the United Nations.' The use of force by one country against another is the repudiation of the principles that every country has committed to uphold. This applies to the present military offensive. It is wrong. It is against the Charter. It is unacceptable (United Nations Secretary General 2022).

The UN High Commissioner for Human Rights, Michelle Bachelet, emphasised that 'the death and destruction … will scar generations to come. … [T]he extent and intensity of fighting, as well as the number of civilian deaths strongly suggest that serious violations of international … law have occurred' (Deutsche Welle 2022a). The EU, geographically sensitive to the war, reacted immediately. On the day of the invasion, the collectively powerful European Council (heads of State or government) issued an unusually explicit condemnation:

> The use of force and coercion to change borders has no place in the 21st century. Tensions and conflict should be resolved exclusively through dialogue and diplomacy. The European Council condemns in the strongest possible terms the Russian Federation's unprovoked and unjustified military aggression against Ukraine. By its illegal military actions, Russia is grossly violating international law and the principles of the UN Charter and undermining European and global security and stability… Russia bears full responsibility for this act of aggression and all the destruction and loss of life it will cause. It will be held accountable for its actions. (Council of the European Union 2022)

Five days later, the Presidents of the European Parliament, the European Commission, and the European Council, as well as the EU's High Representative for Foreign Affairs and Security Policy, met in an extraordinary plenary session where they were exhorted by live video appeals for support from Ukrainian President Volodymyr Zelensky and the Speaker of the Ukrainian Parliament Ruslan Stefanchuk (European Parliament News 2022b). EU Parliament President Roberta Metsola opened the meeting:

> We are here today in the dark shadow cast by Putin's war… An outrageous invasion of a sovereign, independent state… We will not look away when those fighting in the streets for our values face down Putin's massive war machine. We will support the International Criminal Court's jurisdiction and investigation of war crimes in Ukraine. We will hold him accountable. (European Parliament News 2022b)

Broad economic sanctions against Russia followed. Six packages of sanctions against the Russian government as well as companies and individuals responsible for actions that furthered the assault on Ukraine included: the prohibition of certain goods (e.g., technology and energy related) being exported to Russia; a ban on the importation of valuable products from Russia (oil, coal, and steel, for example); the denial of access to EU airports and airspace for Russian planes; the denial of access to EU ports for Russia's maritime fleet; the denial of most Russian bank transactions through the SWIFT system, and more (Council of the EU [ca. 2022]). The EU also blocked Russian media outlets Sputnik and RT/Russia Today, both within or directed toward the EU, until the end of the war, and until the Russian outlets 'cease to conduct disinformation and information manipulation against the EU and its member states' (Council of the EU Press Release 2022).

In a precedent-setting measure, just a week after the invasion the EU invoked the a directive on minimum standards for providing temporary protection in the event of a mass influx of displaced persons and on measures promoting a balance of efforts between Member States in receiving such persons and bearing the consequences thereof (hereafter – the Temporary Protection Directive), permitting fleeing Ukrainians to physically enter the EU, obtain residency rights, access the labour market, and qualify for housing, social welfare assistance, medical or other assistance, and means of subsistence (European Commission 2020b). An estimated six million refugees have since fled Ukraine, exceeding any other refugee crisis in recent years, and the prompt, successful invocation of the Temporary Protection Directive has been hailed by some as a potential tipping point in humanitarian refugee protection (Benton and Selee 2022).

June 2022 saw another politically symbolic and economically significant step: the EU granted Ukraine accelerated EU membership candidate status, 'a bold geopolitical step hailed by Kyiv and the EU itself as an "historic moment"

…a symbol of the EU's intention to reach deep into the former Soviet Union' (Siebold and Melander 2022; Petrequin and Corder 2022). Commission President Ursula von der Leyen stated at the conclusion of the decisive European Council summit on June 24, 2022 that this decision 'strengthens Ukraine, Moldova and Georgia, in the face of Russian imperialism. And it strengthens the EU. Because it shows once again to the world that we are united and strong in the face of external threats' (Parker *et al.* 2022).

Notably, Lithuania enforced EU sanctions strictly in another significant political and economic move in June 2022, when it barred Russian railroad access across its territory for the transport of steel, coal, and other materials to the Russian enclave of Kaliningrad, which unsurprisingly provoked the ire of Russian leaders (Euractiv 2022).

War Crimes

This book also examines the hugely important topic of war crimes. Thus, it is crucial for the reader to understand that international law has undergone a radical transformation over the past century with the outlawing of aggressive war as a means of settling disputes. Following World War I, some fifteen nations signed The General Treaty for Renunciation of War as an Instrument of National Policy (League of Nations 1919), often referred to as the Kellogg-Briand Pact, which flatly forbade aggressive war for the first time in history (Brownlie 2003). The League of Nations followed and failed, and World War II – more destructive than the First – subsequently befell the globe (Lee 1991). The adoption of the Charter of the UN (1945, hereafter – the UN Charter) and the formation of the UN in 1945 became the symbol and substance of a renewed desire by nations to construct a stable order for global peace and prosperity (UN 1945, Prologue; Art. 1). Both the Kellogg-Briand Pact and the UN Charter were grounded in the rejection of war as a legitimate means of settling international disputes, obliging signatories to settle disputes exclusively by peaceful means (Dexter 2000). Article 2, Sections (3) and (4) of the UN Charter explicitly require that:

3. All Members shall settle their international disputes by peaceful means in such a manner that international peace and security, and justice, are not endangered.
4. All Members shall *refrain in their international relations from the threat or use of force against the territorial integrity or political independence of any state* [emphasis added]. (UN 1945)

Russia's 2022 invasion of Ukraine shocked the international order with its brazenness and lack of credible justification. In this rejection of today's fundamental principles of international law lies the essence of this blow to the global legal order.

Furthermore, today international law establishes a broad web of rules for the conduct of hostilities in general (Detter, 2000 p. 166). The general principles of the IHL have largely become accepted, and were most recently articulated in statute form. The widely heralded Rome Statute (hereafter – the Rome Statute) created the ICC (Bassiouni 1998), and today offers a reasonably clear, contemporary definition of the modern-day offenses recognised by the global community.

Part 2, Articles 5 through 8 *bis* of the Rome Statute list and define the various war crimes within the jurisdiction of the Court. Article 5 is straightforward, limiting its scope to 'the most serious crimes of concern to the international community as a whole', namely: '(a) the crime of genocide; (b) crimes against humanity; (c) war crimes; [and] (d) the crime of aggression' (Rome Statute 1998, p. 3). Then, in Articles 6–8 *bis*, the Statute defines those crimes which 'correspond in a general sense to the state of customary international law. The four categories of crimes are drawn from existing definitions and use familiar terminology' (chabas 2017, pp. 77–78). Due to the length of these statutes, short summaries are offered here.

Article 6 defines genocide as it is commonly understood: killing, seriously injuring, and forcibly transferring populations, with the 'intent to destroy, in whole or in part, a national, ethnical, racial group, as such' (Rome Statute, p. 3). Article 7 lists the many core crimes against humanity: murder, extermination, enslavement, imprisonment, torture, crimes of a sexual nature, and similar. Article 8 describes the acts that constitute war crimes as 'any of the following acts against persons or property protected under the provisions of the relevant Geneva Convention (hereafter – GC)': killing; torture or inhuman treatment, wilfully causing great suffering, or serious injury to body or health and similar (Rome Statute, p. 4).

The notion of straightforward application fits many of these crimes. Many of the heinous crimes against humanity targeting civilians that are outlined in Article 7 have been described patently and repeatedly in government and agency reports and the media as part of the systematic attacks that have occurred in Russia's invasion of Ukraine, especially murder, torture, rape, and other inhumane acts of a similar character intentionally causing great suffering or serious injury to physical or mental health.

Likewise, Article 8 invokes the four GCs of 1949 (Best 1994, p. 80) that extended the protection of international humanitarian law to those not taking part in the hostilities (e.g., health workers and civilians) and those no longer participating in hostilities (e.g., prisoners of war and wounded, sick or otherwise incapacitated soldiers) (International Committee on the Red Cross (hereafter – ICRC 2010). For the aforementioned categories of non-combatant victims, the following war crimes would also apply in Russia's invasion of Ukraine: wilful killing, torture or inhuman treatment; causing serious injury; and the extensive destruction of property not justified by military necessity and carried out unlawfully and wantonly.

Prosecution for these crimes in the ICC, or any court, would be possible and likely to succeed with the evidence being gathered and preserved at present. Captured soldiers and their field leaders would be the most common defendants.

As noted above, Article 5 names the crime of genocide first in its list of the 'most serious crimes of concern to the international community as a whole' (Rome Statute 1998, p. 3). The Rome Statute provides the accepted definition of the crime of genocide, copied from Article II of the original 1948 GC (Convention on the Prevention and Punishment of the Crime of Genocide [GC]), and represents a codification of customary international law (Schabas 2017, pp. 88–89).

Article 6 Genocide

For the purpose of this Statute, 'genocide' means any of the following acts committed with intent to destroy, in whole or in part, a national, ethnical, racial or religious group, as such: (a) Killing members of the group; (b) Causing serious bodily or mental harm to members of the group; (c) Deliberately inflicting on the group conditions of life calculated to bring about its physical destruction in whole or in part; (d) Imposing measures intended to prevent births within the group; (e) Forcibly transferring children of the group to another group (Rome Statute 1998, p. 6).

The actions of the Russian army easily qualify as several of the specific acts prescribed in the aforementioned Article. Undoubtedly, Russian soldiers and weapons have killed and caused serious bodily or mental harm to members of the group of Ukrainians. Moreover, they deliberately inflicted on the group conditions of life calculated to bring about its physical destruction, and the forcible transfer of children has been well-reported. Article 6 of the Rome Statute is clear in requiring only 'any of the following acts'; thus, any one of the sub-articles of Article 6 would expose Russia to valid accusations of this most heinous crime.

Finally, the Rome Statute's subsequent Article 8 *bis* articulates the 'Crime of Aggression', the enactment of which was as unexpected as it was revolutionary

(Schabas 2017, pp. 131–139). This crime focuses on the most powerful political and military actors.

The Special Crime of Aggression

Multiple scholars, lawyers, and other leaders have also recommended that the prosecution of the specific international crime of aggression, as articulated in Article 8 *bis* of the Rome Statute, would be especially appropriate and just in the circumstances presented by Russia's publicly orchestrated invasion of Ukraine in 2022 (Ochab 2022). Some also recommend that this act of aggression as a war crime would be most effectively prosecuted in a special hybrid court created by Ukraine in collaboration with one or more European institutions and supported by willing European States.

Judges at the historic Nuremburg trial poignantly captured the significance of this crime:

> War is essentially an evil thing. Its consequences are not confined to the belligerent States alone but affect the whole world. To initiate a war of aggression, therefore, is not only an international crime; it is the supreme international crime differing only from other war crimes in that it contains within itself the *accumulated evil of the whole* [emphasis added]. (*France et al. v. Göring* 1948, p. 433).

One prominent human rights advocate has also aptly urged that, as such a pure form of evil, 'the crime of aggression cannot be left unpunished' (Ochab 2022). '[T]he crime of aggression is the beating heart of this whole issue', another adds; 'at the end of the day, if Putin had not gone to war, none of the other crimes would have taken place' (Roth 2022). A further expert reminds us that preventing 'the scourge of aggressive war' is manifestly the central purpose of the UN Charter, as explicitly stated in the Preamble and Article 1 (1) (Trahan 2022).

The highly focused crime of aggression, then termed 'crimes against the peace', was first prosecuted in the well-known Nuremberg and Tokyo special tribunals after World War II, specifically dedicated to prosecuting the political and military leaders of Germany and Japan. This crime gradually received international acceptance as customary international law, and in 2010 it was included in the litany of crimes named in the Rome Statute (McDougall 2021, pp. 1–3). As its definition, outlined below, illustrates, it is designed for heads of state and top leaders in decision-making positions, and concerns acts that are actually easier to prosecute than the other categories of war crimes (Inglis 2022).

Key legal actors agree that this level of accountability should be pursued. Ukraine's President, Zelensky, has urged more than once that 'existing judicial institutions cannot bring all the guilty parties to justice. Therefore, a special tribunal is needed to address the crime of Russian aggression against Ukraine' (AFP 2022a). In May 2022, 'Ukrainian Foreign Minister Dmytro Kuleba officially requested the support from G7 countries and the Council of Europe for the creation of a special tribunal to judge Russia's 'aggression' against Ukraine: 'This is the first official request from the Ukrainian government', said Anton Korynevych, Zelensky's advisor' (Maupas 2022). Korynevych also named the Hague as a possible site for this special court, hoping for as many other countries as possible to participate in order to strengthen its legitimacy (Majumdar 2022).

The ICC's defining Rome Statute offers the most contemporary articulation of such military aggression against a sovereign State. Article 8 *bis* of the Rome Statute was delicately designed to target the political and military architects of such international law and humanitarian disasters, enduring multiple rounds of contentious negotiations before finally being adopted in 2010 (Barriga and Grover 2011). Article 8 *bis* opens a new chapter and category for the ICC.

The Russian military invasion of Ukraine patently qualifies on every criteria quoted above. Moreover, this extreme and public war begs for the prosecution of its leaders and participants at every level, but especially the top leadership of Russia, who took the pernicious decision to start the killing. The crime fits precisely, and its prosecution should be straightforward. One human rights lawyer also recommends the crime of aggression because it targets those in power who made the decision to attack, rather than those who continue to carry out the order: 'The very fact that you launched the war illegally against another country is enough. It's a much easier crime to prove, and it is much more straightforward in terms of who's responsible because it was announced publicly on television [by Russian President Vladimir Putin]. … It is not a secret who the top generals are who are now executing it' (Schultz 2022).

This Foreword has sought to orient prospective readers to the valuable offerings that follow. So many issues arising from the war in Ukraine require sophisticated inquiry, and these introductory comments are meant only to aid the reader in that task. In the end, many international and intergovernmental organisations will approach the task of ensuring accountability, and courts and rebuilding programs will follow – from the Ukrainian government to the EU, the Council of Europe, the OSCE, the UN, and numerous national governments. A formal judicial decree branding Putin and his generals as war criminals would echo down the halls of history long after – it is hoped – the Russians are driven out of Ukraine (Lacovara 2022). While convictions against individuals are the ideal outcomes of international criminal law, this timely book reveals the many constructive actions and remedies that will help reconstruct Europe after the war in Ukraine.

Patrick R. Hugg
Professor of Law Emeritus
Loyola University College of Law, USA

Acknowledgements

This collective edited book is the result of the efforts of Mykolas Romeris University Law School, which on several occasions analysed the legal aspects of emergency situations previously (the last being the COVID-19 pandemic). Almost immediately after the invasion of 24 February 2022, Mykolas Romeris University academics reacted to the aggression against Ukraine by gathering Lithuanian experts to urgent online discussions on the emergency situation, and on 9 March 2022 – internationally renowned experts of international law to deliver preliminary assessment of the situation. This expertise has led to a wider initiative to gather academics in their respective fields to answer the questions that many of us raise when emergency occurs.

This book is published in the framework of the 2022–2026 Research Program titled *Rule of Law, Sustainability, Technologies* approved by MRU in 2021, which identified five target interdisciplinary domains, including, 'The Transformation of Human Rights', 'Democracy and the Rule of Law', 'The Relations Between Law, Sustainability and Technologies', 'Effective Justice' and 'Security Research'. The aim of the domains titled 'The Transformation of Human Rights' and the 'Democracy and the Rule of Law' is intended to explore the influence of international and regional legal systems on the development of democratic institutions and to address interdisciplinary studies related to the impact of new technologies on law, changes in legal regulation. For this task, over 20 national and international legal scholars contributed to this edited volume.

The editors of this book would like to express gratitude to all authors for their commitment to this initiative, Mykolas Romeris University and Law School administration – for taking care of the publishing and editing procedures, as well as reviewers, proof-readers and other persons involved in this project for their valuable assistance. Particular acknowledgement goes to Ms. Meda Baranauskaitė from the Law School who spent endless hours to proofread the manuscript and organise all the references in a reader friendly manner.

Introduction

Several crises have shocked the world in recent years, reshaping numerous norms that regulate inter-state relations, state and individual relations and even our daily lives in general. Even amongst these events, Russia's aggression against Ukraine has been acknowledged by politicians and observers as a watershed moment in modern history, a turning point comparable in importance to the attacks on the World Trade Centre, the fall of the Berlin Wall, and even the assassination of John F. Kennedy (The Guardian 2022). Undoubtedly, the violence following the Russian invasion of Ukraine on 24 February 2022 has shaken the established international legal order in somewhat unexpected and unwelcome ways. Ukraine has become the crucible of a new global reality overnight, producing a new geopolitical alphabet that spells out a much-altered future (The Guardian 2022). Has it also produced significant change in the approaches of international law, and will this lead to the transformation of the international legal environment? Will it shape national legal developments, forcing them to be better prepared and more resilient in the face of such extraordinary situations?

This peer-reviewed edited book 'The impact of war and extraordinary situations on law in the context of aggression against Ukraine' represents the joint efforts of over 20 authors from Lithuania, Poland, the United States and Ukraine who gathered in spring 2022 under the leadership of Mykolas Romeris University (Lithuania) with a common objective to provide a legal assessment of the events in Ukraine and their potential effects on national and international legal systems.

The research object. This book is primarily designed to address the legal challenges arising for international law and selected fields of national law, both as a result of Russia's war of aggression against Ukraine and more generally other extraordinary situations. The object of the research is the national and international legal framework in selected fields, specifically the transformation of legal norms and changes in their application when encountering emergency situations. The authors test the concepts of the values underlying these laws against the effects of war, challenge existing legal approaches in international law in the face of emergencies, and evaluate the relevance and transformation of the legal regulation of Ukraine insofar as it addresses the changed circumstances in the state and society after the effects of the war.

It should also be noted that the analysis of the transformation of legal regulation in Ukraine cannot be considered fully completed at this stage – after all,

Russia's war against Ukraine continues. As of February 2024, the Ukrainian state is in an extremely difficult situation. The failure of the counter-offensive in the summer of 2023, the lack of funds in the state budget, the reduction of external financial assistance, the problem of mobilisation and outflow of the population from the country, as well as other challenges, allow us to predict that the Ukrainian Parliament will adopt a number of unpopular legal acts in 2024 that will significantly affect the legal status of Ukrainian citizens. Finding a reasonable balance between private and public interests will be a major challenge for Ukraine in the near future.

The research aims and objectives. The book aims to analyse the ways in which national and international legal systems have been affected by Russia's aggression against Ukraine since February 2022 and consider the challenges that lie ahead in this regard. It questions certain approaches that prevail in the international legal order whilst emphasising the importance of upholding international standards of peace, stability and the rule of law. To achieve the aims of the research, the following objectives were established:

1. to determine the relationship between law and moral values such as human dignity and freedom of conscience, assessing the impact of these values on legal interpretation with a view towards elucidating the deep-rooted factors that determine the effectiveness of legal regimes and at the same time outlining potential solutions to the challenges that we face today in national and international legal contexts;
2. to review the relevance of key elements of international law in a changing contemporary context, in particular during war and emergency situations, and to disclose both the need and potential for the transformation of international law or its continued resilience where relevant;
3. to analyse the experiences of Ukraine and selected neighbouring countries with a view towards crystalizing the specificity of the application of legal norms in various fields of law in war and emergency situations on the basis of these experiences.

The methodology of the research. Methodologically, the book follows the process of establishing the immediate and long-term effects of war and emergency situations based on the experiences of Ukraine, on general international legal order and specific fields of law. The research combines an *ex post* evaluation of events in Ukraine following Russia's aggression on 24 February 2022 from a legal perspective with an assessment of the effects of the invasion on various specific fields of law and the future of the national and international legal order.

This begins by examining the underlying preconditions for the effectiveness of law as they relate to value-based systems, and the role of values in the application of law during war and emergency situations. The research then moves to an examination of selected key challenges faced by international law as exemplified by the Ukrainian experience, comparing the situation on the ground with the perspectives of existing standards on the prohibition of the use of force, jurisdictional issues in dispute resolution and international humanitarian law. Building on this, an attempt is made both to uncover elements of resilience and highlight the potential for transformation within international law. Finally, the effects of Russia's war of aggression on selected fields of law are reviewed, outlining how and when the law should adapt to extraordinary emergency situations or remain resilient. Besides an *ex post* evaluation, a horizontal thread runs through the research that seeks to highlight how elements of different legal perspectives will engage with the post-war recovery of Ukraine.

The following questions are addressed by the researchers: What effects has Russia's war of aggression had on international law and specific fields of law? Should these effects lead to a change in the approaches of law and the broader legal order? Has the exigency of the situation compromised the prevalence of law? How can legal systems be better prepared for emergency situations, and where should they remain resilient?

The structure of the book. The book is structured around the general question of the impact of war, aggression and extraordinary situations on national and international law, before then delving into specific issues related to specific fields of law. Chapter 1 of the book looks into the role of values and identity as a joint basis for legal developments during armed conflicts and other emergencies. Chapter 2 of the book reviews the challenges faced by international law in the context of armed conflicts and emergencies by examining the function of the prohibition of the use of force in contemporary settings, selected issues of international humanitarian law, the problem of genocidal intent from a historical perspective and its applicability to the war of aggression against Ukraine, and jurisdictional challenges related to the coastal state rights dispute concerning sovereignty over territories in the context of international dispute resolution. Chapter 3 reviews specific challenges posed in particular fields of law by emergencies and armed conflict situations in order to examine how the law should change – or has already changed – to best address these challenges. Special focus is placed on the fields of criminal proceedings, lay participation in court proceedings, environmental law, the law of elections, administrative procedure law, health law, business and human rights law and cybersecurity law. In addition, a case study involving a neighbouring country affected by Russia's aggression against Ukraine is presented in order to elucidate a more general problem relating to the adaptation of the legislative process to this emergency situation.

On behalf of Mykolas Romeris University Law School, we would like to express our gratitude to all authors, reviewers and editors for their contributions. This book is our tribute to the ongoing debate surrounding the future of the international legal order following the events of February 2022. Through it, we wish to foster awareness of the fact that it is not international law, the rule of law and human rights that falter during emergencies, but ourselves when we fail to uphold them.

Editors
Prof. dr. Lyra Jakulevičienė and Prof. dr. Dmytro Luchenko

Abbreviations

Additional Protocol 1; Protocol I	Protocol of the International Committee of the Red Cross Additional to the Geneva Conventions, and Relating to the Protection of Victims of International Armed Conflicts of 12 August 1949
BHR	Business and Human Rights
CC	Criminal Code
CCP	Code of Criminal Procedure
CEC	Central Elections' Commission
CESCR	Social and Cultural Rights
CJEU	Court of Justice of the European Union
CLC	Collective Legal Consciousness
CSDDD	Directive of the European Parliament and of the Council on Corporate Sustainability Due Diligence and amending Directive (EU) 2019/1937 of 23 February 2022
CSOs	Civil Society Organizations
Directive 2016/343	Directive of the European Parliament and of the Council on the strengthening of certain aspects of the presumption of innocence and of the right to be present at the trial in criminal proceedings (EU) 2016/343 of 9 March 2016
ECHR	European Convention of the Council of Europe for the Protection of Human Rights and Fundamental Freedoms
ECtHR	the European Court of Human Rights
E-court	Electronic Court
EU	European Union
EU Charter	Charter of Fundamental Rights of the European Union
ECCC	Extra-ordinary Chambers in the Courts for Cambodia
Environmental Crime Directive	Directive 2008/99/EC of the European Parliament and of the Council on the protection of the environment through criminal law of 19 November 2008

DNR	Donetsk People's Republic (Rus. Doneckaya Narodnaja Respublika)
FRL	Freedom of Russia Legion (Rus. Legion Svobodnoj Rosii)
ICC	International Criminal Court
ICJ	International Court of Justice
ICCPR	International Covenant of the United Nations General Assembly on Civil and Political Rights of 16 December 1966
ICRS	International Committee of the Red Cross
ICTR	Trial Chamber of the International Criminal Tribunal for Rwanda
ICTY	International Criminal Tribunal for Former Yugoslavia
IDPs	Internally Displaced Persons
IHL	International Humanitarian Law
IICIU	Independent International Commission of Inquiry on Ukraine
IOM	International Organisation for Migration
GA	United Nations General Assembly
GC	A common term to describe Geneva Conventions I-IV on Protection of Victims of War of 12 August 1949
G7	Group of Seven
HRDD	Human Rights Due Diligence
LAP	Law of Ukraine 'On Administrative Procedure'
Law on Fundamentals	the Law of Ukraine 'On Fundamentals of the Legislation of Ukraine on Healthcare' No. 2073-IX of 17 February 2022
LNR	Luhansk People's Republic (Rus. Luhanskaya Narodnaja Respublika)
MGB	Ministry of Security Service (Rus. Ministerstvo gosudarstvennoj bezopasnosti)
MOH	the Ministry of Health of Ukraine
MART	Medically Assisted Reproduction Techniques
MRT	Moldavian Republic of Transdniestria
NATO	North Atlantic Treaty Organisation
NGO	Nongovernmental Organization
NSDC	National Skill Development Corporation

OECD	Organisation for Economic Cooperation and Development
OHCHR	United Nations Office of the High Commissioner for Human Rights
OSCE	Organisation for Security and Co-operation in Europe
PACE	Parliamentary Assembly of the Council of Europe
PMC	Private Military Company
POWs	Prisoners of War
RMF	Russia's Military Forces
Rome Statue	Rome Statute of the International Criminal Court
RBC	Responsible Business Conduct
RDK	Russian Volunteer Corps (Rus. Russkij dobrovolcheskij korpus)
SC	United Nations Security Council
SCSL	Special Court for Sierra Leone
SDGs	United Nations Sustainable Development Goals
SIGMA	Support for Improvement in Governance and Management Project
STL	Special Tribunal for Lebanon
TDF	territorial defence units
Temporary Protection Directive	Council Directive 2001/55/EC on minimum standards for giving temporary protection in the event of a mass influx of displaced persons and on measures promoting a balance of efforts between Member States in receiving such persons and bearing the consequences thereof of 20 July 2001
TEU	Treaty on the European Union
UDHR	Universal Declaration of Human Rights
UFD	Ukraine Defence Forces
UK	United Kingdom
UN	United Nations
UN Charter	Charter of the United Nations

UNESCO	United Nations Educational, Scientific and Cultural Organization
UNGC	Convention of the United Nations General Assembly on the Prevention and Punishment of the Crime of Genocide of 9 December 1948
UNHRC	United Nations Human Rights Committee
UNICEF	United Nations International Children's Emergency Fund
UNCLOS	United Nations Convention on the Law of the Sea of 10 December 1982
UNGA	United Nations General Assembly
UNIAN	Ukrainian Independent Information Agency
USA	United States of America
USSR, Soviet Union	Union of Soviet Socialist Republics
Venice Commission	European Commission for Democracy Through Law
WJP	World Justice Project
WHO	World Health Organization

Chapter 1 Role of Values, Identity and Human Rights in the Context of Armed Conflicts and Emergencies

1.1. Polysemy of Human Dignity in the System of Legal Principles

1.1.1. Context

The doctrine of human rights took shape after the Second World War as a legal instrument to ensure the impossibility of war. The foundational philosophical-legal concept of this doctrine is inherent dignity, the formulation of which brought about much debate and disagreement in the post-war years (Kivistö 2012). According to the Preamble of the Universal Declaration of Human Rights (1948, hereafter – the UDHR), dignity is the foundation of freedom, justice and peace in the world for all members of the human family. Although all the Member States of the UN are parties to at least one of the nine core international human rights treaties monitored by independent expert committees – and 80% are parties to four or more human rights treaties, where it could be assumed that such recognition of the fundamental treaties represents the consolidation of human rights in the normative structure of the international community – humankind has not stopped fighting wars (Hasenclaver 2015, p. 441). The realities of Russia's war of aggression in Ukraine show that the human rights doctrine that has been developed for more than half a century does not safeguard peace, and that its founding principle often remains a theoretical abstraction that is legally ineffective and incapable of withstanding totalitarian threats. It is, therefore, necessary to keep coming back to the origins of this legal category and to the assessment of its significance in the system of legal principles.

Although the idea of human dignity is an old one in philosophical traditions, the first examples of the *expressis verbis* documentation of dignity in positive law are traced back to the 1848 Decree of the Abolition of Slavery in France, the 1944 Declaration of Philadelphia, the UDHR, the 1949 Constitution of the Federal Republic of Germany, the 1966 International Covenants of the General Assembly (hereafter – the GA) of the UN, etc. The Convention for the Protection of Human Rights and Fundamental Freedoms (1950, hereafter – ECHR) does not explicitly mention dignity; however, after two judgments in 1995, the European Court of Human Rights (hereafter – ECtHR) recognised dignity and freedom as the essence of the ECHR (C.R. v. United Kingdom (hereafter – the UK) 1995, para.42). In the Charter of Fundamental Rights of the EU (hereafter – the EU Charter), dignity is the first principle in the framework of principles of this instrument (Art. 1). Hence, human dignity is a recent phenomenon in positive law. Dignity was not *expressis verbis* enshrined in the declarations adopted in the United States of America (hereafter – the USA) or France in the 18th century or in later texts (Fabre-Magnan 2007, p. 3). Scholars argue that, for a long time, positive law was based on the principles of liberty and equality rather than on dignity (Braibant 2001, p. 88). This can be explained by the fact that for a long time the Western legal tradition was predominated by natural law, which views man and society as an organic and purposeful system. According to this theory of law, the nature of human beings and society, as well as the knowledge of purposes supported by the thinking that seeks the truth and the good, makes it possible to deduce specific natural rights that are currently referred to as human rights (Plėšnys 2021, p. 14). The events of the Second World War, the search for a just framework for law and, later, the risks associated with biotechnological advancement – which were addressed, *inter alia*, by the European Convention on Human Rights and Biomedicine – have rekindled interest in natural law and have led to the express recognition of human dignity in a number of key instruments of national and international law (Andorno 2005, p. 96). Legal practice began to rely on dignity as an argument in the second half of the 20th century, especially in Anglo-Saxon countries, in order to emphasise the right of the individual to avoid the use of artificial life-sustaining technologies and the possibility of withdrawing (in the case of a terminal condition, with a doctor's written order) from life-sustaining procedures (Macklin 2003, p. 1419). The subsequent case law of the ECtHR has clarified that the right to life cannot be interpreted as having a negative aspect: i.e., Article 2 of the ECHR cannot be interpreted as conferring a completely opposite right, i.e., the right to die (Pretty v. UK 2002, para.39), and the right of a person to decide how and when their life will end, if they can freely form their will in this matter and act accordingly, is one aspect of the right to respect for their private life (Haas v. Switzerland 2011, para.51). An active philosophical and legal discourse on dignity is *ipso facto* an indication of contestation over fundamental legal concepts and a deconstruction of a coherent legal system (Fabre-Magnan 2007, pp. 5–6). This is reflected in the plurality of interpretations of dignity, with their striking contradictions (Sacks 2021, pp. 225–226) which go as far as extreme forms in which dignity is considered a 'useless concept'. It is argued that wherever the concept of dignity comes across in law (e.g., in the protection of life, genetic technologies, clinical trials or other issues), it does not have anything distinctive apart from what is already provided for by other legal principles and norms (Macklin 2003, p. 1419).

This section seeks to explore the importance of Kant's ideas for the legal concept of dignity and relies on the views of Muriel Fabre-Magnan on the structural status of dignity in law, as well as on the summarising insights on dignity in the case law of the ECtHR. The research object is the legal/philosophical concept of human dignity, with the aim of clarifying the significance and place of dignity in the system of legal principles. This will be achieved by: demonstrating the relevance of the Kantian concept of dignity for law; unfolding the content of dignity as a fundamental legal category (hierarchical aspect); underlining the importance of dignity in the evolution of jurisprudence (dynamic aspect); and assessing the role of dignity in the interaction of the human rights framework with the democratic form of governance.

1.1.2. Kant's Concept of Dignity as the Basis for the Hierarchical and Dynamic Character of Dignity in the System of Legal Principles

Dignity, as the backbone of human freedom and choice associated with the traditions of natural law and the Bible, has been most extensively developed in modern times by Immanuel Kant. His philosophy explores dignity in three main contexts: (1) moral dignity; (2) human dignity; and (3) the dignity of one member of a group in relation to others (Sensen 2021, p. 148).

For Kant, law is a 'moral science'. Moral worth is the highest, and the categorical imperative is 'the universal condition of morality': the absolute basis for scientific knowledge of phenomena and causal relations (Jokubaitis 2021, pp. 78, 81). In this context, dignity for Kant does not imply the unconditional value of a human being – only good will rather than the person *per se* predetermines the 'absolute worth' of human existence (Kant 2019, p. 387). Therefore, dignity should be understood as the 'highest rank' rather than an 'absolute value'. Relative value has a low rank, i.e., price, while the moral value of a good disposition has the highest rank, i.e., dignity (Kant 1980, p. 70). This means that the categorical imperative determines the morality of anyone and any action not because the person is the highest good and an end in itself, but for the person to be such. This determines the specifics of the possibility of invoking dignity. In other words, according to Kant, we may not say that one or another rule of law must be obeyed because the person is the highest good and always an end in itself; instead, rules of law must be followed so that the person can be the highest good and an end in itself. Such a conception allows for the dynamic application of dignity as a legal argument, i.e., when and where it is necessary to promote the rights of the disfavoured members of society, to enrich social rights in order to extend protection to the people, and to attribute priority to certain rights depending on the existing social situation in the field of human rights.

The second context in which dignity comes across in Kant's philosophical writings is human dignity. As a result of human freedom and the ability to behave morally, for Kant, dignity also means the uniqueness of humanity in relation to the rest of nature. Kant refers to this form of dignity as intrinsic dignity. 'Only by being morally good and making proper use of this capacity does man fully realise his initial dignity' (Sensen 2021, p. 149). This Kantian approach is well illustrated by the Constitutional Court of the Republic of Lithuania, which refers to the innate human rights and freedoms established in Article 18 of the Constitution as inalienable from and inherent to an individual, i.e., *ipso facto* innate abilities of an individual (Ruling No. KT-2/98 1998). This is a teleological treatment of human nature in line with the classical tradition of natural law and Kant's approach, which views the innate abilities of human beings as possessing individual and social potential. This view can be traced back as early as the ancient concept of nature. The Platonic and Aristotelian notion of nature (Greek: Φύσις), *natura* in Latin, denoted the *lex naturale* inherent of human nature, indicating man's purpose in the world. The innateness of human abilities is manifested in the fact that, in order to pursue forms of human well-being as principles of practical reason, man has a spontaneous ability to recognise good as desirable and evil as avoidable. 'Human abilities' stimulate the subject to realise their potential and thus provide guidance (Strauss 2017, p. 107).

All of this means that in each person the whole of humanity is represented. The protection of individual rights and freedoms is not limited to subjective rights and freedoms, but also has an objective character. Dignity must be respected not only in relation to others, but also in relation to oneself. For example, no one can legitimately consent to being subjected to acts that violate human dignity. Such consent would also contradict the well-established principle of criminal law: that the consent of the victim is not a circumstance justifying an offence. Where there are expressions of inflated responsibility in a discourse on fundamental rights, such treatment of dignity offers an opportunity to find ways in which to abolish entitlements consisting only of rights and to renew responsibilities and obligations in the fundamental rights vocabulary (Fabre-Magnan 2007, pp. 14–16). Hence, dignity is a binding aspiration that no one can dispense of, either in relation to others or to oneself. The basis for such treatment of dignity is its connection with the teleological nature of natural law, since every human being has an innate quality: the ability to become somebody, regardless of whether this ability is realised.

From the perspective of international law, humanity is enshrined as an object protected by law. The protection of humanity as a species is set out in Article 6 of the Charter of the International Military Tribunal (Nuremberg), which defines crimes against humanity as inhuman acts committed against any civilian population on political, racial or religious grounds and speaks about threats to humanity. The legal protection of humans as a species also includes, for example, the human genome. According to Article 1 of the United Nations Educational, Scientific and Cultural Organization (hereafter – UNESCO) Declaration on the Human Genome and Human Rights, the human genome underlies the individual genes of each person individually and the specifics of the genetic material of the human family.

In light of the above, some court decisions can be criticised for abusing the concept of dignity. Scholars consider the judgment of the European Court of Justice (hereafter – the CJEU) of 14 October 2004 in the *Omega* case as one such example, where the principle of dignity was inappropriately argued. A good example of the application of this aspect of dignity in law involves dwarf-tossing, a game popular in America and Australia. In one case, a court ruled that dwarves cannot perform the function of a ball and must be protected from that role. It should be noted that in this case the dwarf concerned disagreed with the court's view, as he lost his source of income. However, the court's view was that it was not the dwarf himself or even dwarves in general, but the humanity of society that had to be protected (Fabre-Magnan 2007, pp. 18, 23). Thus, each human being represents the whole of humanity and, according to Kant, for a person 'humanity in his person must be holy to him' (2015, p. 192).

Finally, Kant speaks of dignity without a moral link to show the subordinate relations of members of a group (Sensen 2021, p. 149). The dignity of the legislative, executive and judicial branches of a state, for example, expresses a command relationship with those who must obey the established order. 'A state implies the relation of a superior (legislating) to an inferior (obeying)' (Kant 1996, p. 126). In this context, Kant uses the concept of dignity to speak about respect for others.

Thus, for Kant as a moral philosopher, dignity is, first and foremost, a moral concept denoting humanity as an end in itself *par excellence*. This idea is developed in many different formulations of the categorical imperative (Wuerth 2021, p. 68), and the categorical imperative is a way to reconcile the individual and the common good *per se*. Morality deals with the intrinsic goodness of actions, whereas jurisprudence deals with what is right; therefore, the latter relates only to aspects of the power of compulsion rather than intentions. Human dignity as a legal category, therefore, may not be a final principle – it must be treated as a group of ethical requirements that pure reason sets as maxims of action for legislation. For Kant, morality is unshakeable only when it is based not on what is, but on what must necessarily be. The recognition of dignity in the most important instruments of positive law means that the primacy of man is always an end to be aspired to. In other words, the tension between respect for dignity and its effectiveness remains (Sambuc and Le Coz 2012, pp. 232, 237). However, as will be shown later in the chapter, this is the specificity of dignity as a legal matrix that all other legal principles and norms attempt to realise.

1.1.3. Dignity as an Axiom of Law: The Hierarchical Dimension

In the system of legal values, dignity, as the most important value, is usually positioned at the beginning of fundamental legal instruments (constitutions, declarations, conventions, charters). Dignity does not require argumentation or detailing because it is an obvious, necessary and fundamental concept of law. A proposition that people with the right experience and conceptual understanding accept as true and agree with without the need for argument is considered obvious (Finnis, 2014b, p. 64). The Greek *ἄξιος (axios)*, from which the term 'axiom', meaning a social obviousness and a foundational circumstance, derives, means something that is appropriate and valuable, something to be followed. From a legal point of view, dignity is an axiom, a principle/matrix that contributes to the understanding of the entire concept of political and legal reality (Legendre 1983, p. 19).

Dignity as an axiom of law has three characteristics – it is: (a) deductively unprovable (*per se notum*); (b) inviolable (no exceptions or limitations); and (c) not yielding to expression or formulation (Fabre-Magnan 2007, p. 1).

(a) The deductively unprovable character of norms is known and practised in law (Fabre-Magnan 2007, pp. 8–9). Law, like many other hard, experimental sciences, relies on unprovable truths and unquestionable beliefs. Historical examples include the Declaration of Independence of 4 July 1776 of the USA, which recognises the exclusive, special status of certain principles that underpin the legal system. The Declaration begins by stating the 'truth' that 'we hold these truths to be self-evident'.

That is what dignity in the legal system is – not requiring deductive proof. It is the basis of law and not *inter alia* a principle equal to others. Such a character of dignity is recognised in the most important legal instruments. The UDHR, for example, refers to the inherent dignity of all members of the human family as to the foundation of freedom, justice and peace in the world. Similarly, the Preamble to the ECHR integrates dignity into the value system of the Convention not as one of its principles, but as a foundation, since the ECHR explicitly mentions justice and peace which refer to dignity in the UDHR. The EU Charter reveals the fundamental nature of dignity in law. Article 1 of the EU Charter states that 'human dignity is inviolable'. This Article indicates dignity as a fundamental right *per se*, and the true basis of fundamental rights. The CJEU has held that none of the rights set out in the EU Charter can be used to violate the dignity of another person, and stressed that human dignity is an essential part of the EU Charter's rights. The distinction of dignity within the framework of legal principles is also implicit in Article 2 of the Convention on Human Rights and Biomedicine: 'the interests and welfare of the human being shall prevail over the sole interest of society or science'.

Hence, human dignity, as the foundation of the legal system, has supremacy over other rights and freedoms. Dignity, as the fundamental right, does not derive from other rights. According to the Constitutional Court of the Republic of Lithuania, 'human life and dignity, as expressing the integrity and unique essence of the human being, are above law' (Ruling No. KT-2/98 1998). This is a fundamental axiom of a dogmatic character and the ultimate goal of the legal system (Fabre-Magnan 2007, p. 10), which is binding and not subject to axiological debate. Dignity is the basis of any proof, while remaining itself unprovable.

Where such a character of dignity (deductive unprovability) is disregarded, this can lead to practical and epistemological problems of law. Unprovability is part of the legal system, which means that there must be conventional, unquestionable foundational concepts that cannot be turned into deductive logical arguments because they are the foundation of the system. It is impossible to avoid metaphysical discourse if the fundamental worth of human beings is questioned. The fact of proof as such would presuppose the knowledge of the essence and meaning of human life. Such questions, however, rest with metaphysics. Therefore, for scholars, dignity is a transcendental principle (Sambuc and Le Coz 2012, p. 237) that has replaced the sacral (*sacrum* in Latin) (Clément 2005, p. 38).

(b) The second characteristic of dignity as an axiom is *inviolability* (indivisibility). Since dignity is the foundation of the legal framework which 'impregnates' the entire legal system, it cannot be used unreasonably. The larger principles of the legal system cannot take on the functions that can be effectively performed, e.g., by derivative legal principles or by other, i.e., lower-level, legal rules (Finnis, 2014b, p. 202). The unfounded and frequent reliance on the axiom promotes its inflation. The capacious content of the concept should not become a reason to justify the non-necessity of this principle (Andorno 2005, pp. 95–96). It is therefore a subsidiary principle to be used only where necessary to protect the interest that the usual concepts are not sufficient to protect. This is why reliance on human dignity became widespread, in particular in bioethical matters, in the second half of the 20th century. This area, which was new at that time, lacked special legislation (Fabre-Magnan 2007, p. 18). The situation, however, has changed, and calls for the restoration of the inviolability of dignity are increasingly heard. Dignity must be applied with precision and purpose, and, quite often, on a temporary basis, i.e., until there is another technical solution for a new problem.

This second characteristic of dignity as an axiom demonstrates the fundamental difference between dignity and other legal concepts used to protect specific people or groups of people. The subject of dignity, which is sometimes described as a 'third generation' human right[1] and is unlike other rights, is humanity rather than the individual.[2] The recognition of dignity in the most important legal instruments in *expressis verbis* form is associated with the necessity of counterbalancing the law created on the basis of purely subjective human rights (Fabre-Magnan 2007, p. 21). Hence, human dignity not only does not require proof, but is also indivisible and, therefore, is not a subjective or even a human right, but a fundamental principle – an axiom.

(c) The third characteristic of dignity as an axiom is that it 'does not yield itself' to being expressed and formulated. The distinctiveness of dignity as a legal category is linked to the problem of the definition of this concept (Ferrand and Petit 2004, pp. 171–184). To name something means to define a subject, and any naming in law means a legal qualification that triggers the application of the law (Fabre-Magnan 2007, p. 23). Once dignity has become a legal concept, its interpretation no longer allows it to remain ontological. Nevertheless, it would be fair to avoid questioning the fundamental and ultimate basis of the legal system and to consider this axiom as beyond the

1 The first generation of human rights are civil and political rights; the second generation of human rights are social and economic rights.

2 In genetic science, for example, new technologies continue to present more opportunities to go beyond healthcare. The advancement of genetic science presupposes the bi-directional relationship that human beings have with their genes: individual and collective. As a result, law deals with the issues of protection not only of specific individuals, but of the human species.

> law as its foundation. Axioms exist because they cannot be analysed and questioned without limit (Fabre-Magnan 2007, pp. 27–28). Dignity must, therefore, be seen as the moral basis of law, without which law cannot exist. In this case, it may not be asked what criteria should be used to distinguish people from those who they are not. Nor should the issue of human dignity be confused with the definition of the human being in law. A fundamental norm is not identical to other norms and should not be assimilated to a constitutional norm. Only in this way can law fulfil its anthropological function (Fabre-Magnan 2007, pp. 29–30).

Thus, dignity is not part of positive law, but its foundation. This foundation leaves much room for its application – it does not serve as a strict rule, but as a guideline for the fleshing out of legal norms. The more specific the situation, the more difficult the application of primary principles, because specificity brings along more exceptions (Thomas d'Aquin 1935, Ia-IIae, q. 94, a. 4).

1.1.4. Dignity in the Evolution of Jurisprudence: The Dynamic Aspect

The role of the ECHR leads to the reinforcement of the concept of constitutional rights as innate rights based on the democratic values of European culture, and contributes to the promotion of the constitutional values of human rights (Birmontienė 2010, p. 26). Accordingly, the function of the ECtHR is to oversee the development of standards that contribute to a closer European community of nations. Effectiveness is brought to the development of European law through the interpretation of the Convention's norms, and through the interpretation of national legislation. Values and dignity, in particular, help shape the general direction of casuistry and enable the nature of the 'random and unpredictable evocation of dignity' associated with consensus to be understood (Grewe 2014, pp. 10–11).

The combination of hierarchy and dynamism of dignity as a legal category in the jurisprudence of the ECtHR relates to both absolute and relative rights, creating a meaningful approximation between them. Absolute rights underpin the abovementioned Convention, express fundamental values, and reflect the hierarchy in which human dignity, as mentioned, has a special place. Relative rights that are subject to limitations and are subordinated to other rights or interests may appear to be inconsistent with the principle of dignity; however, it is the dynamism of dignity that helps bridge the gap between absolute and relative rights (Grewe 2014, p. 2).

In the context of relative rights (in particular Art. 8, 9, 10 and 11 of the ECHR), references to dignity could be seen as incoherent in terms of the fundamental nature of dignity, as the latter rights are not assessed according to the legal regime of absolute rights. Such an assessment, however, would imply a reassessment of the hierarchical prioritisation of the ECHR and would ignore another function of dignity – to promote the rights of the disfavoured (Grewe 2014, p. 3). Therefore, the dynamic character of dignity is manifested in the fact that this value can be invoked in order to enrich rights and extend their protection. In this way, the jurisprudence of the ECtHR reinforces protection in relation to, for example, the right to life and the prohibition of forced labour or slavery. The scope of this disposition is extended to deportations, extradition, detention conditions, the treatment of mentally ill patients and life imprisonment (Grewe 2014, p. 3). Hence, protection is no longer related only to the obligation of states not to interfere or obstruct, but also to undertake positive, affirmative commitments. This monitors not only compliance with the substance of the law, but also implementation procedures and decision-making by national authorities. On the other hand, Grewe points out that at there is also the evolution of jurisprudence that seeks to introduce another auxiliary argument – dignity – between the differentiation and relativisation of fundamental values, since the most common approach is the introduction of modulations in the protective field in order to affirm that they are unquestionable (Grewe 2014, p. 5).

Thus, on the one hand, the hierarchy inherent in absolute rights must coexist with the principle of indivisibility of rights and must not exclude the possibility that relative rights convey fundamental values (subsidiarity), while on the other hand, it is important to strengthen the legal protection of the most vulnerable groups of society. In complex legal disputes, human dignity therefore becomes a handy argument for enriching rights or giving them social continuation (Grewe 2014, p. 6). In this way, dignity leads to a theoretical bridging of the gap between absolute and relative rights.[3] Hence, taking into consideration the need for the promotion and social development of a right, dignity should either be specifically emphasised or not.

3 Examples of the theoretical blurring of the distinction between absolute and relative rights include the definition of the broad scope of family life or the notion of privacy as encompassing the autonomy of an individual, the storage of identifying data in the virtual environment, etc. (Grewe 2014, p. 7).

1.1.5. The Gap Between Hierarchical and Dynamic Aspects of Dignity as a Characteristic of Democracy

As dignity is at the heart of human rights, it is ultimately important to consider its implications for the interaction between the human rights framework and the democratic form of governance. Human rights and democracy are similar, and both characterise modern developed societies. Respect for human rights would be highly problematic without vigilant public opinion, a multi-party system, freedom of expression and an independent judiciary. Human rights and democracy are also united by a common enemy: dictatorship and totalitarianism (Denquin, 2008, p. 266). Thus, the two concepts clearly interact.

However, 'legal systems or constitutional orders are not deductive arguments. Conclusions do not flow rigorously from premises. We need not think of principles as major premises in a logical sense from which particular rules are ultimately derived' (Mittleman 2018, p. 198). Therefore, there is no confusion between these concepts. It must be acknowledged that human rights and democracy are logically and historically independent. Ancient Greece invented democracy, but did not come up with the idea of subjective rights that could be exercised against the state. Conversely, it was in monarchical Europe, where there was no idea of democracy, that human rights were first conceptualised (Denquin 2008, p. 266). It is therefore important to see dignity as a bridge between the ideal of human rights and democracy as a form of exercising the will of the people, which may not necessarily correspond to the ideal of human rights.

It was shown earlier that dignity is a fundamental legal concept that does not pretend to offer precise solutions, but serves as a reason and a guideline for decision-making. The logic of the case law has shown that this reason can be given different weight in different circumstances. It was also shown that dignity protects humanity itself – in other words, the intrinsic nature of human rights and freedoms – and that it is therefore not possible to separate these rights and freedoms from the human person. It is important to note that this legal status of human dignity already implies an implicit moral stance in the legal system. Since Plato and Aristotle, many philosophers of law have discussed this issue. As Alan Mittleman summarised, rational beings must necessarily find value in themselves and respect their dignity. 'One must already be committed to the concept of human dignity or, more precisely, the dignity of a rational being, for a Kantian argument to acquire traction' (Mittleman 2018, p. 200). John Finnis, responding to Robert Alexy, called this the 'participant's perspective', which is also 'the moral perspective', 'for morality is best (i.e., most reasonably) understood as what reason demands and directs in the open horizon of the whole of human life; what the principles of practical reason taken integrally demand and direct is articulated in the principles and precepts rightly called moral precepts or morality' (Finnis 2014a, p. 94). The concept of human dignity is thus a bridge between morality and law, and 'human communities have a strong presumptive moral responsibility to introduce positive law and to live by and under the rule of law, and to make and keep their positive law in line with justice (that is, with the principles that are morally binding independently of any ratification of them by practice, enactment, or judicial declaration – *ius cogens*)' (Finnis 2014a, pp. 94–95). Human dignity is thus not only a bridge between morality and law, but also between morality and democratic governance. Thus, belief in humanity, long before it becomes a posited right, is a moral attitude that encourages the search for ways to realise and protect humanity. These ways include both content, i.e., the list of human rights, and procedures, i.e., the democratic form of governance. Hence, human rights represent a material absolute that sacralises content, while democracy is a formal absolute in that it sacralises a procedure (Denquin 2008, p. 266). This interpretation not only demonstrates the relationship between dignity and human rights and democratic governance, but also avoids confusion between the two.

However, it cannot be ruled out that the government represents the will of the people, which is at odds with human rights. Nor can the opposite be ruled out: that the government protects and defends human rights while ignoring the will of the people. The fact that democracy does not necessarily coincide with human rights makes it a danger against which we must protect ourselves by extending the powers of judges (Denquin 2008, p. 266). 'To empower courts to protect indeterminate human rights norms is necessarily to empower them to "specify" the concrete meaning of the norms in the various contexts in which the norms are invoked' (Perry 2006, p. 649). Is it a good idea for the citizens of a liberal democracy to empower politically independent courts to protect entrenched human rights – i.e., human rights articulated in entrenched legal texts – against the government? This is a serious and distinct issue in the philosophy of law.[4] We will not develop this question here, but only point out that justice should not be transformed into a transcendent power that maintains loyalty to an ideal in defiance of democratic control.

The essence of this question is well illustrated by the attitude of Socrates towards Thrasymachus in Plato's *Republic*. When Socrates disagrees with Thrasymachus on fundamental principles, he remains convinced that dialectics

4 For more, see Perry (2006, pp. 87–117).

can help to find a solution and tries to convince Thrasymachus with philosophical arguments and to demonstrate the incoherence of his views (Plato 2014, 351c). However, Socrates' discussion with Thrasymachus was generally possible because of the interlocutor's openness to rational arguments. 'To participate in a rational philosophical argument, in good faith at least, is already to eschew violence and to affirm a norm of respect. It is implicitly to concede the premise of human dignity. Dignity here entails respect for the rationality of the other, attention to the other's view as that of a rational being, openness to being persuaded by the rationality of the other, and so forth' (Mittleman 2018, p. 200). Thus, even if one has a correct position that is in line with human rights, conveying it to others not by persuasion but by coercive imposition will always be counterproductive. In a world where the majority of citizens can conceive and (theoretically, at least) express an opinion, it is neither prudent nor legitimate to reinvent a kind of enlightened despotism where self-appointed elites would surreptitiously impose their values, even if they were baptised fundamental rights (Denquin 2008, p. 267).

Democracy is not immune to the old problem in legal philosophy – the gap between 'is' and 'ought', which in law is reflected, *inter alia*, in the hierarchical and dynamic dimensions of dignity. In the view of Immanuel Kant (1996, p. 119), the *status naturalis* in relations between human beings is not peace but the constant threat of a state of war. Therefore, being unprovable, inviolable and inarticulable, human dignity always remains an aspiration of the system of rights and freedoms. Democracy must not be sacrificed for human rights, nor human rights for democracy. Both are necessary, and the tension between them is fruitful. Democracy without human rights can be reduced to the will of the people alone, and human rights without democracy can be reduced to a mere doctrine of an ideal.

The pursuit of total justice – the common good – means, in principle, the good of individuals. The essence of any coexistence is to secure the whole ensemble of conditions necessary for the personal development of each individual. Therefore, common goods are not ends in themselves, but aids and means to help individuals build their own lives and prosperity (Finnis 2014b, pp. 203, 228–229). This is, *inter alia*, the difference between democracy and totalitarianism.

Totalitarianism does not tolerate any deviation from its own principles and objectives. 'Totalitarian lawfulness pretends to have found a way to establish the rule of justice on earth – something which the legality of positive law admittedly could never attain' (Arendt 2022, p. 562). Totalitarianism tends to sacrifice the human being and deny their dignity in the pursuit of these goals and principles. In a free, civil and diverse society, there is always a de facto gap between reality and the ideal of human rights, and this is a characteristic of democracy. A state with the prevailing tendency to weaken the abovementioned guarantors of democratic rule[5] inevitably turns towards totalitarianism, and human rights and freedoms become a practical problem for politics. This suggests that the failure to ensure the protection of the rights and freedoms of Ukrainian civilians, as evidenced by aggression and hostilities, are the result of a breach of *consensus iuris* within the Russian Federation. Overall, the decisions taken by today's Russia under the pretext of legal changes (from amending the Constitution, to brushing away the separation of powers (Birmontienė 2021, pp. 16, 17, 22, 29), to sham referendums in the occupied territory of another state) confirm how a totalitarian regime can proclaim its pursuit of 'good' for humanity, history, the restoration of historical justice, etc., while directly undermining human dignity.

The political narrative of totalitarianism relies on the assumption of a messianic role in the historicist vision of the past and the future. The past, however, can be seen as a history that reminds us of goals for the future. Alternatively, it can be seen as a memory – an intrinsic part of human and social identity that, nonetheless, does not determine the future. The axiom of human dignity, as a legal aspiration that imposes an obligation for common good, keeps the focus on the future and prevents over-indulgence in the correction of the past, protects the individual from the dictates of common ventures, and is the means *par excellence* for avoiding the Procrustean bed.

1.1.6. Interim findings

Law is unable to exist without morality, and morality would remain ineffective without law. This is evident from the character of the principal concepts

5 Analysing the substance of the amendments to the Constitution of the Russian Federation, the Venice Commission, *inter alia*, '182. […] concludes that they have disproportionately strengthened the position of the President of the Russian Federation and have done away with some of the checks and balances originally foreseen in the Constitution. 185. Taken together, these changes go far beyond what is appropriate under the principle of separation of powers, even in presidential regimes. 187. […] Taken together, the amendments to the provisions on the Judiciary amount to a danger to the rule of law in the Russian Federation.' European Commission for Democracy through Law (Venice Commission), Russian Federation. Interim Opinion on Constitutional Amendments and the Procedure for their Adoption, adopted by the Venice Commission at its 126th Plenary Session, Opinion No. 992/2020, 23 March 2021, https://www.venice.coe.int/webforms/documents/default.aspx?pdffile=CDL-AD(2021)005-e.

consolidated in the most fundamental legal instruments, the key to which is human dignity. International law views and recognises dignity as the fundamental philosophical basis of freedom, justice and world peace.

The legal category of human dignity *per se* and the debates arising on its basis are an indication and outcome of the novelty of human rights doctrine. The proper use of dignity in law requires reliance on the philosophy of law, which leads to the principled theses of natural law, as the doctrine of human rights is its modern counterpart. The hypothesis of dignity as an excessive legal category lacks substantiation because it is not a principle of the legal system but its foundation and a legislative maxim, which is understood in the context of the purposefulness of law and in its organic system.

Dignity is not an argument; it requires arguments. According to the Kantian concept, dignity does not imply the unconditional value of a human being, because only goodwill rather than the person *per se* predetermines the 'absolute value' of human existence. Dignity, therefore, does not imply what a person is, but what they ought to be. This conception requires an appropriate legal argumentation on dignity: the point of reference in the application of arguments should not be the person as the highest good and an end in itself, but arguments should be applied in such a way that the person be the highest good and an end in itself.

The positioning of dignity in international legal instruments confers an exceptional hierarchical status of social obviousness to this value, which does not need to be proven, is not subject to exceptions or limitations, and does not 'yield itself' to being defined. This suggests that dignity is not part of positive law but is a foundation from which human rights can be derived; however, dignity as such cannot serve subjective rights. In order to apply dignity in a proper manner and to avoid its devaluation, the principle of subsidiarity must be respected: it must be invoked only when necessary to protect an interest for the protection of which ordinary legal institutes are inadequate.

The hierarchical character of dignity is fully revealed only in its proper interaction with the evolution of jurisprudence (the dynamic aspect of dignity). Dignity as a legal argument can only be applied when it comes to defending humanity and not isolated individuals or their groups of individuals. This avoids the inflation of dignity in relation to subjective human rights. Through the proper interaction between the dynamic and hierarchical aspects of dignity, this value helps bridge the gap between absolute and relative rights, in particular by strengthening the legal protection of the most vulnerable groups in society. Therefore, considering the need to promote and socially develop a certain right, human dignity becomes the *ultima ratio* argument to justify the social continuation and development of human rights.

The gap between the hierarchical and dynamic aspects of dignity is a characteristic inherent in any democratic legal system, maintained by the rule of law and the separation of powers. Dignity, while always remaining an aspiration of law, is a never-ending obligation to keep creating conditions for the common good that ensure the flourishing of individuals and protect against the messianic role of totalitarian regimes in the historicist vision of the past and future.

1.2. The Complexity of the Value-Based Approach in Legal Interpretation

1.2.1. The Necessity of (Re)considering the Value-Based Approach in Legal Interpretation

Certain aspects of the value-based approach in legal interpretation have been repeatedly discussed and debated in the works and research of legal scholars and practitioners. Law is a set of mandatory rules upheld by any society which ensures the survival of the nation as a national community; it is the way of expressing its correct order (Etxabe 2021; Galginaitis 2002; Jimenez 2022; White 2012). Law, as the legal order, is based on a set of values reflecting the preconceptions of the community regarding what is right and wrong and acceptable standards of coexistence. Law changes inevitably alongside changes in the values of society. The concept of a value itself is key in perceiving the application of the value-based approach in legal interpretation. Accordingly, the debate around the nature of the value-based approach in legal interpretation is never-ending, and predominantly surrounds its two main features: consistency and dynamism, deriving from the social phenomenon of law itself.

On the other hand, the need to discuss the content, meaning and application of this approach in legal interpretation arises from the present military challenges in the international legal order, endangering respect for fundamental human rights, legal stability, the rule of law and the democracies of the world. Therefore, in non-democratic regimes, the value-based approach, as a method to interpret the legal norms and principles and implement justice, may be purposefully misused by pressing members of the judiciary to act in favour of the values of the political regime. A lack of freedom of conscience and mind, the inner values and morality of judges, and a dependence on dictators and their political propaganda pervert the meaning and application of the value-based approach in judicial interpretations, and serve against the purposes of democracy. Hence, the urgency of analysing the meaning and application of the value-based approach in judicial interpretation in different political regimes is crucial so as to identify the misuse of it and evaluate the dangerous consequences and impact of this on the international legal order and global democracies.

This chapter refers to the value-based approach in legal interpretation as a method to apply and interpret the law by using the organic combination of a philosophical approach alongside general scientific and special legal research methods (document content, systematic analysis, comparative, historical). The chapter focuses on exploring the content of the value-based approach, the importance of this approach in legal interpretation and its place among other interpretative methods of law, the role of judges regarding the value-based interpretation of law, and specific features of the application of this approach under different political regimes and in emergency situations. It is worth noting that it is not the purpose of this chapter to clarify all of the questions it raises (e.g., the notion of value in philosophical discourse, or the mode of application of the value-based approach in different non-democratic regimes such as authoritarianism, totalitarianism, dictatorships, etc.) because the object of this research is very broad and multi-faceted. Still, it is important to begin and continue such research.

1.2.2. The Variety of Methods of Legal Interpretation and Their Interplay

'Law hardly ever can be just applied as it stands, it has to be interpreted'; hence 'interpretation means it does not have enough content as it stands, to solve the case' (University of Sydney Law School 2009, pp. 10–11). Put differently, 'interpretation derives the legal meaning from the text': the interpreter changes static law into dynamic law, translates ordinary language into legal language, and transforms a linguistic text into a legal norm (Barak 2002-2003, p. 64). Therefore, the statement that legal interpretation, first of all, is an intellectual and cognitive process – one of thinking, creating, explaining, imagining, connecting, deducting, comparing, schematising and much more – is unsurprising. 'Legal interpretation' refers to a wide range of legal practices performed by legal theorists and practicing lawyers (e.g., advocates, judges) 'marked by contrasting labels such as interpreting existing law and creating new law <…>, describing law as it is and prescribing law as it should be, making discourses upon law <…> and making discourses inside law' (Villa 1997, p. 451).

Due to the complexity of both the human mind and the process of legal interpretation itself, it is no surprise that the interpretation of law has presented problems from the earliest times to the present day (Murray 2007). Many legal scholars and practitioners admit that there are indeed many systems of legal interpretation (Barak 2002–2003; Mesonis 2010; Mikelėnienė and Mikelėnas 1999). Legal theorists in countries under the Western law tradition consider there to be from several to several hundred legal interpretative methods, which often overlap. However, there are several main methods of legal interpretation that most point to: linguistic, systemic, historical, teleological (intentional), precedential, comparative, and value-based (Barak 2002–2003; Congressional Research Service 2022; Irving 2015; Mesonis 2010; Mikelėnienė and Mikelėnas 1999). These are the interpretative tools that give meaning to the legal rules which are most appropriate under certain circumstances to solve a legal dispute in a case. The existing variety of methods of legal interpretation and the choices made when applying them are undoubtedly of considerable importance, and may result in different (or sometimes inappropriate) interpretations of the law.

There is no single optimal system of legal interpretation capable of solving any legal dispute, and any interpretative method struggles with the limitations created by the nature of certain characteristics of the method itself (Barak 2002–2003). While interpreting legal rules, the aforementioned interpretative methods, whether collectively or individually, may be applied in cases depending on their complexities – the range of questions of facts and law raised, the abstractness or indeterminacy of the relevant legal rules and general principles of law, the complexity and novelty of legal issues, the demand for new interpretations of relevant legal norms, or the question of grounds for deviation from existing court practice.

1.2.3. The Content of the Value-Based Approach in Legal Interpretation

One of the most composite and complex methods of legal interpretation is the value-based approach, which, like any other interpretative method, has its own limitations. Nevertheless, we chose to discuss the content of this method and its characteristics following a number of legal scholars (Barak 2002–2003; Mesonis 2010; Tripkovic 2018) who determined that it compensates for the limitations of the other interpretative methods, especially in non-clear-cut cases.

Although the grounds for the application of this approach, as for the other aforementioned legal approaches, derive from the indeterminacy, specificity, ambiguities and contradictions of legal norms, the principal demand for this approach in legal interpretation is caused by the incapacity of other legal interpretative methods to provide the contextual and 'just' meaning of a legal text in the scope of a legal dispute. However, the value-based approach in legal interpretation cannot be perceived as (nor is it designed to be) a replacement for other interpretative methods, but may be regarded as a supplementary interpretative method that is used as a last resort when the other interpretative methods are insufficient to support the just solution of a case.

The importance of values is recognised by many scholars because of their determining role in legal interpretation (Mesonis 2010). The category of a value itself may seem to offer explicit and definite guidance for the application of this interpretative approach, but this is somewhat of a fallacy. Considering the meaning of the word value itself – 'the regard that something is held to deserve; the importance or worth; principles or standards of behaviour' (Pearsall 2001) – it carries its own ambiguities. The Greek philosopher Plato urged that the three transcendental values by which the law is measured are truth, justice and beauty (Hickman 2018). So, if a legal rule has the characteristics of either truth, justice or beauty, then it will be in conformity with the transcendental values themselves. Plato and his followers wrote extensively about these values in their philosophical writings; the debate on the notion of a value is never-ending in philosophical discourse, even at present.

If a person must interpret legal provisions containing the character of values, then it follows that they are unable to determine what the provision means without determining the nature and extent of the value that it seeks to establish (Villa 1997). Hence, the valuable character of this interpretative method lies in the objects or interests that the legal rule is meant to protect (Villa 1997). This rises from the very foundation of the law itself, which is a set of values of a community and, as indicated by D. Hume, consists of 'ought' propositions containing characteristics of values (Allsop 2016; Fitzpatrick 2000). Values specify the fundamental benchmarks and the common social ground of a society (Blanc-Fily 2015; Petsche 2010). V. Villa (1997, p. 456) offers the definition of a value-based approach as having 'the function of making an appreciation, whether positive or negative, of a given object and normally expressed through the use of evaluative predicates like good, right, just, beautiful, praiseworthy'. In legal discourse, Villa admits that this appreciation is given in light of certain ethical (e.g., the inviolability of human life or respect for the dignity of the human person) or political values (e.g., justice) (Villa 1997).

The value-based approach (together with the other interpretative methods) is introduced in hard cases, where 'no settled rule dictates a decision either way' (Dworkin 1975, p. 1060) and a judge, in order to settle the legal dispute, has to 'contribute an honest voice to the ceaseless striving for the best expression of the law in relation to a particular case at a particular moment' (Sachs 2009,

p. 145). R. Alexy (2005) underlined several factors that cause difficulty in resolving hard cases when a judgement cannot simply be deduced from existing valid norms: the vagueness and ambiguity of legal language, conflicts of norms, and the lack of an existing valid norm. The very nature of hard (in other words, non-clear-cut) cases contains conflicts and clashes of fundamental values and principles, which are the basis for urging the application of the value-based approach. These cases generally find their way to the highest courts, and the justices deciding them must necessarily make choices based on values (Barak 2002–2003; Chemerinsky 2000).

Consequently, the value-based approach in legal interpretation is based on the entirety of the fundamental values that are upheld by societies as an assurance of the survival of the nation as a community and embodied in the legal order. This method seeks to interpret the legal text in conformity with the general perception of the values existing in particular community at a particular given time. The nature of the value-based approach in legal interpretation is very broad because of the inarticulate and polysemous nature of the notion of value (Blanc-Fily 2015). Therefore, the application of it in interpreting the law is very complex, dense and challenging, demanding an interpreter of broad and comprehensive mind regarding legal, ethical, and philosophical discourses.

1.2.4. The (Im)possibility of Resolving a Conflict of Values

Perceptions of values that thrive among different communities and legal systems, as well as clashes between competing values even within the same legal system or society – or value pluralism, as some legal scholars refer to it (Spicer 2009) – may entail conflicts of values. I. Berlin and M. W. Spicer looked at the moral nature of a human being as having many goals, 'not all of them commensurable, and in perpetual rivalry with one another' (Berlin 1969, p. 171; Spicer 2009), which therefore naturally causes the conflicting perception of values.

Conflicts of values occur at different levels (Spicer 2009), and this must be considered when resolving them. Values 'can come into conflict with one another' (Spicer 2009, p. 537), or one value may be of a different conception in different societies. As S. Hampshire figuratively remarked, value conflicts can happen 'both in the soul and in the city' (2000, p. 5), and the latter is heavily involved with global or regional political issues which cross national borders (Spicer 2009). Russia's ongoing war of aggression against Ukraine clearly illustrates a conflict of values both at the individual (personal) and political (state) levels; likewise, both within Russian society itself and between Russia and most democratic states around the world. Some Russian individuals have strong or even blind faith in the conduct of their political leader and his supporters, while others are struggling with their loyalty both to the state of which they are an integral part and to the democratic values prospering outside it. Most of the world's democracies and their leaders stand firmly for democratic values and against the war in Ukraine, while a few states around the world have not clearly expressed their attitude towards Russia's war of aggression against Ukraine, and to a certain extent still remain in a conflicting international political position.

In present times, value conflicts of an international (regional) character have become crucially sensitive, *inter alia* political, issues, and the means through which they are resolved (if indeed they are resolved) affect coexistence between communities and states. Elaborating the means of resolving value conflicts, the legal literature provides two modes of action: 'using force or violence or, alternatively, more peaceful means' (Spicer 2009, p. 543), such as institutional mechanisms and recognised procedural rules (Hampshire 2000; Popova 2013). It is obvious that even during extraordinary situations of value conflicts 'war, tyrannies, massacres <…> are felt as evils directly and without recourse to the norms of any particular way of life or to any specific set of moral ideas' (Hampshire 2000, p.xii). Consequently, peaceful means and nonviolent resolutions may at least be regarded as rational (Rorty 2007).

Legal scholars sometimes discuss the rules and methods through which value conflicts can be resolved and the ways in which value choices must be reasonably made (Jeutner 2020; Petsche 2010; Simon 1957; Spicer 2009). They suggest that some value conflicts are resolvable 'by determining their 'relative weights' (Simon 1957, p. 61; Spicer 2009, p. 542) and 'by means of proportionality tests (determination of suitability, necessity and proportionality *strictu sensu)*' (Jeutner 2020, p. 457). This implies that the question of which aspects of both conflicting norms (or values) 'should have more weight than others when dealing with a particular case' (Christófolo 2016, p. 47) must be answered. For instance, how does Ukraine's right of self-defence and protectory conduct against Russia's war on and invasion of its territory interplay with the use of violence and force, which is prohibited by the rules of the international community? The prohibition of the use of violence is in conflict with the exercise of a state's right to self-defence, 'even though both norms are largely based on the same value(s)' – the preservation of peace and life of the nation (Petsche 2010, p. 259). In the case of Russia's war in Ukraine, proportionality analysis leads to the consideration that Ukraine's right to self-defence (and in a broad sense its right to use (lawful) force for self-defensive purposes) is justifiable for the protection of the territorial integrity and sovereignty of the Ukrainian nation. On the other hand, it must be noted that the resolution of conflicting values 'is necessarily subjective in the sense that <…>

proportionality assessment is linked to the identity of the legal subject undertaking the assessment' (Jeutner 2020, p. 467). Often, proportionality tests are misused in favour of the rules of dangerous, non-democratic regimes.

However, academics admit that in some cases 'there may be no overriding value or common ethical measuring rod that is available to us to arbitrate such conflicts' (Spicer 2009, p. 537) and no such criteria that are 'always overriding and final'; 'no compelling principle, or rational method, of balancing one value against another' (Hampshire 1983, pp. 24, 118–119) in settling existing value conflicts (Jeutner 2020). Theoretically, such extraordinary situations inevitably demand the sacrifice of some values over others. Nevertheless, if we assume, according to M. Popova, J. Crowe and A. A. Cançado Trindade, that 'the rule of law is universally good' (Popova 2013, p. 215) and that 'human rights constitute the basic foundation of the legal order' (Cançado Trindade 2009, p. 27), then the possibility of resolving conflicts of values would not seem so unachievable. The principle of the rule of law is directly pertinent to other democratic values, and the primary directions in making a choice among conflicting values are quite evident.

1.2.5. The Value-Based Approach in European Jurisprudence

The just meaning of values should be determined not apart from, but in the context of a certain legal system and its traditions. Consequently, courts must use value-based interpretation within the 'ambit of certain constitutional and legal framework so that they are consistent with, and reflect, the values and ethos of the society fashioned by its constitution' (Murray 2007, p. 43). This derives from the perspective that 'value judgments are equated with judgments expressing a – positive or negative – stance on a given legal system, as a whole or in one of its parts' (Villa 1997, p. 450).

In order to frame the content of values in terms of their relationship with the legal system, one should refer to the provisions of national constitutions which form the fundamental, supreme law of the state, where the aspirational direction of the nation and the values binding it are established. As a unique legal document, constitutions enshrine a special kind of norm and stand at the top of the hierarchical normative pyramid. Difficult to amend, these documents are designed to direct human behaviour for years to come (Barak 2002-2003). A constitution 'shapes the appearance of the state and its aspirations throughout history, determines the state's fundamental political views, lays the foundation for its social values, <...> reflects the events of the past and determines how the future will look' (Barak 2002-2003, p. 68). This is clear from the provisions of the preamble of the Constitution of the Republic of Lithuania, which embodies the innate right of human beings and the nation to live and create freely, sets out national concord in the land of Lithuania, and strives for an open, just, and harmonious civil society and a State under the rule of law. Similar values are enshrined in the Constitution of Ukraine – guarantees of human rights and freedoms, worthy conditions of human life, civil harmony on Ukrainian soil, and a democratic, social, law-based state.

The values enshrined in constitutions embody the true meaning of the texts of the law and define the image of what a community seeks to become and stand for in the future. A reference to the constitutional provisions, which embody the core values of the society, is of significant importance in contextualising and framing the set of values in any legal system. Therefore, a value-based interpretation must meet the values and principles embodied in the relevant Constitution.

Besides today's perspective of value-laden constitutions, Plato's truth, justice and beauty may be perceived through the provisions of international legal documents, namely the ECHR, the EU Charter, and the Treaty on the EU (hereafter – the TEU). The legal order of the EU is based on common fundamental values – respect for human rights and freedoms and the rule of law. The aspiration to secure universal human rights, justice and peace in the world alongside effective political democracy is set out in the preambles of these documents. The values which member states of the EU seek to share and their substance are fleshed out in the articles of the aforementioned documents. These provisions clarify (to a certain extent) the content of these universal values through the concept of human dignity, freedom, equality and solidarity, pluralism, non-discrimination, tolerance, and political, social, economic rights.

Nevertheless, the scope of a value still does not eliminate its indeterminacy, and national supreme and constitutional courts along with supranational courts, such as the ECtHR and the CJEU, which for the most part examine borderline cases, are responsible for the interpretation of provisions with a value-based character. These provisions must be interpreted in a manner that promotes and protects the values embodied in the constitution and in relevant international legal documents. For this reason, the presence of the value-based approach as an interpretative method in the highest national and supranational courts is an important cornerstone of their work. In the jurisprudence of the ECtHR (Kjeldsen, Busk Madsen and Pedersen v. Denmark 1976, Soering v. UK 1989) and the CJEU, the specific importance of the value-based approach as a fundamental form of legal interpretation is constantly highlighted when it is used to clarify and define the meaning of provisions of an abstract and open nature (Pollicino 2004). Therefore, the jurisprudence of these courts is an inseparable part of the fundamental legal documents which embody the nature of values in relation to the European legal system and modern conditions.

1.2.6. The Role of the Judge Regarding the Value-Based Interpretation of the Law

The function of judges is to interpret the law, so the question of how judges apply it and what values they bring into a legal dispute is always up for debate (Barak 2002–2003; Sachs 2009). Judges admit that their personal experiences, crucial life events, and beliefs influence their legal interpretations (Sachs 2009), especially in non-clear-cut cases. Hence, the value-based interpretational approach may be of a very subjective nature, and consequently the role of the personal experience of the judge in their legal interpretation directly engages the question of the legitimacy of using the value-based approach (Villa 1997).

The objectivity of the value-based approach lies in the nature of the values held by the society, of which judges are a part, and a key role of judges is to articulate them (Bench-Capon and Sartor 2003). The judge must give 'expression not to his or her own beliefs, but to the deep, underlying values of society' (Barak 2002–2003, p. 51) as they are understood by the community and developed through history in the light and spirit of the constitutional provisions. The judge must 'reflect the fundamental tenets of the people and the national credo rather than his or her personal beliefs' (Barak 2002–2003, p. 51). Thus, judges are intermediaries between society and the legal system it inhabits, embodying the people's understanding of ambiguous or abstract legal norms and principles (Rossum 2022).

All values thriving in society are of a relative nature and change over time because of the law, which is a living structural phenomenon that reflects a society's existential order. If the social reality changes, the law must change accordingly (Barak 2002–2003). Thus, the applicational mode of the value-based approach is subject to change, and changes the outcome of legal interpretation.

Sometimes, changes in a social reality, and therefore in the legal order, are 'drastic, sudden, and easily identifiable, sometimes – minor and gradual, and cannot be noticed without the proper distance and perspective'. Thus, the judge must accordingly 'understand the purpose of law in society and help the law achieve its purpose' (Barak 2002–2003, p. 28). 'The very notion of justice has a profound moral-historical dimension' (Sachs 2009, p. 56), and judges must have the ability to feel the pace and direction of the development of the legal system in which they exercise their duties (Barak 2002–2003). For instance, within the legal framework of the EU, the legal definitions of spouses and marriage have changed over time due to societal changes and contemporary understandings of gender identity and expression, indicating *inter alia* marriages between persons of the same sex. ECtHR, in its case of *Relu Adrian Coman and Others v. Inspectoratul General pentru Imigrări and Ministerul Afacerilor Interne* (2018), while outlining the definition of the words 'spouse' and 'marriage', agreed with the opinion of the Advocate General that 'European Union law must be interpreted in the light of the present day circumstances, regarding to fundamental interests of the society, based on statistical and comparative studies from numerous European jurisdictions regarding the scope of fundamental rights' (Belavusau and Kochenov 2020). Thus, the meaning of a legal rule is adapted to new societal circumstances, changing the meaning of the fundamental right to marriage and family life.

Another important part of the judge's role in regard to the value-based interpretation of the law is their ability to balance conflicting values in a case (Sachs 2009). Laws apply to a community, and this community is held to have common priorities amongst values. It is thus imperative for the judge to articulate these values in order to reach decisions that are just and fair (Bench-Capon and Sartor 2003).

Concerning the mode of prioritising values, R. Dworkin highlighted that values embodied in fundamental principles have weight, and by means of balancing their respective weights it is possible to resolve conflicts between values (Dworkin 1977). The weight of a fundamental principle and therefore the value embodied in it 'reflects its relative social importance, its place in the legal system, and its value within the entire array of social values' (Barak 2002–2003, p. 90). The judge must find the proper balance between different values, and the outcome of legal interpretation must express this balance (Barak 2002–2003). H. L. A. Hart expressed the same view – that a judge has to strike a balance among competing interests (1997). The issue of euthanasia and the human right to die with dignity constitutes an example of a conflict between the individual conception of human dignity and the necessary respect for the right to human life, which cannot be resolved without one of the two rights, or values, involved being set aside in favour of the other (Blanc-Fily 2015). In addition, the weight of values is of a relative nature – the same value may be of a different weight in different cases, and the judge must give appropriate weight to it in each case.

The ability of a judge to identify the just meaning of the values thriving in a society and enshrined in the legal system and then to balance and prioritise them is highly important for the proper application of the value-based approach in legal interpretation and for the achievement of justice.

1.2.7. The Application of the Value-Based Approach in Legal Interpretation and Political Regimes

The application of the value-based approach in legal interpretation differs significantly in different political regimes (democratic and non-democratic) and depends on the values enshrined in the legal system and the political goals of the regime. The political regime itself affects the interpretative system that the judge should apply when interpreting the law and resolving legal disputes (Barak 2002–2003).

Democracy as a political regime is based on the rule of law, the separation of powers and respect for fundamental human rights. Democracies advance justice, fairness, good conscience and equality. From this perspective, democracies are governed by the people themselves through their freely elected representatives, protect the rights and freedoms of human beings, and grant special authoritative powers to the judiciary. The nature of the judiciary and its functioning regarding the rule of law in democracies emphasises its independence and impartiality from the other state authorities. Judges 'give effect to democracy by ruling in accordance with aforementioned democratic values and foundational principles' (Barak 2002–2003, p. 41) and developing a real rule of law with binding scope (Blanc-Fily 2015). The interpretation of law in accordance with respect for democratic values constitutes the proper application of the value-based approach and is implemented to its full normative extent in democracies.

Non-democracies are ruled by the law and involve the restriction of fundamental human rights. Values that are maintained in democracies are reduced in their scope or disrespected in non-democratic regimes. These regimes, wherein positive law is in conflict with democratic values and principles, are based on overall control and power over the society in all areas of life, censorship, and the promotion of the interests of the rulers (elites, dictators, etc.). The judiciary is biased, subordinate to the leader or elite and, according to the regime-related theories developed in its political science, functions as a tool to implement the ideology of the regime rather than seek justice. Political goals are furthered by establishing a dual legal structure in which the ordinary judiciary is largely left to exercise independence in the routine administration of justice; thus, politically sensitive cases are transferred to courts established specifically to hear them (Guarnieri 2010). Accordingly, the application of the value-based approach in legal interpretation to its fullest and most meaningful extent is challenged, which may result in subservient interpretations of legal rules in favour of the rulers. This interpretative approach in legal disputes may be misused to empower dangerous regimes, weaken or even deny fundamental human rights, and control anyone who opposes the rulers or challenges the ideology of the regime.

By way of illustration, judges in Nazi Germany, a regime which lasted from 1933 until 1945, used to implement the ideology of the Nazi Party through their decisions. The Nazis did not actually change the law significantly, but they pressured judges into interpreting or even distorting it by bringing more Nazi political values into the law (University of Sydney Law School 2009). The majority of the judiciary served the Nazi regime by resolving legal disputes and justifying their decisions according to the values of the Nazi Party, especially promoting discrimination on the grounds of national origin and race, which was obviously in contradiction with democratic values. They interpreted the law as prioritising and unconditionally safeguarding the interests of the German nation, which we may now identify as misusing the value-based approach in judicial interpretation. After the collapse of Nazi Germany, Nazi judges were tried for their actions in Nuremberg and in International Military Tribunals.

During the apartheid regime in 20th-century South Africa, the legal system was targeted towards racial discrimination and segregation. Therefore, judges appointed by the government were expected to interpret the law in a way consistent with the policies of the regime. Judges applying the law in legal disputes had to follow the values of the regime, exalting and privileging the white race over black Africans and other non-white race groups living in South Africa. Thus, apartheid judges, instead of implementing justice, fulfilled the policies of the apartheid regime, which, as noted by D. Dyzenhaus, 'led to results disastrous for civil liberties' (Barak 2002–2003, p. 80) and caused violations of substantial and procedural fundamental human rights. Like in the Nazi regime, apartheid judges interpreted the law by reasoning the necessity of protecting white South Africans (Sachs 2009).

Hence, the application of the value-based approach in non-democracies brings significant challenges for the judiciary when it comes to choices relating to the just meaning of values and the freedom of conscience of the judges themselves. In such situations, some judges act as the puppets of the regime, while others try to resist it, challenging the legitimacy of positive law and interpreting the legal rules contrary to established non-democratic values (Sachs 2009). Some scholars argue that the 'extent to which judges are willing to implement the will of the non-democratic rulers depends on how closely their own political ideology is aligned with that of the regime' (Geerling *et al.* 2018, p. 2419). Research by W. Geerling *et al.* (2018, p. 2415) revealed that judges who were ideologically committed to the Nazi Party were more likely to impose the death sentence on those who belonged to the most organised groups of political opposition, those whose acts of treason or high treason involved violent resistance against the state, and those with characteristics to which Nazism was intolerant. Those judges who were against the values of the Nazi regime faced the challenge of standing true and firm to their own values and still performing their duties in an environment of unjust laws by administering as much justice as possible (University of Sydney Law School 2009). This was mostly possible in cases that were not high-profile and not of political interest and relevance to the rulers of the non-democratic regime (e.g., in family law cases) (University of Sydney Law School 2009). In terms of today's judiciaries in non-democratic regimes, the 'Russian judiciary functions fairly well in the less politicised area of civil litigation and when state actors do not have a stake in the outcome of individual cases' (Popova 2013, p. 215). Thus, the value-based approach in legal interpretation may to some extent be a legal tool to resist some of the challenges posed by dictatorships, weaken, albeit to a small extent, their power, and promote democratic values.

The lessons of the 20th century were learned by establishing the ECHR as one of the safeguards of democratic values. This Convention, like some other regional or international legal documents (for example, the UDHR), was created as an instrument to prevent states from sliding back into non-democratic regimes, serving as a functioning bulwark against disrespect for fundamental human rights and the rule of law (Ulfstein 2020). Moreover, in terms of the international legal order, *ius cogens* – peremptory norms of a public, international character that are acknowledged by all or most states as an international community without permitting derogation – are (and should be) the international legal basis that guides national states towards internationally accepted principles of conduct and values. '*Ius cogens* is based on the idea that the international legal system recognizes, or should recognize, a set of fundamental values' (Petsche 2010, p. 258) which derives from fundamental human rights. *Ius cogens*, being of the character of 'fundamental norms' (Petsche 2010, p. 259), prohibit genocide, slavery, torture, aggression, war crimes, terrorism etc., and this list is not exhaustive and may be subject to change due to the political and social circumstances. *Ius cogens* are peremptory norms of hierarchical superiority in international law, and overcome all other sources of law.

Ius cogens interact in a vertical manner – between the international and national legal orders – and national states must validate their domestic laws with respect to them (Cançado Trindade 2009). Accordingly, states are legally obliged by *ius cogens*, and the values thriving within the national state must comply with the fundamental values which the peremptory norms of international law encompass.

Some legal scholars question the practical impact of *ius cogens* in the international community and state that the concept of *ius cogens* remains largely a 'theoretical construct' because of its incoherent application and limited capacity in the international community (Jeutner 2020; Petsche 2010). Nevertheless, they agree that 'it is the vehicle of a particular vision of the international legal order and international law' (Petsche 2010, p. 258), and at least until now it has served as the means for states and communities to coexist, preserve fundamental values, and be led by 'the primacy of law over power politics' (Cançado Trindade 2009, p. 29). M. Petsche adds that 'certain values are fundamental' and 'they do not need to be recognized or confirmed by individual States' as 'they are derived from <…> the rational analysis of the conditions of human existence' (2010, p. 259).

Yet the echoes of radical historical events find their way into today's Russia, where the judiciary and its decisions are subject to non-democratic political pressure. The decisions of the judiciary to imprison critics and opponents of the regime, human rights defenders, and others who publicly promote respect for human rights and the rule of law, obviously suggest that Russian judges interpret and apply the law in a way that is consistent with the values and principles of Russia's authoritarian regime but not in line with democratic values (Solomon and Trochev 2018; Popova 2017). The Constitution of the Russian Federation establishes respect for fundamental human rights, though these rights 'are undermined *de facto* by the Russian courts' (Popova 2017, p. 65). Judges reason their decisions based on the necessity of protecting the Russian nation and Russia's sovereignty against 'threats' arising from the EU and Europeans – and particularly Ukraine. Russia is not an exception in establishing its national identity and interpretation of the law in a way that is contrary to fundamental human rights – the Constitutional Court of Hungary in 2021 delivered a judgment interpreting the right to human dignity of foreigners, including asylum seekers, stating that 'Hungarians have a right to 'constitutional identity', to be interpreted as the right to live in a culturally homogeneous country, essentially associating the arrival of migrants and asylum seekers with a threat to said identity' (Hungarian Helsinki Committee 2022, p. 24; 'V. Mizaras: in times of various crisis…' 2023). This illustrates the inability or rather reluctance of the (in)dependent judiciary to interpret law referring to various changing global circumstances, and suggests that the conflict between the values envisaged in domestic and international law can expand, laying the ground for extreme nationalism ('V. Mizaras: in times of various crisis…' 2023).

Yet, as noted by A. Sachs, 'concepts such as rule of law, fundamental rights and the independence of judiciary', if appropriately used, 'can provide a sense of shape, of dignity, of style, of historical timbre to judicial argument' (2009, p. 57). This is a reminder for the judiciary and the special authoritative state power in democracies, while exercising the power and implementing justice, to 'look beyond the next three years, and look down the pages of history' (University of Sydney Law School 2009, p. 12).

1.2.8. The Application of the Value-Based Approach in Times of Crisis

The application of the value-based approach in legal interpretation demands scrutinous consideration and utmost attention, and is a challenging process for legal interpreters even in times of peace and stability. However, when times of crisis and emergency situations – war/martial law, terrorism, pandemics – arise, what occurs in the perception of the fundamental values of the society, and how is the value-based approach in legal interpretation applied? Is the application of the value-based approach in legal interpretation modified or not? If so, to what extent are there safeguards in place to preserve fundamental values? Are there any legally permissible exemptions?

It is unquestionable that times of crisis present many legal challenges to the powers of the state, its legal system and legal interpretation at the national and international levels. Such extreme situations may cause a threat to national legal systems, the international legal order, and legally enshrined fundamental values (specifically in constitutions and binding international legal documents), and demand urgent, extraordinary responses (Greene 2018). The grounds for the declaration of a state of emergency and any restrictions referring to fundamental human rights and freedoms are usually embedded in national constitutions and detailed in certain domestic legal acts. For example, the Constitution of Ukraine indicates that it shall not be amended, and such constitutional rights and freedoms as the right to life, right to freedom and personal inviolability, right to fair trial, etc., shall not be restricted in conditions of martial law or a state of emergency. In contrast, specific restrictions on the right to private property, the right to privacy, and the right to freely leave the territory of Ukraine may be established for the period of emergency.

In times of crisis, fundamental values may be in conflict to a much greater extent than in times of peace, and from the perspective of legal interpretation this is a determining factor for the application of the value-based approach. In extraordinary situations, the value-based approach must be applied consistently with respect for the rule of law and fundamental human rights. Hence, the principle of proportionality and the rule of balancing weights must still be applied in order to achieve lawful outcomes in a crisis situation. Most likely, the application of the value-based approach in legal interpretation will result in different outcomes during wartime than it would in a time of peace; however, this is justifiable because of the demands posed by the emergency circumstances themselves.

However, the danger of the value-based approach becoming distorted arises particularly keenly in emergency situations of an interstate political character – i.e., war/martial law, unlawful territorial expansion, and the use of force and violence. Political purposes may tend to be prioritised by the members of the judiciary; therefore, the law is interpreted and the actions of state power institutions are justified politically, but not necessarily legally. Ukraine is an emerging, 'weakly institutionalized democracy' (Sanchez Urribarri 2014, p. 1081), yet it retains some intrinsic patterns of a post-Soviet state and has traces of a communist ideology (Zvieriev 2018). This is all the more pronounced in the face of Russia's war of aggression. There is still a significant proportion of the Ukrainian population who are guided by Soviet post-truth ideology, either partly or fully (Zvieriev 2018, p. 93). Therefore, the judiciary is challenged by a complex of extraordinary circumstances and is at risk of misinterpreting the law, advancing political rather than legal justifications and relying on political reasoning. This may, *inter alia*, have a large impact on the independence of the judiciary and the separation of powers. Political interests are very powerful, and whether or not the judiciary will exercise its powers, interpret the constitution independently, and preserve the rule of law depends to a great extent on politicians and their commitment to the values of democracy ('V. Mizaras: in times of various crisis…' 2023).

Still, *ius cogens* and national constitutions, which are compatible with these peremptory norms, are supposed to be the legal cornerstones that prevent departures from the rule of law, safeguarding the protection of fundamental human rights and the justified interpretation of law both in times of crisis and peace. Such constitutions, as living instruments, are able 'to respond and would respond to all the legal challenges and needs that would arise in a crisis situation' ('V. Mizaras: in times of various crisis…' 2023).

1.2.9. Interim findings

The value-based approach in legal interpretation is founded on all fundamental values that are upheld by the relevant society as an assurance of the survival of the nation as a community and that are embodied in the legal order. The nature of the value-based approach in legal interpretation is very broad because of the nature of the notion of a value itself. Therefore, the application of this approach in interpreting the law is very complex, dense and challenging, demanding an interpreter of broad and comprehensive mind in the legal, ethical, and philosophical areas.

Although the grounds for the application of the value-based approach, as for other interpretative methods, derive from the indeterminacy, specificity, ambiguities and contradictions of legal norms, the principal demand for this approach in legal interpretation is caused by the incapacity of other legal interpretative methods to provide the contextual, just meaning of a legal text in the scope of a legal dispute, especially in non-clear-cut cases.

The just meaning of values should be determined not apart from, but in the context of a certain legal system and its traditions. Consequently, courts must use value-based interpretations when referring to the provisions of national constitutions – fundamental, supreme laws of the state where the aspirational direction of the nation and the values binding it are established – and relevant international legal documents such as the ECHR, the EU Charter, and the TEU. The latter are based on common fundamental values: respect for human rights and freedoms and the rule of law. The jurisprudence of the ECtHR and the CJEU is an inseparable part of these legal documents, embodying the nature of these values in relation to the European legal system and present-day conditions.

The ability of judges to identify the just meaning of the values thriving in a society and enshrined in the legal system, and then to balance and prioritise them, is important for the proper application of the value-based approach in legal interpretation and the achievement of justice. Value conflicts are resolvable by determining their relative weights and by means of proportionality tests.

The application of the value-based approach in legal interpretation differs significantly in political regimes (democratic and non-democratic) and depends on the values enshrined in the legal system and the political goals of the regime. The interpretation of law in accordance with respect for democratic values constitutes the proper application of the value-based approach, and is implemented to its full normative extent in democracies. In non-democratic regimes, this interpretative approach in legal disputes may be misused by empowering these dangerous regimes, weakening or even denying fundamental human rights, and controlling anyone who opposes the rulers (elites, dictators, etc.) or challenges the ideology of the regime.

Ius cogens – peremptory norms of a public, international character that are acknowledged by all or most states as an international community without permitting derogation – are (and should be) the international legal basis that guides national states towards the internationally accepted principles of conduct and fundamental values.

In times of crisis, fundamental values may be in conflict to a much greater extent than in times of peace. Nevertheless, in extraordinary situations the value-based approach must be applied consistently with the rule of law and fundamental human rights. The danger of the distortion of the value-based approach is particularly perilous in emergency situations of an interstate political character – i.e., war/martial law, unlawful territorial expansion, and the use of force and violence. In these scenarios, political purposes may tend to be prioritised by the members of the judiciary. Therefore, the law is interpreted and the actions of state power institutions are justified politically, but not necessarily legally.

National constitutions, which are compatible with *ius cogens*, are supposed to be significant legal cornerstones preventing departure from the rule of law and safeguarding the protection of fundamental human rights and the justified interpretation of law, both in times of crisis and peace.

1.3. The War Against Freedom of Conscience*

1.3.1. Freedom of Conscience and Its Contemporary Relevance

From the time of Socrates to the events involving Salman Rushdie, the war against freedom of conscience has always been part of human history. What makes the state of this freedom even more pressing today is that we have recently seen an increase in the erosion of the freedom to hold, express and live according to personal beliefs and commitments through various constraints, including surveillance technology, religious discrimination, white supremacy movements, and re-education camps that inhibit freedom of conscience and other freedoms. Although it has been decades since freedom of conscience as a core human right first appeared under the protection of international law, this fundamental right appears to be an overlooked piece in the universal human rights jigsaw to the extent that it sometimes receives the label of a forgotten right. Why is this? First, what freedom of conscience means more precisely is anything but clear. Second, very little scholarly writing has been devoted to freedom of conscience. Third, it does not play a role in legal practice; thus, its content remains vague. Fourth, surprisingly, in this secular age, freedom of conscience continues to be seen through the rubric of religious freedom.

* This Chapter is written under the Postdoctoral project which has received funding from the Research Council of Lithuania (LMTLT), agreement No. S-PD-22-61.

In 2024, three anniversaries will bring together the global community as all of their dates are connected to the conception of human rights, including the fundamental human right to freedom of conscience, and global security. Both Immanuel Kant's moral system and his understanding of the possibility of a 'perpetual peace', which find their expression in modern human rights principles, are being undermined at the time when the world will witness his 300th birthday. In addition, the EU as a peace project was itself based on the view of minimum, universal freedoms, and when the largest EU enlargement happened 20 years ago, it signified that Central and Eastern Europe also believed in this European identity and its unquestionable attachment to universal values such as individual liberty, democracy, the rule of law and universal human rights, including the right to freedom of conscience. This reality has not stopped the rise of various 'exit' appeals towards illiberal democracy, or the practical suppression of judicial independence, which clearly reflects an entirely different agenda. The question to be posed in the contemporary time is whether the Kantian system and his conception of freedom are at risk of being replaced. If so, what could be the potential consequences for freedom, including freedom of conscience? Can there be a human rights system without the Kantian moral system that seems to be under attack, alongside universal values? As recognised by Kant and others, only a strong legal framework and alliance can bring about global peace. The North Atlantic Alliance was created to uphold freedom and security. NATO, which celebrates its 75th birthday in 2024, is bound to protect individual liberty, democracy, and the rule of law. It also agreed at its 2023 Vilnius summit to tackle global security threats, including food security issues that bring famine and pose a threat to peace across the globe.

The international order that emerged after the Second World War sought to uphold security by defending individual liberty, democracy, the rule of law, and human rights values, including the fundamental right to freedom of conscience. Article 1 of the UDHR, for example, sets out that 'all human beings are born free and equal in dignity and rights' and that 'they are endowed with reason and conscience'. The ECHR guarantees the right to freedom of conscience and its expression in Article 9. The EU Charter explicitly grants the right to conscientious objection in Article 10. Nonetheless, today we live in a world where time-honoured fundamental freedoms, particularly freedom of conscience, are under threat. In his reaction to the Russian war against Ukraine and the lack of action on the part of some Western countries, the President of the Republic of Ukraine, Volodymyr Zelensky, stressed that Ukraine, like any other state, should not be expected to compromise its conscience, sovereignty, territory, or independence. In this statement, the emphasis on conscience as a target in war is of particular importance. Today, the war in Ukraine, conscience conflicts, food and global economic insecurity, global terrorism, and death threats against those exercising free speech all pose a threat to freedom of conscience and give rise to greater insecurity.

Beliefs of a religious or secular nature are a matter of conscience, and freedom of conscience is one of the foundations of contemporary society. The ECtHR has noted several times that freedom of conscience is undoubtedly one of the pillars of a democratic state. The very question of the human rights system – and, in particular, of the right to freedom of conscience – is central to the functioning of democracy itself. However, the contemporary world has recently seen an increase in the erosion of the freedom of conscience, along with various constraints that inhibit religious and other freedoms. The massacre of journalists working at the *Charlie Hebdo* magazine; the murder of a French teacher after a class on freedom of expression and the 'anti-separatism law' that followed these events; the dialogue on COVID-19 vaccination policies; the debate on abortion rights and related Polish legal changes; the refusal to sell a wedding cake to gay couples; the ban on Muslims entering the USA; white supremacist movements in the USA; or even the stabbing of Salman Rushdie on a lecture stage in New York – all of these events involved important aspects of freedom of conscience, and all weakened freedom of conscience worldwide. Although secular law guarantees freedom of conscience, 'conscience wars' (Mancini and Rosenfeld 2018) are on the rise around the world. On many occasions, law has only deepened these problems rather than addressing them. By turning Republican, Christian, Muslim or any other belief or ideology into state law, the fundamental human principles of living in the society are denied. As a result, conflicts of conscience among people lead to disagreements between communities, states or civilisations.

The growing number of examples of oppression directed toward freedom of conscience across the globe in 2023 resulted in two recent UN resolutions being adopted within a 1-month period. On 14 June 2023, the Security Council of the UN (hereafter – the SC) unanimously adopted a resolution urging the prevention of incitement and the condemnation of hate speech, racism, and acts of extremism. This resolution encourages the prevention of the spread of intolerant ideology, the promotion of tolerance, and that the challenges of hate speech be addressed. Another resolution, adopted by the UN Human Rights Council on 11 July 2023, focuses on religious hatred. The resolution on religious hatred was adopted following a request from the countries of the Organisation of Islamic Cooperation in response to a series of acts expressing hatred toward the Quran in Sweden and elsewhere. There was no unanimity regarding this resolution, as a number of Western countries regarded it as potentially restricting the exercise of the right to freedom of expression. The main difference between the West and the East in their outlook toward free speech and respect for religious symbols was more than apparent here. As was observed, freedom over honour with regard to religious symbols prevails in the laws of European liberal democracies, whereas honour and religious dictates are most important for religious Muslims (Akyol 2019). It is very likely that this difference is at the heart of the matter which divides the West and the East (Fradkin 2019), and this division is sensible for the religious identity and the manifestation of freedom of conscience questions for those who live in the West. France – with its recent bans on certificates of virginity and Islamic clothing at schools and the subsequent reactions of various groups of people – represents how far this clash could lead in the future. In the West, where the presumption in favour of liberty dominates, both UN resolutions illustrate that the freedom to hold and act according to one's personal conscience remains an urgent issue (Zucca 2012, p. 26).

1.3.2. Freedom of Conscience and Its Development

In the secular age, it is suggested that conscience be seen as an ecumenical value that can appeal both to religious and secular citizens (Laborde 2017, p. 64). Here, conscience is a personal instinct, a form of moral self-awareness concerning what is or would be right and wrong. Such personal commitments and beliefs come from individual minds, and a secular state should recognise this because it is a question of the sovereignty of the person in their choices of conscience (Maclure and Taylor 2010, p. 21). The conscience is an inner obligation which goes beyond any other kind of norm, whether legal, religious or otherwise. It might be added here that conscience is a process of internal examination; a process in which a balance between inner beliefs and external rules is always sought. Two dimensions are evident in this search, namely: immunity from any enforcement against internal beliefs and values; and the power of self-determination in terms of the right to conscientious objection against any external force. Through conscientious objection, individuals protect their freedom to live according to the orders of their own conscience. However, the approach which suggests that freedom of conscience is equal to conscientious objection is too narrow, and does not enable the full concept of freedom of conscience to be revealed. Conscientious objection makes a person's conscience open and public in the sense that one can dissent from what secular law expects them to do as an obligation. Freedom of conscience is broader than conscientious objection. Thus, both dimensions represent the essence of what individual conscience and personal sovereignty entail.

In liberal societies, personal sovereignty signifies that respect for people includes respect for personal autonomy. Kantian reasoning serves as a conception of moral autonomy, which represents the capacity to deliberate and give oneself a moral law rather than blindly following the injunctions of others, whereas personal autonomy is the capacity to decide and pursue a course of actions in one's life. Here, moral judgments are entitled to respect regardless of whether they are right or wrong, as long as they are central to the self-image and self-respect of the person (Macklem 2006, p. 81). Personal sovereignty in the secular age also means the freedom to hold and express one's core beliefs. In an age in which religion is just one way of seeking good, people are regarded as having the moral capacity to control their own lives under individually chosen belief systems (Tebbe 2021, p. 275). Core moral beliefs and commitments, which are sometimes called 'convictions of conscience', constitute the moral identities of individuals (Maclure and Taylor 2010, p. 13). Moral beliefs and commitments composing one's moral identity are at the heart of the notion of individual conscience. Conscientious duties are particularly weighty demands that constitute and maintain the integrity of individuals as moral persons (Laborde 2017, p. 61). Equal freedom of conscience, as noted by John Rawls, is the only principle that individuals in the original position (the state of nature, to phrase it differently) can acknowledge (1971, pp. 206–207).

Personal freedom, including freedom of conscience, has received its fullest expression in Western societies (Gregg 2019, p. 7). However, if the development of freedom of conscience through the ages is considered, it has undergone many different stages, and there have been many occasions of being misled by false interpretations given by different actors. Freedom of conscience has been a target, and it has been attacked using various instruments including secular laws, religious dictates, heavy guns, propaganda or surveillance technologies. From the time of Socrates to the present war of aggression against Ukraine, it seems that a hostile stance against freedom of conscience has always been part of human history. Conscience under control has always been a sought-after result achieved by implementing a long-term strategy. The entire history of society might be described through the stages that freedom of conscience as a human right has undergone in the face of authority, whether religious or secular, democratic or authoritarian.

Neither the church nor the secular state is totally neutral, and both tend to promote a particular conception of good life in accordance with substantively religious or secular standards (Laborde 2011, p. 104). Immanuel Kant once observed that churches and states alike tend to violate the right to freedom of conscience by rewarding or punishing the expression of beliefs and convictions, as well as by prohibiting or interfering with the critical examination of the beliefs they seek to impose (Wood 2020, p. 199). In the context of the war of aggression against Ukraine, these Kantian words become very relevant when considering the behaviour of Russia towards the mind and conscience of the Russian people – especially toward those who oppose the prevailing ideology and the very idea of the war being waged by Russia. Indeed, religion or state ideology have always had a strong influence on beliefs, and have certainly penalised thoughts and beliefs that did not fit the prevailing world view. For instance, scientific belief or philosophical exploration that challenged established religious thinking could lead to a death sentence in Renaissance Europe (Alegre 2023, p. 30). Russian state ideology, with its message denying the existence of the Ukrainian state and of Ukrainians as a nation, has influenced thousands of Russians by transforming their personal thoughts and collective way of thinking with regard to Ukraine, and those who do not agree with the prevailing ideological message are prosecuted under the letter of the law. Collective conscience might always have a crushing effect on individual freedom. Moreover, even in this secular age the expression of individual beliefs might lead to one being stabbed before a lecture in New York – as was the case with Salman Rushdie in 2022.

It is also important to highlight another idea discussed in this secular age. Although we might see it as a paradox that religious freedom still plays a special role in the legislation and case law, scholars add that, in a liberal democracy, the secular law of religious freedom in general concentrates all attention not to belief as a state of mind, but rather to belief as an activity in the world (Asad 1993, p. 10). More precisely, if religion is in essence a state of mind, it should thus be located in the area of private life, whereas religious activities in public are to be supervised with a close eye based on secular law. Why is this the case? As a result of the concept of religion formulated in the Western secular mind, the concept of religion seems to be biased against non-Protestant religion (Asad 1993, p. 10). This argument suggests that secular modernity in Europe is protestant in its deepest sense (Laborde 2017, p. 22). The secular mode of governance and legislation relies on binary oppositions between divine and civil obligations, between belief and reason, between thought and action, and between mind and body. Thus, as Protestantism rejected Catholic ritualism, true religion according to modern secularism is located on the first side of each opposition mentioned above. In such modern reading, religion is private, individual, and textual. The issue of Islamic veiling, for instance, proves to be an exemplary case of the inevitable conflict between modern Europe based on secular law and those who live in Europe but have a different religious conscience based on the Islamic faith, which has no protestant history.

1.3.3. Freedom of Conscience and Its Relation to Freedom of Thought and Freedom of Religion

Freedoms of thought, religion and conscience are fundamental inner freedoms that allow scientific progress, artistic inspiration, emotional fulfilment, political engagement and spiritual enlightenment – and, as correctly observed, without these freedoms, democracy is meaningless (Alegre 2023, p. 5). Usually, freedom of conscience is enshrined in law alongside clauses relating to freedom of thought and freedom of religion. Commonly, all three are treated together as the right to freedom of thought, conscience and religion. Indeed, freedom of thought and freedom of religion have a very close link in their content to freedom of conscience. However, if we follow the principles of law, each legal term – although they correspond to one another and might even be used interchangeably – always has its own authentic meaning and content. Some authors claim that freedom of thought and conscience should be treated as purely internal human rights, whereas the focus of religious freedom is on the free exercise of religious beliefs (Lindkvist 2017, p. 6). Other authors hold that what makes all three more than similar is the architecture of their freedoms; namely, the similarity in the distinction between unrestricted *forum internum* and the right to external manifestation (Taylor 2005, p. 19). Therefore, it is obvious that freedom of conscience, thought and religion are interrelated, and they all have inevitably unique meanings.

Despite this, freedom of conscience is commonly perceived to be analogous to religious freedom, or is sometimes confused with the other fundamental freedoms, including freedom of expression. For instance, in one of its judgments the Constitutional Court of Romania stressed that 'freedom of conscience presupposes the possibility of individuals to possess and publicly express an outlook about the outside world' (Brodeala and Epure 2021, p. 739). There is no doubt that thoughts, beliefs and commitments find their meaning in acts of expression. Acts of expression are representative, for they consist in presenting to the world what already exists in a mind full of beliefs and commitments. It is true that in order to flourish, freedom of conscience depends on such freedoms as freedom of expression and privacy; however, freedom of conscience differs in a number of aspects from all other freedoms. Nonetheless, it is necessary to return to the question of the tradition of equating freedom of conscience and religious freedom. Timothy Macklem provides an illustrative way in which to capture the essence of the relationship between the domains of freedom of conscience and freedom of religion. Regarding conscientious objection, the examples of military service and medical treatment are common in case law. Take the example of a doctor, cleric, teacher or lawyer who is called on to provide services as part of a public regime in a way that offends their conscience. Macklem argues that only in some of these cases is conscience married to religious conviction: 'in nearly all it is political community has called upon him to do; in every case it is principled and autonomous matter of following the dictates of one's own reasoning rather than the dictates of others' (2006, p. 68). Such a line of thinking reveals the essence of freedom of conscience and its link to religion in a secular age.

Ronald Dworkin suggested that freedom of conscience be redefined from the conventional Western right to religious liberty into the general right to ethical independence (2013, p. 132). There have been many more efforts to define it; however, the paradox of the secular age lies in the fact that although it is characterised by pluralism of beliefs, values, and commitments, special status is still given to religious freedom by presenting it as a liberal right.

1.3.4. The Right to Freedom of Conscience and Legal Regulation

The right to freedom of conscience is enshrined in the main relevant international and national legal acts. It was suggested that the right to freedom of conscience be named as a sacred right by the framers of the UDHR. The final text of the UDHR stipulates that all people are free and equal in dignity and human rights, and that all people 'are endowed with reason and conscience'. These words were to mean that reason and conscience are defining features of the human person, and are protected by international human rights law (Alegre 2023, p. 20). Furthermore, the text of Declaration explicitly mentions the right to freedom of thought, conscience, and religion (Art. 18). Since the Declaration was adopted, according to L. Lindkvist, this article has come to shape the understanding of what it means to speak of religious freedom as a human right (2017, p. 4).

Clauses concerning religious freedom and freedom of conscience might also be found in other significant international human rights treaties, including the International Covenant on Civil and Political Rights of 1966, the UN Declaration on the Elimination of All Forms of Intolerance and of Discrimination Based on Religion or Belief of 1981, and the UN Convention on the Rights of the Child of 1989. The EU Charter also guarantees the right to freedom of thought, conscience and religion (Art. 10). One exceptional aspect of the EU Charter is that, in the second paragraph of Article 10, it recognises the right to conscientious objection. The African Charter on Human and People's Rights notes in Article 8 that freedom of conscience, profession and the free practice of religion is guaranteed. The Universal Islamic Declaration of Human Rights mentions the right to freedom of belief, thought and speech in Article 12. Interestingly, the latter

Declaration adds Article 13, which concerns the right to freedom of religion. It is also necessary to add that freedom of conscience receives some protection by those articles of international treaties that are devoted to freedom of expression, freedom of speech, freedom to private life and so on. However, it is necessary to emphasise that is it is wrong to think that freedom of conscience is adequately protected by these human rights instruments. Even Kant urged that it is a mistake to think that freedom of conscience is adequately protected by freedom of speech or any other right (Wood 2020, p. 199).

The ECHR, adopted in 1950, also incorporates the right to freedom of thought, conscience, and religion (Art. 9). It is important here to emphasise the second paragraph of Article 9, which lays the basis for the justification of limitations on religious freedom. This paragraph speaks about limitations on manifestations of religion or belief, but not on holding these beliefs as such. However, the protection of religious practice implies that the right to hold religious beliefs is implicit in the text of Article 9. Four grounds for limitations are listed in this paragraph, and the list cannot be interpreted in an expansive manner. These grounds are: public safety, the protection of public order, health or morals, and the protection of the rights and freedoms of others. All four notions of limitations lend themselves to a diversity of interpretations. We have plenty of descriptions of what morals or public safety entail, and the same applies to the notions contained in Article 9 – namely, thought, conscience, and religion. The definitions of these concepts, as was mentioned before, are interconnected and differ in content. In order to learn more about the content of the right to freedom of conscience, there is a need to turn to the interpretation formulated by the ECtHR.

1.3.5. Case Law on the Right to Freedom of Conscience

The ECtHR has delivered a considerable number of judgments on Article 9 of the ECHR. The majority of them examine freedom of religion questions, and a small portion of cases discuss the freedom to hold, and to act according to, secular beliefs and commitments. Article 9 of the ECHR contains two strands, namely, to hold and to manifest one's religious and secular belief. In several judgments, the ECtHR noted that Article 9 contains religious as well as secular dimensions; thus, the scope of Article 9 is very wide as it protects both religious and non-religious convictions. If a conviction is to benefit from the right enshrined in Article 9, it must attain, as stated by the ECtHR in *Eweida and Others v. UK*, a certain level of cogency, seriousness, cohesion and importance. For instance, regarding compulsory vaccination cases, the ECtHR in *Vavricka and others v. the Czech Republic* held that the critical opinion of the applicants on vaccination needs always to be tested against the notion of whether a conviction or belief is sufficient in cogency, seriousness, cohesion and importance. It is important to add that the ECtHR pointed out that if the parents (applicants) relied on Article 9 of the ECHR without mentioning any religious reasons for their positions on vaccination, it was not their freedom of religion that was potentially at stake but their freedom of thought and conscience.

The ECtHR has the right to analyse the sincerity of one's belief – namely, as stated in *Skugar and others v. Russia*, the Court has the right to make factual findings as to whether an applicant's religious or secular claims are sincerely held and genuine. The Court has refused to grant the protection of Article 9 to various applicants because of a lack of sincerity regarding their religious or secular convictions. For instance, a father's wish to inflict corporal punishment on his child (Abrahamsson v. Sweden); an applicant's wish, motivated by his Christian belief, to hand out tracts against abortion near an abortion clinic (Van Den Dungen v. Netherlands); the refusal of a driver to fasten his seatbelt while driving a motor car in order to express the view that he should be allowed to choose his own means of protection (Viel v. France); an applicant's wish to walk naked in public on the basis that such behaviour was socially acceptable (Gough v. UK) – all have been refused protection under Article 9.

In a number of judgments, the ECtHR has acknowledged that the safeguards of Article 9 apply to: (i) the 'major' and 'ancient' world religions which have existed for millennia or for several centuries (Jakobski v. Poland; Layla Sahin v. Turkey; X v. UK); (ii) new and relatively new religious or spiritual practices (Mockute v. Lithuania; Boychev and others v. Bulgaria; Romuva v. Lithuania; A. O. Falun Dafa and others v. Moldova); and (iii) various coherent and sincerely held philosophical convictions, such as pacifism (Arrowsmith v. UK), principled opposition to military service (Bayatyan v. Armenia), veganism and opposition to the manipulation of products of animal origin or that are tested on animals (W. v. UK), opposition to abortion (Knudsen v. Norway; Van Schijndel and others v. Netherlands), a doctor's opinions on alternative medicine (Nyyssonen v. Finland), the conviction that marriage is a lifelong union between a man and a woman and the rejection of homosexual unions (Eweida and others v. UK), and attachment to secularism (Lautsi and others v. Italy; Hamidovic v. Bosnia and Herzegovina). All of these secular beliefs and convictions receive the protection of Article 9 regardless of whether they are recognised by the state or not (Mockute v. Lithuania). The Court has made it clear that the right enshrined in Article 9 of the ECHR applies to atheists, agnostics, sceptics and the unconcerned (Kokkinakis v. Greece).

The case law of the ECtHR is not only diverse, but is also constantly developing. The principle of living together revealed by the Court is something that is frequently added to the fully fledged method used by the Court in various cases which usually relate to freedom of conscience. *European consensus* is the method which has been applied by the ECtHR in cases of a sensitive nature, such as those concerning abortion, euthanasia, marriage, sexual relationships and so on. According to some observers, this method poses a threat to the content and limits of freedom of conscience, which is unique in all European countries (O'Hara 2021, p. 93). If one looks into the case law of the ECtHR, the first case that comes to mind is *Otto Preminger Institute v. Austria*, where the Court spoke of a uniform position on the particular question among European countries. The Court had to decide in this case whether a state sanction preventing the screening of a film was in breach of the ECHR, and whether the sanction was justified in the name of the protection of religious feelings. The Court decided that the sanction was justified because the film risked provoking a strong reaction from the Christian community which prevails in Austria. Here, religion received a different treatment, as in this case Austria, a secular state, could barely cope with diversity, let alone safeguard the right to the freedom to hold one's beliefs and express them publicly. According to the Court, the absence of a uniform European position on the significance of religion in society meant that the state was entitled to a certain margin of appreciation in assessing the necessity of imposing a restriction in order to avoid offending religious beliefs.

The notion of European consensus means much more than the idea and practice of settling political conflicts by negotiation and agreement. The effect of the language of consensus can be seen, for example, in the Court's finding in the case of *Stübing v. Germany*. According to the Court's central line of argument, there existed 'a broad consensus that sexual relationships between siblings are neither accepted by the legal order nor by society as a whole'. While in that case the Court provided a picture of Member States' different legal positions on incest, demonstrating that there was in fact no complete agreement on the matter, its references to a 'broad consensus' and 'society as a whole' imply at least some European commonality. It might be said that European consensus as a method of legal interpretation has played a role in shaping the identity and directions of Europe on a particular set of questions.

1.3.6. Freedom of Conscience in the Context of Russia's War of Aggression Against Ukraine

This section seeks to explore whether and to what extent freedom of conscience might turn into the object of war. It seems that the long-term purpose of war for the country which wages it, first of all, is to cause a considerable shift in the collective conscience of a society or particular groups of people. The result of targeting socially significant norms of life, traditions, and the prevailing social set of beliefs and personal convictions could be totally different than if a country were to concentrate their attention on destroying infrastructure and trying to change a government. The Union of Soviet Socialist Republics (hereafter – USSR, Soviet Union) had the aim of changing the religious and other personal convictions of people in Eastern European states by means of law and violence. Trying to reflect how conscience was treated in Soviet times, Aleksandr Solzhenicyn once said that people in the Soviet Union were arrested and prosecuted not so much for the expression of personal beliefs, but rather for holding personal beliefs and convictions altogether (2009, p. 55). Losing the capacity to hold and express one's personal beliefs, and thus to make moral choices, means losing elements of personal identity (Alegre 2023, p. 92). Article 58 of the Criminal Code (hereafter – the CC) of the Soviet Union, which contained a vague description of fourteen crimes and related punishments, was the instrument which permitted the negation of personal identity, the human autonomy sphere, and freedom, including freedom of conscience, for thousands of people. Based on Article 58, 10 years in prison was prescribed as the punishment for the religious teaching of one's own children. However, as Solzhenicyn added, if a person agreed to abandon or change their religion into the prevailing ideology in the courtroom, they were able to safeguard their right to raise their children (2009, p. 56). In both ways, freedom of conscience was totally denied by the regime. This is just one example of what it means to wage war against freedom of conscience in order to fundamentally transform a system of values.

Today, Russia seeks to change the core principles and collective conscience of Ukrainian society. In his reaction to the Russian war of aggression against Ukraine and the lack of action on the part of some Western countries, President Volodymyr Zelensky stressed that Ukraine should not be expected to compromise its conscience, sovereignty, territory, or independence. A country's independence, sovereignty and territory are usually seen as targets of war. However, the collective conscience, which rises from thousands of individual consciences, needs to be treated as yet another strategic objective of this war. A war against freedom, including freedom of conscience, has been waged by Russia in Ukraine while trying to instil a particular ideology which is hostile to the idea of Ukraine as a sovereign state and the Ukrainian people as nation. One of the ways in which the aggressor has sought to achieve this is the deportation of children. From the beginning of the war against Ukraine, the tendency to deport Ukraine's children to Russian lands has been on the rise. Mounting evidence shows that Russia uses the forcible relocation and re-education of Ukraine's children in so-called 'summer camps' as key components of its systematic efforts to suppress Ukraine's identity, history, and the very freedom of conscience of its individuals. In addition, the regime in Russia has permitted fast-tracked Russian citizenship for children from Ukraine, facilitating the fostering of Ukrainian minors by Russian families and paving the way for permanent adoption in a country where the adoption of foreign nationals is not allowed by law. It is obvious that in its war against Ukrainian children, Russia seeks to fundamentally transform their collective way of thinking and to erase Ukrainian identity as such.

The conscience of people in Russia has also been profoundly transformed throughout the regime of President Putin. According to Vladimir Kara-Murza, Russia's regress under Putin has taken on a dramatic pace, to the extent that it has much more in common with the handling of 'enemies of the people' under Joseph Stalin than of dissidents under Leonid Brezhnev. Such a comparison leads to the analysis of certain legal documents. The results of comparative analysis might speak for themselves. For instance, the text of the CC of Stalin's time, particularly Article 58 thereof, has much in common with the current legal norms of the CC of Russia. This resemblance is evident in the general and vague terminology of the legal norms, which provides vast room for manoeuvre when applying them. For Kara Murza, repression and fear are the only ways that the Kremlin is able to keep significant anti-war sentiments in Russian society from translating into open protests. Today, those who oppose the war in Ukraine experience harsh punishment. The very aim of the regime is to instil fear in Russian society and to paralyse any will to challenge it. Kant believed that the use of punishment to influence belief is ineffective or even counterproductive, as motives of hope and fear can influence a person's freedom of conscience only by violating the person's inalienable right to form convictions that are free from such wrongful influences (Wood 2020, p. 199). Indeed, Russians of different backgrounds and vocations have refused to become silent accomplices to the war, even at the cost of personal freedom. This chapter takes a closer look at how, by legal means, Russia has waged a war – both against the freedom to hold personal anti-war beliefs and to act accordingly, and against its own citizens.

To first return to the comparative analysis between legal norms in the CC of Stalin's time and those of Putin's Russia, the country has recently enacted two laws by which it criminalised war reporting, protesting the war, and expressing or even holding any personal beliefs or convictions regarding the war of aggression in Ukraine, Russian state authority and the army. The aim was to suppress all dissent and deny access to any information that contradicts the official Russian narrative. Article 207 (3) (disseminating false information about the actions of the armed forces) was introduced into the Russian CC on 4 March 2022, 10 days after the invasion of Ukraine. On the same day, the Code of Administrative Offences was changed by adding Article 20(3) on discrediting the armed forces. According to Article 207(3) of the CC, public dissemination under the guise of reliable statements of knowingly false information containing data on the use of the Russian armed forces or the exercise by Russian state bodies of their powers outside the territory of Russia for the purposes of protecting the interests of Russia and its citizens, maintaining international peace and security now came to be treated illegal 'Knowingly false information' implies everything that does not come from Russian official sources. Another question is the meaning of the words 'public dissemination' or 'under the guise of reliable information'. What is 'public' is also decided by the authority and, as practice shows, it is possible to receive a fine or imprisonment for 'liking' something on social media or for statements made in private WhatsApp or Viber messages. According to lawyers working in independent media and human rights defence groups, the severity of punishment in modern Russia varies greatly depending on the qualification of each case, the principles of which are often unclear – for almost identical actions, one can receive sentences ranging from 4 months to 19 years. From 24 February 2022 to 27 August 2023, 19,794 arrests are known to have been made in Russia. More than 7,200 people were fined administratively for discreditation and were prosecuted under criminal law. Punishments for spreading knowingly false information range from fines to imprisonment. The dissemination of false information, which results in grave consequences, can lead to imprisonment for up to 19 years. Again, what 'grave consequences' could mean is left to the courts to explain, and Russian courts have broad discretion for interpretation. A further article in the CC speaks of the discreditation of the state authority and the army (Art. 280 (3)). Simply put, this criminalises criticism of the use of the Russian military or the activities of state authorities operating abroad. Article 284 (2) is also important, as it criminalises pleas for the adoption of measures that introduce or prolong sanctions against Russia or its citizens or legal entities.

The abovementioned articles of the CC and the Code of Administrative offences constitute a single system of freedom of conscience restrictions. All of these articles are connected to the beginning of Russia's military aggression against Ukraine. Retaining the power of authority holders and changing the nature of public conscience and its expression could be seen as the most significant aims of the abovementioned legal norms. The CC penalises the public dissemination of deliberately false information regarding the use of the Russian Armed Forces, with punishments ranging from large fines to imprisonment for up to 3 years. Those who allegedly disseminate such information using their official position, or as part of an organised group, or when accompanied by the fabrication of evidence, or when guided by greed, or when motivated by political, ideological, racial, ethnic or religious hatred or hatred against a social group, could face 5–10 years in prison. In the event of grave consequences, the punishment might reach up to 15 years, with a ban on carrying out a profession or certain activities for up to 5 years. Public calls, for instance, for the armed forces to be withdrawn or to stop the war are illegal according to such legal regulation. These legal norms contradict Article 29 of the Russian Constitution and Russia's international obligations, including Article 18 and 19 of the International Covenant on Civil and Political Rights (hereafter – ICCPR); moreover, they contravene the basic principles of law. Any restrictions on fundamental human rights cannot be justified by military censorship. According to the Russian Constitutional Act on Martial Law, under martial law, the law does not impose special restrictions on freedom of speech, opinion, or conscience. It is important to emphasise that there are no legal grounds for such restrictions when martial law is not imposed. The urgent introduction of new legal norms, the rhetoric of officials and the context of their application make the legal norms even more questionable. By making only one source of information truthful – namely, the official channel – and by prohibiting the use of the word 'war' to describe the war, Russian authorities not only restrict freedom of speech, but also wage a war against the freedom to hold, express and act according to one's personal beliefs. Simply speaking, a war against the personal autonomy of Russian citizens is being waged.

A law that defines a crime in vague terms is likely to raise due-process problems. Such laws, first of all, contradict the legal principle of *nulla crimen sine lege* (no crime without law). Laws of vague quality were found in the norms of the Soviet CC, especially the aforementioned Article 58, which was mostly concerned with questions of the conscience of people under the Soviet regime. Two passages from Article 58 should be quoted here in order to illustrate the similarity in the text and its content between Soviet law under Stalin and modern Russian legislation under Putin's regime. Article 58 (10) states: 'Propaganda or agitation containing an appeal to overthrow, undermine or weaken the Soviet authority or to commit individual counter-revolutionary crimes, or dissemination, preparation or possession of literature containing such matter, entails deprivation of liberty for a period of not less than 6 months'. There is a clear resemblance between the vague text and content of the present-day legal norm on the dissemination of information on the state authority or the army and said Article of the Soviet CC. In addition, Article 58 (12) of the Soviet CC stated that 'any omission, by any person having certain knowledge of the matter, to report any counter-revolutionary crime, which is in preparation or has been committed, entails deprivation of liberty for a period of not less than 6 months'. This legal norm, according to Solzhenicyn, affected everyone in the former Soviet Union, and if a person knew of and did not report a violation then it was treated as if they had committed it themselves (2009, p. 81). There was no maximum punishment provided in these two parts of Article 58. Such legal text created a status quo which was described by Solzhenicyn as follows: 'where there is a law, there is a crime' (2009, p. 83). It is very likely that the only thing which separates the criminal law policy of Stalin from that of Putin is that under the authority of the latter, punishments still have an upper limit, at least in the text. However, the remainder of the text bears a striking resemblance. The application of these laws continues steadily, with 182 people persecuted under Article 207 (3) (fakes) and 97 under Article 280(3) (discreditation). The latter number has grown steadily since the beginning of 2023, as more and more people have been fined administratively for discreditation (more than 7,200 as of September 2023) and have been subject to persecution. Sentences under these articles have also changed towards becoming harsher. It is possible to receive a fine simply for 'liking' something on social media, or for statements made in private WhatsApp or Viber messages.

Of course, the right to freedom of conscience is not an absolute right like the majority of other human rights, and it may be restricted under three conditions: the restriction should be provided by law; it should pursue a legitimate aim; and it should be necessary and proportionate to achieve that aim. All of the abovementioned new legal norms are directed towards freedom of conscience, freedom of expression, freedom of speech and so on. In other words, they touch on all of the main aspects of core human freedom. All of these restrictions fail all three parts of the justifiability test. Although these restrictions are written in the letter of law, these laws do not satisfy the qualitative criterion of foreseeability as they are too vague. They are, in fact, so vague that people cannot foresee what kind of speech or text might be regarded as an act against the law. Take, for instance, the words 'grave consequences' from Article 207(3), which, according to this legal norm, might lead to 15 years of imprisonment. It seems that any belief or opinion regarding the army or the state and its oral or written expression might be regarded as unlawful and, thus, punishable harshly because it could create grave consequences. These laws are for suppressing any form of pluralism, dissent, public protest or critical thought. In other words, it is against freedom to think freely and to have personal beliefs and commitments. In this regard, in the case of *Navalny v. Russia*, the ECtHR has already noted that the restrictions stated by these laws were implemented with the aim of suppressing any kind of pluralism and freedom of thought and conscience. These laws are neither necessary nor proportionate, and were issued a little more than a week after the onset of armed aggression against Ukraine. Their restrictions are so general and vague that a person might be imprisoned for wearing a peace sign, quoting the Bible, saying that the armed forces are unprofessional, or even singing the song 'give peace a chance'. Therefore, they have no ground against all three of the abovementioned criteria, and these restrictions grounded in law are unlawful and of a repressive nature. If we take a closer look at Article 58 of the former Soviet CC, all 14 of its passages were considerably vague and general, and remind us well that legal history might be repeated.

By applying all of the aforementioned legal norms, the courts of Russia came to be guardians of the war. In order to illustrate this point, the case of Alexey Gorinov can be analysed. Mr. Gorinov, a deputy of the Council of Deputies of the Krsnoselsky Municipal District, suggested, instead of praising 'the special operation' in Ukraine, that an exhibition of Ukrainian children's paintings be made. Later, Gorinov expressed his views against the war in Ukraine by making these statements public on social media. According to the court, the defendant, using his official position as a deputy and motivated by political hatred, committed public dissemination, and this charge was laid under the guise of reliable reports of deliberately false information containing data on the use of the Armed Forces of the Russian Federation in order to protect the interests of the Russian Federation and its citizens and maintain international peace and security. The court found Gorinov guilty in committing a crime provided for in Article 207 (3) of the CC. The defendant stated that he expressed his personal opinions and beliefs, which he independently concluded, and he did not intend to spread deliberately false information about the actions of the Armed Forces of the Russian Federation in the territory of Ukraine. The court, however, had no doubt that Gorinov acted with direct intent, because, quoting the court of the Russian Federation, 'the defendant was aware of the public danger of his actions, foresaw the inevitability of socially dangerous consequences and desired their onset and guided by the motive of political hatred expressed in a dismissive, unfriendly, aggressive attitude towards the current executive and legislative authorities of the Russian Federation deliberately misled a limited circle of people about the legality of the actions of the Armed Forces of the Russian Federation during a special military operation, creating the appearance of illegal activity violating international legislation of both the Armed Forces of the Russian Federation individually and the state authorities of the Russian Federation as a whole, which led to the undermining of the authority and discrediting of the Armed Forces of the Russian Federation in society, and caused citizens who have seen the above video a sense of anxiety, fear, anxiety and insecurity on the part of the state'.

The court in Gorinov's judgment considered it necessary to note that Article 10 of the ECHR, along with the proclamation of the right of everyone to freely express their opinion, proceeds from the fact that the exercise of such freedom imposes duties and responsibilities and may be associated with certain formalities, conditions, restrictions or sanctions that are provided for in the law and are necessary in a democratic society in order to protect health and morals. The proclaimed right to freely adhere to one's beliefs and the right to freedom of expression, including freedom to seek, receive and disseminate all kinds of information and ideas by any means and regardless of State borders, simultaneously corresponded, as stated by the court in the judgment against Gorinov, 'to the standards enshrined in international legal acts establishing that the exercise of these rights and freedoms may be restricted, in particular, in the interests of security or public order, the prevention of riots or crimes (Art. 18, 19 and 29 (2) of the UDHR, Art. 19 of the ICCPR, Art. 9 and 10 of the ECHR)'.

Freedom in general and freedom of conscience in particular came to be an object of Russia's war against the Ukrainian people and against those Russians who oppose the war. Similarities between the law of Stalin's time and that of the current day are evident. The method of translating the law into an instrument in the war against freedom of conscience is also apparent. It seems that the only difference in this war against freedom is that today there is still an upper limit on the punishments written in the codes. As correctly observed, questioning is good for freedom of conscience, freedom of opinion and its expression, but deep mistrust can be as corrosive for freedom as blind faith (Alegre 2023, p. 86).

1.3.7. Interim findings

Conscience is a person's belief about what is right and what is evil, and freedom of conscience, which is at the heart of human autonomy and identity, is the core human right in a democracy. However, restriction, prosecution and oppression, or a war against freedom of conscience, has been part of human history for aeons. Indeed, freedom of conscience as a human right has received its fullest expression in Western societies; however, the contemporary western approach that freedom of conscience is equal to conscientious objection is too narrow, and does not enable the full concept of freedom of conscience to be revealed. Conscientious objection makes a person's conscience open and public in the sense that one is dissenting from what secular law expects them to do as an obligation. Thus, freedom of conscience is broader than conscientious objection.

Although freedom of conscience is enshrined in contemporary law alongside clauses relating to freedom of thought and freedom of religion, freedom of conscience is interrelated with these two other legal concepts, yet inevitably they each have unique meanings and content. Conscience is a more universal part of human nature than religion; thus, conscience cannot be limited to or mixed with religious conscience. The very basis for religious freedom in the secular age is the idea of the liberty of conscience. The amount case law of the ECtHR regarding Article 9 cases has been and continues to be on the increase. Cases in which secular beliefs come to be under protection via the application of Article 9 imply that freedom of conscience receives a greater amount of attention.

One long-term purpose of a war waged by one country against another is the creation of a considerable shift in the collective conscience of a society or of particular groups of people. A war against freedom, including freedom of conscience, has been waged by Russia against Ukraine by trying to instil a particular ideology which is hostile to both the idea of Ukraine as a sovereign state and the Ukrainian people as a society. Moreover, the freedom of conscience of people in Russia has also been profoundly transformed throughout the regime of president Putin. Today, those who oppose the war in Ukraine experience harsh punishments enshrined in the newest amendments to the CC, which was issued ten days after the invasion of Ukraine. The very aim of the Kremlin regime, via the means of new legislation, is to instil fear in Russian society and to paralyse its will to challenge the regime.

By adopting new criminal and administrative laws, Russia has criminalised war reporting, protesting the war, and expressing or even holding any personal beliefs or convictions regarding the war in Ukraine, the Russian state authority or the army. A resemblance between the new criminal norms in Russia and the CC of Stalin is evident in the general and vague terminology of both sets of legal norms, which provide vast room for manoeuvre when applying them. It is very likely that the only thing which separates the criminal laws of Stalin and Putin is that under the authority of the latter, punishments still have upper limits, at least in the text. However, all other aspects of their texts bear an uncanny resemblance to one another.

1.4. Perspectives on Ukrainian Constitutional Aspirations Regarding European Identity After the War of aggression

1.4.1. The 2019 Constitutional Amendments Introducing Ukraine's European Identity

Recent geopolitical history can be split into two periods: pre- and post-24 February 2022. On that day, the largest ground war in Europe since World War II was launched by the Russian Federation against the independent and sovereign state of Ukraine. Officially, Russia claimed that its citizens residing in Ukraine's territory were in need of protection and defence, and that Ukraine, having expressed its will to join the EU and NATO, presented a threat to Russia's national security. These claims were unfounded and false. Nevertheless, they led to military aggression that has already lasted more than more than two years, without any clearly defined solution that might bring peace to the country.

Russia's recurring fear of losing a zone of influence that it had long held were fulfilled when, on 7 February 2019, the Verkhovna Rada (the Ukrainian Parliament) amended the Constitution of Ukraine and *expressis verbis* confirmed 'the European identity of the Ukrainian people and the irreversibility of the European and Euro-Atlantic course of Ukraine' (Constitution, preamble). After military actions were launched in Ukraine, one of the aggressor's immediate requirements in order to cease hostilities were that the Constitution of Ukraine be reverted, enshrining its neutrality (Belton 2022). Russia insisted that Ukraine give up its goal of joining NATO and the EU. Such rhetoric permits the consideration that the constitutional amendments of 2019 might have been the spark that ignited this military conflict, which for a number of years was smouldering in the East of Ukraine.[6] Of course, in reality this is only one of many unsuccessful attempts to find a justification for unjustifiable actions.

1.4.1.1. The Construction of Ukraine's Identity and Its Determination Towards Western Europe

Ukraine's aspirations for European identity were vivid long before these amendments were made. Although Russia, as its closest neighbour in terms of language, culture and religion, has always been an important actor in the making of the Ukrainian nation (Dragneva and Wolczuk 2015), Europe and Europeanness, as an alternative supranational identity to the Eurasian and Slavic identities, has also played an integral role in the construction of Ukraine's identity (Shulman 2004).

Since the moment at which Ukraine proclaimed its independence from the Soviet Union in 1991, the country has striven to transform itself into a democratic and independent state. This was easier said than done. However, almost at once the EU saw the potential to plant democratic ideas on the eastern border of the union. Although the path to the west has not always been smooth and

6 In February and March 2014, Russia invaded Crimea, and after a sham referendum annexed it to the Russian Federation with the approval of the Constitutional Court of Russia. Concerning the role of the Russian Constitutional Court, see: Leonaite and Zalimas 2015.

straight, the EU has, largely, always been there for Ukraine: it has tried to involve Ukraine in the regional and global trading system; it has spread the ideas of human rights protection, democratic governance, and anti-corruption efforts; and it has fostered the national capacity for Ukraine to chart its own political future and foreign policy directions free from external interference. Ukraine, in its turn, has had ups and downs in its relationship with the EU, having had pro-European and pro-Russian leaders and having had to solve the dilemmas of the compatibility of supranational institutions adopting binding decisions with the national legal system of Ukraine (Moskalenko and Streltsov 2015).

The Orange Revolution in 2004, the Euromaidan in 2013, and the occupation of Crimea in 2014 were critical junctures that helped Ukrainians to finally determine the direction in which they were seeking to go and to abandon the construction of Ukrainian identity as inherently Eastern Slavic. This concept, where Russia is considered as the 'elder brother', is promoted by so-called Russophiles obsessed with the construction of a Russia-centric community. These historical moments, which can be considered 'big bang' events, contributed to the profound transformation of deeply held beliefs and convictions (Risse 2010, p. 2) which can no longer provide valid grounds for problem solving. The deep crises which occurred in the state always created windows of opportunity in which changes in identity could be introduced (Marcussen *et al.* 1999). Therefore, while before the Russian-Ukrainian conflict it was possible to identify three meta-narratives within the Ukrainian national identity – Ukraine as part of Europe, Ukraine as part of the Eastern Slavic tradition, and Ukraine as a nation of two ethnic groups sharing the features of Russia and Europe and seeking Western integration with Russia (Minesashvili 2022, p. 4) – Russia's actions and its expansion of hostilities since 2014 have turned Ukraine to the West, leading it to seek to cement this relationship by obtaining EU candidate status. The case of Ukraine shows that the successful democratic transition of Eastern European countries needs a geopolitical goal that includes support for a democratic order (Reznik 2022). Since the constitutional amendments of 2019, this is no longer merely a political goal; it is now a constitutional value to foster and implement.

Leaving behind all other claims of identity, the discourse that emphasized Ukraine as an inherent part of European civilization – whether on a racial, cultural or historical basis – justified the country's Europeanness through its mental unity with Europe due to common historical experiences which formed a national character in line with European values. This view has prevailed in Ukraine for the last decade. The EU stood as an example of democracy, the rule of law, and good standards of life. Closer relations with, and eventually membership in, the EU and NATO were not only deemed to represent security, independence and development, but were also seen as the only way to escape Russian dominance (Minesashvili 2022, p. 7). The concepts of security and independence being intertwined with the processes of democratization and reforms (Vieira 2020) required changes in the legislation, preferably at the highest level.

In 2014, when the EU-Ukrainian Association agreement was signed and ratified, the need for the constitutional consolidation of principles governing the interrelations between EU law and the national laws of Member States had already been identified. The specific nature of EU law, being a *sui generis* legal system, could not have been introduced without some constitutional compromises. Looking for closer integration with the west while Russia continued its hostilities in the eastern part of Ukrainian territory, the geopolitical context seemed to be favourable for Ukraine to gather the necessary political will to enshrine these changes in the Constitution. There was no longer a group of political elites that opposed the pro-European choice in the legislative body.

On 7 February 2019, 334 of the 385 deputies registered at the session of the Verkhovna Rada voted to amend the Constitution to outline Ukraine's strategic objectives of joining the EU and NATO (Verkhovna Rada 2019). The overwhelming majority of Ukrainian representatives decided to stop looking back at the Soviet period, instead seeking to bring prosperity and wellbeing to the country, with only 35 voting against this amendment. This characterisation is how EU and NATO membership were represented in society. When looking for the European perspective, it is useful to analyse in more detail the construction of constitutional clauses enabling the Europeanisation of Ukraine and their significance to the Ukrainian legal order, as well as their impact on the activities of state institutions.

1.4.1.2. The Importance of the Amended Preamble of the Ukrainian Constitution

The preambles of constitutions are introductions to the constitutional rules, and usually refer to historical moments of the state as well as to certain constitutional values that frames the entire interpretation of the constitution. Nearly all constitutional preambles assert the sovereignty of the nation (Frosini 2012), and the Ukrainian preamble is no exception. Alongside the expression of the sovereign will of the people, it brings the reader back to the centuries-old history of Ukrainian state-building, provides for the recognition of human rights and freedoms, and affirms the determination to build a democratic state based on the rule of law guided by the Act of Declaration of the Independence of Ukraine, adopted on 24 August 1991 and approved by national vote on 1 December in the same year. The legal significance of preambles is increasingly being recognized, and they are now considered equal to the provisions of the constitution. The vivid debate regarding the formulation of the preamble to the Ukrainian Constitution proves that the Ukrainian Parliament treated the preamble not as a mere introduction to the Constitution which does not have any value, but as a provision which reflects the essence and spirit of the Ukrainian state (Frosini and Lapa 2020a, p. 74). The jurisprudence of the Constitutional Court in recognizing the legal value of the preamble and using it as a tool for interpreting and providing a background in order to explain other constitutional provisions only confirms its importance. Therefore, while examining the 2019 constitutional amendments, it should first be noted that the preamble to the Constitution was amended, introducing the confirmation of 'the European identity of the Ukrainian people and the irreversibility of the European and Euro-Atlantic course of Ukraine'.

Although constitutional amendments are a rather ordinary measure for reflecting changes in the social reality, it is not a very common practice to change the preamble of the Constitution. While amendments to constitutional provisions are made only when they are completely unavoidable, in order to preserve the stability of the Constitution, amendments to the preamble are almost non-existent. This is not without reason. Constitutional preambles are regarded as part of the country's heritage, representing the standing, fundamental values upon which the state and nation are based and serving as a constant background for the interpretation of other constitutional provisions. However, the previously prevailing opinion that the preamble of the Constitution has no legal power has changed with the modern acknowledgement that, in fact, it has the same power as other constitutional provisions, or perhaps even greater power (Orgad 2010) as it is used as a tool for understanding the original sense of the Constitution.

The role of preambles should not be underestimated, and changes to the preamble of the Ukrainian Constitution exemplify its importance (Frosini and Lapa 2020b). Some scholars state that because of the significance of preambles to the interpretation of constitutional provisions, states with unstable political environments, like Ukraine, should be careful with use of the constitutional preamble as a tool to implement their convictions (Frosini and Lapa 2020a, p. 85). There is merit to such statements, and the course chosen by Ukraine might have been different. However, taking into account the content of this particular amendment, one has to concede that the choice of Ukraine's Verkhovna Rada to amend not only the main text of the Constitution, but also its preamble, proves the country's strong determination to following a new direction, both now and in the future.

The opinion of the Grand Chamber of the Constitutional Court regarding the 2019 amendments to the Constitution (which were found to be compatible with the Constitution according to the parameters provided in the Constitution itself) contained several separate opinions. These views underlined the importance of the preamble to the Constitution as the cornerstone of the Ukrainian constitutional order, and claimed that amendments to the preamble of the Constitution enshrining the main constitutional values might only have been made by the people of Ukraine, who are the only source of power in the country (this was the separate opinion of Judge Lytvynov). Other opinions stated that the legislator amending the preamble meddled with the history of Ukraine, and that the amendment of certain articles of the Constitution would have been enough.

Having amended the Constitution of Ukraine starting from its preamble, the Verkhovna Rada consolidated in an act of the highest legal power the new geopolitical orientation of the state of Ukraine, and its new strategic objective of full membership in the EU and NATO. Although this was an incredible geopolitical achievement which marked the end of the consideration of which constitutional identity Ukraine belonged to, it was only the first step, and had to be followed by concrete decisions. Taking that into consideration, the legislator amended not only the preamble, but also a number of constitutional provisions.

1.4.1.3. Amendments to the Text of the Constitution

Alongside the alterations to the preamble, several other constitutional provisions were changed. Namely, the Ukraine's pursuit of a Euro-Atlantic direction was attributed to the competence of all state power institutions of Ukraine, amending the relevant articles providing for the authority of the Verkhovna Rada, the President of Ukraine and the Cabinet of Ministers.

First, Article 85 (5), providing for the competence of the Ukrainian Parliament and stating that the Verkhovna Rada determines the principles of internal and foreign policy, was supplemented. Now, next to the simple determination of the principles of foreign policy, the Verkhovna Rada is *expressis verbis* entrusted with the 'realization of the strategic course of the state on acquiring fully fledged membership of Ukraine in the European Union and in the North Atlantic Treaty Organization'. Thus, the competence of the Ukrainian Parliament was extended to cover the goal of acquiring fully fledged membership in these two international organisations.

Secondly, Article 102, defining the place of the institution of the President in the State of Ukraine, was amended by adding part 3 to the article. Thus the President of Ukraine became a guarantor of the implementation of the strategic course of the state: gaining fully fledged membership in the EU and the NATO. The President also acquired the responsibility to do everything in to their constitutional power to implement this new strategic European and trans-Atlantic goal.

Finally, Article 116, which enumerates the powers of the Government and the Cabinet of Ministers, provides for the implementation of the strategic course of the state: gaining fully fledged membership of Ukraine in the EU and the NATO. Article 116 was supplemented by paragraph 1^1 to provide for this new competence of the Cabinet of Ministers.

The analysis of these Ukrainian constitutional provisions clearly shows that not only was the abstract declaration of the chosen geopolitical orientation of the State of Ukraine enshrined in the preamble of the Constitution, but the legal preconditions necessary in order to implement this Euro-Atlantic course – with its very precise measure of acquiring the fully fledged membership of Ukraine in the EU and NATO – were also created. To achieve this objective, the involvement of all state power institutions is necessary and the constitutional obligation to act effectively towards that goal is imposed onto them. The fact that constitutional provisions concerning the legislative as well as executive body were amended does not mean any repartition of previously acquired powers, but rather stresses the need for both to act together towards the common new direction.

The clauses enabling the Europeanisation of Ukraine signify the receptiveness of the Constitution towards specific international cooperation and this specific form of integration. The country's future membership in the EU and NATO should be considered as a constitutional value, giving guidelines to all internal and external politics. Since those amendments came into force, this is no longer only a matter of politics, but also one of constitutional law.

The chosen course towards the EU and NATO is not only a geographical direction, as it also contains strong values-based content. With the amendments of 2019, the existence of common values with the community of Western democratic states was declared. The 'European identity of the Ukrainian people' is a new term in the constitutional discourse of Ukraine, and means that the Ukrainian nation identifies itself with the Western legal tradition and universal constitutional values and principles. This ensures the harmony and integrity of all constitutional principles, values, and provisions. Secondly, the aspiration of integration into that community was expressed. Thus, the constitutional identity of Ukraine does not leave room for ambiguities as to what future awaits the State, as there are no longer any real or alleged contradictions between the national constitutional values and those that are recognized in the Western community. The short passage supplementing the Constitution of Ukraine regarding European identity and the irreversibility of the Euro-Atlantic course actually means that the content of the Constitution itself has also undergone changes.

At the same time, the entire legal system must change together with it, as the principle of Western geopolitical orientation can be regarded as one of the most important coordinative constitutional principles (Žalimas 2019).

The new constitutional principle of Western geopolitical orientation consolidated in the Constitution of Ukraine could contribute to the creation of welfare in the state if, first of all, the Constitutional Court of Ukraine and other legal institutions understand and implement this principle and its potential accordingly. This means that every decision after the amendments to the Constitution in all Ukrainian state institutions must be taken after considering what the new principle requires from them. The appropriate interpretation of the Constitution by revealing its 'living' content and opening it to the influence of European law, including through jurisprudential means, is due (Žalimas 2019). This also concerns the negative perspective of the newly enshrined principle of geopolitical orientation. Although it is not *expressis verbis* noted in the Constitution, any other geopolitical direction that brings the state towards the east and towards less democratic regimes is intolerable, and therefore cannot be undertaken by any state power institution.

According to the Constitution currently in force and the imposition of the obligation to all state institutions to follow the newly chosen course, any law or presidential decree guiding the state in the opposite direction would be recognised as unconstitutional. The role of the Constitutional Court deciding on the constitutionality of state decisions then becomes crucial. If such a case were to occur, in a decision on unconstitutionality the Constitutional Court of Ukraine would almost certainly refer to Article 19 of the Constitution of Ukraine, which states that 'all state and local self-government and their officials are obliged to act only on the grounds, within the limits of authority, and in the manner envisaged by the Constitution and the laws of Ukraine' (Frosini and Lapa 2022). The Constitution can also be violated by the non-implementation of constitutional prescriptions when the legislator omits to regulate what has to be regulated according to the Constitution – i.e., when it fails to adopt legislation necessary to implement Western democratic values belonging to a particular area of legal relations. Naturally, this can only occur if the Constitutional Court itself acts under the provisions of the Constitution and interprets it with receptiveness towards fundamental Western values.

Ukraine's commitment stemming from the Constitution to adopt and implement Western constitutional values, proving that Ukraine deserves to be considered as a plenipotential member of the Western community, has begun to acquire a very concrete shape. In certain areas, it has even overtaken that of more established members. For instance, Ukraine's intention to fully adhere to these constitutional values was proven by the ratification of the Istanbul Convention in 2022. Ukraine even did so prior to the European Parliament inviting all of the countries that had not yet ratified the Convention to do so. The ratification of the Istanbul Convention was rightly emphasized as an important step towards Ukraine's constitutional destination – accession to the EU (EUAM Ukraine 2023).

Another example of Ukraine's institutions working together and seeking systematic change while implementing the strategic course towards European and Euro-Atlantic integration is the adoption of anti-oligarch laws forbidding persons possessing a certain amount of money from financing political parties, owning media or taking part in privatisation (Verkhovna Rada 2021). This also required some sacrifices. Prior to the adoption of this law, the Speaker of the Verkhovna Rada was dismissed by a majority in Parliament after opposing the adoption of the aforementioned law and referring it to the assessment of the European Commission for Democracy Through Law (hereafter – the Venice Commission). Although the latter concluded recently that the new law lacks a systemic approach and is too personalized (Venice Commission 2023b), this still demonstrates the willingness and determination of the state to abandon old relics and mentalities while participating in the creation of a new Europe-orientated Ukraine.

1.4.2. Constitutional Safeguards and the Despicable Proposition to End the War of aggression

The values-based commonness with Western democratic states that serves as the foundation of the geopolitical orientation expressed in the provisions of the Constitution could not have been missed by the Russian Federation, which has always considered its neighbours as a long-held zone of influence. Ukraine's increasingly overt pro-Western foreign policy orientation and step-by-step approach to EU integration provided a pretext for Russia's continued destabilising tactics, and perhaps played a role in paving the path to war (Ramani 2023). Since the first days of the war, Russia has insisted that Ukraine gives up its goal of joining NATO and the EU, as expressed in constitutional provisions from 2019. It might seem from today's perspective that these amendments – clearly expressing values-based commonness with Western legal thought and emphasizing the importance of adhering to the fundamental principles of democracy, the rule of law and the protection of human rights – might have been regarded as the pretext to initiating the war. Controversially, this would mean that those amendments, while pursuing the objectives of better defence and cooperation in securing peace and the independence of Ukraine through closer integration with Europe, caused threats to the nation and the state.

Obviously, this cannot be the case, but, at least theoretically, it must be considered. Could the Russian requirement be fulfilled in an attempt to re-establish peace in Ukraine, protect the people and stop the extremely severe violation of human rights? Could a constitutional amendment to bring the Ukrainian legal order back to its previous state – as demanded by Russia – really contribute to achieving a breakthrough in the conflict? What conditions must be met in order to legitimize secession, which would include not only giving up on euro-Atlantic integration, but also ceding parts of the currently occupied territory of the state, in which Ukrainian citizens reside?

The answer to the first question is no. Ukraine declared a state of martial law on the first day of the conflict. In the Constitution of Ukraine, like in most of constitutions, there is a prohibition on amending the Constitution in the conditions or martial law or a state of emergency (Article 157). Thus, even if Ukraine were to consider believing the Russian promise to end the war for even a second by beginning to initiate the relevant amendments, they would not be constitutional while martial law is in effect.

It is hard to imagine the implementation of the Russian demand even theoretically, as it would change one of the core elements of the newly confirmed Ukrainian constitutional identity. This would mean the birth of a new nation different from the existing one, perhaps with the loss of territory. This is not achievable within the contours of the existing Ukrainian Constitution – nor for that matter, within any nation-building constitution.

The formulation in the provisions of the preamble contains the word 'irreversibility', as the legislator adopting these amendments foresaw an upcoming fight for this aspiration. Thus, the Constitution itself provides a safeguarding formula in case the politicians governing Ukraine were to one day change their minds regarding the geopolitical orientation of the state, precluding a reversal of course by potential future pro-Russian leaders or in the case of external menace. The use of the word irreversibility in relation to the chosen course means that there is (or should be) no turning back; therefore, re-amendments returning Ukraine to its previous state are impossible. If those amendments would be made, it would mean the emergence of a state of Ukraine of different constitutional identity than the one that is being built now.

While considering the preservation of the chosen geopolitical orientation and the European direction, a substantial role is entrusted to the Constitutional Court. There is a requirement in the Constitution of Ukraine that every constitutional amendment (for better or worse) be verified *ex ante* in the Constitutional

Court. The Constitutional Court should pronounce on the conformity of any draft law to amend the Constitution with the requirements of Articles 157 and 158, providing for the procedural and substantial restriction of amendments to the Constitution which, *inter alia*, precludes its amendment during a state of martial law.

In this context, one must note that the Constitution does not provide for any exceptions to constitutional control during a war or during a state of martial law. There is no restriction on challenging acts adopted during this period, nor any limitation on deciding on their constitutionality. Constitutional control is a fundamental pillar of the state acting under the rule of law, and the rule of law is the only legitimate answer to the rule of force. Therefore, it is crucial to ensure control of the constitutionality of all acts adopted during wartime, thus preventing any unconstitutional actions determined by internal of external factors. Having faced the ongoing war, the Constitutional Court did not stop functioning after a period of adjustment to the new reality.

A conclusion of the Constitutional Court was delivered regarding the amendments of 2019, which were found to be compatible with the Constitution (Constitutional Court 2018). Thus, if there were attempts to amend the Constitution by deleting from it the aspiration to move towards the EU and NATO, they would have to be approved by the Constitutional Court. The latter has the obligation not only to ensure that the Constitution is not amended during martial law, but also to verify whether amendments abolish or restrict human rights or freedoms. Obviously, the refusal to be directed towards Western constitutional values would be a significant loss for the promotion of the human rights and freedoms of the Ukrainian people.

Therefore, it must be stated, above all, that constitutional resistance to the Russian demand to abolish the European course is encoded in the text of the Constitution, as there is no legal way to amend it while still preserving the state and the Constitution. There is no way to legitimize the demands of Russia imposed on Ukraine to constitutionally enshrine political neutrality, which means that the Constitution cannot serve as a tool for settling the conflict as it cannot be a tool with which to destroy the state and the nation. Amending Ukraine's Constitution to allow for secession would amount to an unconstitutional amendment and a violation of the eternal values of territorial integrity, national unity (Weill 2022) and the commitment to respect human rights and freedoms. In other words, this would represent the reconstitution of the state and its people into a form that would no longer be the independent state of Ukraine. Ukraine's commitment to constitutional democracy and the rule of law, including its chosen geopolitical orientation, must continue, despite the aggressor's attempts to declare war not only against the independent state of Ukraine, but against its Constitution as well.

1.4.3. A European Perspective for Ukraine After the War of Aggression: Steps Taken and Future Insights

Although the entire ethnic territory of Ukraine has been under the influence of various cultural factors for a long time due to the territorial fragmentation and differing mentalities of the Ukrainian regions (Tsyrfa 2023, p. 51), the Russian-Ukrainian conflict-turned-war has had a crucial ideological impact on Ukraine's national identity. The very meaning of belonging to the Ukrainian nation has changed even more, manifesting itself in increased alienation from Russia and the greater embrace of Ukrainian nationalism as a worldview (Kulyk 2016, p. 607). This has confirmed Ukraine's dedication to European values and the determination to seek its place among European states.

On the one hand, the formation of the European identity of Ukraine is possible only through the perception of Ukraine as a part of Europe by European nations. On the other hand, during the last year it has become clear that Ukrainian security is essential to that of Europe. This war, on the eastern border of Europe against an independent and sovereign state vigorously resisting its aggressor, is an existential threat to the rules-based international order: not since World War II has a war between two states been considered a legitimate way to assert territorial claims. Thus, the importance of Western support has been emphasized since the beginning of this large-scale military invasion, and the gradual acceptance of Ukraine as a European state has led to the fact that in the middle of this war of aggression against it, Ukraine was granted an invitation to become the EU candidate (European Council 2022). Ukraine's accession to the EU is a crucial element of the stability of Eastern Europe. Therefore, it could appear that the goal enshrined in the Constitution – fully fledged EU membership – is within striking distance. A big step ahead has been taken, but the path forward will be a long one.

It is worth recalling that in 2014, when the determination of Ukraine became orientated towards Europe more than ever, four scenarios predicting the future of Ukraine in the EU were drafted. In a highway scenario, Ukraine becomes a full EU member by 2030 and a democratic Ukraine is a reliable player in the region. If Ukraine heads down a road with a speed limit, it has a chance of becoming a candidate state by said year and opening negotiations with the EU. If the bumpy road scenario occurs, Ukraine will still be in the process of implementing the Association Agreement, with little progress down the path to integration by

2030. Finally, in a dead-end scenario, Ukraine finds itself in a regress of democracy, remaining under the strong influence of Russia (for more detailed elaboration see: Meuser and Hett 2014). Today, it might be observed that Ukraine has moved forward in the most optimistic scenario, and a number of factors point to the likelihood that the goal of becoming a full EU member may be achieved even ahead of the most optimistic projections. Ukraine has entered the highest gear while traveling down its highway to Europe.

1.4.3.1. Ukraine's Homework to Be Done Before Accession to the EU

As indicated by the citizens of Ukraine, the most important advantages of the EU are a high level of social security, the rule of law, an advanced democracy, a lower level of corruption, and scientific and technological development (Tsyrfa 2023, p. 59). It is possible that due to the war of aggression against it, Ukraine will benefit from a less bureaucratic scenario than other states have experienced while preparing for EU membership. The mere fact of receiving candidate status within a few months proves the uniqueness of this situation.[7] Paraphrasing a tweet from Ursula von der Leyen, those who are ready to die for the European perspective deserve to live the European dream (von der Leyen 2022).

The EU has shown unprecedent flexibility and determination to achieve compromises. The majority of the EU Member States and their populations, or at least the recent accessions, strongly supported Ukraine's determination to becoming one of them even before the war of aggression began. Such strong support can be explained not only by the recognition of the importance of the EU's enlargement policy for creating a stable and democratic environment, but also by a genuine belief in the need for overcoming post-cold war divisions in Europe and the right of non-EU countries to stability and prosperity, which has changed the region of Central Europe beyond recognition in the last 15 years (Král 2007). The Russian invasion of Ukraine has opened a window of opportunity in the form of widespread support among all Europeans for the idea of Ukraine's accession to the EU.

However, certain fundamental criteria will have to be met as the old Europe preserves itself against the enthusiasm for future enlargements. Ukraine's invitation to become a full member and its treaty of accession to the EU can be accepted only when the country fulfils the conditions necessary for European integration, including, *inter alia*, the Copenhagen criteria, which consist of: the

---

7 Ukraine sent its application for EU membership on 28 February 2022, and by the unanimous agreement of 27 Member States was granted candidate status on 23 June 2022.

stability of institutions guaranteeing democracy, the rule of law, human rights and respect for, and the protection of, minorities; a functioning market economy and the capacity to cope with competition and market forces; and the capacity to enforce the EU *acquis*. Even the state of war and the fact of Ukraine having protected the EU's eastern border for more than a year cannot exempt it from the obligation to follow these procedures.

The European Commission determined seven specific reforms to be implemented before engaging in official negotiation on the membership of Ukraine (European Commission 2022, June 16), some of which are of a constitutional nature. Two of the prescribed reforms are related to the judiciary. Without the effective implementation of these reforms and the fulfilment of its accession conditions, Ukraine's further path to the EU could be called into question.

First, Ukraine should reform the selection procedure for constitutional judges, including a pre-selection process based on the evaluation of their integrity and professional skills. In this vein, Ukraine is to follow the recommendations presented by the Venice Commission. Second, the integrity vetting of candidates for membership of the High Council of Justice and the selection of candidates to establish the High Qualification Commission of Judges should be finalized. Needless to say, the judicial reform ensuring independent tribunals (as they will be charged with implementing EU law at the national level) is of the utmost importance.

The third requirement emphasized by the European Commission is also very specific and particular to Ukraine: strengthening the fight against corruption, in particular at the highest level, including the appointment of a new official – the head of the Specialised Anti-Corruption Prosecutor's Office. The issue of corruption has persisted for many years in Ukraine, finding its roots in the transitional period from a centralized planned economy to a market economy. Here, imperfections and legal gaps in privatization laws created the preconditions for the enormous influence of newly formed oligarchs in all areas of public power. The abuse of entrusted power for illicit private gain negatively affects political stability, democracy and sustainable peace, which is extremely detrimental in war-afflicted states that are trying to maintain the activities of public institutions, restore social trust, and help the economy to survive (Remeikienė *et al.* 2023, p. 503). The common practice of oligarch-friendly legislation cannot be justified anymore according to the new meaning of the Constitution, and even if the first steps have been taken with the adoption of the aforementioned anti-oligarch law, it will take some time to see these changes manifest in reality, not only within the legal framework.

Fourth, efforts must be put into preventing money laundering. Fifth, Ukraine is asked to implement the recently adopted anti-oligarch law to limit the excessive influence of oligarchs in economic, political, and public life, again following the guidelines issued by the Venice Commission. Sixth, Ukraine must finalise the reform of the legal framework for national minorities and adopt immediate and effective implementation mechanisms. This issue has already drawn the attention of the Venice Commission, which criticised the existing legal regulation and called for its revision. Lastly, Ukraine is invited to adopt a media law that aligns the country's legislation with the EU Audiovisual Media Services Directive and empowers the independent media regulator. The ability to execute the reforms determined in these recommendations will allow Ukraine to officially begin the process of negotiation to become a member of the EU.

The constitutional framework for the implementation of the aforementioned reforms is more than favourable, taking into account the constitutionally prescribed obligations of the President of the State, the Parliament and the Cabinet of Ministers to act in a way that ensures that the full EU membership of Ukraine becomes a reality. Therefore, the executive and legislative bodies should engage in the adoption of the necessary legislation without further delay, if necessary by fighting against deep-rooted convictions and behavioural patterns that are not in line with Western values.

1.4.3.2. Ukraine's Endeavours to Comply with European Requirements Concerning the Appointment of Constitutional Judges

The ongoing war of aggression has not prevented Ukraine from taking the actions necessary to engage in the implementation of the abovementioned reforms. Progress in one of them, namely the selection procedure for Constitutional Court judges in Ukraine, is worth examining in more depth as it is a central part of the changes required. The intense attention of Ukraine's European allies concerning the proper functioning of its institution of constitutional control is not difficult to explain.

First of all, the importance of constitutional review within a state striving for democracy is undeniable. Efficient constitutional control over the acts adopted by the legislative or executive body is one of the main pillars which permanently underpins the fundamental values of the rule of law, democracy and the protection of human rights and freedoms. It also secures the separation of powers and ensures that the proper checks and balances are in place. While deciding on issues related to the organization and functioning of state authorities or guaranteeing the protection of human rights and freedoms, the constitutional court preserves the supremacy of the Constitution, ensuring that the people can trust the constitutional order of the state. Ukraine's democratic development and its ability to consolidate its European identity or achieve the goals set in the Constitution will greatly depend on this institution.

Secondly, since the adoption of the constitutional amendments of 2019 prescribing the new Ukrainian constitutional identity and the clear direction towards Western values, the Constitutional Court of Ukraine stumbled when, in 2020, it took an anti-reformist stance and did not uphold anti-corruption reforms (Ruling of 27 October 2020), repealing some parts of the anti-corruption law of 2014 (Verkhovna Rada 2014). In its decision, the Constitutional Court pronounced the closure of the public register of declarations and the abolishment of criminal liability for failing to submit or for falsifying an electronic declaration. In the dissenting opinion of Justice Serhiy Holovaty, it says that the major parts of the Court's argumentation were to be of a non-legal nature. This constitutional decision almost provoked a constitutional crisis in the state, with the President of Ukraine using his decree to revoke the authority of the then-President of the Constitutional Court and one of the judges (which is not provided for in the Constitution), leaving vacancies in the Constitutional Court which could not have been lawfully filled (given that their very existence was contrary to the law).

Thus, in order to prevent possible constitutional crises in the future, to ensure the depoliticization of the constitutional control institution, and to re-establish trust in it, improvements to the procedure of the selection and appointment of constitutional judges are among the priorities set out by European institutions.

The willingness of the Ukrainian state authorities to implement constitutional provisions, to acquire EU membership and to deploy all efforts to achieve significant results in the abovementioned reforms can be demonstrated by the initiative of the Speaker of the Parliament, who addressed the Venice Commission on his own motion and asked the commission to assess the draft law concerning the selection procedure of constitutional judges. The Venice Commission responded to that request, formulating some recommendations in its opinion issued in December 2022 (Venice Commission 2022). One recommendation novel to the Ukrainian legal system outlined the intention to establish an advisory group of experts, and probably found its inspiration in the procedure for the selection of judges to European jurisdictions, namely Committee 255 for the CJEU or the Advisory Panel of Experts for the ECtHR. This should ensure the objectivity of the selection of candidates and their professionalism, moral qualification and integrity, while also guaranteeing the pluralism of views among judges-to-be. If the majority of the previously issued recommendations of the Venice Commission concerning the functioning of the Constitutional Court (for instance, the Opinion on the Draft Law on the Constitutional Court (CDL-AD(2016)03), adopted in 2016, or the Urgent Opinion on the Reform of the Constitutional Court of Ukraine issued pursuant to Article 14a of the Venice Commission's Rules of Procedure, adopted in 2020) were ignored by parliamentarians, disregarding the recommendations of the Venice Commission this time around might prevent the state from achieving its constitutional goal of European integration.

Therefore, the adoption of the Law on Amendments to certain legislative acts of Ukraine to clarify the provisions on the competitive selection of candidates for the position of a judge of the Constitutional Court of Ukraine on a competitive basis did not take long, and was met favourably by the Venice Commission. The latter also appreciated the decision to include international experts in the advisory group (three out of six, according to the initial draft law – one designated by the Venice Commission and two by international organizations who have previously assisted Ukraine while implementing various reforms) tasked with running a preliminary integrity check of candidates for the position of a constitutional judge. However, some improvements were also suggested by the Venice Commission, such as: simplifying the selection of advisory group members in order not to paralyse the selection of judges; adding a seventh member to the advisory group of experts; respecting gender equality while selecting future judges; setting out a timeframe for carrying out the selection procedure; and paying attention to ensuring that the selection procedure as well as the advisors' opinions and the votes cast be made public (for more, see Venice Commission 2022). In a follow up opinion issued on June 2023, the Venice Commission welcomed Ukraine's efforts to move forward with the reforms despite the ongoing war of aggression, especially regarding the clause excluding 'not suitable' candidates from further consideration following both the integrity and professional competence assessments. It also reminded Ukraine of the importance of filling vacant positions in a timely manner (Venice Commission 2023a). Although the adopted law regulating the selection and appointment procedure of constitutional justice is far from perfect, the determination of Ukrainian institutions to cooperate at the European level in order to create an independent, active, bold institution of constitutional control allows for the expectation that the necessary reforms will be implemented sooner rather than later, and the challenges of the past will be overcome. In its most recent follow-up opinion, the Venice Commission finally concluded that the key recommendations it had formulated previously have been followed, and that the members of a new advisory group of experts might be nominated from now on (Venice Commission 2023b).

Russia's aggression has only strengthened Ukraine's determination to keep fighting for the right to decide its own future, to enter into whichever agreements it so wishes, and to thrive as part of the European family of nations, free from foreign domination or domestic dictatorship. Ukraine has proved that it is willing to risk the lives of its people for the European values of democracy, independence and freedom. The solidarity of European and other states with Ukraine should keep the country's spirits high when pursuing these reforms. Ultimately, even if the Ukrainian Prime Minister Denys Shmyhal's ambitious plan 'to join the EU within the next 2 years' sounds rather optimistic (Lynch 2023), being part of the liberal and rules-based Western world, as its Constitution prescribes, is a very realistic objective to be achieved in the nearest future.

1.4.4. Interim findings

Russia's war of aggression against Ukraine started in 2014 with the occupation of Crimea. This meant Ukraine's break-up with Russia and a national renaissance, as well as the determination and self-transformation of a new Ukrainian constitutional identity. The readiness to contribute to democratic change originated in social mobilisation against an authoritarian regime (Kulyk 2016, p. 588). The 2019 amendments to the Constitution, as the constitutional embodiment of the events taking place in Ukraine since Maidan Dignity revolution, introducing the principle of a Western geopolitical orientation, affected the entire constitutional regulation and changed the lives of every state institution. Interpreting the Constitution in light of this new principle will allow Ukraine to overcome the shadows of the past and become a state with a European identity. The clear link between the European aspirations of Ukrainians being enshrined in the Constitution and the behaviour of state institutions adopting decisions to implement and foster democratic values demonstrates the sincerity of the European choice.

Having set this new goal, like many Central and Eastern European countries, Ukraine was obliged to gradually remodel its constitutional system to make it compatible with the *acquis communautaire*. These constitutional changes, introducing new constitutional values and moving the life of the state in a European direction, cannot be seen as merely political tool in the hands of decision-makers – even during a situation as severe as the ongoing war. The constitutional identity of the state cannot depend on the country's political leaders or its geopolitical circumstances. The choice was made by the legitimate representatives of the nation, therefore, even this war cannot initiate new constitutional amendments that would deny previous iterations without destroying the state as it exists today. Ukraine's constitutional aspiration to become part of Europe is set in stone and, being described as irreversible, cannot be easily revoked. The aspiration to renounce the new constitutional identity would mean an endevour to transform the state again; it is not impossible, but it would mean the emergence of a state of Ukraine of different constitutional identity than the one that is being built now.

The Ukraine-Russia crisis that continues to evolve on the geographic boundaries of Eastern Europe at the moment of editing this chapter is more about a fight between ideologies; a fight for democracy which is consolidated in the Constitution. It remains only to hope that, in this battle of good against evil, existing constitutional values will serve as an inspiration for the better futures of subsequent generations. Ukraine's accession to the EU and possibly NATO is a prerequisite for the country's continued survival as an independent entity, constituting a vital obstacle to Russia's further expansionist goals that are no longer even thinly masked. Therefore, it is only a matter of time before Ukraine becomes a member of the EU. Whether this occurs sooner or later will not affect Ukraine's determination to preserving its European identity and working towards the implementation of fundamental constitutional values common to all European states.

Chapter 2. Challenges for International Law Field in the Context of Armed Conflicts and Emergencies

2.1. Understanding the Function of the Prohibition of the Use Force and Its Impact on Seeking Peace

2.1.1. The System

The UN is by no means a perfect instrument, but it is a precious one. I urge you to seek agreement on ways of improving it, but above all of using it as its founders intended – to save succeeding generations from the scourge of war, to reaffirm faith in fundamental human rights, to re-establish the basic conditions for justice and the rule of law, and to promote social progress and better standards of life in larger freedom. The world may have changed… but those aims are as valid and urgent as ever. We must keep them firmly in our sights. (Annan 2003)

It would be hard to find anyone who would argue against the understanding that the UN Charter is the foundation of the existing world order. From the middle of the 20th century, it became 'a document of unassailable legal authority that would eventually gain credence as the secular world's *sacred text* [emphasis in original'] (Johnson 2008, p. 702). Just like all other sacred texts, this supreme legal document – in particular Article 2(4) prohibiting the use of force – has been interpreted in many ways since its inception. All of these interpretations could be summarised as *broadening* or *restricting* the right to resort to force. Needless to say, these approaches are contradictory, and the application of the former would result in different legal conclusions and practical actions than if the latter were to be relied upon.

It is submitted that the UN Charter is the correct foundation for the existing world order. The aims of the UN, as Kofi Annan claims, 'are valid and urgent as ever'. However, the manner of understanding and implementing these aims depends on the content of the collective legal consciousness (hereafter – CLC) of the international community, which has a distinguished quality of liveliness and constant change. Naturally, at a certain moment in time old legal thought must be switched to new. As previous patterns of legal thought are not capable of achieving there aims, it is suggested that there is a pressing need to create new ones.

One of the main characteristics of old legal thought is the predominance of positivism, which is deeply rooted in the CLC of the international community. Even extremely intelligent and talented interpreters, at the theorical level, and exceptionally skilful appliers, at the practical level, willingly use the tools and techniques provided by positivism and ignore extra-positive law (Johnson 2008, pp. 24–25). Such extreme abandonment of *natural law* for decades is one of the factors that led to an unfortunate situation in the international arena, where one cannot see the forest for the trees. Consequently, instead of finding ourselves in a *world of order* with the purpose of *maintaining peace* and focusing on the *creation of peace*, we are witnessing a *world of disorder* (Allott 2022), where the main purpose is to *prevent wider war* and the focus is on *permanently strengthening armed forces*. It is stated that there is an enormous difference between these two worlds and purposes. The occurrence of more than 300 armed conflicts all over the world after 1945 (O'Connell 2019, p. 60), including the ongoing war of aggression against Ukraine, illustrates how massive and painful this difference is – not only in legal or philosophical academic debates, but also in everyday life. Russia's attack on Ukraine and the subsequent events on the international plane have proved once again that old legal thought is capable neither of achieving the aims of the UN, nor of dealing with contemporary challenges.

The importance of the content of dominant legal thought on understanding the prohibition of the use of force and its impact on seeking peace are examined in this chapter. Firstly, the characteristics of old legal thought are addressed. Secondly, the chapter deals with three practical examples in the context of Russia's use of force against Ukraine which reflect the dominance of old legal thought. Lastly, the analysis of the need for new legal thought and its assistance in achieving the aims of the UN is explored.

2.1.2. Old Legal Thought

2.1.2.1. Collective Legal Consciousness

During recent decades, interest in studies regarding the conception and scope of legal consciousness has been growing (Hertogh 2004, p. 457). So far, most trend-setting studies on legal consciousness have focused on certain groups of people for comparative purposes. For example, they have sought to identify how law is understood by different societies in different countries or how law is understood by certain classes of people (Kurkchiyan 2012, p. 371). The conception of a CLC was introduced in 2012 and understood as 'the dominant perception of what law is and how people tend to relate to it in a given society' (Kurkchiyan 2012, p. 366). For the purposes of the current chapter, two notions should be explained: 'dominant perception' and 'society'. What is meant by society? Usually, a society is any group of people of a certain state or region, as well as any group of people united by professional association or a union based on personal interests. The dominant perception is understood as the sum of the most frequently occurring patterns or images of law in a particular society. An international community, composed of the subjects of international law, is also a society which has its own CLC. The focus in this chapter is on the currently existing content of the CLC of the international community. It is stated that CLC is a complex phenomenon, and it is doubtful whether a complete and exhaustive list of components can be identified (Kurkchiyan 2012, p. 366). However, scholars identify different dominant perceptions of law (or justice, or other notions) in the CLCs of different societies. Therefore, it is submitted that in the CLC of the international community a dominant perception of international law exists, and this has a decisive effect on the ideas, decisions and actions in the international arena of the members of the international community.

2.1.2.2. The Characteristics of Old Legal Thought

The dominant perception currently existing in the CLC of the international community rests on certain pillars. They serve as axioms which are taken for granted, although arguably they are no longer capable of coping with contemporary challenges. Therefore, this dominant perception is called 'old legal thought', and some of its most distinctive characteristics are put forward. This is a rather short, illustrative list – not an exhaustive catalogue.

2.1.2.2.1. A State-Centred System

For a long time, states have been the only subjects of international law, and they still have a leading role as the most important actors on the international plane. The history of international law itself is associated with inter-state diplomacy and treaty-making (Johnson 2008, p. 74). Moreover, the principle of sovereignty is treated as the first principle of international law. Old legal thought identifies sovereignty as a primary good and the most important value. As Lauterpacht observed, the doctrine of the sovereignty of states mainly reveals itself in two ways (Lauterpacht 1933, p. 3). The first aspect is reflected in the Statute of the International Court of Justice (hereafter – the ICJ), because only states have a right to determine the future of international law through legally binding sources. The second aspect is related to the canon of international law: that the state accepts the jurisdiction of international tribunals voluntarily. To sum up, states are authorities who have a right to create the rules of international law and at the same time states have all possibilities to avoid direct legal consequences for not obeying these rules. These two aspects, when coupled, give undeniable power to states in comparison to the other subjects of international law. This results in a state-centred international system.

Even under Article 1 of the UN Charter, the purposes of said organisation are directed towards peace, respect, and human rights. However, Article 2, dedicated to the principles which are supposed to help achieve these purposes, seems to be 'designed to protect the sanctity of the state rather than the welfare of society' (Johnson 2008, p. 76). Thus, the state-centred approach is not only obvious through the history of international law, but is also clearly reflected in the provisions of the UN Charter.

2.1.2.2.2. The Primacy of Politics

The political foundations of the existing world order still have a huge impact on the international community. After the end of World War II, the political superpowers decided to create a new world order. An agreement on the first draft of the UN Charter was reached by the four leading states of the world at that time: China, the UK, the USSR, and the USA (Johnson 2008, p. 75). According to the UN Charter, collective security was designed to depend on the decisions of the SC, in which the five great powers (with the inclusion of France) had a veto right and could act without legal limitations (Wright 1963, p. 454). 'Thus, it was assumed that the basic decisions of this body would be *political* rather than *legal* [emphasis in original'] (Wright 1963, p. 454). The fact that the veto power still exists is one piece of evidence which suggests that, regrettably, even now politics prevails over the rule of law in the sphere of collective security and peace-seeking.

2.1.2.2.3. A Focus on Strengthening the Armed Forces

According to old legal thought, the increase of security is primarily associated with the increase of the defence budget of a particular state. Whoever has the largest army with the most up-to-date modern armaments is assumed to be the strongest and the safest. This traditional approach is reflected in the Military Balance assessment of 2022 prepared by the International Institute for Strategic Studies (Military Balance assessment, 2022). The five permanent members of the SC made up five of the six countries at the top of the list of armed forces (or defence budget) spending in 2021.

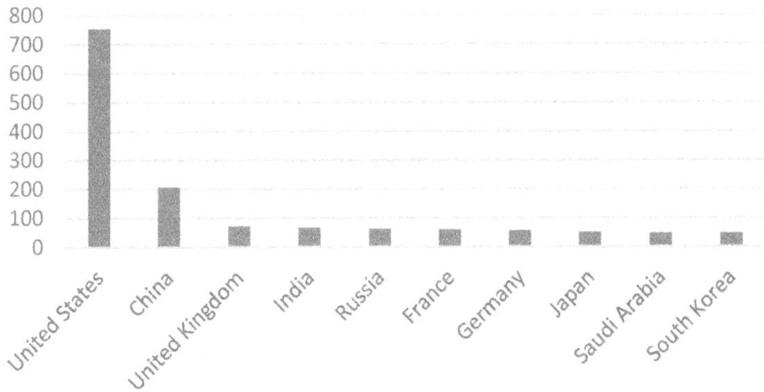

Figure 2.1. International Institute for Strategic Studies in *Military Balance assessment* (2022). Defence budget of top 10 countries, billion USD in 2021.

It is even more interesting to compare the combined defence budget of the five permanent members of the SC against that of the rest of the world. The combined defence budget of the US, China, the UK, Russia, and France amounts to 64 % of the total defence budget of all countries. These five states have a special status in the SC, which bears the primary responsibility for peace and security in the world. Therefore, the approaches to peace and security of these five permanent members are of huge importance and have a direct impact on the international community.

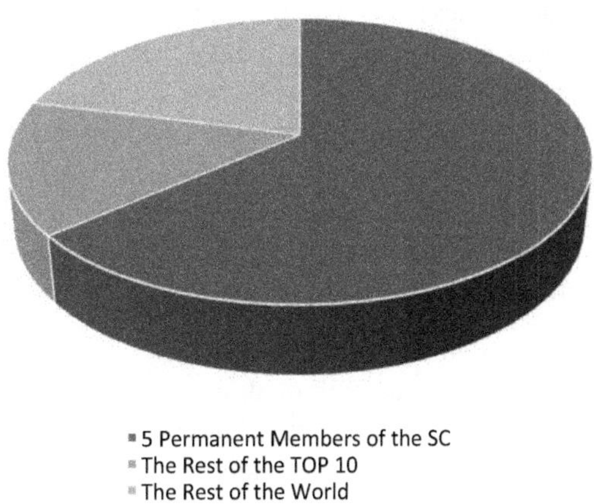

Figure 2.2. International Institute for Strategic Studies in *Military Balance assessment* (2022) Global defence budget of 2021.

If the popular assumption that the largest defence budget leads to the strongest guarantee of security was true, then the safety of our planet – with the five permanent members of the SC spending the largest sums of money on their armed forces and holding primary responsibility for peace and security in the world – would be assured. However, this is not the case, and this axiom is not working.

2.1.2.2.4. The Dominance of Positivism

In the CLC of the international community, legal positivism had already become a dominant perspective by the 1930s (O'Connell 2019, p. 5), and thus had a significant influence on the development of old legal thought. The current realities in the international arena were shaped by the core ideas of this legal thought. Although there are various schools of positivism, the common view of all is that the will of the state is the source of international law, and it always requires material proof of state acceptance (O'Connell 2019, p. 4). This is evident in the mere fact that treaties and customary international law are the two main forms of international law (Statute of the ICJ 1946). Moreover, legal positivism claims that a connection between law and morals is not necessary (Freeman 2014, p. 69). An illustrative example of this feature are the actions of Russia in the SC during the Russian Federation's presidency in 2022 – voting against a draft resolution on ending the Ukraine crisis (UN SC Draft Res 2022) and initiating and upholding a draft resolution which was considered an attempt to justify aggression against Ukraine (UN SC Draft Res 2022).

These four characteristics form the essence of the dominant perception in the CLC of the international community and shape the understanding of concepts such as peace and the prohibition of the use of force. The influence of old legal thought can be observed in the case of the Russian war of aggression against Ukraine.

2.1.3. Courses of Action of the International Community after Russia's Invasion of Ukraine

'No legal order, international or other, is true to its essential function if it fails to protect effectively the ultimate unit of all law – the individual human being' (Lauterpacht 1950, p. 78). There were myriad reactions to the invasion of Ukraine which were reflected in the words and actions of states, international organisations, civil society, individuals, and so on. Three examples are considered for the purposes of the current analysis. First, the (in)action of the SC, as it bears primary responsibility for the maintenance of peace and security. Second, the actions of the ICJ, as it is the most authoritative international court in the UN system. Third, the (re)action of the Nordic countries as they radically changed their position towards collective self-defence.

2.1.3.1. The (In)action of the SC

In the existing world order, the SC bears primary responsibility for the maintenance of peace and security (Charter 1945) in the world. What were the actions of the most authoritative organ of the UN, responsible for peace-making, after Russia's invasion of Ukraine on 24 February 2022?

First, on 25 February 2022, the SC failed to adopt a resolution condemning Russia's aggression in Ukraine. Although 11 of the 15 members of the SC voted in favour of the draft resolution, it was vetoed by a permanent member of the SC, the Russian Federation (UN SC Draft Res 2022). Another permanent member of the SC, China, abstained, along with India and the United Arab Emirates (UN SC Draft Res 2022). Second, on 23 March 2022, the SC was supposed to vote on a draft resolution proposed by four countries: Russia, Belarus, the Democratic People's Republic of Korea, and Syria. From this vote, 13 members of the SC abstained, treating the proposal as an attempt to justify Russia's military actions in Ukraine's territory. However, two of five permanent members – Russia and China – voted in favour (UN SC Draft Res 2022). Third, on 6 May 2022, the President of the SC (the USA for the month of May) made a presidential statement on behalf of the SC, where they 'expressed deep concern regarding the maintenance of peace and security of Ukraine' (UN SC Presidential statement 2022), reminded states of the 'obligation to settle international disputes by peaceful means' (UN SC Presidential statement 2022), and 'expressed strong support for the efforts of the Secretary-General in the search for a peaceful solution' (UN SC Presidential statement 2022). To sum up, from the beginning of Russia's military invasion of Ukraine until the end of 2022, the SC's efforts resulted in: (a) 25 meetings dedicated to the maintenance of peace and security in Ukraine, (b) 1 vetoed resolution, (c) 1 abstained resolution, and (d) 1 presidential statement from the SC. Officially, there is no condemnation of Russia's aggression by the SC as an organ of the UN, nor any other SC resolution addressing the situation in Ukraine. These facts lead to the conclusion that the SC, as an organ of the UN, has demonstrated pure inaction, which shows the institutional disfunction of the existing system.

Because of abuse of the veto power, clear incongruity appears between the established legal obligations of the SC and its existing practice. Unfortunately, this has been an ongoing problem since the beginning of the UN. An attempt to improve the situation was made in 1950, when the Uniting for Peace Resolution shifted power from the SC to the GA (Simma 2012). Such a practice was not intended by the drafters (Tomuschat 2008), but was later confirmed by the ICJ (Certain Expenses of the UN 1962). More than 70 years later, there is still no better solution to this problem. Therefore, after Russia's veto during the SC vote, the GA used its powers on 2 March 2022, relying on Article 11 of the Charter to adopt a resolution condemning 'the aggression by Russian Federation against Ukraine in violation of Article 2(4) of the Charter' (UNGA Res 2022) and demanding 'that the Russian Federation immediately cease it use of force against Ukraine' (UNGA Res 2022). Of the members of the GA, 141 voted in favour, 35 abstained and 5 voted against. This was a way for the international community to express its position and to declare that Russia's use of force is a violation of a *jus cogens* norm.

Why has the SC failed to fulfil its duties according to the UN Charter? The answer to this question depends on one's perspective and its depth.

From the procedural point of view, the reason for this rests in the veto system, which sets no limits to prevent the abuse of the veto power. Russia's invasion of Ukraine is yet another example in a list of cases where the SC was not capable of adopting a resolution because a permanent member referred to its veto power. Questions of the veto system and its possible reform have been discussed on different occasions (Simma 2012, pp. 35–36). Some brilliant legal reasonings have been established to advocate against the existing system (Nollkaemper 2022), and sound arguments have been announced (Trahan 2022), but a few thoughts can be added.

There is a position which suggests that the veto right should not be able to be invoked in cases where the SC votes on issues regarding the breach of a peremptory norm, because that would mean a conflict between a regular rule of international law and a *jus cogens* norm (Trahan 2022). It is true that the substantive/procedural rule distinction has its loyal defenders and furious opponents (Talmon 2012), especially when the discussion turns to the relationship between substantive *jus cogens* rules and procedural rules. It is also true that the ICJ declared in the *Jurisdictional Immunities* case that there is no conflict between a substantive *jus cogens* rule and a rule which is procedural in character because they address different matters (Jurisdictional Immunities of the State 2012). However, there are persuasive arguments in favour of this proposition. First, the dichotomy between substantive and procedural rules serves a certain purpose – namely, substantive rules set goals and procedural rules help achieve them. However, if a state uses its veto power while voting against a peremptory norm, then a procedural rule hinders the application or the enforcement of the *jus cogens* rule. Thus, such a procedural rule does not perform its function, but instead stands in the way of achieving the goal. In this case, the procedural rule is primarily used as a manipulative political tool which allows the will of one to be imposed upon others, and not as a procedural legal rule seeking to reach a common goal. Second, there is a huge difference between the rules of a procedural character appearing in bilateral disputes between individual states and the procedural rules of an international organisation responsible for maintaining peace and security in the world. Even in the *Jurisdictional Immunities* decision there were three dissenting opinions, which confirms that this topic is far from clear cut, yet in the case at hand the question is not simply about a conflict between two opposing states with different interests; the question is about the denial of the main objective of the UN – peace and security in the world. If this objective can be denied by one procedural rule which is used by one state, despite the expressly opposing votes of 141 member states, and this situation is considered to be just or acceptable, then something definitely went wrong with the understanding of justice in the international arena, and this has to be repaired. It is the author's contention that the use of the veto power by a permanent member in such a situation should be considered illegal.

From a broader perspective, the SC failed to perform its duties because it still functions according to the axioms of old legal thought: the state-centred approach and state interests prevail over the fundamental human rights of individuals, and political power is considered to be more important than the rule of law.

2.1.3.2. The Actions of the ICJ

Two days after Russia's invasion of Ukraine, on 26 February 2022, Ukraine initiated proceedings in the ICJ (Order 2022). Ukraine asked the Court to adjudge and declare on six contentions (Order 2022), all of which were based on the request to pronounce that the Russian Federation's illegal actions are based on a false claim of genocide allegedly committed in the Luhansk and Donetsk oblasts of Ukraine (Order 2022). It is clear that this application represented Ukraine's attempt to use available institutional legal tools to stop Russia's use of force by peaceful means.

On 16 March 2022, the ICJ delivered an Order. The Court acknowledged that the Russian Federation's special military operation 'has resulted in numerous civilian deaths and injuries, (…) caused significant material damage, (…) attacks are ongoing (…), many persons have no access to the most basic foodstuffs, potable water, electricity, essential medicines or heating' (Order 2022), therefore suggesting that provisional measures should be indicated, although they were not identical to the requested ones (Order 2022).

The Court declared unanimously that 'both parties shall refrain from any actions which may aggravate or extend the dispute before the Court or make it more difficult to resolve' (Order 2022). Thirteen judges voted in favour of a declaration that Russia 'shall immediately suspend the military operations' (Order 2022) in Ukraine and 'shall ensure that any military or irregular armed units which may be directed or supported by it, as well as any organizations and persons which may be subject to its control or direction, take no steps in furtherance of the military operations referred to in point (1) above' (Order 2022). Vice-President Gevorgian and Judge Xue voted against. Vice-President Gevorgian expressed his position that Ukraine sought to bring a dispute which was about the use of force and not related to the 1948 Convention on the Prevention and Punishment of the Crime of Genocide (hereafter – the UNGC); therefore, the ICJ had no jurisdiction to entertain the case (2022). Judge Xue also raised doubt as to whether the case was about genocide, tending to think that Ukraine brought a case about the 'Russian Federation's recognition of the Luhansk and Donetsk oblasts of Ukraine as independent republics and its military operations in Ukraine' (2022). Both judges appended declarations, not dissenting opinions. Three more judges opted for declarations: Nolte, Bennouna, and ad hoc Judge Daudet. Judge Robinson appended a separate opinion.

Art. 57 of the ICJ's Statute gives a general right to a judge to express their individual views if the 'judgement does not represent in whole or in part the unanimous opinion of judges' (Statute of the ICJ 1946), and Article 95 (2) of the Rules of the Court explains when a declaration can be made. It states that 'a judge who wishes to record his concurrence or dissent without stating his reasons may do so in the form of a declaration' (Rules of the ICJ 1978). To sum up, if a judge adds a dissenting opinion, it is obvious that they oppose the Court's decision, and they then lay down arguments. If a judge gives a separate opinion, they agree with the Court's decision but advocate for different reasoning. However, when a judge pronounces a declaration, they are free from the obligation to state any reasons. Interestingly, in the Court's practice there is an increasing tendency to append declarations rather than separate or dissenting opinions. It is highly doubtful that the frequent use of declarations is a tendency that should be welcomed in the ICJ. Although it is not the purpose of this article to tackle the reasons for this trend, it seems that this shift might be used as a means of encouraging ambiguous, potentially devious attitudes and sitting on the fence, instead of providing more legal certainty and demonstrating leadership by making clear-cut choices and giving authoritative legal reasonings.

'Members of the Court are independent judges' (Rules of the ICJ 1978) and they 'exercise their powers impartially' (ICJ 1945), yet it is impossible to ignore a certain coincidence: the two judges of the ICJ who voted against the Court's Order are of Russian and Chinese nationalities, and the two permanent members of the SC who expressed a different position regarding the illegality of Russia's use of force in the territory of Ukraine are Russia and China. As the judges from these two countries are supposed to be free from the political influence of their states of nationality, one possible assumption is that there are huge differences between the content of the CLC of these two states and that of the other states (Germany, Morocco, Jamaica, France, Slovakia, the USA, Uganda, India, Lebanon, Japan, Australia), and that these two judges, coming from these two legal traditions, reflect existing dissimilarities in their individual opinions.

In conclusion, it is commendable that the ICJ acted quickly by delivering an Order and urging the suspension of the 'military operation'. This institution has proved that it can act rapidly in challenging times. Whether Russia in this case, and states in general, accept and obey these Orders is another question leading to other realms. For now, Russia has chosen to ignore and contravene this Order. This is yet another example in a long line of others which together reflect the outdated standards of old legal thought, which is neither sufficient for contemporary constraints nor helps to achieve the goal outlined by K. Annan: 'to re-establish the basic conditions for justice and the rule of law' (2003).

To accept compulsory jurisdiction and to obey the judgements and orders of the World Court should be prestigious in a world where the rule of law is respected. Unfortunately, the current situation leaves plenty of room for improvement in this field.

2.1.3.3. The (Re)action of the Nordic Countries

On 18 May 2022, Finland and Sweden formally expressed their wish to become part of the NATO and applied for membership. What was the rationale for these formerly neutral states to consider joining the largest military alliance in the world?

After the signing of NATO Accession Protocols, The Foreign Minister of Sweden, Ann Linde, expressly outlined the country's reason: 'The Swedish Government decided to apply for NATO membership against the backdrop of the deteriorated security situation in the Euro-Atlantic area following Russia's unprovoked, illegal, and unjustifiable war against its neighbour – the peaceful, democratic, and military non-aligned state of Ukraine. (…) This Swedish Government's decision has overwhelming political and public support in

Sweden, and we believe that joining NATO is the best way for Sweden to ensure our national security and keep the Swedish people safe' (Linde 2022). Moreover, the representative of Sweden talked not only about national security, but also about the security of the Alliance: 'We are convinced that our membership will strengthen NATO and add to the stability in the Euro-Atlantic area. We will do our part in contributing to NATO's collective defence shoulder to shoulder with the other Allies' (Linde 2022). The Foreign Minister of Finland, Pekka Haavisto, stated: 'The membership of both Finland and Sweden will not only contribute to our security, but to the collective security of the Alliance. (…) Together we are stronger in defending the rules-based international order and the principles of democracy, freedom and rule of law' (2022).

Two thoughts are offered on the Nordic countries' shift from neutrality to joining NATO. First, Russia's illegal actions in Ukraine and behaviour in the SC lead to fear and a sense of insecurity. Russia is seen as an unpredictable aggressor; thus, even such a neutral state as Sweden has decided to become part of a military alliance. Although this is an understandable (re)action in the current situation, it unfortunately reflects a deep-rooted tradition in the CLC of the international community: to spend more money on armaments and not on education or culture, and to focus on competing between 'them' and 'us' and not on creating together. Second, Sweden was neutral for a long time, during which it took a leading role in global nuclear disarmament efforts and acted as a mediator. However, when a state joins a military alliance, it is doubtful whether it is able to continue this course and influence and inspire others, because its own example of neutrality is lost. From now on, these two Nordic governments will inevitably designate more attention, resources, and time to defence and the military industry. Unfortunately, this means that this is going to come at the expense of the active creation of peace. The almost automatic (re)actions of Sweden and Finland confirm that the old belief of concentrating on spending more on armaments is a primary choice of states when seeking peace and security.

2.1.4. New Legal Thought

'The moral claims of today are often the legal rights of tomorrow' (Lauterpacht 1950, p. 74). The same old thinking produces the same old results, and old patterns lead to old failures. Thus, the aims set forward by the UN Charter are left unachieved. In order to create new results, new patterns need to emerge in the CLC of the international community. What could be the features of this new legal thought that could form the dominant perception of the future CLC of the international community? The following list is not a complete and exhaustive catalogue of characteristics, but rather a starting point essential for the switch in individual and collective legal minds.

2.1.4.1. An Individual-Centred System

The domination of the state and the principle of sovereignty should be overridden by a focus on individual and human rights. Impressive ideas on the humanisation of sovereignty were comprehensively outlined by Anne Peters (2009).

This feature is closely linked to the goals quoted in Kofi Annan's speech – the goods of individuals. They can only be fully secured and realised in the context of the international community (Finnis 2011, p. 150). The international community is a group, and it has certain dynamics. J. Finnis provides a definition of a group, which is also applicable to the international community: it 'exists wherever there is a co-ordination of activity by a number of persons, in the form of interactions, and with a view to a shared objective' (2011, p. 153). Two criteria are identified: (i) to have a common goal, and (ii) to co-ordinate the actions of the subjects in the group. When these two conditions are fulfilled, there is evolution and progress on the international plane, but if at least one of them is missing, a crisis occurs. Most of the time, the attention of an international lawyer is on the second element – how to improve the rules, how to make them more effective or convenient. However, the primary task is to agree on shared goals, and this is not a mere political task as there might be significant differences in the understanding of these goals because the same legal concepts mean different things in the distinct CLCs of separate states.

Historically, the concept of sovereignty appeared as a product of political theory and was associated with the internal constitutional power of the state (Jennings and Watts 1996, p. 125); it was associated with the supreme power and authority within the state. In the 20th century, the attempt was made to use this essentially internal concept on the international plane; however, sovereignty as super-norm is inapplicable to the position of states from the international law perspective (Simma 2012, pp. 157–158) because reference to the 'sovereign state' is a description of an 'internal constitutional position rather than (…) legal status on the international plane' (Jennings and Watts 1996, p. 125). Within the international community, the relationship between states is based on equality (Jennings and Watts 1996, p. 125). In the 21st century, the understanding of sovereignty continues to change. It is observed that the 'ongoing process of a humanization of sovereignty is a cornerstone of the current transformation of international law into an individual-centred system' (Peters 2009, p. 514). In new legal thought, the concept of human rights should be one of the key goals of international law, and sovereignty is seen as a tool serving the achievement of this goal.

2.1.4.2. Respect for the Rule of Law

The central ideal of the rule of law is expressed in simple words: 'all need to be ruled, it assumed, not least the rulers' (Postema 2022, p. 3). The rule of law is recognised as the foundation of peace, justice, and human rights (Rule of Law Index 2022). In the words of Ban Ki-moon, 'the rule of law is like gravity. It is the rule of law that ensures that our world and our societies remain bound together and that order prevails over chaos' (2012). Unfortunately, these statements of scholars and representatives of the international institutions are not illustrated by state practice. Conversely, scholars are warning about the erosion of the rule of law, and it is submitted that 'the global rule of law crises reached a new low with the recent attack by Russian forces against Ukraine, which was a blatant violation of international law' (Postema 2022, p. X). Therefore, the international community is not moving closer to the aims of peace, justice and the effective protection of human rights; on the contrary, it is turning away from them.

The recent annual report of the World Justice Project (hereafter – WJP) lists 140 countries according to their adherence to the rule of law (Rule of Law Index 2022). Regrettably, the five permanent members of the SC, having extra powers and being a constant part of the organ which bears primary responsibility for peace in the word, are not leading this list (Table 2.1). Only the UK makes it into the top 20, while the other four countries are left behind. China is ranked 95th and Russia is 107th. It is an unwelcome paradox that respect for the rule of law, which is a foundation of peace and justice, is not exhibited by the permanent members of the SC. As has been correctly observed, 'the problem is not with agreement on the law that applies, but rather with acceptance that the law applies to all, on the basis of equality. The same norm applicable to Russian action in Ukraine applies to French action in Mali. It applies to the USA and the UK action in Syria and Iraq' (O'Connell 2019, p. 101).

The primary concern should switch from politics to international law when seeking the achievement of the main aims of humanity through the SC, and the UN in general. The primacy of politics in the SC's work is an outdated characteristic of old legal thought. There is no room for such a feature in new legal thought if the goal is to operate effectively.

The individual political interests of states are important. However, the primary collective goals of humanity are vital. In order to achieve them, rule of law is essential because 'law recognizes the priority of the will of the whole over that

Table 2.1. The ranking of the five permanent members of the SC in the Rule of Law Index.

Place in Global Rank (2022)	Country (Permanent Member of the SC)	Change in Global Rank (Since 2021)
15	UK	1 position up
21	France	2 positions up
26	USA	1 position up
95	China	3 positions up
107	Russian Federation	6 positions down

Note. World Justice Project, 2022, *Rule of Law Index.*

of the parts; politics seeks to impose the will of each part upon other parts or upon the whole' (Wright 1963, p. 454). The equality of states should be a principle operating in practice, and this is possible only through the rule of law – not through politics, which provides the right to dominate for the most powerful subjects. As G. J. Postema rightly summarises, 'when law rules in a political community, it provides protection and recourse against the arbitrary exercise of power through law's distinctive tools' (2022, p. 18).

Primary responsibly for advocating for the rule of law rests on international lawyers and legal advisers. They could follow the impressive example of Derek Bowett, who not only represented states in front of the ICJ, but also persuaded them to comply with the Court's decisions even if they were not favourable for them (O'Connell 2019, p. 293). For Derek Bowett, persuading Muammar Ghaddafi to comply with a non-beneficial judgment of the ICJ 'was one of his most challenging performances. He succeeded by explaining the honour that accompanies a demonstration of respect for the law. It was a real success for peace in the region' (O'Connell 2019, p. 293). The function of an international lawyer is not only to participate with other professionals of the field in legal or academical processes, but also to clearly and persuasively advocate for the advantages of the rule of law and compliance with international law for non-professionals – first and foremost, politicians and decision makers. The latter task is more demanding, but is of principal importance, yet for such a shift in action to occur it must be preceded by a shift in legal thought.

2.1.4.3. A Focus on Creating Peace

The concentration on defence and stronger armed forces should be replaced with a concentration on creating peace through active action.

According to the UN Charter Commentary, 'Article 1(1), (2), and (3) indicate that peace is *more* than the absence of war [emphasis in original]' (Simma 2012, p. 110). Therefore, in order to enjoy peace, *ongoing* and *positive* actions are required. The proposition is that the *prevention of war* is not the same as the *creation of peace*. While a deep-rooted positivistic position concentrates solely on the prevention of war, natural law stresses that the most important and effective action is to focus on *creating peace*. In 1992, the President of the SC stressed that international peace and security has a broader meaning in times of change: 'the absence of war and military conflicts among States does not itself ensure international peace and security. The non-military sources of instability in economics, social, humanitarian, and ecological fields have become threats to peace and security' (Simma 2012, p. 772). In the post-Cold War period, 'peace and security' was understood more broadly, but was still based on a positivistic approach and concentrated on the prevention of various crises (military as well as economic, humanitarian or ecological). It was proposed that the understanding of peace should shift from constituting mere interstate security towards human security (Simma 2012, p. 772). However, this broader understanding of 1992 is not broad enough for 2022, nor for the 21st century in general. It is suggested that in the new pattern of legal thought, the focus should be shifted from the prevention of war (or economic, humanitarian, ecological crises and so on) to the creation of peace. The caution and evaluation of risks are important, yet insufficient; the international community must broaden its horizons regarding the concept of peace and focus its attention on the creation of peace through continuing and positive action. It is impossible to *win* peace, it is only possible to *create* peace. Article 2(4) and Article 2(3) of the UN Charter are interrelated, the latter being central while the former serves only as a red line which cannot be crossed in international relations. One who focuses on the prohibition of the use force is concentrating on *winning* peace, but one who focuses on the peaceful settlement of disputes is concentrating on *creating* peace. Moreover, the focus on creating a mere civilisation should evolve into a focus on creating culture. This core change in the legal mind must be achieved in order to proceed with new legal thought.

2.1.4.4. The Need for Natural Law

The predominant theory of positivism should be balanced with natural law. The positive law method alone is not capable of explaining peremptory norms (O'Connell 2019, p. 75), including the prohibition of the use force, which is a *jus cogens* norm. Therefore, understanding natural law and its inclusion in international relations is crucial.

Natural law was seen by Lauterpacht as the 'ever-present source for supplementing the voluntary (consent-based) law of nations' (1946, p. 21), which can explain why certain peremptory norms and inherent general principles of law are superior to the consent and will of states. Natural law is necessary when explaining such concepts as universality, equality, justice, peace, inherent human rights (O'Connell 2019, p. 5) and so on. John Finnis deserves recognition for reintroducing natural law to scholarly debates (Finnis 2011). Moreover, several ICJ judges have advocated for the practical application of natural law, including Judge Tanaka (Tanaka 1966), Judge Trindade (Cancado Trindade 2013), and Judge Weeramantry (Weeramantry 2004). Despite these few examples, the small amount of knowledge on natural law that had been generated (and which, arguably, was never fully developed) was abandoned, and consequently the 'sources of human wisdom' in the legal process were lost (O'Connell 2019, p. 88). This has led to unresolved problems and has expanded the distance between the aims set out in UN Charter and the current standpoint of the international community.

As an example, the recent work of the ILC on *jus cogens* norms (International Law Commission 2022) also demonstrates the dominance of positivistic legal thought. Although the ILC acknowledges that *jus cogens* norms are 'hierarchically superior to other rules of international law' (International Law Commission 2022), it fails to outline the source of this superiority. The ILC provides two criteria for the identification of *jus cogens*, namely: '(a) it is a norm of general international law; and (b) it is accepted and recognized by the international community of States as a whole as a norm from which no derogation is permitted and which can be modified only by the subsequent norm of general international law having the same character' (International Law Commission 2022). However, positivism alone can only explain law based on consent, not norms of higher normativity. It is a well-known fact that the prohibition of torture is a *jus cogens* norm. Regrettably, it is also true that the great majority of states systematically engage in torture (Higgins 2007, p. 20). Nevertheless, the prohibition of torture is still acknowledged as a *jus cogens* norm, and the majority would agree with this. Therefore, how, according to positivism, can the prohibition of torture enjoy the special status of a hierarchically superior rule of international law and be considered a *jus cogens* norm if state practice is the opposite? Rosalyn Higgins suggests that the massive and systematic abuse of the prohibition of torture does not trigger the status of this norm simply because the second element of *opinion juris* continues to exist (Higgins 2007, p. 22). This is a perfectly possible formalistic approach of positivism. However, it does not solve the excruciating underlying problem – huge incongruity between the declaration of what international law is and what states do in practice. Moreover, it does not answer the question of why we need these hierarchically superior norms if states can systematically ignore them in everyday life. The criteria in the ILC's conclusions reflect the positivistic understanding that the will or consent of states is the most important factor, and that it is the basis for the emergence of *jus cogens* norms. However, some law is binding regardless of state consent and, in the words of Judge Tanaka, international law needs natural law to achieve 'its supra-national and supra-positive character' (Tanaka 1966). Only natural law, not positivism, holds the explanation of why compliance with the law is a moral good, and why rediscovering and reimposing natural law as part of international law could help to achieve the purposes set out in the UN Charter. It is impossible to achieve aims such as peace or justice when natural law is in exile, because without natural law (or extra-positive law) international law loses the source of its answers to fundamental questions (O'Connell 2019, p. 17).

For a strictly positivistic old legal mind, the four listed features of new legal thought might seem utopian and idealistic. This is due to the fact that a pure positivistic legal mind can generate only pure positivistic ideas; it cannot create different types of solutions. However, the truth is that a purely positivistic legal mind cannot sincerely and fully dedicate itself to the task of achieving the purposes of the UN Charter, such as peace and security in the world, as these are idealistic purposes themselves. Consequently, if the international community wants to make constant progress (i.e., to set goals and achieve them), there are two possibilities: the international community has to either change its idealistic purposes in line with the existing mindset, or change its mindset in line with the existing idealistic purposes. The author strongly supports Kofi Annan's position that the current purposes are correct; the contention is that the old way of thinking is wrong and should be changed in favour of the new.

2.1.5. Interim findings

It is suggested that the purposes stated in the UN Charter – namely, maintaining peace and security, implementing fundamental human rights and re-establishing the rule of law – remain valid in the contemporary world and should be the pillars of the international community.

The constantly changing content of the CLC of the international community forms the dominant legal thought, which shapes our understanding and determines our actions. An illustrative list of the characteristics of the dominant old legal thought is as follows: (i) a state-centred approach, (ii) the primacy of politics, (iii) a focus on strengthening the armed forces, and (iv) legal positivism. These four features condition a mainstream understanding which perceives peace as a state that it is possible to win with a better-equipped army and considers the prohibition of the use force as a norm which can be interpreted in a broad way and used to promote justice.

The manifestation of the characteristics of old legal thought is observed in practice in Russia's attack against Ukraine, which triggered Articles 1(1) and 2(4) of the UN Charter. The (in)action of the SC, the action of ICJ and the (re) action of the Nordic countries all confirm that old legal thought is not capable of achieving the purpose of maintaining peace and security in the world. Therefore, a submission on new legal thought is pronounced.

The proposition is made that new legal thought should consist of the following non-exhaustive list of characteristics: (i) an individual-centred international system as opposed to a state-centred international system, (ii) the priority of the rule of law over politics in international law, (iii) a primary focus on actively creating peace instead of a primary focus on the constant prevention of war on the international plane, and (iv) reintroducing natural law and balancing it with positive legal thought in the CLC. This would lead to a deeper understanding of the substance of the concepts validated in Articles 1(1) and 2(4) of the UN Charter and the relationship between them. Namely, that peace cannot be won, but only created; that the use of force being a *jus cogens* norm serves as a boundary between the world of order and the world of disorder; and that the relationship between peace and the prohibition of the use force is a complex phenomenon, not a dualistic choice.

Progress towards peace can be achieved with the help of a shift in the CLC by abandoning old legal thought and strengthening the characteristics of new legal thought.

2.2. Battlefield Ukraine: Russia's War of Aggression Against Ukraine and Selected Issues of International Humanitarian Law

2.2.1. Context

The present chapter analyses two main issues related to the application of International Humanitarian Law[8] (hereafter – the IHL) during Russia's ongoing war of aggression against Ukraine. First, it analyses the peculiarities and

8 International Humanitarian Law is a specific body of international public law that intends to limit an impact of an armed conflict, in particular, to protect victims of war as well as to limit the application of armed violence, while imposing certain obligations upon the states and non-state actors. It is also known as law of armed conflict, law of war or jus in bello. For more see Kalshoven and Zegveld 2001, pp. 1–3.

typology of the conflict (covering not only the full-scale invasion that began on 24 February 2022, but also the build-up to this situation, from the occupation and annexation of Crimea in 2014 to the hybrid war in the Donbas). In the second part, it discusses particular issues such as the status of the different forces engaged in the conflict (regular forces, irregular forces, volunteers, private military company personnel, etc.) and some interrelated issues regarding the treatment of prisoners of war.

2.2.2. The Qualification of the Conflict: Nomen est Omen

When Henry Dunant – the hero of the relief effort in the aftermath of the Battle of Solferino and one of the founders of the organisation later to be known as ICRC – was awarded the Noble Peace Prize, he was not the sole recipient. The prize was also awarded to Frédéric Passy, founder and president of the first French society for peace, a known and outspoken pacifist. The approach that war is inevitable and that the best humanity can do is to alleviate the suffering of victims has always been met with caution. This view has been attacked both by militarists such as British admiral Lord Fisher, who claimed that the humanisation of war is foolishness, and pacifists advocating for the total outlawing of war (Cooper 1991, pp. 80–82).

The law of war, or the IHL, stood in the middle of these views, and still stands today. In contrast to the law of peace, the IHL has many specificities that are unknown to the public. Moreover, from the first point of view the IHL may seem illogical or simply unfair, e.g., where it mandates the equal treatment of the forces of the aggressor and the defender: 'no matter the inequalities, the parties are equally subject to the principles and rules of the law of war' (Kalshoven and Zegveld 2001, p. 2).

Such feelings of unfairness may even start with the naming of situations, and that is where our analysis begins. Many different terms have described the situation between Russia and Ukraine in recent years, and especially during the years of 2022–2023. The terms 'aggression', 'invasion', 'full-scale invasion', 'war', and 'conflict' are used interchangeably. Some have a particular legal meaning, while some do not. However, even the mere usage of a certain term might lead to disagreements, official protests, etc. It is interesting to observe how legal terminology is being used to avoid the true meaning of these terms (following Russia's example). We must also emphasise that the usage of these terms is important in the application of particular legal regimes. Therefore, we will discuss the usage of different legal terms and their content from the point of view of the IHL and its applicability towards Russia's aggression against Ukraine.

2.2.3. Crimea and the Hybrid War in the Donbas

Russia's first operation against Ukraine was the seizure of the Crimean Peninsula. In 2014, after the success of the Maidan Dignity revolution in overthrowing pro-Russian president Viktor Yanukovich, Russia was quick to mobilise its proxies and troops already stationed in Crimea, which resulted in Ukraine's loss of the peninsula. The seizure involved only a few military clashes, and met almost no resistance from Ukrainian military forces. Russia tried numerous times to justify the seizure by different ways, including: staging a fake referendum, claiming self-defence on different grounds, and not recognising the military forces engaged in the seizure as their own ('orderly people', 'little green men') (Marxsen 2016, pp. 14–15, 24–26). However, the only thing that the IHL is interested in is how the seizure of Crimea can be described in IHL terms. The IHL is quite limited in its terms; therefore, only two are worthy of analysis: armed conflict and occupation.

The IHL provides for two regimes of armed conflicts: international armed conflict and non-international armed conflict. Classic contemporary definition of international armed conflict is found in Duško Tadič case, dealt by the International Criminal Tribunal for Former Yugoslavia (hereafter – the ICTY), and it states that international armed conflict is 'a situation in which there is a resort to armed force between States' (Crawford and Pert 2020, p. 57). Nevertheless, Common Article 2 of the GC provides for additional situations that are equivalent to the regime of international armed conflict: declaring war or issuing any other instrument (as Dinstein puts it, 'war in the purely technical sense' (2017, p. 12)) or partial or total occupation, even as it is worded in Common Article 2 'when met without resistance'. Of course, those terms are not self-explanatory and require some analysis.

First, 'resort to armed forces' raises the issue of what is understood by 'armed forces' as well as what is meant by 'resort' and 'between states'. Generally, the armed forces of the state are understood as military organisations and personnel which are under the control and responsibility of the state. Protocol Additional to the GC of 12 August 1949, and Relating to the Protection of Victims of International Armed Conflicts (Protocol I) (hereafter – Additional Protocol 1) provides the following broad definition that we will use extensively: 'The armed forces of a Party to a conflict consist of all organised armed forces, groups and units which are under a command responsible to that Party for the conduct of its subordinates' (Art. 43 (1)). The crucial words here are 'of a Party'. Nevertheless, in the initial stages of seizure Russia simply denied that its military forces (despite evident facts) were taking part (Maxsen 2016, p. 15). Moreover, as mentioned above, this seizure was met with little resistance and was portrayed by Russia as an act of self-determination. This led to the claim that there was no armed conflict between Russia and Ukraine, and that the only conflict that had arisen was between Crimea's people and the forces of Kiyv (Maxsen 2016, pp. 19–20). Therefore, Russia in the case of Crimea's seizure denied the very existence of the armed conflict itself, both from the 'resort to armed force' and 'party' points of view. In such a case, 'occupation' may not exist either, because only state forces or forces acting in the name of the state can conduct an occupation, 'there is an inextricable tie between this species of occupation and inter-State war' (Dinstein 2009, p. 31). The 'even met without resistance' clause in Common Article 2 this time seems to be irrelevant, because non-resistance was masked under fake referenda and the veil of self-determination.

Despite of all these efforts, the majority of the world did not accept Russia's version of events. The alleged legality of the seizure and annexation of Crimea was not recognised by the UN resolution on the territorial integrity of Ukraine, which was followed by many other international declarations (Grant 2016, pp. 49–50). However, from the point of view of the IHL, the question remains: Can we consider the seizure of Crimea as the start of an armed conflict or occupation, and what legal consequences does it entail?

ICC Prosecutor Fatua Bensouda released a first report on the situation in Ukraine in 2020 (Bensouda 2020). In this report para. 277, 278, the seizure and annexation of Crimea is described as an 'ongoing occupation'. It also emphasises in para. 274 that Russia is still executing effective control over Crimea. This is the exact wording that describes an occupation in the IHL, as Dinstein puts it 'Effective control is a conditio sine qua non of belligerent occupation' (2009, p. 43). Such an evaluation is also shared by international law specialists. (Tsybulenko and Kelichavyi 2018, pp. 277–297), (Geiß 2015, pp. 443–447).

This wording is important from the point of view of the regime of occupation, as it means that the occupier (in our case, Russia) is restricted by the law of occupation, which foresees the substantial limitation of their powers. In reality, Russia has introduced its own laws by annexing Crimea, and has commenced the transfer of its own population to Crimea, which is strictly prohibited by GC IV, Article 49.

The ICC Prosecutor's report also concerns the situation that followed the occupation of Crimea: instigating a conflict in the Donbas by creating the so-called Donetsk People's Republic (Rus. *Doneckaya Narodnaja Respublika*; hereafter – the DNR) and Luhansk People's Republic (Rus. *Luhanskaya Narodnaja Respublika*; hereafter – the LNR). Even though the official parlance from the Russian side (and not only) spoke about 'pro-Russian separatists', there was ample evidence that Russia's political and military forces were engaged in this conflict, despite Russia's constant denial and refusal to take responsibility for its military personnel involved in the fighting (Tsybulenko and Francis 2018, pp. 123–145). The ICC Prosecutor's report is somewhat dubious regarding the exact qualification of the situation, and it describes the Donbas situation both as a possible international and non-international conflict (see paras. 279–281), most likely considering the possibility that specific situations might have different qualifications.

This is a rather interesting phenomenon, but Ukraine's official policy was also somewhat blurred as regards the Donbas situation. On the one hand, all official announcements claimed that Russia was engaged in aggression, but up until 2018 there was no official recognition that Ukraine was in an international armed conflict with Russia. Until 2018, Ukraine officially termed the war in Donbas an 'anti-terrorist operation' (Ponomarenko 2018). Ukraine also did not consider LNR and DNR fighters as members of Russia's armed forces, but as members of terrorist groups; consequently, they were not considered 'proper' prisoners of war, even after the full-scale invasion (ANON, 2022e).

These peculiarities might suggest that Ukraine was also treating this situation as a mix between an international and non-international armed conflict. Such an approach had its own benefits, both politically and legally. From the national legal point of view, it allowed Ukraine to prosecute LNR and DNR fighters and any others involved in the fight as ordinary criminals, without granting them combatant's privileges. From a political point of view, this helped to show that Ukraine was not trying to escalate the conflict.

The national legal view of the facts on the ground is neither compulsory nor obligatory for international law. Therefore, looking from the point of view of the IHL, it is evident that the conflict in the Donbas might have been both international and non-international at the same time, depending on the particular situation. Despite the fact that Russia never recognised its direct involvement in 'separatist' forces, there was ample of evidence of Russia's participation. In our case, however, the most interesting element is that of the control of so-called separatists by Russia and the two self-proclaimed LNR and DNR 'states' (Korotkyi and Hendel 2018, pp. 145–173).

This is not the first 'separatist' movement instigated by Russia. The ECtHR jurisprudence analysed a somewhat analogous situation in one of the post-soviet 'frozen conflicts' in Moldova and the so-called self-proclaimed Moldavian Republic of Transdniestria (hereafter – the MRT). In some cases while analysing the general situation surrounding the MRT the court found 'that Russia continues to exercise *effective control* [emphasis added] and a decisive influence over the MRT authorities' (see Catan and Others v. Moldova and Russia 2012, para.122; Mozer v. Moldova and Russia 2016, para.110), taking into account its military, financial, political support provided to 'separatists'. The term 'effective control' might refer to two important concepts: state responsibility as in Nicaragua v. USA and occupation under the IHL as was already discussed when analysing the seizure of Crimea.

There is enough evidence to suggest that the capture of the Donbas territory by 'separatists' fully corresponds to the same circumstances that were analysed in cases concerning the MRT. (Korotkyi and Hendel 2018, pp. 145–173). Therefore, it is possible to demonstrate that Russia had effective control over the Donbas (DNR/LNR), and we can claim that this situation amounts to occupation by proxy. In such a case, the conflict will be considered an international armed conflict.

2.2.4. Full-Scale Invasion

Events took a turn for the worse on 24 February 2022, when Russia launched its full-scale invasion of Ukraine. Russia titled the invasion a 'special military operation' (McDermott and Bartles 2022); it did not declare war upon Ukraine nor officially acknowledge that it is part of an international armed conflict. Russia's highest authorities have denied that they are waging full-scale war against Ukraine on numerous occasions. However, despite political wording, the facts on the ground play a crucial role towards the application of the IHL. Russia has launched its full military might (land, air, naval), and has conducted – and, at the time of preparing this chapter, continues to conduct – numerous military operations via state forces in the state's name.

Despite its wording, Russia tacitly recognises the applicability of the IHL (although recognition of applicability does not mean that it follows the rules of the IHL). For example, captured Ukrainian military personnel are considered prisoners of war (ANON, 2023d) (at least some of them, in contrast to sailors involved in the Kerch incident (Socor 2019)). Russia is also justifying its strikes on targets in Ukraine in military or at least quasi-military terms (Anon 2022); there are sometimes agreements on humanitarian corridors (Anon 2022), etc. Therefore, one must conclude that all of these word games of not calling invasion a war or an international armed conflict are oriented towards Russian society, and have nothing to do with the IHL.

In summary, the regime of international armed conflict started with the seizure of Crimea in 2014, and continued during the 'conflict in Donbas' in different forms: first belligerent occupation (Crimea), then proxy occupation

(Donbas). During the 'conflict in Donbas' period, it could have been the case that this conflict may have been mixed, and possibly included elements of both non-international and international armed conflict. On 24 February 2022, a full-scale invasion continued this ongoing international armed conflict, only in a more open and much more broad-scale way.

2.2.5. The Status of Persons Involved in the Conflict

Russia's aggression against Ukraine sees a lot of different personnel involved in the conflict or acting within it. First, it involves members of armed forces: both the Armed Forces of Ukraine (Ukraine Defence Forces) (hereafter – UDF), and Russia's military forces (hereafter – RMF). The RMF are also supplemented by using the infamous Wagner private military company (hereafter – PMC). The UDF are supplemented by foreign volunteer units ('International Legion'), coming from different countries to fight alongside Ukrainians. There are also territorial defence forces (hereafter – the TDF) (Ukr. *Teroborona*), national guards (Ukr. *Nacional'naja gvardija*), etc. Numerous organisations of non-military volunteers are supporting the UDF by providing different technologies and materials, from food to sophisticated drones and armament. This part of the chapter will discuss the status of these persons under the IHL and the nature of different parties' obligations towards them.

2.2.6. Armed Forces

In the case of international armed conflict, 'armed forces of the state', under Article 43(1) of Additional Protocol 1, includes 'all organized armed forces, groups and units which are under a command responsible to that Party for the conduct of its subordinates, even if that Party is represented by a government or an authority not recognized by an adverse Party'. Consequently, members of the armed forces are to be considered combatants (Art. 43(2)). The 'black-letter law' is plain and simple; it makes no distinction between drafted or recruited persons and it holds no requirements of nationality. Instead, the main requirement is that various groups and units must be under the command of a party to the conflict.

Regular military forces correspond to this requirement *ipso facto*. In the case of other units, their command link to a party to the conflict must be analysed (Crawford and Pert, pp. 99–100).

2.2.7. The International Legion

Let us start with the status of international volunteers who are fighting on the Ukrainian side. President Volodymyr Zelensky on 27 February 2022 made a public appeal for foreign citizens to come and to fight Russia's invasion on behalf of Ukraine (Zelensky 2022). There are different units, such as: the Canadian-Ukrainian brigade; Belarusian regiments (Pagonya and the Kastous Kalinouski battalion); Georgian National Legion, Free Russia and Russian Volunteer Corps, Chechen battalions, etc. (Pugliese 2023, pp. 46–58).

The International Legion does not operate on its own, neither is a separate unit from UDF. The military service of 'legionnaires' is regulated by the Ukrainian Law on Military Duty and Military Service. By the same law, foreign citizens are accepted for military service. Under this law, foreign volunteers are formally included into UDF as units of foreign fighters. It is considered as part of the Territorial Defence of the Armed Forces of Ukraine.

In contrast to Ukrainian citizens, such service is carried out exclusively on a voluntary basis, under a contract, and in positions overseen by non-officer members of the Armed Forces of Ukraine (i.e., the commanders of volunteers are exclusively Ukrainian servicemen) (Art. 2(2); Art. 4(3), Chapter III-1). The amount of financial support for foreigners serving in the Armed Forces of Ukraine is determined at the same level as that established for servicemen – citizens of Ukraine serving under a contract (Art. 21–1).

Additional details are regulated by the Decree of the President of Ukraine On Military Service of Aliens and Persons Without Citizenship in the Military Forces of Ukraine. Under this Decree volunteers must be present in the territory of Ukraine legally (Chapter II, 17). In order to facilitate and speed up the access of foreigners to this opportunity, a Presidential decree introduced visa-free entry into Ukraine from 1 March 2022 for citizens of foreign countries who wish to join the International Legion of Ukraine, except for citizens of the aggressor state.

As has been shown, foreign volunteers are officially a part of the UDF, which means that they should enjoy combatant status and should be treated as prisoners of war (hereafter – POWs) if captured.

Nevertheless, Russia has made statements suggesting that it would consider international volunteers as mercenaries (Malet 2022). Such claims have no legal ground. Neither these units nor these personnel correspond to the definition of mercenaries as it is understood by international law. Such definition is provided in Article 47 of Additional Protocol 1. Without analysing every criterion embedded in article (for an extended discussion, see below), it is enough to say that a person cannot be considered as a mercenary if they are a member of the armed forces of a party to the conflict (Art. 47, 2(e)), also their remuneration is the same as any other member of UDF (they do not correspond to Article 47, 2(c)).

Despite this, Russia has instituted at least one trial of foreign volunteers that took place in the so-called 'DNR'. In summary fashion, volunteers were accused, tried, and sentenced to being mercenaries and terrorists, without recognition of their combatant and prisoner of war status (Goldman 2022). Such a trial clearly contradicts even the minimal requirements of the IHL, and seems to constitute a war crime by itself (GC III, Art. 130, Rome Statute, Article 8(2)(2)(a)(6)).

2.2.8. Territorial Defence Forces (Teroborona) and levée en masse

As was mentioned, foreign fighters are included in the structures of TDF, but the main personnel of these units are Ukrainian citizens. The status of the TDF is regulated by the Law on the Foundations of National Resistance. The TDF is divided into military units of the Armed Forces of Ukraine and volunteer formations of territorial communities subjected to Armed Forces control. The TDF formations of territorial communities are regulated by the Regulation of the Cabinet of Ministers of Ukraine on the voluntary formation of territorial communities, which foresees procedures and requirements for such formations. Both of these types of units represent part of the state's armed forces. It could therefore be concluded that people who serve in TDF units must also be regarded as combatants because they are part of UDF.

Although the TDF system was systemically built from 2021, the main influx into its units happened during the first days of full-scale invasion (Hessey 2022). The process of joining Teroborona ranks was simplified to the minimum: only ID cards were enough (Belieskov 2023). Such a hasty practice at first glance is more reminiscent of the *levée en masse* phenomenon foreseen both in the Hague Regulations Article 2, attached to the Hague Convention (IV) Respecting the Laws and Customs of War on Land and the GC. GC III, Article 4 provides the following definition of *levée en masse*: 'Inhabitants of a non-occupied territory, who on the approach of the enemy spontaneously take up arms to resist the invading forces, without having had time to form themselves into regular armed units, provided they carry arms openly and respect the laws and customs of war.'

During the first days of the invasion, occupation was expected (and, in fact, happened), and people were ready to defend their cities and territories. However, perhaps this could not be considered as a classic example of *levée en masse* as regards the criteria of spontaneity. As is stated in the Commentary of 2020 to GC III, Article 4, *levée en masse* involves '<...> those who have not had time to form themselves into regular armed units and who have not been organized in advance by organs of the State, are covered'. TDF units and groups were still drawn up with at least some element of state organisation. In other places, there were also classic examples of *levée en masse* – such as the defence of Sumy, where people took up arms to resist without the prior authorisation of the government

(Koshiw 2023). In case of the capture of such persons, they should also be regarded as combatants (and, consequently, POWs) if they followed the two requirements mentioned: carry arms openly and respect the laws and customs of war (Green 2000, p. 107). However, in most cases classic *levée* participants are evaluated on a case-by-case basis. The Russian side announced that it would not consider such fighters as legitimate belligerents in those territories which Russia declared annexed and there are reports that members of TDF were arrested and tortured (Anon 2023).

2.2.9. Rogue Forces

An interesting case is the phenomenon of cross-border raids into Russia's territory by the Freedom of Russia Legion (Rus. *Legion Svobodnoj Rosii*; hereafter – FRL) and Russian volunteer corps (Rus. *Russkij dobrovolcheskij korpus*; hereafter – RDK), which were happening prior to the Ukrainian counter-offensive in the summer of 2023 (Polityuk 2023). These units are reported to consist only of Russian-nationality fighters who are fighting on the Ukrainian side with the aim of ousting Putin's regime. These units captured a few settlements in the Russia-Ukraine border region, fought with Russian forces, and then withdrew. This operation was performed while claiming that the units were acting on their own, with Ukraine not acknowledging any involvement. There was also considerable mocking of Russian propaganda surrounding the seizure of Crimea; for example, Mykhailo Podoliak, an adviser to the President of Ukraine wrote: 'As you know, tanks are sold at any Russian military store, and underground guerrilla groups are composed of Russian citizens' (Roth 2023).

There might be different perspectives from which to discuss these cross-border raids, e.g. from jus ad bellum view (Talmon 2023) but it might also be interesting to look at them from the point of view of the status of the personnel involved.

Officially, both the FRL and RDK are a part of the UDF, so their members have to be considered as members of the armed forces and, consequently, combatants. However, if the government of a party to the conflict denies such a link or the forces are operating in a rogue forces scenario, then this situation might change. First, the adversary would not be obliged to treat such forces as combatants from the point of view of the combatant's privilege, they would be considered as civilians who took up arms illegally. Consequently, such persons could be prosecuted or tried for the very fact of participation in hostilities under ordinary criminal law (marauders, bandits, etc.) (Green 2000, pp. 107–108). This means that under such circumstances, members of such rogue forces find themselves at the legal mercy of the captor. The captor is not obliged to prosecute, but it has the right to do so; therefore, such scenarios are not beneficial towards the members of these units.

2.2.10. An Assessment of the Status of the Wagner Private Military Company

One of the most infamous fighting forces that Russia has used in the war in Ukraine is the Wagner PMC. Wagner forces played an important role in capturing the city of Bakhmut and the Russian offensive of winter/spring 2023 (ANON, 2023c). So-called Wagnerians were also active in Syria, the Central African Republic, Mali, etc., where the group became infamous for its barbaric acts including the killing of journalists, executions, human rights violations, and other crimes (Anon 2022, pp. 21–29). It should be noted that Wagner is not a unified organisation or company, but more of an umbrella term for a network of companies which are engaged not only in military services but also natural resource extraction, etc. (Heinemann-Grüder and Aris 2022, pp. 2–8) However, in the context of the war of aggression against Ukraine, Wagner are referred to primarily as a fighting force and will be discussed from this point of view.

Most often, the personnel (or fighters) of Wagner forces are called Wagner mercenaries because they are specifically recruited for service under contract. During the Russian autumn/winter offensive in 2022–2023, Wagner recruited tens of thousands of prisoners from Russian prisons. (Anon 2023b). Therefore, we first need to clarify whether we can call Wagner forces mercenaries from the point of view of the IHL.

As already discussed, under the IHL mercenaries are considered unprivileged belligerents and war criminals. However, there is a difference between the legal concept of a mercenary and the titles given by journalists and the media. There are a number of definitions of mercenaries in international law, but the most commonly accepted is embedded in Article 47 of Additional Protocol 1. This provides for a cumulative set of criteria to which a person shall correspond in order to be treated as a mercenary:

> A mercenary is any person who: (a) is specially recruited locally or abroad in order to fight in an armed conflict; (b) does, in fact, take a direct part in the hostilities; (c) is motivated to take part in the hostilities essentially by the desire for private gain and, in fact, is promised, by or on behalf of a Party to the conflict, material compensation substantially in excess of that promised or paid to combatants of similar ranks and functions in the armed forces of that Party; (d) is neither a national of a Party to the conflict nor a resident of territory controlled by a Party to the conflict; (e) is not a member of the

armed forces of a Party to the conflict; and (f) has not been sent by a State which is not a Party to the conflict on official duty as a member of its armed forces.

In order for a person to be treated as a mercenary, they should correspond to all of the above criteria (Crawford and Pert 2020, p. 109) Because of this, the definition of a mercenary is frequently criticised (Fallah 2006, pp. 605–606).

Looking at the above criteria, it could be said that most of the Wagner personnel cannot be considered mercenaries. Despite the fact that they are specifically recruited to fight in the conflict, that they take direct part in hostilities, and that they are offered better remuneration than ordinary Russian soldiers, the majority of them are Russian citizens – i.e., citizens of a party to the conflict; therefore, they cannot be considered as mercenaries under the IHL. The situation might be more complicated for those who are not Russian or Ukrainian citizens, but their share in the fighting force is not substantial.

If Wagner personnel are not mercenaries, then what are they? The main problem is that the status of the personnel of PMCs under the IHL is far from clear; neither the GC nor other treaties define it. There are only a few soft-law sources that codify and embed international law and best practices for private military security companies, such as The Montreaux Document on Private Military and Security Companies but they lack an obligatory character. It could be said that PMCs are still operating in a grey area of law; therefore, the status of their members is not clearly defined. In most cases, PMC functions are limited to non-lethal tasks such as reconnaissance, logistics, training, security, protection, etc. It is generally agreed that PMC personnel performing non-lethal functions should be considered as civilians. If such personnel are taking part in hostilities, they lose civilian protection for as long as such participation lasts (Crawford and Pert, pp. 117–119). However, Wagner represents a different case.

In contrast to other contractors, Wagner in Ukraine was a fully-fledged fighting force with heavy machinery (artillery, tanks, MRLS, and even anti-aircraft weapons) performing military operations. Wagner personnel were engaged in performing lethal functions and conducting full-scale hostilities; in other words, they were acting like an armed group – so should they be considered as such? We have already presented the definition of armed forces under Article 43 of the Additional Protocol 1 when analysing different Ukrainian units, so we can now consider whether Wagner fits this definition.

To answer the question of whether Wagner could be considered as a part of the armed forces of a party to the conflict (the Russian Federation) it is very important to define the nature of the link between Wagner and Russia's military forces. One of the criteria to consider when analysing whether a fighting force is part of a state's armed forces is incorporation. This criterion provides that an armed group must be incorporated into the armed forces either legally or actually, 'whether through a formal procedure under national law or *de facto* by being given a continuous combat function' (Melzer 2009, p. 39).

While analysing this criterion, it should be noted that Wagner was not officially considered part of the RMF by the Russian Federation itself. Formally. Wagner is not under the control of Russia's Ministry of Defence or part of Russia's military forces, and Wagner units are not commanded by the active RMF officers, moreover, its leadership was even against such control (Pickrell 2023). On the battlefield, Wagner acted with relative independence on an operational and tactical level. Russia has never taken responsibility for the actions of Wagner, nor instituted any processes against its personnel.

As we can tell from the previous examples, the Wagner PMC was not incorporated into the RMF from a legal point of view. This finding may also be supported by the fact that after Prigozhyn's mutiny (mentioned above), Wagner personnel were offered a choice: to enter into a contract with the RMF, or to go to Belarus, as was allegedly agreed between Prigozhyn and Putin (Clarke 2023). It also may be interesting to note that tensions between Wagner and the RMF were the chief motivator behind the short-lived mutiny of 23–24 June 2023 (Schmitt 2023).

On the other hand, RMF and Russian governmental influence over the Wagner PMC is essential: Russia finances the group (Sauer 2023), while the RMF provides heavy machinery, ammunition, and equipment. Wagner performs military operations that are planned by the RMF, acts in coordination with the RMF, and has strong links with Russia's Military Intelligence (GRU) (ANON, 2020a). It would be impossible to deny that there is a *de facto* link between the RMF and Wagner. Therefore, factually, Wagner corresponds to the incorporation criterion, even though it enjoys some independence.

It therefore seems as if Wagner must be treated as a *de facto* part of Russia's armed forces engaged in the conflict, and Russia must bear responsibility for its actions (which Russia continues to refuse to do). However, some questions remain.

Article 43 of Additional Protocol 1 not only provides that armed forces are 'all organized armed forces, groups and units', but also says that 'Members of the armed forces of a Party to a conflict <...> are combatants, that is to say, they have the right to participate directly in hostilities'. However, the Commentary to Article 43 (par.1671), Additional Protocol 1 provides that said article 'does not invalidate the norms of the Hague Regulations and Article 4 of the Third Convention (GC III, Add.)'. Here we see a tension between the umbrella-like nature of Article 43 and the more specific requirements of Article 4 GC III in the sense that combatant status is a privilege for those who follow the IHL. Wagner is infamous for its breaches of the IHL. There is also another requirement in Article 43 of Additional Protocol 1: that 'armed forces shall be subject to an internal disciplinary system which, 'inter alia', shall enforce compliance with the rules of international law applicable in armed conflict'. There is little evidence of such a system within Wagner, in contrast, reports of their breaches are numerous (see above). Therefore, the question emerges of whether Wagner personnel are entitled to combatant status, or whether they should be treated as unprivileged belligerents (unlawful combatants) despite being *de facto* a part the RMF.

IHL treaties directly provide for only two possible statuses for those involved in conflict: combatants and protected persons (civilians, medical/religious personnel, etc.). It would be absurd to claim that a fighting force that has at its disposal tanks, armoured vehicles, artillery, etc., could be considered civilians. So-called unprivileged belligerency is a blurred concept developed mainly in the USA/Israeli jurisprudence, and has very limited basis in written law (Crawford and Pert 2020, pp. 111–114). Jurisprudence connects this concept with Article 51 (3) of Additional Protocol 1, which provides that 'civilians shall enjoy the protection <…> unless and for such time as they take a direct part in hostilities', and claims that unprivileged belligerents are in fact civilians who do not enjoy combatant privileges but do take part in hostilities. Such 'civilians' also comprise groups that perform constant combat functions (Melzer 2009, p. 39). Wagner doubtless corresponds to the definition of such a group, but, as demonstrated above, they act as a *de facto* part of Russia's armed forces.

Therefore, we face the following problem with Wagner: if a state *de facto* authorises the use of force by certain group, but does not accept responsibility for the group's actions, should the adversary treat members of this group as combatants? From the humanitarian point of view, the answer is affirmative, as Additional Protocol 1 Article 43 leaves little room for discussion: if an armed group is a part of the armed forces of a party to a conflict, its members are considered combatants, and, consequently, prisoners of war, if captured. Even the IHL breaches committed prior to capture cannot be grounds to refuse POW status (Additional Protocol 1, Article 44). However, this victim-centred view has problems when we are dealing with the unwillingness of a party to a conflict to accept responsibility for a group's actions, but still use it as a *de facto* military force.

This creates a burden upon the captor (adversary) to consider personnel differently than the party to whom they belong. Perhaps here there is some room for discussion of the idea that the umbrella formula in Additional Protocol 1, Article 43 was meant also for national liberation wars and not pure inter-state conflicts (Green 2000, p. 111); maybe the old rules on combatancy from the Hague Regulations and the GC can come into play and help to deny combatant status for such forces. What is the rationale behind such a denial, which might seem unhumanitarian? Perhaps this loophole encourages states to act in a grey area, and if such practices are not countered at least by legal means, then recourse to private fighting forces will increase. Nevertheless, the formula of Additional Protocol 1, Article 43 is recognised as part of customary international law in ICRC's Study on the customary IHL, Rule 106 (Henckaerts 2005, p. 207) and perhaps only *ad hoc* approaches in specific cases could solve this issue. For the time being, Ukraine is considering captured Wagner personnel as prisoners of war (Hendrix and Korochulk 2023).

2.2.11. The Treatment of Prisoners of War

Both parties to this war are taking prisoners of war. The exchange of POWs has become a normal routine, happening every month or so. The majority of reports about the mistreatment of POWs are related to the Russian side, and range from misbehaviour to outright atrocities (killings, mutilations, etc.), moreover, Russian side do not grant access to the places where they keep POWs (Anon 2023a, pp. 12–20). It would not be possible to list all of the cases of mistreatment in this short chapter; therefore, here we will only discuss some practices that are not so self-evident as breaches, or that contain other interesting legal elements.

One practice regarding POWs in this war is widespread: filming and posting videos of captured enemy soldiers on social media. Sometimes these soldiers are asked to identify themselves by giving their name, ranks, units, and fighting histories. Sometimes captives are shown calling their relatives, etc. Such practices, even they do not contain evidence of misbehaviour or outright crimes, are highly questionable.

Article 13 of the GC III provides that POWs should always be protected 'against insults and public curiosity'. This rule was drafted a long time ago, before social media, but the modern interpretation of it is rather wide. The content of this prohibition is well-described in the Commentary of 2020 to Article 13 (paras.1623–1627) and such prohibition should cover not only the prohibition of showing-off prisoners of war in kind (the hybrid-war period has seen the old practice of parading prisoners of war through the streets revived on the Russian side), but must also include any new forms of public curiosity. During Operation Desert Storm in 1991, Iraq was condemned for showing POWs on television (Green 2000, p. 200). Social media is based on public curiosity; therefore, even if such a practice may play a positive role (e.g., the relatives of POWs may know that they are alive), it is still controversial an even contrary to the rule, especially if POWs are shown in humiliating manner.

Another practice used by Russians is to keep prisoners of war *incommunicado*, i.e., without any connection with the external environment, where people are not allowed to inform their loved ones about their fate and whereabouts (Anon 2023a, p. 15). Such a practice is in clear contradiction of Article 70 GC III, which clearly provides for the immediate right of POWs to inform relatives about their capture. Such an obligation continues throughout captivity (Article 71), and provides that POWs have a right to send post-cards or letters. As the Commentary of 2020 of Article 71 (para.3181) states, 'It recognizes the right of prisoners of war to maintain, to a certain extent, relations with the outside world. It also represents the default position: prisoners of war must be allowed to send and receive correspondence, without discrimination.' In the modern world, post-cards and letters are falling into almost complete disuse, but the aim of this rule is simple: to enable POWs to communicate with relatives. Therefore, there would not be a breach of this rule if POWs were allowed to communicate by other means (Commentary of 2020 of Article 71, (para.3186): make calls and send messages, communicate through e-mail, etc.)

One extremely interesting case occurred in July 2023 related to commanders of the Azov regiment. This regiment, which initially appeared as a volunteer unit, is regarded by Russia as a terrorist organisation (Anon 2022). During the beginning of full-scale invasion in 2023, Azov was the main defence force of the city of Mariupol, and took a last stand at the Azovstal plant. Being outnumbered and surrounded, they were ordered into surrender. The surrender agreement, brokered by Turkish president Erdogan, foresaw that the garrison should march into captivity, with its commanders relocated to Turkey and kept until the war is over. Specific details of the agreement were not made public (Anon 2023a).

The fate of the captives was different: some experienced harsh captivity and were then exchanged; some were killed in the Olenivka prison attack (Anon 2023a, p. 19); some are perhaps still in captivity; and some are currently facing another sham trial on terrorism charges (Kvitka 2023). However, the commanders unexpectedly returned to Ukraine from Turkey before the Vilnius NATO Summit on 9–11 July 2023. From official statements, it looks as if this was done without Russia's consent. Turkish president Erdogan commented that he released these captives at the request of Ukraine's president, Zelensky, and did not breach any agreement because the initial agreement was between Russia and Ukraine (Anon 2023). Upon their return, these commanders promised to return to the battlefield as soon as possible. (Anon 2023)

It is very hard to evaluate this situation while knowing so few details. Indeed, Article 111 GC III foresees such an option – to transfer POWs to a third, neutral state. Special agreements supplementing protection on an *ad hoc* basis are also foreseen as instruments in the common articles of the GC. Such agreements concerning the transfer of POWs to a third country cannot be concluded without the third country's consent. Therefore, such a turn of events might suggest that either Turkey did not honour the previous agreement or that official statements about the agreement were not true. In the case of Turkey's breach, this might lead to Russia's future unwillingness to conclude agreements of this nature.

2.2.12. Interim findings

Russia's aggression against Ukraine has raised many legal issues. However, some of these issues are clearly artificial, such as Russia's use of the term 'special military operation' rather than 'war' or 'conflict'. Without any doubt, under the IHL, Russia's war against Ukraine is an international armed conflict, and Ukraine's territories (including Crimea) are under military occupation – despite Russia's annexations or the creation of puppet states. Most of the personnel involved in active fighting should be regarded as combatants and, consequently, prisoners of war upon capture. Moreover, Russia's constant attempts to deny combatant rights to international volunteers, the Azov regiment, and members of territorial defence units are illegal. Finally, personnel of the Wagner private military security company should be recognised as part of Russia's armed forces, and Russia must accept responsibility for their actions.

2.3. The Problem of Genocidal Intent: A Historical Perspective for Ukraine

2.3.1. State Responsibility vs Individual Responsibility

This chapter discusses genocidal intent as the *mens rea* for the crime of genocide in light of the UNGC and recent ECHR case law regarding Soviet crimes in Lithuania, analysing relevant recent Russian sources for potential proof of genocidal intent in Ukraine since February 2022. The focus of this chapter is on one element of genocidal intent – the perpetrator state's plan to destroy a national group, in whole or in part, as established in genocidal declarations or speech. The issue of individual criminal responsibility for genocide is not covered in this chapter.

Since 24 February 2022, Russia has violated international law many times, but the massacre at Bucha, which went public on 1 April after Russian forces withdrew from this city near the Ukrainian capital of Kiev, accelerated debates about the ongoing genocide of Ukrainians to the highest level. On the US Senate floor on the evening of 6 April 2022, US Senate Majority Leader Chuck Schumer directly accused Russia of waging a genocidal war in Ukraine (Vytvytsky 2022a). However, not everybody agreed with Schumer's interpretation at that time (Vytvytsky 2022b). Just a few days earlier, in Brussels, NATO Secretary General Jens Stoltenberg and US Secretary of State Antony Blinken demurred when asked the genocide question. Within a week the debate reached its peak, when US President Joe Biden accused Putin of committing genocide in Ukraine on 13 April (Borger 2022a); however, French leader Emmanuel Macron declined to follow Biden's example, arguing that an 'escalation of words' would not help bring peace (Borger 2022b). Another US ally, Australian Prime Minister Scott Morrison, also stopped short of using the term 'genocide', though he said that Putin should be 'held to account' for war crimes and atrocities in Ukraine.

Politicians' caution around declaring the crime of genocide can be affected by many factors; however, the problematic notion of genocidal intent adopted in the UNGC would likely be the main reason from a legal perspective (UN Convention on the Prevention and Punishment of the Crime of Genocide 1951). Article II of the UNGC states that in the present Convention, genocide means 'any of the following acts committed with intent to destroy, in whole or in part, a national, ethnical, racial or religious group, as such.' The intent of the crime of genocide has three basic components, which are challenging to prove: the offender must intend to destroy the group; the offender must intend that the group be destroyed in whole or in part; and the offender must intend to destroy a group that is defined by nationality, race, ethnicity, or religion (Schabas 2000, pp. 228–241).

Clearly, Ukrainians are a national group that the Russian regime is attempting to destroy. However, since 'case law has associated intent with the existence of a State or organizational plan or policy', the question then becomes: does the Russian regime have such a plan or policy? (Motyl 2022). While searching for an answer, one should bear in mind the difference between state responsibility for genocide and individual criminal responsibility for genocide: the latter emphasises the need to prove that the perpetrators themselves acted with genocidal intent; while for the former, no such proof is necessary – demonstrating the collective genocidal intent of the Russian state would be enough (Bosnia and Herzegovina v. Serbia and Montenegro, ICJ 2007). The Court further examines the question of whether it may make a finding of genocide by a State in the absence of a prior conviction of an individual for genocide by a competent court on page 68 of the judgment.

It appears that more and more politicians are convinced that there is such a plan, and thus genocidal intent. Since early spring of 2022, the perception of Russia's violations of international law have changed dramatically due to the emergence of many pieces of evidence. Thus, some countries (Whatcott 2022) have already declared Russia's genocide of Ukrainians, including Lithuania (Anon 2022), Latvia, Estonia (Sytas 2022), Ireland, Poland, Canada (Treisman 2022), and the Czech Republic (Jack 2022). The US Congress also joined this list in June 2022 (Mackinnon 2022). Debates over the claim of genocide are being refreshed with renewed intensity alongside new developments in the war of aggression, such as the International Criminal Court's warrant of arrest (Law 2023) or the anniversary of the war (Hinton 2023). The reason for this is that 'genocide monopolises people's moral imaginations' (Moses 2022).

While political declarations have little impact on the legal debate as genocide cannot be presumed (Harb 2022), the question in the legal field of the genocidal intent of Russia as a state remains open. The problem here is that politicians 'seem to be using the term genocide in a demagogic and provocative manner, a way to stigmatize their enemy in the eyes of public opinion'.(Schabas 2022, p. 854) However, many prominent scholars have already communicated the idea that the war in Ukraine represents potential genocide, including non-legal scholars such as Eugene Finkel (Finkel 2022), Timothy D. Snyder (Snyder 2022a), and Gregory Stanton (Wright 2022), and legal experts such as Otto Luchterhandt (Blyk 2022), and Zakhar Tropin (Trofimov and Marson 2022). A comprehensive report by the Raoul Wallenberg Centre for Human Rights claimed that, along with the acts required to meet the definition of genocide, there is genocidal intent in Ukraine, together establishing genocide (New lines Institute 2022). However, recent legal analysis, i.e., that of William Schabas (2022), Kevin Jon Heller (2023) or Iryna Marchuk and Aloka Wanigasuriya (2022), is not so clear-cut.

In this study, the suggestion is to include the additional historical perspective of Soviet crimes in countries formerly occupied by the USSR (including Ukraine) in an attempt to prove the current Russian genocide in Ukraine. The recent case law of the ECtHR regarding the Soviet genocide against Lithuanian partisans could serve as a background to indicate that at least some elements of genocide exist in the current Russian war of aggression against Ukraine. The main problem in the Lithuanian cases was that the Lithuanian national courts needed to prove Soviet genocidal intent from indirect sources, as one part of the relevant archival data on this issue was destroyed in 1990 and the other part remains in Moscow and is not available to the public. The Lithuanian national courts failed to prove genocide in the first case (2015) but succeeded in the second (2019). It is believed that the strategies of proving the genocidal intent of the USSR in the

Lithuanian cases at the ECtHR could benefit the various ongoing legal investigations into current Russian atrocities in Ukraine (Armstead 2022).

2.3.2. The Challenging Concept of Genocidal Intent: The Role of a Motive

Genocidal intent has been a crucial legal problem since the adoption of the UNGC, and concept is still under crucial development (Ambos 2009, pp. 833–858). From its initial codification in 1948 to its inclusion in the Rome Statue in 1998, the international crime of genocide has been defined as involving the 'intent to destroy, in whole or in part, a national, ethnical, racial or religious group, as such'(Greenawalt 1999, pp. 2259–2294). However, when Lemkin, a Polish lawyer who emigrated to the US, first coined the term *genocide*, there was little emphasis on intent (Goldsmith 2010, p. 247). He saw genocide as a coordinated plan of different actions aiming at the destruction of the essential foundations of the life of a national group:

> Generally speaking, genocide does not necessarily mean the immediate destruction of a nation, except when accomplished by mass killings of all members of a nation. It is intended rather to signify a coordinated plan of different actions aiming at the destruction of essential foundations of the life of national groups, with the aim of annihilating the groups themselves. The objectives of such a plan would be disintegration of the political and social institutions, of culture, language, national feelings, religion, and the economic existence of national groups, and the destruction of the personal security, liberty, health, dignity, and even the lives of the individuals belonging to such groups. Genocide is directed against the national group as an entity, and the actions involved are directed against individuals, not in their individual capacity, but as members of the national group (Lemkin 1944).

Still, from legal perspective the reference to 'intent' in the UNGC indicates that the prosecution must go beyond establishing that the offender meant to engage in the conduct, or meant to cause its consequences. The offender must also be proven to have had a 'specific intent', or *dolus specialis*. Where specific intent is not established, the act remains punishable, but not as genocide – it may be classified as a crime against humanity or it may simply be a crime under ordinary criminal law (Schabas 2000, p. 214). The Trial Chamber of the International Criminal Tribunal for Rwanda (hereafter – the ICTR) in the *Akayesu* judgement described genocidal intent as the 'key element' of an intentional offence, which is 'characterized by a psychological relationship between the physical result and the mental state of the perpetrator' (The Prosecutor v. Jean-Paul Akayesu, ICTR 1998, para.518). The subsequent case law of the ICTR essentially followed the *Akayesu* findings, requiring, in addition, that the aim of destroying one of the protected groups be proven. The case law of ICTY took the same approach. The ICJ also refers, citing the ICTY, to 'special or specific intent' as an 'extreme form of willful and deliberate acts designed to destroy a group or part of a group' (Bosnia and Herzegovina v. Serbia and Montenegro, ICJ 2007, para.188 cited The Prosecutor v. Kupreškić *et al.* ICTY 2000, para.636).

The specific intent necessary for a genocide conviction is very demanding. Unable to rely on the number of victims as evidence of genocidal intent (i.e., the meaning of the definition of the phrase 'in whole or in part'), the prosecution is required to introduce other proof (Bryant and Jones 1975, p. 692). Proof of genocidal intent includes: (a) some sort of genocidal declaration or speech; (b) the context of the crime, its massive scale, and elements of its perpetration that suggest hatred of the group and a desire for its destruction; (c) a very high number of atrocities committed against the group; and (d) proof of attacks directed against cultural institutions or monuments committed in association with killing, which may prove important in establishing the existence of genocidal rather than merely homicidal intent (Schabas 2000, pp. 222–223).

Other indicators to detect the intent to commit genocide could include situations in which: (a) potential perpetrators are agents of the state or rival authorities, for example, military or police units, or militias authorised by the state or by a revolutionary leader; (b) elites and groups linked to them often use hateful propaganda and attack ethnic and political opponents of the state; (c) government repression in response to opposition activities is greatly disproportionate to opposition acts; and (d) authorities and security forces ignore isolated killings and the abuse of ethnic and political group members. In 1996, Genocide Watch Director G. H. Stanton presented eight stages of genocide to explain genocidal intent. He argued that intent can be directly proven from statements or orders by perpetrators, but more frequently it must be deduced from the *systematic pattern* of their acts, a pattern that could only arise out of specific intent. In addition, a plan for genocide does not need to be written out. An act of genocide may arise in a culture that considers members of another group to be less than human, where killing members of that group is not considered murder (Stanton 1996–2023).

The ICTR in *Akayesu* declared that genocidal intent could be inferred from physical acts, and specifically 'the massive and/or systematic nature or their atrocity'. According to the Trial Chamber:

> This is the reason why, in the absence of a confession from the accused, his intent can be inferred from a certain number of presumptions of fact. The Chamber considers that it is possible to deduce the genocidal intent inherent in a particular act charged from the general context of the perpetration of other culpable acts systematically directed against that same group, whether these acts were committed by the same offender or by others.

> Other factors, such as the scale of atrocities committed, their general nature, in a region or a country, or furthermore, the fact of deliberately and systematically targeting victims on account of their membership of a particular group, while excluding the members of other groups, can enable the Chamber to infer the genocidal intent of a particular act (The Prosecutor v. Jean-Paul Akayesu, ICTR 1998, para.477).

Some scholars suggest that the role of motive in the elements of the crime of genocide cannot be dismissed, as it is clear that genocide cannot be committed without a degree of planning and preparation, and it is unlikely that courts will convict in the absence of proof of a plan (Bassiouni and Manikas 1995, p. 527). Genocide is, by its nature, a collective crime that is committed with the cooperation of many participants. It is, moreover, an offence generally directed by the state. The organisers and planners must necessarily have the motive of destroying the target group – that is, a genocidal motive, taken as a whole. Where this is lacking, the crime cannot be genocide (Schabas 2000, p. 255). Individual players may also be driven by a variety of motives, such as monetary gain, jealousy, or political ambition. In other words, hatred of the group must be the driving force behind the crime. Genocide was made a crime in order to be punished as such, not to serve as a proxy for crimes of mass slaughter carried out for other reasons.

The ICTR in *Akayesu* at some point also stated that specific intent is essentially a motive requirement – the members of the victim group were targeted because of their membership in the group:

> On the issue of determining the offender's specific intent, the Chamber considers that intent is a mental factor which is difficult, even impossible, to determine. This is the reason why, in the absence of a confession from the accused, his intent can be inferred from a certain number of presumptions of fact. The Chamber considers that it is possible to deduce the genocidal intent inherent in a particular act charged from the general context of the perpetration of other culpable acts systematically directed against that same group, whether these acts were committed by the same offender or by others. Other factors, such as the scale of atrocities committed, their general nature, in a region or a country, or furthermore, the fact of deliberately and systematically targeting victims on account of their membership of a particular group, while excluding the members of other groups, can enable the Chamber to infer the genocidal intent of a particular act. […] (The Prosecutor v. Jean-Paul Akayesu, ICTR 1998, para.523; Amobs 2009, pp. 833–859).

Thus, the existence of a genocidal plan – and, consequently, of a genocidal purpose – can prove a destructive motive. However, the utility of a plan is evidential; it is not legally required following the definition of genocide. In other words, such a plan or policy is not a formal requirement of genocide: it is simply extremely difficult to prove the necessary specific intent without evidence of a plan or policy.

To sum up, according to relevant legal doctrine the indication of genocidal intent requires strong evidence, but only some types of evidence are assessed in the case law of genocide trials. As the definition of genocide seeks to address systematic actions against a specific group, the majority of potential evidence of genocidal intent leads to the need to prove the existence of a general genocidal plan by the perpetrator state. This can then prove the essence of the crime of genocide: a destructive motive. Historical cases on Soviet crimes in Lithuania could contribute to this cause.

2.3.3. A Lithuanian Strategy to Prove Soviet Genocidal Intent

The issue of Soviet genocidal intent was neglected for decades in academic scholarship, as was the idea of potential Soviet genocide itself. Only in the 2000s did several scholars begin to argue that new genocidal trials could contribute to efforts to identify Soviet crimes as genocide. The ICTY found in the *Jelisić* case that 'genocidal intent can take two forms': on the one hand, the intent to exterminate a very large number of members of a group; on the other, the intent to pursue a more selective destruction targeting only certain members of a group because of the impact that their disappearance would have on the survival of the group as such' (The Prosecutor v. Jelisić, ICTY 1999, para.82; Verdirame 2000, p. 587). As Lauri Malksoo stated regarding the target group, the context of the Soviet repressions in the Baltic states seems to indicate genocidal intent in the second sense, because repressive actions in the Baltic states were directed towards 'liquidating' the people who would be most determined to carry on the will for independent statehood based on 'non-Soviet' principles of government (Mälksoo 2001, pp. 784–785). However, the question of the role of the Soviet leadership in committing genocide is even more complicated due to the absence of direct proof of genocidal intent. In short, evidence from both the Soviet Union and elsewhere suggests that Stalin's deranged personality was probably only a secondary factor in explaining the crimes of his regime (Somin 2010). Moreover, the genocidal intent of the Soviet leadership does not automatically prove that, for instance, a particular official had *dolus specialis* regarding the crime of genocide when obeying their superior's orders, nor the intent to *destroy* a group or a part of it. Such intent must be proven separately in each individual case (Mälksoo 2001, pp. 784–785; Kinetz *et al.* 2022).

In recent ECtHR judgments concerning the killing of Lithuanian partisans by Soviet officers, one of the main issues was the genocidal intent of the particular perpetrators and their link to the general genocidal plan of the USSR in the occupied countries. In the ECtHR case *Vasiliauskas v. Lithuania*, former Ministry of State Security (hereafter – the MGB, 1946–1953) officer Vytautas Vasiliauskas (born 1930) complained that his conviction for genocide by the domestic courts was in breach of Article 7 of the ECHR, in particular because the national courts' broad interpretation of that crime had no basis in international law (Vasiliauskas v. Lithuania, ECtHR 2015). On 2 January 1953, Mr. Vasiliauskas took part in an operation against two Lithuanian partisans who had been hiding in the forest. The goal of the operation was to capture or eliminate the partisans (the Soviets used the phrase 'liquidate the bandits'). Several soldiers were involved and the applicant was part of the operation. During the attempt to apprehend them, the partisans resisted by opening fire on the MGB officers and the Soviet soldiers. The partisans were shot and killed. In this case, the question that the ECtHR had to answer was whether the applicant's conviction for genocide in 2005 by domestic courts was reasonably foreseeable in light of international law as it stood in 1953, when the crime was committed.

The ECtHR Grand Chamber of 17 judges came out split on the outcome, ruling by 9 votes to 8 that the conviction for the genocide of a political and social group according to post-Soviet Lithuanian legislation was not foreseeable and that it was in violation of ECHR Article 7, which states that one cannot be held criminally accountable for something which is not a crime at the time when it is committed. Numerous dissenting opinions criticised the majority, arguing that it ruled too formally and failed to address the justice desired by Soviet victims. In the case of *Drėlingas v. Lithuania*, former KGB (State Security Committee, 1954–1992) officer Stanislovas Drėlingas (born 1931) complained to the ECtHR on the same grounds (Drėlingas v. Lithuania, 2019 ECtHR). In 2014, Mr. Drėlingas was charged by domestic courts with being an accessory to genocide for having taken part in an operation on 11–12 October 1956 during which the last partisan leader, Vanagas (meaning 'The Hawk', a cryptonym), was captured, tortured, sentenced to death and executed. His wife, Vanda, was also captured and sentenced to deportation afterwards. Once again, the main question was whether the applicant could have sufficiently foreseen that he was involved in committing genocide in 1956. In the judgment, which was delivered in March 2019, the ECtHR held that Mr. Drėlingas must have been aware in 1956 that he could be prosecuted for the genocide of a national group for taking part in the detention of two partisans, and that his conviction had been foreseeable. The judgment entered into force on 10 September 2019, when the defendant's request for referral to the Grand Chamber of the ECtHR was rejected.

The Lithuanian national courts in both cases needed to demonstrate the link between the state's ideology, which included some aspects of a genocidal plan, and the officers who executed that plan using a clear methodology and instructions. The intent of Soviet repressions in Lithuania was summarised by the Lithuanian Constitutional Court in 2014, clarifying the goal and the plan of the USSR regarding Lithuanians:

> the repressions against the residents of Lithuania were not in any manner coincidental and chaotic, but rather such repressions sought to exterminate the basis of the political nation of Lithuania, inter alia, the former social and political structure of the State of Lithuania. Those repressions were directed against the most active political and social groups of the residents of the Republic of Lithuania: participants of the resistance against the occupation and their supporters, civil servants and officials of the State of Lithuania, Lithuanian public figures, intellectuals and the academic community, farmers, priests, and members of the families of those groups.

To be precise, during the first Soviet occupation of Lithuania (1940–1941) at least 23 different categories of people were considered a threat to the Soviet regime (Vižulis 1985, p. 101). The Lithuanian Constitutional Court also concluded that actions which took place before the 2003 national legislation and which had been directed against certain political and social groups might constitute genocide if it could be proved that the aim of such actions was to destroy groups that represented a significant part of the Lithuanian nation and whose destruction had an impact on the survival of the entire Lithuanian nation. The Court indicated that Lithuanian partisans constituted such a group, considering their activity during the 1944–1953 partisan war (Sagatienė 2021, p. 781).

However, the Supreme Court of Lithuania's finding that Mr. Vasiliauskas, when taking genocidal actions, had known of the Soviet regime's goal of eradicating all Lithuanian partisans was rejected by the ECtHR. According to the Supreme Court of Lithuania,

> the actions of Vasiliauskas also correspond to the subjective element of genocide – direct intent [lith. *tiesioginė tyčia*]: Vasiliauskas, when taking those actions, had known the goal of the Soviet Government – to eradicate all Lithuanian partisans. He knew that the brothers J.A. and A.A. were partisans, and understood that during the operation they would be killed or arrested and then tortured, tried as 'traitors to the homeland' and [possibly] sentenced to death, and [Vasiliauskas] wished that to happen.

Vasiliauskas was able to assess the partisans as a significant part of the national group because he was an MGB officer, an organisation which had been carrying out these tasks since 1945–1946 against partisans as a national group in order: to eliminate the remains of 'political banditism' and other anti-Soviet activities; to eliminate sabotage intelligence and other enemy groups as well as individuals; to eliminate 'anti-Soviet elements', traitors, traitors to the homeland and other enemy proteges and supporters; to confiscate illegally held weapons; to perform the tasks of the USSR and the MGB-MVD to guarantee the security of USSR; and to protect special objects approved by the MVD (Starkauskas 1998, p. 29). The prosecutor stated that

> He knew that the LSSR MGB's main purpose was to physically eradicate part of the Lithuanian population belonging to a separate political group, namely, the Lithuanian partisans, participants in the resistance to the Soviet occupation. The applicant had been active in fulfilling that main goal of the LSSR MGB by killing some of the inhabitants of Lithuania belonging to the aforementioned political group (Starkauskas 1998, p. 29).

The prosecutor found it to be established that, as of 15 September 1951, the applicant had served as an operational agent in the Kaunas region, Šakiai district branch of the LSSR MGB. For the prosecutor, the applicant's guilt was proved on the basis of his service record, the applicant's superiors' commendation for his persistence when executing search measures, managing the operation and personal participation when apprehending the bandits. The evidence examined by the prosecutor included statements by witnesses, minutes of the meetings of the Šakiai district MGB unit which were obtained from the Lithuanian Special Archive and the Genocide and Resistance Research Centre of Lithuania and translations of those documents, which mentioned the applicant, the tasks he had been assigned with regard to the liquidation of banditry, bandits' assistants and contact persons. Other evidence included [MGB] reports about the liquidated bandits J.A. and A.A.

This argument was further developed in the case of *Drėlingas v Lithuania*, where the ECtHR concluded that national courts brought clarification to the need to establish intent (para.108), and approved the domestic interpretation that

> the annihilation of the participants in the armed national resistance, namely Lithuanian partisans, their connections and supporters, by the occupying power and its repressive bodies, was systematic, consistent, based on a clear methodology and instructions. The acts of repression were directed against the most active and advanced part of the Lithuanian nation as a national, ethnic group. Such extermination had the clear aim of influencing the demographic changes of the Lithuanian nation and its very survival, as well as at facilitating the sovietisation of the occupied Lithuania. The extermination of the resistance participants not only meant the elimination of obstacles to the objectives of the occupying regime; it also had another purpose, namely to intimidate the residents of Lithuania by showing what destiny awaited those who refused to obey the occupying power. (para.25) (Starkauskas 1998, p. 54)

Regarding the applicant's conviction for genocide, the Supreme Court found it established that by 1956, when the crime was committed, the applicant had already been working for the MGB, which he had joined 'consciously and voluntarily', for four years. Before that, he had completed the Vilnius School of MGB Operational Staff Training, where he studied for two years. It was noteworthy that the applicant had studied at the security service school and started his service in the security structure during the period when the national resistance movement against the occupying power was active. He was not an ordinary officer: from 1952 he was a member of the USSR Communist party, and after graduating from the MGB school he was granted the rank of officer-lieutenant. The applicant worked at the Lithuanian MGB/KGB 2-N board, the main function of which was the fight against the national resistance movement. It was also noteworthy that the division where the applicant had worked carried out surveillance of the members and leadership of the Lithuanian national underground movement'.

These ECtHR cases illustrate how closely genocidal intent by a particular officer executing an act of genocide is linked to the general ideology of the perpetrator state. In the case of the USSR, Soviet repressions were part of systematic Sovietization and arose in a much broader ideological context, as the goal of the Soviet regime was to transform human existence and create an entirely new kind of human being – the New Soviet man. Thus, nationality was not important anymore, and a new socialist nation had to emerge (Lebed 1958, pp. 4–5). In mid-June 1940, the USSR presented the Baltic governments with a demand for the total occupation of their territories, backed by a warning that military resistance would be repressed. The Baltic governments capitulated and the Soviet forces invaded. Shortly thereafter, hasty 'elections' were held, in which only candidates approved by the Communist Party could run. The resulting 'parliaments' immediately petitioned Moscow to admit the Baltic states into the Soviet Union, a wish that was promptly granted, and the Baltic states were annexed to the USSR in early August 1940. Thus, 'within three months, the three states had been transformed from independent sovereign republics into union republics, constituent parts of a latter-day empire' (Plakans 2011, pp. 293–307; Kasekamp 2010, pp. 95–105). What happened next had something to do with a particular Soviet interpretation of history (Liivoja 2013, p. 249). The USSR took the view that the post-1917 governments in the Baltic states with which they had negotiated peace treaties in 1920 had not been legitimate, but had instead been Bolsheviks who had been toppled by 'bourgeois democratic' regimes. Accordingly, everyone involved in governing the Baltic states between 1918 and 1940 was seen as having played a role in the illegal usurpation of Soviet power. As a result, Lithuanians, together with Latvians and Estonians, were considered as persons belonging to 'untrustworthy' or 'unreliable' nationalities which interfered with the Soviet plan of successful Sovietization (Anušauskas 1996, p. 385).

In the Baltic states, Sovietization was a systematic and comprehensive project which was comprised of the following elements: (a) the introduction of the USSR's administrative and economic systems; (b) the subjugation of states to the economic and political needs of the USSR; (c) militarisation; (d) the colonisation of states (especially Latvia) by hundreds of thousands of Russian-speaking immigrants; (e) the destruction of the traditional social structure through genocide and Russification; (f) total control over the internal means of communication and contact with foreign countries; and (i) the destruction of established political, economic and cultural traditions (Strods 2005, p. 209). The partisan movement in Lithuania was destroyed by the USSR after almost 10 years using this strategy, which contained a system of various methods delivered by different Soviet organs that were all mobilised to systematically destroy resistance in Lithuania. All of these methods were subordinated towards achieving the ultimate goal: killing the members of the Lithuanian partisan movement.

Thus, the Lithuanian legal strategies at the ECtHR, which mainly followed the ICTR's *Akayesu* formula, demonstrate the importance of the link between a state's ideology and its officers in proving genocidal intent when specific – in this case, Soviet – genocidal declarations are not available. The genocidal intent of the USSR against Lithuanian partisans was mainly proved by clarifying the ideological background of the USSR and the structural system of implementing communist ideology: both the MGB as institution and its individual officers implemented some part of the Sovietization plan in order to destroy undesirable nationalities using clear methodologies and instructions.

2.3.4. Proving Russian Genocidal Intent in Ukraine

As previously mentioned, a genocidal plan can be traced through specific genocidal declarations by the perpetrator state, which in the case of Soviet crimes are still absent from academic discourse. In the context of Russia's crimes in Ukraine, however, they can be observed directly – especially since February 2022. This makes a significant difference for the prosecutor when proving genocidal intent; however, as recent ECtHR case law suggests, even public genocidal declarations by Russian officials may not be sufficient to prove the country's current genocidal intent in Ukraine. ECtHR case law regarding the Soviet genocide against Lithuanian partisans indicates that a strong link between executors and the ideology of the state is crucial in order to establish genocidal intent. The independent report produced by genocide scholars in May 2022 regarding Russian crimes in Ukraine indicated that genocidal intent can be attributed to a state through evidence of a general plan (derived from official statements, documents, or policy), or can be inferred from a systematic pattern of atrocities targeting the protected group (New Lines Institute 2022, p. 2). These scholars argued that genocidal intent can be traced in official or officially endorsed Russian statements denying the existence of the Ukrainian nation, expressing the vague goal of 'denazifying' Ukraine, and characterising a significant undefined segment of the population (or 'them') as Nazis or mortal threats, thus rendering this group a legitimate target for destruction. This report also revealed many public cases of high-ranking Russian officials denying Ukraine's right to exist or calling for its destruction (New Lines Institute 2022, pp. 12–20).

As the legal doctrine indicates that genocidal declarations are the most powerful evidence of genocidal intent, it is useful to analyse them in light of recent ECtHR case law dealing with historical cases of Soviet genocide in order to establish a link between the executors of these crimes and the current Russian ideology towards Ukrainians. Perhaps the most notable high-level public declarations which could be considered as genocidal are the following: (a) Putin's essay of July 2021; (b) Putin's speech before the invasion on 21 February 2022; (c) an RIA Novosti editorial entitled 'What Russia should do with Ukraine' published on 3 April 2022; and (d) a Telegram post by Dmitry Medvedev of 5 April 2022.

In July 2021, Putin published an essay entitled 'On the Historical Unity of Russians and Ukrainians', in which he reasserted that Ukrainians and Russians are 'one people, a single whole', and added that his position is 'not driven by some short-term considerations or prompted by the current political context' (Putin 2022a). In this essay, Putin argued that 'modern Ukraine is entirely the product of the Soviet era' and that the 'true sovereignty of Ukraine is possible only in partnership with Russia'. He further suggested that when the Ukrainian government rejects the idea that Russians and Ukrainians are the same people, they are indulging neo-Nazis and Nazism. On 21 February 2022, 3 days before the start of the full-scale invasion, Putin gave a speech insisting that 'modern Ukraine was entirely created by Russia or, to be more precise, by Bolshevik, Communist Russia', and that Russia was 'ready to show what real decommunisation would mean for Ukraine' (Putin 2022b). In his speech announcing the invasion of Ukraine, Putin urged Ukrainians to reject their elected officials in order to strengthen Ukraine and Russia 'from within as a single whole, despite the existence of state borders' (Putin 2022c).

In an RIA Novosti editorial published on 3 April 2022 entitled 'What Russia should do with Ukraine', author Timofey Sergeytsev referred to Ukrainians in the following terms: 'a considerable portion of the population – very likely, a majority of it – has been subjected to the Nazi regime and dragged into its agenda …', one that is 'a bigger threat … than German Nazism in the style of Hitler'. He also suggested that 'significant part of the masses … are passive Nazis and accomplices', and pointed to 'a nazified bulk of the population' and 'a Nazi society'. In addition, he asserted that Ukraine's elites 'must be liquidated as re-education is impossible', that 'denazification will inevitably include de-ukrainization', and that 'Ukrainism is … a subordinate element of a different and alien civilization' (Rodionov 2022). Putin claims that American-led slaughter shattered Ukraine's national pattern, denying it agency, and that Russian extermination would eradicate this Americanised trend by improving Ukraine's ruined state so that it could become like Russia. Thus, any genocide would simply undo the preceding genocide, and therefore would not be genocide (Etkind 2022).

On 5 April 2022, the deputy chairman of Russia's Security Council, Dmitry Medvedev, posted the following on Telegram: 'Ukrainian-ness, which is fuelled by anti-Russian poison and is consumed by the lie concerning its own identity – this is all one big fake. This phenomenon has never existed in history. And it does not exist now' (2022). Medvedev used fictitious rhetoric – though vivid and detailed, which tends to make it more believable – to justify violence against an entire generation of Ukrainians that he described as Nazis:

> For the past 30 years, a passionate segment of Ukrainians has prayed for the Third Reich. Literally. Nazi symbolism that provokes disgust can be found on photos from practically every military unit in Ukraine taken by our army — there are banners, literature, posters. Even cups with swastikas! … It's no wonder that, having transformed itself into the Third Reich, and having written into its history textbooks the names of traitors and Nazi henchmen, Ukraine will suffer the same fate. This kind of Ukraine gets what it deserves!… These difficult tasks cannot be completed instantaneously. And they will not only be decided on battlefields (2022).

Each of these pieces contribute to establishing the Russian state ideology towards Ukraine, and each can be considered as elements of the Russian genocidal plan. For this reason, the political structure and ideology might be crucial in proving Russian genocide in Ukraine; however, there is still a gap in defining it.

In the West, Putin's system of rule is still often described as a monolithic pyramid. In the eyes of society, Putin manages to present himself as an irreplaceable leader/statesman (a 'tsar', according to the West), solely making key decisions. However, such an understanding of the ruling processes in Russia is one of the main mistakes which prevents deeper insight into the regime's origins and foundations from being obtained. Since 2000, the style of making political decisions (its initial formation was influenced by various factors) has been shifting towards that of the USSR's Politburo (political bureau). Many analysts, public figures and even politicians focused on Russia have long been using the term 'collective Putin'. This fact reflects their belief that decisions in the country are not made by one person, and that Putin is just a symbol of this ruling system – though, obviously, he has not lost his role as an arbiter and moderator (Kasčiūnas *et al.* 2014; Anon 2020). In 2002–2003, a former member of the Council of the Russian

Federation, one of the richest people in the country, said that from 1996 to 2000 all important decisions were made by a small group of people called 'The Family' (Povilaitis 2022). The former Russian billionaire claimed that the so-called 'Family' continued to hold power when Yeltsin resigned as president and named Vladimir Putin as his replacement. Approximately 90 % of decisions were made by its representatives from 2000 to 2004, leaving only 10 % for Putin and his immediate circle, which was made up of old St. Petersburg-based co-workers. Putin has been making the majority of the decisions by himself and consulting with a very small group of individuals since 2012, when he genuinely won the elections.

Since the 2018 presidential election, the Politburo 2.0, an informal decision-making group that has grown around Vladimir Putin since 2012, has remained in place. As Russia's relations with the West continue to deteriorate, the Politburo 2.0 is compelled to choose the option of mobilisation. As a result, the SC's machinery will play a larger role, becoming Putin's fourth 'Big Government' component after the Presidential Administration, the general government, and the major state companies (Minchenko Consulting 2019). Speaking about the war in Ukraine, former supporter L. Nevzlins considered that the plan to attack the country arose in Putin's mind at the end of 2019, during the so-called Normandy Format meeting:

> When E. Macron, A. Merkel, V. Putin, V. Zelensky met, it was expected to sign an agreement on what was already discussed in Minsk. Suddenly V. Zelensky refused to sign; it seems that V. Putin was promised that V. Zelensky would definitely sign the agreement. When this plan failed, it seems that Putin decided that this was his last meeting with Zelensky and that only revenge awaited. And this is revenge not only for V. Zelensky personally, but also for the whole of Ukraine, V. Putin simply cannot do otherwise.

Thus, how can we indicate the current ideology of Russia and link it with the genocidal plan against Ukrainians when so many factors have still not been explored? The neologism of 'Rashism', a portmanteau of Russian fascism (Russian: *русский фашизм*), is a term used by a number of scholars, politicians and publicists to describe the political ideology and social practices of Russian authorities during the rule of Vladimir Putin. It is also used to refer to the ideology of Russian military expansionism (Marayev and Bilyk 2022; Samolenko *et al.* 2021, p. 367; Gaufman 2016, p. 107), and has been used as a label to describe an undemocratic system and nationality cult mixed with ultranationalism and a cult of personality (Snyder 2022c). This transformation was described based on the ideas of the 'special civilizational mission' of Russia, including notions such as Moscow as the third Rome and an expansionism (Gregor 1998, pp. 1–15; Motyl 2015; Stanley

2022) which manifests itself in anti-Westernism and supports regaining Imperial lands by conquest (Marayev and Bilyk 2022). Timothy Snyder believes that the ideology of Putin and his regime was influenced by Russian nationalist philosopher Ivan Ilyin (1883–1954) (Snyder 2022c). Another ideologist, Aleksandr Dugin, through books such as *The Fourth Political Theory*, published in 2009, has been cited as an inspiration for Russian policy in events such as the war in the Donbas region (Saunders 2014).

To conclude, since 2022 many high-level public genocidal declarations can be identified and highlighted as proof of a genocidal plan; however, the clarification of the political ideology in Russia can be also relevant in future legal cases. Having in mind that there is still a lack of definition surrounding the current Russian ideology and the country's governmental structure, prosecutors could be forced to enter the field of political science to develop an interdisciplinary approach to indicate those responsible for the potential crime of genocide against Ukrainians since 2022. Moreover, extra caution must be employed when proving genocidal intent in this particular case to ensure that state leaders do not avoid prosecution, and to avoid a situation where only low ranked Russian officers are accused of committing genocide.

2.3.5. Interim findings

The perpetrator state's unique genocidal declarations – which are observable in the context of Russia's atrocities in Ukraine, particularly from February 2022 – can be used to outline the formation of a genocidal plan, and essentially constitute a destructive motive for genocide. This makes a significant difference in the prosecutor's ability to demonstrate genocidal intent, but as the most recent ECtHR case law suggests, even public confessions of genocidal intent on the part of Russian officials might not be enough to demonstrate its current existence in Ukraine.

The Lithuanian strategy may be useful in demonstrating Russia's intent to commit genocide against the Ukrainian people, as the Soviet Union's intent to commit genocide against Lithuanian partisans was primarily established by demonstrating the ideological foundation of the Soviet Union and the institutional framework for implementing the communist ideology. In this way, both the MGB as an organisation and its individual officers carried out part of the Sovietization plan in order to eradicate undesirable ethnic groups using precise methods and guidelines.

Since 2022, numerous high-level public assertions of genocidal intent have been recognised and cited as evidence of a genocidal scheme; nevertheless, future legal proceedings may also depend on Russia's political ideology and the organisational structure of the country's decision-making process. Prosecutors may be forced to work in the field of political science and develop an interdisciplinary strategy in order to identify those responsible for potential genocidal crimes against Ukrainians since 2022, given that Russia's current ideology and governmental structure have still not been clearly defined.

2.4. A Jurisdictional Challenge in the Coastal State Rights Dispute: Sovereignty Issues over Crimea

2.4.1. The Factual Background of the Coastal State Rights Dispute

On 16 September 2016, Ukraine served the Russian Federation with a Notification and Statement of Claim under Annex VII of the UN Convention on the Law of the Sea (hereafter – the UNCLOS) referring to the *Coastal State Rights Dispute*. This dispute was caused by Russian violations of UNCLOS in the Black Sea, Sea of Azov, and Kerch Strait. The Annex VII arbitral tribunal characterised that this dispute was as a consequence of 'events that occurred in 2014 in Crimea', and from then the parties to the dispute have had different views on these events.

The main disagreements began in March 2014. Firstly, on 11 March 2014, the parliament of the 'Autonomous Republic of Crimea' adopted a resolution entitled 'About Crimean Independence'. This was followed by a controversial referendum on 18 March 2014, where 96.77% of votes were cast in favour of Crimea's reunification with Russia. Several different international institutions and representatives recognised this referendum as invalid, including the Parliamentary Assembly of the Council of Europe (hereafter – the PACE), the presidents of the European Council and the European Commission, the UNGA, the Venice Commission, etc.

The Russian Federation and the 'Republic of Crimea' signed the Treaty on the Admission to the Russian Federation of the Republic of Crimea and the Formation of New Constituent Entities Within the Russian Federation on 18 March 2014. Ukraine reacted negatively to all of these events, claiming that the Russian Federation invaded, occupied and unlawfully annexed Crimea in 2014.

It is important to note that the authors are of the opinion, guided by the resolutions of the GA and the legal analysis of the situation, that Crimea was illegally occupied and that it is currently annexed by the Russian Federation. Such a view is also supported by different scholars including Socher (2021), Gaspani (2021), Nuridzhanian (2018), Buchan and Tsagourias (2017), Grzebyk (2017), Leichtova (2016), Marxsen (2014), and others.

Ukraine, in its Memorial filed on 19 February 2018 to the Annex VII arbitral tribunal, claimed that the Russian Federation had violated:

(a) Ukraine's rights to hydrocarbon resources in the Black Sea and Sea of Azov;
(b) Ukraine's rights to living resources in the Black Sea, Sea of Azov, and Kerch Strait;
(c) Ukraine's rights by embarking on a campaign of illegal construction of the bridge in the Kerch Strait that threatens navigation and the marine environment;
(d) its duty to cooperate with Ukraine to address pollution at sea;
(e) Ukraine's UNCLOS rights and [its] own duties in relation to underwater cultural heritage.

The fact that Ukraine initiated the *Coastal State Rights Dispute* created a valid ground for legal opinions. Robert G. Volterra *et al.* (2018) claimed that this dispute reactivated the discussion on whether and to what extent UNCLOS grants 'jurisdiction to decide law of the sea disputes involving concurrent land sovereignty issues' (p. 616). Nilüfer Oral assumed that '[t]here is no doubt that Ukraine is utilizing UNCLOS and its compulsory dispute settlement mechanism to gain recognition of its sovereignty, even if implicitly, over Crimea through the international adjudicative process' (2021, p. 507).

The jurisdiction of the arbitral tribunal in the *Coastal State Rights Dispute* is provided by para. 1 of Article 288 of UNCLOS, which states that a special arbitral tribunal constituted in accordance with Annex VII shall have jurisdiction over any dispute concerning the interpretation or application of UNCLOS.

The name of the dispute itself offers a challenge to the jurisdiction of the tribunal. As it is possible to observe from the title of the dispute in question, it is a 'Dispute Concerning Coastal State Rights'. Thus, the ruling in this dispute would involve the determination of which country is the coastal state and what its rights are. However, starting from March 2014, after the annexation of Crimea by Russia, there have been a significant number of disagreements between Ukraine and Russia. Due to the disputed status of Crimea, the coastal state in Crimea is not clearly indicated to the tribunal. Thus, maritime zones such as the territorial sea, the contiguous zone, the exclusive economic zone generated by Crimea, as well as the rights of the coastal state over the peninsula, are claimed by two states simultaneously. This obviously incurs the following question: to which state do the sovereignty, sovereign rights and jurisdiction of the maritime zones extend?

Due to this question, several scholars have expressed the view that the recognition of Ukrainian sovereignty over Crimea is one of the challenges to determining jurisdiction in this dispute (Oral 2021; Nuridzhanian 2018; Schatz and Koval 2019; Tzeng 2016, etc).

Recently, there have been two international arbitrations instituted under Annex VII of UNCLOS that have had to answer the question of whether a dispute that involves the determination of a question of territorial sovereignty would fall within the jurisdiction of arbitrations (Silva 2019). The first was the case of *Chagos Marine Protected Area Arbitration* (Mauritius v. UK 2015), and the second was *South China Sea Arbitration* (The Philippines v. China 2016). Both disputes include controversies that were related to the law of the sea but also contained territorial sovereignty issues. Mauritius and the Philippines asked international tribunals to deal within the law of the sea, with elements of contradictory signs over jurisdiction. Following these two disputes, the *Coastal State Rights Dispute* between Ukraine and the Russian Federation became the third dispute instituted under the UNCLOS provisions regarding dispute settlement. This case presents territorial sovereignty issues and issues related to the law of the sea. Unlike the other two disputes, the dispute between Ukraine and Russia is still ongoing. After the publication of the Award on Preliminary Objections in the *Coastal State Rights Dispute* in February 2020, the final award is yet to be delivered.

When Ukraine submitted the dispute, the preliminary objection of the Russian Federation was that Ukraine brought 'a dispute regarding sovereignty over Crimea [...] and this is a matter that falls outside of the dispute settlement provisions of UNCLOS' (2018, para.64).

According to the arbitral tribunal, even if the interpretation and application of UNCLOS in relation to the Russian Federation's actions in the Black Sea, the Sea of Azov, and the Kerch Strait consist of the real objective of Ukraine's claims, a considerable part of Ukraine's claims rests on the premise that Crimea is the territory of Ukraine. Moreover, 'if the legal status of Crimea [...] is not settled in the sense that it forms part of Ukraine's territory [...] the Arbitral Tribunal would not be able to decide the claims of Ukraine insofar as they are premised on the settled status of Crimea as part of Ukraine without first addressing the question of sovereignty over Crimea' (Award on Preliminary Objections 2020, paras.153–154).

To move beyond the sovereignty issue as an obstacle for the jurisdiction of the arbitral tribunal, Ukraine invoked two arguments: firstly, that there is no dispute over sovereignty; secondly, that even if there were to be a dispute, then the arbitral tribunal would have incidental jurisdiction to rule over the determination of a coastal state (Rejoinder of Ukraine on Jurisdiction 2019, paras.26, 51; Schatz 2021).

The arbitral tribunal addressed the nature or character of the dispute submitted by Ukraine with the evaluation of the scope of its jurisdiction under para. 1 of Article 288 of UNCLOS, commenting on the existence *vel non* of a sovereignty dispute over Crimea (Award on Preliminary Objections 2020, para.154). The next two sections of this chapter will elaborate on these matters regarding the analysis of the argumentation of the arbitral tribunal, as well as with respect to the recently published scholarly commentaries of the Award concerning the Preliminary Objections of the Russian Federation.

2.4.1.1. The Scope of the Arbitral Tribunal's Jurisdiction Under para. 1 of Article 288 of UNCLOS

Article 288 of UNCLOS consists of jurisdiction *ratione materiae*. The wording of para. 1 of this article is as follows: 'A court or tribunal referred to in article 287 shall have jurisdiction over any dispute concerning the interpretation or application of this Convention which is submitted to it in accordance with this Part.'

UNCLOS, in its wording, is silent on whether a dispute related to the determination of sovereignty over territory comes under the jurisdiction of the tribunal. However, the judicial practice of decisions under the UNCLOS provisions shows that the tribunal does not have such jurisdiction (Chagos Marine Protected Area Arbitration Award 2015, para.206; The South China Sea Arbitration Award on Jurisdiction and Admissibility 2015, para.153).

In its Award on Preliminary Objections in the *Coastal State Rights Dispute*, the arbitral tribunal considered 'whether a dispute that involves the determination of a question of territorial sovereignty would fall within the jurisdiction of a court or tribunal'. It stated that 'the text of the Convention provides no clear answer to this question' (para.156) – thus, it examined some UNCLOS articles that have provisions related to some aspects of sovereignty. However, considering the provisions of Article 297 and para. 1 of Article 298, sovereignty disputes are not mentioned anywhere in UNCLOS. The argumentation of the arbitral tribunal was as follows:

In light of Article 297, which carves out certain categories of disputes relating to the exercise of sovereign rights and jurisdiction in the exclusive economic zone, and Article 298, paragraph 1, which allows States to exclude three categories of disputes, such as disputes concerning such sensitive matters as the delimitation of maritime boundaries, from compulsory dispute settlement procedures, a sovereignty dispute, which is mentioned in neither provision, may not be regarded a dispute concerning the interpretation or application of the Convention. The fact that a sovereignty dispute is not included either in the limitations on, or in the optional exceptions to, the applicability of compulsory dispute settlement procedures supports the view that the drafters of the Convention did not consider such a dispute to be a dispute concerning the interpretation or application of the Convention. (para.156)

This means that a sovereignty dispute is not considered to be a dispute concerning the interpretation or application of UNCLOS. Thus, the compulsory dispute settlement procedures are not applicable in this regard. In this sense, due to the absence of jurisdiction, it is important that the arbitral tribunal's decisions should not be dependent on the fact of ruling directly or implicitly over the sovereignty issue, nor should anything in its decisions be understood to imply a view with respect to questions of land sovereignty (para.160).

The decision of the arbitral tribunal in the *Coastal State Rights Dispute* that it does not have jurisdiction to rule over the determination of a coastal state was consistent with the existing jurisprudence (Chagos Marine Protected Area Arbitration Award 2015, para.206; The South China Sea Arbitration Award on Jurisdiction and Admissibility 2015, para.153). This decision reaffirms that the jurisdiction of the tribunal does not apply where the arbitral tribunal should first expressly or implicitly render a decision on sovereignty and/or the actual objective of the claim is to create a better position in the existing dispute over sovereignty in order to be able to resolve the submitted claims.

2.4.1.2. *The Existence* vel non *of a Sovereignty Dispute Over Crimea*

The evaluation of the existence of a sovereignty dispute over Crimea has provided a kind of guidance towards a threshold indicating whether or not the sovereignty dispute exists. This evaluation is unique in its nature as it is the first time in a law of the sea dispute under the UNCLOS provisions that such an evaluation has been conducted in respect of the occupied territories.

The core argument of Ukraine is that there is no sovereignty dispute over Crimea: Ukraine is the coastal state of the peninsula, and that is why the arbitral tribunal does not need to decide on sovereignty over Crimea. The argument of Ukraine is that even if the arbitral tribunal were to find that there was a sovereignty dispute over Crimea, the arbitral tribunal would still have the jurisdiction to decide on the dispute itself because the sovereignty dispute is ancillary to the dispute concerning the interpretation or application of the Convention.

The Russian Federation characterised the dispute as representing Ukraine's claim to sovereignty over Crimea (Coastal State Rights Dispute, Preliminary Objection by the Russian Federation 2018, paras.24–65). Ukraine claimed that Russia's claim that the legal status of Crimea had been altered was inadmissible, and that Russia's claim was not plausible (Coastal State Rights Dispute 2018, Ukraine's Written Observations, paras.13–40).

According to the arbitral tribunal's Award on Preliminary Objections, para. 186: 'The exercise of the arbitral tribunal's jurisdictional power in this regard should be limited to assessing the Russian Federation's claim of sovereignty for the sole purpose of verifying whether there exists a dispute as to which State has sovereignty over Crimea.'

Due to this, the arbitral tribunal evaluated and found that the GA's Resolutions on Crimea do not apply the international law requirement of non-recognition, and are not entitled to weight before the tribunal itself (paras.176–178). It also did not support Ukraine's argument that Russia's claim over Crimea was inadmissible as a consequence of the principles of good faith and estoppel (paras.179–182). Regarding plausibility, the arbitral tribunal was not convinced by the plausibility test as argued by Ukraine. However, it did not find 'the threshold of the abuse of rights' as presented by the Russian Federation (paras.183–190).

By rejecting these submissions of Ukraine that supported the core argument of the non-existence of a dispute between the parties over Crimea, the arbitral tribunal then found itself in the position where there was a dispute between parties over the status of Crimea. The jurisdiction of the tribunal within the scope of Article 288 (1) of UNCLOS is not included in a such dispute. The arbitral tribunal thus proceeded to evaluate the arguments of Ukraine suggesting that such a dispute can be considered as an ancillary one that falls under the tribunal's jurisdiction.

The arbitral tribunal answered that the sovereignty dispute over the Crimean Peninsula is not a minor issue ancillary to the dispute concerning the interpretation or application of UNCLOS. Indeed, to adjudge and declare Ukraine's rights in the maritime zones of Crimea would require the determination of the coastal State. Nevertheless, the arbitral tribunal did not close the case, and asked Ukraine to revise its memorial (paras.191–196). Earlier cases have shown that 'such revision is quite feasible, especially in relation to questions concerning the protection and preservation of the marine environment and the determination of the status of maritime features' (Oral 2021; Schatz 2021; Koval 2021).

To conclude, in its Award on Preliminary Objections the arbitral tribunal solved a judicial challenge over the sovereignty claim by applying a neutral position. It recognised 'the existence of a dispute over the territorial status of Crimea'; however, this 'in no way amounts to recognizing any alteration of the status of Crimea from the territory of one Party to the other, or to 'any action or dealing that might be interpreted as recognizing any such altered status'. Neither would it imply that the Russian Federation's actions toward and in Crimea were lawful' (para.178). This conclusion might be considered to suggest the arbitral tribunal indicating that it agrees neither with Ukraine nor with the Russian Federation. Due to this, the question then becomes whether it is possible to change this neutral position. The answer to this question is presented in the following section by providing options as to how it can be solved theoretically and practically, both within and outside of the UNCLOS dispute settlement procedure.

2.4.2. The Settlement of the Sovereignty Dispute Over Crimea Within the UNCLOS Dispute Settlement Procedure

The dispute settlement procedure under UNCLOS is oriented towards, and was aimed during its drafting at solving, disputes related to the law of the sea. UNCLOS does not solve discussions of sovereignty over land territory; instead, its provisions on coastal state jurisdiction accept pre-existing sovereignty (Beckman 2013, p. 142).

It is worth mentioning that Peter Tseng proposed multiple options to solve issues related to the maritime zones generated by the Crimean Peninsula under the UNCLOS dispute settlement procedure.

The first option is to use the additional jurisdiction established under paragraph 2 of Article 288 of UNCLOS.

According to the UNCLOS Commentary edited by Prof. Alexander Proelss, para. 2 of Article 288 represents the 'broadening of subject-matter jurisdiction on the basis of treaties different from the Convention' (p. 1859). The same view was confirmed by the authors of the UNCLOS commentary of the Center for Oceans Law and Policy and the University of Virginia (pp. 47–48).

Peter Tseng directly confirms that 'the text of Article 288(2) expressly grants UNCLOS tribunals jurisdiction over non-UNCLOS disputes. The context supports this interpretation: the language of Article 288(2) parallels that of Article 288(1), which grants UNCLOS tribunals jurisdiction over UNCLOS disputes' (2016, p. 516).

On 14 August 2015, the arbitral tribunal in *The Arctic Sunrise Arbitration* made a decision based on the jurisdiction established by para. 2 under Article 288 of UNCLOS. It recognised that para. 2 of Article 288 could serve as a source of jurisdiction over a non-UNCLOS dispute (para.192, note 184). This implication of this paragraph is possible only upon the existence of an international agreement related to the purposes of UNCLOS, and only if the dispute was submitted in accordance with the mentioned agreement.

In the modern context, it is complicated to talk about new agreements related to the purposes of UNCLOS in the dispute between Ukraine and the Russian

Federation that would involve the UNCLOS provisions and implications that directly depend on the status of Crimea.

Nevertheless, even if it would be practically possible to apply such an agreement, then the question of sovereignty would again arise. Following the tribunal's decisions in this matter, it is most likely that the tribunal would not be able to accept such disputes. The wording of para. 2 is that the tribunal 'ha[s] jurisdiction over any dispute concerning the interpretation or application of an international agreement related to the purposes of this Convention'. Can the issues of sovereignty over the territory be recognised as related to the purposes of UNCLOS? There is no definitive answer so far on this question.

According to the preamble of UNCLOS, when signing it, its States Parties were '[r]ecognizing the desirability of establishing through this Convention, with due regard for the sovereignty of all States, a legal order for the seas and oceans which will facilitate international communication, and will promote the peaceful uses of the seas and oceans, the equitable and efficient utilization of their resources, the conservation of their living resources, and the study, protection and preservation of the marine environment'.

Thus, from one perspective, it is most likely that the determination of the sovereign state over Crimea cannot be considered as a dispute related to the purposes of UNCLOS. However, from the perspective of the violation of coastal state rights over the Crimean Peninsula, a determination is required for establishing the coastal state in this case. Even though sovereignty over land is not governed by UNCLOS, it says that 'matters not regulated by this Convention continue to be governed by the rules and principles of general international law'. Thus, the most important part of that agreement shall be within the purpose of UNCLOS, and it must indicate without doubt the clear willingness of both states to grant supplementary jurisdiction to the arbitral tribunal. From one perspective, the exaggerated expansion of jurisdiction might reduce the number of states joining UNCLOS and enlarge states' refusal to comply with the awards of UNCLOS tribunals. On the other hand, the enormous restriction of jurisdiction might limit the efficiency of the dispute settlement procedure under UNCLOS (Tzeng 2016, p. 515). However, by concluding such an agreement, states give their full consent to grant additional jurisdiction to UNCLOS tribunals without aggravating the question of the exaggerated expansion of jurisdiction for other states. Thus, the agreement according to para. 2 of Article 288 is relevant only to the parties of the agreement.

Based on the background of the case, and in the context of the ongoing war between Ukraine and the Russian Federation, an agreement between these two countries to grant a basis for supplemental jurisdiction is not achievable.

The second option is to solve issues related to the maritime zones generated by the Crimean Peninsula under the UNCLOS dispute settlement procedure by applying conditional decisions. An example of a conditional decision is presented in the *Pedra Branca* case between Malaysia and Singapore. The ICJ in this case stated that 'sovereignty over South Ledge, as a low-tide elevation, belongs to the State in the territorial waters of which it is located' (paras.291–299). This happened because the jurisdiction of the parties to the dispute was given only to establish sovereignty over three maritime features, but not to draw the line of delimitation. The advocate for conditional decisions was Peter Tzeng. According to him, a conditional decision can be a solution to the dispute between Ukraine and the Russian Federation.

Due to the number of submissions of Ukraine depending on the status of Crimea, such a judgement would require too many options to be taken into consideration. Such a conditional decision could cause more controversies between the parties. Moreover, the occupation of the peninsula cannot be tantamount to determining the status of a low-tide elevation. Therefore, this option also does not seem realistic for resolving issues of sovereignty. In accordance with our view, since the dispute settlement procedure under UNCLOS cannot help to achieve the decision over the majority of submissions presented by Ukraine in its initial Memorial, then the search for answers leads to dispute settlement options outside of UNCLOS.

2.4.3. Removing the Judicial Challenge of a Sovereign Dispute Outside of UNCLOS

2.4.3.1. A Decision by the SC

The UN Charter provides the SC, in Article 39, with the power to 'determine the existence of any threat to the peace, breach of the peace, or act of aggression'. SC decisions are legally binding upon all member states of the UN. According to Article 27 of the UN Charter:

'1. Each member of the Security Council shall have one vote.
2. Decisions of the Security Council on procedural matters shall be made by an affirmative vote of nine members.
3. Decisions of the Security Council on all other matters shall be made by an affirmative vote of nine members including the concurring votes of the permanent members; provided that, in decisions under Chapter VI, and under paragraph 3 of Article 52, a party to a dispute shall abstain from voting.'

Thus, the SC decisions, apart from those on procedural matters, are subject to the veto of the permanent members of the UN. The Russian Federation is one of the permanent members along with the USA, China, and the UK. The veto of the Russian Federation regarding the non-procedural decision of the SC is predictable. Thus, it used its veto power in draft resolutions related to Ukraine in 2014, 2015 and 2022. To obtain a SC's decision, there are three options:

(a) the Russian Federation does not exercise its veto in relation to the decision (highly unlikely);
(b) the Russian Federation is deprived of its veto-power and/or its seat in UN Security Council;
(c) the procedure does not include the vote of the Russian Federation as a state of interest.

Within the first option, it is necessary to consider whether the prohibition of threats to the peace, breaches of the peace, or acts of aggression applies to the Russian Federation. Despite this sounding like an absurd statement, it is not. The Russian Federation has insisted that only the SC has the power to determine the existence of aggression, and, within the SC, the Russian Federation enjoys a veto power that allows it to block any decision that is not in favour of the Russian position (Mälksoo 2019; Grzebyk 2017).

Thus, even if the Russian Federation has violated the peace or is carrying out an act of aggression, the SC is unable to determine anything on this subject. While the first option shows the privilege of the Russian Federation, the second and third gives ideas as to how to stop the Russian Federation from abusing its permanent member power within the SC. Thus, the second option addresses the possibility of depriving the Russian Federation of its veto power and/or its seat on the SC. It has already been argued by Joris van de Riet that the refusal or denial of the Russian Federation's succession to the seat of the USSR would be contradictory to consistent and uniform practice. Examples of such practice include Egypt, which succeeded the United Arab Republic in 1961, Singapore from Malaysia in 1969, and Serbia from Serbia and Montenegro in 2006 (Riet 2022).

The third option is based on para. 3 of Article 27 of the UN Charter: '[d]ecisions of the Security Council on all other matters shall be made by an affirmative vote of nine members including the concurring votes of the permanent members; provided that, in decisions under Chapter VI, and under paragraph 3 of Article 52, a party to a dispute shall abstain from voting.'

Firstly, the language of the article includes the word 'shall', which means the direct obligation of the state to follow such provisions. Secondly, Chapter VI of the UN Charter contains provisions regarding the peaceful settlement of disputes, so the SC can 'call upon the parties to settle their dispute' by such means as negotiation, enquiry, mediation, conciliation, arbitration, judicial settlement, resort to regional agencies or arrangements, or other peaceful means of the choice of the parties to the dispute.

The problem with this option is that the determination of acts of aggression is not under Chapter VI but under Chapter VII of the UN Charter. Because of this, the only way available according to the third option is to call on Ukraine and the Russian Federation to solve their dispute within any peaceful means of their choice.

Meanwhile, the SC can request that the ICJ provide an advisory opinion and take measures to ensure compliance with the ICJ award. However, such competencies of the SC 'have been far too rarely used' (Ambassador Sven Jürgenson 2020).

To make such a decision, the consent of all of the permanent members of the SC is necessary because this is not a procedural decision. Since the Russian Federation is likely to veto, it is possible to request an advisory opinion from the ICJ through the GA. In this regard, it is worth mentioning that on 28 April 2022, the PACE adopted Resolution No. 2346 regarding the Russian Federation's aggression against Ukraine. This Resolution aimed at ensuring accountability for serious violations of the IHL and other international crimes. In paragraph 12.5.2, the Parliamentary Assembly called on the UNGA to 'request an Advisory Opinion from the ICJ on possible limits to the veto rights of permanent members of the SC that could be based on the general legal principles of the prohibition of the abuse of rights and the duty of member States of international organisations to exercise their membership rights in good faith.' Considering the abovementioned procedure, receiving a binding decision on the status of Crimea seems difficult, yet the question of whether the ICJ can solve the dispute by itself remains. For this reason, the next sub-section provides an analysis of an ICJ decision as a solution to the judicial challenge in the *Coastal State Rights Dispute*.

2.4.3.2. An Advisory Opinion by the ICJ

The jurisdiction of the ICJ is as follows: firstly, it makes decisions in conformity with international law in disputes submitted to it by States; secondly, it gives advisory opinions on legal questions at the request of the organs of the UN, specialised agencies, or related organisations authorised to make such requests. Neither Ukraine nor Russia have made declarations recognising the jurisdiction of the ICJ as compulsory (ICJ no date). Thus, any decision of the ICJ would not be binding for both of these countries unless they were both to agree otherwise.

A legally binding decision delivered by the ICJ is possible only when Ukraine and the Russian Federation declare their recognition of the jurisdiction of the ICJ as compulsory. Until now, there has been no visible solution to obtaining a legally binding decision regarding the sovereignty dispute over Crimea. However, the mechanism of receiving an advisory opinion of the ICJ provides the possibility to obtain a legally relevant opinion that could influence the status of Crimea within the settlement of the dispute under UNCLOS.

An interesting precedent related to the Advisory Opinion of the ICJ occurred recently when the Judgment on Preliminary Objections in the *Dispute Concerning Delimitation of the Maritime Boundary Between Mauritius and Maldives in the Indian Ocean (Mauritius/Maldives)* became available on 28 January 2021. In para. 246 of the Judgment, the Special Chamber said that 'the Chagos advisory opinion has legal effect and clear implications for the legal status of the Chagos Archipelago' and, moreover, that the Advisory Opinion has 'the authoritative determinations'. Thus, there is a precedent in which the ICJ's advisory opinion was recognised as having a legal effect and authoritative determinations.

The legal status of the Chagos Archipelago was addressed earlier in the *Chagos Marine Protected Area Arbitration* (Mauritius v. UK), where the arbitral tribunal stated that 'the dispute regarding sovereignty over the Chagos Archipelago does not concern the interpretation or application of the Convention' (para.221). In February 2019, Mauritius received an Advisory Opinion of the ICJ concerning the *Legal Consequences of the Separation of the Chagos Archipelago from Mauritius in 1965*. The ICJ evaluated the findings of the previous arbitral tribunal's award and stated that the issues that were determined by it were not the same as those that were before the ICJ in the later case. Thus, the ICJ stated that its opinion was that 'the UK is under an obligation to bring to an end its administration of the Chagos Archipelago as rapidly as possible' (paras.50, 81, 183).

In June 2019, Mauritius instituted arbitral proceedings against the Maldives under Annex VII of UNCLOS in *Dispute concerning the delimitation of the maritime boundary between Mauritius and Maldives in the Indian Ocean*, which later, upon the agreement of the parties, was transferred to a special chamber formed according to Article 15, para. 2, of the Statute of the International Tribunal for the Law of the Sea. The Special Chamber issued its Preliminary Objections Judgment in January 2021. The most significant part of this decision is the fact that the Tribunal admitted its jurisdiction in this case related to the Chagos Archipelago, and that Mauritius was recognised as the coastal state over the Chagos Archipelago even before the process of decolonisation was finished (paras.246, 250, 354).

In the Separate and Dissenting Opinion of Judge Ad Hoc Oxman, he addressed the issue of there being two different approaches regarding the UNGA Resolutions and the ICJ Advisory Opinion. He stated that compulsory jurisdiction under UNCLOS, 'with respect to issues regarding rights to land territory, can be or should be avoided where there is a disagreement regarding the legal effect of a treaty, or judgment, award, or advisory opinion, or resolution of an international organization that addresses such rights' (para.29). If this approach is not followed, then in the *Coastal State Rights Dispute* the UNGA resolutions would be considered correct, and this 'would *ipso facto* imply that the Arbitral Tribunal finds that Crimea is part of Ukraine's territory. However, it has no jurisdiction to do so'.

In the authors' view, the influence of the UNGA resolutions regarding Crimea and the Chagos Archipelago, as well as the ICJ Advisory Opinion on the *Legal Consequences of the Separation of the Chagos Archipelago from Mauritius in 1965*, are not the same. The situation regarding the Chagos Archipelago is considered an unfinished process of decolonisation. Therefore, after receiving the ICJ Advisory Opinion, the UNGA adopted a text calling for Mauritius' complete decolonisation. The Special Chamber in the *Dispute Concerning Delimitation of the Maritime Boundary Between Mauritius and Maldives in the Indian Ocean* noted that '[i]n light of the general functions of the General Assembly on decolonization and the specific task of the decolonization of Mauritius with which it was entrusted, the Special Chamber considers that resolution 73/295 is relevant to assessing the legal status of the Chagos Archipelago' (Preliminary Objections 2021, para.227). With this, the Special Chamber gave certain weight to the resolution when evaluating the legal status of the archipelago. This was only possible via a combination of the UNGA Resolution and the ICJ Advisory Opinion. In the context of Crimea, only UNGA Resolutions were adopted, and no request for an ICJ Advisory Opinion was made.

The level of examination of the dispute is also different within an ICJ Advisory Opinion and the UNGA resolutions. In respect of a UNGA resolution, this level of examination can be noticeable, but '[i]t operates on the political not the legal level: it does not make these resolutions binding in law'. Moreover, 'the effect of factual and legal determination made in UNGA resolutions depends largely on their content and the conditions and context of their adoption. So does the weight to be given to such resolutions by an international court or tribunal'. Based on this, it is possible to say that a UNGA Resolution might obtain more legal weight and consideration together with an ICJ Advisory Decision that 'entails an authoritative statement of international law on the questions with which it deals' (Delimitation of the maritime boundary in the Indian Ocean, Preliminary

Objections 2021, paras.203, 204, 224, 225; Coastal State Rights Dispute, Award on Preliminary Objections 2020, para.174).

Due to this, the option to request and obtain an Advisory Opinion of the ICJ regarding the legal status of Crimea followed by a number of UNGA Resolutions confirming the status of Crimea (preferably adopted unanimously or by full consensus) would give the sovereignty dispute over Crimea clarity within international law. Thus, any court or tribunal within UNCLOS would not be required to rule over the status of Crimea, and would have the option of following the approach taken in the *Delimitation of the maritime boundary in the Indian Ocean* case. For strengthening this argument, it would also make sense to involve other non-binding instruments. For example, this can be achieved by including the Joint Declaration of the International Crimea Platform Participants, where all participants 'underline that any alteration of the status of the Autonomous Republic of Crimea and the city of Sevastopol as an integral part of the sovereign territory of Ukraine is not and will not be recognized, and that Russia's efforts to legitimize the temporary occupation and illegal seizure are unacceptable' (Joint Declaration of the International Crimea Platform Participants no date). This can be used to show the unanimous and full consensus of the international community – in particular, if comparing the support for and votes in favour of this Declaration with the evaluation of votes in the UNGA Resolutions concerning Crimea by the arbitral tribunal in the Preliminary Objection's Award in the *Coastal State Rights Dispute*. The arbitral tribunal in the award concluded that the UNGA Resolutions in question were 'framed in hortatory language' and 'were not adopted unanimously or by consensus but with many States abstaining or voting against them' (para.175). With more states joining this Declaration, the stronger its language and the more unanimously it is supported by the full consensus of other states, the more legal weight it will have within the legal evaluation of this document by courts and/or tribunals.

2.4.3.3. The ICC and/or a Decision of a Yet-To-Be-Established Ad Hoc Tribunal

Another source that could determine the status of Crimea is ICC, as it has the jurisdiction to determine the crime of aggression. The determination of aggression was adopted on 14 December 1974 by GA Resolution 3314 (XXIX), with the Definition of Aggression annexed to it. According to it 'Aggression is the use of armed force by a State against the sovereignty, territorial integrity or political independence of another State, or in any other manner inconsistent with the Charter of the United Nations.' Later, the definition of the crime of aggression was clarified by Resolution RC/Res.6 on 11 June 2010. On 17 June 2018, the jurisdiction of the ICC over the crime of aggression was activated. Thus, the relevant elements of the crime of aggression are provided in para. 2 of Article 8 bis, mirroring the previously adopted definition. However, para. 2(a) of the same article specifies that the act of aggression also includes '[t]he invasion or attack by the armed forces of a State of the territory of another State, or any military occupation, however temporary, resulting from such invasion or attack, or any annexation by the use of force of the territory of another State or part thereof'.

Since the act of aggression was performed by the Russian Federation at the beginning of 2014, a logical question arises: Is the jurisdiction of the ICC applicable to the dispute between Ukraine and the Russian Federation?

Another option is to determine the status of Crimea within the decision of an ad hoc tribunal. This has frequently been discussed among the international community since the escalation of Russia's war of aggression against Ukraine (PACE Calls for an Ad Hoc International Criminal Tribunal to Hold to Account Perpetrators of the Crime of Aggression against Ukraine 2022; European Parliament Resolution 2023; Dannenbaum 2022; Stojanovic 2022; Lerch 2022; Heller 2022a, 2022b; Lemos 2023; Nußberger 2023, etc.).

Moreover, nearly 40 prominent legal and political personalities have signed The Combined Statement and Declaration Calling for the Creation of a Special Tribunal for the Punishment of the Crime of Aggression Against Ukraine. The discussion of whether such an idea is good or bad has already begun (Heller 2022a, 2022b).

However, for the purpose of this publication, the main question is: Will the decision of the ad hoc tribunal have binding power, and will it be capable of determining the status of Crimea starting from 2014? The answer to this question solely depends on the establishing document of such an ad hoc tribunal. This document will be able to provide the jurisdiction of the tribunal as well as the level of acceptance of its decision.

2.4.4. Interim findings

Since the arbitral tribunal in the *Coastal State Rights Dispute* rejected all of Ukraine's claims related to Ukraine as the coastal state over the maritime zones of Crimea due to its lack of jurisdiction, it became necessary to determine the status of Crimea in accordance with international law. Such a definition is necessary so that issues related to the law of the sea in the waters surrounding the Crimean Peninsula can be resolved under the UNCLOS dispute settlement procedure. There are two main directions in which to solve this sovereignty dispute: either apply the UNCLOS provisions or find a solution outside of them.

In relation to the first direction, the possibilities of supplementary jurisdiction and conditional judgments were explored. The option of supplementary jurisdiction under Article 288 (2) of UNCLOS is possible; however, considering the ongoing war between Ukraine and the Russian Federation, the conclusion of an international agreement related to the purposes of UNCLOS is hardly feasible. A conditional decision would mean an overly complicated decision containing a lot of 'ifs', which could create more controversy regarding the interpretation of such a decision than it possessed initially. In addition, such a decision can be considered appropriate in relation to a low-tide elevation, but not to the whole peninsula.

As for the second direction, here the determination of the status of Crimea is more probable. While the SC has the right to announce a binding decision regarding the status of Crimea, due to Russia's veto power the SC cannot practically do so. Starting from 24 February 2022, discussions began on the possibility of depriving the Russian Federation of the right to veto and/or its seat in the SC, as well as the activation of the obligation of the Russian Federation to abstain from voting as an interested state. This could be submitted for clarification and interpretation within the framework of the Advisory Opinion of the ICJ, together with the question of whether the Russian Federation has the obligation or right to abstain from voting in disputes referred to in Article 27 (3) of the UN Charter. However, such a procedure for obtaining a binding decision on the status of Crimea seems overly complicated.

Ukraine and Russia do not recognise the jurisdiction of the ICJ, so there is no option for a binding decision. However, nothing prevents the UNGA from making a request for an Advisory Opinion from the ICJ. As the jurisprudence of the law of the sea shows, the combination of an Advisory Opinion and UNGA resolutions might be enough for a tribunal or court in this dispute regarding the law of the sea to declare that the status of Crimea is resolved.

Finally, an ICC decision and/or a decision of a yet-to-be-created ad hoc tribunal regarding the aggression of the Russian Federation is a possible option. An appropriate definition of the status of Crimea could be created in the context of the definition of aggression as indicated by Russia's military occupation of Crimea since 2014. With this, the matters related to the law of the sea that were rejected because their resolution would require the direct or implicit determination of the status of Crimea would be able to be resolved under the UNCLOS dispute settlement procedure.

Chapter 3. Challenges for Specific Fields of Law in the Context of Armed Conflicts and Emergencies

3.1. The Right of the Accused to Be Informed as a Condition for the Legality of Criminal Proceedings in Absentia in the Context of War Crimes and Crimes Against Humanity

3.1.1. Criminal Trials *in absentia:* Is This Still Relevant?

Trials *in absentia* are a hot topic in Ukrainian legal circles today (Vereshchak 2021, pp. 86, 88). Chapter 24–1 of the Code of Criminal Procedure (hereafter – the CCP) of Ukraine, entitled 'Specific Aspects of Special Pre-trial Investigation of Criminal Offences', deals with the specific features of this type of proceedings (the CCP of Ukraine has been supplemented with Chapter 24–1 in 2014 and amended in 2015, 2017, 2018) and applies in conjunction with the general provisions of the CCP (Art. 88 of the CCP). As indicated in these sources, new transitional provisions were brought in that modified the law on *in absentia* pre-trial investigation and, to a lesser extent, *in absentia* trial proceedings (Trials in absentia: a dilemma for Ukraine, pp. 1–14), and these changes sparked debate. However, it should be stressed that in the history of criminal justice, including international criminal justice, the concept of *in absentia* trials has always sparked active debate. International crimes committed against Ukraine and its population – which may be prosecuted both in the national courts of Ukraine and in other States, in the exercise of universal jurisdiction (KLUWEN 2017, pp. 7–38; Poels 2005, pp. 65–84; Colangelo 2005, pp. 537–604; Rabinovitch 2005, pp. 500–530), and in international judicial bodies – have re-activated legal discussions on the grounds and conditions of proceedings *in absentia*. Individuals accused of international crimes often refuse to appear in court or otherwise avoid criminal proceedings. In the meantime, instruments of international legal cooperation that could ensure the direct or remote participation of the accused person in court are also ineffective because, for example, the State of the accused's nationality not only refuses to extradite its national, but also fails to cooperate in other ways (e.g., Ruling of the Supreme Court of Lithuania in a criminal case no. 2K-7-39-1073/2022; Transcript of the MH17 judgment hearing 2022; Prosecution and trial (MH17 plane crash) 2022). In such a situation, it becomes problematic not only to gather evidence and make substantiated allegations of war crimes or crimes against humanity, but also to properly inform the individual of the charges against them, as well as of the ongoing trial.

At present, this problem is also relevant in practice. According to the data of the UN Office of the High Commissioner for Human Rights (hereafter – the OHCHR), the total number of verdicts of trial courts of Ukraine in 'conflict-related cases' from 1 August 2022 to 31 January 2023 was 777, 71 of which were *in absentia* proceedings (Report on the Human Rights Situation in Ukraine 2023, p. 34). The OHCHR reports that they welcome the efforts of the Government of Ukraine to prosecute war crimes and uphold the rights of victims to truth and effective remedies, but have concerns about the overall fairness of certain proceedings, including trials *in absentia* (Report on the Human Rights Situation in Ukraine 2023, p. 33). Some researchers also state that 'Ukraine's CCP does not ensure sufficient regulation of the procedure of special court proceedings because it does not prescribe the procedure for summoning to court of the accused against whom special pre-trial investigation was conducted' (In Absentia Procedure: the Concept of Amendments to National Legislation Ukraine). Another relevant issue is the right of a person convicted *in absentia* to a new trial. The CCP of Ukraine, as well as the criminal laws of many other States, provides for a rather limited possibility of a new trial after *in absentia* proceedings.

The relevance of analysis of this subject is also demonstrated by the fact that some countries – including Lithuania, Germany, France, Poland, Latvia, Estonia, Norway, Sweden, Slovakia, Switzerland, Spain, Canada, the USA, the UK, etc. – have launched pre-trial investigations into alleged war crimes in Ukraine in the exercise of universal jurisdiction (Universal Criminal Jurisdiction in Ukraine 2022; Germany investigating 'several hundred' possible Ukraine war crimes 2022). Without entering into deep doctrinal debates on universal jurisdiction and proceedings *in absentia* – as well as the difficulties of universal jurisdiction regarding *in absentia* proceedings in practice, including the suboptimal fulfilment of the objectives of criminal law, compromising the right of the accused not to be tried twice, and possibly destabilising international relations (KLUWEN 2017, pp. 28–34; Colangelo 2005, pp. 543–564; Poels 2005, p. 82) – this analysis considers that States asserting absolute universal jurisdiction when prosecuting international crimes do not violate international law (KLUWEN 2017, p. 26). Moreover, the application of universal jurisdiction in the prosecution of international crimes may reduce the impunity of those committing such crimes (KLUWEN 2017, p. 27; Colangelo 2005, pp. 564–578; Poels 2005, p. 78) if proceedings *in absentia* do not violate the right to a fair trial.

Thus, this research is aimed at one of the most problematic conditions of procedures *in absentia* – namely, the right to be informed, non-compliance with which may lead to an infringement of the individual's right to a fair trial. The research raises the question of whether the fairly well-established interpretation of this right in supranational case-law strikes the correct balance between the right to due process of persons accused of international crimes (war crimes and crimes against humanity) and the expectations of victims, society, the State and the international community regarding substantive and procedural justice in such cases. The second problem of this scientific research concerns the legal consequences of a violation of the right of a person who is subject to proceedings *in absentia* to adequate information. The research then raises the question of whether such an infringement can be remedied by granting the individual an unlimited right to a new procedure. Finally, it is considered whether such a right of a person convicted *in absentia* who has not been properly informed of the proceedings can be subject to certain conditions.

This chapter aims to analyse the content of the right to be informed about the criminal procedure and possible peculiarities of ensuring this right in cases of war crimes and crimes against humanity.

The constitutional and international standards followed by national courts in criminal proceedings, including *in absentia* proceedings, form the basis for the application of national criminal procedural law. It is important to note that the right to be informed and the right to a new trial are subject to national regulatory discretion. Supranational courts only lay down certain criteria for securing this right on a case-by-case basis. Hence, this analysis is largely based on ICCPR, the UN Human Rights Committee (hereafter – the UNHRC), the ECHRand the case-law of the ECtHR, as the importance of the presence of the accused as a fundamental safeguard ensuring the fairness of the trial is broadly reflected in the aforementioned international treaties that Ukraine, and Lithuania, has signed. The study is also based on EU law and the case-law of the CJEU. This analysis, due to its limited scope, does not analyse the views of international tribunals on the *in absentia* process. However, the rules applied by international tribunals may be relevant: cases on international crimes dealt with in absentia by national courts may be related to cases which could potentially be dealt with at the ICC (Trials in absentia: a dilemma for Ukraine 2016). It also draws on scientific papers that analyse the *in absentia* process.

It should be noted that any efforts to modify the law, especially criminal law and criminal procedure law, should bring it in line with both international standards and the constitutional and national legal framework. The concern that the provisions are incompatible with Ukrainian domestic law (Report on the Human Rights Situation in Ukraine 2023; Trials in absentia: a dilemma for Ukraine 2016; In Absentia Procedure: the Concept of Amendments to National Legislation

Ukraine; Vereshchak 2021, pp. 85–90) is important, but specific legislative proposals are outside the scope of this research. Therefore, this research deals only with international *in absentia* procedural standards relating to the exercise of the right to be informed.

3.1.2. The Right of the Accused Person to Be Present at the Trial: The Premise of Fair Criminal Proceedings

A defendant's right to be present during their trial is fundamental to due process. In the context of the present problem, it should be noted that the participation of the accused person in the trial (and more generally throughout the criminal proceedings) is not only an essential guarantee of their own procedural rights, but also a guarantee of the fairness of the overall hearing of the case. The participation of the accused person in court is important both for the court hearing the case, whose duty it is to qualitatively examine and evaluate the evidence, and for the other participants in the proceedings, in particular the victims.

This individual right is in particular encapsulated in Article 14 of the ICCPR, which provides that, in the determination of any criminal charge against them, everyone shall be entitled to the following minimum guarantees, in full equality: to be tried in their presence, and to defend themselves in person or through legal assistance of their own choosing (Art. 14(3)(d) of the ICCPR).

Article 6(3)(c) of the ECHR provides that any person accused of committing a crime has the right to defend themselves or with the assistance of a defence counsel. Although the text of the ECHR does not mention the right of a person to appear before a court, the case-law of the ECtHR has established that the right of the accused person to participate in the criminal proceedings in which they have been charged constitutes an essential guarantee of the defendant's rights of defence and of a fair trial, which in principle determines the possibility of exercising other procedural rights conferred on them (Sejdovic v. Italy [GC], paras.81, 84; Jelcovas v. Lithuania 2011, para.106).

This right of the accused is also enshrined in the EU legislation (e.g., Directive (EU) 2016/343 of the European Parliament and of the Council of 9 March 2016 on the strengthening of certain aspects of the presumption of innocence and of the right to be present at the trial in criminal proceedings (hereafter – the Directive 2016/343); Council Framework Decision 2009/299/JHA of 26 February 2009 amending Framework Decisions 2002/584/JHA, 2005/214/JHA, 2006/783/JHA, 2008/909/JHA and 2008/947/JHA, which strengthens the procedural rights of persons and promotes the application of the principle of mutual recognition to decisions rendered in the absence of the person concerned at the trial). This right is also generally recognised in national law.

The value of this right has also been confirmed in many individual cases (KLUWEN 2017, p. 30): from *Hopt v. Utah* before the United States Supreme Court in 1884 (Hopt v. Utah, 110 U.S. 574 (1884), 579; KLUWEN 2017, p. 30; Donaldson 2016, pp. 16–17) to *Colozza v. Italy* at the ECtHR in 1985 (Colozza v. Italy 1985, para.29).

On the other hand, there is a broad consensus (e.g., Trials in absentia: a dilemma for Ukraine, 2016) that despite the apparently mandatory language of the ICCPR and ECHR, no international or regional human rights treaty explicitly prohibits holding proceedings in the absence of the accused (Mbenge v. Zaire 1990, para.14.1; Maleki v. Italy 1999, para.9.3; Colozza v. Italy 1985, para.27).

As noted in the literature, conducting a trial in the absence of an accused person is, in principle, at odds with the general requirements of due process and the right to participate in one's own defence set out in Article 14 of the ICCPR. Article 14 of the ICCPR does not invariably render proceedings *in absentia* as inadmissible (Parry 2021). General Comment No. 13 of the UNHRC states that 'the accused or his lawyer must have the right to act diligently and fearlessly in pursuing all available defences and the right to challenge the conduct of the case if they believe it to be unfair. When exceptionally for justified reasons trials *in absentia* are held, strict observance of the rights of the defence is all the more necessary' (Human Rights Committee 1984, General comment No. 13, Article 14 (Administration of justice)). The Human Rights Committee has acknowledged that exceptional circumstances may apply allowing for trial *in absentia* to proceed in the interest of the proper administration of justice (Mbenge v. Zaire 1990; Maleki v. Italy 1999). The Human Rights Committee has emphasised that 'according to Article 14 (3) of the Covenant, everyone is entitled to be tried in his/her presence and to defend himself/herself in person or through legal assistance. This provision and other requirements of due process established in Article 14 cannot be construed as invariably rendering proceedings *in absentia* inadmissible of the reasons for the accused person's absence' (Mbenge v. Zaire 1990, para.14.1).

The case-law of the ECtHR recognises that the impossibility of holding a trial in the absence of the accused person may paralyse criminal proceedings so that such an examination is not, in itself, incompatible with the requirements of the Convention, and forms the criterion of the right of the individual to participate in the trial on a case-by-case basis. The case-law of the ECtHR shows that neither the letter nor the spirit of Article 6 ECHR prevents a person from waiving – of their own free will, expressly or tacitly – the entitlement to the guarantees of a fair trial. In relation to proceedings in absentia in the context of the prosecution of international crimes, the ECtHR has noted that in such cases, despite the absence of limitation periods, the public interest and the interest of victims in bringing justice are very important, which may also lead to proceedings in the absence of the accused person (Sanader v. Croatia 2015, para.77). Thus, according to the case-law of the ECtHR, a case may be heard in absentia if the defendant has waived their right to be present at the hearing. Such a refusal is subject to the usual requirements of the ECtHR rulings: a waiver of the right to take part in the trial must be established in an unequivocal manner and be attended by minimum safeguards commensurate with its importance. Furthermore, it must not run counter to any important public interest (Sejdovic v. Italy [GC] 2006, para.86; Vilches Coronado and others v. Spain 2018, para.36). Any waiver of the guarantees under Article 6 of the Convention must be in accordance with the test of 'informed and reasonable refusal' laid down in the case-law of the ECtHR (Sejdovic v. Italy [GC] 2006, paras.86–88).

The right to a fair trial is referred to in recital 47 of Directive 2016/343 and is laid down in Article 47 and Article 48 of the EU Charter, which, as stated in the Explanations relating to the EU Charter, corresponds to Article 6 ECHR (CJEU, C-688/18, TX, UW 2020, paras.34–35). Thus, EU law also recognises that, despite the fact that right of suspects and accused persons to be present at the trial is based on the right to a fair trial, 'under certain conditions, suspects and accused persons should be able, expressly or tacitly, but unequivocally, to waive that right' (Recital 33 of Directive 2016/343).

Thus, an analysis of research and case-law suggests that criminal proceedings in absentia are an exceptional procedural form. Trials *in absentia* inevitably entail a certain restriction of the rights of the defendant who is absent, of the other participants in the proceedings and of the procedural possibilities of the court hearing the case. Thus, criminal proceedings in the absence of the accused person may be heard only where the interests of justice so require, and when the procedural requirements to protect the rights of a defendant who is not present and the fairness of the proceedings have been fulfilled. Both UNHRC and ECtHR jurisprudence provide almost identical safeguards: (I) the accused must have notice of the proceedings; (II) the accused must be legally represented in the proceedings and have effective assistance of counsel; and (III) the accused should have the right to retrial or an *ex novo* trial in their presence (IBA Report on the 'Experts' Roundtable on trials in absentia in international criminal justice 2016, p. 5; Human Rights Committee, General Comment No. 32 2007, para.36; Article 6 (3) of the ECHR; Colozza v. Italy 1985; Goddi v. Italy 1984; VanGeyseghem v. Belgium 1999; Lala v. Netherlands 1994; Sejdovic v. Italy [GC] 2006). The recent case-law of the ECtHR and the CJEU, as will be analysed further, suggests that the right to retrial or an *ex novo* trial in the presence of the accused should be guaranteed only in certain cases – that is to say, those three conditions are not cumulative.

Moreover, there is general consensus internationally that the right of an accused to be present at their trial is not absolute and may be subject to certain limited exceptions. However, as regards the national regulation of criminal proceedings *in absentia*, the meaning of the right to be heard can be understood in the context of two distinct legal traditions: namely, the common and civil law systems. The doctrine of criminal proceedings has often highlighted the classic difference between common and civil law: it is argued that, for historical reasons, an *in absentia* court in the former is practically impossible, while in the latter it is possible (Pradel 2001, p. 478; Rabinovitch 2005, p. 526; Karas 2018, p. 292). According to the literature, it is widely accepted that the prohibition of *in absentia* trials is a feature of the adversarial/accusatorial system as a legal tradition of common law regimes (Zakerhossein and De Brouwer 2015, pp. 205–206). On the contrary, the civil law approach tolerates *in absentia* trials to a greater extent. For these jurisdictions, there are two arguments in favour of *in absentia* trials. First, it has been held that in the context of civil law systems the interests of justice may prevail over the interests of the accused. The second argument is related to the issue of the truth: in the context of this system, the primarily responsibility of judges is to establish the truth (Zakerhossein and De Brouwer 2015, p. 206).

However, it has long been observed in comparative law literature that such a distinction is rather artificial, since neither model can ever be found in its pure form anywhere and they must be studied only as ideal types (Pradel 2001, p. 478; Zakerhossein and De Brouwer 2015, p. 205). Modern legal regulation of criminal proceedings, despite the existence of historical models, is largely influenced by international and constitutional human rights standards (Ažubalytė 2010, pp. 281–296). This is because, at present, some European countries do not accept the possibility of trials *in absentia* at all, while other countries regulate them under different regimes (Klip 2016, p. 282) under the influence of the jurisprudence of the ECtHR. According to an analysis of the case-law of the U.S. Supreme Court, in certain exceptional cases a defendant may also waive the right to their presence in the trial (Donaldson 2016, p. 44; Starkey 1979, pp. 733–745).

It should be noted that both the International Military Tribunals (hereafter – IMTs) in Nuremberg and Tokyo recognised total *in absentia* trials. However, this permissive approach to *in absentia* trials changed over time, and other international criminal tribunals and courts – i.e., the ICTY, the ICTR, the Special Court for Sierra Leone (hereafter – SCSL), the Special Panel for Serious Crimes (East Timor) (hereafter – SPSC), the Extra-ordinary Chambers in the Courts for Cambodia (hereafter – ECCC) and the ICC – therefore adopted the opposite approach, holding that *in absentia* trials are not consistent with the accused's fair trial rights and thus are not allowed. Nonetheless, the Special Tribunal for Lebanon (hereafter – STL), reintroduced the concept of *in absentia* trials as a means to preclude suspects of international crimes from avoiding justice (Zakerhossein and De Brouwer 2015, pp. 181–182). In this case, the *in absentia* conditions essentially coincided with the requirements of the case-law of the UNHRC and the case-law of the ECtHR regarding *in absentia* proceedings (Herath 2014, p. 9). However, the latter possibility of prosecution *in absentia* is also criticised in the literature as being in breach of the principles of fair procedure, at least because, as an *ad hoc* institution, the STL cannot and does not effectively guarantee a retrial (Jordash and Parker 2010, pp. 487–510). On the other hand, the ICC concept of not recognising the *in absentia* process is also subject to criticism and suggestions to reinterpret it (Parry 2021), or to change regulation (Shaw 2012, pp. 107–140). The abovementioned different approaches to *in absentia* trials in international criminal justice are actively reflected in the abovementioned works and in other legal research. However, as mentioned above, this legal regulation does not have a direct impact on national criminal procedural law and is therefore not subject to further discussion.

Before examining the conditions of proceedings *in absentia*, it is necessary to define that the expression of an *in absentia* trial includes two instances. In the first instance, it can refer to a total *in absentia* trial, in which the accused is completely absent from the criminal proceedings. This is also called 'trial by default' (Gaeta 2007, pp. 1165, 1169, cited in Zakerhossein and De Brouwer 2015, p. 183). In the second, it can refer to a partial *in absentia* trial, where the accused is absent in one or some specific hearings while they are still under the control of the court in order to receive a sentence, if found guilty. Here, the reasons for the absence of the accused can be various. The accused may waive their right to be present at trial, may be removed from the courtroom due to their disruptive behaviour, or the health status of the accused may impede their presence in the courtroom (Zakerhossein and De Brouwer 2015, p. 183). This analysis supports the scientific position that, in spite of this conceptual distinction, the legal literature tends to group different types of *in absentia* trials together and study them from a normative perspective. This leads to some incoherence and misunderstanding as to the phenomenon (Zakerhossein and De Brouwer 2015, p. 183). This research recognises, however, the above distinction of total and partial *in absentia* trials. The doctrine of *semel preasens simper praesens* (to be once present is to be present always) that is applied by a number of jurisdictions allows trials to continue in case the accused disappears during the proceedings (Zakerhossein and De

Brouwer 2015, pp. 207–208). If the accused person has participated in the proceedings (or part of the proceedings) and is subsequently excluded from the proceedings due to their abuse of rights or no longer participates in the proceedings, their right to be informed is usually perceived to have already been exercised. This study analyses different situations wherein proceedings *in absentia* are conducted on the ground that the accused person has waived their right to participate in the proceedings and therefore did not participate in the proceedings at all. Therefore, one of the conditions of total *in absentia* proceedings – the right of a person to be informed of the proceedings before them – becomes essential.

3.1.3. Proper Notification of the Accused Person – A Condition for the Legality of Criminal Proceedings *in absentia*

The notification requirement (enshrined in both the ICCPR and ECHR) is at the heart of the legality of *in absentia* proceedings (Trials in absentia: a dilemma for Ukraine 2016, p. 6). If a person is duly informed but has waived their right to appear in court, proceedings *in absentia* can take place with effective legal representation and do not in themselves constitute unfair proceedings. If a person has been misinformed or not informed, it is decided what other procedural safeguards can counterbalance the organisation of national criminal proceedings. As a rule, this takes the form of a guarantee of the right to a new criminal procedure, which will be discussed later. Thus, on the basis of scientific research and both international and national case-law, the content and form of the right to be informed is further analysed.

The ECtHR has held that 'to inform someone of a prosecution brought against him/her is a legal act of such importance that it must be carried out in accordance with procedural and substantive requirements capable of guaranteeing the effective exercise of the accused's rights; vague and informal knowledge cannot suffice' (Sejdovic v. Italy [GC] 2006, para.99). The case-law of the ECtHR sets out the essential elements of a person's right to be informed: this is to inform them of the ongoing proceedings and of the accusations made. The ECtHR states that: 'a waiver may be found where it is established that the accused person has been informed of the existence of the criminal proceedings against him or her, is aware of the nature and the cause of the accusation, and does not intend to take part in the trial or wishes to escape prosecution' (Sejdovic v Italy [GC] 2006, para.99; Kounov v. Bulgaria 2006, para.48). In essence, the CJEU shares this view, while emphasising the need to inform the person concerned of the consequences of non-appearance, which means, in particular, informing that person, in due time, 'that a decision might be handed down if he or she does not appear at the trial' (CJEU, C 569/20, IR 2022). The content of the information does not give rise to any major debate, so further analysis of the means of informing the individual or the form of information is carried out.

Article 6 (1) cannot be construed as conferring on litigants the right to obtain a specific form of service of court documents, such as by registered post (Kolegovy v. Russia 2012, para.40; Perihan and Mezopotamya Basın Yayın A.Ş. v. Turkey 2014, para.39; Avotiņš v. Latvia [GC] 2016, para.119). Nonetheless, the Court considers that in the interests of the administration of justice, a litigant should be notified of a court hearing in such a way as to not only have knowledge of the date, time and place of the hearing, but also to have enough time to prepare their case and to attend the court hearing (Kolegovy v. Russia 2012, para.40, Aždajić v. Slovenia 2015, para.48, Korchagin v. Russia 2018, para.65).

Specific knowledge about the charges faced by an accused in any proceedings is a necessary pre-requisite for a decision by the accused to either take part in the proceedings or withdraw from them (Poitrimol v. France 1993, para.31). The ECtHR held that even supposing that the applicant was indirectly aware that criminal proceedings had been opened against them, it cannot be inferred that they unequivocally waived their right to appear at their trial (Colozza v. Italy 1985, paras.27, 29; Poitrimol v. France 1993, para 31). The ECtHR has also held that where a person charged with a criminal offence had not been notified in person, it could not be inferred merely from their status as a 'fugitive' (*latitante*), which was founded on a presumption with an insufficient factual basis, that they had waived the right to appear at the trial and defend themselves (Colozza v. Italy 1985, para.28; Sejdovic v. Italy [GC] 2006, para.87; Sanader v. Croatia 2015, para.73). In any event, objective factors need to be shown to conclude that an accused could have been deemed to have had effective knowledge of the proceedings against them (Yeğer v. Turkey 2022, para.33).

On the other hand, the ECtHR has acknowledged that there may be cases where, even in the absence of an official notification being received by the accused, it may nonetheless still be possible to establish that they have unequivocally waived their right to be present. As the ECtHR stated, 'this may be the case, for example, where the accused states publicly or in writing that he does not intend to respond to summonses of which he has become aware through sources other than the authorities, or succeeds in evading an attempted arrest (Iavarazzo v. Italy 2001), or when materials are brought to the attention of the authorities which unequivocally show that he is aware of the proceedings pending against him and of the charges he faces' (Sejdovic v. Italy [GC] 2006, para.99).

In this context, it should be stressed that according to the CJEU case-law, 'considering whether the way in which the information is provided is sufficient to ensure the person's awareness of the trial, particular attention should be paid to the diligence exercised by public authorities in order to inform the person concerned and to the diligence exercised by the person concerned in order to receive that information' (CJEU, C-569/20, IR 2022, para.50). The CJEU has also stated that 'where it is apparent from precise and objective indicia that the person concerned, while having been officially informed that he or she is accused of having committed a criminal offence, and therefore aware that he or she is going to be brought to trial, takes deliberate steps to avoid receiving officially the information regarding the date and place of the trial that that person may be deemed to have been informed of the trial and to have voluntarily and unequivocally foregone exercise of the right to be present at it. Such precise and objective indicia may, for example, be found to exist where that person has deliberately communicated an incorrect address to the national authorities having competence in criminal matters or is no longer at the address that he or she has communicated' (CJEU, C-569/20, IR 2022, paras.48, 49).

The case-law of the UNHRC also suggests that informing a person is recognised as one of the essential preconditions for the legality of proceedings *in absentia*. When a trial *in absentia* is necessary for the proper administration of justice, the prosecution must show that all due steps have been taken to inform the accused of the charges and proceedings. The UNHRC states that 'proceedings in the absence of the accused may in some circumstances be permissible in the interest of the proper administration of justice, i.e., when accused persons, although informed of the proceedings sufficiently in advance, decline to exercise their right to be present. Consequently, such trials are only compatible with Article 14 (3) (d) if the necessary steps are taken to summon accused persons in a timely manner and to inform them beforehand about the date and place of their trial and to request their attendance' (Mbenge v. Zaire 1990, para.14.1; Maleki v. Italy 1999, para.9.3). According to the UNHRC, 'otherwise, the accused, in particular, is not given adequate time and facilities for the preparation of his defence (Art. 14 (3) (b)), cannot defend himself through legal assistance of his own choosing (Art. 14 (3) (d)) nor does he have the opportunity to examine, or have examined, the witnesses against him and to obtain the attendance and examination of witnesses on his behalf (Art. 14 (3) (e))' (Mbenge v. Zaire 1990, para.14.1). In the case of *Mbenge v. Zaire*, the UNHRC acknowledged 'that there must be certain limits to the efforts which can duly be expected of the responsible authorities of establishing contact with the accused' (para.14.1).

Summarising the requirement of the manner (form) of notification, it must be concluded that adequate information on ongoing criminal proceedings may be represented by any action of the State (the public prosecutor or the court) which demonstrates that the accused actually knows about the trial. Thus, cases in which a person is informed personally, including by serving procedural documents or by informing the person through a lawyer, are well established, and in practice are no longer disputed as ways of properly informing the person. Knowledge can also be established if it is clear from other circumstances (e.g., from the person's own statements) that the person is aware of the process, and this may not necessarily be from official sources – e.g., they were informed by an adult family member, etc.

In order for the accused person to be regarded as having implicitly waived their right to be present at the trial and to defend themselves, it also must be established that they could reasonably have foreseen the legal consequences of their own conduct (Chong Coronado c. Andorre 2020, para.30). Whether a person is to be regarded as having waived the right to participate in the proceedings or as evading the proceedings is, in principle, assessed in the light of the circumstances in which they were informed of the proceedings, the results of that communication, and the subsequent conduct of the person after receiving the relevant information.

However, as already mentioned, in the investigation and handling of cases of war crimes and crimes against humanity, the abovementioned ways of informing the individual may be ineffective and the courts have to address the dilemma as to whether persons tried *in absentia* are aware of the proceedings. According to the ECtHR, the impossibility of holding a trial by default may paralyse the conduct of criminal proceedings in that it may lead to dispersal of the evidence, expiry of the time-limit for prosecution or a miscarriage of justice (Colozza v. Italy 1985, para.29; Sanader v. Croatia 2015, para.77). On the other hand, as pointed out by the ECtHR in *Sanader v. Croatia*, concerning war crimes, 'in the particular circumstances of the case, given the gravity of the crime at issue which, although not susceptible to statutory limitation periods, was commensurate with great public interest and the interest of the victims to see the justice being done, the Court accepts that holding a hearing in the applicant's absence was not itself contrary to Article 6' (Sanader v. Croatia 2015, para.77).

In 2019, Lithuania issued a judgment in a case where 67 persons in total were convicted *in absentia* for crimes against humanity and war crimes committed in 1991 in Vilnius (Vilnius Regional Court pronounced the judgement in the case of the events of January 1991). In the present case, one of the questions raised by the Supreme Court of Lithuania concerned appropriate informing of defendants who are not citizens of the Republic of Lithuania (Ruling of the Supreme Court of Lithuania in a criminal case no. 2K-7-39-1073/2022). The Supreme Court, in response to arguments of the defence concerning the incorrect informing of the sentenced persons, formed certain peculiarities of the State's positive obligation to inform a person about criminal proceedings in cases in which nationals of other States are accused or tried for international crimes (Ruling of the Supreme Court of Lithuania in a criminal case no. 2K-7-39-1073/2022). The Supreme Court, when assessing the efforts of State institutions to inform the defendants, stated, *inter alia*, that 'in such a case, the State has limited possibilities to act actively in the territories of other States – from a procedural point of view, its obligation to take measures to properly inform the person ends by informing the competent authorities of another State under international or bilateral agreements, transferring to them the power to inform about the ongoing criminal proceedings against their nationals (e.g., Art. 66, Art. 218(9) of the Lithuanian CCP). Therefore, in such cases, when assessing the appropriateness of compliance with the obligation to provide information, it is important to determine whether the persons who committed the act have been identified, whether their nationality has been established, their possible place of residence, other personal data necessary to form reports, and whether appropriate channels for the transmission of information have been used to ensure that another State is properly informed of the ongoing prosecution of its citizens or residents' (Ruling of the Supreme Court of Lithuania in a criminal case no. 2K-7-39-1073/2022).

It should be noted that, in the present case, there were other circumstantial indications that the accused were aware of the proceedings, including the defendants having been informed through the media of their countries of nationality and residence, which, taken together, enabled the courts to find that the accused were aware of the ongoing proceedings (Ruling of the Supreme Court of Lithuania in a criminal case no. 2K-7-39-1073/2022). Informing participants or other interested persons about legal proceedings through the media, including social media, is one of the procedural features that apply in civil proceedings as well as in criminal proceedings, e.g., by informing victims of proceedings which do not constitute substantive claims in the case. However, publicising information on criminal proceedings, in particular in the media or on the websites of the authorities, is not generally considered sufficient and appropriate as a method informing a person of criminal proceedings against them.

According to Article 297^5 (1) of the CCP of Ukraine, in an *in absentia* case, e.g., when conducting a special pre-trial investigation, the summons shall be sent to the last known address of residence or temporary residence of the suspect, and shall be published in the national mass media and on the official websites of the agencies conducting pre-trial investigation. The suspect shall be deemed to have been properly informed about the summons content from the moment of its publishing in national mass media. Article 297^5 (2) of the CCP prescribes that copies of the procedural documents to be delivered to the suspect shall be sent to the defence counsel.

Thus, international organisations rightly fear that in cases where, according to the CCP of Ukraine, the courts and prosecutors summon defendants by simply publishing a notice in Ukrainian media or on the courts' websites may constitute insufficient proof that the defendants were notified of trial dates and thus waived their right to be present (Report on the Human Rights Situation in Ukraine 2023, p. 33). This position is also supported by other sources stating that the major assumption that an accused is aware of their trial because the trial is widely publicised in the media is not sufficient (Trials in absentia: a dilemma for Ukraine 2016, p. 5); the publication of a summons in mass media is no guarantee at all of a suspect reading it, and falls far short of meeting the State's obligation to prove that the accused has actual knowledge of the proceedings (Trials in absentia: a dilemma for Ukraine 2016, p. 11). It is therefore to be considered that courts hearing cases in the context of such regulation of pre-trial investigations *in absentia* should take additional measures to inform defendants. This is important because, as will be shown later, the Ukrainian CCP provides for a rather limited right to a new process.

In addition to the content and form of elements of the informing of the defendant, international judicial authorities form a procedural rule that a person may not be subject to the burden of proving that they have not been informed. The ECtHR points out that a person charged with a criminal offence must not be left with the burden of proving that they were not seeking to evade justice, or that their absence was due to *force majeure* (Colozza v. Italy 1985, para.30; Sanader v. Croatia 2015, para.74). At the same time, it is open to the national authorities to assess whether the accused showed good cause for their absence or whether there was anything in the case file to warrant a finding that they had been absent for reasons beyond their control (Medenica v. Switzerland 2001, para.57; Sanader v. Croatia 2015, para.74). In the *Dworzecki* case, the CJEU also pointed out that 'the issuing judicial authority must provide evidence showing that the person concerned was actually aware of that information' (CJEU, C-108/16 PPU, Pawel Dworzecki 2016, para.41). Thus, if a summons was not served directly to the person concerned, but on an adult resident of the same household who undertook to pass it on to the person concerned, and if it cannot be ascertained from the European Arrest Warrant (hereafter – EAW) if and when an adult really passed the summons on, then the conditions set out in Article 4a(1)(a)(i) FD 2002/584 are not satisfied (CJEU, C-108/16 PPU, Pawel Dworzecki 2016, para.54). This means that it is permitted for the executing authority to refuse the execution of the EAW if none of the other guarantees of Article 4a(1) have been complied with (Karas 2019, p. 469). In the case of *Maleki v. Italy*, the UNHRC also stated that the State had to prove that the person was duly informed: 'the State party [...] has failed to show that the author was summoned in a timely manner and that he was informed of the proceedings against him' (Maleki v. Italy 1999, para.9.4). The UNHRC reasoned that it is the obligation of a domestic court to verify that the accused had actual knowledge about a case before commencing a trial *in absentia* (Report on the Human Rights Situation in Ukraine 2023, p. 33).

3.1.4. The Legal Consequences of Failure to Inform the Accused of the Criminal Proceedings Against Them

As already mentioned, in international criminal cases, a situation where a person charged with such crimes cannot be properly informed despite the efforts of the State often arises. In such a case, national CCPs often provide for the possibility of trial *in absentia*. In *Sanader v. Croatia*, the ECtHR held that 'there is no evidence before the Court, nor was it argued by the parties, that the applicant was ever notified of these proceedings, or that the reason for his absence was to escape trial. Indeed, given the conditions of the escalating war in Croatia at the time and the fact that the applicant lived on territory which was outside the control of the domestic authorities it was impossible for them to notify him of the criminal proceedings or to secure his presence, and it was highly improbable that he could have had knowledge of the proceedings and that reason for his absence from Sisak (Croatia) at the time was not being tried. In such circumstances, it was possible under the relevant domestic law to hold a hearing *in absentia* if there were highly important reasons for doing so (Art. 290 of the CCP). In the case at issue these reasons were associated with the need to effectively prosecute the serious war crimes' (Sanader v. Croatia 2015, para.76).

Once a case has been examined *in absentia* and it is established that the convicted person was not aware of the proceedings against them – in other words, there is no reliable indication that they were duly informed and voluntarily waived the right to be present – national courts are normally required to decide which procedural measures may be applied. The right to the new hearing of a case in which a person was convicted *in absentia* is explicitly proclaimed in some instruments within the Council of Europe (European Convention on the International Validity of Criminal Judgments, Art. 24–26; the Second Additional Protocol to the European Convention on Extradition, the Committee of Ministers Resolution (75)11 on the criteria governing proceedings held in the absence of the accused, para. 8). However, this study relies mainly on ECtHR case-law, as well as on the practice of applying the relevant EU regulation. Thus, the case-law of the ECtHR and the CJEU allow a distinction to be drawn between certain criteria for determining whether such a person had an effective opportunity to assert the right to a fair trial.

First of all, it should be noted that neither the Covenant, nor the Convention, nor other international treaties are intended to unify national criminal procedural law. According to the ECtHR, the Convention leaves the Contracting States with wide discretion as regards the choice of the means put in place that ensure that their legal systems are in compliance with the requirements of Article 6 (Medenica v. Switzerland 2001, para.55; Somogyi v. Italy 2004, para.67, Sanader v. Croatia 2015, para.69). In the context of assessing the legality of proceedings *in absentia*, it is noted that 'in particular, the procedural means offered by domestic law and practice must be shown to be effective where a person charged with a criminal offence has neither waived his right to appear and to defend himself nor seek to escape trial' (Medenica v. Switzerland 2001, para.55; Somogyi v. Italy 2004, para.67, Sanader v. Croatia 2015, para.69). The EU rules on the guarantees of *in absentia* proceedings are interpreted, in essence, in the same way. It is acceptable that the CJEU indeed has repeatedly pointed out that the purpose of the legislation was not to harmonise trial *in absentia* in Member States in general (Karas 2019, p. 470), 'but only to lay down common grounds for refusal as regards decisions delivered *in absentia* in criminal matters' (CJEU, C-108/16 PPU, Pawel Dworzecki 2016, para.14; CJEU, (Grand Chamber) C-399/11, Stefano Melloni 2013, para.43). Detailed rules of that kind laid down by national law cannot undermine the aim of safeguarding the fairness of the proceedings, and thus of enabling the person concerned to be present at their trial, which requires that they have the ability to prepare their defence (CJEU, C-564/19, IS 2021, para.128; CJEU, C-569/20, IR 2022). On the other hand, it can be accepted that although the definition of *in absentia* formally applies in the context of international cooperation, this concept will lead to harmonisation in the manner of summoning an accused (Klip 2016, p. 282; Karas 2018, pp. 294–296).

As already mentioned, the duty of the State to guarantee the right of a criminal defendant to be present in the courtroom – either during the original proceedings or at a retrial – ranks as one of the essential requirements of Article 6 of the ECHR (Stoichkov v. Bulgaria 2005, para.56; Sanader v. Croatia 2015, para.71). Accordingly, the refusal to reopen proceedings conducted in the accused's absence without any indication that the accused has waived their right to be present during the trial has been found to be a 'flagrant denial of justice' (Stoichkov v. Bulgaria 2005, paras.54–58; Sanader v. Croatia 2015, para.71). Thus, according to ECtHR case-law, a denial of justice undoubtedly occurs where a such a person convicted *in absentia* is subsequently unable to obtain from the court a fresh determination of the merits of the charge, in respect of both law and fact (Sejdovic v. Italy [GC] 2006, para.82, Sanader v. Croatia 2015, para.68). The jurisprudence of the ECtHR leads to the conclusion that the basic conditions for such a right to arise are that it has not been unequivocally established that the person has waived their right to appear and to defend themselves (Colozza v. Italy 1985, para.29; Einhorn v. France 2001, para.33; Krombach v. France 2001, para.85; Somogyi v. Italy 2004, para.66)), or that they intended to escape trial (Medenica v. Switzerland 2001, para.55).

The CJEU formulates a similar position: 'an accused person whom the competent national authorities, despite their reasonable efforts, do not succeed in locating and to whom they accordingly have not managed to give the information about his or her trial may be tried and convicted *in absentia*, but must be able, after notification of the conviction, to rely directly on the right to secure the reopening of the proceedings or access to an equivalent legal remedy resulting in a fresh examination, in his or her presence, of the merits of the case' (CJEU, C-569/20, IR 2022). Persons who were aware of the proceedings and did not participate in the proceedings in the absence of valid reasons cannot benefit from this guarantee in accordance with Article 6 of the Convention (Mihelj v. Slovenia 2015; Atanasova c. Bulgarie 2017, para.44). According to CJEU case-law, a person may be denied that right if it is apparent from precise and objective indicia that they received sufficient information to know that they were going to be brought to trial and, by deliberate acts and with the intention of evading justice, prevented the authorities from informing them officially of that trial (CJEU, C-569/20, IR 2022). However, it may also be found in the national regulation that the sentenced person is given the possibility to request a new trial automatically (without any conditions) after proceedings *in absentia* (e.g., Art. 438 of the CCP of the Republic of Lithuania provides for the possibility for the sentenced person to lodge an appeal without time-limits, and to require a fresh investigation of all evidence and the resolution of all questions of law).

Hence, according to ECtHR case-law, when domestic law permits a trial to be held notwithstanding the absence of a person 'charged with a criminal offence', that person should, once they become aware of the proceedings, be able to obtain from a court a fresh determination of the merits of the charge, in respect of both law and fact (Colozza v. Italy 1985, paras.27, 29, Sanader v. Croatia 2015, para.78). The domestic legislation should afford the applicant with sufficient certainty regarding the opportunity to appear at a new trial (Sejdovic v. Italy [GC] 2006, para.101, Sanader v. Croatia 2015, para.78).

The retrial offered by the domestic authorities, regardless of its procedural form, should comply with the requirement of effectiveness (Medenica

v. Switzerland 2001, para.55, Sanader v. Croatia 2015, para.78). The right to fresh determination of the case can be realised as a new trial at the same instance as an appeal: the point is that a person can effectively challenge both the facts and the applicable law. A retrial based on new facts and evidence may also be an opportunity to re-examine the case following *in absentia* proceedings. However, this is a general legal avenue for seeking a retrial after a decision convicting a defendant has become final and enforceable, and is open to both those tried *in absentia* and those tried in their presence. Despite this, this remedy is applicable only to a restricted category of cases since the condition for its use is the existence of new evidence or facts usually capable of leading to acquittal or resentencing under a more lenient provision (e.g., Art. 444 of the CCP of Lithuania, Art. 501 (1)(3) of the CCP of Croatia). Those proceedings cannot therefore be regarded as a specific procedural guarantee of the right to due process of a person convicted via *in absentia* proceedings.

Thus, in assessing whether the right to a new procedure is an effective instrument, the case-law of the ECtHR and the CJEU allow the following main criteria to be distinguished: a person is not obliged to appear before the domestic authorities and is entitled to demand a new assessment of the charges, both in fact and in law.

A person who has requested a new hearing must not surrender to the law enforcement authorities, especially when they have been sentenced to imprisonment during *in absentia* proceedings. The requirement of the person's presence under the jurisdiction of the domestic authorities is a very strict condition. The ECtHR has considered that 'the requirement that an individual tried *in absentia*, who has not had knowledge of his prosecution and of the charges against him or sought to evade trial or unequivocally waived his right to appear in court, has to appear before the domestic authorities and provide an address of residence in the State during the criminal proceedings in order to be able to request a retrial, appears disproportionate' (Sanader v. Croatia 2015, para.84). In the case of *Sanader v. Croatia*, the ECtHR stated that this requirement essentially provides that individuals sentenced *in absentia* to imprisonment who do not live in the territory of the State cannot apply for the automatic reopening of the proceedings unless they present themselves to the judicial authorities, which would, in the ordinary course of action, mean that they would be deprived of their liberty based on their conviction (Sanader v. Croatia 2015, para.85). The ECtHR also pointed out that 'even taking into account the particular circumstances of the present case, which concerns serious charges of war crimes, the Court considers that the obligation that an individual tried *in absentia* has to appear before the domestic authorities and provide an address of residence in Croatia during the criminal proceedings in order to be able to request a retrial, is unreasonable and disproportionate' (Sanader v. Croatia 2015, para.89). It follows that an accused cannot be obliged to surrender to custody in order to secure the right to be retried (Sanader v. Croatia 2015, para.87).

At the same time, the State has the right, in the fresh proceedings, to apply all measures envisaged under the relevant domestic law, including detention (Khalfaoui v. France 1999, para.44, Sanader v. Croatia 2015, para.88). However, that would need to have a different legal basis – that of a reasonable suspicion of the applicant having committed the crime at issue, and the existence of 'relevant and sufficient reasons' for their detention (Kudła v. Poland [GC] 2000, para.111; Dragin v. Croatia 2014, para.110; Sanader v. Croatia 2015, para.88).

Another important aspect of the first condition is that a person who has the opportunity to seek a retrial without bearing them to a situation where they would trade that opportunity with their liberty also acquires the responsibility to participate effectively and diligently in the fresh proceedings. The person's failure to do so legitimately has previously led to the discontinuation of the new proceedings (Sanader v. Croatia 2015, para.90).

The second important condition is that a person is entitled to claim a fresh factual and legal determination of the criminal charge. The essence of this requirement is that, in the course of proceedings *in absentia*, the person concerned was unable to exercise the rights of the accused in adversarial proceedings, including the right to present evidence and challenge the evidence of the prosecution, and to express their position on legal issues. According to CJEU case-law, the fresh determination of the merits of the case may lead to the original decision being reversed: 'the Member States must ensure that, where a trial *in absentia* is conducted the person concerned has the right "to a new trial", or to another legal remedy, which allows a fresh determination of the merits of the case and which may lead to the original decision being reversed ("right to a new trial")' (CJEU, C-569/20, IR 2022, para.27).

It should be noted that a number of jurisdictions provide, after a new examination, for ordinary appeals against this decision.

Researchers argue that the scope of human rights protection in the execution of an EAW, in cases of trials *in absentia*, does not seem to fully comply with the guarantees provided in the jurisprudence of the ECtHR (Karas 2018, p. 464; Stan 2020, p. 657). As numerous researchers have pointed out, in the *Melloni* judgment (CJEU, (Grand Chamber) C-399/11 Stefano Melloni 2013, para.41), two guarantees – that the person was informed of the trial and that they were represented and effectively defended by two counsels that they appointed – were sufficient, and actually precluded any additional condition, including the conviction rendered *in absentia*, from being open to review in the presence of the convicted person (Cavallone 2014, p. 30; Karas 2019, p. 464; CJEU, (Grand Chamber) C-399/11 Stefano Melloni 2013, paras 40, 46). According to the aforementioned authors, it seems that the ECtHR (Sejdovic v. Italy [GC] 2006, para.81; Colloza v. Italy 1985, para.29; Hermi v. Italy 2006, para.58) requires that both of these requirements – the right to be represented by a lawyer and the possibility to claim a retrial – be met cumulatively in order to comply with guarantees of the right to fair trial (Cavallone 2014, p. 32; Karas 2019, p. 464). This study takes the view that ensuring the legal representation of a person who does not know about proceedings against them in those same proceedings by the State or family members is not recognised as compensating for the person's absence and denying their right to a new trial. On the other hand, that does not call into question the benefits of such representation in safeguarding the fairness of the proceedings and the rights to defence of the defendant who is not present. Moreover, we take the view that *in absentia* proceedings against a person who is unaware of such proceedings can take place only in the presence of a lawyer (despite the difficulties of the defence, especially in cases where the defendant has no connection with the defender (IBA Report on the 'Experts' Roundtable on trials in absentia in international criminal justice 2016, p. 9)), so that this discussion is not continued.

As already stated, the other possibility of compensating a person convicted *in absentia* is the broadening of the limits on the lodging of an appeal and its handling. The ECtHR has also held that the reopening of the time allowed for appealing against a conviction *in absentia*, where the defendant was entitled to attend the hearing in a court of appeal and to request the admission of new evidence, entails the possibility of a fresh factual and legal determination of the criminal charge, so that the proceedings as a whole could be said to have been fair (Jones v. UK 2003, Sejdovic v. Italy [GC] 2006, para.85; Atanasova c. Bulgarie 2017, para.44).

Those requirements must not only be provided for by law, but, in order to ensure the effective right to a new examination, they must accordingly have been interpreted in the case-law of the domestic courts.

The case-law of international courts presupposes a rather broad discretion of States in regulating the right to retrial. On the other hand, we can agree with the view that it is difficult to assimilate the situation of one who did not actually know about the criminal proceedings pending against them with one who knew it, but avoided the criminal procedure. This is one of the reasons why states provide some filter criteria for retrial procedure which, in some cases, are difficult to fulfil (Stan 2020, p. 667). As can be seen from the provisions of criminal procedure in some States, the right of a person convicted *in absentia* to a review of the case is regulated in very different ways, from an unconditional re-examination to the introduction of certain conditions for a new trial. For example: a person has to make such a request within certain deadlines; the person must provide information that they have not been informed of the criminal proceedings against them; before demanding a new examination, the person must exercise the right of appeal, etc. (Stan 2020, pp. 658–667; Karas 2018, pp. 299–307).

In the context of the Ukrainian legal system, there is a concern that *in absentia* proceedings in Ukraine do not comply with international human rights standards (OHCHR, Report on the human rights situation in Ukraine 16 May to 15 August 2018, para.63). At the same time, various sources suggest solutions that include both substantial and rather technical, albeit very important, regulatory changes in this institute (In Absentia Procedure: the Concept of Amendments to National Legislation Ukraine). The main thread of these approaches, which also responds to the recommendations of international organisations, is to provide for the right of the individual to request a new trial under certain conditions. There are opinions which suggest that the rule which only allows for a retrial if the verdict has not yet been delivered is contrary to the international standards that retrial should be available for defendants at any time after initial proceedings *in absentia* (Views of the Human Rights Committee under Article 5 (4), of the Optional Protocol to the International Covenant on Civil and Political Rights, paras.9.4–9.5). The OHCHR notes that this non-compliance with international human rights standards may lead to rejections of future extradition requests (Report on the human rights situation in Ukraine (16 November 2019–15 February 2020), p. 19). For States participating in the EAW system, non-compliance with the conditions governing the legality of proceedings *in absentia* may also lead to non-transfer of a person (Karas 2019, pp. 459–475). The OHCHR recommended that the CCP of Ukraine be amended to allow for a full retrial of those tried *in absentia* upon their request at any time before or after the verdict in their cases has been delivered (Report on the human rights situation in Ukraine (16 November 2019–15 February 2020). A similar suggestion is to supplement the CCP of the Republic of Ukraine with a special norm for the review of decisions made in the course of *in absentia* proceedings, which is expressed in other sources (In Absentia Procedure: the Concept of Amendments to National Legislation Ukraine; Hloviuk 2015, p. 22).

3.1.5. Interim findings

Criminal proceedings in the absence of the accused person may be heard only where the interests of justice so require, and the procedural requirements for the protection of the rights of the absent defendant and of the fairness of the proceedings have been fulfilled. The right of a person to appear in court is not absolute, but its refusal must meet certain conditions, the fundamental tenet of which is the right to be duly informed of the proceedings.

Total *in absentia* proceedings are based on the fact that the accused person has waived their right to participate in the proceedings and therefore did not participate in the proceedings at all. Whether a person is to be regarded as having waived their right to participate in the proceedings or as evading the proceedings is assessed in the light of the circumstances in which they were informed of the proceedings, the results of that communication, and the subsequent conduct of the person after receiving the relevant information.

The elements of the content of the right to be informed are essentially formed. It is the duty of the State to ensure that the person against whom proceedings are pending is informed in a timely manner of the time and place of the proceedings, of the charges, and of the legal consequences of the person's failure to appear before the court.

The method of notification is not precisely defined; therefore, national courts and law enforcement authorities must constantly decide whether the way in which they choose to inform the person is compliant with the requirements of fair proceedings.

Considering whether the way in which the information is provided is sufficient to ensure the person's awareness of the trial, particular attention should be paid to the diligence exercised by public authorities in order to inform the person concerned and to the diligence exercised by the person concerned in order to receive that information.

Informing a person by serving procedural documents, either personally or through a lawyer who is authorised by the person, are well established ways to properly inform the person, but they are not always effective in cases of international crimes. Therefore, properly informing the defendant is a situation in which it can also be established from other circumstances of the case that the person is aware of the proceedings. Public information about criminal proceedings in the media or on the websites of the law enforcement authorities shall not be considered as adequate information about the criminal proceedings against the accused person.

Along with the requirements of the content and form of informing the accused person, the case-law has established a procedural rule according to which the proper information of a person is an obligation of the State and the burden cannot be placed on the person of proving that they have not been properly informed of the proceedings.

In the interests of justice, criminal proceedings *in absentia,* including cases of war crimes and crimes against humanity, may also take place against an uninformed person, in which case the individual must be guaranteed an effective right to a new trial.

The individual's right to request new proceedings can be guaranteed both in the context of new judicial proceedings and with broad appeal possibilities.

In assessing whether the right to a new procedure is an effective remedy, the case-law of the ECtHR and the CJEU allows the following main requirements to be distinguished: a person is not required to appear before the domestic authorities, and they are entitled to request a new assessment of the charges in terms of fact and law.

3.2. Should Ecocide Be an International Crime?

3.2.1. Background

Critical environmental impacts both during and in the aftermath of conflict can take decades to restore. Climate change, biodiversity and wellbeing are affected by wars. Thus, practical and legal instruments should be used to reduce their environmental impact. Nevertheless, the environment does not feature as part of the main international conventions on the law of war, such as the Hague Conventions of 1899 (Convention for the pacific settlement of international disputes 1899) and 1907 (Convention (IV) respecting the Laws and Customs of War on Land and its annex: Regulations concerning the Laws and Customs of War on Land 1907) or the GC of 1949. In fact, the word 'environment' does not even appear in these treaties. International law does, however, recognise that parties to a conflict are responsible for protecting the environment and minimising harm to it. This obligation is codified in a few international legal instruments, including the additional protocols to the GC of 1949 and the Protection of Victims of International Armed Conflicts (Protocol I) of 1977, which address the protection of the natural environment during armed conflict.[9]

---

9 'Article 55 – Protection of the natural environment:

1. Care shall be taken in warfare to protect the natural environment against widespread, long-term and severe damage. This protection includes a prohibition of the use of methods or means of warfare which are intended or may be expected to cause such damage to the natural environment and thereby to prejudice the health or survival of the population.

2. Attacks against the natural environment by way of reprisals are prohibited.'

The ICC, which is the principal international judicial body to investigate and prosecute individuals for the gravest crimes of concern to the international community, currently recognises four core international crimes:

1. Genocide as acts committed with the intent to destroy, in whole or in part, a national, ethnical, racial, or religious group.
2. Crimes against humanity as widespread or systematic attacks against civilian populations, including acts such as murder, torture, enslavement, and others.
3. War crimes as grave breaches of the laws and customs of international armed conflicts.
4. The crime of aggression as the planning, preparation, initiation, or execution of an act of aggression by a state against another state.

While the ICC can prosecute for environmental crimes, this is only possible within the context of these four crimes mentioned above, and only during war. It does not place any legal restrictions on legal harms that occur during times of peace. In 1998, the destruction of the environment was proposed as an international crime against peace, but ultimately was not adopted as part of the Rome Statute (1998) due to political factors (the reluctance of major powers to stop various weapons tests). The latter document includes genocide, crimes against humanity, war crimes and the crime of aggression.

At the moment, the concept of ecocide is not formally recognised as an international crime under the framework of international law. However, there has been growing interest and discussion around the idea of recognising ecocide as an international crime to hold individuals and corporations accountable for environmental harm.[10] Efforts to recognise ecocide as a fifth core international crime are based on the belief that environmental harm should be considered on a par with other international crimes due to its potentially catastrophic impact on humanity and the planet.

In December 2019, at the ICC in the Hague, Vanuatu's ambassador to the EU formally proposed to amend the Rome Statute (Statement by H. E. John H. Licht

10 In 2021, the European Commission produced a proposal for a Directive of the European Parliament and of the Council on the protection of the environment through criminal law and replacing Directive 2008/99/EC, In 2023 In 2023 the European Parliament's Committee on Legal Affairs made a report on the proposal for a directive of the European Parliament and of the Council on the protection of the environment through criminal law and replacing Directive 2008/99/EC with an amendment of the new Article 3a: ecocide https://www.europarl.europa.eu/doceo/document/A-9-2023-0087_EN.html.

2019), the treaty that established the International Criminal Court, to include ecocide as the fifth international crime. The proposed amendment aims to hold individuals, including corporate executives, accountable for actions that cause severe environmental damage. Changing the Rome Statute would require a two-thirds majority among the 123 countries that have ratified the treaty (according to the ICC 2023 data), so many countries' political will and international cooperation are required, which poses a challenge.

3.2.2. The Concept of Ecocide

The term *ecocide* is derived from the Greek word *oikos* (house or environment) and the Latin word *caedere* (to kill or destroy). It was first coined in the 1970s by Arthur Galston, an American plant biologist and chair of the Department of Botany at Yale University, in the context of discussing the use of herbicides in warfare and their impact on the environment at the Conference on War and National Responsibility in Washington (Weisberg, B., 1970). Ecocide in Indochina. Canfield Press, San Francisco.). The term *ecocide* became widely recognised in 1972 at the UN Stockholm Conference on the Human Environment, when Olof Palme, then the Prime Minister of Sweden, called the Vietnam War an example of ecocide in his opening speech (Björk, 1996, p. 15). In 1973, Richard A. Falk proposed his draft Ecocide Convention. In this convention, the following definition of ecocide was proposed – 'any of the following acts committed with intent to disrupt or destroy, in whole or in part, a human ecosystem:

(a) The use of weapons of mass destruction, whether nuclear, bacteriological, chemical, or other;
(b) The use of chemical herbicides to defoliate and deforest natural forests for military purposes;
(c) The use of bombs and artillery in such quantity, density, or size as to impair the quality of soil or to enhance the prospects of diseases dangerous to human beings, animals or crops;
(d) The use of bulldozing equipment to destroy large tracts of forest or cropland for military purposes; The use of techniques designed to increase or decrease rainfall or otherwise modify weather as a weapon of war;
(e) The forcible removal of human beings or animals from their habitual places of habitation to expedite the pursuit of military or industrial objectives' (Falk 1973, p. 12).

In April 2010, a proposal for an international ecocide law was submitted to the UN Law Commission by UK-based lawyer Polly Higgins (2010), who proposed to define the Crime of Ecocide as:

> 'Acts or omissions committed in times of peace or conflict by any senior person within the course of State, corporate or any other entity's activity which cause, contribute to, or may be expected to cause or contribute to serious ecological, climate or cultural loss or damage to or destruction of ecosystem(s) of a given territory(ies), such that peaceful enjoyment by the inhabitants has been or will be severely diminished.

1. To establish seriousness, impact(s) must be widespread, long-term or severe' (Higgins, ca. 2010).

David Zierler's 2011 book, *The Invention of Ecocide*, also gives a historical account of how the use of herbicidal warfare in the Vietnam War resulted in a movement of scientists who advocated for ecocide to be recognised as an international crime.

In 2017, Laurent Neyret *et al.* proposed a Draft Convention against and offered the following definition:

'1. For the purposes of the present Convention, Ecocide means intentional acts committed as part of a widespread or systematic attack on the security of the planet, as follows:
   a. release of radioactive ('ionising') substances;
   b. transport or disposal of waste;
   c. factory production of dangerous substances;
   d. production, transport, etc. of radioactive substances;
   e. destruction, possession or capture of wild flora or fauna, whether protected or not;
   f. other acts of a similar nature which threaten the security of the planet.'

Thus, the term *ecocide*, without one coherent definition, has been well understood since the 1970s.

In 2023, several notable mentions of ecocide were not purely theoretical and involved individuals other than scientists and environmentalists. In June 2023, Ukrainian President Volodymyr Zelensky called the destruction of the Nova Kakhovka damn an example of brutal ecocide. Suddenly, ecocide became an international issue discussed in many countries, as well as in international organisations such as EU institutions. Therefore, there was another chance to discuss it as a necessary norm of international law.

3.2.3. The Path Towards International Law Recognising Ecocide as an International Crime

As discussed above, the framing of environmental damage known as ecocide can be traced back to the 1970s, when it emerged in response to the environmental atrocities caused by the use of herbicides such as Agent Orange in the Vietnam War. Since then, attempts to respond to large-scale environmental destruction have included Professor Richard A. Falk's draft of an International Convention on the Crime of Ecocide in 1973. Debates over whether to criminalise environmental destruction in the report of the International Law Commission entitled 'Draft Code of Crimes Against the Peace and Security of Mankind' (1996) were developed in the 1990s (this document was eventually to become the Rome Statute, adopted in 1998 and entering into force on 1 July 2002).

Until now, perhaps the most significant initiative to create a new norm of international law occurred in 1991; then, the International Law Commission created the Draft Code of Crimes Against the Peace and Security of Mankind. This contained twelve crimes, which included an environmental crime:

> '*Article 26 Willful and Severe Damage to the Environment*
> An individual who willfully causes or orders the causing of widespread, long-term and severe damage to the natural environment shall, on conviction thereof, be sentenced.'

However, this article was withdrawn from the final version of the Draft Code of Crimes Against the Peace and Security of Mankind. It did not become part of the Rome Statute or an international crime due to the abovementioned political reasons.

Given the likely political challenges associated with actually introducing and implementing a new international crime into the Rome Statute (i.e., this will depend on the political consensus of more than 120 countries – the signatories and parties of the Rome Statute), it is worth reviewing how prosecuting the crime of ecocide could be possible in the International Criminal Court.

For example, in 2008, the ICC prosecutor charged Omar Al-Bashir (*Prosecutor v. Omar Hassan Ahmad Al Bashir* (2010) para. 34) with genocide under Article 6(c) of the Rome Statute,[11] noting the connection between genocide and the deliberate destruction of the environment by systematically destroying properties and vegetation, leading to the pollution of water sources by the militia and the Janjaweed in Darfur.

In the jurisprudence of the ICC, the possibility to frame environmental crimes as crimes of aggression, or the 'use of armed force by a State against the sovereign territorial integrity or political independence of another State' can also be identified. The initial inquiry into NATO's bombing campaign against Serbian military positions in 1999 examined aggression-related environmental harm (Final

11 '(c) Deliberately inflicting on the group conditions of life calculated to bring about its physical destruction in whole or in part.'

report to the Prosecutor 2000), but no criminal case followed, and the ICC did not assess what kind of environmental damage can be considered excessive.

On 22 June 2021, a group known as the Independent Expert Panel for the Legal Definition of Ecocide officially launched what they described as a 'practical and effective definition of the crime of ecocide'. The twelve members of this panel – lawyers from around the world with backgrounds in criminal, environmental, and climate law – expressed their hope that the 'proposed definition might serve as the basis of consideration for an amendment to the Rome Statute of the International Criminal Court'. As they argued, 'the time has come to extend the protections for serious environmental harm'. Ecocide, as they envisioned it, would form a new distinct international crime, defined thus: 'For the purpose of this Statute, ecocide means unlawful or wanton acts committed with knowledge that there is a substantial likelihood of severe and either widespread or long-term damage to the environment being caused by those acts' (Stop Ecocide Foundation 2021, p. 5).

Jérôme de Hemptinne summarised three reasons in support of marking ecocide as the 'fifth international crime':

> First, the 'safety of the planet' is increasingly recognised as being among the core 'supranational' values and interests that must be protected internationally. This is evidenced by the fact that Ecocide is often referred to as being 'of concern to the international community as a whole'. Second, the massive exploitation and destruction of natural resources usually transcend national borders by involving or affecting the interests of several States. To stop these exploitation and destruction, coordinated action at the international level is required. Third, committing environmental criminality on a massive scale usually threatens peace and security, like any other international crime. (Hemptinne 2022)

However, even if many states and politicians agree with the abovementioned reasons, introducing a new crime to the Rome Statute is not straightforward. Furthermore, it would be frivolous to assume that criminalisation will offer an effective response to environmental destruction by itself, as the criminalisation of the current four core international crimes (genocide, crimes against humanity, war crimes, and crimes of aggression) does not prevent them entirely.

Another aspect of the popularity of codifying ecocide could be its criminalisation through national laws. Individual countries have their own rules and regulations to prevent such harm (ecocide is officially a crime in 10 countries). Vietnam, as a consequence of its experiences during the harmful Vietnam War, was the first country to include the crime of ecocide in its domestic law; other countries also have domestic ecocide laws, including France, Ecuador, Ukraine and Russia. Certainly, there is an amplified interest in ecocide crimes at the national level. However, this interest is still limited, and very little or no judicial practices concern the investigation and prosecution of ecocide perpetrators.

At the level of the EU, in its resolutions on Human Rights and Democracy in the World 2019 and the EU Biodiversity Strategy for 2030, the European Parliament voted to urge 'the EU and the Member States to promote the recognition of Ecocide as an international crime under the Rome Statute of the International Criminal Court' (European Parliament resolution of 20 January 2021, para. 1) and the European Commission proposed the revision of the Directive 2008/99/EC on the protection of the environment through criminal law (hereafter – the Environmental Crime Directive) (Proposal for a Directive of the European Parliament and of the Council on the protection of the environment through criminal law and replacing Directive 2008/99/EC of the European Parliament and of the Council of 19 November 2008 on the protection of the environment through criminal law). Here, ecocide is defined as 'any conduct <...> committed with intent, which may cause, or substantially contribute to causing, severe and long-term damage or severe and irreparable or irreversible damage to an ecosystem or ecosystems in the natural environment'.

While definitions have differed due to authors, eras or circumstances, proponents of the specific crime of ecocide have been united by the belief that existing criminal laws are insufficient to address environmental crimes. Environmental activists, ecocide campaigners and others concerned about the global environment argue that mass environmental destruction (in biodiversity destruction wars, such as the hostilities in the Democratic Republic of the Congo (UN Environment Programme 2018), the Republic of Côte d'Ivoire (UN Environment Programme 2015), Ukraine (UN Environment Programme 2023; Pereira *et al.* 2022) or Gaza (Environment Programme 2021)) will continue until a global law is in place. While there may be variations in specific definitions, it could be summarised that ecocide generally refers to large-scale environmental impacts that result from harmful activities that cause profound or irreversible damage. The most important parts of the term ecocide could be divided into three: first, the environmental impact; second, activity that causes damage to nature; and third, the damage to nature itself. This is a complex and multifaceted concept with various definitions and interpretations, but its core idea is the severe harm or destruction of ecosystems due to human actions.

3.2.4. *Ecocide as a Crime of the State*

The idea of ecocide as a crime of the state would involve holding governments and their representatives accountable for actions or omissions that result in extensive environmental impact.

Using the ICC system to prosecute ecocide has a significant disadvantage – only individuals can be charged with crimes under the Rome Statue. In wartime situations mentioned above (in the Democratic Republic of the Congo, the Republic of Côte d'Ivoire or Ukraine) or in times of peace (for example, oil extraction in Canada (Stockholm Environment Institute 2020) and mining in Venezuela (Unit 2023)), the crime of ecocide was or is being committed by corporations or even states.

Another disadvantage is that the jurisdiction of the ICC does not cover the whole world – only 123 states have accepted its jurisdiction. Some of the largest countries have not, such as China, the USA, India, and Russia. For instance, in the context of the destruction of the Nova Kakhovka damn (Ukraine) by Russia, it would be exceedingly difficult to hold the Russian government and its representatives accountable.

Without the international legal norm of ecocide, it is difficult to see how a state could be prosecuted at the international level as a perpetrator of ecocide. National laws or even the proposals of international organisations (for example, the European Commission's proposal for revising the Environmental Crime Directive) include only the liability of natural and legal persons. At the same time, the increasing number of activities that entail risks of environmental damage with transboundary and global impacts (e.g., pollution) raise questions about principles and criteria governing states' responsibility for environmental damage. There is a need to identify, harmonise and develop the principles of international law applicable to responsibility and liability in the context of environmental damage.

There are other ways in which a state could potentially be prosecuted for environmental damage, such as diplomatic efforts to resolve the matter amicably. This can include negotiations, discussions, or diplomatic pressure to encourage the state to rectify its actions. However, it is tough to foresee whether diplomatic means would be effective and how long they would take; this would also depend on states' relationships and past events. Diplomatic and economic sanctions can be used as pressure tactics to compel a state to address its environmental crimes.

Regarding environmental disputes involving states, the ICJ can hear cases in which one state alleges that another state has violated its international legal obligations concerning the environment (Statute of the ICJ 1945, Art. 34). This might involve issues such as transboundary pollution, disputes over shared natural resources, or disagreements regarding the interpretation and application of international environmental agreements. However, it is important to understand that the role of the ICJ is to resolve disputes between states, and it can only do so if both parties involved agree to its jurisdiction. States are sovereign entities that can choose whether to participate in proceedings. Additionally, ICJ decisions are typically related to providing remedies for disputes, such as compensation or injunctive relief, rather than imposing criminal sanctions.

Another way in which state responsibility arises from regional agreements is, for example, if an EU Member State is responsible for environmental damage in another Member State. These actions might breach EU environmental laws. Those cases could potentially fall within the jurisdiction of the CJEU; this would be resolved similarly in other regional organisations.

Another option may involve one state prosecuting another at the national level, but this is a complex and often politically sensitive procedure. The principles of state sovereignty and international law play a significant role in these cases. Therefore, such prosecutions are relatively rare and involve cases of extreme gravity, such as acts of aggression or gross human rights violations. Additionally, specific legal procedures and requirements can vary widely among countries. First of all, in order to initiate proceedings against another state there must be a legal basis under domestic law for doing so; national laws must permit the prosecution of foreign states or their officials for the alleged offences. Then, the state must clearly define the offences or actions for which it is seeking prosecution, gather substantial evidence to support these allegations, and determine the appropriate legal jurisdiction to hear the case. In some cases, this may be the state's domestic criminal courts, while in others, it may involve specialised courts or tribunals explicitly established for certain types of offences. After a court or tribunal renders a judgment that a state has violated the national legislation of another state, the most challenging part can be enforcing that judgment due to state sovereignty and political or other motives.

Another possibility is to mobilise wide public attention and international civil society organisations to raise awareness about the environmental crimes committed by the state; this could be used to stop a state.

3.2.5. Interim findings

After evaluating possible definitions of ecocide, another new option could be proposed that covers all of its essential aspects: ecocide is the wilful and systemic act of severe harm, damage, or destruction of natural ecosystems, including but not limited to terrestrial, aquatic, and atmospheric systems, resulting from human activities, whether direct or indirect, that significantly disrupt the ecological balance, endanger the continuity of species, or threaten the well-being of present and future generations. Of course, ecocide encompasses actions that violate international environmental agreements, customary international law, and the fundamental principles of environmental protection.

In order to recognise ecocide as a crime under international law, it is necessary to ensure the following main aspects:

(a) Advocacy and awareness: environmental activists and organisations, such as the Stop Ecocide Foundation, have been working to raise awareness of ecocide and promote its recognition as an international crime. Public support and engagement are crucial to driving this initiative forward.
(b) Legal formulation: proposals and draft codes have been put forward to define and codify ecocide as a crime under international law. The draft law should outline ecocide, ensuring accountability for state and corporate actors, addressing issues of sovereignty and jurisdiction, and providing potential penalties for those found guilty.
(c) Political will and international cooperation: the recognition of ecocide as an international crime requires support and cooperation from the international community. Countries must come together to agree on the legal framework.
(d) Ratification and enforcement: if an agreement is reached and a legal framework is established, countries need to ratify and incorporate this new law instrument into their national legal systems. Effective enforcement and exercise would then become a key aspect of making ecocide a meaningful deterrent against large-scale environmental destruction.

3.3. Lay Participation in Ukrainian Court Proceedings During Russian Aggression: Constitutional Aspects

3.3.1. Context

Article 1 of Ukraine's Constitution states that 'Ukraine is a sovereign and independent, democratic, social, and state which upholds the rule of law' (Constitution of Ukraine 1996). Thus, the constitutional principle of the rule of law is enshrined in the Ukrainian Constitution, which implies that states have a duty to guarantee human rights and freedoms. One way to help ensure this is through the establishment and functioning of a transparent and efficient judiciary. Such a judicial system is one of the means of achieving justice, which is, among other things, an integral part of the fundamental principle of the rule of law. It is noteworthy that the core function of the judiciary in Ukraine, which is to protect human rights and freedoms, is carried out by judges together with *lay* judges (a mixed court model) in the administration of justice, who, among other things, do not have a legal education. The Constitution of Ukraine uses the term *присяжні*, which can be translated into English as either *lay judges* or *jurors*, depending on the context (Wegen and Shepel 2020, p. 21).

It is worth mentioning that the Republic of Lithuania also intends to introduce a form of lay participation, i.e., lay judges (a mixed court model), into its system of justice (Draft Law on Amendments of the Constitution of the Republic of Lithuania 2019). Thus, the identification of the most optimal and rational modern model of general lay participation in response to the real intention to introduce a form of lay participation in Lithuanian court proceedings determines the need to analyse the models of other countries. In the present case, it is expedient to analyse the legal regulation of a state defending itself against aggression with regard to lay participation and to assess the functioning of this institute in such a context.

Although a lot of research has been carried out as regards the institute of lay participation in Ukraine (Tytych 2022, Dronova 2015, Savva 2021, Wegen and Shepel 2020), the constitutional and ordinary regulation of lay participation has been studied insufficiently, and the lay participation model has not been duly identified. Moreover, little research has been carried out regarding the functioning of this institute in the conditions of the current war of aggression. It is noteworthy that most of the constitutions of the member states of the Council of Europe, including Ukraine, enshrine some form of lay participation in the administration of justice. In this regard, it is worth noting again that Lithuania intends to introduce a form of lay participation, i.e., lay judges (a mixed court model). Various authors have analysed the involvement of lay participation in the administration of justice in Ukraine. However, there is a lack of assessment of the constitutional and ordinary regulation of lay judges (often referred to as *jurors*) during times of aggression, and, respectively, the functioning of the model of lay participation in the administration of justice in such circumstances. Therefore, in order to find the most optimal and rational model of lay participation, a study of a legal system such as that of Ukraine, which is defending its sovereignty in the context of aggression, is appropriate, including a detailed analysis of the legal regulation. This context is what determines the novelty and necessity of such research in legal science, and that which is presented in this chapter. Thus, it is doubly noteworthy to emphasise the importance of this research because – according to Vitaliy Tytych (2022), an expert, attorney at law, insider and witness to the situation in Ukrainian courts during this aggression – there is an urgent need to introduce a real and effective mechanism for involving the people in the administration of justice, which has long been the focus of Ukrainian experts. This need is caused by a new aspect that has emerged: future trials in cases of international crimes related to Russia's aggression (war crimes, genocide, etc.).

This chapter analyses the lay participation model in Ukraine in order to reveal its functioning in the context of aggression. It examines the constitutional and ordinary regulations for lay participation in Ukraine, further assesses its strengths and weaknesses, and, lastly, provides an overview of the practical functioning of the lay participation model in the context of aggression. The chapter looks into the data obtained from scientific research on lay participation in the administration of justice, which is based on qualitative research, thematic analysis, document selection for data collection, and document content analysis.

Firstly, the Ukrainian lay participation model will be analysed, highlighting its positive and negative elements; secondly, cases related to lay participation in the administration of justice during aggression will be examined.

3.3.2. The Model for the Participation of Lay Judges in the Administration of Justice in Ukraine

It would be appropriate to start with the observations of the model for the participation of lay judges in the administration of justice in Ukraine by considering Tytych (2022), the abovementioned expert, insider and witness to the situation in Ukrainian courts during this aggression. According to him, national law indicates that trials in Ukraine are conducted by *jurors*: they are the institute of democracy in Ukraine enshrined in the Constitution and in the Law on the Judicial System and the Status of Judges (2010, hereafter – Law on the Judicial System). Although such a trial is called a *jury trial*, indeed this is not in the sense of case/common law, i.e., it is not a classic *jury trial* as in the USA or the UK, where the system operates with separate panels, the jury independently renders a verdict to the accused, and the judge determines the sentence. A *jury trial* in Ukraine is conducted by joint panels, i.e., the decision is made by jurors together with professional judges.

These observations provided by Tytych can be objected to in one aspect, i.e., that the term *присяжні* enshrined in the Constitution of Ukraine corresponds to the concept of jurors (jury trial). It can be assumed that, as stated by Shepel, *присяжні* can be translated into English as either *lay judges* or *jurors*, depending on the context (Wegen and Shepel 2020, p. 21). However, a closer look at the Ukrainian lay participation model shows that lay participation in Ukraine is more in line with the institute of *lay judges* (mixed court) than that of *jurors* (jury trial). A *mixed court* containing *lay judges* normally hears cases with judges in the panel, and decides on both matters of fact and the application of the law.

Jurors or a *jury trial*, where jury members are not part of the judicial panel, has jurors sit separately from the judge and make decisions only on specific issues of fact, usually in establishing guilt. *Inter alia*, Tytych (2022; Blacksmith *et al.* 2018, p. 37) also confirmed that such *jury trials* are, in fact, complete copies of the Soviet courts, which contained people's assessors or lay assessors. Thus, it can be concluded that, in fact, the Ukrainian court system does not have jurors, but has the institute of lay judges, who are sometimes called lay assessors (people's assessors). Other researchers, e.g., Savva, support the latter position (Blacksmith *et al.* 2018, p. 9). Thus, the term *lay judges* is further used in this chapter to reveal the form of lay participation in Ukraine.

Articles 124(5), 127(1), and 129(4) of the Constitution of Ukraine prescribe that justice should be administered by lay judges (*присяжних*) in cases determined by law. Thus, as can be seen, lay participation in the administration of justice is a constitutional principle. These provisions are also incorporated into the Law on the Judicial System (Art. 1(2), 5(3), and 15(1)).

The Law on the Judicial System provides a chapter not only for judges, but also for lay judges (i.e., Chapter III), which sets out the requirements for them and describes their status, rights and duties, and the procedure of their selection. Thus, according to Article 65, a lay judge must: be a citizen from 30 to 65 years of age (a questionably justifiable restriction), speak Ukrainian, and permanently reside in the territory to which the jurisdiction of the relevant district court extends. Nevertheless, to ensure impartiality, it is prohibited to hold certain positions, such as in the state service, advocacy, notary office, law enforcement, local administration, or military service. A lay judge's health must also allow them to perform their duty, e.g., the person must have full legal capacity, and must not suffer from chronic, mental, or other illnesses. It is obvious that such a person must be of impeccable reputation, i.e., must not have an unexpunged criminal record or any administrative sanctions that were imposed during the previous year for any corruption offence.

It is noteworthy that in the case of Ukrainian judges, the concept of their impeccable reputation is understood differently than that of lay judges, i.e., judges must declare that they have committed no corruption offences (Art. 62(2)(3)), including not having administrative sanctions for corruption offences. Thus, unlike lay judges, a judge cannot have a criminal record at all, regardless of whether it is expunged or not. On the other hand, as can be seen, a lay judge can be sentenced for a corruption offence, but it is important that this was not during the previous year; i.e., 1 year after their conviction, such a person has the opportunity to participate in justice. This is an important distinction between the legal status of a judge and a lay judge.

It is generally accepted in the countries of the Western legal tradition that the statuses of judges and lay judges should be equal, including that both should have an impeccable reputation. This avoids judgments by the ECtHR involving a violation of Article 6 of the ECHR (1950, ECHR). However, an innovative approach towards the legal status of lay judges is emerging in modern society. Danish scholars note that there is a problem in terms of legal certainty when people are convicted by those who do not represent the population (Minke 2023, p. 32). To avoid the problem of legal uncertainty for citizens, it is necessary that lay judges should come predominantly from the social groups that usually end up in court (Bonnez 2023, p. 33). This is particularly important when there is no hard evidence in a case, because different rules of conduct apply in different walks of life and the judge must understand what is happening in that society (Bonnez 2023, p. 32). The legal uncertainty created by such actions may violate the constitutional principle of the rule of law, which threatens states which uphold the rule of law (Minke 2023, p. 31).

It should be noted that according to Article 64(1) of the Law on the Judicial System, a list of lay judges who meet the abovementioned requirements of Article 65 of this law and have given their consent to serve as lay judges is approved by the local councils upon the submission of the Judicial Administration. According to Article 64(5), after the list of lay judges has been approved, it shall be sent to the respective district court by post, and also in electronic form. It is noticeable that the duties of lay judges are voluntary. Furthermore, the fact that the selection of one of the members of the judicial panel, i.e., lay judges, involves the participation of *local councils*, the election of which is a political process through which local political power is administered, may lead to a risk of the violation of the principle of the independence of the judiciary, and of judges. The fact that only the law, not also the Constitution, guarantees the independence and inviolability of lay judges when they administer justice, can also contribute to the risk of violation of the principle of the independence of the judiciary, and of judges.

Accordingly, only those citizens who are included in the list approved for three years by the decision of the relevant local council can administer justice. According to Article 67(2) of the Law on the Judicial System, the selection of citizens to be invited to participate in the administration of justice as lay judges shall be carried out by means of an automated system. It should be explainable that such lists are forwarded to the court, where the personal composition of the judicial panel in proceedings with lay judges' participation should be defined by the court's automatic system of random document circulation (Dronova 2015). Article 63(1), which establishes the status of lay judges, states that a lay judge, in cases defined by the procedural law, and with their consent, decides cases as part of the court together with the judge. Article 68(1–4) establishes the guarantees of lay judges' rights. Lay judges shall be remunerated for the time spent performing their duties in the court, with compensation calculated on the basis of the salary rate of a local court judge, and taking into account the hours actually worked in the manner prescribed by the Judicial Administration. Lay judges shall be reimbursed for travel and accommodation expenses, and shall be paid a *per diem* allowance. Lay judges shall keep all guarantees and privileges provided by law at the place of their principal employment for the duration of their duties in the court. Time spent by lay judges performing their duties in the court shall count towards all types of employment records. A lay judge may not be dismissed or transferred to another position without their consent while performing their duties in court. Statutory guarantees of the independence and immunity of judges shall apply to lay judges for the duration of their duties in the administration of justice. Upon a reasoned request by a lay judge, they may benefit from security measures even after completing their duties.

In addition to legally guaranteed rights, lay judges also have duties. Article 63 (2) of the Law on the Judicial System states that lay judges shall perform the duties specified in Article 56 (7) (1), (2), (4–6). The duties of lay judges set out in these provisions of the Law on the Judicial System relate to: fairness, impartiality, and obedience to the law in considering cases; observance of the rules of judicial ethics; respect for the participants in the judicial process; respect for the principle of confidentiality; and, as mentioned above, anticorruption activities. Obviously, these are not the only duties of lay judges, as they also have to appear at the court hearing earlier than other attendees, because the non-appearance of a lay judge without valid reasons is considered contempt of court (Art. 67 (6)). They also have to submit an annual electronic declaration of assets and income. It should be noted that lay judges must obtain an electronic digital signature in advance in order to fill out the declaration. Deliberate non-declaration of information or the publication of inaccurate information is a corruption offence for which administrative and criminal liability is provided (Art. 366[1] of Law on Prevention of Corruption 2014; *Електронне декларування присяжними* 2022).

In order to further clarify the content of the model of lay participation in Ukraine, it is appropriate to provide an analysis of the legislative regulation on the grounds and procedure for the dismissal of lay judges provided for in Article 66 of the Law on the Judicial System, as well as an analysis of the duties of the latter in the course of the court proceedings provided for in Article 67 of the Law on the Judicial System. Article 66 of this law establishes grounds and procedures for relieving lay judges from their duties. Undoubtedly, a person shall be relieved from the duties of a lay judge upon their request submitted before they begin performing these duties (Art. 66 (3)), as well as in the case as a result of recusal (self-recusal) in a particular case in the manner prescribed by procedural law or upon a proposal of the presiding judge (Art. 66 (4)). It is clear that the chairperson of the court has the right to dismiss a lay judge who does not meet the requirements mentioned above as established in Article 65. Moreover, the chairperson of the court shall relieve a lay judge from their duties in the following cases: a person who is on maternity leave, or childcare leave, as well as a person who has children of preschool or primary school age or supports children with disabilities or elderly family members; a person who is the head or deputy head of a local authority; a person who, due to their religious beliefs, finds it impossible to participate in the administration of justice; or any other person, if the chairperson of the court finds the reasons offered by them compelling (Art. 66 (1)).

Article 67 of the Law on the Judicial System establishes the involvement of lay judges in performing their duties in the court. The court shall involve lay judges in the administration of justice in turns, for a period not exceeding 1 month per year, except in cases where the extension of this period is due to the need to complete hearings in a case that started with their participation (Art. 67(1)). The court shall send to the lay judge a written invitation to participate in the administration of justice not later than seven days before the beginning of the court hearing. The invitation shall contain information on the rights and obligations of the lay judge, the requirements which they must meet, as well as the grounds for being relieved from their duties. Simultaneously, when sending the invitation, a written notice shall be sent to the employer about the individual being involved as a lay judge (Art. 67(3)). Involving lay judges in performing their duties in court and summoning them shall be carried out in the manner prescribed by procedural law (Art. 67(4)). The employer shall be obliged to grant the lay judge a leave of absence while they are performing their duties in the administration of justice. Refusal to provide a leave of absence shall be deemed to constitute contempt of court (Art. 67(5)).

After having reviewed the model of lay participation in Ukraine, we can see the weaknesses of this model related to the system of *selection* of lay judges, when the local political authorities participate in the selection of lay judges. The unequal legal status of lay judges compared to judges can also be observed, which affects the independence of the courts and the effort to restore trust in this branch of governance, i.e., the power of the judicial branch. One of the essential requirements for ensuring the independence of the courts is the procedure for appointing judges or lay judges. An independent judicial body, i.e., the Council of Judges (Ukr. *Ради суддив*), should take part in the selection of *присяжні*.

In democracies, this independent judicial body, as a counterweight to the executive (the President), is usually involved in the selection of judges. Therefore, the constitutional regulation could be improved by *enshrining this institution in the Constitution* and by wording the constitutional provision as follows: 'the appointment and dismissal, legal status, and guarantees of independence of *lay participants* shall be established by law'. Such a constitutional amendment is necessary in order to ensure the equal legal status of judges and lay judges in judicial proceedings. Currently, lay judges have the status of officials, which is provided in criminal law. Moreover, the Constitution should not provide for a specific form of lay participation in court proceedings (lay judges/jurors), i.e., *присяжні*, as is currently the case in the Ukrainian Constitution. The reason for this proposal – i.e., the participation of the citizens of the Republic of Ukraine in the administration of justice in accordance with the procedure established by law – is that if there was a need to improve or change the model of lay participation and the Constitution, it would not provide for a specific form, including its extent (i.e., in what cases and at which instance lay participants should take part in the proceedings), then there would be no need to amend the Constitution. On the other hand, an important positive aspect is that the institution of lay participation in Ukraine is regulated at the legislative level, with a distinct regulation specific to it. Having discussed the model for the participation of lay judges in the administration of justice in Ukraine, the following sub-chapter will reveal the legal regulation of cases involving the participation of lay judges in court proceedings during the current aggression, focusing on several examples.

3.3.3. The Participation of Lay Judges in the Administration of Justice in Ukraine During Russian Aggression

First of all, it is necessary to emphasise the importance of research on the participation of lay judges in the administration of justice in Ukraine during the current aggression. As has been mentioned above, according to Tytych (2022), an attorney at law, insider, and witness to the situation in Ukrainian courts during this period of aggression, the need to introduce a real and effective mechanism for involving the people in the administration of justice has long been the focus of Ukrainian experts. Presently, a new aspect of the participation of lay judges in the administration of justice in Ukraine has emerged, i.e., the future administration of justice in cases of international crimes related to Russian aggression (i.e., war crimes, genocide, etc.).

Thus, this sub-chapter discusses the participation of lay judges (*присяжних*) in the administration of justice in Ukraine during this aggression. It should also be emphasised that Article 64(2) of the Law on the Judicial System mentions the possibility of involving lay judges in *commercial cases*, i.e., 'A list of lay judges for hearing commercial cases shall be approved in the manner prescribed by law from among the persons who meet the requirements of Article 65 and have given their consent to serve as lay judges'. However, according to Tytych (2022), there is currently no legislation establishing such a procedure. In fact, lay judges work exclusively in *criminal proceedings*.

It is important to note that, as mentioned by Tytych (2022), there is no separate legal regulation for commercial cases (e.g., bankruptcy cases, cases in disputes between business entities, cases in disputes concerning the privatisation of property, etc. in the Commercial and Procedural Code of Ukraine (1991, Artcile 20). However, in fact, lay judges, together with judges in the panel, decide civil cases – including such cases during this period of aggression. There are no specific norms in the Civil Code of Ukraine (2003) that establish the institute of lay judges, but there are two relevant norms in the Civil Procedural Code of Ukraine (2004). According to Article 34(2), in the cases established by this Code, civil cases in the courts of first instance shall be considered by a panel of one judge and two lay judges, who shall enjoy all the rights of a judge in the administration of justice.

Thus, such a composition of the panel hears civil cases, e.g., on: the restriction of the civil dispositive legal capacity of an individual, which is, *inter alia*, an extension of the period of validity to recognise a person as incapacitated (e.g., *The Lviv Shevchenkiv District Court of Lviv*, Case No. 466/7097/17); the recognition of an individual as incapable (e.g., *The Sokal District Court of the Lviv Region*, Case No. 454/2322/21; *The Khortytskyi District Court, Zaporozhye*, Case No. 337/1428/22; *The Tyvriv District Court of the Vinnytsia Region*, Case No. 145/207/22); the restoration of the civil dispositive legal capacity of an individual, including issues of appointment/dismissal of a guardian (e.g., *The Kamianets-Podilskyi City District Court of Khmelnytskyi Region*, Case No. 676/1501/22); the recognition of an individual as missing (e.g., *The Haysynsky District Court of Vinnytsia Region*, Case No. 129/1573/20) or declaring them deceased (e.g., *The Horodotsky District Court of Lviv Region*, Case No. 441/1858/21; *The Leninsky District Court of the city of Poltava*, Case No. 553/3316/21); adoption (e.g., *The Uzhhorod City District Court of the Transcarpathian Region*, Case No. 308/4709/22; *The Desnyan District Court of the city of Kyiv*, Case No. 754/18888/21); providing a person with compulsory psychiatric care (e.g., *The Khmelnytskyi City District Court Khmelnytskyi Region*, Case No. 686/7071/22; *The Odessa Suvorovsky District Court of Odesa*, Case No. 523/3984/22; *The Shevchenkivskyi District Court of Chernivtsi*, Case No. 727/1911/22); and compulsory hospitalisation in an anti-tuberculosis facility (Art. 293(4)). Obviously, at the request of the lay judges, they are released from the duties of a lay judge in connection with military service and mobilisation, from 24 July 2022 until its end. In this case, they are replaced by another lay judge by automatically selecting from the list lay of judges (e.g., *The Kotovsky City and District Court of Odesa Region,* Case No. 505/928/22; *The Vasylkiv District Court of Dnipropetrovsk Region,* Case No. 191/3557/21; *The Krynychanskyi District Court of the Dnipropetrovsk Region,* Case No. 178/425/22). There are cases when, due to the absence of citizens who agreed to be lay judges of a particular court, the city council was not able to approve the list of lay judges. Under such circumstances, it is impossible to form a court composition to consider the above cases. Therefore, the court transfers the case to the closest court territorially (e.g., *The Zhovtovod City Court of the Dnipropetrovsk Region,* Case No. 176/950/22). Recusal issues regarding lay judges are decided upon the basis of Articles 36 and 40 of the Commercial and Procedural Code of Ukraine, which establishes the grounds and procedure for the recusal of judges (e.g., *The Vyzhnytsky District Court of the Chernivtsi Region,* Case No. 713/1098/22, *The Pyryatinsky District Court of the Poltava Region,* Case No. 544/2074/21). Thus, as can be seen, lay judges participate not only in criminal, but also in civil proceedings.

Regarding commercial cases, as mentioned above, it has to be noted that, according to Shepel (2019, pp. 4, 7), it is desirable to change the function of lay judges in commercial cases, i.e., to change the term 'lay judges for consideration of economic affairs' into 'sworn arbitrators' or 'lay judges-arbiters'. Shepel claims that such lay judges should be highly trusted; therefore, it is suggested that the list of potential lay judges should not be long (up to 30 people), there should be only one for the whole country, and it should include generally recognised and well-known specialists. Moreover, according to Shepel, the requirements for lay judges should include higher legal education, work experience in the field of law for more than ten years, and experience of participation in the consideration of cases in international arbitration or an arbitral tribunal. The administration of the formation of the list should also take place via the voting of business representatives. Finally, the minimum fee for one lay judge for the decision of a case would amount to 38,420 UAH (1,028.56 EUR), plus an award (Shepel 2019, pp. 4, 7).

Other sources state (Wegen and Shepel 2020, p. 21) that in the process of a dialogue on the models of a mixed composition court for resolving *commercial* disputes, and as a result of the study of the potential effect of a decision, the following proposals of experts and business representatives regarding the respective legislative regulation were identified: (a) lay judges resolving commercial disputes should be professional lawyers who have competences in various areas of legal support for commercial activity (experience in resolving disputes in international arbitration must be an advantage), who are well-known experts, and who have an impeccable reputation; (b) only disputes with a significant property interest where there is a high risk that untrustworthy parties may influence the court (corruption risk or possible political influence) should be resolved by a mixed court with lay judges in its composition; (c) the reviewing of cases by a mixed court with lay judges in its composition should be conducted in courts of the appellate instance – this, according to the abovementioned authors, will decrease the motivation for using unlawful influence on the court of the first instance on the one hand; on the other hand, it will significantly simplify the hearing of the cases with the participation of lay judges as it will not require their second involvement for reviewing cases; and d) in case of the cassation or revision of a decision adopted with the participation of lay judges, the court should not have the right to cancel the decision and adopt the new one, and only in case there are grounds for cancelling the decision can they direct the case for a second hearing to the appellate court with a different composition of lay judges (Wegen and Shepel 2020, p. 21).

Further, it would be appropriate to continue the discussion about lay judges' participation in criminal proceedings. As stated in Article 31(3) of the CCP of Ukraine, criminal proceedings in a court of the first instance in respect of crimes for the commission of which the punishment of life imprisonment is envisaged shall be conducted by a panel of three judges, and upon the request of the accused, by a panel consisting of two judges and three lay judges (*присяжних*). If a criminal case is heard against several accused, upon the request of at least one of the accused, the entire case is heard by a panel consisting of two judges and three lay judges.

It would be necessary in this respect to distinguish the circumstances under which a person cannot be sentenced to life imprisonment. Life imprisonment shall not be imposed on: persons who committed offences while under eighteen years of age; persons over sixty-five years of age; and women who were pregnant at the time of the offence or at the time of sentencing; as well as in the cases stipulated by Article 68(4) as provided of in Article 64(2) of the CC of Ukraine.

Furthermore, life imprisonment for the preparation for a crime and the attempt to commit a crime shall not apply, except in cases of committing crimes against the foundations of the national security of Ukraine as provided for by Articles 109–114, against the peace and security of mankind, and against the international rule of law provided for by Articles 437–439, Article 442(1) and Article 443 as provided of in Article 68(4) of the CC of Ukraine. It is noteworthy that the murder or attempted murder of a judge, lay judge, or their close relatives in connection with their activity related to the administration of justice shall be punishable by, *inter alia*, life imprisonment (Art. 379). War crimes punishable by imprisonment are those that involve: trespass against the country's territorial integrity and its inviolability (Art. 110(3)); acts of terrorism (Art. 258); the violation of the rules of warfare (Art. 438(2)); the use of weapons of mass destruction (Art. 439(2)); the use of mercenaries (Art. 447(3)) if they caused the death of people or resulted in any other grave consequences; trespasses against the life of a statesman or a public figure (Art. 112); actions connected with the premeditated murder of a commander or another person performing military service duties (Art. 404(5)); and genocide (Art. 442).

Thus, lay judges administer justice exclusively in criminal cases in which the accused are punishable by life imprisonment in Ukraine. Such legal regulation allows us to conclude that lay judges hear complex (resonant) cases. No doubt, solving such cases requires good professional training and relevant character qualities (Myshchak 2020, pp. 18–19). Vovk (in Zakharchenko 2020) emphasises that it is necessary to create special commissions that would test candidates for the presence of logical and critical thinking, a level of basic legal knowledge, and skills for stress management. Psychologists and lawyers should work with lay judges, help them work effectively, and explain the details of the legal process and the rights of all of its participants. A detailed analysis of the information surrounding a person must be performed before allowing them to participate in the legal process as a lay judge (Zakharchenko 2020).

Article 30(2) of the Ukraine's CCP establishes the conditions and procedures for criminal proceedings in the court of the first instance in trials by lay judges, the procedure for forming a list of lay judges (summoning/selection, deliberation, and voting for the jurors), and their rights and duties. Article 65(1)(7) establishes that lay judges cannot be interrogated as witnesses regarding the discussion that arose in the deliberation room during the adoption of the court decision, except for in criminal proceedings in cases related to the adoption of a judgment or ruling deemed by the judge(s) to be unjust. In addition, the CC criminalizes attempts on the life, property, etc., of lay judges. Tytych (2022) confirmed that, as of the end of 2022, there has been no participation of lay judges in courts on war crimes charges (Art. 438 of CC). As mentioned above, Article 438 CC provides for liability for the violation of the laws and rules of war. According to Anisimov, Article 438 should be applied from the moment of aggression in 2014, and it is not sufficient to apply it only to actions undertaken after the declaration of martial law in accordance with Presidential Decree No. 64/2022 (2022) 'On the introduction of martial law in Ukraine' of 24 February

2022 (Anisimov 2022). It should be noted that this insight by Anisimov was accurate. By the decision of the ECtHR Grand Chamber of 2023 in the case of *Ukraine and the Netherlands v. Russia*, a resolution was taken to hear the case brought by the Netherlands against Russia for the downing of civilian aircraft MH17 in 2014 and the 2 (two) cases brought by Ukraine against Russia for crimes against civilians and children in 2014. Russia is accused of human rights violations, such as violations of the right to life, torture, and inhuman treatment. These three cases have been consolidated into one. Thus, by accepting these cross-border cases, the ECtHR simultaneously acknowledged that the relevant part of the Donbas was already occupied by Russia in 2014 and that these alleged violations were therefore within its jurisdiction. This ECtHR case is likely to serve as a starting point for international tribunals to rule on the criminal responsibility of Russian officials for aggression against Ukraine and war crimes against the Ukrainian population as early as 2014 (an insight based on an opinion issued on the personal social media profile of international law professor Dainius Žalimas on 26 January 2022).

Article 35(1–3) of the Ukraine's CCP establishes that an automated court document management system (*Автоматизована система документообігу суду*) (hereafter – court's automatic system) shall function in the court to ensure, *inter alia*, the selection of lay judges for judicial proceedings from among the persons in the list of lay judges (*списку присяжних*). For further reference, more specific information can be found online, as all the cases are provided in the *Unified State Register of Court Decisions and the Status of Proceedings*. In addition, some cases are discussed in more detail further in this sub-chapter.

Article 75(1) (1–5) of the Ukraine's CCP establishes in which cases lay judges do not participate in criminal proceedings, i.e., in the presence of circumstances that cast doubt on the judge's impartiality. Article 75(2) additionally specifies that the composition of the court which conducts a judicial proceeding shall not include individuals who are related to each other. Moreover, a lay judge may not take part in the proceedings if the procedure for appointing them to hear a case, as is provided by Article 35(3) and Article 75(1)(5), has been breached. Further, the examples of cases illustrating the grounds for determining the removal of lay judges, regulated by Articles 75–76, 80(1), 387(2–7), and 390, are provided. Failure to inform the court of a lay judge's absence from a court session due to their participation in the war does not constitute grounds for removing them, as the duty to defend the homeland is a constitutional duty. However, the very fact of participating in the defence of the homeland leads to the impossibility of administering justice, because it is incompatible with the duties of lay judges (Law on the Judicial System Article 65(1)(1) (e.g., *The Boryspil City District Court of Kyiv*

Region, Case No. 359/3962/20). In one case, the lay judges themselves decided on the question of removing the presiding judge, because the judge, in the opinion of the accused, being not indifferent to the pro-Russian political party, unreasonably dismissed questions to the witness, etc. However, the lay judges decided that, in accordance with Article 321 of the Ukraine's CCP, the judge had the right to exclude questions from the witness that were obviously not related to the case, and the accused had the opportunity to state their arguments in the appeal (e.g., *The Pyryatinsky District Court of Poltava Region*, Case No. 532/308/15-k). Other removal issues relate to political party membership and the age limit up to which lay judges can serve, i.e., up to 65 years old (65(1)(6) of the Law on the Judicial System) ('Суд по делу убийства Вороненкова отобрал присяжных Громадское телевидение' 2018).

Hereinafter, the legislation for lay judges in criminal proceedings is analysed in more detail, as such an analysis contributes, among other things, to the search for an optimal model. Lay judges shall be impanelled at the local general court of the first instance (Art. 361(2) of the Ukraine's CCP). Upon the selection of principal lay judges, two reserve lay judges shall be selected (Art. 387(8–10)). Article 388 of the Ukraine's CCP establishes administering the oath of the lay judges. Upon completion of the selection of principal and reserve lay judges, they shall occupy the seats indicated by the presiding judge. The text of the oath shall be read out by each lay judge, after which they shall confirm that their rights, duties, and competence are understood (Art. 388(1–2)). Article 384(1) of the Ukraine's CCP establishes the duty of the prosecutor and the court to explain to those accused of an offence punishable by life imprisonment their right to be tried in the presence of lay judges, and specific aspects related to this. The public prosecutor's written explanations given to the accused regarding the possibility, specific aspects, and legal implications of hearing the case shall be attached to the indictment and the register of pre-trial investigation records, which shall be submitted to the court. It should be noted that if the prosecutor does not comply with these requirements, the detected deficiency indicates a significant violation of the provisions of the criminal procedural law when drawing up and approving the indictment, and makes it impossible to set a trial. Therefore, the indictment against the person is subject to return to the prosecutor. In addition, the court stated in one case that the Ukraine's CCP does not provide for the possibility of the prosecutor to attach a written explanation to the accused about the opportunities, peculiarities, and legal consequences of consideration of criminal proceedings by lay judges at the stage of a preparatory court session or trial. Therefore, such a request of the prosecutor must be refused (e.g., *The Shevchenkivskyi District Court of the Kyiv*, Case No. 761/7319/22).

In another case, the court also took the same position, finding that the right to consider criminal proceedings by lay judges is an integral part of the accused's right to defence, and violation of this right indicates non-compliance by the prosecutor and the court with the requirements of Article 6 of the ECHR. The panel of judges noted that the prosecutor's written explanation to the accused about the possibility, peculiarities, and legal consequences of consideration of criminal proceedings by lay judges was not attached, which deprived the accused of the opportunity to make an informed decision about the feasibility of implementing such rights. The judicial review of the case is appointed precisely on the basis of the indictment drawn up in accordance with the law, and the court cannot eliminate the shortcomings that were admitted at the pre-trial investigation stage of the criminal proceedings, since the judicial branch of government is entrusted with the function of the administration of justice, and not the performance of duties placed on the side of public prosecution. The panel of judges returned the indictment to the prosecutor since the prosecutor's failure to comply with the requirements of Article 384 of the Ukraine's CCP can significantly affect the rights of the accused regarding ensuring the right to a fair trial and the violation of the right to the defence of the accused (e.g., *The Kostopil District Court of Rivne Region,* Case No. 572/879/22).

However, in another case the court arrived at the conclusion that there was no reason to return the indictment to the prosecutor. The court noted that the right to a trial before a court established by law, including cases involving lay judges, is more important than the untimeliness of such a request. As mentioned above, a request for a trial in the presence of lay judges must be made at the pre-trial stage of the investigation. However, there are cases where the accused does so at a preparatory hearing. Even so, the court, considering that the right to a fair trial outweighs the observance of the procedure for the submission of the applications in question, satisfies the applications of the accused. Thus, given that both judges and lay judges are selected for a specific case only by the court's automatic system, the courts will then refer the case to the automated appointment of a panel (e.g., *The Kostopil District Court of Rivne Region,* Case No. 572/879/22). In conclusion, a person charged with an offence punishable by life imprisonment has the right to request, at the preparatory hearing, that the case be heard in the presence of lay judges (Art. 384(2) of the Ukraine's CCP). However, such a request cannot be granted during the court hearing (e.g., *The Uzhhorod District Court of the Transcarpathian Region,* Case No. 308/13185/17).

Further, it would be expedient to discuss the procedure for preparing for a court hearing involving lay judges. Article 385(1–4) of the Ukraine's CCP establishes the summoning of lay judges. After scheduling the date of hearing the case in a mixed tribunal, the presiding judge shall give instructions to the court clerk to summon seven lay judges who shall be selected by the court's automatic system from the citizens provided on the list of lay judges. The citizens who are listed in the array of lay judges and can be summoned to the court in the capacity of lay judges shall be selected in compliance with the abovementioned Law on the Judicial System of Ukraine. The written summons shall be served to a lay judge against receipt not later than five days before the date of the court session. The summons shall indicate the date, time, and place of holding the court session, the rights and duties of a lay judge, the list of requirements for lay judges, as well as the grounds for their dismissal from lay judges' duty, the order of their appearance in court, and the obligation of a lay judge (or another person who has received the summons to be handed over to a lay judge) to immediately notify the court of the reasons for their unavailability in the court. On the basis of written summons, an employer shall grant a lay judge a leave of absence for the period in which they have to fulfil their duties related to the administration of justice.

At this point, for an even more detailed disclosure of the content and structure of the model of lay judges, it makes sense to examine and describe the legal regulation of Ukraine related to the rights and duties of lay judges in criminal court proceedings. Article 386 of the Ukraine's CCP establishes the rights and duties of lay judges, such as the participation of lay judges in the examination of all information and evidence in the course of a court session, the right to ask the judge to explain the provisions of law that are subject to the application when deciding certain issues, legal terms and definitions, the content of the documents read out in the course of a court session, elements of the crime of which the defendant is accused, etc. Article 389(1) establishes the inadmissibility of exerting illegal influence on a lay judge.

It should be noted that Article 331 of the Ukraine's CCP establishes that only the judge decides on imposing, revoking, or changing the measure (e.g., restraining order). Another exception states that an on-site inspection shall not be conducted during court proceedings by lay judges (Art. 383(1)). All other issues related to the trial are decided by the panel of the judge and lay judges (Art. 383(3)). The lay judges together, with the judge, also hear cases in which the accused has minor children, disabled parents, etc., who are in need of financial assistance and have been left without supervision. In such cases the court is obliged, simultaneously with the adoption of the sentence, to raise the issue with a separate decision for the establishment of custody and care for such persons (Art. 378) (e.g., *The Shevchenkivskyi District Court of the Zaporizhzhia,* Case No. 336/5497/20).

As an example, we can mention the *Maidan* case, which had great repercussions in Europe. On 20 February 2014, police officers killed 48 protesters and injured several hundred more in the centre of Kyiv (Lukashova 2020; Andreykovets 2022; Pryhno 2021). The case was still pending at the end of 2022, and justice is being administered by a panel of judges and lay judges. However, the interim issue of measures of restraint was decided on exclusively the presiding judge (Sobenko and Kolomiets 2022). The defenders of the accused, following the then fresh judgment of the Constitutional Court (e.g., case No. 7-p/2019), appealed against the ruling to extend the measures of restraint (custody) of the accused. According to Article 176(5) of the Ukraine's CCP, the only measure of restraint for persons accused of crimes against national security was custody. However, the Constitutional Court stated that such a norm, according to which, for crimes related to a threat to national security, the accused cannot be subject to other measures of restraint, like personal commitment, personal warranty, bail, or house arrest (Art. 176(5) (1) – (4)), contradicts the Constitution because it violates the principle of the rule of law and limits the individual's right to freedom and personal immunity. Such a norm allows the application of measures of restraint (custody) on the basis of a purely formal court decision, which violates the principle of the rule of law. It should be emphasised that the 20 February 2014 protest was inspired, *inter alia*, by people's frustration with justice, when the courts were included in the mechanism of illegal repression against protest participants from 21 November 2013 to 21 February 2014. According to Tytych, more than 330 judges made repressive decisions on the basis of forged documents against hundreds of innocent protest participants, and even random persons who did not participate in the protests. This led to the need to change the legal regulation in order to restore trust in the judiciary, which had essentially been lost completely. The representatives of the legislative power concluded that the effectiveness of the courts depends primarily on the authority of the judiciary. Public confidence in the judiciary is far more important than the perfection of laws or legal procedures (Blacksmith *et al.* 2018, p. 30).

Another example of a case in which lay judges administered justice together with judges but did not participate in the decision-making on the issue of measures of restraint is the high-profile case of the murder of journalist Pavel Sheremet (*Павел Шеремет*) ('Дело Шеремета: суд оставил Антоненко и Кузьменко под ночным домашним арестом – подробности' 2022; Lukashova 2020). This journalist was known for reporting on political attacks in Belarus, and this case illustrates the importance of the participation of reserve lay judges, where their presence ensures the more prompt and smooth hearing of the case when, for certain reasons, it is necessary to replace one of the lay judges ('На суде по делу об убийстве Павла Шеремета сменили присяжного' 2020). As mentioned above, according to Article 387(10) of the Ukraine's CCP, reserve lay judges always remain in the seats specified for them during the hearing and may be included in the main group of lay judges, until the judgment is passed, if one of the lay judges cannot continue the hearing. The panel of judges and lay judges makes a decision on the replacement of the absent main lay judge with a reserve lay judge (e.g., *The Dnipro Samara District Court of Dnipropetrovsk*, Case No. 206/11/17; *The Odesa Primorsky District Court of Odesa*, Case No. 504/4242/19).

Another high-profile case – the murder of pro-Russian journalist Oles Buzina (Ukr. *Олесь Бузина*) (Lukashova 2020) – was heard by a mixed court. In this case, the journalist was shot on 16 April 2015, in the yard of his own house in Kyiv. The case gained a high profile when two fighters – members of the *Правого сектора* organisation, which is banned in Russia, who volunteered to defend their country (i.e., Ukraine), Europe, and the whole civilized world against Russian aggression – were suspected of the murder ('Судья по делу Бузины взял самоотвод' 2022). As the above examples demonstrate, jury trial (in a mixed court) will be in demand in Ukraine in the future, with a high probability of its use in the consideration of the most high-profile cases (Myshchak 2020, p. 19).

Article 391(1) – (4) of the Ukraine's CCP establishes the procedure of *deliberation* and *voting* in a mixed court. Lay judges' deliberation shall be directed by the presiding judge who shall sequentially pose questions to be discussed listed in Article 368(1) – (5), and shall conduct open voting and the counting of votes (part 1). All issues shall be resolved by the vote of the majority. The presiding judge shall be the last to vote (part 2). No one of the lay judges may abstain from voting, except for when a decision is made on assigning a punishment and the judge or a lay judge voted for the acquittal of the accused. In this case, the vote of the lay judge who has abstained shall be added to the votes for the decision that is most favourable for the accused. If there are differences of opinion on which decision is the most favourable for the accused, the issue shall be resolved by voting (part 3). Each lay judge shall have the right to express in writing their dissenting opinion, which shall not be subject to an announcement in the court session but shall be attached to the case records and made open to perusal (part 4). Where there are no judges on the panel that rendered a decision, the presiding judge shall provide assistance to lay judges with the drafting of the court decisions (part 5). It is important to note that in one case, the judges did not agree with the motives that guided the lay judges in reaching the judgment; therefore, they expressed a separate opinion on the judgment of the lay judges.

In the opinion of the judges, there was no direct evidence in the case to support the guilt of the accused. The judges stated that an accusation cannot be based on illegally obtained evidence or on assumptions. Any doubt as to the guilt of the person proved shall be construed in their favour. In these circumstances, the judges decided that it was necessary to interpret all doubts about the accused person's proven guilt in their favour and to acquit them (e.g., *The Kryukiv District Court of Kremenchuk,* Case No. 536/1112/19).

According to Article 615(10) of the Ukraine's CCP, Section IX[1] 'Special Rules of Pre-Trial Investigation During Martial Law, Emergency or in the Area of Anti-Terrorist Operation', criminal proceedings in the court of first instance regarding crimes punishable by life imprisonment are carried out exclusively by a panel of three judges, with the exception of criminal proceedings in a court in which, before the introduction of martial law and the entry into force of this part, criminal proceedings were carried out by a panel with the participation of lay judges. Fomin (*Сергій Фомін*) (2022) noted that Article 615(10) in fact suspended the possibility of creating a mixed court during the period of aggression, when on 1 May 2022 this norm entered into force.

Consequently, criminal proceedings in the court of first instance regarding crimes punishable by life imprisonment are carried out by only three judges, except for criminal proceedings in a court which, before the introduction of martial law and the entry into force of this norm, were heard by a panel of judges and lay judges (e.g., *The Boryspil City District Court of Kyiv Region,* Case No. 359/3962/20; *The Kyiv District Court of Poltava,* Case No. 552/2173/22; *The Shishatskyi District Court of the Poltava,* Case No. 583/2641/21). Thus, after the introduction of martial law in Ukraine and the entry into force of the discussed amendment, all criminal cases are assigned exclusively to judges (e.g., *District Court of Kyiv Region,* Case No. 552/2173/22; *The Sviatoshyn District Court of the Kyiv,* Case No. 759/4623/22). It can be assumed that this change in the law is due to martial law, where citizens become obliged to defend their homeland and, therefore, there is no longer a sufficient number of them to administer justice.

It is obvious that due to the aggression against Ukraine, and due to the inability of lay judges to participate in the judicial process and the need to replace them with new ones, cases were not being processed smoothly (i.e., *The Vasylkivskyi City District Court of the Kyiv Region,* Case No. 362/1064/21). There were cases where lay judges did not appear in the hearing twice in a row, which led to a situation where the accused chose to completely refuse lay judges such that the case would be headed exclusively by three judges (e.g., *The Boryspil District court of Kyiv Region,* Case No. 367/6693/20). Such a possibility is available if the case has not yet commenced consideration in a court session (e.g., *The Holosiivskyi District Court of Kyiv,* Case No. 757/33903/21-k).

In addition, according to Article 336 of the Ukraine's CCP, court proceedings can be carried out in the mode of a video conference broadcast from another room which is located outside the court premises (i.e., remote court proceedings) if it is necessary to take such measures for the efficiency of the court proceedings (e.g., *The Gorodotsky District Court of the Lviv Region Yavorsk,* Case No. 944/5877/19). In times of martial law, for the safety of the participants in the proceedings, efforts have been made to increase the frequency with which participants participate in proceedings online. Court hearings had to be interrupted because of air raid warnings, for example, and justice must be administered primarily for the safety of people and in accordance with the requirements of the Law About the Legal Regime of Martial Law (2000). The electronic court (hereafter – e-court) has played an important role in these times of aggression, during which the *Дия* e-court services portal was integrated. This provides citizens with additional opportunities to be informed about the time and place of hearings and to receive certain documents (Tkachuk and Kalarash 2022).

It should be pointed out that until 11 July 2022 only three Russian soldiers had been convicted of killing civilians in Ukraine (Hyde 2022). The first case directly related to war crimes, when 21-year-old Russian soldier Vadim Shyshimarin (*Вадим Шишимарин*) was sentenced to life imprisonment under Article 438 of CC for violating the rules of warfare by the judgment of the Solomyanskiy District Court of Kyiv on 23 May 2022. V. Shyshimarin was convicted of killing an unarmed Ukrainian civilian when he was shot in the head through an open car window. It is worth mentioning that when starting the trial against V. Shyshimarin, the abovementioned norm (Art. 615(10) of the Ukraine's CCP) regarding the non-participation of lay judges during the period of aggression was not yet valid; however, the accused refused a mixed court (Askew 2022).

Thus, it should be concluded that, as has already been mentioned above, Article 124 of the Constitution of Ukraine establishes that 'The people directly participate in the administration of justice through *присяжні*'. However, at the time of preparing this contribution in 2023, there was no real jury trial in the country. *Присяжні* played the role of so-called *people's assessors* in former Soviet court proceedings. Presently, in criminal cases, decisions are made together by two judges and three lay judges; in civil cases, decisions are made together by one judge and two lay judges. It should be pointed out that decisions are made including the legal aspects of the case. For example, the abovementioned panel of judges and lay judges (mixed court) decide together whether the accused is guilty, clarify the legal intricacies of the case together, and write the judgment together. Here it is obvious that judges have the opportunity to influence the opinion of their non-professional colleagues, which is not compatible with the individual's right to a fair trial. However, this is not the case with jurors (jury trial), when they make their own decisions on the issue of fact (i.e., guilt) and the legal aspects of the case are decided by the judge(s) (for example, Judicial Commission of New South Wales 2002).

It is noteworthy that the recent *draft laws of Ukraine* (a planned optimal model for Ukraine, which, if implemented, would involve jurors in the trial instead of lay judges) are aimed at implementing the Anglo-Saxon model of a jury trial consisting of one judge and seven jurors. The fundamental difference between the proposed jury trial model and the current one is that the jury renders a verdict independently, without the participation of a judge. It is also worth mentioning that research shows that verdicts depend on the number of jurors, i.e., a smaller panel's verdicts are less predictable, but they yield more convictions, while a larger panel of jurors makes fewer mistakes. Furthermore, jurors are not volunteers, as they are now in the *присяжні* (lay judges) role, because jurors perform their civic duty and are chosen randomly. A jury trial is only used in criminal cases that carry a penalty, such as more than 10 years in prison, and this does not require a motion by the accused. At the request of the accused, the jury trial may be replaced by a trial composed of three professional judges. During the trial, the juror's task is reduced to answering the following three main questions: Is the fact of the crime proven? Is it proven that the accused committed it? Is their guilt for the crime committed established? In the case of the verdict of guilt, the judge decides what punishment should be imposed. If the judge recognises that the verdict of guilt has been issued against the innocent, then a decision is made to dissolve the jury and the criminal case is sent for a new trial by another court. Thus, judges could be called 'judges of law', and jurors could be called 'judges of fact' (Blacksmith *et al.* 2018, pp. 7, 9). The classic jury trial (i.e., the Anglo-Saxon model) is suitable for countries with relatively low legal cultures and a basic level of democracy. In this model, the local authorities are removed from the process of forming jury lists. In Ukraine, this duty is entrusted to the State Judicial Administration of Ukraine and its territorial administrations using the information contained in the State Register of Voters (Savva 2021).

It is agreed that the automatic procedure for appointing a juror is more in the interests of fairness in court. It is important to emphasise that the judicial system must be independent; therefore, as mentioned above, its members must not be selected via political processes. Moreover, when non-professionals participate in the judicial process, this makes the process more understandable to the general public. Zakrevska stated that a jury trial, to some extent, cleans the judicial process from casuistry and clerical work, procedural abuses, and formalism (Blacksmith *et al.* 2018, p. 23). According to Tytych, the *Principles for Juries and Jury Trials* of the American Bar Association do not have a universal character and are not binding for Ukraine; however, they cannot be ignored during the construction of a new modern system of jury trial in Ukraine (Blacksmith *et al.* 2018, p. 37). It should be pointed out that, according to Shepel, in the event of opening the possibility of changes to the Constitution of Ukraine, it is necessary to amend Article 124, which will allow the use of other forms of lay participation in the judicial system, such as commercial (lay) judges or arbitrators (Wegen and Shepel 2020).

The specific performance of the institute of lay judges in court proceedings during the Russian aggression against Ukraine is worth emphasising once again at this point. Based on the contextual analysis above, it can be concluded that lay judges administer justice together with judges in both criminal and civil cases of the first instance in Ukraine. Lay judges participated in criminal cases during the aggression; however, from 1 May 2022 they have administered justice together with judges *only* in civil cases. As has already been stated, in civil cases, a panel of one judge and two lay judges with equal voting rights hears cases, such as in cases involving: the restriction of civil dispositive legal capacity of an individual, *inter alia*, an extension of the validity period to recognise a person as incapacitated; recognition of an individual as incapable; restoration of civil dispositive legal capacity of an individual, including issues of appointment/dismissal of a guardian; recognition of an individual as missing or declaring them as deceased; adoption; providing a person with compulsory psychiatric care; and compulsory hospitalisation in an anti-tuberculosis facility. However, due to the extraordinary situation of aggression, at the request of lay judges, they are released from the duties of a lay judge in connection with military service and mobilisation from 24 July 2022 until its end. Thereby, they are substituted by another lay judge by automatically selecting from the list of lay judges. There are cases where, due to the absence of citizens who agreed to be lay judges of a particular court, the city council could not approve the list of lay judges. In these cases, it is impossible to form a complete court panel to hear civil cases. As a consequence, the court transfers the civil case to the closest court territorially. Thus, it can be noted again that, in the circumstances of aggression against Ukraine, and due to the inability of lay judges to participate in the judicial process and the need to replace them with substitutes, the hearings of civil cases proceed non-operatively. At the same time, if it is necessary to take measures for the efficiency of court proceedings and for the safety of participants in times of martial law, they can be carried out online for the purpose of avoiding the interruption of court hearings because of air raid warnings. The 'Дия' e-court services portal was created to fulfil the abovementioned needs and goals in the conditions of aggression. This also secures the fact that the process participants receive all necessary information and documents related to the hearing. Though these extreme conditions of aggression in the country have induced a lot of unexpected situations as discussed above, which evoke challenges for keeping to the law and carrying out hearings, these were the only additional reasons for changing and introducing appropriate modifications in the model of lay participation in Ukraine.

3.3.4. Interim findings

Considering the aim of this sub-chapter to analyse the lay participation model in Ukraine and to reveal its functioning during the time of aggression, the following conclusions can be drawn.

The analysis of the constitutional and ordinary regulation of lay participation in Ukraine, assessing its strengths and weaknesses, revealed first that lay participation in the administration of justice is a constitutional principle in Ukraine. The term *присяжні*, enshrined in the Constitution of Ukraine, corresponds to the concept of lay judges (mixed court), but not jurors (jury trial). Thus, lay participation in Ukraine is more in line with the institute of *lay judges* (mixed court) than with *jurors* (jury trial). *Lay judges* (or a *mixed court*) normally hear cases together with judges in the panel, and decide on both matters of fact and the application of the law. *Jurors* or *jury trials*, which are not part of the judicial panel, sit separately from the judge and make decisions only on a specific issue of fact, usually in establishing guilt. However, the legislative amendments initiated in this context are aimed at changing the model of lay participation and introducing a classical jury trial in Ukraine. Provisions related to lay judges are also incorporated into the Law on the Judicial System and the Status of Judges.

The review of the model of lay participation in Ukraine allows some weaknesses and strengths of this model to be revealed. One of the negative aspects of the model concerns the selection of *присяжні* and the way in which the local authorities are involved in the political process. Another negative aspect is the unequal legal status of judges and *присяжні*. The concept of the impeccable reputation of judges means that, among other things, a judge cannot have a criminal record at all, regardless of whether it has been expunged or not. Meanwhile, a lay judge can be sentenced for a corruption offence, but it is important that this did not occur during the previous year. Currently, lay judges have the status of officials, which is provided in criminal law. These negative factors affect the independence of the judiciary and efforts to restore confidence in this branch of state governance, i.e., the power of the judicial branch. One of the essential requirements for ensuring the independence of the judiciary is the procedure for appointing judges or lay judges in court proceedings. In Ukraine, the selection of lay judges should not involve representatives of the political process, and the Judicial Council (Ukr. *Ради суддив*) should be involved by ensuring the participation of such an institution at the constitutional level. The Constitution should provide that, for both judges and *присяжні*, 'appointment and dismissal, their legal status and guarantees of independence shall be established by law'. Such an amendment would ensure that judges and lay judges have the same legal status. On the other hand, the Constitution should not prescribe the specific form (i.e., lay judges or jurors) and extent (i.e., in which cases and at which instance) of lay participation in the judicial process. If there was a need to improve or change the model of lay participation, the Constitution would not need to be amended. Meanwhile, a significant positive aspect is that the institution of lay judges is enshrined in a specific law, with regulations specific to this institute. Moreover, it is noticeable that when non-professionals participate in the judicial process it makes the process more understandable to the general public.

The analysis of the negative and positive aspects of the lay participation model in the administration of justice in Ukraine allowed for an analysis that looked into and provided an overview of the practical functioning of lay judges in the context of aggression. Firstly, it should be emphasised that Article 64(2) of the Law on the Judicial System and the Status of Judges provides for the possibility of involving lay judges in commercial cases. However, it is important to note that the Commercial and Procedural Code of Ukraine does not contain a separate legal regulation for commercial cases (e.g., bankruptcy cases, cases involving disputes between business entities, cases involving disputes on the privatisation of property, etc.). In addition, in practice, lay judges together with the judge in the panel hear civil cases, not commercial cases, including in times of aggression. On the other hand, the Civil Code of Ukraine does not contain specific norms establishing the institute of *присяжні*. Only the Civil Procedure Code of Ukraine contains two norms, i.e., Article 34(2) and Article 293(4), which provide for the institute in question in civil proceedings, where certain cases in courts of the first instance are heard by a panel consisting of one judge and two lay judges, who have all the rights of a judge in the administration of justice. However, the performance of the institute of lay judges in court proceedings during the Russian aggression against Ukraine is specific. Due to the extraordinary situation of aggression, lay judges at their own request can be released from the duties of a lay judge in connection with the mobilisation of military service from 24 July 2022 until its end, and can be substituted by another lay judge. In cases when it is impossible to form a complete court panel to hear civil cases, e.g., when the city council has no chance to approve the list of lay judges due to their shortage, the court transfers the civil case to the closest court territorially. Additionally, the efficiency of the court proceedings and the safety of the participants in extreme conditions of aggression require that measures be taken to move hearings online, which also ensures the timely and efficient delivery of all the necessary information and documents related to the hearing to all the participants. Thus, the challenges of the court in civil cases during Russian aggression add extra reasons for the need to modify the model of lay participation in Ukraine.

The participation of lay judges in criminal cases is governed by the Ukrainian CC and the Ukraine's CCP, under which judges exclusively hear criminal cases unless the accused is punishable by life imprisonment. In that case, at the request of the accused, the case shall be heard by a panel of two judges and three *присяжні*. Thus, as can be seen, in Ukraine, the legislature has established the institute of *присяжні* only in high-profile cases. However, as of the end of 2022, lay judges do not participate in cases involving war crimes (Art. 438 of the CC), even though they are punishable by life imprisonment under the law. Following the imposition of martial law in Ukraine and the amendment to Article 615(10) of the Ukraine's CCP, which entered into force on 1 May 2022, all criminal cases are heard exclusively by judges.

3.4. Organising Elections During Wartime: The Case of Ukraine

3.4.1. The Context of Elections Taking Place in Ukraine

One of the central institutes of democracy is elections (Lenarčič 2005, p. 1; Šileikis 2005, pp. 160). They are a vital form of citizens' participation in the governance of the state, are protected by international human rights law instruments (UN 2021), and are a necessary element in forming the state's political representative institutions (Constitutional Court of Lithuania 2004).

Elections allow citizens to participate in political life, express their opinions, and choose between candidates and political parties who may have different policies, platforms, and visions for society, in return for which citizens expect accountability (Merloe 2008, pp. 17–21). This ensures that the people's will is reflected in the government. If officials do not perform their duties effectively, they can be voted out of office in the next election.

Ukraine, a sovereign, independent, democratic, social, rule of law-based state (Art. 1 of the Constitution 1996) according to its legal acts, also holds several types of elections which are crucial to its system of governance:

(a) *Presidential elections.* The president of Ukraine is the head of state. The citizens elected the president for a 5-year term based on universal, equal, and direct suffrage by secret ballot (Art. 103 of the Constitution of Ukraine).
Regular elections for the position of president shall be held on the last Sunday of March in the 5th year of the president's mandate (Art. 103(5) of the Constitution). In case of early termination of the term of the president, presidential elections shall be held within 90 days from the day of termination of the president's authority (Art. 103(5) of the Election Code 2019). The president exercises their powers until the newly elected president assumes office (Art. 108(1) of the Constitution).
(b) *Parliamentary elections.* The constitutional composition of the Verkhovna Rada consists of 450 members who are elected for 5-year terms based on universal, equal, and direct suffrage by secret ballot (Art. 76(1) of the Constitution). This is based on an open, proportional electoral system (Art. 133 of the Election Code).
Regular elections to the Verkhovna Rada shall be held on the last Sunday of October in the 5th year of the term of the Verkhovna Rada. The president can schedule extraordinary elections to the Verkhovna Rada, which shall be held within 60 days from the day of publication of the decision on the early termination of the powers of the Verkhovna Rada (Art. 77 of the Constitution; Proskurina 2023).
(c) *Local elections.* The Constitution states that a village, settlement, city, district, and oblast council are composed of deputies elected for 5-year terms by the residents of a village, settlement, city, district, or oblast based on universal, equal, and direct suffrage by secret ballot. The term of authority of the village, settlement, city, district, or oblast council whose deputies are elected at regular elections is 5 years (Art. 141 of the Constitution, Art. 3 of the Election Code).

3.4.2. The Implementation of the Principle of Regular Elections

The standard principles (Katuoka 1989) of European constitutional heritage (ECtHR 2007) which form the basis of any genuinely democratic society frame the right to vote in terms of the possibility to cast a vote in universal, equal, free, secret and direct elections held at regular intervals (ECtHR 2017). Despite variations in their form, content, and qualities, regular elections are arguably not only one of the defining characteristics of a democracy (Dahl 2014) that are embedded into many conceptualisations of electoral integrity (Norris 2014), but are also the only tool that upholds the 'democratic' label of a government (Moniruzzaman 2018).

The principle of regular elections as a fundamental aspect of democratic governance or the right to periodic elections means that elections are held at established intervals according to a predetermined schedule or timeframe. This is an essential component of democratic governance, promoting political stability, accountability, and the active participation of citizens in shaping their societies.

Several aspects can be distinguished in relation to the principle of regular elections:

(a) Predictability and stability. Regular elections provide a predictable and stable framework for exercising political power. By having fixed intervals for elections, citizens and political actors can anticipate when elections will occur and plan their strategies and campaigns accordingly.
(b) Accountability and renewal. Regular elections enable citizens to hold their elected representatives accountable for their actions (Shapland 2015) and decisions. This allows citizens to express their satisfaction or dissatisfaction with incumbents' performance and make informed choices about new candidates or political parties.
(c) Legitimacy and democracy. Regular elections contribute to the legitimacy of political systems and the democratic process. By allowing citizens to participate in elections express their preferences, and have their votes counted, regular elections uphold the democratic principles of sovereignty, political equality, and majority rule.
(d) Participation and inclusion. Regular elections encourage citizens' engagement and participation in the political process. They provide a platform for individuals and groups to express their political views, compete for office, and contribute to shaping public policies.
(e) Transparency and fairness. Regular elections should be conducted transparently and fairly, adhering to established rules and procedures. This includes ensuring equal access to information, an impartial electoral administration, proper voter registration, transparency in campaign financing, and mechanisms to prevent electoral fraud or manipulation.

Regular elections are a fundamental principle recognised and emphasised in various international documents and instruments that apply to Ukraine. While their exact phrasing and interpretation may vary, the focus is generally on the regular and periodic holding of elections as a crucial aspect of democratic governance. For instance:

(a) Article 21 of the UDHR states that 'the will of the people shall be the basis of the authority of government' and emphasises the right to take part in the government; this will be expressed in periodic and genuine elections, which shall be by 'universal and equal suffrage' (Charity 2015). The reference to 'periodic and genuine elections' emphasises the need for elections to be held at regular intervals.

(b) Article 25 (1) of the ICCPR provides the right of every citizen to 'take part in the conduct of public affairs, directly or through freely chosen representatives' (May 2017), including the right to elect and to be elected in 'genuine periodic elections'. Regular elections enable citizens to exercise their right to participate in public affairs and choose their representatives.

(c) Article 3 of Protocol No. 1 of the ECHR (1952) provides that 'the High Contracting Parties undertake to hold free elections at reasonable intervals by secret ballot, under conditions which will ensure the free expression of the opinion of the people in the legislature's choice' (ECtHR 2007; Karimi 2012).

The principle of regular elections is also stated in the American Convention on Human Rights (1969, Art. 23(1.b)), the African Charter on Democracy, Elections and Governance (2007, Art. 3), the Human Rights Declaration of the Association of Southeast Asian Nations (2012), etc. (European Parliament 2020).

It is worth mentioning that the Venice Commission, an advisory body of the Council of Europe (Culik 2016), has developed the Code of Good Practise in Electoral Matters, which also stresses the importance of regular elections and that they should be held at fixed intervals to ensure democratic legitimacy.

The Guidelines on Elections adopted by the Venice Commission at its 51st Plenary Session in 2002 also state that 'elections must be held at regular intervals' (Para. No. 1) (Guidelines on elections) and 'a legislative assembly's term of office must not exceed 5 years' (Para. No. 5; The Charter Center 2016); 'general elections are usually held at 4- or 5-yearly intervals, while longer periods are possible for presidential elections, although the maximum should be 7 years' (Para. 57; The Charter Center 2016).

In various commitments and declarations, the OSCE also notes the importance of regular and periodic elections. For instance, the 1990 Document of the Copenhagen Meeting of the Conference on the Human Dimension of the CSC (now the OSCE) (Bernard 2009) states 'the participating States declare that the will of the people, freely and fairly expressed through periodic and genuine elections, is the basis of the authority and legitimacy of all government' (OSCE 1990). Also, the Charter of Paris for a New Europe states that 'democratic government is based on the will of the people, expressed regularly through free and fair elections' (D'Aspremont and Brabandere 2011).

Thus, while these legal acts of international organisations do not provide a specific timeframe for the regularity of elections, they establish the fundamental principle that elections should be held regularly to ensure democratic governance, popular participation, and the accountability of elected officials.

The ECtHR has also noted that elections must be regular (*Gitonas and Others v. Greece* (1997); *Py v. France* (2005); *Russian Conservative Party of Entrepreneurs and Others v. Russia* (2007); *Doyle v. UK* (2007); *Krasnov and Skuratov v. Russia* (2007); *The Georgian Labour Party v. Georgia* (2008); *Sarukhanyan v. Armenia* (2008). However, the court has not indicated what specific deadlines for the organisation of elections should be considered reasonable, and in which periods elections must be organised (so that such a deadline is not too short or too long).

Only the European Commission of Human Rights has spoken out in this regard, noting that too short an interval between elections may impede political planning for the implementation of the will of the electorate, which is the basis of governmental legitimacy. Too long an interval can lead to the petrification of political groupings in parliament, which may no longer bear any resemblance to the prevailing will of the electorate (Timke 1995).

The precise intervals and procedures for holding elections are typically defined by national legislation, and practises are determined by the principles outlined in international legal instruments.

In Ukraine, various legal acts, including the Constitution (Art. 76–77, 136(2) for the parliamentary elections and Articles 103, 108 for presidential elections) and the Election Code, outline the specific intervals and timing of elections. According to the Constitution, there cannot be a situation in which elections are not held or are held outside of the periods provided for in the Constitution. For instance, parliamentary elections shall be organised in the 5th year of the Verkhovna Rada of Ukraine. This means that the next parliamentary elections should be held on 29 October 2023. Assuming the last presidential election was on 31 March 2019 and the president's term is 5 years, the next presidential election is expected in 2024.

The organisation of local self-government elections at certain intervals is also stated in the legal acts. Considering that the last local elections were in 2020 and the local self-government term is 5 years, new regular local elections should take place in autumn 2025, according to the Constitution.

In other countries, the leading legal acts also enshrine the periodicity of elections and establish that regular elections must be held regularly. For instance, the Constitution of the Republic of Lithuania (1992) also includes guarantees for the periodicity of elections – the exact time of the ordinary parliamentary elections (both to the Seimas and the ordinary elections of the president of the republic) are determined: ordinary elections to the Seimas are held on the second Sunday of October in the year when the powers of the members of the Seimas expire (Art. 57 of the Constitution); ordinary presidential elections are held on the last Sunday 2 months before the end of the term of office of the president (Art. 80 of the Constitution of Lithuania). Regarding elections to municipal councils, the Constitution does not contain information as to when regular municipal council elections must be held; here, the powers granted to the legislator are determined by the Election Code (Pukanasytė 2014).

Thus, the constitutional provisions providing for the organisation of presidential, parliamentary, and local self-government elections every 5 years ensure that elections should not be arbitrary or *ad hoc*. Instead, they are conducted according to a predetermined schedule and held at regular intervals, providing for periodic renewal and providing citizens with the opportunity to regularly express their political preferences and participate in the democratic process.

3.4.3. The Impact of Martial Law on Elections

Regular elections are an essential feature of democratic practices (James and Alihodzic 2020). According to international human rights law, participating in government and voting in 'periodic, genuine elections' is a well-established right (Commonwealth Parliamentary Association 2021). Without elections – according to Bjørn Berge, the deputy secretary general of the Council of Europe, and Martin Candinas, president of the Swiss National Council – democracy is impossible (Council of Europe 2023).

Although laws generally provide that rights are usually protected and cannot be restricted and that elections are held regularly, certain circumstances can affect election timing.

Political rights, including voting rights, can be temporarily restricted under a minimal set of circumstances – for instance, in emergencies (Global Citizenship Observatory 2020), on public safety grounds, during significant crises such as world or civil wars, natural or humanitarian disasters, or as a result of technical delays related to logistical issues (Commonwealth Parliamentary Association 2021).

It should be emphasised that all restrictions must respect the standards of legality, necessity, proportionality and temporariness. Moreover, according to the Siracusa Principles adopted by the former UN Commission of Human Rights, which explain the relevant ICCPR provisions, 'the burden is upon a state imposing limitations so qualified to demonstrate that the limitations do not impair the democratic functioning of the society'(European Parliament 2020).

However, each situation is unique in practice and needs to be adequately assessed (Maryunani 2019) based on the circumstances (Elections Canada). Sometimes, elections can be held under challenging conditions, and sometimes the situation can be too risky for those participating.

There are many reasons as to why elections might not take place (James and Alihodzic 2020). This is perfectly illustrated by the decision of the Supreme Council of Turkey 1966, which decided that elections could be postponed following an earthquake that hit the country's eastern provinces 2 days ahead of the vote, making it impossible to hold elections (Soylu 2023). Another example is Nigeria. The 2019 Nigerian presidential and national assembly elections were postponed by the Independent National Electoral Commission 3 days before the scheduled elections 'following a careful review of the implementation of the logistics and operational plan' (Mckenzie and Wails 2019; James and Alihodzic 2020). This decision was announced only 5 hours before polls were due to open, and the election was put back a week. Of course, election-related delays can sometimes be longer. For instance, the Bosnian post-war elections in 1996 were postponed for 3 months due to technical delays (James 2020): the 1991 census was to be used as an electoral register, but mistakes were made in scanning the data. Meanwhile, voter identification was hampered by the problem of issuing documents to IDP (Hadziabdic 2019).

This chapter focuses on one reason for the postponement of elections: the declaration of martial law.

Martial law should be declared only via the law, and authorised only in the case of a threat to the nation's life, where measures compatible with the Constitution and laws in force are inadequate to address the situation (The Charter Center 2016).

The imposition of martial law is intended to be a temporary measure implemented in exceptional circumstances such as *war, invasion, insurrection, rebellion, riot or any* violent resistance to law (Phillimore 1900, pp. 45–72), primarily to address threats to the country's territorial integrity, independence, or constitutional order.

Declaring martial law is a complex process that requires the consensus of several branches of government. Ukraine is no exception. Under Article 106 (21) of the Constitution of Ukraine, the president may 'adopt a decision, by law, on the general or partial mobilization and the introduction of martial law in Ukraine or its particular territories in the event of a threat of aggression or danger to the independence of Ukraine' (КримSOS 2021). However, this decision only enters into force after approval by the parliament.

Similar regulation regarding martial law is in force in other countries. For instance, Article 29 of the Constitution of Poland (Buamah 2018) states that 'in the case of external threats to the State, acts of armed aggression against the territory of the Republic of Poland or when an obligation of common defence against aggression arises by international agreement, the president of the republic may, on request of the Council of Ministers, declare a state of martial law in a part of or upon the whole territory of the State' (Constitution of Poland 1997). Article 71(5) of the Constitution of Georgia also states that 'in cases of an armed attack, or a direct threat of armed attack on Georgia, the president of Georgia shall, upon recommendation by the prime minister, declare martial law' (Constitution of Georgia 1995). However, in some countries, martial law is declared only by parliament. For instance, according to Article 142 of the Constitution of the Republic of Lithuania, martial law is introduced by parliament (the Seimas) (Constitution of Lithuania).

Martial law typically involves suspending or limiting certain civil liberties and fundamental rights – for instance, involving restrictions on freedom of assembly, freedom of speech, freedom of the press, and the right to political participation. Such limitations can impede the ability of political parties, candidates, and voters to engage in election-related activities, participate in the election campaign, express their views, or access the information necessary for informed voting.

The specific measures and limitations imposed during martial law, including any impact on voting rights, are determined by the relevant legislation and decrees enacted by the government during that period.

As in many other countries, the introduction of martial law in Ukraine is inevitably associated with the restriction of specific rights. The president, with the consent of the Verkhovna Rada, can impose not only martial law but also restrictions on certain constitutional rights and freedoms, which may include limitations on the right to vote.

The Constitution of Ukraine does not explicitly state that elections are not organised or that certain elections are not organised during martial law. On the other hand, the Constitution provides that if the term of the Verkhovna Rada expires while martial law is in effect, its mandate shall be extended until the day of the first meeting of the first session of the Verkhovna Rada of Ukraine elected after the cancellation of martial law or the state of emergency (Art. 83 (4) of the Ukraine Constitution).

Moreover, such a restriction or prohibition is detailed at the level of the laws governing the martial law regime. For instance, according to Article 19 entitled 'Guarantees of Legality Under Martial Law' of the Law of Ukraine 'On the Legal Regime of Martial Law' (2015), in a period of martial law, it is prohibited to conduct: elections for the president of Ukraine, the Verkhovna Rada of Ukraine, the Verkhovna Rada of the Autonomous Republic of Crimea, and local self-government bodies; all-Ukrainian and local referenda; and strikes, mass meetings, and actions. In other words, the Law 'On the Legal Regime of Martial Law' directly prohibits holding all types of elections during martial law.

It should be noted that martial law also affects any election process that has already started. The election process stops after the announcement of elections and the introduction of martial law in all of Ukraine or its separate territories. Under Article 20 of the Election Code, 'in the event of martial law or a state of emergency being imposed in Ukraine or its separate territories, the election process of national elections and/or local elections held in these territories, or their parts shall be terminated from the date of entry into force of the respective decree of the president of Ukraine'. The Code provides that 'after the entry into force of the decree of the president, the Central Elections' Commission (hereafter – CEC) shall decide to terminate the election process throughout Ukraine or in its separate territories and determine the rules for completing election procedures initiated in the framework of the election process'.

The Election Code establishes a deadline for calling elections where the electoral process was suspended or failed to start due to the introduction of martial law. Article 20 of the Election Code establishes that after the cessation or abolition of martial law, any electoral process which has been suspended in connection with this shall begin again. The decision on calling elections which had their electoral process suspended or which did not begin due to the imposition of martial law shall be adopted by the subject of their appointment no later than 1 month from the date of the termination or abolition of martial law. If the law does not require a separate decision on the appointment for holding the elections, the CEC shall announce the start of the election process no later than 1 month from the date of the termination or abolition of martial law (Art. 20 of the Election Code). However, this does not seem realistic, because 'the Verkhovna Rada of Ukraine, no later than 90 days from the date of termination or cancellation of martial law, if regular or special elections to the relevant bodies were to be held during the period during which martial law was imposed, shall decide on the appointment of elections for deputies of the Verkhovna Rada Autonomous Republic of Crimea, local elections' (Kliuchkovskyi and Volodymyr 2022).

3.4.4. The Influence of the War of Aggression on the Organisation of Elections in Ukraine in 2023–2024

According to the Ukrainian Constitution, regular parliamentary and presidential elections must be held in 2023–2024. In 2019, for the first time in independent

Ukraine, extraordinary elections to the Verkhovna Rada were held in the summer, on 21 July 2019. The Verkhovna Rada acquired powers on 29 August 2019. Considering that, according to the Constitution of Ukraine, parliamentary elections are held on the last Sunday of October of the 5th year of the parliamentary term, the next parliamentary elections should take place on 29 October 2023.

Since presidential elections are also held every 5 years and the last election was held in March 2019, the next elections are scheduled for 31 March 2024, i.e., 6 months after the parliamentary elections.

However, this time, holding elections within the deadlines set by the Constitution of Ukraine and ensuring compliance with the principle of regular elections may be difficult, or even impossible.

On 24 February 2022, the Russian Federation launched large-scale armed aggression against Ukraine (National Security and Defense Council of Ukraine Report 2022). To resist the aggressor and to protect the sovereignty and territorial integrity of the state, based on the proposal of the National Security and Life Council of Ukraine and Article 106 (20) of the Constitution of Ukraine and the Law of Ukraine 'On Martial Law' of 24 February 2022, martial law was introduced by presidential decree No. 64/2022.

On the same day, the Verkhovna Rada approved the presidential decree allowing the imposition of the legal regime of martial law for 30 days (Decree Art. 1). Later, in connection with the ongoing military aggression of the Russian Federation against Ukraine, the decrees of the president of Ukraine 'On the Extension of Martial Law in Ukraine' were adopted. At the time of preparing this chapter, under the president's decree, the period of martial law has been extended until 14 February 2024.

Following the declaration of martial law in Ukraine by presidential decrees, restrictions on human rights were introduced, regarding which the Ukrainian government, according to the ICCPR and the ECHR, notified the European Council (Democracy Reporting International 2023). Restrictions on human rights included a ban on holding any mass events, election campaigns, or elections, which have been an integral part of Ukraine's political system throughout its years of independence.

Ukraine has been successfully holding regular parliamentary and presidential elections since its independence with the exception of 2004, which led to the Orange Revolution. However, this time, due to the full-scale invasion of the Russian Federation into Ukraine, the occupation of part of the Ukrainian territories (Oliinyk 2023) and the declaration of martial law throughout the country, as long as martial law continues, national and local elections, whether ordinary, extraordinary, or by-elections, cannot be held and should be postponed.

Many constitutions of foreign countries also provide for postponement or the opportunity to postpone elections during emergencies, for example by extending the term of the parliament. This is the case in Croatia, Italy, Germany, Greece, Poland, Lithuania, Slovenia, Spain, Hungary and Canada.

In other countries' constitutions, an emergency precludes the dissolution of the parliament, e.g., Germany, Spain, Portugal, Poland, Hungary (European Parliament 2020).

However, there are also countries whose legal acts do not stipulate that elections are not organised during wartime. For instance, the USA Constitution does not provide in express language any authority for a federal official or institution to 'postpone an election' under any circumstances. If there is time for elections, they should be held at that time. Many elections in US history illustrate this well. For example, presidential elections were held during the War of 1812, the Civil War (1864) (Ho 2020), World War II (1944), the Vietnam War (1964, 1968, 1972), and the wars in Iraq and Afghanistan (2004, 2008, 2012, 2016) (The National Task Force on Election Crises 2003). Interestingly, the Civil War lasted 48 months, and in at least half of those months major elections occurred in the North. 'On average, the North witnessed a major election every other month of the war (White 2020).'

Election postponements represent a departure from the normal democratic procedure and hold the potential to compromise or destabilise democracy. Such postponements can diminish institutional certainty (James and Alihodzic, 2020) by altering the expectation of power transfer (Plutowski 2022). Postponing a vote also entails political risks: leaders (European Parliament 2020) and representatives who are not necessarily doing a good job will remain in office for longer, and citizens will be temporarily denied their right to shape public policy – perhaps at exactly the moment they need to (Maury 2020). Therefore, although election postponement can be a democratic process (James and Alihodzic 2020), this remedy should be chosen when all other options have been exhausted (Maury 2020). In addition, extraordinary measures such as election postponement must comply with all international standards for such derogations, and not threaten democracy itself (ICCPR).

3.4.5. Cases in Which Elections Can Be Held

Elections are prohibited in Ukraine during martial law. Therefore, in order for the elections to take place within the terms stipulated in the Constitution and not be postponed, there are several alternatives: (a) to change the legal acts that determine the specific date of the elections; or (b) to amend the legislation relating to the declaration of martial law in the country.

The dates of parliamentary and presidential elections are set in the Constitution. Therefore, for parliamentary or presidential elections to take place on a day other than that provided for in the Constitution, amendments to the Constitution should first be initiated. The Constitution can be changed if there is an objective judicial necessity for this and the Constitution's norms, principles, and stability are not violated as a result (The Constitutional Court of Lithuania 2014). The nation can change the Constitution directly or through democratically elected representatives, but only according to the rules established in the Constitution (Lithuanian Constitutional law 2017). However, in this case, considering that a state of war was declared in Ukraine, the Constitution cannot be changed (Art. 157(2) of the Constitution).

Another option is to change legislation prohibiting elections during times of war or emergency.

Under the Ukrainian Constitution, sole legislative power belongs to the Verkhovna Rada (Art. 75 of the Constitution). The Verkhovna Rada's legislative authority continues during martial law, i.e., the Ukrainian Constitution does not delegate legislative powers to the president under these circumstances. Given this, the parliament could initiate amendments to legislation, such as the emergency law prohibiting elections during wartime and others.

Another alternative to elections is to reverse martial law. For example: (1) end martial law if there is no longer a threat (this can be done by the president by a decree on the proposal of the SC or parliament); (2) do not renew martial law after the expiration of its term (if a new request for its extension is not submitted); or (3) introduce martial law only in part of Ukraine's territories.

Notably, on 28 November 2018, martial law was introduced in Ukraine for 30 days for the first time (Human Rights Watch Report 2018). However, it was not valid across the entire Ukrainian territory, but only in 10 of the 25 regions on the border with Russia and Moldova (Daren and Way 2018). Since the presidential decree on the imposition of martial law was not extended, on 31 March 2019, presidential elections took place as planned.

3.4.6. The Announcement of Elections after the End of Martial Law

Elections are a political process during which political representative institutions are formed, i.e., institutions whose decisions are of decisive importance for the life of the state and society; therefore, it is important that this process is based on the Constitution (Pukanasytė 2013, p. 633).

Article 136 (2) of the Election Code, which regulates time frames for the organisation of elections for members of the Ukrainian parliament, states that in ordinary elections, the regular election process shall begin 60 days before the day of voting.

The Central Elections Commission must announce the start of the election no later than one full day before it begins. Theoretically, if the armed actions had ended by mid-August 2023 and martial law was not extended beyond 18 August 2023, it would have been possible to plan parliamentary elections in 2023. In other words, the requirement provided for in Article 77 of the Constitution would have been fulfilled (Opora analysis 2023). On the other hand, the organisation of elections immediately after this state of war is ambiguously assessed by Ukrainians. As surveys of the population show, respondents' opinions on 'when Ukraine should hold the first elections after the end of martial law' differ. In general, 16 % believe that elections should take place immediately, 28 % suggest waiting for 3–6 months, 30 % think that they should happen in around a year, another would 13 % prefer to wait a few years, and 2 % have other opinions (Opora analysis 2023).

A short deadline of a few months for holding elections is also stated in the constitutions of other countries. For instance, according to Article 37 (3) of the Constitution of Georgia, 'if the election date coincides with a state of emergency or martial law, elections shall be held no earlier than the 45th day and no later than the 60th day after the state of emergency or martial law has been revoked' (Constitution of Georgia). In some countries – for instance, in Lithuania – a longer deadline is provided for the conduct of elections organised after the end of the state of emergency. Article 143 of the Constitution of the Republic of Lithuania stipulates that 'elections must be called not later than 3 months after the end of the war'(Constitution of Lithuania).

However, the reasons and circumstances for martial law may be different. Therefore, assessing whether a 2–3-month period in which to hold new elections after the introduction of martial law is sufficient is quite difficult. In one case, a state of war may be introduced to strengthen the defence of the country, taking into account growing foreign threats; in another case, it may be a response to an armed attack by a foreign state, a violation of territorial integrity, etc. Accordingly, depending on the consequences, in one case, 2 months may be enough to hold new elections; in another case, serious obstacles may be encountered in election preparation. This applies especially in cases where the country's political situation is not stabilised after the end of the state of war, political parties and candidates are not ready to participate in the elections, and there is no possibility to prepare the necessary infrastructure for the elections or to ensure the safety of the persons participating in the process.

On the other hand, holding elections immediately after martial law has several advantages.

Firstly, if martial law in the country was not extended, then ensuring that the parliamentary and presidential elections in Ukraine would take place within the terms set by the Constitution would be helpful. This would partially correspond to the position of the president of the PACE, Tiny Kox: that holding parliamentary and presidential elections in Ukraine is a duty under the Council of Europe Charter (Europeiska Pravda 2023), and elections must be held even while martial law is in effect (Pohorilov 2023). The positions of the representatives of Ukraine and the Council of Europe are radically different in this respect, as Ukrainian officials, responding to the position expressed by the representative of the Council of Europe, have noted that Ukraine has its own Constitution and laws which they must observe. This means that election matters must be decided according to the laws in force in their country, which do not grant the right to organise elections while martial law is in effect. Meanwhile, although the representative of the Council of Europe admitted that the Ukrainian Constitution does not allow elections to be held while martial law is in effect, he stated that Ukraine must find a solution. According to the representative, they cannot say how it is to be achieved, but free and fair elections must be held because that is an obligation under the statute and conventions (Pohorilov 2023). The representative also observed that winning the war and surviving the invasion are incredible challenges, but in order to restore, strengthen, and rebuild the country while observing the rules of democracy, the rule of law, and human rights, this challenge will remain with Ukraine for many years. Nonetheless, Ukraine must overcome it (Zubkova 2023). According to the PACE president, organising elections under these conditions will be extremely difficult; however, there are examples from other countries – particularly Turkey, which managed to hold elections after a devastating earthquake (Zubkova 2023). Because the constitution prohibits elections during martial law, the position of the PACE president that elections should be held anyway can be analysed in more detail.

Organising elections during martial law would violate the principle of the supremacy of the constitution. An essential requirement of a democratic legal state is that it does not allow anyone to violate the constitution, meaning that the constitutional order must be defended. Among other things, a violation of this principle would mean that the principle of the constitutional state is also violated, a universal principle that underpins the entire legal system and the constitution itself (The Constitutional Court of the Republic of Lithuania 2002).

Secondly, the defence of human rights is critical for any democracy (International Institute for Democracy and Electoral Assistance 2022) – even more so for a country that is fighting for its territorial integrity. Ever since Ukrainians decided to make their country more democratic in the Maidan revolution of 2014 and to freely choose their own foreign policy direction, the Russian government has responded with warfare. The full-scale Russian invasion of 24 February 2022 marked only the latest step in the escalation of a war the Kremlin launched in 2014 (Democracy Reporting International 2023).

If Ukraine succeeds in holding democratic and well-organised elections, it will send an important message to the world about unity and commitment to democracy and democratic renewal (Democracy Reporting International 2023). This is reflected in Ukrainian polling – for instance, one poll in August 2022 found that 95 % of Ukrainians believe that it is essential that Ukraine become a fully functioning democracy (Democracy Reporting International 2023).

Thirdly, by organising elections under challenging conditions, Ukraine would also show the world that it is a unique state that, even during a full-scale war for its freedom and independence, does not forget about democracy. This would be a powerful signal that the state does not deviate from democratic standards and the political rights of citizens under any conditions.

Although the organisation of elections immediately after the end of the state of war would bring a lot of added value to the country, certain disadvantages can also be observed.

Firstly, infrastructural challenges may be encountered when organising elections. During the state of war, the infrastructure intended for elections (the work of election commission members, polling stations, etc.) may suffer or need to be improved, and it may be difficult and sometimes downright impossible to restore it in a relatively short time.

Secondly, challenges of voter awareness and participation in elections may be encountered. During martial law, it is not uncommon for voters to relocate and be isolated from information. Over 6 million Ukrainians are currently abroad. Therefore, informing them about elections and their right to participate in state governance may take a lot of time and effort.

Thirdly, there may be some security challenges, as war can cause instability or discord between different groups in society. There may be threats to the organisation of elections and the persons participating in them, starting with members of election commissions, spreading to voters and ending with candidates. Meanwhile, elections as a democratic institute are only possible where a secure environment can be guaranteed so that there is no threat to the safety of any participant. In addition, as Leendert Verbeek, the president of the Council of Europe

Congress of Local and Regional Authorities, observed, governments should ask themselves whether elections may be held and consider different aspects of elections, including voters' security (Democracy Reporting International 2023). Democratic elections cannot be organised and held where people must take care of their survival and meet only their basic needs (safety, health care, food, hygiene, etc.) (Council of Europe Needs Assessment Report 2022).

Fourthly, there may be some challenges related to the restoration of democracy and democratic principles, especially since democracy is unthinkable without a credible electoral process. This includes not only voting, but also equal possibilities to campaign for all candidates, freely exercising the right of assembly, participating collectively in the political process and ensuring pluralism of ideas. As stated by the ECtHR – for example in the cases of *Stefan Stankov v. Bulgaria* (2015) and *Karacsony and Others v. Hungary* (2016) – freedom of expression, assembly, and association are essential foundations and are among the paramount values of a democratic society (Briefing of European Parliament 2020).

Elections should make voting possible, but it is much more essential to create conditions where voters can freely form their will and then express it by voting in elections (Kliuchkovskyi and Venher 2022). Meanwhile, the threat of political manipulation and corruption influencing election results may arise after military action. This can undermine confidence in the electoral system and the authorities. Additionally, organising free and fair elections in some territories may be impossible due to occupation or other territorial disputes.

Finally, it can be challenging to meet international democratic standards in such circumstances (Parliamentary Conference 2023). Ukraine has long been an example of democratic progress in the region, and already has experience in organising fair and free elections (Erben and Kokakhidze 2022). Thus, lowering election standards in the post-war period could lead to a high degree of degradation of the political system. Losing the dynamics of democratic progress is a daunting prospect that could unbalance the trust that has been formed between the citizens and the state of Ukraine (Opora 2023).

3.4.7. The Extension of the Mandate

Suppose the military actions in Ukraine were to continue, and martial law continued to apply. In that case, the mandates of both members of parliament and the president may expire during martial law, i.e., when no election could be held. However, the fact that the mandate of representatives of the nation elected by the citizens expired during a particular situation, such as martial law, would not mean that the country would remain without a parliament or a person holding the office of the president.

The Law 'On the Legal Regime of Martial Law' and the Constitution specify that if the term of authority of the Verkhovna Rada of Ukraine expires while a state of martial law is in effect, its powers are valid until the day when the Verkhovna Rada elected after the cancellation of the state of martial law convenes its first meeting of the first session (Art. 83(4) of the Constitution). Very similar regulation also exists in other countries – for instance, Article 53(3) of the Constitution of Greece states 'in case of war, the parliamentary term shall be extended for the entire duration thereof. If parliament has been dissolved, elections shall be postponed until the termination of the war and the parliament dissolved shall be recalled *ipso jure* until that time' (Constitution of Greece, 1974). Article 63(3) of the Constitution of North Macedonia states 'the term of office of the Representatives to the Assembly can be extended only during states of war or emergency' (Constitution of Macedonia, 1991). Very similar regulation is found in Article 143 of the Constitution of Lithuania, which provides that if a regular election must be held in a time of war, either the Seimas or the president of the republic shall adopt a decision to extend the term of powers of the Seimas, the president of the republic, or municipal councils (Constitution of Lithuania). This means that one of the two leading institutions of the country – the parliament or the president of the republic – must extend the powers of the nation's representatives. There is no freedom to extend the powers of the people's elected officials or hold new elections according to the Constitution of the Republic of Lithuania. Article 131 of the Constitution of Estonia also states that 'the Riigikogu, the president, and representative bodies of local authorities may not be elected, nor may their authority be terminated during a state of emergency or war. If the term of office of the Riigikogu, the president or representative bodies of local authorities should expire during a state of emergency or a state of war that term is extended' (Constitution of Estonia, 1992).

As polls show, many Ukrainians support such legal regulation during times of martial law. For example, according to sociological surveys in which Ukrainians were asked how the authorities should act in a situation of martial law when, according to the Constitution of Ukraine, no elections are possible, the vast majority (61.6 %) spoke in favour of extending the powers of the current Verkhovna Rada of Ukraine until the end of martial law, no matter how long it lasts. Only 11.7 % of the surveyed respondents were comfortable with suspending martial law and holding a shortened election campaign and elections in October

2023, while 26.7 % were unsure and could not answer the question (Vedernikova 2023). Therefore, in this case, if martial law in Ukraine was extended and then the mandate of the members of parliament was to end, a situation would arise in which the current term of office of the deputies of the Verkhovna Rada would be the longest in the history of Ukraine so far.

However, the legal regulation in this case is not precise. For instance, specific questions could be raised in cases where, during martial law, members of parliament would themselves refuse their mandate (resign) or lose it on the grounds provided for in legal acts.

Currently, the Election Code provides that 'the election of members of parliament of Ukraine shall be held according to the proportional system with unified lists of members of parliament candidates in the nationwide election district, based on which regional lists of members of parliament candidates shall be formed from parties' (Art. 130). The members of the Verkhovna Rada of the current term were elected according to a mixed election system: half of the members of the parliament were elected based on a proportional system, with closed party lists in one multi-member constituency; the other half of the members of parliament were elected in a single-member constituency under a plurality system in a single round (first-past-the-post) (The Office for Democratic Institutions and Human Rights 2019).

The termination of the powers of a member of the Verkhovna Rada of Ukraine elected in a single-mandate constituency will result in a vacant mandate in parliament, which cannot be filled during martial law as by-elections in individual constituencies – established in Article 106 of the Law of Ukraine 'On Elections of People's Deputies of Ukraine' – can be held only after the termination (lifting) of martial law (Council of Europe 2022).

However, if there were many such vacancies, the Verkhovna Rada of Ukraine would have fewer than 300 elected members. There is a risk that the Verkhovna Rada of Ukraine would then lose its powers on the grounds stipulated in the Constitution. For instance, Article 82(2) of the Constitution states that 'The Verkhovna Rada of Ukraine shall be legally constituted provided that at least two-thirds of its constitutional composition has been elected' (Constitution of Ukraine). A method through which to control this situation under the conditions of martial law is not provided, although such a situation should be described in detail in the law.

According to the Law 'On Elections of People's Deputies of Ukraine' (2004), the decision on calling by-elections for a member of the Verkhovna Rada in a single-mandate constituency shall be made by the Central Election Commission within 10 days following the early termination of powers of a People's Deputy elected in a particular constituency.

However, regarding calling Verkhovna Rada by-elections in individual constituencies, no special regulations are adapted for the period after the termination of martial law. For instance, there is no procedure for replacing members of the Verkhovna Rada who have died during the Russian invasion (Constitution of Ukraine). Therefore, legislative instructions shall be provided regarding the timeframe for the by-elections of people's deputies of Ukraine in individual single-mandate constituencies where the grounds for calling and holding by-elections arise during martial law or immediately after it is lifted. Moreover, parliamentary by-elections cannot be designated by the CEC during the 5th year of power of the Verkhovna Rada (Art. 16(7) of the Law 'On Elections of People's Deputies of Ukraine') (Venice Commission 2005). Lithuania's experience can also be relied on here. For instance, the Election Code of the Republic of Lithuania stipulates that repeated elections must be held no later than 15 days from the day on which the grounds for holding these elections arose. Repeated elections must be held no later than 3 months from their announcement (Art. 14(2)) of the Election Code of the Republic of Lithuania (2022).

Similar regulation as in the case of the expiration of the mandate of the members of parliament also applies to the expiration of the powers of the president of Ukraine during a state of war. The Law 'On the Legal Regime of Martial Law' prescribes the extension of the authority of the president of Ukraine if the constitutional term of their mandate expires during martial law. In other words, the election of the president of Ukraine can be called only after the termination of martial law. However, in the event of the early termination of the mandate of the president of Ukraine, the discharge of the president's duties is vested with the speaker of the Verkhovna Rada (Art. 112 of the Constitution).

3.4.8. The Organisation of Elections in Occupied and De-Occupied Territories

When preparing this chapter, some parts of Ukraine's territory were occupied and some were de-occupied. Holding elections in occupied territories where hostilities are occurring is impossible (Council of Europe 2022). Despite this, in sociological surveys (Vedernikova 2023), 46.8 % of respondents who were asked 'Should voters living in the occupied territories take part in the parliamentary elections' answered positively. While 24.6 % found it difficult to answer, 28.7 % of respondents answered that there is no need to hold parliamentary elections because they are not yet relevant.

On the other hand, holding elections during or in the aftermath of a public emergency brings challenges (UN 2021).

Firstly, the security challenge is relevant. De-occupied territories often face lingering security concerns that pose many challenges. For instance, the presence of armed groups, unresolved conflicts, or the risk of reprisals can create an environment that is not conducive to conducting elections smoothly and safely. Without adequate security guarantees, even calling elections is a risk (Council of Europe 2022). Therefore, ensuring the safety of election officials, candidates, and voters could become crucial, requiring well-thought-out decisions. Second, infrastructure and logistics present concerns: elections are enormous, complex logistical events requiring resources, laws and staff (James 2011, pp. 37–52). In de-occupied territories, infrastructure, communication, and other networks are often damaged (LB.ue 2023), and the rebuilding of essential infrastructure can pose logistical challenges for organising elections. Third, population displacement is relevant: the occupation of a specific territory or part of it means the relocation of the population living in it, or the movement of these people to other places. In the case of de-occupation, some residents may return to their homes, but there may also be those who will not return to their former residential areas due to destroyed infrastructure, negative memories, and other factors. In this way, the place of residence of some residents who left occupied territories may be known, but there will be many whose places of residence are unknown. Therefore, ensuring that residents are involved in electoral processes can be difficult (Radio Free Europe 2023), as there are too many challenges for the State Voters Register. Fourth, legitimacy is difficult: establishing the legitimacy of the electoral process in de-occupied territories can be challenging as citizens may distrust election processes, the candidates participating, and election results, which might exacerbate rather than resolve political conflicts.

Fifth, rebuilding trust is key: usually, de-occupied territories are marked by deep political divisions and fractured societal relationships. Rebuilding trust among the locals, fostering reconciliation efforts, and creating an environment encouraging participation in the electoral process can be complex and time-consuming.

Lastly, international involvement and support is decisive. Organising elections in de-occupied territories may require international involvement and support, as international organisations and peacekeeping missions may play a role in facilitating the electoral process, providing technical assistance, or monitoring the fairness and transparency of the elections.

3.4.9. The Importance of Securing Elections During the Application of Martial Law

Elections held amid ongoing armed conflicts are rare, as it is nearly impossible to meet international democratic standards in such circumstances (Council of Europe 2023). On the other hand, ensuring regular elections during wartime is vitally essential for several reasons:

(a) Democratic legitimacy: regular elections provide a mechanism for peaceful power transfer and the establishment of legitimate governments. They allow citizens to express their preferences, choose representatives, and participate in the democratic process. By conducting regular elections during wartime, the legitimacy of the government and its decisions can be maintained, fostering democratic principles and upholding the people's will.
(b) Accountability and transparency: regular elections hold governments accountable for their actions, policies, and decision-making (Cutler 2004), even during wartime. Elections allow citizens to evaluate the performance of implemented policies and express their approval or disapproval through the ballot box (Topaloff 2017). This helps to ensure that those in power remain responsive to the needs and concerns of the people, promoting transparency and accountability in governance.
(c) Stability: regular elections can contribute to stability and social cohesion during conflicts. By allowing citizens to have a say in the political process, elections provide an outlet for the peaceful expression of differing views and conflict resolution through democratic means. They can help promote dialogue, reconciliation, and a shared vision for the future.
(d) The protection of human rights: regular elections, even during wartime, help safeguard fundamental human rights. Elections allow citizens to exercise their right to participate in public affairs (UN 2018), including suffrage. Elections contribute to protecting civil and political rights, promoting inclusivity, and empowering individuals to have a voice in shaping their society.

While organising elections during wartime may pose logistical and security challenges, regular elections remain essential for upholding democracy, maintaining government legitimacy, ensuring accountability, and promoting stability. They contribute to the long-term resolution of conflicts and the establishment of a more inclusive and prosperous society.

3.4.10. Interim findings

Because Ukraine has held regular elections since the restoration of its independence, except for in 2004 when the Orange Revolution occurred, postponing the elections would represent a deviation from standard democratic procedure. Therefore, this measure should be chosen responsibly and not threaten democracy itself.

As armed conflict continues in Ukraine, there are several alternatives to holding elections within the term based on the Constitution: (1) lifting martial law; (2) the non-extension of the state of war after its termination; or (3) the extension of martial law only in some regions of the country.

The Election Code stipulates that elections must be held within 90 days of martial law ending. However, such a deadline may be too short to prepare for smooth elections meeting democratic election principles and international standards.

By organising elections even under challenging conditions, Ukraine would show the world that it is a unique state that does not forget democracy even during a large-scale war for its freedom and independence, and this would be a powerful signal that the state does not deviate from democratic standards and the political rights of citizens under any conditions. On the other hand, holding elections in wartime can make it challenging to adhere to international democratic standards. Given that Ukraine has long been a model of democratic progress in the region, the post-war lowering of electoral standards could lead to the significant degradation of the political system.

In organising elections during wartime, various challenges could be faced, such as: the absence or lack of adequate infrastructure for elections; a lack of voter awareness regarding elections and low voter turnout; multifaceted security issues; political manipulation and corruption; the inability to hold elections in occupied territories, etc.

The Constitution or other legal acts do not describe in detail how to address the situation when, during a state of war, the Verkhovna Rada of Ukraine consists of fewer than the 300 members provided for in Article 82 of the Constitution.

3.5. The Administrative Procedure Act in Ukraine: Recent Development, Challenges, and Solutions

3.5.1. The Concept of an Administrative Procedure

This chapter reveals the concept of an administrative procedure and the development of the Law of Ukraine on Administrative Procedure (2005); provides for the analysis of the key novelties of the Law, the core guaranties for private persons in relations with public administration entities and the main obligations of public servants; and analyses possible challenges and solutions in the practical realisation of the Law in both present and post-conflict Ukraine.

Administrative procedure is a crucial element of good administration. In certain European countries, legal regulation of the administrative procedure tradition goes back almost 100 years. For example: in Spain and Germany, the first laws governing administrative procedures were passed in the 19th century; the Austrian Administrative Procedure Act was passed in 1925; in Poland, the issue of administrative procedures was settled in 1928; and the rules on administrative procedures in Czechoslovakia were first laid down in 1928 (Janowicz 1970, p. 121). These legal acts enshrined modern principles (the right to be heard, publicity, oral proceedings, economy, and efficiency) and institutes of administrative procedure. However, in some countries, legislation of this magnitude was only adopted fairly recently. In Ukraine, the Law on Administrative Procedure was adopted after several decades of deliberations and discussions at the most painful time for this country – during the full-scale aggression of the Russian Federation against Ukraine.

The concept of an administrative procedure is explained in the doctrine of administrative law, according to which an administrative procedure refers to a sequence of procedural actions performed by the public administration or other entities to resolve an administrative case in the form of an administrative decision, as well as procedural actions performed to verify an administrative decision. Some scholars define an administrative procedure as the formally regulated path (a 'number of steps known in advance') which an administrative body should follow in order to take an administrative action (Adamiak and Borkowski 2014; Rusch 2009). Moreover, we can find yet more global understandings of administrative procedures – for example, some scholars assume that '[A]dministrative procedure is a universal way of deciding on rights and obligations of persons in the field of public administration and administrative law', and that, '[A]t present, we will probably not be able to administrate public affairs without administrative procedure and it will not be possible to completely replace it' (Potěšil *et al.* 2021). Other scholars have summarised the doctrine and legal provisions of administrative procedures by giving a general definition: 'administrative procedure is a part of public administration activity, during which a public administration entity, performing the functions assigned to it in its field of competence, using general or special legal measures, makes an administrative decision (act) or concludes an administrative contract, thus completing the administrative procedure that has been started' (Deviatnikovaitė and Bareikytė 2021, p. 189).

3.5.2. The Historical Context of the Law of Ukraine on Administrative Procedure

The current administrative legislation in Ukraine does not have a special legal act on general administrative procedure. Even the terms 'public administration', 'administrative procedure', and 'administrative act' are still doctrinal ones. Different administrative procedures are regulated by numerous legal acts, composed of laws and regulations approved by different public administration entities. As emphasised in the explanatory note to the draft Law on Administrative Procedure No. 3475, 'the majority of the procedural elements of the relations of the bodies of executive power and local self-government bodies, their officials and other subjects empowered by law to execute power managerial functions, with citizens are not regulated by the legislation at all, or regulated by the by-laws' (Explanatory note to the draft Law of Ukraine 'On Administrative Procedure' 2000).

The Concept on Administrative Reform in Ukraine approved by the Decree of the President of Ukraine (1998) outlined the necessity of approving a separate Administrative Procedure Code of Ukraine (Concept on Administrative Reform in Ukraine). However, at that time it was not clear what the subject of the regulation of such a code should be. The first working group for the development of the Administrative Procedure Code was established in 1999 under the supervision of Prof. Vadym Averianov.

The process of development, consideration, and approval of the Law on Administrative Procedure took 22 years. During this long period, several attempts were made to approve such a law, and several draft laws (from draft Administrative Procedure Codes to a draft Administrative Procedure Law) were registered at the Verkhovna Rada of Ukraine.

Logically, it was expected that the Administrative Procedure Code would have been approved first in order to regulate the administrative decision-making procedure. However, there was no clear understanding regarding the unification of general procedure rules at that time. Therefore, the Code on Judicial Administrative Proceedings of Ukraine was approved on 6 July 2005 – before the Law on Administrative Procedure. As a compromise, the provisions of part 2 of Art. 2 of the Code on Judicial Administrative Proceedings of Ukraine include a set of general principles of administrative decision-making, the fulfilment of which shall be assessed by the administrative courts.

The successful draft Law of Ukraine 'On Administrative Procedure' (hereafter – the LAP) No. 3475 was registered with the Parliament on 14 May 2020, approved in its first reading on 2 September 2020, and finally approved by the

Parliament on 16 November 2021. On 8 December 2021, the Law was returned to the Parliament with the proposals of the President of Ukraine, and on 17 February 2022 it was finally approved by the Parliament. On 13 June 2022 (this process took more time under the conditions of martial law), the President of Ukraine signed the LAP, which was published on 15 June 2022 (Law 'On Administrative Procedure').

The adoption of the LAP was a result of the multiannual work of professionals from the public administration (first, the Ministry of Justice of Ukraine), academic, and civil society spheres. European experts (in particular, from the SIGMA project – Support for Improvement in Governance and Management) contributed significantly in the process of development and consideration of the draft LAP at different stages via the analysis of the draft Law, the provision of recommendations, and sharing progressive foreign experience (Minenko 2021). The process of development of both the Ukrainian doctrine on administrative procedure and the draft LAP was significantly influenced by the German doctrine of Administrative Law (Bojko *et al.* 2017).

As stated in the explanatory note to draft LAP No. 3475, 'this draft Law was written in order to encourage efficient and quality level of the legislative regulation of the procedures of external governmental activity of the bodies of executive power and local self-government bodies, their officials and other subjects that are empowered by law to execute authorities' managerial functions, and protection of rights and legal interests of natural and legal persons in relations with the state'.

It is expected that the LAP, together with the Code on Judicial Administrative Proceedings of Ukraine (2005), would establish an efficient legal framework for the protection of the rights, freedoms, and legal interests of private persons in relations with public administration entities.

3.5.3. The Law of Ukraine on Administrative Procedure: Analysis of Key Provisions

3.5.3.1. The Structure and Scope of the LAP and Its Relationship to Other Laws

The LAP consists of 9 chapters and 100 articles that define the main rules on general administrative procedure. It should be noted that the structure of the Law is very similar to the codes on judicial proceedings in Ukraine.

The LAP regulates relations between public administration entities and private persons (natural persons and legal entities of private law) on the consideration and resolution of administrative cases by means of the adoption and execution of administrative acts.

Considering that the Law regulates only procedures that lead to issuing administrative acts, the rule-making procedure (which is traditionally considered one of the key types of administrative procedure in the Ukrainian doctrine of administrative law) and the procedure on the conclusion of administrative contracts are not subject to this Law. As to the rule-making procedure, the draft Law on Rule-Making Activity was approved on an initial basis in the first reading by the Verkhovna Rada of Ukraine on 16 November 2021. At the time of preparing this chapter, professionals are discussing the idea of drafting a law on the procedure for administrative contracts. This could take the form of an amendment to the Law of Ukraine on Administrative Procedure or a separate Law on Administrative Contracts.

There are still special laws that regulate certain administrative procedures. These administrative procedures are regulated by the LAP in the areas that are not regulated by special laws. For instance, the Law of Ukraine 'On Regulation of Construction Activity' does not regulate the procedure of the revocation of administrative acts in the construction sector (in particular, construction permits). In this area, the LAP shall be applied.

Thus, the LAP shall be considered a general legal act on administrative procedure, whereas other legal acts on certain administrative procedures are considered special laws on administrative procedure.

3.5.3.2. The Novelties in the Categorial Apparatus of the LAP

The LAP uses categories comprehensively elaborated by administrative law doctrine, in particular: administrative authority; administrative act; administrative case; administrative procedure; administrative proceedings; and functions of public administration.

The term 'administrative authority' is new for Ukrainian legislation. At the time of preparing this chapter, the terms 'subject of power', 'public authorities', and 'bodies of executive power' are used in relation to public administration entities. An administrative authority is defined by the LAP as 'a body of executive power, a body of power of the Autonomous Republic of Crimea, a local self-government body, their public official, or other subject empowered by law to perform public administration functions' (Art. 2, part 1, point 1). Thus, 'administrative authority' reflects the doctrinal term 'public administration entity'.

An administrative act is considered 'a decision or legally significant action of individual character approved (made) by an administrative authority in order to resolve a concrete case and aimed (directed) at obtaining, change, termination, or realisation of rights and/or obligations of a concrete person (persons)' (Art. 2, part 1, point 3). The following features of an administrative act can be distinguished on the basis of the provisions of the LAP:

(a) it is issued by the competent public administration entity (an administrative authority) in the frames of its competence;
(b) it is a result of the consideration of an individual (concrete) administrative case;
(c) it is a ground for obtaining, changing, terminating, or realising the rights and/or obligations of concrete persons;
(d) its addressees are clearly defined;
(e) it is valid until its execution (single-use validity);
(f) it is externally vectored.

Whereas the administrative procedure is understood as the procedure for the consideration and resolution of an administrative case, administrative proceedings are understood to represent the scope of the procedural actions taken by the administrative authority and the approved procedural decisions on the consideration and resolution of the case that leads to the approval and, in necessary cases, execution of the administrative act. A procedural action is defined as an action of the administrative authority made during the consideration of a case which does not lead to the final resolution of the case; a procedural decision is a decision of the administrative authority approved during the consideration of a case which does not lead to the final resolution of the case.

The LAP is based on the approach to the definition of the administrative process that dominated in the Ukrainian doctrine of administrative law for many decades. In contrast with the other types of legal processes – e.g., civil, criminal, and economic, which are judicial – the administrative process was broadly considered, and included both judicial and non-judicial (procedural) proceedings. Proceedings were considered to be within the scope of administrative stages, whereas these stages fall within the scope of administrative actions (administrative actions are the smallest element of administrative proceedings). After the approval of the Code on Judicial Administrative Proceedings of Ukraine, the administrative process started to be considered by some professionals as a purely judicial process, whereas the procedural activity of public administration entities was seen as an administrative procedure. At the time of preparing this chapter, this approach prevails. However, the structure of the administrative process within the scope of administrative proceedings was extrapolated to the structure of the administrative procedure.

The LAP uses the term 'functions of public administration'. This is the first example of the term 'public administration' being used in any legal act in Ukraine. The following functions of public administration are defined by this Law: rendering administrative services, inspecting (control, supervision) the performance of these activities, and resolving other cases upon the application of the person or upon the initiative of the administrative authority.

The Code on Judicial Administrative Proceedings of Ukraine operates with other terms, and its provisions shall be provided in accordance with the Law on Administrative Procedure. For instance, the term 'subject of powers' should be replaced with the term 'public administration entity' (or 'administrative authority' in certain cases), 'individual act' with 'administrative act', and 'power managerial functions' with 'functions of public administration'. The term 'administrative case' is used in both laws. To avoid misinterpretation, it would be better to make changes in the Code on Judicial Administrative Proceedings of Ukraine in order to replace the term 'administrative case' with, for example, the term 'judicial administrative case' (or 'administrative dispute').

3.5.3.3. The Key Principles of the Administrative Procedure

One of the key peculiarities of the LAP is the character of its framework. It does not simply provide for a list of the key principles of the administrative procedure and their definitions – it is a set of principles by itself. The principles of the administrative procedure are reflected in every provision of the Law.

The LAP is based on the following principles: the rule of law, legality and legal certainty, equality before law, reasonability, fairness (impartiality) of an administrative authority, integrity and prudence, proportionality, openness, timeliness and reasonable term, effectiveness, presumption of the legitimacy of the actions and requirements of a person, formality, safeguards for the right of a person to participate in an administrative proceeding, and safeguards for effective remedies (Art. 4–18). The administrative authority is governed by the principle of the rule of law, which means that human rights and freedoms are the highest values and determine the content and direction of the state activity (Art. 5).

While defining the principle of legality, the LAP introduces into the legislation the term 'discretionary powers' and stipulates the requirements on the use of discretionary powers by administrative authorities (Art. 6, part 3).

The principles of administrative procedure defined by the LAP are compatible with the modern European principles of administrative procedure elaborated, in particular, by: the Committee of Ministers of the Council of Europe in Resolution (77) 31 of 28 September 1977 on the protection of the individual in relation to the acts of administrative authorities (namely, the right to be heard, access to information, assistance and representation, statement of reasons, and indication of remedies); Article 6 of the ECtHR (1950) on the 'Right to a fair trial' (timeliness and reasonability of the consideration of administrative cases); and Article 41 of the EU Charter (2000) on the 'Right to good administration'.

The principles of administrative procedure are applicable not only to administrative procedures regulated by this Law. As already mentioned, the LAP regulates only the general administrative decision-making procedure. Certain administrative procedures are regulated by other legal acts (special laws). Administrative activity is also not limited only to administrative decision-making. Thus, the principles of administrative procedure defined by the LAP are applicable to all administrative procedures and other types of administrative activities of public administration entities, even though such activities are not regulated by this Law (Art. 4 part 2).

3.5.4. Administrative Proceedings Under the Law on Administrative Procedure

3.5.4.1. The Subjects of Administrative Proceedings

The subjects of administrative proceedings include administrative authorities, participants of the administrative procedure, and persons that contribute to the consideration of the administrative case.

It should be noted that the administrative authority responsible for the consideration of the administrative case is a compulsory subject of the administrative procedure. However, it is not a participant of the administrative procedure according to the LAP.

According to the Constitution of Ukraine (Art. 19, part 2), all public authorities, bodies of local self-government and their officials shall act on the basis, in the framework of, and by the means stipulated by the Constitution and laws of Ukraine (Constitution of Ukraine) Administrative authorities are bound by their competence, as defined by the Constitution and laws of Ukraine. The LAP regulates the competence dispute between administrative authorities (Art. 21).

To minimise the negative impact of frequent changes (reorganisation and liquidation of public authorities) to the system of public administration on the realisation and protection of the rights and interests of private persons in relations with public administration entities, the Law establishes the rules on the legal succession of an administrative authority (Art. 25).

The following persons are defined as participants of the administrative procedure: the addressee of the administrative decision and the interested person. The addressees of administrative decisions are the persons whose issue on the right, freedom, legal interest or obligation is resolved in the administrative act, including applicants, complainants, and persons regarding whom the administrative authority initiated the administrative proceedings. The interested person means any other person whose right, freedom, or legal interest is or could be negatively influenced by the administrative action. The category of persons that contribute to the consideration of an administrative case includes witnesses, experts, specialists, and interpreters.

Human-centrism is a key aspect of the LAP. The Law (Art. 28) stipulates the scope of very important rights of participants of administrative proceedings – in particular, the rights:

(a) to be heard before a negative decision is made;
(b) to have access to administrative case materials;
(c) to be informed about the administrative decision and its grounds;
(d) to be informed about the appeal procedure and to submit an appeal at any stage of the administrative procedure.

The right to be heard at any stage of the administrative procedure is crucial for the participants of the administrative procedure, especially when a negative decision can be made by the administrative authority. According to the Law, a participant of the administrative proceedings has the right to submit to the administrative authority their explanations, objections or evidence at any stage of the administrative procedure before the administrative act is issued. In case of hearings, this may occur by the day of or during the hearings.

The right to be informed about a decision and grounds of the decision is another important novelty of the Law that requires significant changes in the behaviour of public servants, who do not usually follow this principle in their activity. One could observe that such an obligation on the part of public servants will lead to the increase in their workload. However, on the one hand this will serve as a very important guarantee of the rights of private persons in the administrative procedure; on the other, it will simplify the tasks of public servants when proving the legality of their decisions if they are challenged in an administrative or judicial procedure.

The right of private persons to appeal against administrative action/inaction/decision and the possibility of its realisation at any stage of the administrative procedure will serve as a guarantee of the prompt protection of their rights, freedoms, and legal interests.

According to the LAP (Art. 28), the participants of administrative proceedings can request documents or data necessary for the consideration and resolution of their case. There is a corresponding obligation of the administrative authority to request documents and information from other authorities. In such cases, an administrative authority can request administrative collaboration (Art. 26), involving another administrative authority making one or several administrative actions within administrative proceedings based on the principles of reasonability and efficiency. This is a crucial provision of the Law, because previously the obligation to submit all necessary documents and data available from other public authorities was imposed on private persons, which made the administrative procedure longer and more complicated for them.

A person can participate in administrative proceedings in person and/or via their representative (except in cases defined by law) (Art. 31).

3.5.4.2. *The Stages of Administrative Proceedings*

Based on the provisions of the LAP, the following stages of administrative procedure can be defined:

(a) initiation of the administrative procedure;
(b) beginning of the administrative proceedings and preparation of the case for consideration;
(c) research of merits and assessment of evidence;
(d) consideration and resolution of the case;
(e) issuing the administrative act;
(f) execution of the administrative act;
(g) administrative complaint consideration (non-compulsory stage).

3.5.4.2.1. *The Initiation of Administrative Proceedings*

Two types of administrative procedure can be defined on the basis of the subject of their initiation:

(a) an administrative procedure initiated by an administrative authority (in particular, within their inspection, control or supervision powers) (intervening procedure); and
(b) an administrative procedure initiated by a private person – an applicant (declarative procedure).

The right of the administrative authority to initiate an administrative procedure differentiates administrative proceedings from judicial administrative proceedings, where the administrative courts do not have such a right. The following grounds for administrative procedure are defined by the LAP (Art. 37):

(a) the execution of the powers defined by law by the administrative authority;
(b) an event defined by law as a ground for issuing the administrative act has occurred;
(c) the violation of the human rights, freedoms, and legal interests of a person or a public interest has been detected by the administrative authority.

As to an event as a ground for issuing an administrative act, such an event shall be stipulated only by the law (not by the regulation). This is applicable, in particular, during a state of martial law. According to the Law of Ukraine 'On Legal Regime of Martial Law' (para. 19, Art. 8 (1)), the responsible public authorities can issue a decision on the evacuation of the population in case of an emergency situation or the risk of the emergence thereof, as well as from zones of armed conflict (areas of possible military action) to safe regions. This evacuation procedure is stipulated by Regulation of the Cabinet of Ministers of Ukraine No. 841 of 30 October 2013 (with amendments). This application can be submitted in oral or written form.

The LAP defines that the administrative procedure shall be completed within a reasonable time; however, this term cannot exceed 30 calendar days (or 45 days in case of hearings). The terms of certain administrative procedures can be defined by law. In case of the administrative complaint procedure, the administrative complaint shall be considered within 30 calendar days.

The LAP stipulates the principle of acquiescence in cases when an approval or opinion is needed. Thus, as referred to in Art. 58 of the Law, in order to obtain the approval or opinion of another administrative authority, the administrative authority contacts such an authority for this purpose and defines the reasonable time period for the reply. If the administrative authority is not provided with a rejection of approval, it shall be considered that approval was provided. It should be noted that the principle of acquiescence is not new for Ukrainian legislation. As referred to in Art. 45 of the LAP, the application is not subject to consideration if:

(a) it is an anonymous application (it is not possible to determine the applicant from its content);
(b) it is a repeated application (an application submitted to the same administrative authority by the same applicant on the same issue) where the previous application was considered on its merits, except in changes of circumstances (conditions) essential for the consideration of the case;
(c) it is an application regarding an issue that is the subject of judicial consideration at the moment of its submission to the administrative authority, or

regarding which there is a negative judgement, except in changes of circumstances (conditions) essential for the consideration of the case;
(d) the application relates to social relations that are not subject to this Law;
(e) the application does not contain the applicant's requests or includes non-normative lexicon and or/offensive statements;
(f) the application includes calls for the liquidation of the independence of Ukraine, forced changes to the constitutional regime, the violation of the sovereignty and territorial integrity of the state, state security, the unlawful seizure of the state power, war propaganda, acts of force, stirring interethnic, racial, or religious hostility, or the violation of human rights and freedoms or human health.

Another important provision of the LAP is related to the definition of the day of initiation of the administrative procedure. The application shall be registered by the administrative authority on the day of its submission. In case of irregularities or incomplete documents, the application shall be abandoned. However, if the applicant rectifies defects of documents in due time, the application shall be considered as submitted on the day of registration. This is especially important now, when IDP face difficulties in the registration and payment of social aid.

Due to the full-scale aggression of the Russian Federation, many people have had to move to safer territories inside Ukraine and have obtained the status of IDP. The public authorities had to find mechanisms to support these people. The Procedure of providing aid to IDP approved by Regulation of the Cabinet of Ministers of Ukraine No. 3232 of 20 March 2022 (which came into force on 22 May 2022) stipulates that in order to receive aid, the internally displaced person submits an application via the Diia portal. Many IDP from temporarily occupied territories registered in the Diia application in order to receive state aid. However, due to technical problems, many applications were not submitted from Diia to the social security authorities. When those people contacted the social security authorities, they were advised to submit their documents again. However, in such a situation, those people would receive money only from the new date of submission. The public authorities worked on technical problems and stated that all people would receive money from the date of their registration in Diia, despite the lack of such a norm in the current legislation of Ukraine (Dorosh 2022). In order to resolve this problem, the procedure mentioned above was amended with the following provision: if the lists of IDP registered for the state aid lack necessary information or include incorrect information, the social security authority, in case of the availability of communication, informs the internally displaced person included in the list prepared by the Ministry of Digital

Transformation of Ukraine regarding the necessity of submitting the necessary information in order to receive aid for certain periods. If the list lacks information about the person, the person additionally submits the information saved on their devices that confirms the fact of submission of the application via the Diia portal (p. 6 of the Procedure mentioned above). With the entry into force of the LAP, this situation will have a legal solution and these concerns will be avoided.

3.5.4.2.2. The Beginning of Administrative Proceedings and the Preparation of the Case for Consideration

Administrative proceedings begin from the date when:

(a) the responsible administrative authority receives the application;
(b) the responsible administrative authority approves the decision on the beginning of the administrative proceedings upon its own initiative or takes the first procedural action in the case. At this stage, the administrative authority shall check if all necessary materials are provided and make all necessary preparatory actions – in particular, requesting additional documents and data (Art. 47 of the LAP).

The involvement of the interested person and the peculiarities of proceedings involving a large number of persons (usually, more than 10 persons) are novelties of this Law. The lack of such provisions in the legislation has led to violations of the rights of persons that are not participants of concrete administrative procedures; however, their rights, freedoms, or legal interests are influenced or can be influenced by an administrative act issued within such an administrative procedure. Construction permits requested according to the Law of Ukraine 'On Regulation of Construction Activity' (2009) can be provided as an example of such violations: in many cases, inhabitants of houses situated near to new construction projects are not informed in advance about the construction, and cannot influence the administrative procedure in cases when they consider their rights violated by a positive decision regarding construction. With the entry into force of the LAP, they will be able to protect their rights within the administrative procedure, whether directly or indirectly (via their representatives or the representatives of civil society organisations).

3.5.4.2.3. The Examination of Merits and the Assessment of Evidence

According to the LAP, any factual data on the basis of which the administrative authority can define the existence or absence of circumstances important for the consideration of a case are considered as evidence in the administrative proceedings. The following are defined by the LAP (Art. 53 (2)):

(a) explanations of the participants of the administrative proceedings;
(b) documents;
(c) data from certain national electronic informational resources;
(d) electronic assessment outcomes;
(e) real evidence;
(f) explanations of the witnesses;
(g) the conclusions of experts, consultations, or the interpretations of specialists.

The Law introduces the institute of witnesses in the administrative procedure; this was not previously used in administrative proceedings. It is stipulated that upon the application of the participant of the administrative proceedings or from their personal initiative, as well as in cases defined by law, the administrative authority involves a person that supports the consideration of the case in the administrative procedure – in particular, a witness (Art. 29, part 2). The explanations of witnesses are defined among possible evidence (Art. 53, part 2, p. 6). The explanations of the witness are reports of a person about the circumstances known to them that are important for the consideration of the case. If the witness cannot provide the source of their information regarding certain circumstances, or their explanations are based on the report of another person, such witness explanations cannot be considered as evidence. It is not possible to establish on the basis of the explanations of a witness a circumstance or fact that, according to the legislation, should be reflected in a certain document. Other circumstances (facts) that cannot be established on the basis of the explanations of a witness are defined by the legislation. The witness can reject the submission of explanations regarding themselves, family members or close relatives that can lead to legal liability for themselves, their family members or close relatives.

3.5.4.2.4. Case Consideration and Resolution

According to the LAP (chapter 4), the following types of case consideration are prescribed:

(a) non-delayed case consideration and resolution (for simple cases);
(b) case consideration and resolution in written administrative proceedings (if non-delayed case consideration and resolution is impossible);
(c) case consideration and resolution with court hearings;
(d) case consideration and resolution in the automatic regime.

The LAP stipulates the requirements regarding the use of informational technologies in the administrative procedure (in particular, regarding the submission of the application in electronic format, the communication of participants with the administrative authority at different stages of the administrative proceedings, the use of evidence in electronic format, the fixation of administrative actions, issuing administrative acts in electronic format, the submission of complaints in electronic format, etc.).

The administrative authority shall inform the participant of the administrative procedure regarding the possible negative consequences of their absence in the proceedings and the non-submission of explanations and/or objections in the case – in particular, in case of submitting an administrative complaint.

The Supreme Court in its Ruling on administrative offences (*The Ruling of the Supreme Court*, Case No. 482/17), concluded that a person shall be duly informed about the time and place of the consideration of their case by the responsible public official. The multiplicity of ways of communication allows the public official to choose one or several methods that encourage the awareness of the person.

According to Art. 32 of the LAP, the participant of administrative proceedings, i.e., the person that supports the consideration of the case, shall be duly informed regarding the consideration of the case, and the administrative authority shall be ready to prove this.

According to Art. 66 of the LAP, the administrative authority can decide on the organisation of case hearings to encourage the impartial, objective, and fast consideration of a case. Hearings are conducted upon the request of the participant of the administrative proceedings if the participants of the administrative proceedings have adverse interests, or in other cases defined by law. The LAP (Art. 63 and 66) defines the circumstances where hearings cannot be conducted.

The LAP stipulates the procedural rights of the participants of the hearings (e.g., to submit oral and written explanations and/or objections on issues related to the case, to raise questions related to the case resolution, to submit documents and evidence, etc.).

The LAP defines the reasons for the stay (Art. 64) and termination of proceedings (Art. 65). When discussing the reasons for the stay of proceedings, it should be emphasised that according to Art. 10 of the LAP the participants of the administrative proceedings shall use their rights in good faith and not abuse them (in particular, in order to make the administrative proceedings longer).

3.5.4.2.5. The Issuance of the Administrative Act

The consideration of the case is completed by issuing the administrative act. The administrative act, in the meaning of the LAP, is characterised by the following features:

(a) it is issued by the administrative authority;
(b) it is issued as a result of the resolution of a concrete individual administrative case;
(c) it establishes rights, freedoms, legal interests, or imposes duties of concrete private persons;
(d) it contains expressions of a one-sided will (in contrast with administrative contracts);
(e) it has an external direction (outside the system of public administration; the addressees are private persons);
(f) it is issued according to the administrative procedure rules.

The administrative act is mostly issued in the written (electronic or paper) form. In cases defined by law, including the necessity of preventing risks to life, the health of citizens, property or public security, the administrative act can be issued in oral form (Art. 70 of the LAP). The oral form for an administrative decision is defined, in particular, by the Code of Ukraine on Administrative Offences (1984), which stipulates that a verbal warning can be used in cases of minor offences (Art. 22). The customs authorities of Ukraine can use the oral form for their decision in accordance with the law (Art. 19[1] of the Customs Code of Ukraine (1984)). Interim procedural decisions that do not lead to the approval of a final administrative act could be delivered in oral form following the principle of efficiency, in order to make the procedure simpler and faster, and in order to spend fewer resources. As to the use of the oral form for administrative decisions aimed at the prevention of risks to life, the health of citizens, property, or public security, it can be used by supervisory/control authorities and law enforcement authorities in particular. During the COVID-19 pandemic, a verbal request from responsible public officials to wear a face mask, if a person satisfied this request, could be considered as an appropriate form of administrative decision that did not require a subsequent written form. The oral form of administrative decision is especially relevant during the state of martial law, when the public authorities need to rapidly adopt decisions in emergency situations (in particular, a request to leave a building or vehicle, to change a route, etc.). In order to prevent abuses of power during the usage of the oral form for administrative decisions, the LAP establishes the obligation of public authorities to inform the addressee of the administrative decision that they may request the administrative decision in written form, which shall be done within 5 working days. One of the most important questions for citizens during the state of martial law is the form of administrative decisions while crossing the border. The migration authorities can allow or bar individuals from crossing the border based on the restrictions stipulated by the law (in particular, those applicable to men aged 18–60). According to the Ukrainian legislation (Art. 14 of the Law of Ukraine 'On Border Control' (2009)), the migration authority can refuse permission for crossing the border only via the approval of a decision in written form that shall include reasoning. The form of such a decision was recently changed by Decision of the Ministry of Internal Affairs of Ukraine No. 457 of 5 June 2023.

The Law defines strict requirements on the content of an administrative act (Art. 71). Thus, a written administrative act or an oral administrative act confirmed in written form shall be composed of the following parts: introductory part, statement of reasons, operative part, and conclusive part.

According to Art. 72 of the LAP, the statement of reasons for the administrative act in written form shall encourage the person to understand this act correctly and realise their right to challenge the administrative act. The administrative act, in particular, shall provide: the facts of the case; the content of documents and data considered during the consideration of the case; references to evidence or other case materials that are the basis for the conclusions of the administrative authority; the detailed legal assessment of the circumstances detected by the administrative authority; and the clear provision of conclusions developed on the basis of such a legal assessment of the circumstances.

It should be noted that the statement of reasons is not required in the administrative act if the administrative authority satisfied the application of the act; if the administrative act is not related to the rights, freedoms or legal interests of other persons; or if the administrative authority did not detect any violations of the legislation during the execution of its inspection (control, supervisory) powers.

As to the last exception, the current legislation of Ukraine (in particular, the Tax Code of Ukraine (2010)) also does not request the statement of reasons in such cases.

3.5.4.2.6. The Validity, Termination, and Nullity of an Administrative Act

As referred to in Art. 74 of the LAP, an administrative act enters into force regarding the participant of the administrative proceedings from the day when the respective person was informed about it, if another term of entering into force is not prescribed by law or by this administrative act. There are different methods of promulgation of the administrative act stipulated by the administrative authority according to law and depending on the number of addressees (Art. 75, part 1), including: hand delivery or sending by postal service (recommended as a letter with receipt); sending via e-mail or transferring via other means of electronic communication; a public announcement or promulgation according to legislative requirements; and oral communication in cases defined by law.

An administrative act involving a large number of persons (which is new in the Ukrainian legislation) shall be promulgated to such persons via the official website of the administrative authority and/or via the publication in print media of the information on the content of the decision, the procedure of familiarisation with the act, and the complaint procedure.

The LAP establishes the grounds and requirements for the termination of the administrative act that are specific for lawful and unlawful administrative acts, and provides the public authority that issued the administrative act with the opportunity to eliminate the mistake or to react to the changing situation. In particular, the administrative act can be terminated via the revocation of a lawful administrative act by the administrative authority that issued it, and this is new in the Ukrainian legislation.

As referred to in Art. 77 of the LAP, an administrative act is null if it includes clear significant drawbacks, in particular related to the necessary data, standardised form, lack of powers, or objective impossibility of execution.

The nullity of an administrative act can be recognised by the administrative authority at any time, or the person can request the recognition of the nullity of the administrative act directly from the administrative authority that issued the act, or can challenge it before the court. A null administrative act will not enter into force.

3.5.4.2.7. The Administrative Complaint Procedure

At the time of preparing this chapter, the main legislative provisions related to the administrative complaint procedure are included in the Law of Ukraine 'On Citizens' Petitions' (1996), primarily, Art. 16–19).

The regulations provided by the new LAP are more complex and detailed. The right to administrative complaint is held by a person who considers that their right, freedom or legal interest was infringed or can be infringed by the issued administrative act, or their right, freedom, or legal interests are influenced by the procedural decision, action, or inactivity of the administrative authority. Thus, it is possible to challenge not only final but also interim decisions – however, only in cases defined by the LAP. Administrative complaints regarding other interim procedural decisions and actions will be considered only after the approval of the administrative act.

An administrative complaint shall be submitted in written (electronic or paper) form; oral form is possible only in cases defined by law. The content of an administrative complaint is regulated by the LAP. The petition of a person that does not correspond to the legislative requirements regarding their form or content, but is related to the complaint by its content, shall be considered according to the rules of the administrative complaint (Art. 81, part 4).

The submission of the complaint shall suspend the administrative act upon the request of the complainant (except in cases defined by law). The same approach is used by the Tax Code of Ukraine (Art. 56, point 56.15). The Law of Ukraine 'On Citizens' Petitions' does not include such a provision. According to the Code on Judicial Administrative Proceedings of Ukraine, the submission of a complaint does not automatically lead to the suspension of the execution of the individual act being challenged. The suspension of the execution of the challenged individual act is defined as a method of provisional protection (Art. 117 of the Code). It is the right of the court to use this method upon the request of the complainant of the proceedings, or upon its own initiative based on the requirements stipulated by the Code. The Supreme Court in its ruling (*The Ruling of the Supreme Court,* Case No. 3Д/460/2/20), stated that the court shall assess the reasonability of the arguments of the complainant regarding the use of concrete methods of provisional protection with the consideration of the following aspects: the reasonableness, reasonability, and adequacy of the requirements of the complainant concerning the provisional protection; the encouragement of the balancing of interests of parties, as well as other participants of judicial proceedings; the existence of a connection between the concrete method of provisional protection and the subject of the complaint requirements, in particular, if such a method is able to encourage the real execution of the judgement in case of the satisfaction of the claim; the possibility of problems with the execution or non-execution of the judgement if the security of the complaint would not be ensured; and the prevention of the infringement of the rights and legal interests of persons and participants of these judicial proceedings connected with the use of such methods. The position of the Supreme Court is based on the provisions of the Code on Judicial Administrative Proceedings, as well as on Recommendation No. R (89) 8 of the Committee of Ministers to Member States on Provisional Court Protection in Administrative Matters (Adopted by the Committee of Ministers on 13 September 1989 at the 428th meeting of the Ministers' Deputies).

An administrative act can be annulled only as a result of the administrative complaint procedure or administrative judicial proceedings. It can be annulled as a whole or in part in case of the violation of the norms of substantive law; however, as to the procedural norms, only severe violations (including competence) can lead to the annulation of the administrative act. An administrative act can also be annulled because of the incorrect or incomplete detection of the circumstances of the case that led to the approval of an unlawful administrative act (Art. 85, part 2 of the LAP). The lack of the motivation element in the administrative act (when it is compulsory according to the law) is the reason for the annulation of the administrative act (Art. 85, part 3 of the LAP).

3.5.4.2.8. The Revocation of the Administrative Act or Its Recognition as Invalid

The issue of whether the individual acts of local-self-government bodies are subject to future changes was subject to consideration by the Constitutional Court of Ukraine and the Supreme Court. The Constitutional Court of Ukraine, in its Decision of 16 April 2009 No. 7-рп/2009, concluded that 'non-normative legal acts of local-self-government bodies are valid until their execution; therefore, they cannot be annulled or changed by the local-self-government authority after their execution'. The Supreme Court followed this approach in a number of rulings (e.g., *The Ruling of the Supreme Court*, Case No. 21- 64a13; *The Ruling of the Supreme Court*, Case No. 21-5459a15; *The Ruling of the Supreme Court*, Case No. 182/2428/16-a2-a/0182/102/2016) and concluded that 'the local-self-government bodies cannot annul their previous decisions, amend them if the legal relations connected with the realisation of certain subjective rights and legal interests arose on their basis, and subjects of certain legal relations are against their amendments or termination'.

According to the LAP, the administrative authority that issued the administrative act has a right to revoke it or to recognise it as invalid in order to renovate legality and/or protect the public interests in the cases and according to the procedure defined by the law. It shall be emphasised that a lawful administrative act can be revoked and an unlawful act recognised as invalid.

There are the following peculiarities of the revocation procedure regarding administrative acts:

(a) it can be used only in relation to a lawful administrative act;
(b) it can be used only by the administrative authority that issued such an act;
(c) it can be initiated by the administrative authority that issued the administrative act or by an addressee of the administrative act;
(d) as a general rule, an administrative act can be revoked only for the good of a private addressee of the administrative act (except of cases defined by law);
(e) it can be used only before the completion of the execution of the administrative act;

(f) it can be used retroactively;
(g) it cannot be used if the same administrative act needs to be approved again or if revocation is against the law.

An example of the revocation of a lawful act that can be provided is a possible situation with the revocation of lawful construction permits issued to private persons for the purposes of construction of temporary dwellings for IDP (public interests prevail).

The administrative act is unlawful if it does not correspond to the requirements defined by the law, in particular:

(a) if it was issued by an incompetent administrative authority or this authority unlawfully used discretionary powers;
(b) if it contradicts the legislative requirements regarding the form and content of an administrative law;
(c) if it violates the norms of substantive law;
(d) if it does not follow the principles of administrative procedure (Art. 87, part 2 of the LAP).

For instance, based on such provisions of the LAP, a construction permit issued with violations of the legislative requirements can be recognised as invalid.

3.5.4.2.9. The Execution of the Administrative Act

The legislation of Ukraine (first of all, the Law of Ukraine 'On Enforcement Proceedings' (2003)) mostly concentrates on the execution of judgements.

The LAP regulates the execution of administrative acts. If an administrative act was not voluntarily executed by the addressee of the administrative act, the administrative authority shall decide on the use of the following enforcement actions (in the order provided):

(a) taking actions at the expense of the obligated person by another person;
(b) imposing a monetary penalty for the non-execution of the administrative act;
(c) direct impact.

If an administrative decision was not executed by the obligated person and there is not another person that can execute this decision at the expense of the obligated person, the administrative authority shall impose a fine on the obligated person according to the requirements established by the law (minimum and maximum fines are established by the LAP for natural persons and legal entities separately). At the same time, the administrative authority defines the new term for the execution of the administrative act. If the administrative act is not executed again, the administrative authority will impose a fine in the same amount or at a double rate. An administrative decision on imposing a fine is considered as an enforcement order and is subject to the enforcement procedure established by the enforcement legislation (Art. 96).

A decision on imposing enforcement actions can be challenged by the obliged person in an administrative complaint procedure or before the court.

3.5.5. The New Administrative Procedure: Possible Challenges and Solutions

The revocation of a lawful administrative act is a novelty of the LAP, and the efficiency of certain legislative provisions will be assessed only in practice. There are protection mechanisms for the rights of private persons in case of the revocation of a lawful administrative act for the prejudice of the person in the LAP; however, the risk of negative consequences for the private person in this case still exists, especially in case of usage of the revocation procedure for the protection of public interests.

An efficient administrative complaint procedure is an essential part of the legal mechanism for the protection of human rights, freedoms, and legal interests in relations with public administration entities, and has many benefits for private persons in comparison with judicial dispute resolution. It is faster, less harmful, and free of charge, helps to decrease the court workload and saves money for private persons which would otherwise be spent on court fees. However, all of these benefits would be eliminated in case of the inefficiency of the administrative complaint procedure.

Some of the rights of private persons in the administrative complaint procedure are prescribed by the legislation in force. E.g., certain aspects of the right to be heard are stipulated by laws; however, applicants can only seldom enjoy this. In particular, the Law of Ukraine 'On Petitions of Citizens' (Art. 18) stipulates that the complainant in the administrative complaint procedure has the rights: to personally express their arguments to the person that assessed the application or the complaint and participate during the assessment of the complaint or the application; to access the files of the assessment; to submit additional materials or to insist on their request by the authority responsible for the consideration of the application or the complaint; and to be present during the consideration of the application or the complaint. However, they are not guaranteed in practice (e.g., within the tax complaint procedures, even if the complainant requests to be provided with the opportunity to be present during the consideration of the complainant, the tax authority of a higher level can simply ignore this request and the complainant will receive only a decision on the consideration of the complaint)

According to the LAP, the complaint shall be submitted to the administrative authority that approved the administrative act or procedural decision and/or performed the procedural action, or that has been inactive. Then, the complaint, together with the case materials, is to be sent by this administrative authority to the subject responsible for its consideration (Art. 82, part 2). In the current legislation of Ukraine, there are different approaches to the definition of the subject the complaint is to be submitted to – to the authority that issued the administrative act/performed an action or was inactive, or to the authority of the higher level. In particular, according to the Law of Ukraine 'On Licensing of Types of Economic Activity' (2015), complaints are to be submitted to the Expert Appellate Council in licensing, which is the permanent collegial authority of the special competent licensing authority. The abovementioned approach is based on the argument that the body that issued the challenged decision/performed the challenged action has to prepare the case for consideration and submit it to the higher-level body for consideration. It is expected that such a procedure will save the time for the consideration of the complaint. However, in this case there is a risk that the administrative authority that issued the challenge decision/performed the challenged action will try to influence the consideration of the case in a non-appropriate manner.

As referred to in Art. 7, part 4 of the Law of Ukraine 'On Citizens' Petitions', it is prohibited to send citizens' complaints to the bodies or public officials that performed the actions or issued the decisions that are being challenged. The Tax Code of Ukraine (Art. 56) also defines that a complaint on the decisions of tax authorities shall be submitted to the tax authority of a higher level, not to the tax authority that approved the decision under question. The LAP goes further. As was mentioned, the administrative authority that issued the challenged administrative act can be even the subject of the consideration of the administrative complaint. This is possible if there is no administrative authority of a high level and the administrative complaint consideration commission is established by the administrative authority that issued the challenged administrative act (Art. 79, part 3 of the LAP). However, the commission is not a complaint consideration authority; its decisions have only a recommendatory character. Thus, the final decision regarding the complaint will be issued by the same authority that issued the challenged administrative act. There is a strong doubt as to whether such a decision will be in favour of the complainant. Considering the above, it is highly debatable that the new administrative complaint procedure regulation is adequately regulated by the LAP.

During the state of martial law in Ukraine, some principles and instruments defined by the LAP could be applicable to protect private and public interests. In particular, some restrictions were approved regarding rendering administrative services. The terms of rendering administrative services in the fields of the state registration of legal entities, natural persons and entrepreneurs, the state registration of property rights on real estate and their restrictions, the state registration of the acts of civil status by subject that act during the state of martial law, administrative services by subjects of their rendering, and terms of issuing permission documents (with the exception of administrative services in the field of construction defined by the Law of Ukraine 'On Construction Regulation') were terminated by Regulation of the Cabinet of Ministers of Ukraine No. 165 of 28 February 2022. Special provisions regarding the state registration and functioning of the single and state registers maintained by the Ministry of Justice of Ukraine during martial law were included in Regulation of the Cabinet of Ministers of Ukraine No. 209 of 6 March 2022. These restrictions will be valid during the period of martial law and one month after its termination.

3.5.6. Interim findings

The approval of the LAP is a significant step towards the systematisation of administrative procedural legislation in Ukraine. It provides a general legal framework for decision-making, and is expected to become an effective instrument for the protection of the rights of private persons in relations with administrative authorities and to play a vital role in the organisation of public administration activities after the end of the war of aggression in order to protect citizens' rights, rebuild the ruined economy, and attract investment in Ukraine.

The scope of rights of private persons in relations with public administration entities has been broadened and specified in the Law, in comparison with the current legislation. Special attention is paid to the right to be heard, the right to access to the case records, and the right to submit an administrative complaint.

The LAP introduces some new important institutes – in particular, competence dispute resolution, the legal succession of administrative authority, the discretionary powers of administrative authorities, and the revocation of an administrative act.

The LAP provides detailed regulation of each stage of administrative procedure, including the peculiarities of the execution of administrative decisions (which is of high importance considering that the current law enforcement legislation mostly aims at the execution of judgements).

Despite positive changes that will be brought to the Ukrainian legislation by the LAP, there are also challenges that should be taken into consideration. In particular, the institutes of witnesses in administrative procedures and the revocation of a lawful administrative act by the administrative authority, which are new, require serious attention to stimulate the protection of the human rights and legal interests of the participants of administrative procedures.

The administrative authority that issued a challenged administrative decision can be the subject of the consideration of a complaint regarding this act if there is no administrative authority of a higher level and the administrative complaint consideration commission is established by such an authority. However, the decisions of such a commission are of a recommendatory character, which means that the final decision in administrative complaint proceedings is to be issued by the administrative authority that issued the challenged administration act.

The LAP is not a single act that would regulate administrative procedures. Still, the special laws that govern certain types of administrative procedure would remain in force. This means that some overlapping and divergent interpretations could arise after the LAP becomes applicable.

The main provisions of the Law of Ukraine on Administrative Procedure enter into force on 15 December 2023. Until then, the responsible public authorities shall amend and issue their normative legal acts according to this law and approve the regulations necessary for its implementation. Considering the large number of legislative acts that regulate administrative procedures at the time of preparing this chapter, significant work is to be done to eliminate drawbacks and to minimise problems during the implementation of the Law in practice. This adaptation period shall be also used for the purposes of raising the awareness of both public officials and private persons regarding the rights and obligations stipulated by this Law.

The emergency situation that arose in Ukraine due to the full-scale aggression of the Russian Federation led to difficulties in the realisation of the rights and legal interests of private persons in relations with public administration authorities (e.g., regarding the registration of IDP for the purposes of receiving state aid or obtaining documents, restricted access to administrative services, etc.). During the state of martial law, the principles and mechanisms of the LAP will be applicable with some necessary restrictions (e.g., measures for the protection of objects of critical infrastructure, or restrictions regarding free movement, choice of place of residence, protection of state secrets, etc.) stipulated in accordance with the Constitution of Ukraine (Art. 64), the Law of Ukraine 'On Legal Regime of Martial Law' (e. g., Art. 8, 12–1, 20), and Decree of the President of Ukraine No. 64/2022 'On Introduction of Martial Law' of 24 February 2022.

3.6. Ensuring and Protecting Human Rights in Healthcare in Times of War: The Ukrainian Experience

3.6.1. The Context

An individual's health status greatly influences their life expectancy and quality of life, along with the possibility of their self-fulfilment. The health status of a population is an important factor of state-building and national security (Svintsytsky 2013, pp. 7–13), success, and the sustainable development of a state. The place of the right to health among other human rights has, therefore, become more prominent, and its connection with civil and political rights, as well as with other social, economic, and cultural rights, has become even closer.

The protection of the right to health is a key task of national health systems. At the same time, the implementation of this task requires ensuring other rights, the exercise of which is connected with healthcare.

In times of health emergencies – especially war, which is regarded as a public health emergency (Goto *et al.* 2022) – ensuring and protecting human rights within healthcare acquires a special significance and faces particular difficulties. The Ukrainian experience of overcoming such difficulties may be of importance not only for Ukraine, which must rebuild its healthcare system after the consequences of the full-fledged war of aggression unleashed by the Russian Federation against Ukraine, but also for other countries whose healthcare systems operate in a volatile and unstable world and, unfortunately, may be confronted with armed conflicts, natural disasters, and other public health emergencies.

This study considers the current human rights landscape of Ukrainian healthcare, attempts to assess some of the measures taken by the Ukrainian government and other institutions and organisations to respond to war-induced challenges for the protection of human rights in healthcare, and ponders the prospects of such protection.

3.6.2. The Right to Life and the Right to Personal Integrity in the Context of Human Rights in Healthcare

War always brings death, injury, devastation, and other tragic consequences. The evil that has been unleashed in Ukraine by Russia's aggression is the most significant seen in Europe since World War II. The most vital, non-derogable rights to life and to the integrity of a person are closely connected with the right to health, and they are also the rights that are most severely violated during war. The death and suffering of children are the most horrible consequences of war. As of 29 October 2023, 510 Ukrainian children were dead, 1,139 wounded,

1,995 missing, and 19,546 deported or forcibly displaced. As mentioned on the Children of War (2023) platform, 'it is impossible to establish the exact number of injured children due to active hostilities and the temporary occupation of a part of Ukrainian territory'. Based on the information of the Mariupol City Council (relocated to territory under Ukrainian Government control), the Ukrainian Independent Information Agency (hereafter – the UNIAN) reports that at least 147 children were killed by Russia's occupiers during the siege of the city of Mariupol in the Donetsk oblast, which lasted until May 2022 (Andalitska 2023).

The Independent International Commission of Inquiry on Ukraine (hereafter – the IICIU), which investigated the events in the regions of Kyiv, Chernihiv, Kharkiv and Sumy in late February and March 2022 pursuant to UN Human Rights Council Resolution S-34/1, found that since March 2022, violations of human rights and the IHL had been committed against people's personal integrity in the towns and settlements occupied by Russian armed forces, including: summary executions, torture, ill-treatment, sexual and gender-based violence, unlawful confinement and detention in inhumane conditions, and forced deportations (IICIU 2022).

Unleashing this war of aggression and conducting hostilities resulted in the loss of life and immense suffering of many Ukrainians, and the Russian Federation has violated fundamental rules of international law. Such rules include but are not limited to those stipulated in Article 6 of the International Covenant on Civil and Political Rights safeguarding the right to life, because, as stated in para. 70 of the UNHRC General Comment No. 36, 'parties engaged in acts of aggression as defined in international law, resulting in deprivation of life, violate ipso facto Article 6 of the Covenant' (UNHRC 2019).

On 2 March 2022, the UNGA adopted resolution A/ES-11/L.1, whereby it deplored in the strongest terms the aggression by the Russian Federation against Ukraine and demanded that the Russian Federation immediately, completely and unconditionally withdraw all of its military forces from the territory of Ukraine within its internationally recognised borders. Despite the requirements of international law and calls from the international community, the Russian Federation continues its war of aggression against Ukraine. Among other hardships and grievances, the war has caused 'persistent and intensifying public health challenges' (Simoneau and Khan 2022).

Despite all of these challenges, Ukraine has performed its positive obligations to protect human lives and personal integrity deriving from the International Bill of Human Rights, the ECHR, and other international instruments to which Ukraine is a party. Such obligations extend to certain 'health-related' duties, e.g., the duty to undertake measures 'to fight the stigmatization associated with disabilities and diseases, including sexually transmitted diseases, which hamper access to medical care', measures for 'improving access to medical examinations and treatments designed to reduce maternal and infant mortality', and other measures required to comply with the obligations enshrined in General Comment No. 36 (UNHRC 2019). Indeed, health-related violations often endanger individuals' lives and personal integrity and require measures pertaining to the healthcare domain. The inverse is also true: violations of the right to life and the right to personal integrity (or attempts to commit such violations) also infringe upon a person's health.

3.6.3. Ensuring the Resilience of the Healthcare System as a Prerequisite for Protecting Human Rights in Healthcare

3.6.3.1. No Derogation From the Right to Health During the Period of Martial Law

The commitment of the state to ensuring the right to health is the key issue arising in the public health context in times of war when normal legal regulation gives way to a special legal regime (that of martial law) and to wartime legal mechanisms.

In connection with the military aggression of the Russian Federation against Ukraine, on 24 February 2022, the President of Ukraine issued a decree imposing martial law in Ukraine that was then approved by the relevant law as required by the Constitution of Ukraine. Afterwards, the martial law period was extended several times.

The Constitution of Ukraine includes articles that provide for rights and freedoms which may *not* be temporarily limited under the conditions of martial law or a state of emergency. Article 49 of the Constitution of Ukraine, which guarantees the right to healthcare and medical assistance, is *not* included in said list. Thus, the Constitution of Ukraine does *not* prohibit the temporary limitation of the right to healthcare and medical assistance in case of the imposition of martial law.

It is notable, however, and should be positively assessed, that *no derogation* from said right has taken place. Thus, the Order of the President of Ukraine 'On the Imposition of Martial Law' did not impose any limitations on the right to healthcare and medical assistance for the period of martial law. The Ukrainian state has done much to ensure the provision of practical opportunities for exercising the abovementioned right.

3.6.3.2. *The Underlying Determinants of the Right to Health During Wartime and Their Protection in Ukraine*

The right to health – as provided for by international instruments, particularly the International Covenant on Economic, Social and Cultural Rights – unfolds itself through health determinants, i.e., health services-related and non-medical factors affecting individual and population health. Pursuant to the interpretation given by the UN Committee on Economic, Social and Cultural Rights (hereafter – the CESCR) in General Comment No. 14, 'The Right to the Highest Attainable Standard of Health (Art. 12)', the right to health shall be understood as 'an inclusive right extending not only to timely and appropriate health care but also to the underlying determinants of health, such as access to safe and potable water and adequate sanitation, an adequate supply of safe food, nutrition and housing, healthy occupational and environmental conditions, and access to health-related education and information, including on sexual and reproductive health' (CESCR 2000).

Russia's war against Ukraine has negatively affected all determinants of health, which has consequently resulted (and will continue to result) in the deterioration of the health of many individuals and of the population.

For example, according to the United Nations International Children's Emergency Fund (hereafter – the UNICEF), 1.4 million people were left without access to safe water, and 4.6 million people experienced limited access to it within the first 7 weeks of the full-fledged invasion of Ukraine by the Russian Federation (UNICEF 2022). In Ukraine, difficulties with access to safe water were experienced even before the war, but they have become more perceptible since its onset.

On 21 February 2022, just a few days before Russia's full-fledged invasion, the draft Law of Ukraine 'On the Nationwide target program 'Potable water of Ukraine' for 2022–2026', adopted by the Supreme Rada (parliament) of Ukraine, was submitted to the President of Ukraine for signature. It has now become evident that this draft law needs improvements accounting for new challenges, as emphasised by experts, civil society activists and representatives of municipal authorities (Ukrainian Climate Network 2022). It should be noted that the Ukrainian government and municipal authorities closely cooperate with international organisations (WHO, UNICEF, etc.) to resolve the water supply problem. As of June 2023, UNICEF has provided access to safe water for 4,649,974 people, including almost 1 million children, since the beginning of the full-fledged war (UNICEF 2023).

One should mention the deterioration of environmental conditions and the damage inflicted to the environment of Ukraine by the acts of Russia's invaders that constitute a blatant violation of the rules of international law. Not only Ukraine, but also the entire international community shuddered at the destruction of the Kakhovsky dam committed by Russia's occupiers, resulting in damage to soil and soil cover, water pollution, the destruction of the flora and fauna of the flooded area, changes to the Black Sea climatic region, damage to the Ukrainian agricultural sector, etc. (Malashchuk and Smolenska 2023, pp. 104–106). This act created serious threats to the epidemiological safety of both the flooded region and the entirety of Ukraine (Pavlenko 2023, p. 85). There are grounds to believe that the restart of the epidemiological system created by the newly adopted Law of Ukraine 'On the Public Health System' will contribute to reducing the abovementioned threats. In turn, laying down foundations of the public health system that, together with the system of provision of medical care, form the Ukrainian healthcare system, shall foster the resilience of the latter.

3.6.3.3. Measures to Ensure the Resilience of the Ukrainian Healthcare System in the Context of Human Rights Protection

The vitality of the Ukrainian healthcare system during Russia's aggression against Ukraine will certainly be thoroughly examined by scholars and healthcare managers. While facing the war, the healthcare system has proven its persistence, manageability, and ability to adapt to the challenging conditions and to generally ensure the healthcare servicing of the population.

The factors that conditioned the resilience of the healthcare system and the possibility to protect the right to health and other health-related human rights during wartime include: the practice of functioning in non-optimal conditions; the experience of struggling with COVID-19; the steps taken towards reforming the Ukrainian healthcare system both before and during the full-fledged war of aggression; other appropriate legislative and administrative solutions, including the simplification of regulatory procedures; the close interaction of the healthcare sector with other sectors of the national economy and spheres of activity; the heroism of Ukrainian healthcare workers, as well as the efforts of a considerable part of society; and strong international support.

Since the first days of the full-fledged war, the Ministry of Health of Ukraine (hereafter – the MOH) has managed to ensure due health governance by ensuring the uninterrupted work of its departments, the National Health Services of

Ukraine,[12] the State Service of Ukraine on Medicines and Drugs Control,[13] and the state enterprises and institutions that belonged to the MOH's area of governance. Healthcare facility managers were required to ensure the uninterrupted provision of medical services during the martial law period.

On 24 February 2022, the first day of Russia's full-scale invasion, the MOH of Ukraine established temporary measures to be introduced at healthcare institutions in order to ensure their preparedness for the provision of medical services to the injured. The relevant MOH order prescribed that state and municipally owned healthcare facilities should ensure the full provision of emergency care, prepare additional surgical teams for providing medical aid to the injured, suspend planned hospitalisations (except in cases stated therein), increase the part of healthcare services provided with the use of telemedicine, etc. In less than a month, planned hospitalisations and operations were renewed in many regions of Ukraine based on amendments to said order and on the situation at healthcare facilities (Slovo i Dilo 2022).

Such a rapid renewal of the provision of routine healthcare services certainly contributed to the proper exercise of the right to health. However, similarly to the peak of the COVID-19 pandemic, the problem of pent-up demand for healthcare services, especially in areas of active warfare, has remained. Notably, the majority of the above-mentioned measures were introduced at the beginning of the COVID-19 pandemic. Ukrainian healthcare officials point out that the struggle against COVID-19 prepared the Ukrainian healthcare system to respond to any emergency (Husak 2022).

Since the beginning of the full-fledged war, Russian aggressors have attacked healthcare infrastructure and personnel on numerous occasions. As of 30 November 2023, 1,419 attacks on the Ukrainian healthcare system were registered in the World Health Organization (hereafter – the WHO) Surveillance

---

12 The National Health Services of Ukraine is a central executive body, the main functions of which *inter alia* include the implementation of state policy in the sphere of state financial guarantees for the heathcare servicing of the population and the performance of the function of the purchaser of medical services and pharmaceutical products under the program of state financial guarantees.

13 The State Service of Ukraine on Medicines and Drugs Control is a central executive body that implements state policy in the sphere of quality control and safety of medicines, including medical immunobiological medicines, medical equipment and pharmaceutical products, as well as the circulation of narcotic drugs, psychotropic substances and precursors, counteractions to their illicit trafficking, and state policy in the sphere of the donation of blood and its components.

System, including 1,252 attacks that impacted healthcare facilities, 189 attacks that impacted healthcare transport, and 123 attacks that impacted healthcare personnel (WHO 2023).

The war has been extremely hard on healthcare facilities located in active war zones. Many healthcare facilities have experienced an influx of patients – both servicepersons and civilians – with bullet and shrapnel wounds. Healthcare professionals working at such facilities have had to perform their duties in difficult conditions, often with risk to their lives. For instance, medical workers at Kyiv city clinical hospital No. 7 – which is located near Kyiv suburbs in which there was fierce fighting at the beginning of the full-fledged war, and which was itself hit by Russian rocket fire – dwelled in the hospital for a month and a half, providing medical services to patients even in bomb shelters (Kyiv City Council, Kyiv City State Administration 2022). Most healthcare professionals stayed in their posts, though some (mostly female) moved to safer regions of Ukraine or fled abroad, evacuating their children. Immediate legal and public administration responses were provided to ensure healthcare workforce capacity.

The MOH of Ukraine allowed foreign medical professionals and intern doctors to become involved in the provision of medical care to the injured. Measures were taken to send volunteer medical workers to municipal healthcare institutions located in active war zones. These interim solutions, however, were questionable from the viewpoint of compliance with the existing laws and the rules of legal technique. The majority of outstanding issues were substantially resolved by adopting the Law of Ukraine 'On Introducing Changes to Some Laws of Ukraine Regarding the Increase of Accessibility of Medical and Rehabilitation Care During the Martial Law Period' on 29 July 2022, which, *inter alia*, extended legislative opportunities for involving volunteers (including foreign healthcare professionals) in the provision of medical and rehabilitative care and using telemedicine for the provision of such care during the period of martial law.

The situation in safer regions of Ukraine was also difficult, as the need to ensure access to healthcare to people who moved there from active war zones and neighbouring areas (internally displaced persons, hereafter – IDPs) appeared. According to the results of a general population survey conducted by the International Organisation for Migration (hereafter – IOM), 'as of 16 March 2022, 14.7 % of the general population are currently internally displaced within Ukraine, equivalent to 6.48M individuals' (IOM 09–16.03.2022). Accounting both for the Ukrainians who returned to their places of permanent residence and for new internal migrants, the IOM estimated the number of IDPs at over 6.64 million individuals as of 23 July 2022 (IOM 17–23.07.2022).

Discussing the issue of ensuring the access of IDPs to healthcare, it is necessary to mention that the Ukrainian healthcare system has been in a state of transformation. The ongoing healthcare reform that, *inter alia*, reformatted primary care, allows individuals to select a primary care physician by submitting the relevant declaration to the primary care provider regardless of the place of permanent residence of the patient. The chosen primary care physician then performs diagnostics and treatment of the most common diseases, carries out vaccination, monitors the patient's health, and sends them for specialised care to be provided at the expense of the State budget if needed for medical reasons. In March 2022, the MOH provided that rendering primary care, care in emergency conditions, and vaccination (according to the vaccinations calendar) to IPDs shall not require the resubmission of declarations on physician selection by such patients (Order of the MOH of 17.03.2022 No. 496 'Some Issues of the Provision of Primary Medical Care under the Conditions of Martial Law'). This appears to have been helpful, especially in cases when the patients and/or their attending primary care physicians have changed their place of residence, though the procedure for changing the selected physician is not difficult. Thus, the steps taken during the healthcare reform and the use of the possibilities that it provided largely contributed to the resilience of the Ukrainian healthcare system. The head of the National Health Services of Ukraine, N. Husak, pointed out that the Ukrainian healthcare system has survived the challenge of the war due to said transformation (Interfax-Ukraine 06.05.2022).

Under the conditions of martial law, especially at the beginning of the full-fledged war, the simplification of bureaucratic procedures was the key regulatory trend. This particularly related to the right to conduct medical practice, the accreditation of healthcare providers, etc. This contributed to ensuring the largely normal work of healthcare institutions (to the extent that this possible during the wartime period) which, in turn, positively influenced the rights of patients and healthcare professionals.

3.6.4. Patients and Healthcare Professionals' Rights in Times of War: A Few Considerations

Ukrainian legislation provides for a list of patients' rights that is nearly as complete as that recognised globally and at the European level – particularly by the World Medical Law Association Declaration of Lisbon on the Rights of the Patient, the European Charter of Patients' Rights, etc. These rights are stipulated by the Civil Code of Ukraine, the Law of Ukraine 'On Fundamentals of the Legislation of Ukraine on Healthcare' (hereafter – the Law on Fundamentals), the Law of Ukraine 'On the State Financial Guarantees of Healthcare Servicing of the Population', and other laws, including special laws governing the provision of certain types of healthcare (e.g., the Law of Ukraine 'On Psychiatric Care').

In Ukraine, the low level of systematisation of patients' rights, the lack of effective procedures for the exercise of such rights, and insufficient practice in their implementation pose an issue. Certain steps to improve the situation have been taken, though they have been somewhat fragmented. Notably, efforts to properly ensure patients' rights did not stop with the beginning of the war full-fledged war; only the needs and priorities changed, though some issues became more evident.

The main challenge was to ensure the right to access healthcare services, especially for vulnerable categories of patients. People with disabilities – who, as of 1 January 2021, constituted 2.703 million persons (Radio Svoboda 2021) – are among the most vulnerable parts of the population. At the beginning of the war, many people with disabilities, especially those who appeared to be in territories experiencing active hostilities, faced grave problems with access to healthcare and other basic services, and their lives were exposed to additional risks because of their low mobility or other health conditions.

Ukrainian authorities and the personnel of hospitals and boarding houses took efforts to evacuate persons with disabilities who stayed or lived there. The evacuation of people with disabilities (including children) who lived with their families, however, sometimes became the business of such families, volunteers, or persons with disabilities themselves (Ratsybarska 2022). The fate of persons with disabilities (especially those who stayed in psychiatric hospitals, psycho-neurological boarding houses, etc.) located in the territories temporarily occupied by the Russian Federation often appeared tragic.

According to the Law of Ukraine 'On Ensuring Rights and Freedoms of Internally Displaced Persons', such persons are entitled to the full extent of necessary medical care to be provided by state or communal healthcare institutions, although in practice, especially at the beginning of the full-fledged war, some persons with disabilities found themselves without the medicines or medical products they needed (OHCHR 2022).

The Ukrainian government has taken measures to ensure uninterrupted access to essential medicine and necessary treatment to patients with chronic diseases during the period of martial law. Thus, for example, according to information of the National Health Service of Ukraine, in 2022, persons who lived with diabetes could receive insulin drugs as they were among the 72 drugs included in the Drugs Reimbursement Registry within the program of state financial guarantees (where 45 insulin drugs are provided completely free of charge). This program is implemented by nearly 11,000 drug stores throughout Ukraine in accordance with the prescription of an endocrinologist or a primary care physician, regardless of the place of location of such a physician and/or the institution by which they are employed (Kyiv Oblast Military Administration 2022).

At the same time, the Ukrainian Parliament Commissioner for Human Rights, Dmytro Lubinets, pointed out in his annual Report on the Observance and Protection of Human Rights and Freedoms in Ukraine in 2022 that the program of state financial guarantees 'does not fully represent packages of the priority services that are of paramount importance during the war and post-war period' (Lubinets 2022).

With all of this, considerable progress has been made in the inclusion of drugs and treatment methods, including innovative solutions, in the program of state financial guarantees. For instance, in 2022–2023, an expanded neonatal genetic screening method allowing 21 hereditary and/or rare diseases to be detected in newborns was included in the program of state financial guarantees (Order of the MOH of Ukraine of 04.08.2022 'On Introducing Expanded Neonatal Screening in Ukraine').

Another example of ensuring patients' access to healthcare that is recognised as a core component of the right to health (WHO 2023) and promoting the right to innovations is legislative support for building the transplantation system, which derives from a number of rules of various laws. Changes to relevant laws and the issuance of sub-legislative acts related to transplantation that became effective in 2022–2023 were among the factors that made transplantation a field of medicine that dynamically evolved in spite of the war. Thus, 406 organ transplantations were performed during 9 months of 2023, while 384 transplantations were performed in 2022. The number of hematopoietic stem cell transplantations is also increasing: 251 transplantations during 9 months of 2023 versus 223 transplantations in the whole of 2022 (Ukrainian Centre for Transplant-Coordination 2022).

Attention is paid to the protection of patients' rights in the course of the receipt of certain types of medical treatment. In addition to transplantation and blood donation, one should mention the provision of medical services with the use of medically assisted reproduction techniques (hereafter – the MART) – a field that has boomed in Ukraine, particularly due to the MART-friendly legislative approach. Since the beginning of the war, a number of issues related to the protection of the rights of participants of in vitro fertilisation programs and surrogacy motherhood programs have become extremely topical. It is, therefore, natural that the elaboration and adoption of the law on the MART is envisaged as a task to be accomplished in the course of Ukraine's recovery process that has already been started, without waiting for the post-war period (The National Council for the Recovery of Ukraine 2022).

Special focus has also been placed on the protection of the rights of people in need of or receiving psychiatric or phycological care and rehabilitation. War cannot but negatively affect mental health. According to Minister of Health of Ukraine Victor Liashko, speaking at a mental health meeting in June 2022, at that stage of war, approximately 15 million Ukrainians needed psychological care, of whom 3–4 million will require pharmaceutical treatment (Liashko 2022). The longer the war lasts, the worse its impact on mental health will be. This is why Mrs. Olena Zelenska, the first lady of Ukraine, initiated the elaboration of the national mental health and psychosocial support program (MOH 2022).

Notably, these individuals are not only patients, but also healthcare professionals who suffer from the consequences of the war. Under such circumstances, the proper protection of their rights has become increasingly important, especially because the protection of healthcare professionals' rights is a prerequisite for the protection of the rights of patients.

The situation with the protection of healthcare professionals' rights largely resembles that concerning the rights of patients. The current legislation of Ukraine, including Article 77 of the Law on Fundamentals, provides for a wide range of professional and social rights and privileges of medical and pharmaceutical workers, but the real state of their protection deserves to be better. The reasons for this include imperfect institutional foundations, inadequate implementation mechanisms, insufficient financing, low social trust in healthcare and its professionals, as well as insufficient awareness by healthcare professionals of their rights and the absence of the practice of healthcare professionals demanding that their rights be observed.

These issues have been exacerbated by the war, and new challenges have appeared. The afore-mentioned challenges *inter alia* include: the necessity of differentiating between civil and military medicine and properly determining the legal status of civil and military healthcare personnel; the implementation of the medical neutrality concept; the utilisation of labour and professional rights by medical and pharmaceutical workers; the improvement of the healthcare standardisation landscape being performed by the healthcare profession rather than by the regulator, etc. A number of legislative and health governance interventions are required to resolve these issues.

The introduction of healthcare professionals' self-governance is a clear example of such solutions. The MOH prepared the relevant draft law to be submitted by the Cabinet of Misters of Ukraine to the Supreme Rada (Ukrainian Parliament) for consideration. The introduction of healthcare professionals' self-governance should help empower medical and pharmaceutical workers to decide on issues pertaining to their professional activities and enhance ethical and performance standards of healthcare professionals to increase public trust in the Ukrainian health system (Sorbie *et al.* 2023). Like many other legislative interventions, the adoption of the relevant draft law is envisaged by the draft Ukraine Recovery Plan stipulating that its implementation should begin as soon as possible that will help Ukraine in winning the war and modernising its healthcare.

It is also worth mentioning that, besides legislative and governance support for ensuring human rights in healthcare, court protection of such rights also takes place. In Ukraine, the practice of applying to the court for the protection of violated healthcare rights is less widespread than that in the USA or the EU states, but Ukrainian courts have considered civil, administrative, and criminal health-related cases even during the martial law period (Supreme Court 2023).

3.6.5. Interim findings

Ensuring and protecting human rights in healthcare during times of emergency, particularly in times of war, is a challenging task. It can, however, be accomplished, as has been proven by the Ukrainian experience of the protection of such rights during the full-fledged war of aggression unleased by the Russian Federation against Ukraine.

Being committed to performing its international law and constitutional obligations to protect the non-derogable rights to life and personal integrity extending to certain health-related duties, Ukraine has also managed to ensure the protection of the right to health. Despite the fact that the Constitution of Ukraine allows the right to healthcare and medical assistance to be temporarily limited under the conditions of martial law, no derogation from that right has taken place.

Several measures have been undertaken by the Ukrainian government, the healthcare profession, and civil society – not only to ensure the provision of timely and appropriate healthcare, but also to reduce the damage to the determinants of health (e.g., access to safe water, adequate housing, etc.) caused by the war. Some of these measures were among the factors that ensured the resilience of the Ukrainian healthcare system and the possibility to protect human rights in healthcare in the country.

The war highlighted existing issues of the protection of the rights of patients and healthcare professionals, and brought a new set of problems (e.g., difficulties in ensuring the right to access healthcare services, especially for vulnerable patients; the increased need for mental healthcare and rehabilitation; the necessity of properly differentiating between civil and military medicine; the need for the improvement of the standardisation of the healthcare service landscape to be performed by the healthcare profession rather than by the regulator, etc.). At the same time, efforts to increase the level of protection of the rights of patients and healthcare professionals were not stopped by the war. The notion that such efforts are to be extended and launched in the nearest future derives from the draft Ukraine Recovery Plan.

3.7. Business and Human Rights in the Recovery Agenda for Ukraine*

3.7.1. Social Expectations of Corporate Responsibility and Respect for Human Rights

In their first lectures, first-year law students hear the following: 'Jurisprudence is the science of how it should be'. This idea can also be found in the book *Jurisprudence: Themes and Concepts* (Veitch *et al.* 2006, p. 21). The authors of this book mention that there is a constant dynamic and tension within law due to the fact that our expectations – based on the principles of equality, freedom and justice – do not match the existing experience:

> The discrepancy between the way things are now and the way things might be if they were better in the future can be described as a discrepancy between 'social experience and social expectations' (De Sousa Santos 2002, p. 2). The desire to make the social experience better by living up to these expectations is the source of energy that drives us to improve our social life. <…> This desire for improvement creates a constant tension that underlies modernity <…>. Expectations usually give rise to a demand for release from problems they are currently facing, e.g. from hunger, oppression, discrimination. Where people's expectations remain unfulfilled, the discrepancy requires resolution through advances in knowledge or in more sophisticated ways of organizing things and people. However, if such aspirations are to be consciously realised, they must be provided for in a reasonably orderly manner. This is where regulation comes into play: regulation ensures consistent compliance with the expectations of society as a whole. (Veitch *et al.* 2006, p. 12)

* The author would like to acknowledge the financial support from the MSCA4Ukraine project, which is funded by the European Union, and assisted in preparation of this Chapter.

The business and human rights (hereafter – the BHR) framework has become just another manifestation of the development of social expectations of justice. Just like the struggle against discrimination or other injustice, the BHR field goes through the same stages: the experience of injustice accumulates and the awareness of vulnerability occurs; because of this, the demand for release from problems and a more perfect reality is formed; finally, on the basis of this, a request for new regulation arises. We can find confirmation of this in John Ruggie's (2008) framework: the corporate responsibility to respect human rights is the baseline expectation that society has of all companies in all situations (Protect, Respect and Remedy).

At the same time, the formation of this request for new legal regulation in the case of the development of the BHR concept is significantly different from previous experience, since it has as its addressees not only the state, but also non-state actors. The case of Ukraine is an illustration of how appropriate social expectations are addressed to businesses in times of such global emergency as a war of aggression. After all, 'how business enterprises operate in a conflict and post-conflict context will affect the dynamics that enable or undermine sustainable peace and respect for human rights. However, the role of business in conflict prevention and peacebuilding programmes, and in particular the contribution that effective management of business-related human rights impacts can play, has largely been overlooked' (OHCHR 2019).

In this chapter, we reveal the understanding of responsible business conduct (hereafter – the RBC) and its role in the post war recovery of Ukraine. The starting point of this review is the question of business as a direct addressee of human rights demands, since it seems that one of the determining reasons for the emergence of social expectations which was embodied in the BHR framework was the inability – or, in a number of cases, the conscious unwillingness – of the state to ensure respect for human rights by corporate actors. In times of global emergency such as war and the challenges of post-war reconstruction, the state is very limited in its ability to fulfil its human rights obligations. This, in turn, raises questions about the correlation between the powerful influence of business on human rights and the need to revise the concept according to which private subjects are equal participants in their relations. The powerful nature of the influence of business also means that there is a revision of the social contract, the parties to which were previously considered to be society and the state. This therefore creates the need to legitimise such corporate power in substantive and procedural ways. Global emergencies increase the intensity of the social expectation of solidarity. Therefore, all of the above-mentioned issues are considered through the prism of the solidarity approach.

3.7.2. The Solidarity Approach to Rethinking the Business and Human Rights Framework

We live in a time in which the demand to transform the existing economic order into one of sustainable lifestyles (UNFCCC) based on care, community and cooperation is no longer discussed. All of us are advocates for a just and sustainable new economic order, but there is still a discussion on the most effective way in which to make such a transformation a reality: How can we transform our economy and society to maintain quality of life in a sustainable way? How will people living in relatively poorer socio-economic conditions be able to catch up with and/or be included in the transitions that we deem necessary to sustain our economy and our environment? How, if at all, should we incorporate our legal and ethical responsibility for past, present and future resource use vis-à-vis future generations and the rest of the world (van Zeben 2020, p. 302)?

The answers to these questions depend on the basic question of who will wield power under this transformed society: 'we must change how we structure power if we are to reset our priorities and radically improve our *collective* choices [emphasis added]' (Hill 2002, p. 2).

A hard reality is that the current model of (economic) development is still not rights-based, and business models are still not oriented towards human rights. This leaves the profit-maximisation mantra of modern shareholder value-oriented corporations untouched, and even extends it as a guiding ideal to tackle a variety of social and environmental issues, providing an opportunity for governments to privatise public problem-solving and retreat from essential public domains. There is a need to reorient the role and purpose of corporations in society (Wettstein 2020, p. 13) based on the intrinsic normative force of human rights. All society feels this especially acutely in times of crisis and emergencies, but vulnerable individuals, groups and communities live with this understanding every day.

In June 2021, the UN High Commissioner for Human Rights, Michelle Bachelet, called for a 'human rights-enhancing economy' in her speech to the Human Rights Council (OHCHR n.d. c), but there is still a feeling that we live in a world of an economy enhanced by human rights. In many cases, even the sustainability argument seems like a business case argument, with a focus on sustainable economic growth which can only work when creating win-win solutions. The truth is that situations with no win-win solutions in sight, highlighting the fragility of our world and the fragmentation of development, are routine. Moreover, the idea of respect for human dignity as a key idea of the human rights concept does not need to be substantiated by a sustainability argument: it is valuable in itself, and it should stay as a core determination of all kinds of social regulation.

The situation in Ukraine during the first months of the war of aggression illustrated this well. Thus, small businesses, particularly grocery stores, in some cases demonstrated higher resilience compared to large businesses that were unable to quickly rebuild supply chains to adequately take into account the local context. In the following months of aggression, many small companies stopped operating because they did not have a financial cushion (as large companies usually have) and went bankrupt, but they saved people from hunger under the most exceptionally difficult conditions. The key factors determining why small local companies were able to realise this include their deep understanding of the local context (as they are part of it) and the nature of their supply chains, which are established with a focus on local suppliers (usually involving similarly small companies). This makes them different from the large all-Ukrainian companies whose supply chains were disrupted by the war. The role of these small local stores proved to be critical in minimising the effects of the war on human rights.

Despite the collective nature of the challenges of sustainable development, the Western legal tradition (with its huge influence on the global legal framework) remains predominantly individualistic. The modern understanding of human rights and the concept of neoliberalism developed simultaneously, providing, in many cases, an ideological basis for each other. Neoliberalism believes that the global competitive market would be the most effective method to ensure international economic harmony, and therefore the role of governments was confined to creating and defending markets. There is an emphasis on individual responsibility based on the belief that if everyone has unimpeded access to the market, everyone will benefit equally from it. While classical liberalism sought to free the economy from the state – or, more precisely, to establish sufficient freedoms for the economy – in neoliberalism the market becomes the mode of rationality for both state and society. Neoliberalism thus raises 'the market to a principle of all life and of government' (Moyn 2014, p. 396).

For modern societies, there is a consensus that the 'main values are equity/fairness/diversity; democracy/freedom; community/caring; and sustainability/thriving ecosystems' (Hill 2022, p. 171). This means that the existing model of the organisation of society and its economic order does not correspond to the values professed by this society, and there is thus a need to shift to a solidarity society (Uvarova 2023, p. 3). Based on the Draft declaration on the right to international solidarity (2017), solidarity could be defined as a fundamental principle taking as its foundation a spirit of unity among all social actors encompassing the union of interests, purposes and actions, and the recognition of different needs and rights to achieve common goals.

There are moral (discretionary solidarity) and legal (mandatory solidarity) dimensions of the corporate responsibility to respect solidarity. From the legal perspective, the duty barriers of solidarity are the same as those relating to human rights. In a situation of crisis and emergency, or in any case of people's vulnerability, the reasonable expectation of society consists of enhanced corporate responsibility.

BHR developments are engendering a paradigmatic shift in human rights law. The process of merging public human rights law and private business law into one holistic organism must consider different sides of these issues. Corporate practices must incorporate sustainable business practices within all levels of governance. This requires a mentality shift on the basis of the ideals of social solidarity. These arguments are particularly forceful in vulnerable societies, societies with weak rule of law infrastructures or political instability, and conflict-affected societies.

The BHR approach is important when attempting to systematise the question of when and how a company has an obligation to do something more than merely provide respect or do no harm. The example of Ukraine is especially telling because it creates the urgency to do something. A coherent understanding of solidarity has a clear link with the concept of dignity, but also arguably has transnational and transgenerational dimensions.

3.7.3. Business as a Human Rights Duty Bearer

In jurisprudence, the state is traditionally considered a human rights duty bearer. The precursor to this is history: from the 17th century, states played a 'dominant role in most global legal decision-making processes' (Lung-chu 1989, p. 25; Klabbers 2003, p.p. 354–357; Cismas c.a. 2005, p. 72), acting as 'the basis of the community' (Cassese 1989, p. 71; Heffes 2015, p. 55). This is how the generally recognised thesis that 'human rights correspond to the state's obligations regarding non-interference in the sphere of individual freedom, respect for human rights, their provision, protection and promotion' (Khrystova 2012, p. 54) was formed.

This construction is not theoretical – it is the basis of the international human rights protection system. The question of whether it was a good idea to impose human rights obligations on states is perhaps one of the most difficult in modern jurisprudence, and is extremely rarely addressed – both because of the complexity of the issue itself and because of the feeling that there is no alternative to it. Among those who are still looking for an answer to it, two main positions stand out. The first is that such an approach is justified, at least during the formation of the modern international human rights protection system, because only then did states have sufficient powers to ensure respect for and the fulfilment of human rights. The second observes that states themselves are often the most significant perpetrators of human rights violations: 'It's like entrusting the fox to guard the hen house' (O'Neill 2020, p. 136).

There is a third approach that is of interest in the context of this chapter, according to which the state-centric approach to building a human rights protection system – and, in a more general context, to understanding the nature of human rights – was fully justified in the middle of the 20th century. According to O. O'Neil, this period saw the peak of state power. However, since that point, globalisation has transformed the configuration of power in ways that have often made it difficult for the state to ensure respect for and the fulfilment of human rights. There are several reasons for this: situations illustrating states' inability to effectively protect human rights from corporate abuses; human rights violations by states and business contributing to such violations; and the expansion of spheres of social life that are outside of state regulation.

The ability of states to adequately ensure the implementation of human rights is limited by the powerful influence of non-state actors (Caney 2006, p. 44; O'Neil 2016, p. 71). First of all, this concerns transnational corporations. In 1998, a book by Raymond Vernon, who is sometimes called a pioneer in the study of transnational corporations (his first works on this subject were published in the 1970s), entitled 'In the Eye of the Hurricane: Problematic Perspectives on Transnational Corporations' was published. His decision to write the book, as he states in the preface, 'grew out of the feeling that the world was entering a period in which the inevitable clashes between multinational enterprises and nation-states could become more frequent and intense, finding a response in the society, both in public and in the private sector, which can significantly worsen their functioning' (Vernon 1998, pp. vii–viii).

The global nature of business today is such that regardless of size or model – whether multinational corporations or small and medium-sized enterprises – companies impact people both in their home countries and around the world. One example of this impact can be seen in the proliferation of complex supply chains in many business sectors. A single company's supply chains may span several countries with very different legal frameworks (Human Rights Watch 2016). According to the International Labour Organisation, at least one in five jobs is linked to global supply chains (Human Rights Watch 2016). Inclusion in such a global society has significant advantages for businesses (International Labour Organisation 2018), providing access to new labour markets and new technologies while allowing them to reduce the cost of production. At the same time, being a powerful economic, social and political entity, businesses can also be a force for good in society. Companies provide goods and services, create jobs and can contribute to the alleviation of poverty (World Bank Group 2015); they can create, disseminate or build on best practices and international standards

(Bank for International Settlements 2017). However, the risk of negative business impact is also significant.

Global emergency situations are a significant factor in increasing people's dependence on the conduct of businesses. International human rights law initially considers emergency situations as situations in which, objectively, the ability of the state to perform its functions in order to ensure the common good ('the life of the nation' (Art. 15), 'the independence or security of the state' (Art. 27)) is significantly limited. In this regard, international human rights law allows states to derogate from many human rights obligations in proportion to the looming threat (UN Human Rights Committee 2001). However, derogation does not change the volume/content of the human right, and the value of respect for human dignity does not lose its relevance. On the contrary, in situations of war (or other emergencies) the dependence of individuals (rightsholders) on the ability to realise a particular human right can significantly increase and become critical. Under these conditions of the limited ability of the state to ensure human rights and the critical importance of this right for a person, the scope of the human rights obligations of non-state actors can proportionally increase. This also corresponds to Shue's concept, which provides a plausible account of what the criteria should be for determining who should bear positive obligations. In his view, 'two factors must be considered in this regard: first, means-end reasoning must establish what needs to be done in order for a right to be fulfilled and, in light of this, it must be determined who best can perform those tasks. Secondly, the allocation of duties also depends upon what burdens are reasonable and fair to place upon specific agents… it is clear that, in many instances, corporations will be able to play an important role in helping to realise fundamental rights' (Deva and Bilchitz 2018).

The explanation of the social expectations placed on companies in these situations is based on the fact that when operating as a supplier in an emergency situation, a business performs not just a private function, but also a public one (Mende 2022, p. 42; Fuchs 2013, p.p. 77–78; Scherer *et al.* 2016, p. 274). According to liberal theory, only states are considered as public actors. Companies belong exclusively to the private sphere, and therefore they do not need legitimisation by society. This approach 'conceptualizes corporations as apolitical and corporate responsibility as purely private' (Wettstein 2020, p. 38), but it ignores the real state of affairs: the activities of companies can significantly affect public interests, companies do not always operate purely in the private space given to them by the state, and states are not always able to exercise effective control over such activities. Companies play an important role in ensuring the minimum necessary access to essential goods and services – not only in the private interest of a particular person, but also in the general interest of the whole of society, since such actions ensure societal sustainability which is a requisite for respect for human dignity, and the latter is a minimum requirement of humanity.

Accordingly, in the second half of the 20th century, human rights theory was based on a model where the state was considered the primary human rights duty bearer (the vertical effect of human rights). This theory was also designed to protect human rights from violations by third parties who act as secondary human rights duty bearers (the horizontal effect of human rights), but it often showed its ineffectiveness in practice. From a substantive point of view, this approach is objectionable, as it makes the understanding of human rights state-centric: 'The initial assumption that states are the primary agents of justice sees states and only states as having the will and ability to implement, delegate, or distribute all obligations to ensure justice. The problem with state-centric approaches is not that they seek to allocate obligations that are consistent with human rights, but that they allocate them in ways that may not work. Despite the expected realism of those who impose obligations on the state, their approach is often completely unrealistic' (O'Neill 2001, p. 185).

Recognising the status of non-state actors as the primary human rights duty bearers does not mean that we allow such actors to completely supplant the state. Their main difference from the state is that they cannot establish a legal order within the entire society, and their ability to influence the behaviour of other participants in social relations in order to ensure their compliance with human rights is limited.

3.7.4. The Human Rights Obligations of Business: The Vertical Dimension

As was already indicated in the previous section, the main goal of legal human rights is traditionally considered to be the establishment of rules of relations between the person and the state (the vertical effect of human rights); however, human rights can also be addressed to other persons and require certain behaviours from non-state actors – that is, have a so-called direct horizontal effect.

However, this approach, in fact, does not go beyond the state-centric (when we talk about both the vertical and the horizontal effect of human rights, we are talking about the obligations of the state) model in the first case regarding its own actions (the vertical effect). In the second case, it does not exceed the state-centric model regarding the actions of third parties which affect human rights (the horizontal effect). In other words, the horizontal effect of human rights takes place when the state remains the primary human rights addressee – when it is required to ensure the effectiveness of human rights in relations between two private entities over which the state has authority. This means that the horizontal effect indicates not so much the relations between the two actors themselves (e.g., a rightsholder and corporate actor, even when their relations are subordinated, such as by an employer and an employee), but rather the fact that their equality before the law is ensured by the state, and they can equally count on its intervention in case of the violation of human rights by one of the parties. The fact that the horizontal dimension of human rights is based on the same state-centric approach is confirmed by J. Knox (2008, pp. 1–47) and, in practice, we also find confirmation in the jurisprudence of European courts.

However, can we talk about the horizontal effect of human rights in situations where the state does not fulfil the role of the addressee of human rights demands (due to its incapacity or undemocratic nature, or because the relationship objectively exists outside the sphere of the state's regulation or in an emergency situation)? For example, when the COVID-19 pandemic began, businesses tried to minimise losses. Among other things, major brands resorted to cancelling orders or suspending them for a period until the situation improved and demand increased. Such actions led to large-scale dismissals of employees, the massive non-payment of wages, and the termination of the activities of individual suppliers. This situation most often occurred between North American and EU companies in contracts with suppliers from countries with low labour standards (often featuring large brands). At the same time, these companies acted within the scope of their contracts – they used the contracts' clauses, which gave them the right to refuse the contract at any time, and which placed the counterparties and their employees in an extremely vulnerable position (where civil society organization (hereafter – the CSO) called on governments).

According to the UN Guiding Principles on the BHR (2011), companies have an obligation to 'do no harm'; they have a corporate responsibility to respect human rights. This requires any company to carry out human rights due diligence (hereafter – the HRDD) procedures and, in this way, identify, prevent and respond to any negative impacts on human rights in the process of the functioning of the company and in its supply chains. In the above example, respect for human rights means that companies that cancel or change their orders should assess the impact of their decisions on workers and suppliers and try to minimise such negative impacts as much as possible (Workers Rights Consortium 2023). The demand for such due diligence is especially heightened when it comes to situations which present the obvious de facto inequality of formally equal parties to a contract, since suppliers are forced to agree to a contract condition that gives a company/customer the right to cancel an order at any time before delivery, and are completely dependent on the good faith behaviour of the counterparty without having any leverage over them.

Michael Sandel, in his classic work *Justice: What's the Right Thing to Do* (2009), cites examples of contractual relations in which, due to the unequal position of their parties, the effect of human rights is not horizontal. For example, as a result of Hurricane Charlie, people were forced to buy goods and use services which were in some cases priced ten times higher than normal, and this can be explained only by the vulnerable position of people to whom the choice of whether or not to enter into a contract, and on what terms, existed only formally.

The situation of the dependence of the local population on the behaviour of corporate actors significantly increased during the war of aggression in Ukraine, and will be critical during post-war reconstruction. This can be illustrated by an example. The start of aggression against Ukraine was particularly dramatic in the first two months, as Ukrainian cities were drastically transformed from areas of peace to warzones subject to massive shelling, with more than 20 % of the territory of the whole country occupied in the first week of the conflict alone. In this situation, food security became exceptionally challenging. Cities with hundreds of thousands of people found themselves in situations where many grocery stores ceased operating on the first day of the war, and supply chains for delivering food to stores were disrupted. Queues formed in front of the few stores that remained open, and there were instances of people being killed by shelling while standing in line for food on the street. Older people, people with disabilities, and people with small children were in particularly vulnerable positions (Uvarova 2022, p. 5).

The situations listed above are examples of when a business entity and a person (or group of people) whose rights are affected by the activities of such an entity are not equal. This inequality in the ability to influence the other party determines the requirement for the party which is endowed with such a powerful influence to respect human rights and exercise due diligence in order to avoid having a negative influence on their counterparty.

In other words, non-state actors, which in another context are secondary addressees of human rights demands, may find themselves in a situation where they become the primary human rights duty bearers. The opinion of the UN Guiding Principles on the BHR phrases this in more concrete terms: 'Appropriate action will vary according to: Whether the business enterprise causes or contributes to an adverse impact, or whether it is involved solely because the impact is directly linked to its operations, products or services by a business relationship' (Guiding Principle 19(b)).

3.7.5. Requesting the Legitimacy of Corporate Actors

Business legitimacy is a prerequisite for a company's license to operate in society and conduct relations with various internal and external stakeholders, including investors, shareholders, employees, customers, consumers, suppliers, local communities, the state and the international community. 'Just a few decades ago, the legitimacy of the company was determined to a greater or lesser extent by general norms, control and centralized regulation by the state. Today, legitimacy is ensured in fundamentally new forms of political governance'. This is an important feature of BHR, which takes this field beyond the boundaries of Western neoliberal capitalism. The latter recognises the need for the social responsibility of business, but considers this to be private responsibility. According to liberal theory, only states are considered as public actors. Companies belong exclusively to the private sphere, and therefore they do not need legitimisation by society. This approach 'conceptualizes corporations as apolitical and corporate responsibility as purely private' (Wettstein 2020). However, this approach also ignores the real state of affairs: the activities of companies can significantly affect public interests, companies do not always operate purely in the private space 'given to them by the state', and states are not always able to exercise effective control over such activities. This indicates the need to recognise companies as subjects of public responsibility whose authority is subject to legitimisation by society. This statement is especially relevant for providers of essential goods and services, which can be illustrated by examples of handling human rights challenges during the COVID-19 pandemic. Companies, urged not to interrupt their activities because of their importance for local residents or more globally, were supposed to demonstrate that they had taken all appropriate measures to ensure the highest possible levels of occupational health and safety for their employees.

The privatisation of the provision of essential goods and services does not deprive them of an element of public function (meaning that ensuring the minimum necessary access to essential goods and services is not only in the private interest of a particular person, but the general interest of the whole of society, since such actions ensure societal sustainability and are required in the provision of respect for human dignity, which itself is a minimum requirement of humanity). The public nature of goods and services emphasises the role of the state in providing access to them: in peacetime, the state establishes regulation aimed at ensuring access to essential services for the most vulnerable groups, monitoring the quality of services and more; in times of war and post-war reconstruction, the state becomes the main addressee of the demand to provide access to essential goods and services, either on its own or through the increased regulation of service providers and closer interaction with them. The BHR framework calls on the state to provide recommendations to business on what risks war entails for human rights, what actions should be taken by businesses to minimise the risks of a negative impact on human rights, and what forms of interaction between business and the state can be ensured to minimise such risks and secure access to essential goods and services. At the same time, businesses have their own responsibility to make all possible efforts to secure human rights. In the situation of essential goods and services during the war of aggression or in the post-war period, the state's ability to provide access to them and/or adequately regulate private actors' conduct to ensure accessibility can be extremely limited. This means that additional positive requirements beyond the baseline responsibility to respect rights may be imposed on companies. The second pillar of the Guiding Principles – the responsibility of business to respect human rights – applies regardless of how governments meet their obligations, and indeed applies in all contexts. The development of social relations and the role of business in this process have led to the fact that today the idea of a new social contract which considers business as one party along with the state and society is increasingly heard. Business, as a bearer of public power in a certain way, is also the addressee of requests for legitimacy. It should be noted that the concept of a new social contract has accompanied the UN Guiding Principles on the BHR since the moment they were conceived – J. Raggi (2013) indicated the expectations directed at corporations as part of a collective social contract (Protect, Respect and Remedy).

At the same time, the question of the legitimacy of the government goes far beyond the law. Rather, law provides procedural tools of legitimation, thereby promoting greater certainty and pre-empting potential disputes. The concept of the BHR also offers procedures aimed, in fact, at legitimising the activities of companies in society. First of all, this concerns HRDD – an ongoing *process* which includes assessing actual and potential human rights impacts, integrating and acting upon the findings, tracking responses, and communicating how impacts are addressed (McCorquodale and Nolan 2021, p. 455). However, the procedural component has no independent meaning as it is always aimed at securing the *substantive* goal. The development of a particular procedure is not the purpose as such, and the procedure is determined by the purpose that should be achieved via this procedure (Deva 2023, p. 390). In the case of HRDD, such a purpose is not to ensure the result (no human rights abuses/no harm), but to ensure that businesses respect internationally recognised human rights and take all reasonable measures to prevent, stop and redress human rights harm emanating from their operations or their business relationships.

Ensuring HRDD is a way to ensure the legitimacy of business in society. The need for business legitimacy also dictates the need to comply with rule of law requirements, and the rule of law is applicable to both state and non-state regulation. In particular, rules of conduct established by non-state actors should not lead to human rights abuses, and should prevent them. Therefore, for example, non-state regulation should not be discriminatory; the fact that such regulation is carried out by a private entity cannot serve as justification for limiting human rights on the basis of gender, race, origin, age, nationality, etc. – except when there is a legitimate aim for such a limitation (for example, restricting access to certain content based on age), it is clearly provided for in established rules that are available for review, and it is proportionate (Sander 2020, 935). Guarantees of the rule of law include the possibility to use 'effective means of legal protection at the operational level'.

3.7.6. Heightened Human Rights Due Diligence

The international community is increasingly setting expectations for RBC through international sustainability initiatives (Sjåfjell and Taylor 2019; Ahlström and Sjåfjell 2022). This includes the UN Sustainable Development Goals (hereafter – the SDGs), the Organisation for Economic Cooperation and Development's (hereafter – the OECD) Guidelines for Multinational Enterprises (1976), and most importantly the UN Guiding Principles for Business and Human Rights.

In recent years, the EU has introduced a range of regulatory initiatives which, in different ways, seek to address the impacts that businesses have on the observance of human rights (Danish Institute for Human Rights 2022, p. 10). Key among them are: the European Green Deal (2021), a suite of policy and legislative initiatives announced in 2019 aimed at achieving no net emissions of greenhouse gases by 2050; the 2020 European Pillar of Social Rights and the accompanying action plan; the Corporate Sustainability Reporting Directive; the Sustainable Finance Disclosure Regulation; the Green Taxonomy; the Conflict Minerals Regulation; the Timber Regulation; a proposed ban on goods produced with forced labour; proposed regulation on deforestation-free products; the General Data Protection Regulation; the Public Procurement Directive; and the proposal of the Corporate Sustainability Due Diligence Directive. On 10 March 2021, the European Parliament adopted a resolution with recommendations to the European Commission regarding the approval of a legislative proposal on mandatory supply chain due diligence (the draft of the Directive was published on 23 February 2022 and voted on by the European Parliament on 1 June 2023).

RBC principles and standards set out the expectations for how businesses should prevent and address adverse impacts of their operations and supply chains while also contributing to sustainable development in the countries where they operate. RBC can help to inform companies as to how they should respond to the war in Ukraine in the immediate and medium term – notably by providing a due diligence framework to help them gain visibility over the main human rights and integrity risks present in their supply chains, including those that have emerged or been made worse by the war. Conducting effective supply chain due diligence can help to support both the resilience of Ukraine's economy in the short term as well as its later reconstruction.

In the context of the war of aggression and the post-war period of reconstruction, companies should provide heightened HRDD that requires them to ask themselves whether they make all possible efforts to minimise the negative impact of the emergency situation on human rights, balancing individual human rights (such as employees' safety) and the public interest (such as ensuring access to essential goods and services). Any understanding of heightened HRDD as identifying potential and actual impacts on people (human rights) as well as on the context (the situation of the war) should be supplemented with one more component, i.e., preventing or minimising the impact of the emergency situation on people (human rights). This emergency situation could significantly change the scope of the corporate responsibility to respect human rights. This not only concerns a company's impact on human rights, but also social expectations of its role in responding to human rights challenges that the emergency situation creates.

The concept of heightened HRDD is attracting increasing attention in the BHR studies and policy-making. In 2020, the Report of the Working Group on the issue of human rights and transnational corporations and other business enterprises entitled 'Business, Human Rights and Conflict-Affected Regions: Towards Heightened Action' was published. In 2022, 'with powerful influence in mind UNDP and the UN Working Group on the BHR developed the practical roadmap for action: "Heightened Human Rights Due Diligence for Business in Conflict-Affected Contexts: A Guide"'. It notes that 'heightened human rights due diligence means identifying potential and actual impacts on people (human rights) as well as on the context (conflict)'. Therefore, heightened HRDD involves identifying and assessing not only companies' actual or potential adverse impacts on human rights, but also their actual or potential adverse impacts on the conflict itself. As the summary of the Guide notes: 'The Guide recognises that businesses invariably impact the dynamics of a conflict and that they therefore need to adopt conflict-sensitive practices to account for, and mitigate, these impacts.'

In the first week of the Russian invasion of Ukraine, the European Commission published a proposal for mandatory the HRDD legislation – the *Corporate Sustainability Due Diligence Directive* (2022, hereafter – the CSDDD) – *that* requires companies to identify and mitigate risks for human rights connected to their global operations and business relations. The concept of mandatory HRDD for companies is gaining momentum in Europe. These legislative initiatives suggest imposing significant challenges and severe liabilities on companies that procure their products through supply chains. There are relevant legislative steps in France, the Netherlands, Germany and, as already mentioned, at the EU level. In August 2022, a group of 51 civil society organisations and academics active in the field of the BHR issued a joint statement calling upon EU policymakers to include specific provisions on RBC in conflict-affected areas in the CSDDD. This statement was based partly on research by the Business & Human Rights Resource Centre on companies' due diligence response to the escalating conflict in Ukraine, which showed that the large majority of companies struggle with managing the situation responsibly. On 25 January 2023, the Commission published a proposal for the CSDDD stating that

> in conflict-affected and high-risk areas, <...> should undertake heightened due diligence following the guidance on heightened human rights due diligence for business in conflict-affected contexts developed by the UNDP and other relevant international bodies. This includes complementing standard due diligence with a conflict analysis, based on stakeholders' engagement, *aimed at understanding the root causes, triggers and parties driving the conflict and the impact of the company's business activities on the conflict* [emphasis added].

Finally, the updated OECD Guidelines for Multinational Enterprises on the RBC (2023) also pay attention to situations of armed conflict. In particular, they mention that enterprises should respect the standards of the IHL. In the context of armed conflict or heightened risk of gross abuses, enterprises should conduct enhanced due diligence in relation to adverse impacts, including violations of the IHL.

Many companies in Ukraine demonstrate responsible conduct. They have a number of good practices that have ensured human rights for their employees since the war of aggression started. At the same time, the following can be observed regarding the lack of integration of a human rights approach into companies' policies and processes: (a) companies do not have human rights policies that meet the expectations of the UNGPs, and there is no publicly available commitment to respect human rights, reflections on war-related human rights risks, or IHL; (b) companies are not aware of heightened human rights and conflict-sensitive due diligence, and the correct steps that they take occur because of their good intentions rather than because of an incorporated human rights-based approach (whether concerning employees' safety, the process of making decisions, labour rights, the work, family and volunteering balance, mental health aid, the impact on local communities, grievance mechanisms and tools to communicate with stakeholders, companies' assistance to the armed forces of Ukraine, or responsibly returning to liberated territories or home offices); (c) there is a lack of capability when it comes to tracking human rights risks in tech companies' downstream and upstream supply chains (the Know The Chain methodology could be used for self-assessment); (d) the due diligence process that companies use is based only on a 'risks for companies' approach, without taking into consideration a 'risks for human rights' approach; (e) companies are interested in employees and pay attention to their needs, but at the same time there is an extreme lack of attention paid to companies' possible impact on local communities (because of the lack of capacity to make decisions through the lens of human rights), consumers, or employees in supply chains (this could be the next step in implementing HRDD); (f) companies give priority to avoiding reputational risks because of the conflict (in particular, by leaving risky relationships and/or territories) without assessing the impact of their exit on human rights, in particular the human rights of local communities, and, as a result, without developing a responsible exit strategy; (g) some companies demonstrate good practices of communication with their employees, but most of these tools of communication are oriented towards collective communication (group chats, staff meetings, etc.) and there is a lack of instruments that enable individual communication, especially in situations of marginalisation or regarding the problem of gender-based violence.

3.7.7. Interim findings

In recent years, scientific developments regarding BHR have formed a new prism through which the human rights obligations of corporate actors can be viewed. However, such scientific developments are mainly presented in the Western European and Anglo-Saxon legal tradition (Deva and Birchall 2020; Baumann-Pauly and Nolan 2016). Eastern European scholars have largely failed to participate in this scientific discourse. Moreover, such scientific developments often still present manifestations of the concept of 'business OR human rights' (Deva and Birchall 2020, p. 3), and in post-socialist societies these views prevail. One of these manifestations involves an emphasis on the economic justification (the so-called business justification) of the corporate responsibility to respect human rights – i.e., on arguments concerning why it is economically profitable for businesses to behave responsibly (Carroll and Shabana 2010, p. 85). Finally, existing developments almost entirely fail to take into account the requirements of social solidarity, instead placing their emphasis on individual human rights.

The Ukrainian recovery plan should be based on the RBC approach. For these purposes, following the UNGPs, the governmental agencies responsible for providing financial funds and other forms of cooperation with the private sector as part of the Ukraine's recovery effort should guide companies towards:

(a) publicly affirming their support for democracy, the rule of law, solidarity, fundamental human rights and territorial integrity;
(b) publicly committing to exercising their leverage responsibly, both within their value chains (supporting business partners in building human rights capacities) and in governmental relations (ensuring that companies do not lobby for policies that protect their operations while shifting burdens onto the most vulnerable), in particular by including in the company's human rights policy the commitment not to influence the political and regulatory sphere in an irresponsible way;
(c) having a responsible exit strategy as part of their human rights policy based on consultations with workers and external stakeholders, with disengagement as a last resort;
(d) developing and adopting policies on the work, family and volunteering balance.

In the recovery agenda of Ukraine, the BHR approach is important as it can provide a systematic framework for when and how a company has an obligation to do something more than simply provide respect or do no harm. The example of Ukraine is particularly telling because it creates a real sense of urgency to do something. In this regard, a coherent understanding of solidarity has a clear link with the concept of dignity, but also, arguably, a transnational and transgenerational dimension. This understanding should be reflected by all governmental recovery actions in Ukraine. In particular, ensuring competitive access to funding and growing value by adding sectors of the economy should be seen as critical projects in the recovery plan, which itself should be based on the RBC approach.

3.8. The Role of Cyber Defence and the Problems It Faces in the Context of Aggression

3.8.1. The Concept of Cybersecurity in the Conditions of War Within the Geopolitical Processes of Today

Cybersecurity (along with which the terms *cyber defence* and *cyber protection* are used interchangeably) is a relevant and extremely important component of the modern national security of every state. In the modern world, in which the digital space has become a necessity for the functioning of all spheres of society as well as an object of interest for potential threats, the issues of cybersecurity and countering cybercrime acquire special importance. In the context of Ukraine, which is experiencing geopolitical instability and fighting for its territorial integrity in the conditions of a war of aggression, the problems of cyber defence become extremely urgent and difficult.

Cyber threats evolve constantly. Thus, understanding the problems of cyber defence and its role in Ukraine can determine the further direction of policy in this area and contribute to the preservation of national security and the country's sovereignty.

This analysis starts by assessing global cyber defence problems, including in Ukraine, before identifying modern threats, outlining the main challenges that Ukraine faces, and assessing the role and functions of cyber defence in managing these challenges at the legislative level, taking into account current norms and gaps in the legal framework.

The problem of cybercrime in Ukraine has been studied by many researchers. In particular, V. K. Kharchenko, O. M. Klymchuk, O. G. Korchenko, and Yu. P. Travnikov paid special attention to cyber terrorism and cybersecurity. I. O. Chernukhin, O. D. Dovgan, and V. M. Bogush studied the organisational and legal principles that underlie the organisation of the cyberattack protection systems that guard critical infrastructure.

Some aspects of the regulatory framework for combating cybercrime were studied and discussed in publications by K. Beliakov, V. Butuzov, A. Volevodz, D. Havlovskyy, V. Holubev, V. Huslavskyy, D. S. Klyotskin, M. Litvinov, E. Ryzhkov, V. Rozovskyy, T. Tropyna, V. Tsymbaliuk, O. Yukhno and others.

This part of the study aims to analyse and comprehensively investigate the problems of cyber defence by first assessing the insecurity associated with gaps in the current legislation and the crucially important role of cyber defence in war conditions. It then attempts to determine the possibilities of countering cybercrime in wartime conditions through the prompt exchange of experience at the international level and the improvement of current legislation.

3.8.2. Modern Concepts of the 'fourth branch of government' and Its Impact on the Global Social and Political Climate, Legal Control and the Regulation of the Virtual World

Concepts related to digital and electronic communications are closely intertwined with the global information infrastructure. More and more specialists, lawyers, scientists and politicians are turning to issues of state cybersecurity. This is not surprising, since this is a new sphere of social relations in which the participants – the state and society – are inextricably linked. Regarding the definition of cyberspace, at the 32nd session of the UNESCO General Conference (2003), the Recommendation concerning the Promotion and Use of Multilingualism and Universal Access to Cyberspace was adopted, according to which cyberspace was defined as a virtual world of digital and electronic communication related to the global information infrastructure.

In global law enforcement practice, the concept of cyberspace began to appear at the end of the 20th century. In this context, the definition of cyberspace provided by the Supreme Court of the United States is indicative: this is a unique medium known to its users as cyberspace, which is not located in a certain territory but is accessible to everyone in any part of the world via the Internet (*Reno v. ACLU* 1997).

Finally, in 2013, the NATO published the Tallinn Manual on International Law on Methods of Conducting Cyber Warfare, which defines cyberspace as an environment made up of physical and non-physical elements and characterised by the use of computers and the electromagnetic spectrum to store, modify and exchange data using computer networks (Tallinn Manual on the International Law Applicable to Cyber Warfare 2013).

Therefore, cyberspace can be characterised as a specific environment, which, although created by a human, has received such significant and rapid development due to its globalisation that new forms of legal relations arise in it, which are currently insufficiently researched and regulated in either international or national law.

In recognising cyberspace as an environment for the application of geostrategies and the 'fifth bridgehead' for conducting hostilities, along with land, sea, air and space, more and more attention is paid to the development and protection of information resources, as well as opportunities to influence the information resources of other countries, which in general is described as a problem of ensuring the cybersecurity of the state. Now, the use of cyber armies and cyber weapons, cyber defence, cyber operations and cyberattacks by states is perceived as commonplace.

The analysis and generalisation of the approaches of the world's scientific institutions to the problems of the use of cyberspace allows us to state that the assessment of the capabilities of each country is carried out according to seven factors: (1) the presence of a national cybersecurity strategy; (2) the availability of structures responsible for incidents and their ability to respond to them; (3) the presence of a law enforcement cyber structure and the state of law enforcement practice; (4) the availability of an information exchange system; (5) the availability of a system of personnel training, research and testing; (6) diplomacy and trade; and (7) defence and the availability of structures responding to crisis situations. The USA is identified as the leading country in the development of cyber capabilities around the world across all indicators.

Since 2014, Ukraine has been forced to retaliate against hybrid Russian armed aggression, including in cyberspace. State policy in the field of cybersecurity addresses a number of concerns. The main challenges relate to the legislative framework – namely, the inconsistency or lack of definition of cybersecurity terms, which creates problems in the regulation of such crimes in the legal field. Another important issue is the lack of progress on the part of the state in cyberspace defence systems, along with the lack of cooperation between the state and the private sector in the above-mentioned area. A rather important element of this lack of progressive development is the lack of initiative on the part of the state to create highly qualified personnel in the field of IT. Insufficient interest in the education of personnel leads to an outflow of personnel to foreign countries.

For a fully fledged analysis of this situation, it is also appropriate to recognise that today, along with unresolved personnel, financial, logistical and regulatory problems, there is another, more complex issue regarding the strengthening of the state's cyber defence and the creation of effective Cyber Troops of the Armed Forces of Ukraine. This problem concerns the rejection of the comprehensive consideration of cyber defence issues, mostly through the prism of the implementation of cyber protection and cybersecurity measures of the Armed Forces of Ukraine and their acquisition of capabilities to fulfil the tasks of the comprehensive defence of the state – primarily its cyber defence both within and through cyberspace (Ternovyy *et al.* 2023).

Cyber defence was recognised as an important new component of Ukraine's defence only in the Cybersecurity Strategy of Ukraine (2016). With the introduction of the new National Security Strategy of Ukraine (2020), a start was made on the preparation of drafts of a number of strategic documents, one of which is the Cybersecurity Strategy of Ukraine. This strategy, which was adopted by Presidential Decree No. 447/2021 (2021), implemented the decision of the National Skill Development Corporation (hereafter – NSDC) 'On the Cybersecurity Strategy of Ukraine' (NSDC 2021).

The Cybersecurity Strategy of Ukraine determines: the priorities of national interests in the field of cybersecurity; existing and potential cyber threats; the goals and tasks of ensuring the cybersecurity of Ukraine with the aim of creating conditions for the safe functioning of cyberspace; and the use of cybersecurity in the interests of the individual, society and the state (NSDC 2021).

This Strategy notes that 'ensuring cybersecurity is one of the priorities in the national security system of Ukraine. The implementation of the specified priority is carried out by strengthening the capacities of the national cybersecurity system to counter cyber threats in the modern security environment' (NSDC 2021). The implementation of the norms of the Strategy involved: the improvement of the operation of cyberspace; its control with the help of high-tech, innovative technical means and mobile responses in the preparation, processing and entry into force of improved norms, both in the current legislation and through the development of new normative legal acts in the area of cyber protection; ensuring maximum control; the implementation of the perfect means of deterrence; countermeasures; and the detection of criminals and bringing them to justice (NSDC 2021).

This Strategy is based on the provisions of the Constitution of Ukraine, the laws of Ukraine 'On the National Security of Ukraine' (2018) and 'On the Basic Principles of Ensuring Cybersecurity of Ukraine', the ECHR, the Convention on Cybercrime, the National Security Strategy of Ukraine, approved by the Decree of the President of Ukraine No. 392 (2020), the Concept of Combating Terrorism in Ukraine, approved by the Decree of the President of Ukraine No. 53 (2019), and other normative legal acts.

Thus, the Strategy provides for:

(1) the regulation of electronic evidence issues at the legislative level, using the best practices on these issues of the USA and EU Member States and taking into account modern challenges and trends in the field of cybersecurity;
(2) the regulation at the legislative level of the legal status of cryptocurrencies;
(3) the settlement at the legislative level of the issue of the comprehensive involvement of the private sector and civil society in the implementation of measures to curb destructive activities in cyberspace;
(4) the regulation at the legislative level of the issue of public-private partnership in the field of cybersecurity, determining the forms and methods of implementing such a partnership, strengthening mutual trust and foreseeing the possibility of introducing experimental projects in this area (Hutsalyuk 2023, p. 110)

The National Cybersecurity Manual of the NATO Cooperative Cyber Defence Centre of Excellence summarises the understanding of cybersecurity by NATO member states (Klimburg 2012).

In general, the term cybersecurity is understood to represent maintaining a state of readiness to repel potential threats with high intensity and the adoption of appropriate countermeasures. Experts from the NATO Cyber Defence Centre consider the militarisation of the Internet as one of the main and most dangerous trends in the development of global cyberspace: 'Modern military structures are ready to use the information space as a "parallel battlefield" in future conflicts'. At the same time, confidence is expressed that a cyberattack 'in its pure form' is unlikely (Zavhorodnya 2022, p. 64).

In October 2017, the Law of Ukraine 'On the Basic Principles of Ensuring the Cybersecurity of Ukraine' entered into force, in which two key terms were established for the first time. Before this, there were no legal definitions of the terms *cybersecurity* and *cyber protection* in the current legislation of Ukraine. In accordance with the norms of this law, cybersecurity provides for the protection of the vital interests of a person, citizen, and society in cyberspace, and must ensure the sustainable development of the information society and digital communication environment. The legislator paid careful attention to the importance of a prompt response, the timeliness of detection, and the neutralisation of both real and potential threats to the national security of Ukraine in cyberspace.

The legislator formulates cyber defence as a set of measures aimed at preventing cyberattacks in cyberspace aimed at ensuring the protection of the sovereignty and defence capability of the state, preventing armed conflicts and repelling armed aggression.

In this way, a base of terms was systematised in accordance with those generally accepted on a global scale. The entry into force of this law has opened up great opportunities for the exchange of experience at the international level. Moreover, joining the global anti-terrorist movement has brought about the symbiosis of various fields in the legal space, since the fight against cybercrime is not the exclusive prerogative of law enforcement agencies.

Cybersecurity is provided by cybersecurity entities that take measures to prevent the use of cyberspace for military, intelligence-subversive, terrorist, manipulative, and other illegal and criminal purposes, identify and respond to cyber incidents and cyberattacks, eliminate their consequences, conduct information exchange regarding actual and potential cyber threats, develop and implement preventive, organizational, educational and other measures in the field of cybersecurity, cyber defence and cyber protection, ensure information security audits, including at subordinate facilities and facilities belonging to the sphere of their management, carry out other measures on ensuring the development and security of cyberspace (Potiy *et al.* 2021, p. 142).

This definition has a direct relationship with the legal and operational framework, as it defines the subjects and their functions in the field of cybersecurity. The above definition also indicates that cybersecurity actors must provide measures to prevent the use of cyberspace for various negative, illegal or criminal purposes. They must also respond to cyber incidents and cyberattacks, perform information sharing on cyber threats, and develop and implement cyber protection, cyber defence and cyber security measures. At the same time, they must conduct information security audits and carry out other measures to ensure the development and security of cyberspace.

In order to increase the attention paid to cyber defence, in October 2017 the Law of Ukraine 'On the Defence of Ukraine' No. 1932-XII (1991) was amended, providing for the preparation of the state for defence in peacetime, during which measures regarding cyber defence (active cyber defence) should be implemented in order to protect the sovereignty of the state, ensure its defence capacity, prevent armed conflicts and repel armed aggression. In the future, the Law of Ukraine 'On National Security of Ukraine' No. 2469-VIII (2018) will become an equally important national regulatory act for guaranteeing cybersecurity. Its principles partially revealed the peculiarities of the Cybersecurity Strategy of Ukraine.

The Law contains only general provisions that do not contain specific measures. This led to shortcomings in the sphere of the security and defence of Ukraine, as a result of which disruptions in the work of the state authorities, private businesses, etc. took place and continue to do so. Therefore, in order to specify measures for the defence of the Ukrainian state and, in particular, cyber defence, the relevant Regulation was approved by the Decree of the President of Ukraine No. 23/2019 'On Regulations on the General Staff of the Armed Forces of Ukraine' (2019).

Thus, analysing the main tasks of the General Staff of the Armed Forces of Ukraine and the corresponding provisions, the following observations can be made:

1. With regard to the organisation of information protection and cyber protection, the General Staff of the Armed Forces of Ukraine are responsible for organising the deployment, management and functional existence of the information protection and cyber protection system in the information and telecommunication systems of the Ministry of Defence of Ukraine and the Armed Forces of Ukraine.
2. Concerning participation in the national cybersecurity system, the General Staff participate in the creation and review of the national cybersecurity system on a periodic basis.
3. The planning and implementation of cyber defence measures in order to prepare the state to repel military aggression in cyberspace (cyber defence) is also one of the tasks of the General Staff.

4. The coordination of the implementation of cyber defence tasks is also performed by the General Staff, overseeing the executive authorities, local self-government bodies and other components of the defence forces.
5. The tasks of the General Staff to ensure information security and counter cyber threats aim to ensure information security in the Armed Forces of Ukraine and counter systematic and large-scale actions against the interests of Ukraine in cyberspace, in particular by foreign states and their cyber units with special cyber weapons.

These provisions testify to the importance of interaction, coordination and active cybersecurity measures to ensure the national security and defence capacity of Ukraine in cyberspace. In addition, by Decree of the President of Ukraine No. 473/2021 'On the decision of the National Security and Defence Council of Ukraine' (2021) and 'On the Strategic Defence Bulletin of Ukraine' (2021), the next Strategic Defence Bulletin of Ukraine was approved. This defence planning document normalised the concepts of: military aggression in cyberspace, actions in cyberspace, cyber threats of a military nature, cyber warfare, cyber actions, cyber intelligence, cyber weapons, and cyber infrastructure. The Decree also emphasises that in order to counter the forces and means of the enemy, actions aimed at radio-electronic warfare and confrontation in cyber and information spaces must be combined.

The peculiarity of cyber defence, in contrast to cyber protection, is the presence of an active phase, where the vulnerabilities found in one's own system should become a projection of targets in similar enemy systems. Thus, in mission-critical systems during war, it is important to have procedures for monitoring the state of the system, scanning networks for vulnerabilities, deploying the infrastructure of false targets, and constantly exchanging information with active cyber defence forces. Therefore, the main task of cyber defence is to ensure the continuity of the functioning of systems of critical importance to critical infrastructure objects with the use of active countermeasures against the enemy (Davydiuk 2022, p. 51).

Since 2018, the Security Service of Ukraine has been operating the Cybersecurity Situation Centre. This structure was created with the help of the NATO, and technical equipment and software for the work of the Centre were provided as part of the implementation of the first stage of the Agreement on the implementation of the Ukraine-NATO Cybersecurity Trust Fund. The information security event management system operates on the basis of the Situation Centre, which monitors events in real time and allows the state of information security to be analysed. Moreover, this makes it possible to promptly detect, respond to, and warn of threats in national cyberspace (Security Service of Ukraine, 2022). Every day, cybercriminals use dozens of new schemes and methods of personal enrichment at the expense of other citizens and businesses around the world via the Internet. According to Article 1(8) of the Law of Ukraine 'On the Basic Principles of Ensuring Cybersecurity of Ukraine', cybercrime (computer crime) is a socially dangerous criminal act in cyberspace, the responsibility for which is provided by the Code on Criminal Responsibility (hereafter – CCU) of Ukraine and is recognised as a crime by international treaties of Ukraine.

It should be noted that at the beginning of April 2022, Ukraine was accepted into the Joint Centre for Advanced Technologies in NATO Cyber Defence as a contributing member (Onyshchenko and Hlushko 2022, p. 16).

As recent events show, a war in the information space causes no less damage than a war on the battlefield. Understanding all this, in the first 2 months of hostilities, the Parliament of Ukraine promptly and unanimously optimised the legislation around criminal proceedings. It also improved the grounds and procedural mechanisms for bringing all cybercriminals to criminal responsibility. These changes were concentrated in several laws.

For instance, the law 'On Amendments to the Criminal Code of Ukraine to Increase the Effectiveness of Combating Cybercrime in the Conditions of Martial Law' No. 2149-IX (2022) aims to: strengthen the capabilities of the national cybersecurity system and optimise it to counter cyber threats; implement effective criminal and legal mechanisms for countering cybercrime; and ensure the reliability and safety of using digital services. This Law also provides that interference in the work of information and communication systems and electronic communication networks will not be considered unauthorised if such interference is carried out in accordance with the procedure for searching and identifying potential vulnerabilities of such systems or networks, the exact text of which the State Special Communications was working on at the time of preparing this Chapter.

Secondly, the Law 'On Amendments to the Criminal Procedural Code of Ukraine and the Law of Ukraine "On Electronic Communications" regarding increasing the effectiveness of pre-trial investigation "on hot tracks" and countering cyberattacks' No. 2137-IX (2022), albeit fragmentary, makes necessary and generally positive changes. Among other things, these changes introduced the terms *computer data* and *computer systems* in criminal proceedings and provided a new public investigative (search) action – the taking of evidence from technical devices and technical means that have the functions of photo and video recording. In addition, the name of the law has been changed and the legal regulation of the procedural issues for the implementation of such secret investigative (search) actions as removing information from electronic communication networks and establishing the location of radio equipment (radio-electronic means) has been improved (Maltseva *et al.* 2022, pp. 37–44).

In early April, the Cabinet of Ministers of Ukraine issued resolution No. 299 on 'Some issues of response of cybersecurity entities to various types of events in cyberspace' (2023). This resolution defined the procedure for responding to cyber incidents and cyberattacks. The new resolution will allow for timely responses and the planning of cyber protection measures. It is normatively established that responding to cyber incidents/cyberattacks is carried out by cybersecurity entities by: taking cyber protection measures aimed at the rapid detection of and protection against cyber incidents/cyberattacks; gathering proper information about them; preventing minimising and eliminating negative consequences; correcting vulnerabilities; and restoring the stability and reliability of the functioning of electronic communication, information and communication, and technological systems and other objects of cyber protection (Krasnikov 2023, p. 122).

At the legislative level, the limits of the national police's activity in countering cyber fakes and threats in the information space, as well as the investigation of cybercrimes, provided for in Articles 361 and 361[1] of the CC, were expanded. It can be stated that the strengthening of sanctions, the additional criminalisation of certain acts related to the detection of fakes in social networks, and the prevention of cyberattacks are measures that are able to partially deter potential criminals from committing these and other crimes. State policy in the field of the legal regulation of cybersecurity is determined by the priority of national interests, aims to prevent the realisation of threats to information, and is carried out by implementing the provisions specified in the legislation (Kolesnyk and Plakhotnyy 2023, p. 51).

Behind the strategic steps and the legislative framework of cybersecurity is the need to interact with the private sector, which is an important actor in this space. In the context of general strategies and laws, the private sector, which includes businesses and organisations, is also becoming an object of increasing risk from various cyber threats in the conditions of the war in Ukraine. From cyberattacks on corporate networks to cyber fraud, businesses and industrial entities are currently facing various challenges and threats in the digital environment. Effective protection against these threats requires the private sector not only to comply with established norms and standards, but also to actively participate in the implementation of innovative solutions and technologies for cyber protection. Thus, the interaction between the state, the public sector and private business is a key element in creating a sustainable and secure digital ecosystem.

Legal aspects of interdepartmental and public-private interaction in the national cybersecurity system provide for the establishment of mechanisms for cooperation and information exchange in detecting and responding to cyber incidents. Legislation can establish procedures for joint analysis and response to cyberattacks, the exchange of technical information about new threats and vulnerabilities, as well as the coordination of measures to prevent and neutralise cyber threats.

It is quite obvious that cyber threats are not diminishing. In fact, new cyber threats emerge every day, and cybercriminals will always find new ways to break into systems and steal information. It is for this reason that cybersecurity is becoming increasingly important and companies need to be aware of existing threats in order to understand how to better protect their organisation. Below are just a few main examples of the latest cybersecurity threats, of which we are likely to see more this year.

3.8.2.1. Phishing and SMiShing

Phishing is one of the most commonly reported cybercrimes in the USA, resulting in countless financial losses every year. The goal here is to steal sensitive data and credentials, such as login credentials or credit card details, and trick people into allowing malware to be installed. Phishing techniques can disable security controls while an attacker browses company data undetected.

Smishing works on the same principles as phishing, but the decoy messages are sent via SMS rather than email. An attacker poses as a trusted person and targets mobile devices to gain access to sensitive information. When these mobile devices connect to the company's network, an attacker gains access, stealing customer and employee data and the organisation's source (Art. 200 of the CC of Ukraine).

3.8.2.2. Malicious Software

Malware (malicious software) comes in many forms. Attackers develop malware to create permanent, hard-to-detect backdoor access to company devices. They can then remotely control the device and use it to steal data, explore the local network, or send spam from the infected device. A staggering 91 % of cyberattacks start with a phishing email, so phishing and malware often go hand in hand (Art. 361 of the CC of Ukraine).

3.8.2.3. Ransomware

This form of malware can cause catastrophic damage to a business. Once the malware enters a system, it locks it down and deprives the owner of access to critical data until they pay a ransom to retrieve their sensitive information and regain control of their systems (Art. 189 of the CC of Ukraine).

3.8.2.4. Compromise of Corporate e-Mail

Also known as email account compromise, Business Email Compromise (hereafter – BEC) is one of the costliest cybercrimes. This is manifested in attackers compromising corporate emails to defraud companies (Art. 182 of the CC of Ukraine).

3.8.2.5. Internal Threats

Many people in a company have access to sensitive information. Whether stemming from current or former employees, partners or contractors, 25 % of data breaches are due to insider threats. Bad actors act out of greed, or sometimes disgruntled employees act out of bitterness. In any case, their dissemination of important information can cause significant financial losses (Art. 147–263 of the CC of Ukraine).

According to Article 190 of the CC of Ukraine, fraud committed on a large scale (from 250,000–300,000 hryvnias, approx. 6,250–7,500 EUR) with the use of electronic computing equipment is punishable by imprisonment from 3 to 8 years. If Internet fraud is committed by an organised group or in particularly large amounts (from 635,000 hryvnias), it is punishable by imprisonment for a term of 5 to 12 years with confiscation of property.

A criminal case on fraud is initiated if the amount involved exceeds a minimum of 0.2 of the tax-free income of citizens. If the fraud involved is less than this amount, an administrative penalty is applied.

After the open aggression of the Russian Federation in 2022, new challenges related to cyber warfare emerged. It should be noted that the Russian Federation began the active phase of the hybrid war in the information space of Ukraine after the annexation of Crimea. After 2014, cyberattacks performed by various cyber groups supported by the government structures of the aggressor state began to be carried out on the critical infrastructure of Ukraine (Leonov and Seryogin 2019, p. 57).

It is possible to state that many cyberattacks organised by Russian hacker groups began even before the start of the large-scale war – that is, before 24 February 2022. The first phishing campaigns against Ukraine were recorded by Google specialists back in April 2021. In 2022, the number of cyberattacks on Ukraine increased by 3.5 times compared to 2020, and the number of attacks on NATO countries quadrupled. Google analysts reported that Ukraine and NATO countries were mainly being cyberattacked by five hacker groups: Frozen Lake, Coldrive, Summit, Frozen Barentz and Frozen Vista, some of which cooperate with the FSB and the GRU (the Main Intelligence Directorate) of the Russian Federation. All of these groups, according to the US Treasury Department, are part of the Trickbot cybercriminal group, which was engaged in the development and implementation of computer viruses that were used to steal financial data.

If the actions of these groups are directed against Ukraine or NATO countries, the following aspects of responsibility are possible:

1. International reaction: cyberattacks, especially those with international implications, can provoke a response from NATO and other allies. This could include diplomatic measures, economic sanctions, or even a cyber response.
2. Legal responsibility: if the individuals or organisations responsible for cyberattacks can be identified, legal liability may be considered. They may be charged with cybercrimes or violations of cybersecurity laws.
3. International discussions: states can conduct discussions and consultations in international forums, including the UN or the EU, in order to respond to cyber threats and develop international standards in the field of cybersecurity.
4. Cooperation in the field of cybersecurity: states can strengthen cooperation in the field of cybersecurity by sharing information and developing measures to increase cyber resilience and protect critical infrastructure.

It is important to note that identifying and establishing responsibility for cyberattacks is a complex task and may require time for careful analysis and investigation.

From a technical point of view, the aggressor state systematically implements the latest developments in order to spread malicious software in domestic cyberspace. For example, the Nodaria hacker group, which is closely associated with the Russian Federation, actively uses new malicious software during cyberattacks aimed at Ukraine. The Graphiron malware program is a modern piece of spyware development. This malware system was distributed to collect a wide range of information from infected computers, including system information, credentials, screenshots, and access to individual files. The program uses filenames designed to masquerade as legitimate Microsoft Office files and is similar to other TA471 tools such as GraphSteel and GrimPlant. Previously, they were used as part of a phishing campaign specifically targeting Ukrainian government bodies, in particular in January 2022.

Graphiron is designed to extract much more data, including screenshots and Secure Socket Shell (hereafter – SSH) private keys (Poliakov 2023, pp. 125–138). The information presented may be relevant from the point of view of demonstrating the diversity, high sophistication and seriousness of the harmful effects of enemy cyberattacks. New methods of such crimes emerge every day in cyberspace. Thus, the current legal norms of any country, and even more so of Ukraine, which is in a state of war, should anticipate, identify, resist and provide safeguards in the fight against such a serious global crime more promptly and flexibly.

In March 2023, the State Special Communications Service presented an analytical report on Russia's cyber aggression against Ukraine 'Russia's Cyber Tactics: Lessons Learned 2022' (2022).

Based on the results published by the State Intelligence Service, it is possible to state the main trends and dynamics of the Russian cyber threat. Cyberattacks are a fully fledged component of the Russian war against Ukraine. The goals of Russian hackers correspond to the overall goals of Russian military aggression. Civilian infrastructure is the primary target of Russian cybercriminals, and the hackers' priorities throughout the full-scale invasion have shifted according to military needs. Although state structures have consistently remained key targets of cyberattacks, media and telecoms were important targets early in the invasion, as Russian authorities counted on a quick victory and hoped to influence and intimidate Ukrainians through the media (Analytical report of the State Intelligence Service on the year of Russia's full-scale cyber war against Ukraine 2023, p. 30).

During 2022, Ukraine faced 7,000 cyberattacks on its information infrastructure. In addition, from 24 February to the end of 2022, the government's CERT-UA computer emergency response team processed 2,194 cyber incidents. Of these incidents, 120 were related to the financial sector, 156 to commercial organisations, and 92 to the telecommunications and software development sector. At the same time, since the beginning of 2023 (compared to the fourth quarter of 2022), cyberattacks from pro-Russian groups have decreased, but they remain systematic and intense. During 2023, in addition to banks, cybercriminals attacked insurance companies and bank software developers.

The State Security Service suggests that the increase in phishing attacks and account compromises targeting the Ukrainian banking system indicates that the Russians are planning to hack commercial organisations and attack them in order to steal resources (European Business Association, 2023).

Despite numerous public calls for the peaceful use of cyberspace in the interests of all people and nations, the governments of many leading countries have actively joined the cyber arms race, recreating the classic security dilemma on a qualitatively new basis. This means that against the background of complex and contradictory global processes of political, economic and social development, cyberspace is playing host to a new Cold War – that is, it is serving as the basis of a new confrontation between key geopolitical actors (Horinov and Drapushko, p. 268). However, Ukraine is forming its own model of strengthening the state of cybersecurity in the conditions of war, which requires, first of all, that the development and approval of relevant normative acts that meet the conditions of today is hastened. In early April 2023, the Cabinet of Ministers of Ukraine issued a resolution defining the procedure for responding to cyber incidents and cyberattacks.

The new Resolution of the Cabinet of Ministers of Ukraine No. 299 on 'Some issues of response of cybersecurity entities to various types of events in cyberspace' (2023) will allow for the timely response to and planning of cyber protection measures.

This Resolution approved the Procedure for the response by cybersecurity entities to various types of events in cyberspace. The algorithm for the response of cybersecurity entities to cyber incidents/cyberattacks begins with the preparation stage, during which measures are taken to research modern types of cyber incidents/cyberattacks and develop methods and mechanisms for preventing and countering possible cyber incidents/cyberattacks.

It is also important to note that the EU has supported Ukraine in countering cyberattacks by launching a cyber dialogue between the EU and Ukraine in 2021, strengthening the operational capacity of Ukraine's telecommunications services and helping to combat disinformation. In addition, at the request of the Ukrainian government, for the first time in an operational context, the EU activated rapid response teams for cyber incidents within the framework of PESCO (Committee on Digital Transformation, Information management 2022). Cybersecurity experts help identify, recognise and mitigate threats. Earlier, in July 2020, the EU introduced the first ever sanctions against the organisers of cyberattacks, including NotPetya. The recently approved Strategic Compass aims to strengthen the cyber resilience of the EU (proposing, in particular, a new law on cyber resilience and the further strengthening of the cyber diplomacy toolkit) and the EU's Eastern partners through cooperation in countering hybrid and cyber threats, as well as disinformation (Y. Pshetachnyk *et al.* 2022). In February 2022, the US Cyber Command team assisted cyber incident response teams in searching for active threats. For its part, the USA has allocated 40 million dollars since 2017 for the development of the IT sector of Ukraine. NATO member states are also investing in Ukraine's cyber defence through information sharing and support at the local level. In March 2022, Ukraine became a contributing member of NATO's Joint Advanced Technologies Centre for Cyber Defence. In addition, private companies such as Microsoft, Amazon, and Google are assisting Ukraine in detecting and countering cyberattacks during the invasion. The European Centre of Excellence for Countering Hybrid Threats has also increased cooperation with Ukraine since the beginning of the war, monitoring the situation and organising training on identifying, stopping, destroying and countering cyber threats, creating new ways of countering them.

Therefore, the key legal aspects that relate to the abovementioned context require legal regulation in various fields.

Firstly, at level of international law, the assistance that the USA and NATO member countries provide to Ukraine falls under the principles of international law – in particular, in the case of cooperation between countries or military blocs. This covers arrangements, agreements or certain standards of interaction in the field of cybersecurity.

Secondly, the allocation of financial resources from the USA and other countries for the development of cyber infrastructure in Ukraine falls under laws on development financing, trade and investment.

Thirdly, partnerships in the field of cybersecurity may involve joint agreements and principles for ensuring security in the digital space. This may include mutual assistance and information sharing to detect and counter cyber threats.

Fourthly, legislation on cybersecurity and data protection that is specific to each country is needed in this field.

Fifth, as concerns the private sector and cybersecurity, the involvement of private companies such as Microsoft, Amazon and Google in cybersecurity may take into account laws and standards regarding the protection of confidential information and cooperation with governmental structures in the field of cybersecurity.

Sixth, with regard to international organisations, Ukraine's participation in NATO's Joint Advanced Technologies Centre for Cyber Defence may be subject to regulation by the organisation's regulations and agreements.

Lastly, in the context of hybrid war and threats of a hybrid nature, the legal framework for cooperation in the field of cybersecurity can be supplemented by international standards and conventions on cybersecurity.

Considering all these aspects, the legal context of cooperation in the field of cybersecurity can be explored and defined at different levels: national, international and multilateral. Therefore, in its Resolution the European Parliament called for the immediate and full implementation of all decisions that will strengthen the EU's contribution to strengthening Ukraine's defence capabilities, including in the field of cybersecurity. In addition, the Parliament called on the EU, NATO and other interested partners to strengthen assistance to Ukraine in the field of cybersecurity. MEPs called for the full application of the EU cyber sanctions regime against individuals, legal entities and institutions responsible for or involved in cyber attacks against Ukraine (European Parliament, 2022, pp. 27–30).

Ukraine, taking into account the importance of interagency and public-private cooperation in the field of cybersecurity, is constantly improving its legal framework. The process of development and implementation of new legal acts is aimed at creating a favourable and effective system of cooperation between state bodies and private entities in the field of cybersecurity. For Ukraine, there are only two main problems in the field of cybersecurity: internal and external.

The internal problem is that commercial structures and individuals are not aware of cyber problems. First of all, it is necessary to work on the interaction between law enforcement agencies and those commercial organisations that can provide this service to overcome problems during attacks, hacks, etc. In addition, there should be reforms in the field of education to ensure the sufficient awareness and professional literacy of university graduates. It is clear that cybersecurity professionals will be able to explain the need for cyber protection, and accordingly will develop cybersecurity services. The presence of such specialists is important from the point of view of the protection of state objects and state secrets, in connection with the low level of implementation of innovative technologies in the field of the protection of information of state importance. In the context of foreign policy in this regard, the protection of state objects and state secrets should also be supported by fundamental informational provisions regulated by the laws and by-laws of the state (Bilenchuk and Obikhod 2018, p. 238).

From a legal point of view, among the tasks of the state in the conditions of martial law in the field of cybersecurity there are several key aspects that could be emphasised. Firstly, regarding the creation and optimisation of the national cybersecurity system, possible legal measures could include the development and implementation of legislation aimed at ensuring effective cybersecurity. This may include the creation of security standards, the regulation of cyber protection and cyber defence, and mechanisms for cooperation between the public and private sectors.

Legal measures may also provide for the creation of a legal environment for the development and maintenance of the necessary cyber capabilities. This may include financial incentives, tax breaks and other measures to support cybersecurity initiatives. The creation of prerequisites for mastering modern forms and methods of preparing and holding events is also relevant. This may include the regulation of cybersecurity training programs, certifications, and licensing. Requirements for conducting regular training and activities in the field of cybersecurity may also be established.

A timely response to current threats is also needed. Legal remedies can provide mechanisms for the timely detection, response and elimination of cyber threats. This may include developing standards for sharing information about cyber threats and implementing procedures to coordinate the actions of various actors. Lastly, the creation of effective management and cooperation systems is necessary. Legal measures can define mechanisms for creating effective cybersecurity management systems and ensuring cooperation between various national security actors, as well as with international partners.

The overall goal of such legal measures is to create a transparent, effective and well-coordinated mechanism for the protection of cyberspace under martial law. It is also important to ensure that these measures comply with the principles of human rights and privacy protection.

3.8.3. Interim findings

Cybercrime is a completely new type of crime which is constantly being updated, transformed, and has no permanent features, and against which standard approaches do not work.

As Interpol notes, cybercrime is currently developing at an incredible speed, and cybercriminals can coordinate a complex attack in a matter of minutes. This is why it is important for law enforcement officers to stay abreast of new technologies while understanding the opportunities they create for criminals and the potential for their use to combat cybercrime. A comprehensive approach which includes measures of both a legal and an educational, scientific nature is needed.

The regulation of cybercrime is usually based on a combination of national legislation and international agreements and standards. As cybercrime is becoming increasingly complex and global, regulation must meet these challenges. Many states are parties to the Convention on Cybercrime (Budapest Convention), which defines cybercrime and sets standards for cybercrime and extradition legislation. The EU also develops and implements strategies and legislative measures to ensure the cybersecurity of its members.

International organisations such as Interpol conduct joint operations and provide a platform for information sharing between countries. Some countries are creating special cyber police units and centres to fight cybercrime, and cybercriminals can now be tried and prosecuted by national and international courts either under the laws of the country in which they commit crime or in the country which apprehends them.

In this direction, Ukraine has undertaken positive steps in the legal field, including by defining cybercrime in its CC (including articles about unauthorised access to computers, spreading viruses, the theft of electronic information and other types of cybercrime) and adopting cybersecurity strategies and policies. Because cybercrime is of a flexible nature, the process of improving the legislation should be continuous and prompt.

Ensuring the effective fight against cybercrime requires the constant updating of legislation and technological measures and the cooperation of national and international organisations, taking into account the global nature of cyber threats.

In the conditions of martial law and given the accelerated development of digital technologies, cyber defence should be considered comprehensively. After all, the loss of funds and the leakage of information are only two examples of scenarios that the implementation of a cyberattack could create, and critical elements of the country's infrastructure are under threat. For these reasons, the prevention and elimination of threats to the digital transformation of cyber defence is the basis of both the competitiveness of business activity and the success of the state in general.

Considering the situation in the international arena and the constant improvement of the skills of Russian cybercriminals and hackers, it is necessary to pay sufficient attention at the state level to the issues of strengthening cybersecurity and data protection. Resilience against hacking and cyberattacks is important in any field, and digital security will only continue to grow in importance in the coming years. The state is taking important steps to strengthen cybersecurity at both the regulatory and methodological levels, which will allow the response to various types of events in cyberspace to be regulated and will significantly strengthen the protection of information resources and objects critical to the information infrastructure against cyberattacks. In order to ensure the cybersecurity of Ukraine, it is necessary to strengthen the interaction between the main subjects of the national cybersecurity system and to establish constructive cooperation. Strengthening the state of cybersecurity also involves the implementation and adaptation of EU legislation into national standards in the field of cybersecurity. Further efforts are also needed with regard to active work with the private sector, creating partnerships to share information and jointly fight cybercrime.

3.9. Legislative Challenges in Neighbouring Countries as a Consequence of the War of Aggression Against Ukraine: The Example of Poland

3.9.1. General Remarks

The Russian aggression against Ukraine which began on 24 February 2022 has had a demolishing effect on the Ukrainian state. The population has been critically affected, with people seeking refuge *en masse* in the territory of third countries, and much of the country's infrastructure will need to be rebuilt. The war of aggression has also caused Ukraine's economy to collapse. However, the scale of the war has meant that its impact has not been limited to Ukraine and Russia, as Russia's aggression has also seriously affected third countries, including, in particular, the Republic of Poland, Ukraine's neighbour. This Chapter reviews the impact of the war on modern states, in particular, in the field of constitutional law. The Chapter analyses the effects of the war in Ukraine on the legislative process of the Republic of Poland as a direct consequence. Firstly, it is established which matters required a legislative response and which legislative solutions were implemented in the face of the war of aggression in the territory of the neighbouring state. Secondly, the analysis answers the question of how the wartime circumstances influenced the procedural aspects of the enactment of these laws, especially in terms of the timing of their preparation and enactment. Thirdly, the question of the relations between the key political forces in the Polish parliament in regard to this legislation is explored, which is particularly important in the context of the exceptionally polarised Polish political climate, where two political options antagonised against each other have majorities in the chambers of Parliament. Fourthly, it is examined whether the enacted laws subsequently required amendments, which provides an answer to the question of whether the timing of the enactment of the laws caused legislative defects or whether any amendments were driven by the need to adapt the laws to changing circumstances.

3.9.2. The Substantive Scope of New Regulations

The war of aggression taking place just across the border in Ukraine was a determining factor for the introduction of legislative changes in Poland, the aim of which was to provide legal solutions that would, on the one hand, strengthen Poland's security, and on the other regulate the legal situation of persons fleeing aggression in Ukraine. The new laws adopted primarily concerned three spheres: the defence and security of Poland, assistance to the citizens of Ukraine, and sanctions imposed on the aggressor.

The first sphere where an immediate response was required due to the invasion taking place so close to the territory of Poland concerned the defence and security of Poland. The aggression against Ukraine provided the impetus for the rapid completion of the Act on the Defence of the Homeland, which was enacted on 11 March 2022. It is noteworthy that the previous act – the Act on the Universal Duty to Defend the Republic of Poland of 21 November 1967 – despite several amendments, contained archaic regulations based on principles tailored for another system, and was incompatible with the current needs of an independent army in a sovereign state (Nowak 2019, pp. 77–103; Filip 2020, pp. 257–268). The new Act, which has more than 820 Articles across more than 450 pages, consolidated and tidied up all regulations concerning the Armed Forces for the first time (replacing 14 laws previously in force). As emphasised in the explanation to the bill, the new law was to lay the foundations for building a stronger and better-equipped Polish Army that would be able to repel even the most dangerous attacks and fulfil its primary duty to defend the country effectively.

The main objectives of the Homeland Defence Act were: to strengthen the Polish Army via its technical modernisation; to increase the number of soldiers from 164,000 (as of 31 December 2022 – according to the data provided by the Ministry of Defence) to around 300,000 (250,000 of whom are to be professional soldiers, the remainder territorial defence troops); as well as to significantly increase state expenditure on military purposes. It also aimed to attract military recruits. In addition to the existing professional military service and territorial military service, the law introduced 1-year voluntary basic military service. The regulation on compulsory basic service, which is to last 9 months, was not removed from the law. However, the decision on its reinstatement was left in the hands of the President. The law specified the constitutional duty of every Polish citizen to defend the homeland (Art. 85 of the Constitution of the Republic of Poland (1997)) not only by providing standardisation on issues related to military qualifications and the course of the recruitment process for military service, but also by indicating the defence duties of citizens and other entities not directly related to military service – e.g., the performance of tasks by entrepreneurs for the benefit of the Armed Forces. At the same time, the new law modified the organisation and composition of the Armed Forces, as well as the authorities competent in matters of national defence and their tasks. To achieve the above objectives, the law provides for an increase in the defence budget, which shall be financed annually with expenditures from the state budget of no less than 2.2 % of GDP in 2022 and at least 3 % of GDP in 2023 and subsequent years. This expenditure was previously regulated in the Act on Reconstruction and Technical Modernisation and Financing of the Armed Forces of the Republic of Poland of 25 May 2001. The new Act also provides for the creation of a new source of funding (the Armed Forces Support Fund).

The second, very broad field of legislative response concerned the issue of the residence of and assistance provided to numerous Ukrainian citizens who fled the war of aggression and arrived in Poland. The huge pressure under which Poland found itself as an EU Member State in the context of the influx of people from Ukraine can be compared with the European migration crisis of the last decade (Zdanowicz 2021, pp. 85–103). According to the Polish Border Guard, 9,677,248 people crossed the border into Poland from Ukraine in 2022, while 7,611,722 people left Poland for Ukraine in the same period, an increase of 121 % compared to the previous year (strazgraniczna.pl 2023). In view of such a large number of refugees in need of support (it is pointed out that the aggression of the Russian Federation against Ukraine has caused the largest refugee movement in Europe since years during and immediately after the Second World War (Żołędowski 2022, pp. 4–9)), the existing provisions governing the legal status of foreigners, including social assistance for refugees (Laskus 2016, pp. 61–74), proved to be insufficient. The right to obtain refugee status in Poland is a constitutional right guaranteed by Article 56(2) of the Constitution, which provides that 'Foreigners who, in the Republic of Poland, seek protection from persecution, may be granted the status of a refugee in accordance with international agreements to which the Republic of Poland is a party'. The procedure for granting international protection should take 6 months, but it is often prolonged to last even double this period. Each foreigner who submits an application is issued a temporary certificate of their identity, which entitles them to temporarily stay in Poland. However, the foreigner is not allowed to work in Poland during the first 6 months. The decision to grant refugee status is taken by the Head of the Office for Foreigners.

In response to the exceptional situation of Ukrainian people fleeing the war of aggression, Polish authorities decided to simplify procedures as much as possible and offer additional assistance so that anyone from Ukraine seeking refuge in Poland could effectively receive it. Ukrainian citizens have been provided with assistance and facilitation measures at the border. For example, they no longer need to have the necessary identity documents, nor are they required to register at reception points or worry about formalities. Any Ukrainian citizen wishing to cross the Polish border is admitted, and those Ukrainians who were already present in Poland at the time of the invasion can extend their legal stay so that they are not forced to leave the country. All of these issues were addressed by the Act on Assistance to Ukrainian Citizens in Connection with the Armed Conflict on the Territory of Ukraine of 12 March 2022. The law entered into force on the same day as it was accepted, and its provisions had a retroactive effect from the date of the commencement of Russian aggression against Ukraine on 24 February 2022. This is a special law, existing alongside other legal acts regulating the area of migration and asylum – in particular the Act on Foreigners of 12 December 2013 and the Act on Granting Protection to Foreigners on the Territory of the Republic of Poland of 13 June 2003.

The new law has established requirements for documents issued to Ukrainian people by the Polish authorities in regard to their entitlements to enter and stay within the territory of the Republic of Poland, as well as other key aspects related to their legal status (rights and obligations) in Poland. Thus, it includes special rules for: the employment of Ukrainian citizens; the entitlements of Ukrainian citizens who are students, teachers or research workers entering from the territory of Ukraine; the education, upbringing and care of children and pupils who are Ukrainian citizens, including support for local self-government units in the implementation of additional educational tasks in this area; undertaking and carrying out economic activity by Ukrainian citizens; various forms of material and non-material assistance provided to Ukrainian citizens; and the creation of an Assistance Fund to fully or partly subsidise the implementation of measures aimed at assisting Ukrainian citizens.

It should be noted that on 20 July 2001, the Council of the EU adopted the Temporary Protection Directive. On 4 March 2022, just 1 week after Russia's military invasion of Ukraine, the Council of the EU unanimously decided to trigger this directive for the first time in order to provide quick and effective assistance to people fleeing Ukraine (Council Implementing Decision (EU) 2022/382). The package of rights under the Temporary Protection Directive includes, *inter alia*, the right to a residence permit and free movement in EU countries, as well as access to employment, suitable accommodation or housing, social welfare, medical care, education and child-care services.

The abovementioned extraordinary Polish regulations concerning the legal status of Ukrainian refugees fleeing war to a large extent implement the Temporary Protection Directive, although there are also reservations in this respect. First, not all of the family members of Ukrainian citizens can count on the assistance set out in the special law. The law is addressed to Ukrainian nationals (and their spouses who do not have Ukrainian citizenship) who have come to Poland from the territory of Ukraine in connection with the war on the territory of that country, and Ukrainian nationals who have the Card of the Pole and who, together with their immediate families, have come to Poland because of the war. Therefore, the children of Ukrainian citizens who do not have Ukrainian citizenship, for example, are in principle excluded from the scope of the Act. Second, Ukrainian citizens and other persons fleeing the war in Ukraine cannot effectively appeal if the Polish authorities wrongly refuse to recognise them as beneficiaries of temporary protection. It should be mentioned that between March 2022 and the end of April 2023, more than 18,000 people were refused entry at the Polish-Ukrainian border (Official Polish Border Guard data). As evidenced by data made available by the Border Guard Association to the Legal Intervention Association (Stowarzyszenie interwencji prawnej – interwencjaprawna.pl, 2023), the main reasons for refusal were, in the first instance, exceeding the permitted period of stay in the EU under the visa-free regime and, in the second instance, the lack of a valid visa or residence permit. Several persons were considered a threat to national security.

The third area of the legislative response of the Republic of Poland concerned issues related to national security in the face of the war taking place so close to the border. To regulate this, the Act on Special Solutions to Prevent Support for Aggression against Ukraine and to Protect National Security of 13 April 2022, the so-called Sanctions Act, was adopted. This law is closely linked to EU sanctions imposed on the Russian Federation as early as 2014 in response to the incursion of the armed forces of the Russian Federation into Crimea, and intensified in connection with the Russian aggression against Ukraine which began on 24 February 2022. The Polish Sanctions Act, which entered into force on 16 April 2022, provides for the creation of a list of persons and entities against whom sanctions are to be applied. These sanctions include, *inter alia*, freezing financial and economic resources, exclusion from public procurement procedures, and inclusion on a list of foreigners whose stay in the territory of the Republic of Poland is undesirable. The list is maintained by the minister responsible for internal affairs, and the law provides for severe penalties for violations of EU and Polish sanction provisions. The law was a response to the need to adapt Polish law to the regulations introduced by the EU in view of the unlawful aggression of the Russian Federation against Ukraine and the involvement of Belarus in activities in support of the Russian Federation between 24 February 2022 and 15 March 2022 (e.g. Council Implementing Regulation (EU) 2022/300 of 24 February 2022). While some of these sanctions could be applied directly, some provisions still needed clarification.

3.9.3. Procedural Aspects of Enacted Laws

When considering the consequences of the war of aggression for neighbouring countries, it is important to note its impact not only on the substantive content of law, but also on procedures, including the legislative procedure. Acting in a state of imperative necessity, often under time pressures, the mode of procedures provided for in peacetime may be inadequate. This does not mean, however, that by invoking a state of emergency, state authorities may act outside the limits of the law. To verify this thesis, the case of Poland can be analysed in order to determine how aggression taking place in the territory of a neighbouring state has affected the procedural aspects of the enactment of the abovementioned laws, particularly in terms of the limited time of their preparation and enactment. Although it is not necessary to present the Polish legislative procedure at that point in detail, further analysis requires that its most important elements be pointed out. In order to answer the research question posed in the introduction, it is necessary to analyse the minutes of the sittings of the parliamentary chambers as well as other documents illustrating the course of legislative proceedings.

The key point in this context is that, according to the Articles 118–120 of the Constitution of the Republic of Poland, statutes must be passed by the Sejm in the procedure of three readings. Pursuant to Article 121(1) of the Constitution, the bill is then referred to the Senate, which, within 30 days of the submission of the bill, may adopt it without amendment, adopt amendments, or resolve upon its complete rejection. If, within 30 days following the submission of the bill, the Senate fails to adopt an appropriate resolution, the bill shall be considered adopted according to the wording submitted by the Sejm. If the Senate passes amendments or passes a resolution rejecting the law in its entirety, the law goes back to the Sejm, which, pursuant to Article 121(3) of the Constitution, may reject the position of the Senate by an absolute majority of votes in the presence of at least half of the statutory number of deputies. Upon completion of the proceedings in the chambers, the Marshal of the Sejm presents the enacted law to the President of the Republic for their signature, who shall sign it within 21 days and who orders its publication in the Official Journal of Laws of the Republic of Poland (Rytel-Warzocha 2022, pp. 69–80).

Referring to the first of the enacted laws, the Homeland Defence Act, despite the comprehensiveness of the draft, the time for the required procedural reconciliation within the government was very short, but a number of entities nevertheless submitted comments (Borski 2018, pp. 42–44; Brzęk, pp. 203–222). This is significant because an analysis of the work on the projects of laws within the government shows that these reconciliations usually take several weeks or even several months (Mreńca 2016). The Council of Ministers, at its meeting on 22 February 2022, adopted the draft law and decided to refer it to the Sejm. The procedure within the Sejm was very dynamic – the bill was received by the Sejm on 28 February 2022, and on 11 March 2022 the third reading was held at the plenary sitting, during which the Sejm adopted the bill. In this process, it should be emphasised that the procedures were followed; however, a number of exceptional regulatory solutions were used to accelerate the proceedings. This case involved the application of the exception provided for in Article 37(4) of the Rules of Procedure of the Sejm (c.a. 1992), according to which the first reading may take place no earlier than on the seventh day after the printed version of the draft is delivered to the deputies, unless the Sejm or a committee decides otherwise. Accordingly, a debate was held on 3 March 2022, after which the Homeland Defence Act was referred to the parliamentary National Defence Committee. Another example was the application of the exception provided for in Article 44(3) of the Rules of Procedure of the Sejm, according to which the second reading may take place no earlier than on the seventh day after the committee's report is delivered to deputies unless the Sejm decides otherwise, as the agenda of the plenary sitting of the Sejm was supplemented in order to conduct the second reading. Three days after enactment, the new law was referred to the Senate, which passed it without amendments on 17 March 2022, and on the same day the law was sent to the President for signature. It is noteworthy that in the parliamentary chambers, the majority of votes belong to two different political forces in conflict with each other, and more often than not, the second chamber submits a significant number of amendments to laws passed by the Sejm. In the case of these proceedings, the need to pass this law was so significant that the Senate did not submit any amendments. Moreover, the President of the Republic, without any delay, signed the law the very next day (Królikowski 2023, pp. 74–75).

With regard to the Law on Assistance to Ukrainian Citizens in Connection with the Armed Conflict on the Territory of Ukraine of 12 March 2022, again, the draft law was also brought to the Parliament by the Government (Borski 2018, pp. 39–56). The draft was prepared by the Ministry of Internal Affairs and Administration on 2 March 2022, and on 7 March the Council of Ministers adopted the draft and decided to refer the bill to the Sejm. An analysis of the course of the Government's work on this project shows that the need to prepare this bill quickly was very apparent. For example, this is evidenced by the fact that the draft was processed in a special procedure, which allowed for bypassing the obligation to submit the draft to consultation, opinion, public consultation and consideration by the Legislative Committee. Within 24 hours, the Standing Committee of the Council of Ministers received 15 letters with comments on the proposed legislation (submitted, *inter alia*, by the Prime Minister's Office, the Ministry of State Assets, the Ministry of Family and Social Policy, the Ministry of Justice and the Ministry of Agriculture and Rural Development). During work on the bill in the Sejm, a number of measures were used to allow the law to be passed as quickly as possible. The speed of this work is evidenced by the fact that while in the Sejm the bill was immediately referred to the first reading, which took place on 8 March 2022 (Koksanowicz 2012, pp. 17–18), the law was passed the very next day. Such an exceptional pace of work was possible because the committee had a very short deadline for submitting a report, and after just 10 hours of work the Committee presented a report in which it recommended the adoption of the bill. Other provisions were also applied, allowing the next stages of the procedure to proceed immediately. In accordance with the legislative procedure set out in the Constitution, the Marshal of the Sejm forwarded the bill to the Senate on 10 March 2022 (Wronkowska 2000, pp. 76–83). On the next day, the bill was presented at the plenary session of the Senate, which adopted it with amendments. Still on the same day (11 March), the Senate's resolution on the bill was submitted back to the Sejm, which considered it on 12 March. Of the 60 amendments proposed by the Senate, the Sejm's committee recommended that 43 be rejected and 17 accepted. It should be pointed out that such a fast-tracked legislative procedure is an exception to the general rules. The bill was forwarded to the President of the Republic on 12 March 2022, who exercised neither the right of veto nor the possibility to refer the bill to the Constitutional Tribunal for the examination of its constitutionality, and signed it on the same day.

The third law that is important in the analysed context is the Act on Special Solutions for Counteracting Support for Aggression against Ukraine and Serving to Protect National Security of 13 April 2022. As in the case of the two laws mentioned above, the draft law was brought by the government, which passed it on 29 March 2022 – just 4 days after receiving the original version prepared by the Minister of Internal Affairs and Administration. Again, special provisions of the Rules of Procedure of the Council of Ministers (ca. 1992) were used, which allowed the omission of a number of legislative actions that normally apply. The bill was submitted to the Sejm on 30 March 2022, and the very next day it was referred to the first reading at a plenary session of the Sejm that took place on 6 April 2022 (again the exception provided for in Article 37(4) of the Sejm's Standing Order (ca. 1992) was used). In the meantime, a rather extensive governmental auto-amendment was submitted to the Sejm, prepared by the Minister of the Interior and Administration. By taking advantage of the provisions of the rules of the chamber and the extraordinarily efficient work of the committee, on 7 April 2022 the third reading was held, during which the Sejm passed this Act. On 8 April 2022, the law was passed to the Senate, which voted on it on 12 April 2022, introducing 30 amendments. On the same day, the law was passed back to the Sejm. On 13 April 2022, the Sejm accepted some of the amendments and adopted the law. On 14 April 2022, it was submitted to the President, who signed it on the same day.

The analysis of the legislative proceedings concerning the above laws allows several conclusions to be drawn. Firstly, in all cases bills were proposed to the Sejm by the Government, which was most reasonable from the point of view of the relationship of these laws to the foreign policy of the state, which, according to the Constitution, is carried out by the Council of Ministers. This was also justified from the point of view of the multifaceted nature of these laws, their fundamental impact on the domestic situation and many areas of life, as well as their massive financial impact on the state budget, for the implementation of which the Council of Ministers is also responsible. Secondly, it should be noted that the legislative procedures were conducted at an extraordinarily fast pace. Almost every time, the exceptions provided for by the provisions of the Rules of Procedures of the Council of Ministers, as well as the Standing Orders of the Sejm and the Senate, allowing for the acceleration of the procedures or possibly skipping some of their stages, were used. Thirdly, cooperation between the respective bodies at different stages of the legislative procedures was extremely efficient, as can be seen in particular in the work of the committees, which were often able to prepare a report on their work, including recommendations to the chambers, on the same day. Fourthly, the leadership and advisory bodies in both chambers of Parliament prioritised the procedures of these laws, each time composing the agenda of the sittings in such a way that the chambers could make an immediate decision.

3.9.4. The Impact of the War of Aggression on Political Interactions in the Legislative Process

Another important issue in the context of Polish legislation that is closely linked to the war of aggression against Ukraine is the relationship between the key political forces in the Polish Parliament at the moment of the adoption of this legislation. This is particularly important in the context of the extremely bipolar Polish political climate at that time, and the fact that the ruling party had an absolute majority in Sejm (the lower Chamber of the Polish Parliament) while the opposition had an absolute majority in the Senate. The majority of seats being held by the Law and Justice parliamentary party, supported by the individual votes of MPs from smaller parliamentary groups, allowed for fairly stable support for the Government, resulting in positive voting on Governmental bills (the opposition included Civic Coalition, represented by 126 MPs, the coalition of left parties, represented by 44 MPs, and the Polish Coalition parliamentary party, with a leading role for the Polish People's Party, represented by 24 MPs, and Poland 2050, represented by 8 MPs). The balance of political forces in the Senate was different. Despite the fact that Law and Justice was the most numerous party in the Senate (46 senators), it remained in opposition to other senators who, thanks to a broad political coalition, formed a majority. This resulted in a situation unique in Polish political history and parliamentary practice to date, in which entities forming a majority in one chamber were in opposition in the other chamber.

This provided an interesting background against which to analyse the extent to which political forces which significantly differed in their programmes cooperated in the legislative process in the face of the threat of aggression. In order to assess the behaviour of individual political groups in the process of passing these laws, the minutes and transcripts of the sittings of parliamentary chambers and other documents providing information on the course of parliamentary work were analysed.

With regard to the Homeland Defence Act of 11 March 2022, it should be noted that even before the bill was submitted to the Sejm, representatives of the opposition signalled their willingness to pass this law quickly by declaring their openness to cooperate outside current political disputes. However, throughout the course of the legislative procedure, this was accompanied by disputes and numerous mutual accusations often articulated in debates. In the third reading, when the Sejm voted to pass the bill, in some cases votes were divided, in some cases a significant part of the opposition, not wanting to vote against the bill, abstained, and in some cases amendments were passed almost unanimously. However, in the final vote on the adoption of the bill as a whole, out of the 455 MPs voting, 450 were in favour, 5 MPs abstained and there were no votes against. There was even greater unanimity in the adoption of the Senate's resolution to adopt the law without amendments, as all votes were cast in favour.

At the same session (No. 50), work also took place on the Law on Assistance to Ukrainian Citizens in Connection with the Armed Conflict on the Territory of Ukraine of 12 March 2022. As in the case of the Act on Homeland Defence and the mutual resentments expressed in the debate, the opposition did not take advantage of the procedural provisions of the rules of procedure, which would have caused the work to be prolonged or obstructed. The bill was supported almost unanimously both during committee work (out of 40 committee members, 38 MPs voted in favour of the Act) and in the third plenary reading, when the bill was voted on (Out of 454 MPs voting, 439 were in favour, 3 abstained and 12 were against). Similarly, in the Senate, where the opposition had a majority, although there were differences of opinions on specific solutions to the bill and votes on individual amendments were divided, in the end the Senate also passed it almost unanimously (some of the amendments introduced by the Senate were subsequently accepted by the Sejm).

With regard to the Act on Special Solutions for Counteracting the Promotion of Aggression against Ukraine and Serving to Protect National Security of 13 April 2022, it should be pointed out that despite the numerous political disputes during legislative work on this law, the vast majority of MPs agreed to speed up the proceedings. In the debate, the draft received the support of all political forces (except the Confederation). In the committee, the bill received unanimous support (81 MPs voted in favour, none against and none abstained). Despite the fact that individual opposition groups criticised the bill's detailed solutions and tabled some amendments, it was passed almost unanimously in a vote for the bill as a whole (out of 456 MPs voting, 445 were in favour, none against and 11 abstained). In the Senate vote, despite disagreements regarding individual amendments to the bill, the Senate was unanimous in its vote, with all 99 senators voting in favour.

The above comments on the political circumstances of the laws passed allow us to conclude that despite the fact that legislative deliberations were often held in an atmosphere of contention and mutual resentment, almost all political forces (with the exception of the Confederation in two cases) showed a proper understanding of the geopolitical circumstances that gave rise to the accelerated procedure of adoption of these laws. This leads to the conclusion that the rules defining the legislative process are flexible enough to allow instant law-making in certain factual circumstances, such as those that occurred in this case, when there is sufficient political will in Parliament. This is evidenced by the aforementioned elements of the legislative process, but also by other elements of the legislative procedure. The fundamental issue is, of course, the passage of these laws themselves (which took place each time by an overwhelming majority), but this was also reflected at the level of the Convention of Seniors, which each time gave a unanimous positive opinion on the changes to the agenda that allowed the laws to proceed immediately. This is also evidenced by the work of the parliamentary committees, which, because they were able to agree on a unanimous position on the bills under consideration, were able to quickly present appropriate recommendations to the Sejm. The constitutional and procedural rules defining the stages of work on bills in the Senate were also applied in a responsible and appropriate manner given the geopolitical situation at the time. Thus, in the Senate, where the majority of members belong to entities in opposition in the Sejm, every procedural opportunity was used to take a position as soon as possible.

3.9.5. The Quality and Stability of the Laws Enacted Under the Circumstances of the War of Aggression

The next question is whether the rapid method of passing laws in the face of the circumstances of war in a neighbouring country undermines the stability of the enacted laws. The extra-coordinated, extremely fast mode of enactment of these Acts can also make them prone to legislative defects. To address these issues, it should be considered whether the new legislative acts were driven only by the need to adapt the law to the changing geopolitical circumstances, which were the key impetus for their enactment, or whether there were other requirements for these amendments.

The first law enacted, the Homeland Defence Act of 11 March 2022, has been amended twice so far – firstly by the Act on Medical Devices (2022), and secondly by the Act Amending the Homeland Defence Act and the Public Finance Act of 5 August 2022. The first amendment concerned minor changes in three articles from the scope of medical law, which should be considered a normal legislative practice (Bulira, pp. 388–393, 564–570, 605). With the second amendment, five articles of the law were changed and one article was added (Art. 45a). The amendments introduced some modifications to the sources of supply to the Armed Forces Support Fund, broadening their catalogue, and were also aimed at removing provisions raising doubts as to their interpretation (Seredyński and Królikowski 2023, pp. 152–172).

The second law under review, the Law on Assistance to Citizens of Ukraine in Connection with the Armed Conflict on the Territory of Ukraine of 12 March 2022, has already been amended 13 times. An analysis of the individual amendments shows that they were of different natures and took place for different reasons.

Firstly, it is necessary to point out the amendments for which the need arose from the application of the enacted law. This is because in certain aspects there were solutions that could improve and better organise the activities of the public administration in implementing the provisions of the Act. For example, the Act on amending the Law on Assistance to Ukrainian Citizens in Connection with the Armed Conflict on the Territory of Ukraine of 23 March 2022 concerned the possibility of keeping, in the ICT system, records of underage Ukrainian citizens who arrived in the territory of the Republic of Poland unaccompanied by persons having actual custody of them, and underage Ukrainian citizens who arrived in Poland and, prior to their arrival, were placed in foster care in Ukraine (Kozłowska 2022, pp. 10–16; Kwaśniewska-Sadowska 2022, pp. 184–217; Uścińska 2022, p. 10). This category can also include the Act on amending the Law on Assistance to Ukrainian Citizens in Connection with the Armed Conflict on the Territory of Ukraine and the Law on Informatization of Activities of Entities Performing Public Tasks of 12 May 2022, allowing the minister responsible for information technology to create an ICT system to facilitate contact between employers and job-seeking Ukrainian citizens (Kacprzak-Szymańska 2022, pp. 162–171; Drembkowski 2022, pp. 138–147). The experience with social benefits granted to refugees resulted in the Act on amending the Law on Assistance to Ukrainian Citizens in Connection with the Armed Conflict on the

Territory of Ukraine of 27 April 2022, which extended to 120 days the period for which cash benefits for the provision of housing and food to Ukrainian citizens could be granted, and also allowed the collection of data on those for whom applications had been submitted, which is necessary to monitor the expenditure of public funds for these cash benefits and eliminate possible abuses in this regard (Walczak 2022, pp. 25–36; Kacprzak-Szymańska 2022, pp. 95–111; Martyniuk-Placha and Drembkowski 2022, pp. 77–79). Also noteworthy is an amendment passed just 2 weeks after the law was enacted. This was prompted by the need to clarify some of its provisions, as well as to supplement issues omitted from the current law. The amendment was multifaceted and extremely extensive, introducing approximately 40 amendments to dozens of provisions of the Act on amending the Law on Assistance to Ukrainian Citizens in Connection with the Armed Conflict on the Territory of Ukraine and certain other laws of 8 April 2022. The 8 June 2022 amendment was of a similar nature.

Secondly, some amendments supplemented the scope of statutory regulation with new matters. This was the legislative response to current events and new problems arising from factual circumstances. Such was the nature of the Act on amending the Law on Assistance to Ukrainian Citizens in Connection with the Armed Conflict on the Territory of Ukraine and the Law on Higher Education and Science of 23 March 2022, which allowed the law to also cover citizens of Ukraine who arrived in the territory of the Republic of Poland from the territory of Ukraine in connection with the hostilities conducted in the territory of Ukraine not directly, but after fleeing to another country, only subsequently arriving in Poland and then expressing their intention to stay in Poland (Klaus 2022, p. 22; Słubik 2022, pp. 30–40; Drembkowski and Suwaj 2022, pp. 3–26; Ciszek, 2022, pp. 27-34). This was also the nature of the amendment (Act on amending the Act on professions of nurse and midwife and some other laws of 5 August 2022) which expanded the possibility of providing assistance (Princ 2022, pp. 73–86; Martyniuk-Placha 2022, pp. 52–68), including medical care, to persons who were injured as a result of hostilities conducted in the territory of Ukraine and were transported to Poland for health care services, and who did not meet the conditions for receiving it under the provisions of the law in force until then (Kacprzak-Szymańska 2022, pp. 258–262; Wasilewska 2022, pp. 237–243).

Thirdly, some amendments were in the realm of legislative corrections. Amendments in the field of legislative technique, unifying terms used in the law, correcting erroneous references and clarifying terms used in the law, were found in most of the aforementioned amendment laws. While making substantive amendments, the legislature was simultaneously concerned with the correctness and legislative quality of the law.

The third analysed law – the Act on Special Solutions in the Field of Counteracting Support for Aggression to Ukraine and Serving to Protect National Security of 13 April 2022 – was amended three times before the end of November 2023 by: the Act on Amending the Act on Special Solutions in the Field of Counteracting Support for Aggression to Ukraine and Serving to Protect National Security and the Act on National Fiscal Administration of 5 August 2022; the Act amending the Law on Assistance to Citizens of Ukraine in Connection with the Armed Conflict on the Territory of Ukraine and Certain Other Laws of 13 January 2023; and the Act amending the Act on export insurance guaranteed by the State Treasury and certain other acts of 13 July 2023. These amendments were aimed at supplementing the Act with provisions introducing the institution of temporary management and ensuring support for employees providing work for sanctioned entities.

The analysis of amendments presented above shows that the Polish legislator reacted relatively quickly to its experience resulting from the application of these Acts. It also seems legitimate to conclude that the extra-coordinated mode of their enactment meant that it was impossible to avoid provisions that had to be subsequently clarified or supplemented, but, given the scale of the matter, the legislative quality of these acts was at a satisfactory level. It is also noteworthy that all the amendments made, brought on the initiative of the Government (or, less frequently, on the initiative of the majority party), turned out to be justified in the opinion of the Sejm and were accepted almost unanimously, which testifies to the continuing political consensus on legislation concerning the war of aggression against Ukraine.

3.9.6. Interim findings

The analysis presented above allows for the conclusion that the Polish legislator reacted relatively quickly to the new challenges faced by Europe, and in particular by the states directly neighbouring Ukraine when it was attacked by the Russian Federation on 24 February 2022. The need to introduce new legal regulations concerned various spheres, including, first and foremost, ensuring the security of Polish citizens and the Polish state and strengthening the state's defence potential in the event of possible aggression by an unpredictable Russian aggressor. In order to implement international standards for the protection of human rights and freedoms, it was necessary to provide a legal basis for the entry and stay in the Polish territory of Ukrainian citizens fleeing the war, and to regulate their legal situation by granting them a range of rights. The third area of the new legislation was a response to the need to provide the effective implementation of sanctions imposed on the Russian Federation and Russian citizens in connection with its aggression against Ukraine. As indicated, some of these regulations were determined by the EU, mainly the Council's Decision on the activation of the Temporary Protection Directive and several Regulations on sanctions. The swift enactment of the aforementioned acts through an extraordinary (fast-tracked) mode can be justified by the urgent need for an immediate response to an extraordinary situation. Despite some provisions requiring subsequent clarification or supplementation, the overall legislative quality of the measures in response to the war of aggression against Ukraine was deemed satisfactory. Notably, all amendments proposed by the Government, and occasionally by the majority party, received unanimous support from all political parties. This consensus underscores the political unity in addressing legislation related to the conflict in Ukraine, even in the face of significant divisions within the Polish political landscape.

Conclusions

Having explored the role of values and identity as a basis of legal developments during armed conflict situations and other emergencies, this research concludes that:

1. Firstly, law is unable to exist without morality, and morality would remain ineffective without law. This is evident from the character of the principal concepts consolidated in the most fundamental legal instruments, the key to which is human dignity. International law views and recognises dignity as the fundamental philosophical basis of freedom, justice and world peace. The legal category of human dignity *per se* and the debates arising on its basis are an indication and outcome of the novelty of human rights doctrine. The proper use of dignity in law requires reliance on the philosophy of law, which leads to the principled theses of natural law, as the doctrine of human rights is its modern counterpart. The hypothesis of dignity as an excessive legal category lacks substantiation because it is not a principle of the legal system but its foundation and a legislative maxim, which is understood in the context of the purposefulness of law and in its organic system. According to the Kantian concept, dignity does not imply the unconditional value of a human being, because only goodwill rather than the person *per se* predetermines the 'absolute value' of human existence. Dignity, therefore, does not imply what a person is, but what they ought to be. This conception requires an appropriate legal argumentation on dignity: the arguments should be applied in such a way that the person be the highest good and an end in itself.
2. The positioning of dignity in international legal instruments confers an exceptional hierarchical status of social obviousness to this value, which does not need to be proven, is not subject to exceptions or limitations, and does not 'yield itself' to being defined. This suggests that dignity is not part of positive law but is a foundation from which human rights can be derived; however, dignity as such cannot serve subjective rights. In order to apply dignity in a proper manner and to avoid its devaluation, the principle of subsidiarity must be respected: it must be invoked only when necessary to protect an interest for the protection of which ordinary legal institutes are inadequate.
3. The hierarchical character of dignity is fully revealed only in its proper interaction with the evolution of jurisprudence (the dynamic aspect of dignity).

Dignity as a legal argument can only be applied when it comes to defending humanity and not isolated individuals or their groups of individuals. This avoids the inflation of dignity in relation to subjective human rights. Through the proper interaction between the dynamic and hierarchical aspects of dignity, this value helps bridge the gap between absolute and relative rights, in particular by strengthening the legal protection of the most vulnerable groups in society. Therefore, considering the need to promote and socially develop a certain right, human dignity becomes the *ultima ratio* argument to justify the social continuation and development of human rights.

4. The gap between the hierarchical and dynamic aspects of dignity is a characteristic inherent in any democratic legal system, maintained by the rule of law and the separation of powers. Dignity, while always remaining an aspiration of law, is a never-ending obligation to keep creating conditions for the common good that ensure the flourishing of individuals and protect against the messianic role of totalitarian regimes in the historicist vision of the past and future.
5. Secondly, the value-based approach in legal interpretation is founded on all fundamental values that are upheld by the relevant society as an assurance of the survival of the nation as a community and that are embodied in the legal order. The nature of the value-based approach in legal interpretation is very broad because of the nature of the notion of a value itself. Therefore, the application of this approach in interpreting the law is very complex, dense and challenging, demanding an interpreter of broad and comprehensive mind in the legal, ethical, and philosophical areas. Although the grounds for the application of the value-based approach, as for other interpretative methods, derive from the indeterminacy, specificity, ambiguities and contradictions of legal norms, the principal demand for this approach in legal interpretation is caused by the incapacity of other legal interpretative methods to provide the contextual, just meaning of a legal text in the scope of a legal dispute, especially in non-clear-cut cases.
6. The just meaning of values should be determined not apart from, but in the context of a certain legal system and its traditions. Consequently, courts must use value-based interpretations when referring to the provisions of national constitutions – fundamental, supreme laws of the state where the aspirational direction of the nation and the values binding it are established – and relevant international legal documents such as the ECHR, the EU Charter, and the TEU. The latter are based on common fundamental values: respect for human rights and freedoms and the rule of law. The

jurisprudence of the ECtHR and the CJEU is an inseparable part of these legal documents, embodying the nature of these values in relation to the European legal system and present-day conditions. The ability of judges to identify the just meaning of the values thriving in a society and enshrined in the legal system, and then to balance and prioritise them, is important for the proper application of the value-based approach in legal interpretation and the achievement of justice. Value conflicts are resolvable by determining their relative weights and by means of proportionality tests.

7. The application of the value-based approach in legal interpretation differs significantly in political regimes (democratic and non-democratic) and depends on the values enshrined in the legal system and the political goals of the regime. The interpretation of law in accordance with respect for democratic values constitutes the proper application of the value-based approach, and is implemented to its full normative extent in democracies. In non-democratic regimes, this interpretative approach in legal disputes may be misused by empowering these dangerous regimes, weakening or even denying fundamental human rights, and controlling anyone who opposes the rulers (elites, dictators, etc.) or challenges the ideology of the regime.
8. In times of crisis, fundamental values may be in conflict to a much greater extent than in times of peace. Nevertheless, in extraordinary situations the value-based approach must be applied consistently with the rule of law and fundamental human rights. The danger of the distortion of the value-based approach is particularly perilous in emergency situations of an interstate political character – i.e., war/martial law, unlawful territorial expansion, and the use of force and violence. In these scenarios, political purposes may tend to be prioritised by the members of the judiciary. Therefore, the law is interpreted and the actions of state power institutions are justified politically, but not necessarily legally. National constitutions, which are compatible with *jus cogens*, are supposed to be significant legal cornerstones preventing departure from the rule of law and safeguarding the protection of fundamental human rights and the justified interpretation of law, both in times of crisis and peace.
9. Thirdly, although the freedom of conscience is enshrined in contemporary law alongside clauses relating to freedom of thought and freedom of religion, and is interrelated with these two concepts, yet inevitably they each have unique meanings and content. One long-term purpose of a war waged by one country against another is the creation of a considerable shift in the collective conscience of a society or of particular groups of people. A war against freedom, including freedom of conscience, has been waged by

Russia against Ukraine by trying to instil a particular ideology which is hostile to both the idea of Ukraine as a sovereign state and the Ukrainian people as a society. Moreover, the freedom of conscience of people in Russia has also been profoundly transformed throughout the regime of its president. Today, those who oppose the war in Ukraine experience harsh punishments enshrined in the newest amendments to the Criminal Code. The very aim of the Kremlin regime, via the means of new legislation, is to instil fear in Russian society and to paralyse its will to challenge the regime.

10. Fourthly, the research emphasised Ukraine's national renaissance, determination and self-transformation of a new Ukrainian constitutional identity. The 2019 amendments to the Constitution, as the constitutional embodiment of the events taking place in Ukraine since Maidan Dignity revolution, introducing the principle of a Western geopolitical orientation, affected the entire constitutional regulation and changed the lives of every state institution. Interpreting the Constitution in light of this new principle will allow Ukraine to overcome the shadows of the past and become a state with a European identity. The clear link between the European aspirations of Ukrainians being enshrined in the Constitution and the behaviour of state institutions adopting decisions to implement and foster democratic values demonstrates the sincerity of the European choice.
11. Having set this new goal, Ukraine was obliged to gradually remodel its constitutional system to make it compatible with the *acquis communautaire*. These constitutional changes, introducing new constitutional values and moving the life of the state in a European direction, cannot be seen merely as political tool in the hands of decision-makers – even during a situation as severe as the ongoing war. The constitutional identity of the state cannot depend on the country's political leaders or its geopolitical circumstances. Therefore, even this war cannot initiate new constitutional amendments that would deny previous iterations without destroying the state as it exists today. Ukraine's constitutional aspiration to become part of Europe is set in stone and, being described as irreversible, cannot be easily revoked. The aspiration to renounce the new constitutional identity would mean an endevour to transform the state again; it is not impossible; however it would mean the emergence of a state of Ukraine of different constitutional identity than the one that is being built now.
12. Ukraine's accession to the EU and possibly NATO is a prerequisite for the country's continued survival as an independent entity, constituting a vital obstacle to Russia's further expansionist goals that are no longer even thinly masked. Therefore, it is only a matter of time before Ukraine becomes

a member of the EU. Whether this occurs sooner or later will not affect Ukraine's determination to preserving its European identity and working towards the implementation of fundamental constitutional values common to all European states. At the outset, this research identified and analysed a number of challenges that international law faces in the context of Russia's aggression against Ukraine and concluded that:

13. With regard to the prohibition of the use of force, the purposes stated in the UN Charter – namely, maintaining peace and security, implementing fundamental human rights and re-establishing the rule of law – remain valid in the contemporary world and should be the pillars of the international community. The constantly changing content of the CLC of the international community forms the dominant legal thought, which shapes our understanding and determines our actions. An illustrative list of the characteristics of the dominant old legal thought is as follows: (i) a state-centred approach, (ii) the primacy of politics, (iii) a focus on strengthening the armed forces, and (iv) legal positivism. These features condition a mainstream understanding that perceives peace as a state that it is possible to win with a better-equipped army and considers the prohibition of the use force as a norm which can be interpreted in a broad way and used to promote justice. The manifestation of the characteristics of old legal thought is observed in practice in Russia's attack against Ukraine, which triggered Articles 1(1) and 2(4) of the UN Charter. The (in)action of the SC, the action of ICJ and the (re)action of the Nordic countries all confirm that old legal thought is not capable of achieving the purpose of maintaining peace and security in the world. Therefore, a submission on new legal thought is pronounced.
14. The proposition is made that new legal thought should consist of the following non-exhaustive list of characteristics: (i) an individual-centred international system as opposed to a state-centred international system, (ii) the priority of the rule of law over politics in international law, (iii) a primary focus on actively creating peace instead of a primary focus on the constant prevention of war on the international plane, and (iv) reintroducing natural law and balancing it with positive legal thought in the CLC. This would lead to a deeper understanding of the substance of the concepts validated in Articles 1(1) and 2(4) of the UN Charter and the relationship between them. Namely, that peace cannot be won, but only created; that the use of force being a *jus cogens* norm serves as a boundary between the world of order and the world of disorder; and that the relationship between peace and the prohibition of the use of force is a complex phenomenon, not a dualistic

choice. Progress towards peace can be achieved with the help of a shift in the CLC by abandoning old legal thought and strengthening the characteristics of new legal thought.

15. In the context of the IHL, Russia's aggression against Ukraine has raised many legal issues. However, some of these issues are clearly artificial, such as Russia's use of the term 'special military operation' rather than 'war' or 'conflict'. Without any doubt, under the IHL, Russia's war against Ukraine is an international armed conflict, and Ukraine's territories (including Crimea) are under military occupation – despite Russia's annexations or the creation of puppet states. Most of the personnel involved in active fighting should be regarded as combatants and, consequently, prisoners of war upon capture. Moreover, Russia's constant attempts to deny combatant rights to international volunteers, the Azov regiment, and members of territorial defence units are illegal. Finally, personnel of the Wagner private military security company should be recognised as part of Russia's armed forces, and Russia must accept responsibility for their actions.
16. As concerns the perpetrator state's unique genocidal declarations – which are observable in the context of Russia's atrocities in Ukraine, particularly from February 2022 – they can be used to outline the formation of a genocidal plan, and essentially constitute a destructive motive for genocide. This makes a significant difference in the prosecutor's ability to demonstrate genocidal intent, but as the most recent ECtHR case law suggests, even public confessions of genocidal intent on the part of Russian officials might not be enough to demonstrate its current existence in Ukraine.
17. From a historical perspective, the Lithuanian strategy may be useful in demonstrating Russia's intent to commit genocide against the Ukrainian people, as the Soviet Union's intent to commit genocide against Lithuanian partisans was primarily established by demonstrating the ideological foundation of the Soviet Union and the institutional framework for implementing the communist ideology. In this way, both the MGB as an organisation and its individual officers carried out part of the Sovietization plan in order to eradicate undesirable ethnic groups using precise methods and guidelines.
18. Since 2022, numerous high-level public assertions of genocidal intent have been recognised and cited as evidence of a genocidal scheme; nevertheless, future legal proceedings may also depend on Russia's political ideology and the organisational structure of the country's decision-making process. Prosecutors may be forced to work in the field of political science and develop an interdisciplinary strategy in order to identify those responsible

for potential genocidal crimes against Ukrainians since 2022, given that Russia's current ideology and governmental structure have still not been clearly defined.

19. In terms of international dispute resolution, since the arbitral tribunal in the *Coastal State Rights Dispute* rejected all of Ukraine's claims related to Ukraine as the coastal state over the maritime zones of Crimea due to its lack of jurisdiction, it became necessary to determine the status of Crimea in accordance with international law. Such a definition is necessary so that issues related to the law of the sea in the waters surrounding the Crimean Peninsula can be resolved under the UNCLOS dispute settlement procedure. There are two main directions in which to solve this sovereignty dispute: either apply the UNCLOS provisions or find a solution outside of them. In relation to the first direction, the option of supplementary jurisdiction under Article 288 (2) of UNCLOS is possible; however, considering the ongoing war between Ukraine and the Russian Federation, the conclusion of an international agreement related to the purposes of UNCLOS is hardly feasible. A conditional decision would mean an overly complicated decision containing a lot of 'ifs', which could create more controversy regarding the interpretation of such a decision than it possessed initially. In addition, such a decision can be considered appropriate in relation to a low-tide elevation, but not to the whole peninsula. As for the second direction, here the determination of the status of Crimea is more probable.
20. While the UN Security Council has the right to announce a binding decision regarding the status of Crimea, due to Russia's veto power the UN Security Council cannot practically do so. Starting from 24 February 2022, discussions began on the possibility of depriving the Russian Federation of the right to veto and/or its seat in the UN Security Council, as well as the activation of the obligation of the Russian Federation to abstain from voting as an interested state. This could be submitted for clarification and interpretation within the framework of the Advisory Opinion of the ICJ, together with the question of whether the Russian Federation has the obligation or right to abstain from voting in disputes referred to in Article 27 (3) of the UN Charter. However, such a procedure for obtaining a binding decision on the status of Crimea seems overly complicated.
21. Ukraine and Russia do not recognise the jurisdiction of the ICJ, so there is no option for a binding decision. However, nothing prevents the UN General Assembly from making a request for an Advisory Opinion from the ICJ. As the jurisprudence of the law of the sea shows, the combination

of an Advisory Opinion and UN General Assembly resolutions might be enough for a tribunal or court in this dispute regarding the law of the sea to declare that the status of Crimea is resolved. Finally, an ICC decision and/or a decision of a yet-to-be-created ad hoc tribunal regarding the aggression of the Russian Federation is a possible option. An appropriate definition of the status of Crimea could be created in the context of the definition of aggression as indicated by Russia's military occupation of Crimea since 2014. With this, the matters related to the law of the sea that were rejected because their resolution would require the direct or implicit determination of the status of Crimea would be able to be resolved under the UNCLOS dispute settlement procedure. Challenges in specific fields of law in the context of armed conflicts and emergencies range from environmental to health law, and, as the case study of some of Ukraine's neighbouring countries demonstrates, require adaptations to the general legislative procedures during emergencies as well as the specific application of laws and legal procedures, in particular:

22. In the context of criminal justice, which is already relevant, criminal proceedings in the absence of the accused person may be heard only where the interests of justice so require, and the procedural requirements for the protection of the rights of the absent defendant and of the fairness of the proceedings have been fulfilled. The right of a person to appear in court is not absolute, but its refusal must meet certain conditions, the fundamental tenet of which is the right to be duly informed of the proceedings. Total *in absentia* proceedings are based on the fact that the accused person has waived their right to participate in the proceedings and therefore did not participate in the proceedings at all. Whether a person is to be regarded as having waived their right to participate in the proceedings or as evading the proceedings is assessed in the light of the circumstances in which they were informed of the proceedings, the results of that communication, and the subsequent conduct of the person after receiving the relevant information.
23. The elements of the content of the right to be informed are essentially formed. It is the duty of the State to ensure that the person against whom proceedings are pending is informed in a timely manner of the time and place of the proceedings, of the charges, and of the legal consequences of the person's failure to appear before the court. The method of notification is not precisely defined; therefore, national courts and law enforcement authorities must constantly decide whether the way in which they choose to inform the person is compliant with the requirements of fair proceedings. Considering whether the way in which the information is provided is

sufficient to ensure the person's awareness of the trial, particular attention should be paid to the diligence exercised by public authorities in order to inform the person concerned and to the diligence exercised by the person concerned in order to receive such information. Informing a person by serving procedural documents, either personally or through a lawyer who is authorised by the person, are well established ways to properly inform the person, but they are not always effective in cases of international crimes. Therefore, properly informing the defendant is a situation in which it can also be established from other circumstances of the case that the person is aware of the proceedings. Public information about criminal proceedings in the media or on the websites of the law enforcement authorities shall not be considered as adequate information about the criminal proceedings against the accused person. Along with the requirements of the content and form of informing the accused person, the case-law has established a procedural rule according to which the proper information of a person is an obligation of the State and the burden cannot be placed on the person of proving that they have not been properly informed of the proceedings.

24. In the interests of justice, criminal proceedings *in absentia,* including cases of war crimes and crimes against humanity, may also take place against an uninformed person, in which case the individual must be guaranteed an effective right to a new trial. The individual's right to request new proceedings can be guaranteed both in the context of new judicial proceedings and with broad appeal possibilities. In assessing whether the right to a new procedure is an effective remedy, the case-law of the ECtHR and the CJEU allows the following main requirements to be distinguished: a person is not required to appear before the domestic authorities, and they are entitled to request a new assessment of the charges in terms of fact and law.
25. As concerns lay participation in court proceedings, the review of the model of lay participation in Ukraine allows some weaknesses and strengths of this model to be revealed. One of the negative aspects of the model concerns the selection of *присяжні* and the way in which the local authorities are involved in the political process. Secondly, the unequal legal status of judges and *присяжні*. The concept of the impeccable reputation of judges means that, among other things, a judge cannot have a criminal record at all, regardless of whether it has been expunged or not. Meanwhile, a lay judge can be sentenced for a corruption offence, but it is important that this did not occur during the previous year. Currently, lay judges have the status of officials, which is provided in criminal law. These factors might affect the independence of the judiciary and efforts to restore confidence in

this branch of state governance, i.e., the power of the judicial branch. One of the essential requirements for ensuring the independence of the judiciary is the procedure for appointing judges or lay judges in court proceedings. In Ukraine, the selection of lay judges should not involve representatives of the political process, and the Judicial Council (Ukr. *Ради суддив*) should be involved by ensuring the participation of such an institution at the constitutional level. The Constitution should provide that, for both judges and *присяжні*, 'appointment and dismissal, their legal status and guarantees of independence shall be established by law'. Such an amendment would ensure that judges and lay judges have the same legal status. Among the positive aspects, it is noticeable that when non-professionals participate in the judicial process it makes the process more understandable to the general public.

26. The analysis of the negative and positive aspects of the lay participation model in the administration of justice in Ukraine allowed for an analysis that looked into and provided an overview of the practical functioning of lay judges in the context of aggression. Firstly, it should be emphasised that Article 64(2) of the Law on the Judicial System and the Status of Judges provides for the possibility of involving lay judges in commercial cases. However, the Commercial and Procedural Code of Ukraine does not contain a separate legal regulation for commercial cases (e.g., bankruptcy cases, cases involving disputes between business entities, cases involving disputes on the privatisation of property, etc.). In addition, in practice, lay judges together with the judge in the panel hear civil cases, not commercial cases, including in times of aggression. On the other hand, the Civil Code of Ukraine does not contain specific norms establishing the institute of *присяжні*. Only the Civil Procedure Code of Ukraine contains two norms, i.e., Article 34(2) and Article 293(4), which provide for the institute in question in civil proceedings, where certain cases in courts of the first instance are heard by a panel consisting of one judge and two lay judges, who have all the rights of a judge in the administration of justice. However, the performance of the institute of lay judges in court proceedings during the Russian aggression against Ukraine is specific. Due to the extraordinary situation of aggression, lay judges at their own request can be released from the duties of a lay judge in connection with the mobilisation of military service from 24 July 2022 until its end, and can be substituted by another lay judge. In cases when it is impossible to form a complete court panel to hear civil cases, e.g., when the city council has no chance to approve the list of lay judges due to their shortage, the court transfers the civil case to the

closest court territorially. Additionally, the efficiency of the court proceedings and the safety of the participants in extreme conditions of aggression require that measures be taken to move hearings online, which also ensures the timely and efficient delivery of all the necessary information and documents related to the hearing to all the participants. Thus, the challenges of the court in civil cases during Russian aggression add extra reasons for the need to modify the model of lay participation in Ukraine.

27. Regarding the participation of lay judges in criminal cases, judges exclusively hear criminal cases unless the crime is punishable by life imprisonment. In that case, at the request of the accused, the case shall be heard by a panel of two judges and three *присяжні*. Thus, as can be seen, in Ukraine, the legislature has established the institute of *присяжні* only in high-profile cases. However, as of the end of 2022, lay judges do not participate in cases involving war crimes (Article 438 of the CC), even though they are punishable by life imprisonment under the law. Following the imposition of martial law in Ukraine and the amendment to Article 615(10) of the CCP, which entered into force on 1 May 2022, all criminal cases are heard exclusively by judges.
28. In the area of environmental law, having evaluated the possible definitions of ecocide, in order to recognise ecocide as a crime under international law, it is necessary to ensure:
    (a) Advocacy and awareness: environmental activists and organisations, such as the Stop Ecocide Foundation, have been working to raise awareness of ecocide and promote its recognition as an international crime. Public support and engagement are crucial to driving this initiative forward.
    (b) Legal formulation: proposals and draft codes have been put forward to define and codify ecocide as a crime under international law. The draft law should outline ecocide, ensuring accountability for state and corporate actors, addressing issues of sovereignty and jurisdiction, and providing potential penalties for those found guilty.
    (c) Political will and international cooperation: the recognition of ecocide as an international crime requires support and cooperation from the international community. Countries must come together to agree on the legal framework.
    (d) Ratification and enforcement: if an agreement is reached and a legal framework is established, countries need to ratify and incorporate this new law instrument into their national legal systems. Effective enforcement and exercise would then become a key aspect of making

ecocide a meaningful deterrent against large-scale environmental destruction.

29. In the area of elections, a number of challenges have been analysed. Firstly, because Ukraine has held regular elections since the restoration of its independence, except for in 2004 when the Orange Revolution occurred, postponing the elections would represent a deviation from standard democratic procedure. Therefore, this measure should be chosen responsibly and not threaten democracy itself. As armed conflict continues in Ukraine, several alternatives to holding elections within the term based on the Constitution were explored: (a) lifting martial law; (b) the non-extension of the state of war after its termination; or (c) the extension of martial law only in some regions of the country. Secondly, the Election Code stipulates that elections must be held within 90 days of martial law ending. However, such a deadline may be too short to prepare for smooth elections meeting democratic election principles and international standards. Thirdly, by organising elections even under challenging conditions, Ukraine would show the world that it is a unique state that does not forget democracy even during a large-scale war for its freedom and independence, and this would be a powerful signal that the state does not deviate from democratic standards and the political rights of citizens under any conditions. On the other hand, holding elections in wartime can make it challenging to adhere to international democratic standards. Given that Ukraine has long been a model of democratic progress in the region, the post-war lowering of electoral standards could lead to the significant degradation of the political system. In organising elections during wartime, various challenges could be faced, such as: the absence or lack of adequate infrastructure for elections; a lack of voter awareness regarding elections and low voter turnout; multifaceted security issues; political manipulation and corruption; the inability to hold elections in occupied territories, etc.
30. In the field of administrative procedure law, significant developments have occurred. The approval of the Law on Administrative Procedure was a significant step towards the systematisation of administrative procedural legislation in Ukraine. It provides a general legal framework for decision-making, and is expected to become an effective instrument for the protection of the rights of private persons in relations with administrative authorities and to play a vital role in the organisation of public administration activities after the end of the war of aggression in order to protect citizens' rights, rebuild the ruined economy, and attract investment in Ukraine. The scope of rights

of private persons in relations with public administration entities has been broadened and specified in the Law, in comparison with the current legislation. Special attention is paid to the right to be heard, the right to access to the case records, and the right to submit an administrative complaint. The LAP introduces some new important institutes – in particular, competence dispute resolution, the legal succession of administrative authority, the discretionary powers of administrative authorities, and the revocation of an administrative act.

31. Despite positive changes that will be brought to the Ukrainian legislation by the LAP, there are also challenges to consider. In particular, the institutes of witnesses in administrative procedures and the revocation of a lawful administrative act by the administrative authority, which are new, require serious attention to stimulate the protection of the human rights and legal interests of the participants of administrative procedures. The administrative authority that issued a challenged administrative decision can be the subject of the consideration of a complaint regarding this act if there is no administrative authority of a higher level and the administrative complaint consideration commission is established by such an authority. However, the decisions of such a commission are of a recommendatory nature, which means that the final decision in administrative complaint proceedings is to be issued by the administrative authority that issued the challenged administration act. The LAP is not a single act that would regulate administrative procedures, as the special laws that govern certain types of administrative procedure would remain in force. This means that some overlapping and divergent interpretations could arise after the LAP becomes applicable.
32. The emergency situation that arose in Ukraine due to the full-scale aggression of the Russian Federation led to difficulties in the realisation of the rights and legal interests of private persons in relations with public administration authorities (e.g., regarding the registration of IDP for the purposes of receiving state aid or obtaining documents, restricted access to administrative services, etc.). During the state of martial law, the principles and mechanisms of the LAP will be applicable with some necessary restrictions (e.g., measures for the protection of objects of critical infrastructure, or restrictions regarding free movement, choice of place of residence, protection of state secrets, etc.) stipulated in accordance with the Constitution of Ukraine (Art. 64) and the relevant martial laws.
33. Ensuring and protecting human rights in healthcare during times of emergency, particularly in times of war, is a challenging task. It can, however, be accomplished, as has been proven by the Ukrainian experience

of the protection of such rights during the full-fledged war of aggression unleased by the Russian Federation against Ukraine. Being committed to performing its international law and constitutional obligations to protect the non-derogable rights to life and personal integrity extending to certain health-related duties, Ukraine has also managed to ensure the protection of the right to health. Despite the fact that the Constitution of Ukraine allows the right to healthcare and medical assistance to be temporarily limited under the conditions of martial law, no derogation from that right has taken place. Several measures have been undertaken by the Ukrainian government, the healthcare profession, and civil society – not only to ensure the provision of timely and appropriate healthcare, but also to reduce the damage to the determinants of health (e.g., access to safe water, adequate housing, etc.) caused by the war. Some of these measures were among the factors that ensured the resilience of the Ukrainian healthcare system and the possibility to protect human rights in healthcare in the country.

34. The war highlighted existing issues of the protection of the rights of patients and healthcare professionals, and brought a new set of problems (e.g., difficulties in ensuring the right to access healthcare services, especially for vulnerable patients; the increased need for mental healthcare and rehabilitation; the necessity of properly differentiating between civil and military medicine; the need for the improvement of the standardisation of the healthcare service landscape to be performed by the healthcare profession rather than by the regulator, etc.). At the same time, efforts to increase the level of protection of the rights of patients and healthcare professionals were not stopped by the war. As it derives from the Ukraine Recovery Plan, such efforts are to be extended and launched in the nearest future.
35. In recent years, scientific developments regarding business and human rights have formed a new prism through which the human rights obligations of corporate actors can be viewed. The Ukrainian recovery plan should be based on the RBC approach. For these purposes, following the UNGPs, the governmental agencies responsible for providing financial funds and other forms of cooperation with the private sector as part of the Ukraine's recovery effort should guide companies towards:
    (a) publicly affirming their support for democracy, the rule of law, solidarity, fundamental human rights and territorial integrity;
    (b) publicly committing to exercising their leverage responsibly, both within their value chains (supporting business partners in building human rights capacities) and in governmental relations (ensuring that companies do not lobby for policies that protect their operations while

shifting burdens onto the most vulnerable), in particular by including in the company's human rights policy the commitment not to influence the political and regulatory sphere in an irresponsible way;

(c) having a responsible exit strategy as part of their human rights policy based on consultations with workers and external stakeholders, with disengagement as a last resort;

(d) developing and adopting policies on the work, family and volunteering balance.

36. In the recovery agenda of Ukraine, the BHR approach can provide a systematic framework for when and how a company has an obligation to do something more than simply provide respect or do no harm. The example of Ukraine is particularly telling because it creates a real sense of urgency to do something. In this regard, a coherent understanding of solidarity has a clear link with the concept of dignity, but also, arguably, a transnational and transgenerational dimension. This understanding should be reflected by all governmental recovery actions in Ukraine. In particular, ensuring competitive access to funding and growing value by adding sectors of the economy should be seen as critical projects in the recovery plan, which itself should be based on the RBC approach.

37. The context of war increases the risk of cybercrime. The regulation of cybercrime is usually based on a combination of national legislation and international agreements and standards. As cybercrime is becoming increasingly complex and global, regulation must meet these challenges. International organisations such as Interpol conduct joint operations and provide a platform for information sharing between countries. Some countries are creating special cyber police units and centres to fight cybercrime, and cybercriminals can now be tried and prosecuted by national and international courts either under the laws of the country in which they commit crime or in the country which apprehends them. In this direction, Ukraine has undertaken positive steps in the legal field, including by defining cybercrime in its ĊC (e.g., articles about unauthorised access to computers, spreading viruses, the theft of electronic information and other types of cybercrime) and adopting cybersecurity strategies and policies. Because cybercrime is of a flexible nature, the process of improving the legislation should be continuous and prompt.

38. Ensuring the effective fight against cybercrime requires the constant updating of legislation and technological measures and the cooperation of national and international organisations, taking into account the global nature of cyber threats. In the conditions of martial law and given the accelerated

development of digital technologies, cyber defence should be considered comprehensively. After all, the loss of funds and the leakage of information are only two examples of scenarios that the implementation of a cyberattack could create, and critical elements of the country's infrastructure are under threat. For these reasons, the prevention and elimination of threats to the digital transformation of cyber defence is the basis of both the competitiveness of business activity and the success of the state in general.

39. Considering the situation in the international arena and the constant improvement of the skills of Russian cybercriminals and hackers, it is necessary to pay sufficient attention at the state level to the issues of strengthening cybersecurity and data protection. Resilience against hacking and cyberattacks is important in any field, and digital security will only continue to grow in importance in the coming years. The state is taking important steps to strengthen cybersecurity at both the regulatory and methodological levels, which will allow the response to various types of events in cyberspace to be regulated and will significantly strengthen the protection of information resources and objects critical to the information infrastructure against cyberattacks. In order to ensure the cybersecurity of Ukraine, it is necessary to strengthen the interaction between the main subjects of the national cybersecurity system and to establish constructive cooperation. Strengthening the state of cybersecurity also involves the implementation and adaptation of EU legislation into national standards in the field of cybersecurity. Further efforts are also needed with regard to active work with the private sector, creating partnerships to share information and jointly fight cybercrime.
40. The Polish case study demonstrates that legislators are capable of reacting relatively quickly to the new challenges faced by Europe, and in particular by the states directly neighbouring Ukraine when it was attacked by the Russian Federation on 24 February 2022. The need to introduce new legal regulations concerned various spheres, including: a) first and foremost, ensuring the security of Polish citizens and the Polish state and strengthening the state's defence potential in the event of possible aggression by an unpredictable Russian aggressor; b) providing a legal basis for the entry and stay in the Polish territory of Ukrainian citizens fleeing the war, and regulating their legal situation by granting them a range of rights; c) effective implementation of sanctions imposed on the Russian Federation and Russian citizens in connection with its aggression against Ukraine. Some of these regulations were determined by the EU, mainly the Council's Decision on the activation of the Temporary Protection Directive and several Regulations

on sanctions. The swift enactment of the aforementioned acts through an extraordinary (fast-tracked) mode can be justified by the urgent need for an immediate response to an extraordinary situation. Despite some provisions requiring subsequent clarification or supplementation, the overall legislative quality of the measures in response to the war of aggression against Ukraine was deemed satisfactory. Notably, all amendments proposed by the Government, and occasionally by the majority party, received unanimous support from all political parties. This consensus underscores the political unity in addressing legislation related to the conflict in Ukraine, even in the face of significant divisions within the Polish political landscape.

Summary

'Resort to the violence of armed conflict, with all its usual chances and accidents, its frequent furies and inhumanities, its lists of casualties, trails of desolation, and legacies of hatred, looks like the antithesis of everything comprised in that ark of civilization's covenant, the rule of law' (Best, 1994, p. 3).

The 2022 Russian invasion of Ukraine has produced the most publicized and transparent, deadly military conflict in history. Pursuit of legal recourse has been initiated by multiple international institutions and national governments, and their respective courts. Organs of the UN, the Council of Europe, the EU, a score of national governments and NGOs have set in motion investigations and prosecutions for the array of war crimes alleged, from classic war crimes and crimes against humanity, to genocide. Evidence of these war crimes began to be gathered on an unprecedented scale as events unfolded. Prosecutions for war crimes have begun and will redouble as legal processes advance. Russian combatants and military leaders are being and will be called to justice.

One further, fundamental degree of accountability will require exceptional measures. Even today's advanced array of investigations and prosecutions that follow will leave the most culpable national political leaders immune from reach, and especially from the most properly tailored crime of aggression. Observing the unique visibility and provability of the hostile acts on the battlefield and in the presidential war rooms some advocates have proposed the establishment of a new *ad hoc* criminal tribunal, perhaps a hybrid court in coordination with Ukraine and other institutions, for the prosecution of Russian political and military leaders, as one effective avenue to restore justice and credibility to the international system, in the face of this manifest aggression (European Parliament 2022). Consolidating the major war crimes prosecutions in this special *ad hoc* court may produce the most effective results.

The dramatic circumstances in this war of aggression, featuring the unprecedented publicity, documentation, and aggressive investigations from the scenes of battle will unavoidably produce a new model for the promotion of human rights accountability, setting higher standards for human rights protection and vindication than at any time in the past.

The first part of the book looks into the role of values and identity as a basis of legal developments during armed conflicts and other emergencies in the countries. Firstly, it explores the polysemy of human dignity in the system of legal principles. Taking into account the relative novelty of human dignity as a category of positive law and the plurality of its interpretations, the first part of the book analyses the hierarchical and dynamic aspects of dignity in the system of legal principles. It follows Kant's concept of dignity and relies on fundamental legal instruments to substantiate the character of dignity as the highest moral category in the system of principles of law, where dignity is sustained as not requiring deductive proof – as untouchable and undefinable in concrete terms. On the other hand, it unfolds the threat of totalitarianism and the importance of the dynamism of dignity in the context of the need for the social development of human rights. Dignity is distinct from other legal principles as a supreme moral category and a legislative maxim that dynamically impregnates the entire legal system and requires that humanity always be guaranteed as an end in itself. The gap between the hierarchical and dynamic aspects of dignity is revealed as a characteristic inherent in any democratic legal system, maintained by the rule of law and the separation of powers and as a safeguard against the messianic role of totalitarian regimes in the historicist vision of the past and future.

Secondly, the authors analyse the value-based approach to legal interpretation, the way in which it interplays among other interpretative methods of law, its content, and the question of what determines the meaning of 'value', as well as whether there are any legal tools that can be used to resolve a conflict of values. This includes an exploration of whether the application of the value-based approach differs in democracies and non-democracies and in times of peace and crisis – and, if so, how. The role of the judiciary in implementing this approach to judicial interpretation in different political regimes is also delved into. These issues are addressed by examining the concept of the value-based approach to legal interpretation through the determination of the meaning of value and specific features of the application of this approach under different political regimes and in emergency situations. The research reveals that this approach in legal interpretation is based on all fundamental values that are upheld by societies and is subject to change due to the changing character of societies and their living order. Its application in interpreting the law is very complex, dense and challenging, urging judges to identify these changes as well as to balance conflicting values in legal disputes. The authors assert that the application of the value-based approach in legal interpretation differs significantly across different political regimes and depends on the values enshrined in the legal system and the political goals of each regime. The character of the regime affects the interpretative system that the judge should adopt. National constitutions, which are compatible with the *ius cogens*, are supposed to be legal cornerstones that prevent departures from the rule of law, the protection of fundamental human rights and the justified interpretation of law both in times of crisis and peace.

Thirdly, the place and role of freedom of conscience in the system of values during emergencies is analysed. From the time of Socrates to the events involving Salman Rushdie, the war against freedom of conscience has always been part of human history. What makes the state of this freedom even more pressing today is that we have recently seen an increase in the erosion of the freedom to hold, express and live according to personal beliefs and commitments through various constraints, including surveillance technology, religious discrimination, white supremacy movements, and re-education camps that inhibit freedom of conscience and other freedoms. Although it has been decades since freedom of conscience as a core human right first appeared under the protection of international law, this fundamental right appears to be an overlooked piece in the universal human rights jigsaw to the extent that it sometimes receives the label of a forgotten right. The authors first examine recent scholarship, international legal regulation and case law in order to reveal the concept of freedom of conscience. The treatment of freedom of conscience which has prevailed through the years is also taken into consideration in order to illustrate the thesis that the aim has always been to make individuals rethink prevailing beliefs and commitments, instil an ideology and transform a collective way of thinking. Later, the authors explore the specific ways in which freedom of conscience appears to be under attack in the context of the war of aggression in Ukraine.

The fourth perspective that this part of the book delves into is the possible impact of identity on Ukraine's European aspirations, providing an insight into future developments that are getting underway at present despite the ongoing aggression against the country. The amendments to the Ukrainian Constitution in 2019, confirming the European identity of the Ukrainian people and declaring the irreversibility of the Euro-Atlantic course of Ukraine, prove Ukraine's aspiration to become a member of the Western democratic community. The clauses enabling the Europeanisation of Ukraine signify the receptiveness of the Constitution towards international cooperation and a specific form of integration – fully fledged membership in the EU and NATO. The values-based commonness between Ukraine and Western democratic states as the foundation of the geopolitical orientation expressed in the provisions of the Ukrainian Constitution provoked Russia to impose a condition for ending this unprovoked war: the aggressor required that the Constitution of Ukraine be changed, enshrining the country's neutrality as a condition to cease hostilities on Ukrainian soil. The research aims to ascertain whether a peace treaty that requires that the core of the Constitution be changed can be considered democratically acceptable. Can the Constitution defend itself against unconstitutional amendments that lead the state towards the destruction of its newly chosen course? Construction of constitutional clauses enabling the Europeanisation of Ukraine and their significance to the Ukrainian legal order are explored, as well as their impact on the activities of state institutions. Further, it considers whether the requirement to change the core of the Constitution can be considered even theoretically acceptable in a democratic sense, notwithstanding that it could bring the desired peace to the state and its people. The role of the Constitutional Court during this war of aggression, when martial law has been declared, is considered. Finally, Ukraine's perspective on joining the EU after this war of aggression is evaluated as the Constitution prescribes it, and the steps taken in this direction.

Chapter 2 of the book reviews the challenges faced by international law in the context of armed conflicts and emergencies by examining the function of the prohibition of the use of force in contemporary settings, selected issues of the IHL, the problem of genocidal intent from a historical perspective and its applicability to the war of aggression against Ukraine, and jurisdictional challenges related to the coastal state rights dispute concerning sovereignty over Crimea in the context of international dispute resolution.

At the outset, the research argues that progress towards peace can be achieved with the help of a shift from old to new legal thought in the collective legal consciousness of the international community. It is considered that the purposes stated in the UN Charter – namely, maintaining peace and security, implementing fundamental human rights and re-establishing the rule of law – remain valid in the contemporary world. However, these purposes will not be achieved if the old legal thought shaping understanding and determining actions continues to be the dominant perception. A list of the characteristics of this old legal thought can be identified as follows: (i) a state-centred approach, (ii) the primacy of politics, (iii) a focus on strengthening the armed forces, and (iv) legal positivism. These characteristics manifest in practice in the case of the Russian Federation's war of aggression against Ukraine. Furthermore, the proposition is made that new legal thought should consist of the following non-exhaustive list of characteristics: (i) an individual-centred international system as opposed to a state-centred international system, (ii) the priority of the rule of law over politics in international law, (iii) a primary focus on actively creating peace instead of a primary focus on the constant prevention of war on the international plane, and (iv) reintroducing natural law and balancing it with positive legal thought. This change of the dominant perception would lead to a change of understanding regarding the substance of Articles 1(1) and 2(4) of the UN Charter and the relationships between them. Namely, that peace cannot be won, but only created; that the use of force is a *jus cogens* norm and serves as a border between the world of order and the world of disorder; and that the relationship between peace and the prohibition of the use force is a complex phenomenon, not a dualistic choice.

Further, the authors contend that Russia's war of aggression against Ukraine has raised a number of legal issues related to the application of the IHL. In official statements, Russia is constantly denying the very fact of this full-scale invasion as war, masking it by using the term 'special military operation'. Such a term has no ground in the IHL; therefore, Russia's actions have to be evaluated as international armed conflict, and the captured Ukrainian territories, including Crimea, should be treated as territories under belligerent occupation, despite Russia's annexations. An important issue is the status of the fighting forces, where Russia is again keen to deny combatant status to a number of Ukrainian units, such as the members of the Azov regiment, fighters from the so-called International Legion, and even territorial defence forces. In most cases, such denial is unlawful. One particular issue is the status of the fighters of Russia's Wagner PMC, which was engaged in the war against Ukraine. Despite the fact that Russia is not accepting responsibility for their actions, they must be considered as part of Russia's armed forces and Russia must bear responsibility. This war is also seeing large numbers of prisoners of war captured and mistreated, especially by Russia, which is a significant issue that is also briefly considered in the research.

Thirdly, the second part of the book discusses genocidal intent as the *mens rea* for the crime of genocide in light of the 1948 Genocide Convention (UNCG) and the case law under the European Convention for the Protection of Human Rights and Fundamental Freedoms (ECHR) regarding Soviet crimes in Lithuania, analysing relevant recent Russian sources for potential proof of genocidal intent in Ukraine since February 2022. The research focuses on one element of genocidal intent – the perpetrator state's plan to destroy a national group, in whole or in part, as established in genocidal declarations or speech. It does not cover the issue of individual criminal responsibility for genocide.

In the following sub-chapter, the authors evaluate jurisdictional challenges related to the coastal state rights dispute concerning sovereignty over Crimea. This dispute remains unresolved, and this research examines the options for determining the status of Crimea in accordance with international law so that issues related to the law of the sea in the waters surrounding the Crimean Peninsula can be resolved by the UNCLOS dispute settlement procedure. Firstly, the factual background of the *Coastal State Rights Dispute* and the findings of the Annex VII arbitral tribunal in its Award on Preliminary Objections are considered. Secondly, such options to solve the dispute within the UNCLOS dispute settlement procedure as supplemental jurisdiction and conditional decisions are addressed. Thirdly, alternative options to overcome a jurisdictional challenge in the *Coastal State Rights Dispute* regarding sovereignty over Crimea are evaluated: receiving a SC decision on the occupation and annexation of Crimea, obtaining an advisory opinion from the ICJ, or hearing the decision of the ICC or an ad hoc tribunal on the crime of aggression committed by the Russian Federation.

Chapter 3 of the book reviews specific challenges raised in particular fields of law by emergencies and armed conflict situations, with a view toward examining how the law should or has changed to address these challenges. Issues arising in the law of criminal proceedings, lay participation in court proceedings, environmental law, the law of elections, administrative law, health law, BHR law and cybersecurity law are examined in detail. In addition, a case study involving a neighbouring country affected by the aggression against Ukraine is presented, with regard to a more general problem relating to the adaptation of the legislative process to this emergency situation.

Russia's aggression against Ukraine will one day be adjudicated over, and this will entail the issue of the responsibility of the aggressor state. However, numerous issues related to bringing individuals to justice have already begun to arise. Among these are criminal proceedings in absentia, which involve several conditions, including the right to be informed, non-compliance with which may lead to an infringement of the individual's right to a fair trial. This research raises the question of whether the fairly well-established interpretation of this right in supranational case-law strikes the correct balance between the right to due process of persons accused of international crimes (war crimes and crimes against humanity) and the expectations of victims, society, the State and the international community regarding substantive and procedural justice in such cases. The second problem considered in this regard concerns the legal consequences of a violation of the right of a person who is subject to proceedings *in absentia* to be adequately informed. The research raises the question of whether such an infringement can be remedied by granting the individual the unlimited right to a new procedure, or whether such a right can be subject to certain conditions. The study concludes that the implementation of the right to information in cases concerning war crimes and crimes against humanity is *de facto* quite complex. The method of notification of the accused person is not precisely defined; therefore, national courts and law enforcement authorities must constantly decide whether the way in which they choose to inform the accused person is compliant with the requirements of fair proceedings. Thus, particular attention should be paid to the diligence exercised by public authorities in order to inform the person concerned and to the diligence exercised by the person concerned in order to receive that information. In the interests of justice, criminal proceedings *in absentia,* including cases of war crimes and crimes against humanity, may also take place against an uninformed person, in which case the individual must be guaranteed the effective right to a new trial.

The constitutional principle of the rule of law enshrined in the Constitution of Ukraine presupposes the duty of the state, among other things, to guarantee human rights and freedoms, even during aggression. One of the ways to ensure this is a transparent and efficient judicial system. Such a judicial system is one of the means of achieving justice, which is, *inter alia*, an integral part of the fundamental principle of the rule of law. Thus, another aspect related to the system of justice is lay participation and its constitutional place. The core function of the courts in Ukraine – to protect human rights and freedoms – is achieved by administering justice by judges together with citizens without any legal education (i.e., lay judges) in some cases. The Constitution of Ukraine uses the term *присяжні*, which can be translated into English as either *jurors* or *lay judges*, depending on the context. The research investigates the lay participation model in Ukraine and its functioning during Russia's war of aggression. Firstly, the constitutional and ordinary regulations related to lay participation in Ukraine are analysed and its practical operation during this war of aggression is examined. A detailed analysis of legal regulation is presented in order to identify the most optimal and rational modern model of lay participation.

Aggression against Ukraine has affected the application and implementation of several areas of law. The research notes that many wars have played a significant role in shaping environmental law and policies. Recognising the environmental consequences of wars has spurred efforts to protect the environment during wartime, preserve cultural and natural heritage, hold individuals accountable for environmental crimes, and promote sustainable development in a post-war context. At the same time, the environment was considered an unavoidable war casualty for a long time, but the war against Ukraine poses important environmental challenges, adversely affecting climate change, biodiversity and wellbeing. New international norms to safeguard the environment during conflict are urgently needed. These challenges directly and indirectly impact fundamental rights guaranteed at the international and European levels. War has a tremendous negative impact on air, water, and soil. The existing rules under the IHL and international criminal law, as the example of the war against Ukraine demonstrates, are not sufficient to ensure environmental protection and have been largely ineffective and inappropriate. The growing awareness of the importance of environmental protection and the effects of war on the environment raises more questions about the effective protection of fundamental rights and the responsibility and accountability of states. This research concludes that in order to effectively protect the environment, assessing the impact of existing international mechanisms and possibly introducing new legal norms, such as by including ecocide as an international crime, is necessary.

Emergency situations also affect the law of elections, and this will become very relevant for Ukraine. The research considers the issue of elections in Ukraine and the implementation of the principle of regular elections in legal acts. The authors analyse how the martial law introduced in Ukraine on 24 February 2022 affects the organisation of both presidential elections and elections to the Verkhovna Rada of Ukraine. The analysis focuses on the types of elections that could be held, the gaps in legal acts, and potential issues that Ukraine will face in organising elections after the end of martial law.

In the administrative procedure, this research looks into the newest legislative developments in this field and explores if and how they should be influenced by the emergency situation. Research reveals the concept of administrative procedure, development of the Law of Ukraine on Administrative Procedure, provides for the analysis of the key novelties of the Law, core guaranties for the private persons in relations with public administration entities, the main obligations of the public servants, explores possible challenges and solutions in practical realization of the Law in current and post-conflict Ukraine. Administrative procedure is a crucial element of good administration. In certain European countries legal regulation of the administrative procedure tradition goes back to a hundred years. The legal acts in many countries enshrine modern principles (right to be heard, publicity, oral proceedings, economy, efficiency) and institutes of administrative procedure. However, in some countries, legislation of this magnitude has been adopted quite recently. In Ukraine, the Law on Administrative Procedure was adopted after several decades of deliberations and discussions at the most painful time for this country, during the full-scale aggression of the Russian Federation against Ukraine. This study examines the concept of administrative procedure in the doctrine of administrative law and the relevance of the new legal provisions both during and after the state of emergency in Ukraine.

Further, the study discusses the issues of ensuring and protecting human rights in healthcare based on the Ukrainian experience accumulated during the full-fledged war of aggression. Special attention is paid to the protection of the right to health in conjunction with the non-derogable rights to life and to personal integrity that have been severely violated during this aggression. Despite constitutional permission to do so, no derogation from the right to healthcare and medical assistance has taken place during this period of martial law, which is commendable. Some of the measures taken to ensure not only the timely and appropriate rendering of healthcare services but also the reduction of damage to underlying health determinants (e.g., access to safe water, provision of adequate housing, etc.) caused by the war of aggression are also considered. The research also outlines the factors that conditioned the resilience of the Ukrainian healthcare system and the possibility to protect the right to health during wartime. Some legislative and governance measures aimed at ensuring the resilience of the healthcare system, which is a prerequisite for the protection of human rights within healthcare, are reviewed. This research focuses its attention on the problems of and solutions to ensuring and protecting patients and healthcare professionals' rights in times of war. New challenges (e.g., ensuring access to healthcare, especially for the vulnerable, the increased need for mental healthcare and rehabilitation, etc.) have appeared, in addition to pre-existing ones (in particular, the lack of effective mechanisms for exercising the rights of both patients and healthcare professionals). Some legislative interventions aimed at responding to such challenges are discussed. It is pointed out that the war has not stopped legislative efforts directed at increasing the level of protection of patients and healthcare professionals' rights. Moreover, even during these times, a degree of progress has been made in terms of legislative and institutional support via the protection of these rights, especially in certain spheres (e.g., transplantation). A number of measures (e.g., the introduction of healthcare professionals' self-governance) need to be undertaken within the framework of Ukraine's recovery process to help Ukraine recover, modernise its healthcare system, and better protect human rights in healthcare. It is emphasised that the legal protection of patients and healthcare professionals' rights is ensured even during martial law.

Another important aspect is touched on by this research concerns the importance of a human rights-based approach when rebuilding Ukraine. For its implementation, different stakeholders play critical roles. In this regard, the role of business actors – both international and Ukrainian – should be taken into consideration. The international community is increasingly setting expectations for responsible business conduct through international sustainability initiatives. This includes the UN Sustainable Development Goals, the OECD Guidelines for Multinational Enterprises, and the UN Guiding Principles for BHR. This research explores how business and the concept of human rights define the role of corporate actors in the recovery agenda for Ukraine. It is argued that a universal, one-size-fits-all model of business conduct that meets social expectations of corporate responsibility and respect for human rights in times of post-war recovery is not possible. Instead, there is a need for the heightened, vulnerability-sensitive and solidarity-oriented implementation of HRDD. This requires the joint efforts of the state, local municipalities, investors, academia, civil society organisations and corporate actors, with an ongoing understanding of the rapidly changing context. Companies and investors should build their internal capacities to undertake HRDD and embed human rights throughout their operations to implement responsible business conduct in a concrete manner. This approach should be implemented as a cross-cutting component of all governmental recovery actions in Ukraine.

Moving to another field, this research further evaluates the most critical aspects of cyber defence in Ukraine and the role of cybersecurity in the country. It particularly focuses on issues related to cybercrime within the context of ongoing warfare. In the modern world, cybersecurity has become a vital component of national security. Ukraine, constantly facing cyber threats and attacks, especially against the backdrop of Russia's aggression, is no exception. The research highlights Ukraine's ongoing battles against constant cyberattacks targeting its critical infrastructure, communication networks, and vital economic assets. Cyberattacks can have severe repercussions for the country's economy and security, including data destruction, the theft of confidential information, and the disruption of critical systems. It delves into the role and significance of cyber defence in Ukraine's national defence system. Cyber defence plays a crucial role in countering cybercrime and safeguarding national infrastructure. Cybersecurity experts employ modern technologies and strategies to detect, prevent, and respond to cyberattacks, offering support to Ukrainian military and law enforcement agencies in the realm of cybersecurity. Special attention is given to studying the task of countering cybercrime in Ukraine during wartime. In this context, it is crucial to develop and enhance cyber defence tools and strategies, as well as collaborate with international partners for information exchange and assistance in detecting and mitigating cyber threats.

As an integral component of national security, cyber defence requires constant improvement and cooperation to ensure the country's resilience against cyber threats. It demands a comprehensive approach, encompassing technical measures, policy decisions, and collaboration with national and international entities. Protecting national cybersecurity is the responsibility of all citizens and organisations, necessitating ongoing attention and investment to maintain the country's stability and security.

Cybercrime is a relatively new type of crime that is under constant development. Its negative impact in the context of war and extraordinary situations is increasing and the mechanism of combating cybercrime is being developed with the help of new technologies, as well as through the prompt adoption of new legal norms. The fight against cybercrime in the field of law is urgent and complex, and it is necessary to respond promptly to existing manifestations, anticipate possible variations, harmonise the internal legislation of countries and enter into a common international legal space. The research explores the strengths and weaknesses of countering cybercrime through legal and operational mechanisms, and suggests possible mechanisms for their improvement.

The book ends with a case study of Poland, analysing the adaptability of the legislative process to emergency situations. The war of aggression against Ukraine has had numerous effects on law-making in Poland, which, as a neighbouring state, has been particularly affected by the massive influx of Ukrainians seeking refuge. In this case study, the issues that required a legislative response are examined and the most important solutions adopted by the Polish legislature in the fields of defence and state security, refugee assistance and sanctions against the aggressor are analysed. Special legislative procedures under which the above regulations were enacted are reviewed, noting the dynamics of the legislative process, the impact of the circumstances on political relations between the parliamentary majority and the opposition during the enactment of laws, as well as the quality and stability of the enacted laws. The study shows that the Polish legislator responded quickly to emerging challenges in Europe after 24 February 2022. The rapid implementation of new legal regulation in various areas in Poland took place in emergency (fast-tracked) mode, justified by the need for an immediate response to an exceptional situation. Importantly, these measures received unanimous support from all political parties. Some of these regulations were influenced by the EU, in particular the decision of the Council Commission launching the Temporary Protection Directive and several regulations on sanctions.

Bibliography

ADAMIAK, B. & J. BORKOWSKI. 2014. *Postępowanie administracyjne i sądowoadministracyjne* [Administrative and Administrative Judicial Procedure]. Warszawa: Wolters Kluwer.

AHLSTRÖM, H. & SJÅFJELL, B. 2022. Why Policy Coherence in the European Union Matters for Global Sustainability. *Environmental Policy and Governance*, 33(3), 272–287. Available: https://doi.org/10.1002/eet.2029 [Accessed on 16 January 2024].

AKYOL, M., 2019. *Islam, Blasphemy, and the East-West Divide* [online via Law & Liberty]. Available from: https://lawliberty.org/forum/islam-blasphemy-and-the-east-west-divide/ [Accessed 10 January 2024].

ALEGRE, S., 2023. *Freedom to Think: Protecting a Fundamental Human Right in the Digital Age*. London: Atlantic Books.

ALEXY, R., 2005. *Teisinio argumentavimo teorija* [A Theory of Legal Argumentation]. Vilnius: Teisinės informacijos centras.

ALJAZEERA, 2022a. *Russian forces launch full-scale invasion of Ukraine* [Online]. Available from: https://www.aljazeera.com/news/2022/2/24/putin-orders-military-operations-in-eastern-ukraine-as-un-meets [Accessed 21 February 2022].

ALJAZEERA, 2022c. *World reacts to Russia's attack on Ukraine* [Online]. Available from: https://www.aljazeera.com/news/2022/2/24/world-reaction-putin-orders-military-operation-in-ukraine [Accessed 21 February 2022].

ALLOTT, P., 2022. *Anarchy and Anachronism: An Existential Challenge for International Law* [online]. Available from: https://www.ejiltalk.org/anarchy-and-anachronism-an-existential-challenge-for-international-law/ [Accessed 26 July 2022].

ALLSOP, J., 2016. *Values in Law: How they Influence and Shape Rules and the Application of Law* [online]. Available form: https://www.fedcourt.gov.au/digital-law-library/judges-speeches/chief-justice-allsop/allsop-cj-20161020 [Accessed 15 January 2023].

AMBOS, K., 2009. *What does 'intent to destroy' in genocide mean?*. International Review of the Red Cross 91(876).

AMNESTY INTERNATIONAL, 2023. *EU: European Parliament's Vote for New Corporate Due Diligence Legislation Should Strengthen Human Rights* [online].

Available from: https://www.amnesty.org/en/latest/news/2023/06/eu-european-parliaments-vote-for-new-corporate-due-diligence-legislation-should-strengthen-human-rights/ [Accessed 17 January 2024].

ANDALITSKA, INNA, *Occupiers killed at least 147 children during the siege of Mariupol*, - city council (photo). UNIAN. 19.08.23. Available from: https://www.unian.ua/war/za-chas-oblogi-mariupolya-okupanti-vbili-shchonaymenshe-147-ditey-miskrada-foto-12365811.html [Андаліцька, Інна. За час облоги Маріуполя окупанти вбили щонайменше 147 дітей, - міськрада (фото). УНІАН. 19.08.23. URL: https://www.unian.ua/war/za-chas-oblogi-mariupolya-okupanti-vbili-shchonaymenshe-147-ditey-miskrada-foto-12365811.html.]

ANDORNO, R., 2005. La notion de dignité humaine est-elle superflue en bioéthique? [Is the Notion of Human Dignity Superfluous in Bioethics?]. *Revue Générale de Droit Médical*, 16, 95–102.

ANISIMOV, H., 2022. Під час кваліфікації дій особи як порушення законів та звичаїв війни важливим є встановлення контекстуального аспекту [When Qualifying a Person's Actions as a Violation of the Laws and Customs of War, It Is Important to Establish the Contextual Aspect] [online]. *Scientific and Abstract Online Journal*, ISSN 2521–1463. Available from: https://expertize-journal.org.ua/zovnishni-novyny/6877-pid-chas-kvalifikaciyi-dij-osobi-yak-porushennya-zakoniv-ta-zvichayiv-vijni-vazhlivim-ye-vstanovlennya-kontekstualnogo-aspektu) [Accessed 20 February 2023].

ANNAN, K., 2003. *Speech Delivered at the GA, 58th Session* [online]. Available from: https://www.un.org/sg/en/content/sg/statement/2003-09-23/secretary-generals-address-general-assembly [Accessed 25 November 2023].

ANON, 2014a. *Договор между Российской Федерацией и Республикой Крым о принятии в Российскую Федерацию Республики Крым и образовании в составе Российской Федерации новых субъектов* [Treaty between the Russian Federation and the Republic of Crimea on the Admission of the Republic of Crimea to the Russian Federation and the Establishment of New Entities within the Russian Federation] [online]. Available from: http://kremlin.ru/events/president/news/20605 [Accessed on 18 July 2022].

ANON, 2014b. *Парламент Крыма принял Декларацию о независимости АРК и г. Севастополя* [The Crimean Parliament Adopted the Declaration of Independence of the ARC and Sevastopol] [online]. Available from: https://www.rada.crimea.ua/news/11_03_2014_1 [Accessed on 24 July 2022].

ANON, 2020a. *Band of Brothers: The Wagner Group and the Russian State* [online via csis.org]. Available from: https://www.csis.org/blogs/post-soviet-post/band-brothers-wagner-group-and-russian-state. [Accessed 15 December 2023].

ANON, 2020b. *Who Rules Russia – FSB Intelligence Is the "second government"?* [online via LRT]. Available from: https://www.lrt.lt/naujienos/pasaulyje/6/1188568/kas-valdo-rusija-fsb-zvalgyba-yra-antroji-vyriausybe [Accessed 28 November 2023].

ANON, 2022a. *Ukraine: Russia Agrees Need to Create Humanitarian Corridors* [online via bbc.com]. Available from: https://www.bbc.com/news/world-europe-60611470 [Accessed 15 December 2023].

ANON, 2022b. *Lavrov Defends Russian Attacks on Ukraine's Infrastructure* [online via aljazeera.com]. Available from: https://www.aljazeera.com/news/2022/12/1/lavrov-defends-russian-strikes-on-ukraines-infrastructure [Accessed 15 December 2023].

ANON, 2022c. *Lithuania Recognises War in Ukraine as Genocide, Russia as Terrorist State* [online via LRT]. Available from: https://www.lrt.lt/en/news-in-english/19/1691202/lithuania-recognises-war-in-ukraine-as-genocide-russia-as-terrorist-state [Accessed 28 November 2023].

ANON, 2022d. *Rapport sur les évènements de Moura du 27 au 31 mars 2022* [Report on events at Moura from 27 to 31 March 2022] [online]. Available from: https://www.ohchr.org/sites/default/files/documents/countries/mali/20230512-Moura-Report.pdf [Accessed 15 December 2023].

ANON, 2022e. *Two 'LNR' Machine Gunners Sentenced to Prison* [online via kyivpost.com]. Available from: https://www.kyivpost.com/post/1347 [Accessed 15 December 2023].

ANON, 2022f. *Russian Supreme Court Labels Ukrainian Azov Military Regiment A 'Terrorist' Organization* [online via rferl.org]. Available from: https://www.rferl.org/a/russia-labels-ukraine-azov-military-regiment-terrorist/31970480.html [Accessed 15 December 2023].

ANON, 2023a. *Azovstal Leaders Freed in Prisoner Swap Promise to Return to the Battlefield in Ukraine* [online via cnn.com]. Available from: https://edition.cnn.com/2023/07/09/europe/azovstal-leaders-return-ukraine-intl-hnk/index.html [Accessed 15 December 2023].

ANON, 2023b. *Ukraine's Zelenskyy Brings Home Azovstal Commanders from Turkey* [online via aljazeera.com]. Available from: https://www.aljazeera.com/news/2023/7/8/ukraines-zelenskyy-returns-azov-commanders-released-to-turkey [Accessed 15 December 2023].

ANON, 2023c. *Wagner Chief Says 20,000 of Its Troops Killed in Bakhmut Battle* [online via aljazeera.com]. Available from: https://www.aljazeera.com/news/2023/5/25/wagner-chief-says-20000-of-its-troops-killed-in-bakhmut-battle [Accessed 15 December 2023].

ANON, 2023d. *Report on the Treatment of Prisoners of War and Persons hors de combat in the Context of the Armed Attack by the Russian Federation Against Ukraine 24 February 2022 to 23 February 2023* [online via ohchr.org]. Available from: https://www.ohchr.org/sites/default/files/2023-10/23-03-24-ukraine-thematic-report-pows-en.pdf [Accessed 15 December 2023].

ANON, 2023e. *Russian Federation: UN Experts Alarmed by Recruitment of Prisoners by "Wagner Group"* [online via ohchr.org]. Available from: https://www.ohchr.org/en/press-releases/2023/03/russian-federation-un-experts-alarmed-recruitment-prisoners-wagner-group [Accessed 15 December 2023].

ANON, 2023f. *Turkish President Explains Why He Handed over Azovstal Commanders to Ukraine Despite Russia's Stance* [online via Pravda.com.ua]. Available from: https://www.pravda.com.ua/eng/news/2023/07/12/7411040/ [Accessed 15 December 2023].

ANON, 2023g. *Russia and Ukraine Announce Prisoner Exchange* [online via reuters.com]. Available from: https://www.reuters.com/world/europe/russia-ukraine-announce-prisoner-exchange-2023-07-06/ [Accessed 15 December 2023].

ANON, 2023h. *Нам нужно освобождать и Крым, и Донбасс – херсонский волонтер, переживший пытки и плен в Севастополе* [We Need to Liberate Both Crimea and Donbass – Kherson Volunteer Who Survived Torture and Captivity in Sevastopol] [online via ru.krymr.com]. Available from: https://ru.krymr.com/a/khersonskiy-volonter-igor-kurayan-nam-nado-osvobozhdat-i-krym-i-donbass/32375886.html [Accessed 15 December 2023].

ANON, [no date]. *Can the President Cancel or Postpone the General Election? National Task Force on Election Crises* [online]. Available from: https://static1.squarespace.com/static/5e70e52c7c72720ed714313f/t/5f22c800c516197500f1c997/1596114945315/ElectionTimingGuide.pdf [Accessed 15 December 2023].

ANON, [no date]. *Combined Statement and Declaration* [online]. Available from: https://gordonandsarahbrown.com/wp-content/uploads/2022/03/Combined-Statement-and-Declaration.pdf [Accessed 29 July 2022].

ANON, [no date]. *Explanations relating to the Charter of Fundamental Rights.* OJ 2007 C 303. In: ANON, *Absentia Procedure: The Concept of Amendments to National Legislation Ukraine.*

ANUŠAUSKAS, A., 1996. *Lietuvių tautos sovietinis naikinimas 1940–1958 metais* [Soviet Destruction of the Lithuanian nation in 1940–1958]. Vilnius: Mintis.

ARENDT, H., 1951. *The Origins of Totalitarianism.* Berlin: Schocken Books.

ARENDT, H., 2022. *Totalitarizmo ištakos* [The Origins of Totalitarianism]. Vilnius: Tyto alba.

ARISTOTLE, 2009. *Politika* [Politics]. Vilnius: Margi raštai.

ARMSTEAD, J. H., 2022. *Justice Demands the Arraignment of Russia's Guilty Men* [online via CEPA]. Available from: https://cepa.org/justice-demands-the-arraignment-of-russias-guilty-men/ [Accessed 17 January 2024].

ASAD, T., 1993. *Genealogies of Religion: Discipline and Reasons of Power in Christianity and Islam.* Baltimore: Johns Hopkins University Press.

ASAD, T., 2003. *Formations of the Secular: Christianity, Islam, Modernity.* Stanford University Press.

ASKEW, J., 2022. *Russian Solider, 21, on Trial for Murdering Civilian in Ukraine War* [online via Euronews]. Available from: https://www.euronews.com/my-europe/2022/05/13/russian-solider-21-on-trial-for-murdering-civilian-in-ukraine-war [Accessed 20 February 2023].

AZAROVA, V., 2018. An Illegal Territorial Regime? On the Occupation and Annexation of Crimea as a Matter of International Law. In: SAYAPIN, S. & TSYBULENKO, E. eds., *The Use of Force against Ukraine and International Law: Jus Ad Bellum, Jus In Bello, Jus Post Bellum.* Hague: T.M.C. Asser Press.

AŽUBALYTĖ, R., 2010. Tendencies of the Development of the Lithuanian Criminal Procedure. *Jurisprudencija*, 1(119), 281–296.

BAĞLAYAN, B., 2018. *Good Business: The Economic Case for Protecting Human Rights* [online via SSRN]. Available from: https://ssrn.com/abstract=3304959 [Accessed 17 January 2024].

BANK FOR INTERNATIONAL SETTLEMENTS, 2017. *Understanding Globalisation* [online]. Available from: https://www.bis.org/publ/arpdf/ar2017e6.pdf [Accessed 28 November 2023].

BARAK, A., 2002. *Foreword: A Judge on Judging: The Role of a Supreme Court in a Democracy* [online via Hein Online]. Available from: https://heinonline.org/HOL/LandingPage?handle=hein.journals/hlr116&div=16&id=&page= [Accessed 28 November 2023].

BARRIGA, S. & GROVER, L., 2011. *A historic breakthrough on the crime of aggression. American Journal of International Law*, 105(3), 517-533.

BASSIOUNI, M.C. & MANIKAS, P., 1995. *The Law of the International Criminal Tribunal for the Former Yugoslavia. Irvington-on-Hudson*, NY: Transnational Publishers.

BASSIOUNI, M. C., 1998. *Historical Survey: 1919–1998, A Documentary History.* Transnational Publishers.

BAUMANN-PAULY,, D., and Nolan, J. *Business and Human Rights. From Principles to Practice*, Routledge, 2016.

BECKMAN, R., 2013. The UN Convention on the Law of the Sea and the Maritime Disputes in the South China Sea. *American Journal of International Law*, 107(1), 142–163.

BELAVUSAU, U. & KOCHENOV, D. V., 2020. After the Celebration: Marriage Equality in EU Law Post-Coman in Eight Questions and some Further Thoughts [online via Sage Journals]. *Maastricht Journal of European and Comparative Law*, 27(5). Available from: https://doi.org/10.1177/1023263X20962749 [Accessed 19 January 2024].

BELTON, C., 2022. *Russia Will Stop "in a moment" If Ukraine Meets Terms – Kremlin* [online via Reuters]. Available from: https://www.reuters.com/world/kremlin-says-russian-military-action-will-stop-moment-if-ukraine-meets-2022-03-07/ [Accessed 28 November 2023].

BENCH-CAPON, T. & SARTOR, G., 2003. A Model of Legal Reasoning with Cases Incorporating Theories and Values [online]. *Artificial Intelligence*, 150(1–2). Available from: https://doi.org/10.1016/S0004-3702(03)00108-5 [Accessed 19 January 2024].

BENSOUDA F., 2020. *Report on Preliminary Examination Activities – Ukraine. 14 December 2020* [online]. Available from: https://www.icc-cpi.int/sites/default/files/itemsDocuments/2020-PE/2020-pe-report-ukr-rus.pdf [Accessed 15 December 2023].

BENTON, M. & SELEE, A., 2022. *The Ukrainian conflict could be a tipping point for refugee protection* [Online]. Available from: https://reliefweb.int/report/world/ukrainian-conflict-could-be-tipping-point-refugee-protection [Accessed 19 January 2024].

BERKELEY, J., 2013. *Leaders, Towards the End of Poverty* [online via the Economist]. Available from: https://www.economist.com/leaders/2013/06/01/towards-the-end-of-poverty [Accessed 28 November 2023].

BERLIN, I., 1969. *Four Essays on Liberty*. New York: Oxford University Press.

BERNARD, A., 2009. *Banding with Brothers: Authorising Force Through a Concert of Democracies* [online]. Available from: https://core.ac.uk/download/46709821.pdf [Accessed 28 November 2023].

BIELIESKOV, M., 2023. *Ukraine's Territorial Defence Forces: The War So Far and Future Prospects* [online]. Available from: https://rusi.org/explore-our-research/publications/commentary/ukraines-territorial-defence-forces-war-so-far-and-future-prospects [Accessed 15 December 2023].

BIIJ, 2014. The International Rule of Law in a Human Rights Era [online]. *Global Business & Development Law Journal*, 28(1) [online]. Available from: https://core.ac.uk/download/303871780.pdf [Accessed 28 November 2023].

BILENCHUK, P. D. & OBIKHOD, T. V., 2018. Cybersecurity and Means of Preventing and Countering Cybercrime and Cyberterrorism. *Law Review of the Kyiv University of Law*, 3.

BILEVIČIŪTĖ, E. *et al.*, 2017. *Lietuvos konstitucinė teisė* [Lithuanian Constitutional Law]. [online]. Vilnius: Mykolas Romeris University. Available from: https://www.registrucentras.lt/bylos/dokumentai/literatura/Lietuvos%20konstitucinė%20teisė.pdf [Accessed 6 February 2024].

BILYK, D., 2022. *Expert: Russian Actions in Mariupol Can Be Called Genocide* [online via DW]. Available from: https://www.dw.com/ru/nemeckij-jekspert-dejstvija-rf-v-mariupole-mozhno-nazvat-genocidom/a-61247449 [Accessed 28 November 2023].

BIRMONTIENĖ, T., 2010. The Development of Health Law as a Way to Change Traditional Attitudes in National Legal Systems. The Influence of International Human Rights Law: What Is Left for the National Legislator? [online]. *European Journal of Health Law.* Available from: https://brill.com/view/journals/ejhl/17/1/article-p23_3.xml [Accessed 19 January 2024].

BIRMONTIENĖ, T., 2021. *2020 m. Rusijos Konstitucijos pataisos ir konstitucinės jurisprudencijos labirintai* [The 2020 Amendments to the Russian Constitution and the Labyrinths of Constitutional Jurisprudence]. *Jurisprudencija*, 28(1), 9–32.

BJÖRK, T., 1996. *The Emergence of Popular Participation in World Politics: United Nations Conference on Human Environment 1972* [online]. Available from: http://www.folkrorelser.org/johannesburg/stockholm72.pdf [Accessed 19 January 2024].

BLANC-FILY, CH., 2015. *Les Valeurs dans la Jurisprudence de la Cour Européenne des Droits de L'homme. Essai Critique sur L'interprétation Axiologique su Juge Européen* [The Values in the Case Law of the European Court of Human Rights. Critical Essay on the Axiological Interpretation of European Judge] [online]. Available from: http://www.revuedlf.com/theses/les-valeurs-dans-la-jurisprudence-de-la-cour-europeenne-des-droits-de-lhomme-essai-critique-sur-linterpretation-axiologique-du-juge-europeen/ [Accessed 20 February 2023].

BOJKO, I. V., O. T. ZYMA, & O. M. SOLIVJOVA, 2017. *Administratyvna procedura: konspekt lekcij* [Administrative Procedure: A Conspect Lectures]. Kharkiv: Pravo, 132, 6. Available from: https://pravo-izdat.com.ua/image/data/Files/292/1-19.pdf [Accessed 16 November 2023].

BORSKI, M., 2018. Przygotowywanie projektów ustaw przez Radę Ministrów – wybrane zagadnienia [Drafting of Laws by the Council of Ministers – Selected Issues]. *Roczniki Administracji i Prawa*, 18(2), 39–56.

BOUCHER, F. & LABORDE, C., 2016. Why Tolerate Conscience? *Criminal Law, Philosophy*, 10, 493–514.

BUAMAH, C., 2018. *Legal Pluralism and the Implementation of International Human Rights Law in Africa: The Case of the Convention of the Rights of Persons with Disability (CRPD) in Ghana* [online]. Available from: 2018, https://core.ac.uk/download/216958085.pdf [Accessed 19 January 2024].

BUCHAN, R. & TSAGOURIAS, N., 2017. The Crisis in Crimea and the Principle of Non-Intervention. *International Community Law Review*, 19(2–3), 165–193.

BULIRA, J., 2023. Commentary on Articles 203, 288, 306. In: KRÓLIKOWSKI, H. ed., *Obrona Ojczyzny. Komentarz*, Warszawa: Wolters Kluwer.

BURGORQUE-LARSEN, L., 2010. *La dignité saisie par les juges en Europe*. Paris. Sorbonne: Anthemis, Bruylant.

BURY, J., 2007. *A History of Freedom of Thought* (2nd ed.). United States: Idebate Press.

BRAIBANT, G., 2001. *La Charte des droits fondamentaux de l'Union Européenne*. Paris, Le Seuil: Points-Essais.

BRODEALA, E. & EPURE, G., 2021. Nature versus Nurture: 'Sex' and 'Gender' before the Romanian Constitutional Court. A Critical Analysis of Decision 907/2020 on the Unconstitutionality of Banning Gender Perspectives in Education and Research. *European Constitutional Law Review*, 17, 724–752.

BROWNLIE, I., 2003. *Oxford Principles of Public International Law* (6th ed.). Oxford Publishing.

BRYANT, B. & JONES, R., 1975. Codification of Customary International Law in the Genocide Convention. *Harvard International Law Journal*, 16.

BRZĘK, W., 2014. Konsultacje publiczne w rządowej procedurze legislacyjnej [Public Consultation in Government Legislative Procedure]. In: SITEK, M., I. NIEDZIÓŁKA, & A. UKLEJA, *Bezpieczeństwo informacji państwa i biznesu* [State and business information security]. Józefów: Wydawnictwo Wyższej Szkoły Gospodarki Euroregionalnej. Alcide De Gasperi w Józefowie, 203–222.

CANÇADO TRINDADE, A. A., 2009. *Jus Cogens: The Determination and the Gradual Expansion of Its Material Content in Contemporary International Case-Law* [online]. Available from: https://www.oas.org/dil/esp/3%20-%20cancado.lr.cv.3-30.pdf [Accessed 17 January 2024].

CANCADO TRINDADE, A. A., 2013. *International Law of Humankind: Towards a New Jus Gentium*. Leiden: Martinus Nijhoff Publishers.

CANEY, S., 2006. Justice Beyond Borders: A Global Political Theory [online via Choice Reviews]. *Choice Reviews Online*, 43(05), 3062. Available from: https://doi.org/10.5860/choice.43-3062 [Accessed 17 January 2024].

CARROLL, A. B. & SHABANA, K. M., 2010. The Business Case for Corporate Social Responsibility: A Review of Concepts, Research and Practice [online via Oxford Academic]. *International Journal of Management Reviews*, 12(1), 85–105. Available from: https://academic.oup.com/jicj/article/10/5/1452/817170 [Accessed 17 January 2024].

CASINI, L., 2012. Realising Utopia: The Future of International Law [online via Oxford Academic]. *Journal of International Criminal Justice*. Available from: https://doi.org/10.1093/jicj/mqs067 [Accessed 17 January 2024].

CAVALLONE, G., 2014. European Arrest Warrant and Fundamental Rights in Decisions Rendered in Absentia: The Extent of Union Law in the Case C-399/11 Melloni v. Ministerio Fiscal. *European Criminal Law Review*, 4(1), 19–40.

CCDCOE, 2017. *The Tallinn Manual 2.0.* [online]. Available from: https://ccdcoe.org/tallinn-manual.html [Accessed 30 October 2023].

CHARITY, MATTHEW H., 2015. Unmistakably Clear: Human Rights, the Right to Representation, and Remedial Voting Rights of People of Color [online]. *Touro Law Journal of Race, Gender, & Ethnicity & Berkeley Journal of African-American Law & Policy*, 200–215. Available from: https://core.ac.uk/download/231063423.pdf [Accessed 17 January 2024].

CHEN, L., 1989. *An Introduction to Contemporary International Law: A Policy-Oriented Perspective* [online]. Available from: https://ci.nii.ac.jp/ncid/BB18325640 [Accessed 17 January 2024].

CHEN, L., 1989. *An Introduction to Contemporary International Law*: A Policy-Oriented Perspective, Yale University Press.

CHEREMINSKY, E., 2000. The Jurisprudence of Justice Scalia: A Critical Appraisal [online via AP News]. *University of Hawai'i Law Review*, 22(385), 385–401. Available from: https://scholarship.law.duke.edu/cgi/viewcontent.cgi?article=2130&context=faculty_scholarship [Accessed 17 January 2024].

CHILDREN OF WAR. Platform. 2023. [online]. Available from: https://childrenofwar.gov.ua/en/

CHOMSKY, N. & HERMAN, E. S., 2017. *The Political Economy of Human Rights* [online]. Available from: https://doi.org/10.2307/j.ctt18fsb9g.9 [Accessed 17 January 2024].

CHRISTÓFOLO, J. E., 2016. *Solving Antinomies between Peremptory Norms in Public International Law*. Zurich: Schulthess.

CISMAS, I., 2015. Religious Actors and International Law [online]. *Human Rights Law Review*, 15(4), 787–790. Available from: https://doi.org/10.1093/hrlr/ngv032 [Accessed 23 January 2024].

CISZEK P.., 2022. *Legalizacja pobytu i pracy osób wysiedlonych z Ukrainy [Legalisation of residence and work for displaced persons from Ukraine]*. *In:* *Florczak,*

I. ed., *Pobyt i zatrudnienie cudzoziemców w Polsce. Rozwiązania wynikające z ustawy o pomocy obywatelom Ukrainy* [Residence and employment of foreigners in Poland. Solutions resulting from the Act on Assistance to Citizens of Ukraine], Warszawa: Wydawnictwo C.H. Beck, 27-50.

CLARKE, C. P., 2023. *Following Prigozhin's Aborted Mutiny, What Will Happen to the Wagner Group?* [online]. Available from: https://www.fpri.org/article/2023/07/following-prigozhins-aborted-mutiny-what-will-happen-to-the-wagner-group/ [Accessed 15 December 2023].

CLÉMENT, J-M., 2005. *Les grands principles du droit de la santé* [The Main Principles of Health Law]. Bordeaux-Centre: Les études hospitalières éditions.

COE, 2022. *PACE Calls for an Ad Hoc International Criminal Tribunal to Hold to Account Perpetrators of the Crime of Aggression against Ukraine* [online]. Available from: https://www.coe.int/en/web/portal/full-news/-/asset_publisher/y5xQt7QdunzT/content/pace-calls-for-an-ad-hoc-international-criminal-tribunal-to-investigate-war-crimes-in-ukraine [Accessed 5 February 2024].

CONGRESSIONAL RESEARCH SERVICE, 2022. *Statutory Interpretation: Theories, Tools, and Trends* [online]. Available from: https://crsreports.congress.gov/product/pdf/R/R45153 [Accessed 17 January 2024].

COOPER, S. E., 1991. *Patriotic Pacifism: Waging War on War in Europe, 1815–1914.* Oxford University Press.

CORDER, M., 2022. *ICC Prosecutor Launches Ukraine War Crimes Investigation* [Online]. Available from: https://apnews.com/article/russia-ukraine-genocides-crime-war-crimes-europe-499d7b6a9e955f659284b2edc6f1c508 [Accessed 17 January 2024].

COUNCIL OF EUROPE, 2022. *Organisation and Holding Elections in Post-War Ukraine. Prerequisites and Challenges. Needs Assessment Report* [online]. Available from: https://rm.coe.int/en-organisation-and-holding-of-elections-in-post-war-ukraine-net-2769-/1680a8e995#:~:text=The%20legal%20regime%20of%20martial,be%20called%2C%20let%20alone%20held [Accessed 6 February 2024].

COUNCIL OF EUROPE, 2023. *Elections in Times of Crisis: Challenges and Opportunities»: Post-War Elections in Ukraine in Focus of Discussions at the Parliamentary Conference in Bern* [online]. Available from: https://www.coe.int/en/web/kyiv/-/«elections-in-times-of-crisis-challenges-and-opportunities»-post-war-elections-in-ukraine-in-focus-of-discussions-at-the-parliamentary-conference-in-bern [Accessed 6 February 2024].

COUNCIL OF THE EU PRESS RELEASE, 2022. *EU Imposes Sanctions on State-Owned Outlets RT/Russia Today and Sputnik's Broadcasting in the EU* [online].

Available from: https://www.consilium.europa.eu/en/press/press-releases/2022/03/02/eu-imposes-sanctions-on-state-owned-outlets-rt-russia-today-and-sputnik-s-broadcasting-in-the-eu/ [Accessed 17 January 2024].

CPA, 2021. *Democracy Looks Different: Postponed Elections* [online]. Available from: https://www.cpahq.org/knowledge-centre/blogs/blog-post-democracy-looks-different-how-the-pandemic-changed-commonwealth-democracies/postponed-elections/ [Accessed 6 February 2024].

CRAWFORD, E. & PERT, A., 2020. *International Humanitarian Law* (2nd ed.). Cambridge: Cambridge University Press.

CRIMEA PLATFORM, [no date]. *Joint Declaration of the International Crimea Platform Participants* [online]. Available from: https://crimea-platform.org/en/samit/deklaraciya [8 June 2022].

CULIK, J., 2016. *The Dangers of 'illiberal' Democracy* [online]. Available from: https://core.ac.uk/download/42373182.pdf [Accessed 6 February 2024].

CUTLER, F., 2004. Government Responsibility and Electoral Accountability in Federations [online]. *Oxford University Press*, 34(2). Available from: https://www.jstor.org/stable/3331205 [Accessed 6 February 2024].

DA SILVA, A., 2019. International Arbitration under Annex VII of the United Nations Convention on the Law of the Sea and the Mixed Disputes: Analysis of Recent Cases. *Brazilian Journal of International Law*, 16(1), 90–105.

DAHL, R., 1971. Polyarchy: Participation and Opposition. New Haven, Yale University Press. In: PRZEWORSKI, A. ed., *Minimalist Conception of Democracy: A Defence*. Cambridge: Cambridge University Press.

DANNENBAUM, T., 2022. *Mechanisms for Criminal Prosecution of Russia's Aggression Against Ukraine* [online via Just Security]. Available from: https://www.justsecurity.org/80626/mechanisms-for-criminal-prosecution-of-russias-aggression-against-ukraine/ [Accessed 17 January 2024].

DAREN, K. & AHMAD W. L., 2018. *Why Did Ukraine Impose Martial Law?* [online via Washington Post]. Available from: https://www.washingtonpost.com/news/monkey-cage/wp/2018/11/29/why-did-ukraine-impose-martial-law/ [Accessed 6 February 2024].

D'ASPREMONT, J. & DE BRABANDERE, E., 2011. The Complementary Faces of Legitimacy in International Law: The Legitimacy of Origin and the Legitimacy of Exercise [online]. *Fordham International Law Journal*, 34(2). Available from: https://core.ac.uk/download/144226380.pdf [Accessed 6 February 2024].

DAVYDIUK, A. V., 2022. Cyber Protection and Cyber Defence of Critical Infrastructure. In: PUKHOV YE, H. ed., *Energy Cybersecurity, Scientific and Practical Conference of the Institute of Modelling in Energy Engineering of the*

National Academy of Sciences of Ukraine. Kyiv: National Academy of Sciences of Ukraine.

DE BROUWER, A. M., 2015. Diverse Approaches to Total and Partial in Absentia Trials by International Criminal Tribunals. *Criminal Law Forum*, 26(2), 537–604.

DE RECHTSPRAAK, 2022. *Transcript of the MH17 Judgment Hearing* [online]. Available from: https://www.courtmh17.com/en/insights/news/2022/transcript-of-the-mh17-judgment-hearing/ [Accessed 5 February 2024].

DE SOUSA SANTOS, B., 2002. *Toward a New Legal Common Sense* [online]. Available from: https://openlibrary.org/books/OL28488609M/Toward_a_New_Legal_Common_Sense [Accessed 17 January 2024].

DENQUIN J.-M., 2008. *Democratie*. Paris: Dictionnaire des droits de l'Homme, PUF, 262–267.

DESA, U., 2018. *Transforming Our World: The 2030 Agenda for Sustainable Development* [online via Springer Pub]. Available from: https://doi.org/10.1891/9780826190123.ap02 [Accessed 17 January 2024].

DEUTSCH WELLE, 2022a. *Ukraine: Mariupol 'Horrors' Suggest International Law Violations, Says UN – As It Happened* [Online]. Available from: https://p.dw.com/p/4Cl8w [Accessed 17 January 2024].

DEVA, S., 2023. Mandatory Human Rights Due Diligence Laws in Europe: A Mirage for Rightsholders? [online]. *Leiden Journal of International Law*, 1–26. Available from: https://doi.org/10.1017/s0922156522000802 [Accessed 17 January 2024].

DEVA, S. & BILCHITZ, D., 2018. *Building a Treaty on Business and Human Rights: Context and Contours* [online]. Available from: https://researchers.mq.edu.au/en/publications/building-a-treaty-on-business-and-human-rights-context-and-contou [Accessed 17 January 2024].

DEVA, S. & BIRCHALL, D., 2020. Research Handbook on Human Rights and Business [online]. *Edward Elgar Publishing eBooks*. Available from: https://doi.org/10.4337/9781786436405 [Accessed 17 January 2024].

DEVIATNIKOVAITĖ, I. & BAREIKYTĖ, S. 2021. Administracinė procedūra: Čekijos ir Lietuvos patirtis [Administrative Procedure: Experience of the Chezh Republic and Lithuania]. *Teisės apžvalga*, 1(23), 186–213. Available from: https://www.vdu.lt/cris/entities/publication/bca13924-dd1d-4714-87c0-6ae4b8603421/details [Accessed 16 November 2023].

DIEHN, S. A., 2022. 5 *Ways the Ukraine War Has Changed the World* [Online via DW]. Available from: https://p.dw.com/p/4CAiq [Accessed 17 January 2024]

DINSTEIN, Y., 2009. *The International Law of Belligerent Occupation*. Cambridge: Cambridge University Press.

DINSTEIN, Y., 2017. *War, Aggression and Self-Defence* (6th ed). Cambridge: Cambridge University Press, 2017.

DONALDSON, T., 2016. Sentry or Insensible? A Criminal Defendant's Right to Be Present at a Confrontation Forfeiture Hearing. Accord. *Legal Journal for Practitioners*, 6(1), 1–46.

DOROSH S., 2022. *Chomu pereselentsdi dosi ne otrymaly groshej i na shcho jim spodivatysia* [Why Displaced Persons Have Not Received Money Yet and What They Should Expect]. [online via BBC News]. Available from: https://www.bbc.com/ukrainian/features-62321972 [Accessed 16 November 2023].

DRAGNEVA, R. & WOLCZUK, K. 2015. *Ukraine between the EU and Russia: The Integration Challenge.* New York: Palgrave Macmillan.

DREMBKOWSKI, P., 2022. Commentary on Articles 22a – Art. 22h. In: DREMBKOWSKI, P. ed., *Ustawa o Pomocy Obywatelom Ukrainy. Komentarz z Wzorami Dotyczącymi Pobytu, Dostępu do Rynku Pracy, Świadczeń Społecznych, Edukacji i Opieki Zdrowotnej* [Law on Assistance to Citizens of Ukraine. Commentary with Templates Concerning Residence, Access to the Labour Market, Social Benefits, Education and Health Care]. Warszawa: Wydawnictwo CH. Beck, 138–147.

DREMBKOWSKI, P., & SUWAJ, J. P. [no date]. Commentary on Articles 1–4. In: DREMBKOWSKI, P. ed., *Ustawa o Pomocy Obywatelom Ukrainy. Komentarz z Wzorami Dotyczącymi Pobytu, Dostępu do Rynku Pracy, Świadczeń Społecznych, Edukacji i Opieki Zdrowotnej* [Law on Assistance to Citizens of Ukraine. Commentary with Templates Concerning Residence, Access to the Labour Market, Social Benefits, Education and Health Care]. Warszawa: Wydawnictwo CH. Beck, 3–26.

DRI, 2023. *Ukraine's Democratic Institutions During the War: A Check-Up* [online]. Available from: https://democracy-reporting.org/en/office/ukraine/publications/ukraines-democratic-institutions-during-the-war-a-check-up [Accessed 23 January 2024].

DRONOVA, K., 2015. *Jury in Ukraine* [online via VoxUkraine]. Available from: https://voxukraine.org/en/jury-in-ukraine [Accessed 20 February 2023].

DUDKO, O., 2022. A Conceptual Limbo of Genocide: Russian Rhetoric, Mass Atrocities in Ukraine, and the Current Definition's Limits, *Canadian Slavonic Papers*, 6(2–3).

DWORKIN, R., 1975. Hard Cases [online via JSTOR]. *Harvard Law Review*, 88(6), 1057–1109. Available from: https://doi.org/10.2307/1340249 [Accessed 17 January 2024].

DWORKIN, R., 1977. *Taking Rights Seriously.* Cambridge, Massachusetts: Harvard University Press.

DWORKIN, R., 2013. *Religion Without God.* Harvard, The US: Harvard University Press.

EBA, 2023. *Top 10 Business Cybersecurity Threats in 2023* [online]. Available from: https://eba.com.ua/top-10-zagroz-kiberbezpetsi-biznesu-u-2023-rotsi/ [Accessed 29 October 2023].

ECIPE, 2018. *The Economic Benefits of Globalisation for Business and Consumers* [online]. Available from: http://ecipe.org//app/uploads/2018/01/Globalisation-paper-final.pdf [Accessed 4 May 2023].

EEAS, 2022a. *A Strategic Compass for Security and Defence* [online]. Available from: https://www.eeas.europa.eu/eeas/strategic-compass-security-and-defence-0_en [Accessed 29 October 2023].

EEAS, 2022b. *Joint Statement of Participants in the International Crimea Platform* [online]. Available from: https://www.eeas.europa.eu/delegations/ukraine/joint-statement-participants-international-crimea-platform-26-february-2022_en?s=232 [Accessed 17 January 2024].

ELECTIONS CANADA, [no date]. *Postponing an Election* [online]. Available from: https://www.elections.ca/content.aspx?section=vot&dir=bkg&document=pos&lang=e [Accessed 6 February 2024].

ENNEKING, L., GIESEN, I., SCHAAP, A.-J., RYNGAERT, C., KRISTEN, F. & ROORDA, L., eds., 2020. *Accountability, International Business Operations, and the Law: Providing Justice for Corporate Human Rights Violations in Global Value Chains.* London: Routledge.

EOS, [no date]. *Election Standards* [online]. Available from: https://eos.cartercenter.org/quotes/10 [Accessed 6 February 2024].

ERBEN, P. & KOKAKHIDZE, G., 2022. *Winning the Peace Through Democratic Progress in Post-War Ukraine* [online]. Available from: https://www.atlanticcouncil.org/blogs/ukrainealert/winning-the-peace-through-democratic-progress-in-post-war-ukraine/ [Accessed 6 February 2024].

ETKIND, A., 2022. *Ukraine, Russia, and Genocide of Minor Differences. Journal of Genocide Research*, 25(3–4), 384–402.

ETXABE, J., 2021. *Conversations with Legal Thinkers* [online]. Available from: https://allard.ubc.ca/about-us/blog/2021/conversations-legal-thinkers [Accessed 17 January 2024].

EU ADVISORY MISSION UKRAINE, 2023. *"Ratification of the Istanbul convention is an important step towards the EU accession" – EUAM Ukraine* [online]. Available from: https://www.euam-ukraine.eu/news/ratification-of-the-istanbul-convention-is-an-important-step-towards-the-eu-accession/ [Accessed 17 January 2024].

EURACTIV, 2022. *Security body OSCE ends eight-year Ukraine mission after Russian veto* [Online]. Available from: https://www.euractiv.com/section/global-europe/news/security-body-osce-ends-eight-year-ukraine-mission-after-russian-veto/ [Accessed 17 January 2024].

EUROINTEGRATION, 2023. *Parye, Ukrayina musyt' provesty vil'ni i chesni vybory, navit' yakshcho vony budut' ne ideal'ni* [online]. Available from: https://www.eurointegration.com.ua/news/2023/05/16/7161795/ [Accessed 6 February 2024].

EUROPEAN BUSINESS ASSOCIATION RESEARCH, 2023.04.05 https://eba.com.ua/top-10-zagroz-kiberbezpetsi-biznesu-u-2023-rotsi

EUROPEAN COMMISSION, 2021. *European Green Deal* [online]. Available from: https://commission.europa.eu/strategy-and-policy/priorities-2019-2024/european-green-deal_en [Accessed 17 January 2024].

EUROPEAN COMMISSION, (2022, June 16). *Commission Opinion on Ukraine's application for membership of the European Union*. COM(2022) 407 final. Retrieved from: https://neighbourhood-enlargement.ec.europa.eu/system/files/2022-06/Ukraine%20Opinion%20and%20Annex.pdf

EUROPEAN COMMISSION, 2022a. *Commission Opinion on Ukraine's Application for Membership of the European Union* [online]. Available from: https://neighbourhood-enlargement.ec.europa.eu/system/files/2022-06/Ukraine%20Opinion%20and%20Annex.pdf [Accessed 17 January 2024].

EUROPEAN COMMISSION, 2022b. *European Just and Sustainable Economy: Commission Lays Down Rules for Companies to Respect Human Rights and Environment in Global Value Chains* [online]. Press corner. Available from: https://ec.europa.eu/commission/presscorner/detail/en/ip_22_1145 [Accessed: 23 November 2023].

EUROPEAN COMMISSION, 2023. *Proposal for a Directive of the European Parliament and of the Council on the Protection of the Environment Through Criminal Law and Replacing Directive 2008/99/EC* [online]. Available from: https://www.europarl.europa.eu/doceo/document [Accessed 17 January 2024].

EUROPEAN COMMISSION, [no date]. *Conflict Minerals Regulation: The Regulation Explained.* [online]. Available from: https://policy.trade.ec.europa.eu/development-and-sustainability/conflict-minerals-regulation/regulation-explained_en [Accessed 4 May 2024].

EUROPEAN COMMISSION, [no date]. *Corporate Sustainability Reporting* [online]. Available from: https://policy.trade.ec.europa.eu/development-and-sustainability/conflict-minerals-regulation/regulation-explained_en [Accessed 4 May 2023].

EUROPEAN COMMISSION, [no date]. *Employment, Social Affairs & Inclusion* [online]. Available from: https://ec.europa.eu/social/main.jsp?catId=1226&langId=en [Accessed 4 May 2023].

EUROPEAN COMMISSION, [no date]. *EU Taxonomy for Sustainable Activities* [online]. Available from: https://finance.ec.europa.eu/sustainable-finance/tools-and-standards/eu-taxonomy-sustainable-activities_en [Accessed 17 January 2024].

EUROPEAN COUNCIL, 2022. *European Council Meeting – Conclusions* [online]. Available from: https://www.consilium.europa.eu/media/57442/2022-06-2324-euco-conclusions-en.pdf [Accessed 17 January 2024].

EUROPEAN PARLIAMENT, 2020a. *Coronavirus and Elections in Selected Member States. Briefing of European Parliament* [online]. Available from: https://www.europarl.europa.eu/RegData/etudes/BRIE/2020/651969/EPRS_BRI(2020)651969_EN.pdf [Accessed 17 January 2024].

EUROPEAN PARLIAMENT, 2020b. *Impact of the Pandemic on Elections Around the World. From Safety Concerns to Political Crises* [online]. Available from: https://www.europarl.europa.eu/RegData/etudes/BRIE/2020/652017/EPRS_BRI(2020)652017_EN.pdf [Accessed 17 January 2024].

EUROPEAN PARLIAMENT, 2021a. *Resolution on Human Rights and Democracy in the World and the European Union's Policy on the Matter – Annual Report 2019 (2020/2208(INI))* [online]. Available from: https://www.europarl.europa.eu/doceo/document/TA-9-2021-0014_EN.html [Accessed 17 January 2024].

EUROPEAN PARLIAMENT, 2021b. *Resolution on the EU Biodiversity Strategy for 2030: Bringing Nature Back Into Our Lives* [online]. Available from: https://www.europarl.europa.eu/doceo/document/TA-9-2021-0277_EN.html [Accessed 17 January 2024].

EUROPEAN PARLIAMENT, 2022a. *European Parliament resolution of 19 May 2022 on the Fight Against Impunity for War Crimes in Ukraine* [online]. Available from: https://www.europarl.europa.eu/doceo/document/TA-9-2022-0218_EN.html [Accessed 17 January 2024].

EUROPEAN PARLIAMENT, 2022b. *Opinion of the Committee on Foreign Affairs for the Committee on Legal Affairs on the Proposal for a Directive of the European Parliament and of the Council on Corporate Sustainability Due Diligence and Amending Directive (EU) 2019/1937 (COM (2022)0071 – C90050/2022 – 2022/0051(COD))* [online]. Available from: https://www.europarl.europa.eu/doceo/document/AFET-AD-736653_EN.docx [Accessed 17 January 2024].

EUROPEAN PARLIAMENT, 2022c. *Russia's War against Ukraine: Chronology of Cyberattacks* [online]. Available from: https://www.europarl.europa.eu/RegData/etudes/BRIE/2022/733549/EPRS_BRI(2022)733549_XL.pdf [Accessed on: 29 October 2023].

EUROPEAN PARLIAMENT, 2023. *Resolution of 19 January 2023 on the Establishment of a Tribunal on the Crime of Aggression against Ukraine* [online]. Available from: https://www.europarl.europa.eu/doceo/document/TA-9-2023-0015_EN.html [Accessed 17 January 2024].

EUROPEAN PARLIAMENT, [no date]. *Proposal for a Ban on Goods Made Using Forced Labour* [online]. Think Tank. Available from: https://www.europarl.europa.eu/thinktank/en/ [Accessed 17 January 2024].

EUROPEAN PARLIAMENT'S COMMITTEE ON LEGAL AFFAIRS, 2023. *Report on the Proposal for a Directive of the European Parliament and of the Council on the Protection of the Environment Through Criminal Law and Replacing Directive 2008/99/EC* [online]. Available from: https://www.europarl.europa.eu/doceo/document/A-9-2023-0087_EN.html [Accessed 17 January 2024].

FABRE-MAGNAN, M., 2007. La dignité en Droit: un *axiome* [Dignity in law: an axiom]. *Revue interdisciplinaire d'études juridiques*, 58, 1–30 [online]. Available from: https://doi.org/10.3917/riej.058.0001 [Accessed 19 January 2024].

FALK, R., 1973. Environmental Warfare and Ecocide – Facts, Appraisal and Proposals. *Security Dialogue*, 4(1), 80–96.

FALLAH, K., 2006. Corporate Actors: The Legal Status of Mercenaries in Armed Conflict. *International Review of the Red Cross*, 88(863).

FELDMAN, N., 2021. *Freedom of Religion Means Freedom to Say No for Vaccines* [online]. Available from: https://www.psdispatch.com/opinion/op-ed/77423/noah-feldman-freedom-of-religion-means-freedom-to-say-no-to-vaccines [19 January 2024].

FERRAND, J. & PETIT, H., 2004. *Fondations et naissances des Droits de l'homme*. France: L'harmattan.

FILIP Z., 2020. Świadczenia obywateli na rzecz obrony – prawda i mity [Citizens' Contributions to Defence – Truth and Myths]. *Studia de Securitate*, 10(1), 257–268.

FINKEL, E., 2022. *What's Happening in Ukraine Is Genocide. Period* [online via the Washington Post]. Available from https://www.washingtonpost.com/opinions/2022/04/05/russia-is-committing-genocide-in-ukraine/ [Accessed 28 November 2023].

FINNIS, J., 2011. *Natural Law and the Natural Rights.* Oxford: Oxford University Press.

FINNIS, J., 2014a. Law as Fact and as Reason for Action: A Response to Robert Alexy on Law's 'Ideal Dimension' [online]. *The American Journal of Jurisprudence*, 59(1), 85–109. Available from: https://doi.org/10.1093/ajj/auu007 [Accessed 16 February 2024].

FINNIS, J., 2014b. *Prigimtinis įstatymas ir prigimtinės teisės* [Natural Law and Natural Rights]. Vilnius: Aidai.

FITZPATRICK, J., 2000. *Hume's "Is-Ought" Problem: A Solution* [online via JSTOR]. *New Blackfriars*, 81(951), 216–225. Available from: http://www.jstor.org/stable/43250445 [19 January 2024].

FRADKIN, H., 2019. *Honour versus Freedom* [online]. Available from: https://lawliberty.org/forum/honor-versus-freedom/ [19 January 2024].

FREEMAN, M. D., 2014. *Lloyd's Introduction to Jurisprudence.* London: Sweet & Maxwell.

FROSINI, J. O., 2012. *Constitutional Preambles. At a Crossroads between Politics and Law.* Maggioli: Santarcangelo Di Romagna.

FROSINI, J. & LAPA, V., 2020a. Historical and Legal Significance of Constitutional Preambles: A Case Study on the Ukrainian Constitution of 1996. In: BIAGI, F., FROSINI, J. O. & MAZZONE, J. eds., *Comparative Constitutional History. Principles, Developments, Challenges.* Brill (1), 60–88.

FROSINI, J. & LAPA, V., 2020b. *NATO'S Aspirations in the Constitutional Preamble of Ukraine: Distorting Historical Roots of the Constitution or Reflecting Societal Changes?* [online]. Available from: https://blog-iacl-aidc.org/2020-posts/2020/6/30/natos-aspirations-in-the-constitutional-preamble-of-ukraine-distorting-historical-roots-of-the-constitution-or-reflecting-societal-changes [19 January 2024].

FROSINI, J. & LAPA, V., 2022. *Would Ukraine Breach Its Own Constitution If It Dropped Its NATO Bid?* [online]. Available from: https://doi.org/10.17176/20220219-001043-0 [19 January 2024].

FUCHS, D., 2013. *Theorizing the Power of Global Companies* [online]. Available from: https://doi.org/10.1002/9781118326152 [19 January 2024].

GAETA, P., 2007. To Be (Present) or Not to Be (Present). 5 Journal of International Criminal Justice. In: ZAKERHOSSEIN, M. H. & DE BROUWER, M. A., 2015, *Diverse Approaches to Total and Partial in Absentia Trials by International Criminal Tribunals. Criminal Law Forum*, 26(2), 181–224.

GALGINAITIS, J., 2002. Teisinė sistema ir pagrindinės jos subsistemos kaip lyginamosios teisėtyros objektas [The Legal System and Its Main Subsystems as an Object of Comparative Legal Studies]. *Teisė*, 44, 31–41.

GASPARINI, A., 2021. Do Not Forget the Crimean Crisis: Why Russia 'Annexed' the Peninsula? A (pro-) Western-European Perception. *Global Affairs*, 7(3), 405–410. Available from: https://doi.org/10.1080/23340460.2021.1948800 [Accessed 29 January 2024].

GAUFMAN, E., 2016. Security Threats and Public Perception: Digital Russia and the Ukraine Crisis. *Palgrave Macmillan Cham*, 107.

GAVER, C. D., 2021. Dispute Concerning Delimitation of the Maritime Boundary Between Mauritius and Maldives in the Indian Ocean (Mauritius/Maldives). *American Journal of International Law*, 115(3), 519–526. Available from: https://doi.org/10.1017/ajil.2021.24 [Accessed 29 January 2024].

GEERLING, W., MAGEE, G., MISHRA, V. & SMYTH, R., 2018. Hitler's Judges: Ideological Commitment and the Death Penalty in Nazi Germany [online]. *The Economic Journal*, 128(614), 2414–2449. Available from: https://doi.org/10.1111/ecoj.12497 [Accessed 19 January 2024].

GEIß, R., 2015. Russia's Annexation of Crimea: The Mills of International Law Grind Slowly but They Do Grind. *International Law Studies*, 91.

GEVORGIAN, K. 2022. *Declaration* [online]. Available from: https://www.icj-cij.org/public/files/case-related/182/182-20220316-ORD-01-01-EN.pdf [Accessed 23 November 2023].

GLOBAL CITIZENSHIP OBSERVATORY, 2020. *When Is It Democratic to Postpone an Election? Elections during Natural Disasters, Covid-19, and Emergency Situations* [online]. Available from: https://globalcit.eu/when-is-it-democratic-to-postpone-an-election-elections-during-natural-disasters-covid-19-and-emergency-situations/ [Accessed 23 November 2023].

GLOBAL STATE OF DEMOCRACY, 2022. *Supporting Ukraine's Democracy after the War. Key Issues, Comparative Experience and Best Practices* [online]. Available from: https://www.idea.int/sites/default/files/publications/supporting-ukraines-democracy-after-the-war.pdf [Accessed 19 January 2024].

GOLDMAN, R., 2022. *'Show' Trial of Foreign Fighters in Donetsk Breaks with International Law – and Could Itself Be a War Crime* [online]. Available from: https://theconversation.com/show-trial-of-foreign-fighters-in-donetsk-breaks-with-international-law-and-could-itself-be-a-war-crime-184899 [Accessed 15 December 2023].

GOLDSMITH, K., 2010. The Issue of Intent in the Genocide Convention and Its Effect on the Prevention and Punishment of the Crime of Genocide: Toward a Knowledge-Based Approach. *Genocide Studies and Prevention: An International Journal*, 5(3).

GOTO R, GUERRERO APS, SPERANZA M, FUNG D, PAUL C, SKOKAUSKAS N. *War is a public health emergency.* Lancet. 2022 Apr 2;399(10332):1302. doi: 10.1016/S0140-6736(22)00479-2. Epub 2022 Mar 21. PMID: 35325603. [online]. Available from: https://pubmed.ncbi.nlm.nih.gov/35325603/

GRANT, T. D. (2016). *Three Years after Annexation: Of Frozen Conflicts and How to Characterize Crimea.* German Yearbook of International Law, 59

GRC, 2016. *Trials in Absentia: A Dilemma for Ukraine. Trials in Absentia Are a Hot Topic in Ukrainian Legal Circles Today. Whilst They Have* [online]. Available from: https://lawsdocbox.com/Legal_Issues/71685510-Trials-in-absentia-a-dilemma-for-ukraine-trials-in-absentia-are-a-hot-topic-in-ukrainian-legal-circles-today-whilst-they-have.html [Accessed 19 January 2024].

GREEN, L. C. 2000. *The Contemporary Law of Armed Conflict* (2nd ed.). Manchester University Press.

GREENE, A., 2018. *Permanent States of Emergency and the Rule of Law: Constitutions in an Age of Crisis*. Oxford: Hart Publishing.

GREENAWALT, A.K., 1999. Rethinking Genocidal Intent: The Case for a Knowledge-Based Interpretation. *Columbia Law Review*, 99(8).

GREGG, S., 2019. *Reason, Faith, and the Struggle for Western Civilization*. Washington, the US: Regnery Publishing.

GREGOR, A.J., 1998. Fascism and the New Russian Nationalism. *Communist and Post-Communist Studies*, 31(1).

GRENVILLE, P. G., 1990. Marital Law in Rebellion [online]. *Journal of the Society of Comparative Legislation*, 2(1), 45–72. Available from: https://www.jstor.org/stable/752117 [Accessed 6 February 2024].

GREWE, C., 2014. La dignité de la personne humaine dans la jurisprudence de la Cour européenne des droits de l'homme [The Dignity of the Individual in the Case Law of the European Court of Human Rights] [online]. *Revue générale du droit, Etudes et réflexions* 3, 1–12. Available from: https://www.revuegeneraledudroit.eu/wp-content/uploads/ER2014_3.pdf [Accessed 19 January 2024].

GRZEBYK, P., 2017. *The Annexation of Crimea in the Light of the Definition of Aggression. Does Prohibition of Aggression Apply to Russia?* [online via SSRN Scholarly Paper]. Rochester, NY: Social Science Research Network. Available from: doi.org/10.2139/ssrn.3442237 [Accessed 19 January 2024].

GUARNIERI, C. 2010. Judicial Independence in Authoritarian Regimes. In: PEERENBOOM R. ed., *Judicial Independence in China: Lessons for Global Rule of Law Promotion*. Cambridge: Cambridge University Press.

GUTMANN, A., 2003. *Identity in Democracy*. Princeton: Princeton University Press.

HAAVISTO, P., 2022. *Press Conference by NATO Secretary General Jens Stoltenberg, the Minister of Foreign Affairs of Finland, Pekka Haavisto, and the Minister of Foreign Affairs of Sweden, Ann Linde Following the Signature of the NATO Accession Protocols for Finland and Sweden* [online]. Available from: https://www.nato.int/cps/en/natohq/opinions_197761.htm?selectedLocale=en [Accessed 23 July 2022].

HADZIABDIC, I., 2019. Transitional Elections in Bosnia and Herzegovina, 1996–2002. In: ALIHODŽIĆ, S., MATATU, N. & RAFFOUL, A. eds., *Timing and Sequencing of Transitional Elections: Case Studies*. Stockholm: International IDEA.

HAMPSHIRE, S., 1983. *Morality and Conflict*. Cambridge: Harvard University Press.

HAMPSHIRE, S., 2000. *Justice Is Conflict*. Princeton: Princeton University Press.

HARB, A., 2022. *Ukraine: As Russia Faces 'genocide' Charge, Experts Urge Caution* [online]. Available from: https://www.aljazeera.com/news/2022/4/6/ukraine-as-russia-faces-genocide-charge-experts-urge-caution [Accessed 28 November 2023].

HART, H. L. A., 1997. *The Concept of Law* (2nd ed.). New York: Oxford University Press.

HASENCLEVER, A., 2014. *Human Dignity and War. Interdisciplinary Perspectives* [online]. United Kingdom: Cambridge University Press. Available from: https://doi.org/10.1017/CBO9780511979033.054 [Accessed 23 January 2024].

HAVRYLETS, S., 2023. *Ukraine Extends Martial Law, Ruling Out October Parliament Vote* [online]. Available from: https://euromaidanpress.com/2023/05/02/ukraines-parliament-extends-martial-law-and-mobilization-until-august-2023/ [Accessed 17 January 2024].

HEINEMANN-GRÜDER, A. & ARIS, S., 2022. Wagner Group [online]. *Russian Analytical Digest*, 290. Available from: https://doi.org/10.3929/ethz-b-000588677 [Accessed 15 December 2023].

HELLER, K. J., 2022a. *Creating a Special Tribunal for Aggression Against Ukraine Is a Bad Idea*. [online]. Available from: https://opiniojuris.org/2022/03/07/creating-a-special-tribunal-for-aggression-against-ukraine-is-a-bad-idea/ [Accessed 28 November 2023].

HELLER, K. J., 2022b. *The Best Option: An Extraordinary Ukrainian Chamber for Aggression* [online]. Available from: https://opiniojuris.org/2022/03/16/the-best-option-an-extraordinary-ukrainian-chamber-for-aggression/ [Accessed 28 November 2023].

HELLER, K. J., 2023. *Can International Law Bring a Measure of Justice to Ukraine?* [online]. Available from: https://www.russiamatters.org/analysis/can-international-law-bring-measure-justice-ukraine [Accessed 28 November 2023].

HEMPTINNE, J., 2022. *Ecocide: An Ambiguous Crime?* [online]. Available from: https://www.ejiltalk.org/ecocide-an-ambiguous-crime/ [Accessed 19 January 2024].

HENCKAERTS J., M., 2005. Study on Customary International Humanitarian Law: A Contribution to the Understanding and Respect for the Rule of Law in Armed Conflict. *International Review of the Red Cross* 87, 857.

HENDRIX, St. & KOROLCHUK S., 2023. *Bloodied Wagner Fighters Captured in Ukraine Recount Path from Prison to War* [online]. Available from: https://www.washingtonpost.com/world/2023/02/23/wagner-mercenaries-captives-war-ukraine/ [Accessed 15 December 2023].

HERATH, E., 2014. Trials in Absentia: Jurisprudence and Commentary on the Judgment in Chief Prosecutor v. Abul Kalam Azad in the Bangladesh International Crimes Tribunal. *Harward International Law Journal Features*, 55 [online]. Available from: https://harvardilj.org/wp-content/uploads/sites/15/2014/06/HILJ-Online_volume-55_Herath.pdf [Accessed 15 December 2023].

HERTOGH, M., 2004. A European Conception of Legal Consciousness: Rediscovering Eugen Ehrlich. *Journal of Law and Society*, 31(4).

HESSEY, K., 2022. *Behind the Lines of Kyiv's Territorial Defence Force* [online]. Available from: https://globalnews.ca/news/8727949/behind-the-lines-kyiv-territorial-defence-force-ukraine/ [Accessed 15 December 2023].

HICKMAN, L., 2018. The Good, the True and the Beautiful: Imagining an Ethico-Political Future for the Philosophy of Religion [online]. *Palgrave Commun*, 4(125), 1–10. Available from: https://doi.org/10.1057/s41599-018-0180-y [Accessed 23 November 2023].

HIGGINS, P., [no date]. *Ecocide Crime. Ecocide Law* [online]. Available from: https://ecocidelaw.com/polly-higgins-ecocide-crime/ [Accessed 23 November 2023].

HIGGINS, R., 2007. *Problems & Process: International Law and How We Use It*. Oxford: Oxford University Press.

HIGGINS, P., 2010. *Eradicating Ecocide: Laws and Governance to Prevent the Destruction of Our Planet*. London: Shepheard-Walwyn.

HILL, M. T., 2022. *Building a Solidarity Society: Power, People, and Planet*. Springer Nature Switzerland AG.

HINTON. A., 2023. *A Year on, We Have Clear Evidence of Genocide in Ukraine* [online]. Available from: https://thehill.com/opinion/international/3859439-a-year-on-we-have-clear-evidence-of-genocide-in-ukraine/ [Accessed 28 November 2023].

HLOVIUK, I., 2015. Criminal Proceeding in Absentia of a Suspect or an Accused in the System of Criminal Justice of Ukraine. *Law of Ukraine: Legal Journal*, 7, 16–25.

HORINOV, P. V. & DRAPUSHKO, R. H., 2023. Modern Challenges of the Administrative and Legal Foundations of Cybersecurity of Ukraine in the Conditions of Martial Law. *Legal Scientific Electronic Journal*, 1, 267–270.

HORTON, J. & MENDUS, S., 1991. *A Letter Concerning Toleration in Focus*. London: Routledge.

HRW, 2018. *Important that Ukraine Respects Human Rights under New Martial Law* [online]. Available from: https://www.hrw.org/news/2018/11/27/important-ukraine-respects-human-rights-under-new-martial-law [Accessed 6 February 2024].

HUMAN RIGHTS WATCH, 2016. *Human Rights in Supply Chains: A Call for A Binding Global Standard on Due Diligence* [online]. Available from: https://www.hrw.org/sites/default/files/report_pdf/human_rights_in_supply_chains_brochure_lowres_final.pdf [Accessed 19 January 2024].

HUNGARIAN HELSINKI COMMITTEE, 2022. *Country Report: Hungary* [online]. Available from: https://asylumineurope.org/wp-content/uploads/2023/04/AIDA-HU_2022-Update.pdf [Accessed 19 January 2024].

HUSAK NATALIIA, 2022. Now is the very time to care about health [інтерв'ю з Н. Гусак. .Зараз саме час дбати про здоров'я]. [Online via ZAXID.NET] Available from: https://zaxid.net/medichna_dopomoga_pid_chas_viyni_v_ukrayini_2022_vidpovidi_n1542721. [Accessed 10 October 2024].

HUTSALYUK, M., 2023. Peculiarities of Combating Cybercrime during Martial Law. *Information and Law*, 3(46), 108–117.

IBA, 2016. *Report on the 'Experts' Roundtable on Trials in Absentia in International Criminal Justice'* [online]. Available from: https://www.ibanet.org/document?id=Experts-roundtable-trials-in-absentia [Accessed 5 February 2024].

ICC, 2010. Official Records of the Review Conference of the Rome Statute of the International Criminal Court [online]. *International Criminal Court Publication*, RC/11, part II. Available from: https://treaties.un.org/doc/source/docs/RC-Res.6-ENG.pdf [Accessed 5 February 2024].

ICC, 2019. *Crime of Aggression – Amendments Ratification* [online]. Available from: https://asp.icc-cpi.int/crime-of-aggression [Accessed 29 January 2024].

ICC, [no date]. *Declarations Recognizing the Jurisdiction of the Court as Compulsory, International Court of Justice* [online]. Available from: https://www.icj-cij.org/en/declarations [Accessed 2022 July 25].

ICC, [no date]. *The States Parties to the Rome Statute* [online]. Available from: https://asp.icc-cpi.int/states-parties [Accessed: 23 November 2023].

ICCPR, 1990. *Selected Decisions of the Human Rights Committee under the Optional Protocol* [online]. Available from: https://www.ohchr.org/sites/default/files/Documents/Publications/SelDec_2_en.pdf [Accessed 5 February 2024].

ICIR, 1987. *Commentary of 1987 on Protocol Additional to the Geneva Conventions of 12 August 1949, and Relating to the Protection of Victims of International Armed Conflicts (Protocol I), 8 June 1977, Article 43* [online]. Available from: https://ihl-databases.icrc.org/en/ihl-treaties/api-1977/article-43/commentary/1987?activeTab=1949GCs-APs-and-commentaries [Accessed 15 December 2023].

ICIR, 2020. *Commentary of 2020 on Convention (III) Relative to the Treatment of Prisoners of War. Geneva, 12 August 1949* [online]. Available from: https://ihl-databases.icrc.org/en/ihl-treaties/gciii-1949?activeTab=1949GCs-APs-and-commentaries [Accessed 15 December 2023].

ICJ, 1978. *Rules of the International Court of Justice* [online]. Available from: https://www.icj-cij.org/en/rules [Accessed 28 July 2022].

ICJ, 2012. *Jurisdictional Immunities of the State (Germany v. Italy: Greece Intervening)* [online]. Available from: https://www.icj-cij.org/case/143/judgments [Accessed 28 July 2022].

ICJ, 2019. *Legal Consequences of the Separation of the Chagos Archipelago from Mauritius in 1965* [online]. Available from: https://www.icj-cij.org/case/169 [Accessed 15 December 2023].

ICJ, [no date]. *Jurisdiction* [online]. Available from: https://www.icj-cij.org/jurisdiction [Accessed 5 February 2024].

ICRC, *The Montreux Document on Private Military and Security Companies* [online]. Available from: https://www.icrc.org/en/publication/0996-montreux-document-private-military-and-security-companies [Accessed 15 December 2023].

IMRAN, M., 2021. *International Humanitarian Law and Non-State Actors: Debates, Law and Practice*. The Hague, Netherlands: TMC Asser Press.

INTERFAX UKRAINE, 2022. *The Ukrainian healthcare system withstood the war shock due to the transformation – the NHSU head.* [Online via interfax.com.ua.] Available from: https:interfax.com.ua/news/pharmacy/830169.html [Accessed 20 October 2024].

INTERNATIONAL LABOR ORGANISATION, 2015. *World Employment and Social Outlook 2015: The Changing Nature of Jobs* [online]. Available from: http://www.ilo.org/wcmsp5/groups/public/---dgreports/---dcomm/---publ/documents/publication/wcms_368626.pdf [Accessed 23 November 2023].

INTERNATIONAL LABOUR ORGANISATION, 2016. Decent work in global supply chains.

INTERNATIONAL LAW COMMISSION, 1996. *International Law Commission's Draft Code of Crimes against the Peace and Security of Mankind with Commentaries* [online]. Available from: https://legal.un.org/ilc/texts/instruments/english/commentaries/7_4_1996.pdf [Accessed 23 November 2023].

INTERNATIONAL LAW COMMISSION, 2022. [online]. Available from: https://legal.un.org/ilc/texts/instruments/english/commentaries/1_14_2022.pdf [Accessed 28 July 2022].

INTERNATIONAL CRIMINAL COURT, 2023. *Situation in Ukraine: ICC judges issue arrest warrants against Vladimir Vladimirovich Putin and Maria Alekseyevna Lvova-Belova* [online]. Available from: https://www.icc-cpi.int/news/situation-ukraine-icc-judges-issue-arrest-warrants-against-vladimir-vladimirovich-putin-and [Accessed 28 November 2023].

IOM, Displacement Tracking Matrix, Ukraine — *Internal Displacement Report — General Population Survey Round 2* (9 — 16 March 2022). [online]. Available from: https://displacement.iom.int/reports/ukraine-internal-displacement-report-general-population-survey-round-2-9-16-march-2022.

IOM, *Displacement Tracking Matrix, Ukraine — Internal Displacement Report — General Population Survey Round 7* (17 — 23 July 2022). [online]. Available from: https://displacement.iom.int/reports/ukraine-internal-displacement-report-general-population-survey-round-7-17-23-july-2022

IRVING, H., 2015. Outsourcing the Law: History and the Disciplinary Limits of Constitutional Reasoning [online]. *Fordham Law Review*, 84, 957–967. Available from: https://ir.lawnet.fordham.edu/flr/vol84/iss3/4 [Accessed 23 November 2023].

ITLOS, 2021. *Special Chamber Finds That It Has Jurisdiction to Adjudicate upon the Dispute Concerning the Delimitation of the Maritime Boundary and that Mauritius' Claim in This Regard Is Admissible* [online]. Available from: https://www.itlos.org/fileadmin/itlos/documents/press_releases_english/PR_313_EN.pdf [Accessed 5 February 2024].

IVICEVIC KARAS, E., 2018. Reopening of Proceedings in Cases of Trial in Absentia: European Legal Standards and Croatian Law. *EU and Comparative Law Issues and Challenges*, 2(2), 291–309.

IVICEVIC KARAS, E., 2019. Decisions Rendered in Absentia as a Ground to Refuse the Execution of a European Arrest Warrant: European Legal Standards and Implementation in Croatian Law. *EU and Comparative Law Issues and Challenges*, 3, 459–475.

IWPR, 2022. *Universal Criminal Jurisdiction in Ukraine 2022* [online]. Available from: https://iwpr.net/global-voices/universal-criminal-jurisdiction-ukraine [Accessed 5 February 2024].

IZHUTOVA, I., 2019. Ukrainian Strategic Communications and Martial Law [online]. *Journal of Scientific Papers Social Development and Security*. Available from: https://doi.org/10.33445/sds.2019.9.5.8 [Accessed: 19 January 2024].

JACK, V., 2022. *Czech Republic lawmakers brand Russian actions in Ukraine as genocide* [Online]. Available from https://www.politico.eu/article/czech-senate-recognize-russia-actions-ukraine-genocide/ [Accessed 28 November 2023].

James, Toby S. 2011. "*Fewer 'costs,' more votes? UK Innovations in Electoral Administration* 2000-2007 and their effect on voter turnout." Election Law Journal, 10, (1), p. 37-52.

JAMES, T.S. & ALIHODZIC,, S. (2020). "*When Is It Democratic to Postpone an Election? Elections During Natural Disasters, COVID-19, and Emergency Situations*". In Election Law Journal, 19 (3), 344-362. New Rochelle: Mary Ann Liebert, Inc., publishers.

JANOWICZ, Z. (1970). Rozwój ogólnego postępowania administracyjnego [Development of general administrative procedure]. Ruch Prawni-czy, Ekonomiczny i Socjologiczny, 3, 121–139.

JENNINGS, R. & A. WATTS, 1996. *Oppenheim's International Law*. New York City: Longman.

JEUTNER, V., 2020. Rebutting Four Arguments in Favour of Resolving ius cogens Norm Conflicts by Means of Proportionality Tests [online via Brill]. *Nordic Journal of International Law*, 89, 453–470. Available from: https://brill.com/view/journals/nord/89/3-4/article-p453_453.xml?language=en [Accessed: 23 November 2023].

JEUTNER, V., 2020. Rebutting Four Arguments in Favour of Resolving ius cogens Norm Conflicts by Means of Proportionality Tests [online via Brill]. *Nordic Journal of International Law*, 89, 453–470. Available from: https://brill.com/view/journals/nord/89/3-4/article-p453_453.xml?language=en [Accessed: 23 November 2023].

JIMENEZ, F., 2022. Legal Principles, Law, and Tradition [online]. *Yale Journal of Law & the Humanities*, 33(1), 59–91. Available from: https://openyls.law.yale.edu/bitstream/handle/20.500.13051/18173/2_Jimenez_Legal%20Principles_PRINT_20220426.pdf?sequence=1&isAllowed=y [Accessed: 23 November 2023].

JOHANNESEN, S., 2023. *„Djøfbladet", Dømt af eliten* [online]. Available from: https://bibliotek.dk/eng/moreinfo/netarchive/870971-tsart%253A38363093 [Accessed 20 February 2023].

JOHN, H. E. & LICHT, H., 2019. *Statement by H. E. John H. Licht Ambassador of the Republic of Vanuatu to the European Union* [online]. Available from: https://asp.icc-cpi.int/sites/asp/files/asp_docs/ASP18/GD.VAN.2.12.pdf [Accessed 23 January 2024].

JOHNSON, D. M., 2008. *The Historical Foundations of World Order: The Tower and the Arena*. Leiden: Martinus Nijhoff Publishers.

JOKUBAITIS, A., 2021. Immanuel Kant and the Question of Certainty in Politics [online]. *Problemos*, 100, 75–86. https://doi.org/10.15388/ [Accessed: 23 November 2023].

JORDASH, W. & PARKER, T., 2010. Trials in Absentia at the Special Tribunal for Lebanon. *Journal of International Criminal Justice*, 8 (2), 487–510.

JUDICIAL COMMISSION OF NEW SOUTH WALES, 2002. *Criminal Trial Courts Bench Book* [online]. Available from: https://www.judcom.nsw.gov.au/publications/benchbks/criminal/the_jury.html#d5e10406 [Accessed 20 February 2023].

KACPRZAK-SZYMAŃSKA, E. 2022a. Commentary on Articles 22a – 22h. In: KLAUS, W. ed. *Ustawa o pomocy obywatelom Ukrainy w związku z konfliktem zbrojnym na terytorium tego państwa. Komentarz* [Law on Assistance to Citizens of Ukraine in Connection with the Armed Conflict on the Territory of That Country. Commentary]. Warszawa: Wolters Kluwer Polska, 162–171.

KACPRZAK-SZYMAŃSKA, E., 2022b. Commentary on Article 37. In: KLAUS, W. ed. *Ustawa o pomocy obywatelom Ukrainy w związku z konfliktem zbrojnym na terytorium tego państwa. Komentarz* [Law on Assistance to Citizens of Ukraine in Connection with the Armed Conflict on the Territory of That Country. Commentary]. Warszawa: Wolters Kluwer Polska, 258–262.

KACPRZAK-SZYMAŃSKA, E., 2022c. Commentary on Articles 13–13a. In: KLAUS, W. ed. *Ustawa o pomocy obywatelom Ukrainy w związku z konfliktem zbrojnym na terytorium tego państwa. Komentarz* [Law on Assistance to Citizens of Ukraine in Connection with the Armed Conflict on the Territory of That Country. Commentary]. Warszawa: Wolters Kluwer Polska, 95–111.

KALSHOVEN, F. & ZEGVELD L., 2001. *Constraints on the Waging of War: An Introduction to International Humanitarian Law* (4th ed.). Geneva: International Committee of the Red Cross

KANT, I., 1980. *Dorovės metafizikos pagrindai* [Groundwork of the Metaphysics of Morals]. Vilnius: Mintis.

KANT, I., 1996. *Į amžinąją taiką. Politiniai traktatai* [Perpetual Peace: A Philosophical Sketch]. Vilnius: Aidai.

KANT, I., 2015. *Praktinio proto kritika* [Critique of Practical Reason]. Vilnius: Margi raštai.

KANT, I., 2019. *Sprendimo galios kritika* [Critique of the Power of Judgment]. Vilnius: Margi raštai.

KARIMI, A., 2012. *Iran, Democracy, and International Law* [online]. Available from: https://core.ac.uk/download/56359448.pdf [Accessed 6 February 2024].

KASEKAMP, A., 2010. *A History of the Baltic States*. Basingstoke: Palgrave Macmillan.

KASČIŪNAS, L. *et al.*, 2014. *Vladimir Putin's Pyramid of Rule: Who Really Governs Russia?* [online via Delfi]. Available from: https://www.delfi.lt/en/politics/vladimir-putins-pyramid-of-rule-who-really-governs-russia.d?id=65432116 [Accessed 28 November 2023].

KHRYSTOVA 2012, Христова Г. О. Негативні та позитивні зобов'язання держави у сфері прав людини: до постановки проблеми // Правові засади гарантування та захисту прав і свобод людини і громадянина (23 листопада 2012 р.). Збірник наукових статей та тез наукових повідомлень за матеріалами міжнародної науково-практичної конференції. – Полтава, 2012.

KHRYSTOVA, H., 2019. *Doktryna pozytyvnykh zobo"yazan' derzhavy u sferi prav lyudyny* [online]. Available from: https://dspace.nlu.edu.ua/bitstream/123456789/16853/1/Khrystova_2019.pdf [Accessed 28 November 2023].

KI-MOON, B., 2012. *Speech* [online]. Available from: https://www.un.org/sg/en/content/highlight/2012-09-25.html [Accessed 28 July 2022].

KIVISTÖ, A.M., 2012. The Concept of 'Human Dignity' in the Post-War Human Rights Debates. *Res Publica: Revista de Filosofía Política*, 27, 99–108.

KINETZ, E. *et al.*, 2022. *How Russian Soldiers Ran a 'cleansing' Operation in Bucha* [online] Available from: https://apnews.com/article/bucha-ukraine-war-cleansing-investigation-43e5a9538e9ba68a035756b05028b8b4 [Accessed 28 November 2023].

KLABBERS, J., 2003. *(I Can't Get No) Recognition: Subjects Doctrine and the Emergence of Non-State Actors* [online]. https://doi.org/10.1163/9789004482043_020 [Accessed 28 November 2023].

KLAUS W., 2022. Commentary on Article 1. In: KLAUS, W. ed., *Ustawa o pomocy obywatelom Ukrainy w związku z konfliktem zbrojnym na terytorium tego państwa. Komentarz* [Law on Assistance to Citizens of Ukraine in Connection with the Armed Conflict on the Territory of That Country. Commentary]. Warszawa: Wolters Kluwer Polska, 19–29.

KLIMBURG, A., ed., 2012. *National Cybersecurity Framework Manual.* Tallinn: NATO CCD COE. Available from: https://ccdcoe.org/uploads/2018/10/NCSFM_0.pdf [Accessed 29 October 2023].

KLIP, A. *European Criminal Law. An Integrative Approach.* Intersentia, 2016.

KLIUCHKOVSKYI, Y. & VENHER, V., 2022. *Organisation and Holding of Elections in Post-War Ukraine. Prerequisites and Challenges* [online]. Available from: https://rm.coe.int/en-organisation-and-holding-of-elections-in-post-war-ukraine-net-2769-/1680a8e995 [Accessed 6 February 2024].

KLUWEN, T., 2017. Universal Jurisdiction in Absentia before Domestic Courts Prosecuting International Crimes: A Suitable Weapon to Fight Impunity. *Goettingen Journal of International Law*, 8(1), 7–38.

KNOX, J. M., 2008. Horizontal Human Rights Law [online]. *American Journal of International Law*, 102(1), 1–47. Available from: https://doi.org/10.1017/s0002930000039828 [Accessed 28 November 2023].

KOKSANOWICZ, G. 2012. *Nadawanie biegu inicjatywom ustawodawczym w świetle postanowień regulaminu Sejmu* [Transmission of Legislative Initiatives in the Light of the Provisions of the Rules of Procedure of the Sejm], *Przegląd Prawa Konstytucyjnego*, 1(9), 13–27.

KOLESNYK, V. A. & PLAKHOTNYY, A. P., 2023. *Combating Cybercrime under Martial Law. In Combating Cybercrime and Human Trafficking*. Kharkiv.

KOROTKYI, T. & HENDEL, N., 2018. The Legal Status of the Donetsk and Luhansk "Peoples' Republics". In: SAYAPIN, S. ed., *The Use of Force against Ukraine and International Law*. T.M.C. Asser Press.

KOSHIW, I., 2023. *How Sumy's Residents Kept Russian Forces Out of Their City* [online]. Available from: https://www.theguardian.com/world/2023/jan/02/how-sumy-residents-kept-russian-forces-out-of-their-city [Accessed 15 December 2023].

KOVAL, D., 2021. The Award Concerning Jurisdiction in the Coastal State Rights Dispute Between Ukraine and Russia: What Has Been Decided and What to Expect Next [online]. *Lex Portus*, 7(1), 7–30. Available from: https://doi.org/10.26886/2524-101X.7.1.2021.1. [Accessed 28 November 2023].

KOZŁOWSKA, A., 2022. *Nadawanie numeru Powszechnego Elektronicznego Systemu Ewidencji Ludności obywatelom Ukrainy oraz obowiązek prowadzenia ewidencji* małoletnich [Numbering of the Universal Electronic Population Registration System for Ukrainian citizens and obligation to keep records of minors]. In: LACHIEWICZ, A. KOZŁOWSKA, W., OLECH, M., PIETRZYKOWSKA, D., PROCHOPIEŃ, G., ROGOWSKI, Ł. & WALCZAK, P. eds., *Pomoc obywatelom Ukrainy. Zadania samorządu terytorialnego i ich finansowanie* [Assistance to the Citizens of Ukraine. Tasks of Local Self-Government and Their Financing]. Warszawa: Wydawnictwo C.H. Beck, 10–16.

KRÁL, D., 2007. *Ukraine and the EU – Membership or Partnership? The Czech Perspective* [online]. Available from: http://pdc.ceu.hu/archive/00003096/01/ukraine_and_the_eu.pdf [Accessed 28 November 2023].

KRASNIKOV, S., 2023. Ways to Strengthen the State of Ensuring Cybersecurity in the Conditions of Martial Law. *Information and Law*, 3(46), 118–128.

KREß, C. & BARRIGA, S., 2016. *The Crime of Aggression: A Commentary*. Cambridge: Cambridge University Press [online]. Available from: https://doi.org/10.1017/9781139058360 [Accessed 28 November 2023].

KREß, C. & BARRIGA, S, 2018. On the Activation of ICC Jurisdiction over the Crime of Aggression [online]. *Journal of International Criminal Justice*,

16(1), 1–17. Available from: https://doi.org/10.1093/jicj/mqy007 [Accessed 28 November 2023].

KREß, C., HOBE, S. & NUßBERGER, A, 2023. *The Ukraine War and the Crime of Aggression: How to Fill the Gaps in the International Legal System* [online via Just Security]. Available from: https://www.justsecurity.org/84783/the-ukraine-war-and-the-crime-of-aggression-how-to-fill-the-gaps-in-the-international-legal-system/ [Accessed 2 February 2024].

KRIMSOS, 2021. *Analysis of the Draft Law of Ukraine "On the Principles of the State Policy of Transition Period"* [online]. Available from: https://krymsos.com/en/pravozahysnyky-proanalizuvaly-zakonoproyekt-minreintegracziyi-pro-perehidne-pravosuddya/ [Accessed 6 February 2024].

KRÓLIKOWSKI, H. 2023. *Ustawa z 11.03.2022 r. o obronie Ojczyzny – od projektu do podpisu Prezydenta Rzeczypospolitej Polskiej* [Law of 11.03.2022 on the Defence of the Homeland – From the Draft to the Signature of the President of the Republic of Poland]. In: KRÓLIKOWSKI, H. ed., *Obrona Ojczyzny. Komentarz*, Warszawa: Wolters Kluwer, 73–78.

KULYK, V., 2016. National Identity in Ukraine: Impact of Euromaidan and the War. *Europe-Asia Studies*, 68(4), 588–608.

KURKCHIYAN, M., 2012. Perceptions of Law and Social Order: A Cross-National Comparison of Collective Legal Consciousness. *Wisconsin International Law Journal*, 29(2).

KURSANI, S., 2022. Beyond Putin's Analogies: The Genocide Debate on Ukraine and the Balkan Analogy Worth Noting. *Journal of Genocide Research.*

KVITKA, K., 2023. Russia's Sham Trial of Ukrainian Prisoners of War [online]. Available from: https://www.hrw.org/news/2023/07/06/russias-sham-trial-ukrainian-prisoners-war [Accessed 15 December 2023].

KWAŚNIEWSKA-SADKOWSKA, A., 2022. Commentary on Articles 25–27. In: KLAUS, W. ed., *Ustawa o pomocy obywatelom Ukrainy w związku z konfliktem zbrojnym na terytorium tego państwa. Komentarz* [Defending the Fatherland. Comment]. Warszawa: Wolters Kluwer Polska, 184–217.

KYIV CITY COUNCIL, 2022. *Віталій Кличко показав, як працювали столичні медики від початку широкомасштабної агресії росії (+фото, відео).* [Vitaliy Klichko showed how medical professionals of the capital had worked since the beginning of the russia's full-fledged aggression (+photo, video)] [online]. Available from: https://kyivcity.gov.ua/news/vitaliy_klichko_pokazav_yak_pratsyuvali_stolichni_mediki_vid_pochatku_shirokomasshtabno_agresi_rosi_video/ [Accessed 20 October 2024].

THE KYIV INDEPENDENT, 2022. *Putin Declares War on Ukraine* [Online]. Available from: https://kyivindependent.com/national/putin-declares-war-on-ukraine [Accessed 17 January 2024].

LABORDE, C., 2011. *Critical Republicanism: The Hijab Controversy and Political Philosophy*. Oxford University Press.

LABORDE, C., 2017. *Liberalism's Religion*. England: Harvard University Press.

LACOVARA, P. A., 2022. *Putin and his generals must be tried for war crimes, even in absentia* [Online via the Hill]. Available from: https://thehill.com/opinion/judiciary/3269331-putin-and-his-generals-must-be-tried-for-war-crimes-even-in-absentia/ [Accessed 28 November 2023].

LANDO, M. & ORAL, N., 2021. Jurisdictional Challenges and Institutional Novelties – Procedural Developments in Law of the Sea Dispute Settlement in 2020 [online]. *The Law & Practice of International Courts and Tribunals* 20(1). Available from: https://doi.org/10.1163/15718034-12341444 [Accessed 28 November 2023].

LAUDE, A., MATHIEU, B. & TABUTEAU, D., 2012. *Droit de la santé*. Presses Universitaires de France. Paris: Édition du Kindle.

LAUTERPACHT, H., 1933. *The Function of Law in the International Community*. Oxford: Oxford University Press.

LAUTERPACHT, H., 1946. The Grotian Tradition in International Law. *British Yearbook of International Law*, 23.

LAUTERPACHT, H., 1950. *International Law and Human Rights*. London: Stevens & Sons Limited.

LASKUS K., 2016. Pomoc społeczna dla uchodźców. *Kontrola państwowa*, 2(367), 61–74.

LAW. T., 2023. *Is Russia Committing Genocide in Ukraine? Here's What Experts Say* [online]. Available from https://time.com/6262903/russia-ukraine-genoc ide-war-crimes/ [Accessed 28 November 2023].

LE COZ, P. & SAMBUC, C., 2012. La dignité humaine kantienne: une justification théorique des transplantations d'organes? [Kantian Human Dignity: A Theoretical Justification for Organ Transplants?]. Raison Publique, [Rennes]. *Presses universitaires de Rennes*, 17, 219–238.

LEBED, A., 1958. Genocide as a Means of Creating a Unified Socialist Nation. In: INSTITUTE FOR THE STUDY OF USSR, eds., *Genocide in the USSR*. New York, NY: The Scarecrow Press.

LEICHTOVA, M. B., 2016. Why Crimea Was Always Ours: Legitimacy Building in Russia in the Wake of the Crisis in Ukraine and the Annexation of Crimea. *Russian Politics*, 1(3), 291–315.

LEITER, B., 2013. *Why Tolerate Religion?* Princeton: Princeton University Press.

LEGENDRE, P., 1983. *Leçons II, L'empire de la vérité, Introduction aux espaces dogmatiques industriels* [Lessons II, The empire of truth, Introduction to industrial dogmatic spaces]. Paris: Fayard.

LEMKIN, R., 1944. *Axis Rule in Occupied Europe*, 79. Clark NJ: Lawbook Exchange Ltd.

LEONAITE, E. & ZALIMAS, D., 2015. The Annexation of Crimea and Attempts to Justify It in the Context of International Law. *Lithuanian Annual Strategic Review*, 14, 11–63.

LEONOV B. & SERYOGIN V., 2022. Problems of Legal Provision of Anti-sabotage Protection of Critical Infrastructure Objects under Martial Law. *Information and Law*, 3(42).

LEMOS, M., 2023. *The Law of Immunity and the Prosecution of the Head of State of the Russian Federation for International Crimes in the War against Ukraine* [online]. Available from https://www.ejiltalk.org/the-law-of-immunity-and-the-prosecution-of-the-head-of-state-of-the-russian-federation-for-international-crimes-in-the-war-against-ukraine/ [Accessed 23 January 2023].

LENARČIČ, J., 2005. *Supplementary Human Dimension Meeting on Challenges of Election Technologies and Procedures* [online]. Available from: https://www.osce.org/files/f/documents/7/9/14385.pdf [Accessed 6 February 2024].

LERCH, M., 2022. *Russia's War on Ukraine in International Law and Human Rights Bodies: Bringing Institutions Back In*. 12.

LIASHKO 2022, Міністерство охорони здоров'я України. Вплив війни на психічне здоров'я – колосальний, - Віктор Ляшко. Урядовий портал. 7 червня 2022 р. The Ministry of Health of Ukraine. The impact of war on mental health is enormous, Viktor Liashko. Government portal. 7 June 2022]. [online]. Available from: https://www.kmu.gov.ua/news/vpliv-vijni-na-psihichne-zdorovya-kolosalnij-viktor-lyashko.

LIIVOJA, R., 2013. Competing Histories: Soviet War Crimes in the Baltic States. In: HELLER, K. ed., *The Hidden Histories of War Crimes Trials*. Oxford: Oxford University Press.

LINDE, A., 2022. *Press Conference by NATO Secretary General Jens Stoltenberg, the Minister of Foreign Affairs of Finland, Pekka Haavisto, and the Minister of Foreign Affairs of Sweden, Ann Linde following the signature of the NATO Accession Protocols for Finland and Sweden* [online]. Available from: https://www.nato.int/cps/en/natohq/opinions_197761.htm?selectedLocale=en [Accessed 23 July 2022].

LINDKVIST, L., 2017. *Religious Freedom and the Universal Declaration of Human Rights*. Cambridge: Cambridge University Press.

LISOVSKA, YU. P., 2019. *Cybersecurity: Risks and Measures: Training Manual. Kyiv: Condor Publishing House.*

LUBINETS, D., 2022. *Report on the Observance and Protection of Human and Civil Rights and Freedoms in Ukraine in 2022.* [online]. Available from: https://ombudsman.gov.ua/report-2022/sotsialna-derzhava. [Accessed 20 October 2024].

LUKASHOVA, S., 2020. *Як працює в Україні суд присяжних, що вирішить долю справи Шеремета* [How the jury that will decide the fate of Sheremet's case functions in Ukraine. [online via Ukrainska Pravda] [online]. Available from: https://www.pravda.com.ua/articles/2020/09/10/7265894/ [Accessed 20 February 2023].

LYNCH, S., 2023. *Ukraine Wants to Join EU Within Two Years, PM Says* [online via Politico]. Available from: https://www.politico.eu/article/ukraine-eu-membership-two-years-prime-minister-denys-shmyhal/ [Accessed 28 November 2023].

MACKINNON, A., 2022. *Congress Seeks to Declare Putin's War Genocide* [online]. Available from: https://foreignpolicy.com/2022/06/24/congress-declare-ukraine-russia-war-genocide/ [Accessed 28 November 2023].

MACKLEM, T., 2006. *Independence of Mind.* Oxford: Oxford University Press.

MACKLEM, T., 2017. *Law and Life in Common.* Oxford: Oxford University Press.

MACKLIN, R., 2003. *Dignity Is a Useless Concept. British Medical Journal* 327, 1419.

MACLURE, J. & TAYLOR, C., 2010. *Secularism and Freedom of Conscience.* London, England: Harvard University Press.

MADISON, M., 2017. *The Changing Status of Women in Politics and Society: Ghana.* [online]. Available from: https://core.ac.uk/download/541073653.pdf [Accessed 6 February 2024].

MAJUMDAR, A., 2022. *Ukraine calls for special international tribunal to hold Putin accountable for war crimes* [Online]. Available from: https://www.republicworld.com/world-news/russia-ukraine-crisis/ukraine-calls-for-special-international-tribunal-to-hold-putin-accountable-for-war-crimes-articleshow.html [Accessed 28 November 2023].

MALASHCHUK O., SMOLENSKA L.. *Ecological consequences of destruction of Kakhovsky hydroelectric power plant. Modern trends of development of geodesy, land management, and environmental management: International scientific and practical conference* (c. Odessa, 07-09 July 2023). Pp. 104-106.]. [online]. Available from: http://lib.osau.edu.ua/jspui.

MALET, D., 2022. The Risky Status of Ukraine's Foreign Fighters [online]. Available from: https://foreignpolicy.com/2022/03/15/ukraine-war-foreign-fighters-legion-volunteers-legal-status/#:~:text=On%20March%203%2C%20the%20Russian,status%20of%20prisoners%20of%20war… [Accessed 15 December 2023].

MÄLKSOO, L., 2001. Soviet Genocide? Communist Mass Deportations in the Baltic States and International Law. *Leiden Journal of International Law*, 14(4).

MÄLKSOO, L., 2019. The Annexation of Crimea and Balance of Power in International Law. *European Journal of International Law*, 30(1), 303–319.

MALTSEVA, I. R., CHERNYSH, YU. O. & SHTONDA, R. M., 2022. Analysis of Some Cyber Threats in the Conditions of War. *Cybersecurity: Education, Science, Technology*, 4(16), 37–44.

MANCINI, S. & ROSENFELD, M., 2018. *The Conscience Wars: Rethinking the Balance between Religion, Identity, and Equality*. Cambridge: Cambridge University Press.

MANENT, P., 2021. *Prigimtinis įstatymas ir žmogaus teisės* [Natural Law and Human Rights]. Valstybingumo studijų centras. Vilnius.

MARAYEV, V. & BILYK, J., 2022. *Rashism or Why Russians Are the New Nazi* [online]. Available from: https://voxukraine.org/en/rashism-or-why-russians-are-the-new-nazi [Accessed 28 November 2023].

MARCHUK, I. & WANIGASURIYA, A., 2022. Beyond the False Claim of Genocide: Preliminary Reflections on Ukraine's Prospects in Its Pursuit of Justice at the ICJ. *Journal of Genocide Research*.

MARCUSSEN, M., RISSE-KAPPEN, T., ENGELMANN-MARTIN, D., KNOPF, H. J. & ROSCHER, K., 1999. Constructing Europe? The Evolution of French, British and German Nation State Identities. *Journal of European Public Policy*, 6(4), 614–633.

MARES, R., 2020. COVID-19: *Labour Rights in Global Supply Chains – Impacts and Responsibilities* [online]. Available from: https://rwi.lu.se/blog/covid-19-labour-rights-in-global-supply-chains-impacts-and-responsibilities/ [Accessed 17 January 2024].

MARTYNIUK – PLACHA J., 2022. Commentary on Article 12. In: DREMBKOWSKI, P., *Ustawa o pomocy obywatelom Ukrainy. Komentarz z wzorami dotyczącymi pobytu, dostępu do rynku pracy, świadczeń społecznych, edukacji i opieki zdrowotnej* [Law on Assistance to Citizens of Ukraine. Commentary with Models on Residence, Access to the Labour Market, Social Benefits, Education and Health Care]. Warszawa: Wydawnictwo CH. Beck, 52–68.

MARTYNIUK – PLACHA, J. & DREMBKOWSKI, P., 2022. Commentary on Articles 13–13a. In: DREMBKOWSKI, P. ed., *Ustawa o pomocy obywatelom Ukrainy. Komentarz z wzorami dotyczącymi pobytu, dostępu do rynku pracy, świadczeń społecznych, edukacji i opieki zdrowotnej* [Law on Assistance to Citizens of Ukraine. Commentary with Models on Residence, Access to the Labour Market, Social Benefits, Education and Health Care]. Warszawa: Wydawnictwo CH. Beck, 77–79.

MARXSEN, C., 2014. The Crimea Crisis – An International Law Perspective, *SSRN Scholarly Paper.*

MARXSEN, C., 2016. The Crimea Crisis from an International Law Perspective. *Kyiv-Mohyla Law and Politics Journal* 2.

MARYUNANI, WORO P., *et al.*, 2019. *The Study of Temperature Changes on Asphalt Concrete Wearing Course (AC-WC) Mixing Process on Marshall Characteristics* [online]. Available from: https://doi.org/10.1063/1.5098209 [Accessed 6 February 2024].

MAUPAS, S., 2022. *Ukraine calls for the creation of a special tribunal on the crime of aggression* [Online]. Available from: https://www.lemonde.fr/en/international/article/2022/05/22/ukraine-calls-for-the-creation-of-a-special-tribunal-on-the-crime-of-aggression_5984275_4.html [Accessed 28 November 2023].

MCCORQUODALE, R. & NOLAN, J., 2021. The effectiveness of human rights due diligence for preventing business human rights abuses [online]. *Netherlands International Law Review*, 68(3), 455–478. Available from: https://doi.org/10.1007/s40802-021-00201-x [Accessed 28 November 2023].

MCDERMOTT R., N. & BARTLES Ch, K., 2022. *Defining the "Special Military Operation* [online]. Available from: https://www.ndc.nato.int/research/research.php?icode=777 [Accessed 15 December 2023].

MCKENZIE, D., SWAILS, B. & SPARK, S., 2019. *Nigerian Parties Condemn Lastminute Election Delay* [online]. Available from: https://edition.cnn.com/2019/02/15/africa/nigeria-elections-delayed/index.html [Accessed 6 February 2024].

MEDVEDEV, D., 2022. *About Fakes and Real History* [online via Telegram]. Available from: https://t.me/medvedev_telegram/34 [Accessed 28 November 2023].

MELZER N., 2009. *Interpretive Guidance on the Notion of Direct Participation in Hostilities under International Humanitarian Law.* Geneva: International Committee of the Red Cross.

MENDE, J., 2022. Business Authority in Global Governance: Companies beyond Public and Private Roles [online]. *Journal of International Political Theory*, 19(2), 200–220. Available from: https://doi.org/10.1177/17550882221116924 [Accessed 28 November 2023].

MERLOE, P., 2008. *Promoting Legal Frameworks for Elections: An NDI Guide for Developing Election Laws and Legal Commentaries*, 17–21.

MESONIS, G., 2010. *Konstitucijos interpretavimo metodologiniai pagrindai* [Methodological foundations of the interpretation of the Constitution]. Vilnius, Lithuania: VĮ Registrų centras.

MEUSER, S. & HETT, F., 2014. *The Future of EU-Ukraine Relations. Four Scenarios. Scenario team EU-Ukraine 2030* [online]. Berlin: Friedrich-Ebert-Stiftung. Available from: https://library.fes.de/pdf-files/id-moe/10608.pdf [Accessed 28 November 2023].

MFA OF UKRAINE, 2014a. *Regarding the Resolution "About Crimean Independence" Adopted on March 17, 2014* [online]. Available from: https://mfa.gov.ua/en/news/19773-komentar-mzs-ukrajini-shhodo-postanovi-pro-nezalezhnisty-krimu-vid-17-bereznya-2014-roku [Accessed 5 February 2024].

MFA OF UKRAINE, 2014b. *Statement of the MFA of Ukraine on Russia's Recognition of Self-Proclaimed Republic of Crimea* [online]. Available from: https://mfa.gov.ua/en/news/19853-zajava-mzs-ukrajini [Accessed 5 February 2024].

MICHAEL HILL and PETER HUPE (2002), Implementing Public Policy, Sage Publications.

MIKELĖNIENĖ, D. & MIKELĖNAS, V., 1999. *Teismo procesas: teisės aiškinimo ir taikymo aspektai* [Judicial Process: Aspects of Legal Interpretation and Application]. Vilnius, Lithuania: Justitia.

MILITARY BALANCE ASSESSMENT, 2022. *The International Institute for Strategic Studies.* [online]. Available from: https://www.iiss.org/blogs/analysis/2022/02/military-balance-2022-further-assessments [Accessed 23 July 2022].

MINCHENKO CONSULTING, 2019. *Politburo 2.0 and the Anti-Establishment Wave* [online]. Available from: https://minchenko.ru/netcat_files/userfiles/PB_2.0_summer_2019_ENG.pdf [Accessed 28 November 2023].

MINENKO, K., 2021. Projekt zakonu pro administratyvnu proceduru – krok nazustrich gromadianam [Draft Law on Administrative Procedure – A Stop Towards Citizents]. *Jurydychna gazeta online*, 24 March 2021. Available from: https://yur-gazeta.com/dumka-eksperta/proekt-zakonu-pro-administrativnu-proceduru--krok-nazustrich-gromadyanam.html [Accessed 16 November 2023].

MINESASHVILI, S., 2022. Before and after 2014: Russo-Ukrainian conflict and its impact on European identity discourses in Ukraine. *Southeast European and Black Sea Studies*, 1–27.

MOH, 2022. *Деякі питання надання первинної медичної допомоги в умовах воєнного стану: Наказ МОЗ України 17.03.2022 № 496* [Some Issues of the Provision of Primary Medical Care under the Conditions of Martial Law: Order of the Ministry of Health of Ukraine of 17.03.2022 No. 496]. [online]. Available from: https://zakon.rada.gov.ua/rada/show/v0496282-22#Text. [Accessed 2024 October 20]

MOH, 2022a. *Про залучення медичних працівників-іноземців до надання допомоги постраждалим в умовах воєнного стану: Наказ МОЗ України від* 26.02.2022 № 383. [*On the Involvement of Medical Workers – Foreign Citizens in the Provision of Medical Care to the Injured Under the Conditions of Martial Law: Order of the MOH of Ukraine of* 26.02.2022 No. 383]. [online]. Available from: https://zakon.rada.gov.ua/rada/show/v0383282-22#Text. [Accessed 20 October 2024].

MOH, 2022b. *Про залучення лікарів-інтернів та деяких інших осіб до виконання заходів, пов'язаних із наданням медичної допомоги особам, які постраждали під час надзвичайної ситуації, яка виникла в період воєнного стану в Україні: Наказ МОЗ України від* 27.02.2022 № 385. [*On the Involvement of Intern Doctors and Some Other Persons in Taking the Measures Connected with the Provision of Medical Care to the Persons Injured During the Emergency Occurred Within the Period of Martial Law in Ukraine: Order of the MOH of Ukraine of* 27.02.2022 No. 385]. [online]. Available from: https://dmu.edu.ua. [Accessed 20 October 2024].

MOH, 2022c. *Про залучення до надання медичної допомоги в закладах охорони здоров'я комунальної форми власності, розміщених на території Київської, Харківської, Дніпропетровської, Запорізької, Чернігівської, Миколаївської, Одеської, Сумської областей медичних працівників з інших адміністративно-територіальних одиниць в період дії воєнного стану: Наказ МОЗ України від* 16.04.2022 № 649 [*On the Involvement in the Provision of Medical Care in Municipally-Owned Healthcare Facilities Located on the Territory of Kyiv, Dnipropetrovsk, Zaporizhzhia, Mykolayiv, Odessa, and Sumy Regions of Medical Workers from Other Territorial Communities during the Period of Martial Law: Order of the MOH of Ukraine of* 16.04.2022 No. 649]. [online]. Available from: https://zakon.rada.gov.ua/rada/show/v0649282-22#Text. [Accessed 20 October 2024].

MOH, 2022d. Безоплатні ліки для людей із діабетом. Київська обласна військова адміністрація. 17 листопада 2022 [MOH: *Free medicine for people living with diabetes. Kyiv oblast military administration.* 17 November 2022]. [online]. Available from: https://koda.gov.ua/moz-bezoplatni-liky-dlya-lyudej-iz-diabetom. [Accessed 20 October 2024].

MITTLEMAN, A., 2018. Dignity and Democracy: Defending the Principle of the Sanctity of Human. In: *Is Judaism Democratic? Reflections from Theory and Practice Throughout the Ages* [online]. Purdue University Press, 197–217. Available from: https://www.jstor.org/stable/j.ctvhhhd72.16 [Accessed 16 February 2024].

MIZARAS, V., 2023. *Man įvairių krizinių situacijų kontekste yra ramu dėl Konstitucijos* [In Times of Various Crises, I Am Sure about the Power of the

Constitution] [online via IQ]. Available from: https://iq.lt/advokatas/v-mizaras-man-ivairiu-kriziniu-situaciju-kontekste-yra-ramu-del-konstitucijos/278324 [Accessed 28 November 2023].

MOH, 2022e. *Про самоврядування в сфері охорони здоров'я в Україні: проєкт Закону. 9 вересня* 2022. [*On Self-Governance in the Sphere of Health Care in Ukraine: draft law.* 9 September 2022]. [online]. Available from: https://umj.com.ua/uk/novyna-233345-rozrobleno-zakonoproyekt-pro-samovryaduvannya-v-sferi-ohoroni-zdorov-ya-v-ukrayini. [Accessed 20 October 2024].

MONIRUZZAMAN, M. D., 2018. *Electoral Legitimacy, Preventive Representation, and Regularization of Authoritarian Democracy in Bangladesh* [online]. Available from: https://www.intechopen.com/chapters/63563 [Accessed 6 February 2024].

MOSES A.D, 2022. The Ukraine Genocide Debate *Reveals the Limits of International Law [Online]. Available from* https://www.lawfaremedia.org/article/ukraine-genocide-debate-reveals-limits-international-law [Accessed 28 November 2023].

MOSKALENKO, O. & STRELTSOV, V., 2015. Constitutional Perspective of the EU-Ukraine Association Agreement Application: Ukrainian Problems. *Studia Europejskie – Studies in European Affairs*, 2(74), 121–137.

MOTYL, A. J., 2015. *Is Putin's Russia Fascist?* [online]. Available from: https://www.atlanticcouncil.org/blogs/ukrainealert/is-putin-s-russia-fascist/ [Accessed 28 November 2023].

MOTYL, A. J. 2022. *Is Putin Committing Genocide in Ukraine?* [online]. Available from: https://www.tabletmag.com/sections/news/articles/is-putin-committing-genocide-in-ukraine [Accessed 28 November 2023].

MOYN, 2014. A Powerless Companion: Human Rights In The Age of Neoliberalism. *Law and Contemporary Problems Law and Neoliberalism*, 77(4), 147–169.

MREŃCA, E., 2016. *Procedura przygotowywania rządowych projektów ustaw w Trzeciej Rzeczypospolitej* [The Procedure for Preparing Government Bills in the Third Republic]. Warszawa: Wyższa Szkoła Finansów i Zarządzania.

MURRAY, J. L., 2007. *Methods of Interpretation – Comparative Law Method* [online]. Available from: https://curia.europa.eu/common/dpi/col_murray.pdf [Accessed 28 November 2023].

MYSHCHAK, I., 2020. *Реформування Суду Присяжних в Україні Як Важливий Елемент Підвищення Довіри до судової гілки влади* [Reforming the Jury System in Ukraine as an Important Element of Increasing Confidence in the Judiciary] [online]. Available from: http://nbuviap.gov.ua/images/dumka/2020/18-19.pdf [Accessed 20 February 2023].

NATO, 2022. *Declaration on Standing with Ukraine* [online]. Available from: https://www.nato-pa.int/document/2022-declaration-standing-ukraine-111-sesp-22 [Accessed 23 January 2023].

NETHERLANDS PUBLIC PROSECUTION SERVICE, 2022. *Prosecution and Trial* [online]. Available from: https://www.prosecutionservice.nl/topics/mh17-plane-crash/prosecution-and-trial [Accessed 10 January 2023].

NEW LINES INSTITUTE, 2022. *An Independent Legal Analysis of the Russian Federation's Breaches of the Genocide Convention in Ukraine and the Duty to Prevent* [online]. Available from: https://newlinesinstitute.org/russia/an-independent-legal-analysis-of-the-russian-federations-breaches-of-the-genocide-convention-in-ukraine-and-the-duty-to-prevent/ [Accessed 28 November 2023].

NEYRET, L. *et al.*, 2017. 'Draft Convention against Ecocide'. *Ecocrimes to Ecocide: Protecting the Environment through Criminal Law.*

NDERITU A. W., 2022. *Special Adviser on the Prevention of Genocide on the Order of the International Court of Justice of 16 March 2022* [online]. Available from: https://www.un.org/en/genocideprevention/documents/Statement-by-Special-Adviser-Nderitu-on-the-Order-of-the-International-Court-of-Justice-of-16-March-2022.pdf [Accessed 28 November 2023].

NOLLKAEMPER, A., 2022. *Three Options for the Veto Power After the War in Ukraine* [online]. Available from: https://www.ejiltalk.org/three-options-for-the-veto-power-after-the-war-in-ukraine/ [Accessed 10 January 2023].

NORRIS, P., 2014. *Why Electoral Integrity Matters.* New York: Cambridge University Press.

NOWAK, D., 2019. Służba wojskowa jako element powszechnego obowiązku ojczyzny [Military service as part of the universal duty of the fatherland]. Wiedza Obronna, 268(3), 77-103.

NURIDZHANIAN, G., 2018. Crimea in International Courts and Tribunals: Matters of Jurisdiction [online]. *Max Planck Yearbook of United Nations Law Online*, 21(1), 378–403. Available from: doi.org/10.1163/13894633_021001013 [Accessed 10 January 2023].

NUSSBAUM, M., 2008. *Liberty of Conscience: In Defense of America's Tradition of Religious Equality.* New York: Basic Books.

O'CONNELL, M. E., 2019. *The Art of Law in the International Community.* Cambridge: Cambridge University Press.

OCHAB, E. U., 2022. Is there progress in addressing Putin's crime of aggression? [Online]. Available from: https://www.forbes.com/sites/ewelinaochab/2022/05/23/is-there-progress-in-addressing-putins-crime-of-aggression/?sh=28e234e36c41 [Accessed: 23 November 2023].

O'HARA, C., 2021. Consensus, Difference and Sexuality: Que(e)rying the European Court of Human Rights' Concept of 'European Consensus'. *Law and Critique*, 32, 91–114.

OECD, 1976. *OECD Guidelines for Multinational Enterprises* [online]. Available from: https://www.oecd.org/corporate/publicationsdocuments/legalactsstandards/5/ [Accessed 19 January 2024].

OECD, 2023. *Responsible Business Conduct Implications of Russia's Invasion of Ukraine* [online]. Available from: https://www.oecd-ilibrary.org/docserver/f222a4d1-en.pdf?expires=1686128555&id=id&accname=guest&checksum=3821962557BB6EDA5277CA22E280FFBC [Accessed 19 January 2024].

OECD, [no date]. *2023 Update of the OECD Guidelines for Multinational Enterprises on Responsible Business Conduct* [online]. Available from: https://mneguidelines.oecd.org/targeted-update-of-the-oecd-guidelines-for-multinational-enterprises.htm [Accessed 19 January 2024].

OHCHR, 1984. *General comment No. 13: Article 14* [online]. Available from: https://www.ohchr.org/sites/default/files/Documents/HRBodies/TB/HRI-GEN-1-REV-9-VOL-I_en.doc [Accessed 19 January 2024].

OHCHR, 2018a. *Guidelines for States on the Effective Implementation of the Right to Participate in Public Affairs* [online]. Available from: https://www.ohchr.org/sites/default/files/Documents/Issues/PublicAffairs/GuidelinesRightParticipatePublicAffairs_web.pdf [Accessed 2024 February 7].

OHCHR, 2018b. *Report on the Human Rights Situation in Ukraine 16 May to 15 August 2018* [online]. Available from: www.ohchr.org/Documents/Countries/UA/ReportUkraineMay-August2018_EN.pdf [Accessed 5 February 2024].

OHCHR, Business after conflict: respecting human rights to help sustain peace, 2019.

OHCHR, 2021. A Handbook on International Human Rights Standards on Elections [online]. *Professional Training Series* No. 2/Rev. 1. New York and Geneva. Available from: https://www.ohchr.org/sites/default/files/Documents/Publications/Human-Rights-and-Elections.pdf [Accessed 6 February 2024].

OHCHR, 2022. *Situation with human rights in Ukraine in the context of the armed attack by the Russian Federation, 24 February to 15 May 2022* [online]. Available from: https://www.ohchr.org/en/documents/country-reports/situation-human-rights-ukraine-context-armed-attack-russian-federation [Accessed 20 October 2024].

OHCHR, 2023a. *Russian Federation: UN experts Alarmed by Recruitment of Prisoners by "Wagner Group"*. Available from: https://www.ohchr.org/en/press-releases/2023/03/russian-federation-un-experts-alarmed-recruitment-prisoners-wagner-group [Accessed 15 December 2023].

OHCHR, 2023b. *Report on the Human Rights Situation in Ukraine. 1 August 2022 to 31 January 2023.* [online]. Available from: https://www.ohchr.org/sites/default/files/documents/countries/ukraine/2023/23-03-24-Ukraine-35th-periodic-report-ENG.pdf [Accessed 5 February 2024].

OHCHR, [no date]. *Business after Conflict: Respecting Human Rights to Help Sustain Peace* [online] Available from: https://www.ohchr.org/en/stories/2019/12/business-after-conflict-respecting-human-rights-help-sustain-peace [Accessed: 23 November 2023].

OHCHR, [no date]. *Reports* [online]. Available from: https://www.ohchr.org/en/special-procedures/wg-business/reports [Accessed: 19 January 2024].

OHCHR, [no date]. *Seeding Change for an Economy That Enhances Human Rights – The Surge Initiative* [online]. Available from: https://www.ohchr.org/en/sdgs/seeding-change-economy-enhances-human-rights-surge-initiative [Accessed: 19 January 2024].

OLIINYK, I., 2023. *Parliamentary Elections Will Not Be Held in Ukraine Due to the Martial Law. And When Will They Be? And What Will the De-occupied Territories Look Like?* [online]. Available from: https://zaborona.com/en/parliamentary-elections-will-not-be-held-in-ukraine/ [Accessed 6 February 2024].

ONYSHCHENKO, S. & HLUSHKO, A., 2022. Analytical Measurement of Ukraine's Cybersecurity in the Context of Growing Challenges and Threats. *Scientific journal Economy and Region*, 1(84), 13–20.

O'NEILL, O., 2001. Agents of justice [online]. *Metaphilosophy*, 32(1–2), 180–195. Available from: https://doi.org/10.1111/1467-9973.00181 [Accessed: 19 January 2024].

O'NEILL, MARTIN,Social Justice and Economic Systems. Philosophical Topics, 2020, 48(2), 130-189.

OPEN DEMOCRACY, 2020. *Big Brands and Cheap Clothes in the West Are Bad News for Ukrainian Workers* [online]. Available from: https://www.opendemocracy.net/en/odr/ukraine-global-brands-cheap-clothing/ [Accessed 28 November 2023].

OPORA, 2023. *During the Postwar Elections in Ukraine Participants, Data and Information Must Be Protected at the Highest Level* [online]. Available from: https://www.oporaua.org/en/news/vybory/24701-pid-chas-povoiennikh-viboriv-v-ukrayini-uchasniki-dani-ta-informatsiia-povinni-buti-zakhishcheni-na-naivishchomu-rivni [Accessed 6 February 2024].

ORAL, N., 2021. Ukraine v. The Russian Federation: Navigating Conflict over Sovereignty under UNCLOS. *International Law Studies* 97.

ORGAD, L., 2010. The Preamble in Constitutional Interpretation. *International Journal of Constitutional Law* (I-CON), 8(4), 714–738.

OSCE, 1990. *Commitments on Elections* [online]. Available from: https://www.osce.org/files/f/documents/3/3/16815.html [Accessed 6 February 2024].

OSCE, 2019. *Ukraine Early Parliamentary Elections 21 July 2019 ODIHR Election Observation Mission Final Report* [online]. Available from: https://www.osce.org/files/f/documents/6/9/439634_0.pdf [Accessed 17 January 2024].

PARLIAMENTARY ASSEMBLY, 2022. *Recent Developments in Ukraine: Threats to the Functioning of Democratic Institutions* [online]. Available from: http://assembly.coe.int/nw/xml/xref/xref-xml2html-en.asp?fileid=20873&lang=en [Accessed 5 February 2024].

PARLIAMENTARY ASSEMBLY, 2023. *Parliamentary Conference on "Elections in Times of Crisis: Challenges and Opportunities" Final Declaration* [online]. Available from: https://www.senat.ro/POZE/2023/5/11/c7cf1bad-5e86-4c96-b339-e5ca89ed4b7d/Adopted%20declaration_Bern%20conference%2010%20May%202023.docx.pdf [Accessed 6 February 2024].

PARRY, A., 2021. The Absconding Accused and the ICC: An examination on the Legitimacy and Capacity of the International Criminal Court to Hold *in absentia* Trials. [online]. *PKI Global Justice Journal 36.* Available from: https://globaljustice.queenslaw.ca/news/the-absconding-accused-and-the-icc-an-examination-on-the-legitimacy-and-capacity-of-the-international-criminal-court-to-hold-in-absentia-trials [Accessed 5 February 2024].

PAVLENKO, T.A. *Certain issues of epidemiological safety under the conditions of war. Legal regulation of epidemiological safety under the conditions of war and post-war reconstruction: materials of the international round table of* 29 June 2023; electronic scientific edition / compilers: T.O. Mykhailychenko, P.P. Noha, A.V. Salashna; Academician *Stashis Scientific Research Institute for the study of crime problems at the National Academy of Law Sciences of Ukraine* [et al]]. – Kharkiv: Pravo, 2023. – 140 p. – Pp. 83-87]. [online]. Available from: https://ivpz.kh.ua.

PEARSALL, J., 2001. *The Concise Oxford Dictionary.* Oxford, England: Oxford University Press.

PEREIRA, P., BAŠIĆ, F., BOGUNOVIC, I. & BARCELO, D., 2022. *Russian-Ukrainian War Impacts the Total Environment. Science of The Total Environment*, 1(837), 155865.

PERRY, M.J., 2006. Protecting Human Rights in a Democracy: What Role for the Courts? In: *Toward a Theory of Human Rights: Religion, Law, Courts.* Cambridge University Press, 87–117.

PETERS, A., 2009. Humanity as the Alpha and Omega of Sovereignty. *European Journal of International Law*, 20(3).

PETREQUIN S. & CORDER, M., 2022. *Ukraine Is Granted European Union Candidate Status* [Online via Time]. Available from: https://time.com/6190557/ukraine-eu-membership-candidacy/ [Accessed: 22 January 2024].

PETSCHE, M., 2010. Jus Cogens as a Vision of the International Legal Order [online]. *Penn State International Law Review*, 29(2), 233–273. Available from: https://elibrary.law.psu.edu/cgi/viewcontent.cgi?article=1161&context=psilr [Accessed 22 January 2024].

PICKRELL, R., 2023. *Russian Military Leaders Can't Seem to Get Wagner and Its Boss, Prigozhin, to Fall in Line, and It's a Mess That Goes Beyond Dysfunction* [online]. Available from: https://www.businessinsider.com/russian-military-cant-control-wagner-and-its-a-big-problem-2023-6 [Accessed 15 December 2023].

PIRIE, F., 2021. *The Rules of Laws: A 4,000 – Year Quest to Order the World.* New York: Basic Books.

PLAKANS, A., 2011. *A Concise History of the Baltic States.* Cambridge: Cambridge University Press.

PLATO, 2014. *Valstybė* [Republic]. Vilnius: Margi raštai.

PLĖŠNYS, A., 2021. Introduction in: Manent, P., Prigimtinis įstatymas ir žmogaus teisės. [Natural law and human rights]. Vilnius: Valstybingumo studijų centras. 11-16.

PLUTOWSKI, L., 2022. *Tolerance for Postponing Elections in Crisis Conditions* [online]. Vanderbilt University. Revista Latinoamericana de Oninión Pública. Available from: https://revistas.usal.es/cuatro/index.php/1852-9003/article/view/26934/28614 [Accessed 6 February 2024].

POELS, A, 2005. Universal Jurisdiction in Absentia. *Netherlands Quarterly of Human Rights*, 23(1), 65–84.

POHORILOV, S., 2023. *No Elections Can Be Held in Ukraine While Martial Law in Effect – National Security and Defence Council* [online]. Available from: https://www.pravda.com.ua/eng/news/2023/05/16/7402519/ [Accessed 6 February 2024].

POLIAKOV, O. M., 2023. Modern Trends in Detecting and Countering the Use of Spyware and Malware. *Information and Law*, 2(45), 125–138.

POLITYUK, P., 2023. *Russia Fights Cross-Border Raid That Ukraine Says Is Russian Opposition* [online]. Available from: https://www.reuters.com/world/europe/ukraine-says-it-advances-bakhmuts-flanks-entrap-russians-2023-05-22/ [Accessed 15 December 2023].

POLLICINO, O., 2004. Legal Reasoning of the Court of Justice in the Context of the Principle of Equality Between Judicial Activism and Self-restraint [online]. *German Law Journal* 5(3), 283-317. Available from: https://doi:10.1017/S2071832200012438 [Accessed: 22 January 2024].

PONOMARENKO, I., 2018. *Goodbye, ATO: Ukraine Officially Changes Name of Donbas War* [online]. Available from: https://archive.kyivpost.com/ukraine-politics/goodbye-ato-hello-taking-measures-ensure-national-security-defense-repulsing-deterring-armed-aggression-russian-federation-donetsk-luhansk-oblasts.html [Accessed 15 December 2023].

POPOVA, M., 2013. Response to Justin Crowe's Review of Politicized Justice in Emerging Democracies: A Study of Courts in Russia and Ukraine [online]. *Perspectives on Politics*, 11(1), 215–216. Available from: https://www.jstor.org/stable/43280701 [Accessed: 22 January 2024].

POPOVA, M., 2017. Putin-Style "Rule of Law" & the Prospects for Change [online]. *Daedalus*, 146(2), 64–75. Available from: https://www.jstor.org/stable/48563061 [Accessed: 22 January 2024].

POSTEMA, G. J., 2022. *Law's Rule: The Nature, Value, and Viability of the Rule of Law.* Oxford: Oxford University Press.

POTĚŠIL, L., K. ROZSNYAI, J. OLSZANOWSKI, & HORVAT, M. 2021. Simplification of Administrative Procedure on the Example of the Czech Republic, Poland, Slovakia, and Hungary. *Administrative Sciences* 11. Available from: https://www.mdpi.com/2076-3387/11/1/9/htm [Accessed on 16.11.2023].

POTIY, O., SEMENCHENKO, A., BAKALYNSKYY, O. & MIALKOVSKYY, D., 2021. Public Management of Institutional Development in the Field of Cyber Protection. *Scientific Bulletin: State Administration*, 3(9), 136–162.

PRADEL, J, 2001. *Lyginamoji baudžiamoji teisė* [Comparative Criminal Law]. Vilnius: Eugrimas.

PRINC, M., 2022. Commentary on Article 12. In: KLAUS, W. ed., *Ustawa o pomocy obywatelom Ukrainy w związku z konfliktem zbrojnym na terytorium tego państwa. Komentarz* [Law on Assistance to Citizens of Ukraine in Connection with the Armed Conflict on the Territory of That Country. Commentary]. Warszawa: Wolters Kluwer Polska, 73–86.

PROELSS, A., *et al.*, 2017. *United Nations Convention on the Law of the Sea: A Commentary.*

PROSKURINA, A., 2023. *Future Elections and Local Direct Democracy in Ukraine: Interview with Julia Kyrychenko* [online]. Available from: https://www.democracy.community/stories/future-elections-and-local-direct-democracy-ukraine-interview-julia-kyrychenko [Accessed 6 February 2024].

PSHETACHNYK, Y. & TARPOVA, S., 2022. *Research Service of the European Parliament.* 733.549. Russia's War against Ukraine: Chronology of Cyber Attacks.

PSZCZÓŁKOWSKI, M., & ROGOZIŃSKA Ż., 2022. Commentary on Articles 25–27. In: DREMBKOWSKI, P. *Ustawa o pomocy obywatelom Ukrainy. Komentarz z wzorami dotyczącymi pobytu, dostępu do rynku pracy, świadczeń społecznych, edukacji i opieki* zdrowotnej [Law on Assistance to Citizens of Ukraine. Commentary with Models on Residence, Access to the Labour Market, Social Benefits, Education and Health Care], Warszawa: Wydawnictwo CH. Beck, 175–204.

PUGLIESE, M., 2023. The International Legion of Ukraine: Exploring the Background and Motivations of Foreign Volunteers. *The RUSI Journal*, 168(3).

PUKANASYTĖ, I., 2013. Stability of Legal Regulation during the Election Process – An Important Condition for Democratic Elections. *Societal Studies.* Vilnius: Mykolas Romeris University.

PUKANASYTĖ, I., 2014. *Election Law in the Jurisprudence of the Constitutional Court of the Republic of Lithuania and the European Court of Human Rights* [online]. Available from: http://talpykla.elaba.lt/elaba-fedora/objects/elaba:2119951/datastreams/MAIN/content [Accessed 6 February 2024].

PUKELSHEIM, F., 2018. *Compositional Proportionality among European Political Parties at European Parliament Elections* [online]. Available from: https://core.ac.uk/download/230591724.pdf [Accessed 6 February 2024].

PUTIN, V., 2022a. *On the Historical Unity of Russians and Ukrainians* [online]. Available from: http://en.kremlin.ru/events/president/news/66181 [Accessed 28 November 2023].

PUTIN, V., 2022b. *Address by the President of the Russian Federation* [online]. Available from: http://en.kremlin.ru/events/president/news/67828 [Accessed 28 November 2023].

PUTIN, V., 2022c. *Address by the President of the Russian Federation* [online]. Available from: http://en.kremlin.ru/events/president/news/67843 [Accessed 28 November 2023].

RABINOVITCH, R., 2005. Universal Jurisdiction in Absentia. *Fordham International Law Journal*, 28(2), 500–530.

RADIO SVOBADA 2021,Радіо Свобода. У Держстаті розповіли, скільки в Україні людей з інвалідністю. Радіо Свобода. 24 червня 2021. [Radio Svoboda. The State Statistics Service of Ukraine reported of how many people with invalidity lived in Ukraine. Radio Svoboda. 24 June 2021]. [online]. Available from: https://www.radiosvoboda.org/a/news-ukraina-invalidnist-statystyka/31324501.html.

RADZIKOVSKY, S., KIZLO, L., DUDAR, E. & TROTSENKO, O., 2022. The Military Aspect of Achieving Significant Capabilities in Cyberspace to Ensure State Defence. In: *Materials of the International Scientific and Technical Conference Geoforum-2022.*

RAMANI, S., 2023. *Putin's War on Ukraine.* London: Hurst Publishers.

RASTYBARSKA, Y., 2022. *Якби не добрі люди, ми б не змогли.. Як справляються з викликами війни люди з інвалідністю. Радіо Свобода.* 15 травня 2022. ["If it were not for good people, we could have failed." [online via Radio Svobada]. Available from: https://www.radiosvoboda.org/a/viyna-lyudy-z-invalidnistyu/31849561.html. [Accessed on 2024 October 20].

RAWLS, J., 1971. *A Theory of Justice.* Cambridge: Harvard University Press.

REAMIMACIJNY PAKET REFORM, 2021. *Zakon pro administratyvnu proceduru nablyzyt' Ukrajinu do eurostandartiv* [Reanimation Package of Reforms. The Law on Administrative Procedure Will Put Ukraine Closer to the European Standards]. Available from: https://rpr.org.ua/news/zakon-pro-administratyvnu-protseduru-nablyzyt-ukrainu-do-ievrostandartiv-eksperty/ [Accessed 16.11.2023].

RELIEFWEB, 2022. *EU Should Include Provisions on Conflict in Due Diligence Directive* [online]. Available from: https://reliefweb.int/report/world/eu-should-include-provisions-conflict-due-diligence-directive [Accessed 17 January 2024].

REMEIKIENĖ, R., GASPARĖNIENĖ, L. & VĖBRAITĖ, V., 2023. Corruption in Ukraine: Within the Scope of the Martial Situation. In: DAVULIS, T. & GASPARĖNIENĖ, L. eds., *The Challenges and Opportunities in Law: Ukrainian Case Under the Conditions of War.* Księgarnia Akademicka Publishing.

REZNIK, O., 2022. *Ukrainians' European Integration Aspirations: From Ambivalence to Expression* [online via Democratic Initiatives Foundation]. Available from: https://dif.org.ua/en/article/ukrainians-european-integration-aspirations-from-ambivalence-to-expression [Accessed 17 January 2024].

RINGEN, S., 2008. Robert A. Dahl: Defender of Democracy. Society. 45. 283-287.

RISSE, T., 2010. *A Community of Europeans? Transnational Identities and Public Spheres.* Ithaca: Cornell University Press.

RODIONOV, I., 2022 *Что Россия должна сделать с Украиной [What Russia Should Do with Ukraine] [online via РИА Новости].* Available from: https://ria.ru/20220403/ukraina-1781469605.html [Accessed 28 November 2023].

RORTY, R., 2007. *Philosophy as Cultural Politics: Philosophical Papers,* 4. New York: Cambridge University Press.

ROSSUM, R. A., 2022. *The Textualist Jurisprudence of Justice Scalia* [online via Claremont Mcenna College]. Available from: https://www.cmc.edu/salvatori/publications/the-textualist-jurisprudence-of-justice-scalia [Accessed 8 February 2023].

ROTH, A., 2023. *Anti-kremlin Militia Freedom of Russia Legion Overrun Russian Border Village Kozinka* [online]. Available from: https://www.theguardian.com/world/2023/may/22/anti-kremlin-militia-freedom-of-russia-legion-overrun-russian-border-village-kozinka [Accessed 15 December 2023].

RUGGIE, J. G., 2008. Protect, Respect and Remedy: A Framework for Business and Human Rights [online via MIT Press Direct]. *Innovations*, 3(2), 189–212. https://doi.org/10.1162/itgg.2008.3.2.189 [Accessed 17 January 2024].

RULE OF LAW INDEX, 2022. [online]. Available from: https://worldjusticeproject.org/rule-of-law-index/downloads/WJPIndex2022.pdf [Accessed 17 April 2023].

RUSCH, W., 2009 *Administrative Procedures in EU Member States* [online]. Available from: https://www.sigmaweb.org/publicationsdocuments/42754772.pdf [Accessed 16 November 2023].

RYTEL – WARZOCHA, A., 2022. *Polish Constitutional Law*. Brussels: Larcier.

SACHS, A., 2009. *The Strange Alchemy of Life and Law*. Oxford, England: Oxford University Press.

SACKS, J., 2021. *Moralė: Bendrasis gėris permainų laikais* [Morality: Restoring the Common Good in Divided Times]. Vilnius: Tyto Alba.

SAGATIENĖ, D., 2021. The Debate about Soviet Genocide in Lithuania in the Case Law of the European Court of Human Rights. *Nationalities Papers* 49(4).

SAMOILENKO, S.A. *et al.*, 2021. *Routledge Handbook of Character Assassination and Reputation Management*. Routledge: Taylor & Francis.

SANCHEZ URRIBARRI, R. A., 2014. Politicized Justice in Emerging Democracies: A Study of Courts in Russia and Ukraine by Maria Popova [online via Oxford Academic]. *International Journal of Constitutional Law*, 12(4), 1080–1083. Available from: https://doi.org/10.1093/icon/mou075 [Accessed 17 January 2024].

SANDEL, M. J., 2009. *Justice: What's the Right Thing to Do?* [online]. Available from: https://www.readinggroupguides.com/printpdf/reviews/justice-what's-the-right-thing-to-do [Accessed 17 January 2024].

SANDER, B., 2020. Freedom of Expression in the Age of Online Platforms: The Promise and Pitfalls of a Human Rights-Based Approach to Content Moderation [online]. *Fordham International Law Journal* 43(4), 939. Available from: https://ir.lawnet.fordham.edu/cgi/viewcontent.cgi?article=2787&context=ilj [Accessed 17 January 2024].

SANGAL, A., WAGNER, M., VOGT, A., MACAYA, M., PICHETA, R., SAID-MOORHOUSE, L., UPRIGHT, E., CHOWDHURY, M., & ALFONSO III, F., 2022. February 24, 2022, Russia-Ukraine news [Online via CNN]. Available from: https://www.cnn.com/europe/live-news/ukraine-russia-news-02-24-22-intl/index.html [Accessed 17 January 2024].

SAUER, P. 2023. *Putin Tells Security Staff They Prevented Civil War as Prigozhin Lands in Belarus* [online]. Available from: https://www.theguardian.com/world/2023/jun/27/jet-linked-yevgeny-prigozhin-flies-belarus-fsb-drops-investigation-russia-wagner [Accessed 15 December 2023].

SAUNDERS, D., 2014. *Has Putin Bought into These Dangerous Ideas?* [online via the Globe and Mail]. Available from: https://www.theglobeandmail.com/opinion/has-putin-bought-into-these-dangerous-ideas/article17610287/ [Accessed 28 November 2023].

SAVVA, M., 2021. *Аналітична довідка до законопроектів 4190, 4191, 4192 щодо впровадження суду присяжних* [Analytical Note to the Draft Laws 4190, 4191, 4192 on the Introduction of Jury Trial] [online]. Available from: https://ccl.org.ua/posts/2021/12/analitychna-dovidka-do-zakonoproektiv-4190-4191-4192-shhodo-vprovadzhennya-sudu-prysyazhnyh/ [Accessed 20 February 2023].

SAYAPIN, S., 2014. The Crime of Aggression in the Rome Statute of the International Criminal Court. In: SAYAPIN, S. ed., *The Crime of Aggression in International Criminal Law: Historical Development, Comparative Analysis and Present State*. The Hague: T.M.C. Asser Press, 253–320. Available from: doi.org/10.1007/978–90–6704–927–6_5 [Accessed 17 January 2024].

SC, 2014. *69th Year: 7138th Meeting, Saturday, 15 March 2014, New York* [online]. Available from: https://digitallibrary.un.org/record/767358 [Accessed 8 July 2022].

SC, 2015. *70th Year: 7498th Meeting, Wednesday, 29 July 2015, New York* [online]. Available from: https://digitallibrary.un.org/record/798358 [Accessed 8 July 2022].

SC, 2022. *77th Year: 8979th Meeting, Friday, 25 February 2022, New York* [online]. Available from: https://digitallibrary.un.org/record/3963720 [Accessed 8 July 2022].

SCHABAS, W. A., 2000. *Genocide in International Law: The Crime of Crimes*. New York, NY: Cambridge University Press.

SCHABAS, W. A., 2022. Genocide and Ukraine: Do Words Mean What We Choose them to Mean? *Journal of International Criminal Justice*, 20(4).

SCHATZ, V. J. & KOVAL D., 2019. Russia's Annexation of Crimea and the Passage of Ships Through Kerch Strait: A Law of the Sea Perspective. *Ocean*

Development & International Law, 50(2–3), 275–97. Available from: doi.org/10.1080/00908320.2019.1605677 [Accessed 18 July 2022].

SCHATZ, V. J., 2020. *The Award Concerning Preliminary Objections in Ukraine v. Russia: Observations Regarding the Implicated Status of Crimea and the Sea of Azov* [online via EJIL: Talk!]. Available from: https://www.ejiltalk.org/the-award-concerning-preliminary-objections-in-ukraine-v-russia-observations-regarding-the-implicated-status-of-crimea-and-the-sea-of-azov/ [Accessed 18 July 2022].

SCHATZ, V. J., 2021. The Status of Crimea and the Sea of Azov as a Jurisdictional Hurdle in Ukraine v. Russia: A Comment on the UNCLOS Annex VII Arbitral Tribunal's Award Concerning Preliminary Objections. *Review of Central and East European Law*, 46(3–4). Available from: doi.org/10.1163/15730352-bja10053 [Accessed 18 July 2022].

SCHERER, A. G., RASCHE, A., PALAZZO, G. & SPICER, A., 2016. Managing for Political Corporate Social Responsibility: New Challenges and Directions for PCSR 2.0 [online via Wilwy Online Library]. *Journal of Management Studies*, 53(3), 273–298. https://doi.org/10.1111/joms.12203 [Accessed 17 January 2024].

SCMITT, 2013. The Tallinn Manual on the International Law Applicable to Cyber Warfare: https://doi.org/10.1017/CB09781139169288 Cambridge University Press, 2013

SCHMITT, M. N., 2023. *Was Russia at War with the Wagner Group?* [online]. Available from: https://lieber.westpoint.edu/was-russia-war-wagner-group/ [Accessed 15 December 2023].

SCHULTZ, T., 2022. European prosecutors join forces to bring justice for Ukraine [Online Deutsche Welle]. Available from: https://www.dw.com/en/european-prosecutors-join-forces-to-bring-justice-for-ukraine/a-62026318 [Accessed 17 January 2024].

SELLARS, K., 2013. "Crimes against Peace" and International Law [online]. *Cambridge Studies in International and Comparative Law*. Cambridge: Cambridge University Press. Available from: doi.org/10.1017/CBO9781139236980 [Accessed 5 February 2024].

SENSEN, O., 2021. Dignity. In: WUETRH, J. ed., *Cambridge Kant Lexicon*. Cambridge University Press, 148–149.

SEREDYŃSKI F. & KRÓLIKOWSKI, H., 2023. Commentary on Articles 41–45a. In: KRÓLIKOWSKI, H. ed., *Obrona Ojczyzny. Komentarz* [Defending the Fatherland. Comment]. Warszawa: Wolters Kluwer, 152–171.

SHAPLAND, C., 2015. *Explaining Variations in Political Interest and Participation Amongst Countries: A Cross-National Comparison* [online]. Available from: https://core.ac.uk/download/pdf/54847489.pdf [Accessed 23 January 2024].

SHARMA, D. H., [no date]. *Human Rights Due Diligence Legislation in Europe – Implications for Supply Chains to India and South Asia* [online]. Available from: https://www.dlapiper.com/en-ae/insights/publications/2021/03/human-rights-due-diligence-legislation-in-europe [Accessed 19 January 2024].

SHAW, G. J., 2012. Convicting Inhumanity in Absentia: Holding Trials in Absentia at the International Criminal Court. *George Washington International Law Review*, 44(1), 107–140.

SHEPEL, T., 2019. *The Concept of the Formation of Mixed Courts with the Participation of Jurors Delegated by the Business Community (Lay Judges) on the Basis of the Commercial Court.* Available from: https://drive.google.com/file/d/1CXF4-OqSn339MeNs9gcgMdeolbYC6tTv/view [Accessed 15 December 2023].

SHUHALII, A., 2023. *Strategic Goals of the State Regulation of Foreign Economic Activity of Industrial Enterprices of Ukraine in the Context of the European Vector of Development* [online]. Available from: https://doi.org/10.30525/2661-5169/2023-2-6 [Accessed 6 February 2024].

SHER, G., 2021. *A Wild West of the Mind.* Oxford: Oxford University Press.

SHULMAN, S., 2004. The Contours of Civic and Ethnic National Identification in Ukraine. *Europe-Asia Studies*, 56(1), 35–56.

SIEBOLD, S. & MELANDER, I., 2022. *EU grants Ukraine candidate status, 'beginning a long journey together'* [Online via Reuters]. Available from: https://www.reuters.com/world/europe/wind-change-europe-path-eu-opens-ukraine-2022-06-23/ [Accessed 17 January 2024].

SIGMA, [no date]. *SIGMA at a Glance* [online]. Available from: https://www.sigmaweb.org/about/ [Accessed on 16 November 2023].

SIMMA, B., KHAN, D. E. NOLTE, G. & PAULUS, A. eds., 2012. *The Charter of the United Nations*: A Commentary. Oxford: Oxford University Press.

SIMON, H. A., 1957. *Administrative Behavior: A Study of Decision-Making Processes in Administrative Organization* (2nd ed.). New York: Macmillan.

SIMONEAU M, KHAN H. War amid a Pandemic: *The Public Health Consequences of Russia's Invasion of Ukraine. The Center for Strategic and International Studies.* April 22, 2022. [online]. Available from: https://www.csis.org/analysis/war-amid-pandemic-public-health-consequences-russias-invasion-ukraine

SJÅFJELL, B. & TAYLOR, M. P., 2019. *Clash of Norms: Shareholder Primacy vs. Sustainable Corporate Purpose* [online via Social Science Research Network].

Available from: https://doi.org/10.2139/ssrn.3444050 [Accessed 17 January 2024].

SLOVO I DILO, In Ukraine, *Planned Medical Operations Are Renewed – In Which Regions They Will Not Be Conducted*, 29 April 2022. [online]. Available from: https://www.slovoidilo.ua/2022/04/29/novyna/suspilstvo/ukrayini-vidnovyly-planovi-operacziyi-yakyx-rehionax-yix-ne-provodytymut.[Слово і діло, В Україні відновили планові операції – у яких регіонах їх не проводитимуть, 29 квітня 2022]

SŁUBIK K., 2022. Commentary on Articles 2–3. In: KLAUS, W. ed., *Ustawa o pomocy obywatelom Ukrainy w związku z konfliktem zbrojnym na terytorium tego państwa. Komentarz* [Law on Assistance to citizens of Ukraine in Connection with the Armed Conflict on the Territory of That Country. Commentary]. Warszawa: Wolters Kluwer Polska, 30–40.

SNYDER, T. D., 2022a. *Russia's Genocide Handbook* [online via the Washington Post]. Available from: https://www.washingtonpost.com/opinions/2022/04/05/russia-is-committing-genocide-in-ukraine/ [Accessed 28 November 2023]

SNYDER, T. D., 2022b. *6 Steps to Prove Russian Genocide in Ukraine: Putin and Hitler Act Similarly* [online via YouTube]. Available from: https://www.youtube.com/watch?v=5wUWN2am8QI [Accessed 28 November 2023].

SNYDER, T. D., 2022c. *We Should Say It. Russia Is Fascist.* [online]. Available from: https://www.nytimes.com/2022/05/19/opinion/russia-fascism-ukraine-putin.html [Accessed 28 November 2023].

SOBENKO, N., KOLOMIETS D., 2022. *Справа Майдану: Для п'ятьох ексберкутівців просять довічне ув'язнення* [The Maidan Case: Five ex-Berkut Members Are Being Sentenced to Life Imprisonment]. Available from: https://suspilne.media/260570-sprava-majdanu-prokuratura-prosit-dovicne-uvaznenna-dla-patoh-eksberkutivciv/ [Accessed 20 February 2023].

SOCHER, J., 2021. Russia, the Right to Self-Determination and Annexation. *Russia and the Right to Self-Determination in the Post-Soviet Space.* Oxford: Oxford University Press, 146–176. Available from: https://doi.org/10.1093/oso/9780192897176.003.0005 [Accessed 17 January 2024].

SOCOR, Vladimir. *Kerch Strait Incident: Ukraine Wins Court Ruling Against Russia* [online]. Available from: https://jamestown.org/program/kerch-strait-incident-ukraine-wins-court-ruling-against-russia/ [Accessed 15 December 2023].

SOLOMON, P. H. & TROCHEV, A., 2018. *Authoritarian Constitutionalism in Putin's Russia: A Pragmatic Constitutional Court in a Dual State. Communist and Post-Communist Studies*, 51(3), 201–214. Available from: https://www.jstor.org/stable/48610508 [Accessed on 20 October 2024].

SOLŽENYCIN, A., 2009. *Gulago archipelagas* [The Gulag Archipelago]. Vilnius, Lietuva: Leidykla „Žara".

SOMIN, I., 2010. *Did Joseph Stalin Commit Genocide?* [online]. Available from: http://volokh.com/2010/11/23/did-joseph-stalin-commit-genocide/ [Accessed 28 November 2023].

SORABJI, R., 2017. *Moral Conscience Through the Ages: Fifth Century BCE to the Present.* Chicago, US: University of Chicago Press.

SORBIE, A. et al., 2023. T*owards Self-Governance for Healthcare Professions in Ukraine: Policy brief.* [online]. Available from: https://www.law.ed.ac.uk/research/research-projects/exploring-legal-ethical-and-public-administration-implications-governance. [Accessed 20 October 2024].

SOYLU, R. 2023. *Turkey Earthquake: Could Elections Be Postponed?* [online]. Available from: https://www.middleeasteye.net/news/turkey-earthquake-could-elections-be-postponed [Accessed 6 February 2024].

SPICER, M. W., 2009. Value Conflict and Legal Reasoning in Public Administration [online via Taylor & Francis Online]. *Administrative Theory & Praxis*, 31(4), 537–555. Available from: https://doi.org/10.2753/ATP1084-1806310405 [Accessed 28 November 2023].

SSSCIP, 2023. *Russia's Cyber Tactics: Lessons Learned 2022* [online]. Available from: https://cip.gov.ua/ua/news/russia-s-cyber-tactics-lessons-learned-in-2022-ssscip-analytical-report-on-the-year-of-russia-s-full-scale-cyberwar-against-ukraine [Accessed on: 30 October 2023].

STAN, A., 2020. Remedies for the Trial in Absentia. The Recent Romanian Experiences. *EU and Comparative Law Issues and Challenges Series*, 4, 650–669.

STANLEY, J., 2022. *The Antisemitism Animating Putin's Claim to 'denazify' Ukraine* [online via the Guardian]. Available from: https://www.theguardian.com/world/2022/feb/25/vladimir-putin-ukraine-attack-antisemitism-denazify [Accessed 28 November 2023].

STANTON G. H., 1996–2023. *The Ten Stages of Genocide* [online via Genocide Watch]. Available from: https://www.genocidewatch.com/tenstages [Accessed 28 November 2023].

STARKAUSKAS, J., 1998. *Čekistinė kariuomenė Lietuvoje 1944–1953. Metais Vilnius: Lietuvos Gyventojų Genocido Ir Rezistencijos Tyrimo Centras* [Czekist army in Lithuania 1944–1953. Vilnius: Genocide and Resistance Research Center of the Population of Lithuania].

STARKEY, J. G. (Summer 1979), Trial in absentia. St. John's Law Review 53(4), 721-745.

STARKEY, J. G. 1997. Trial in absentia. *St. John's Law Review*, 53(4), 721–745.

STOCKHOLM ENVIRONMENT INSTITUTE, 2020. *Report Examining risks of new oil and gas production in Canada* [online]. Available from: https://www.sei.org/wp-content/uploads/2020/06/examining-risks-of-new-oil-and-gas-production-in-canada.pdf [Accessed 17 January 2024].

STOJANOVIC, M., 2022. *Ukraine Tribunal Could Try Russian Leaders for Aggression* [online via Balkan Insight]. Available from: https://balkaninsight.com/2022/04/07/ukraine-tribunal-could-try-russian-leaders-for-aggression-expert/ [Accessed 17 July 2022].

STOP ECOCIDE FOUNDATION, 2021. *Independent Expert Panel for the Legal Definition of Ecocide: Commentary and Core Text* [online]. Available from: https://static1.squarespace.com/static/5ca2608ab914493c64ef1f6d/t/60d7479cf8e7e5461534dd07/1624721314430/SE+Foundation+Commentary+and+core+text+revised+%281%29.pdf [Accessed 17 January 2024].

STOP ECOCIDE FOUNDATION, [no date]. *Stop Ecocide International* [online]. Available from: https://www.stopecocide.earth/ [Accessed: 23 November 2023].

STRAUSS, L., 2017. *Prigimtinė teisė ir istorija* [Natural Right and History]. Vilnius: Tyto Alba.

STRODS, H., 2005. Sovietization of Latvia 1944–1991, In: CAUNE, A. *et al.* eds., *Symposium of the Commission of the Historians of Latvia*. Riga: Institute of the History of Latvia.

SULLIVAN, W., 2018. *The Impossibility of Religious Freedom.* Princeton: Princeton University Press.

SUPIOT, A., 2005. *Homo Juridicus, Essai sur la fonction anthropologique du Droit.* France: Seuil.

SUPREME COURT, 2023. Court Statistics. Judicial Power of Ukraine. *[Судова статистика. Судова влада України. 2023]* [online]. Available from: https://supreme.court.gov.ua/supreme/pokazniki-diyalnosti/sud_statistika [Accessed 20 October 2024].

SVINTSITSKYY AS, 2013. Population health as an important factor of state-building and national security. Practicing physician, 2, 7-13. [Свінцицький А.С. Здоров'я населення як важливий чинник державотворення та національної безпеки. Практикуючий лікар. № 2. 2013]

SYTAS, A., 2022. *Latvian and Estonian Parliaments Say Russia Committed Genocide in Ukraine* [online]. Available from: https://www.reuters.com/world/europe/latvian-estonian-parliaments-say-russia-committed-genocide-ukraine-2022-04-21/ [Accessed 28 November 2023].

ŠILEIKIS, E., 2005. *Alternative Constitutional Law.* Vilnius: *Legal Information Center.*

TALMON, S. A., 2012. Jus Cogens after Germany v. Italy: Substantive and Procedural Rules Distinguished. *Leiden Journal of International Law* (25).

TALMON, S., 2023. *Ukraine's Involvement in Cross-Border Raids by Russian Paramilitary Groups: Illegal Use of Force and Intervention or Lawful Self-Defence?* [online]. Available from: https://www.ejiltalk.org/ukraines-involvement-in-cross-border-raids-by-russian-paramilitary-groups-illegal-use-of-force-and-intervention-or-lawful-self-defence/ [Accessed 15 December 2023].

TANAKA, K., 1966. *South West Africa Cases, Judgement of 18 July 1966, Dissenting Opinion.* [online]. Available from: https://jusmundi.com/en/document/opinion/en-south-west-africa-ethiopia-v-south-africa-dissenting-opinion-of-judge-tanaka-monday-18th-july-1966#opinion_1391 [Accessed 23 July 2022].

TANNEN, M., 2020. *Should Elections Be Postponed Because of Coronavirus?* [online]. Available from: https://theconversation.com/should-elections-be-postponed-because-of-coronavirus-133819 [Accessed 6 February 2024].

TAYLOR, P., 2005. *Freedom of Religion: UN and European Human Rights Law and Practice.* Cambridge: Cambridge University Press.

TAYLOR, C., 2007. *A Secular Age.* London, England: Harvard University Press.

TEBBE, N., 2021. The Principle and Politics of Equal Value. *Harvard Law Review*, 135 (1).

THE PROMISE INSTITUTE FOR HUMAN RIGHTS, 2020. *The Report of the Expert Workshop on International Criminal Law & the Protection of the Environment* [online]. Available from: https://promiseinstitute.law.ucla.edu/wp-content/uploads/2022/02/Report-of-the-Expert-Workshop-ICL-and-environment-v2.pdf [Accessed 17 January 2024].

THE DANISH INSTITUTE FOR HUMAN RIGHTS, 2022. *How do the Pieces Fit in the Puzzle? Making Sense of EU Regulatory Initiatives Related to Business and Human Rights* [online]. Available from: https://www.humanrights.dk/publications/how-do-pieces-fit-puzzle-making-sense-eu-regulatory-initiatives-related-business-human [Accessed 17 January 2024].

THE MINISTRY OF HEALTH OF UKRAINE. *Office of First Lady, Ministry of Health and partners launch National Mental Health and Psychosocial Support Program. Government portal.* 20 June 2022]. [online]. Available from: https://www.kmu.gov.ua/en/news/ofis-pershoyi-ledi-moz-ta-partneri-zapuskayut-nacionalnu-programu-psihichnogo-zdorovya-ta-psihosocialnoyi-pidtrimki.

THOMAS D'AQUIN, 1935. *Somme Théologique.* Paris, Tournai, Rome: Luteiae Parisiorum, Kalendas Maii.

TIMKE v. Germany (dec.), no. 27311/95, European Commission of Human Rights, 11 September 1995.

TISDALL, S., 2022. *How Ukraine Has Become the Crucible of the New World Order* [online]. Available from: https://www.theguardian.com/world/2022/mar/12/how-ukraine-has-become-the-crucible-of-the-new-world-order [Accessed 8 February 2024].

TKACHUK, O & KALARASHH, A., 2022. "Останнім часом покращилась якість обґрунтування касаційних скарг, що подаються до суду представниками сторін", https://supreme.court.gov.ua/supreme/pres-centr/news/1296244/ [Accessed 20 October 2024].

TOMUSCHAT, C., 2008. *Uniting For Peace* [online]. Available from: https://legal.un.org/avl/pdf/ha/ufp/ufp_e.pdf [Accessed 25 July 2022].

TOPALOFF, LIUBOMIR K., 2017. Elite Strategy or Populist Weapon? *Journal of Democracy* [online]. Available from: https://doi.org/10.1353/jod.2017.0051 [Accessed 15 December 2023].

TRAHAN, J., 2022. Why the Veto Power Is Not Unlimited: A Response to Critiques of, and Questions About, Existing Legal Limits to the Veto Power in the Face of Atrocity Crimes. *Case Western Reserve Journal of International Law* 54(1).

TREISMAN, R., 2022. *Canada's House Backs a Motion Recognizing Russia's Actions in Ukraine as Genocide* [online via npr]. Available from https://choice.npr.org/index.html?origin=https://www.npr.org/2022/04/28/1095272683/canada-russia-genocide-ukraine [Accessed 28 November 2023].

TRIPKOVIC, B., 2018. *The Metaethics of Constitutional Adjudication.* Oxford, England: Oxford Academic.

TROFIMOV, Y. & MARSON, J., 2022. *Russian Forces Kill Civilians, Loot for Supplies in Occupied Ukraine, Residents Say* [online]. Available from https://www.wsj.com/articles/russian-forces-kill-civilians-loot-for-supplies-in-occupied-ukraine-residents-say-11647267560 [Accessed 28 November 2023].

TROPER, M., 2018. *La Philosophie du Droit.* Presses Universitaires de France. Humensis.

TSYRFA, I., 2013. The Formation of the European Identity of Ukraine: Key Factors and Principles. *Lithuanian Foreign Policy Review*, 30, 43–63.

TSYBULENKO, E. & FRANCIS, J. A., 2018. Separatists or Russian Troops and Local Collaborators? Russian Aggression in Ukraine: The Problem of Definitions. In: Sayapin, Sergey & Tsybulenko, Evhen eds., *The Use of Force against Ukraine and International Law.* T.M.C. Asser Press.

TSYBULENKO, E. & KELICHAVYI, B., 2018. International Legal Dimensions of the Russian Occupation of Crimea. In Sayapin, S. & Tsybulenko, E. ed., *The Use of Force against Ukraine and International Law*. T.M.C. Asser Press.

TZENG, P., 2016a. Supplemental Jurisdiction under UNCLOS. *Houston Journal of International Law*, 38(2), 499–575.

TZENG, P., 2016b. *The Doctrine of Indispensable Issues: Mauritius v. United Kingdom, Philippines v. China, Ukraine v. Russia, and Beyond*. [online via EJIL Talk]. Available from: https://www.ejiltalk.org/the-doctrine-of-indispensable-issues-mauritius-v-united-kingdom-philippines-v-china-ukraine-v-russia-and-beyond/ [Accessed 17 July 2022].

UILA, *Germany Investigating 'several hundred' Possible Ukraine War Crimes* [online]. Available from: https://uila.ie/category/universal-jurisdiction/ [Accessed 17 January 2024].

UKRAINIAN CLIMATE NETWORK, 2022. *Without water: Resolving water supply issues under the conditions of war*. [online]. Available from: https://ucn.org.ua [Accessed 20 October 2024].

UKRAINIAN CENTER FOR TRANSPLAN-COORDINATION, 2023. *місяців трансплантацій виконано більше, аніж за попередній рік*. [More transplantations have been performed for 9 months than for the whole previous year]. [online]. Available from: https://utcc.gov.ua/za-9-misyatsiv-transplantatsij-vykonano-bilshe-anizh-za-poperednij-rik/. [Accessed 20 October 2024].

UKRINFORM, 2023. *The USAID Will Provide Ukraine with $60 Million to Strengthen Cybersecurity* [online]. Available from: https://www.ukrinform.ua/rubric-economy/3668574-usaid-vidilit-60-miljoniv-na-posilenna-kiberbezpeki-ukraini.html [Accessed 29 October 2023].

ULFSTEIN, G., 2020. *Final Report on the European Court of Human Rights*. International Law Association [online]. Available from: https://ila.vettoreweb.com/Storage/Download.aspx?DbStorageId=24293&StorageFileGuid=180841d4-9418-4259-bc86-395fc1a02cbf [Accessed 17 January 2024].

UN, 2014. *General Assembly Adopts Resolution Calling upon States Not to Recognize Changes in Status of Crimea Region*. Available from: https://www.un.org/press/en/2014/ga11493.doc.htm [Accessed 17 January 2024].

UN, 2019a. *General Assembly Adopts Resolution Urging Russian Federation to Withdraw Its Armed Forces from Crimea, Expressing Grave Concern about Growing Military Presence* [online]. Available from https://www.un.org/press/en/2019/ga12223.doc.htm [8 July 2022].

UN, 2019b. *General Assembly Welcomes International Court of Justice Opinion on Chagos Archipelago, Adopts Text Calling for Mauritius' Complete*

Decolonizzation [online]. Available from: https://press.un.org/en/2019/ga12146.doc.htm [Accessed 17 January 2024].

UN, 2022. *Security Council Fails to Adopt Text Demanding Civilian Protection, Unhindered Humanitarian Access in Ukraine, as 13 Members Abstain* [online]. Available from: https://press.un.org/en/2022/sc14838.doc.htm [Accessed 28 July 2022].

UNESCO, 1997. *Universal Declaration on the Human Genome and Human Rights* [online] Available at: http://portal.unesco.org/en/ev.php-URL_ID=13177&URL_DO=DO_TOPIC&URL_SECTION=201.html [Accessed 28 November 2023].

UNDP, [no date]. *Heightened Human Rights Due Diligence for Business in Conflict-Affected Contexts: A Guide* [online]. Available from: https://www.undp.org/publications/heightened-human-rights-due-diligence-business-conflict-affected-contexts-guide [Accessed: 23 November 2023].

UNFCCC, 2022. *Sharm el-Sheikh Implementation Plan* [online via UNFCCC]. Available from: https://unfccc.int/documents/624444 [Accessed 23 November 2023].

UNGA, 2001. *Report of the Human Rights Committee* [online]. Volume I, General Assembly, Fifty-sixth Session, Supplement No. 40(A/56/40), United Nations, New York. Available from: https://ccprcentre.org/files/hr_committee/annual_report/A_56_40Vol-I_en.pdf [Accessed on 8 February 8, 2024].

UNICEF. *1.4 million people without running water across war-affected eastern Ukraine [Press Release]. UNICEF.* 15 April 2022. [online]. Available from: https://www.unicef.org/press-releases/14-million-people-without-running-water-across-war-affected-eastern-ukraine.

UNICEF. UNICEF *helps to repair Ukrainian water supply system.* UNICEF. 5 June 2023. [online]. Available from: https://www.unicef.org/ukraine/en/stories/unicef-helps-repair-water-supply-system

UNICEF. *Children's Rights and Business Principles* [online via Pluto Press]. Available from: https://childrenandbusiness.org/ [Accessed 17 January 2024].

UNIT, V. I., 2023. *Venezuela Security Policy: Illegal Mining and Deforestation* [online via InSight Crime]. Available from: https://insightcrime.org/news/criminal-threats-venezuela-illegal-mining/ [Accessed 17 January 2024].

UNITED NATIONS, 2001. *General Comment No. 29 State of Emergency (Art. 4): International Covenant on Civil and Political Rights* [online]. Available from: https://digitallibrary.un.org/record/451555 [Accessed 19 January 2024].

UNITED NATIONS, 2008. *Protect, Respect and Remedy: a Framework for Business and Human Rights Report of the Special Representative of the Secretary-General on the Issue of Human Rights and Transnational Corporations and Other Business Enterprises* [online]. Available from: https://digitallibrary.un.org/record/625292/files/A_HRC_8_5-EN.pdf?ln=ru [Accessed 19 January 2024].

UNITED NATIONS, 2011. *Guiding Principles on Business and Human Rights* [online]. Available from: https://www.ohchr.org/documents/publications/guidingprinciplesbusinesshr_en.pdf [Accessed 19 January 2024].

UNITED NATIONS, 2020. *Concerned about Ongoing Militarization of Crimea, Human Rights Violations in Eastern Ukraine, Speakers Tell General Assembly Minsk Agreements Must Be Fully Implemented* [online]. Available from: https://www.un.org/press/en/2020/ga12241.doc.htm [Accessed 29 January 2024].

UN COMITEE ON ECONOMIC, SOCIAL AND CULTURAL RIGHTS, 2000. *The right to the highest attainable standard of health (article 12 of the International Covenant on Economic (22nd sess. : 2000 : Geneva).* [online]. Available from: https://digitallibrary.un.org/record/425041 [Accessed 20 October 2024].

UNITED NATIONS, [no date]. *Final Report to the Prosecutor by the Committee Established to Review the NATO Bombing Campaign Against the Federal Republic of Yugoslavia* [online]. Available from: https://www.icty.org/en/press/final-report-prosecutor-committee-established-review-nato-bombing-campaign-against-federal [Accessed 28 November 2023].

UNITED NATIONS ENVIRONMENT PROGRAMME, 2015. *Côte d'Ivoire: Post-Conflict Environmental Assessment* [online]. Available from: https://www.unep.org/resources/assessment/cote-divoire-post-conflict-environmental-assessment-0 [Accessed 17 January 2024].

UNITED NATIONS ENVIRONMENT PROGRAMME, 2018. *Why We Need to Protect Biodiversity from Harmful Effects of War and Armed Conflict* [online]. Available from: https://www.unep.org/news-and-stories/story/why-we-need-protect-biodiversity-harmful-effects-war-and-armed-conflict [Accessed 17 January 2024].

UNITED NATIONS ENVIRONMENT PROGRAMME, 2021. Report *State of Environment and Outlook Report for the Occupied Palestinian Territory* [online]. Available from: https://wedocs.unep.org/bitstream/handle/20.500.11822/35162/Doc3%20Revel%20EnglishK2100501.pdf?sequence=1 [Accessed 17 January 2024].

UNITED NATIONS ENVIRONMENT PROGRAMME, 2023. *The Toxic Legacy of the Ukraine War* [online]. Available from: https://www.unep.org/news-and-stories/story/toxic-legacy-ukraine-war#:%7E:text=Water%20infrastructure%2C%20including%20pumping%20stations,solvents%20to%20ammonia%20and%20plastics [Accessed 17 January 2024].

UNHRC 2019. *Report of the Independent International Commission of Inquiry on Ukraine to the UN General Assembly. IICIU.* 18 October 2022. [online]. Available from: https://www.ohchr.org/en/hr-bodies/hrc/iicihr-ukraine/index

UNITED NATIONS. INTERNATIONAL HUMAN RIGHTS INSTRUMENTS (2008). HRI/GEN/1/Rev.9 (Vol. I). General comments adopted by the Human Rights Committee (1984). General comment No. 13: Article 14 (Administration of justice), 186-190. https://www.ohchr.org/sites/default/files/Documents/HRBodies/TB/HRI-GEN-1-REV-9-VOL-I_en.doc

UNITED NATIONS SECRETARY GENERAL, 2022. Statement by the Secretary-General – on Ukraine [Online]. Available from: https://www.un.org/sg/en/content/sg/statement/2022-02-24/statement-the-secretary-general-%E2%80%93-ukraine [Accessed 17 January 2024].

UNIVERSITY OF SYDNEY LAW SCHOOL, 2009. *Judicial Values: Should Judges Apply the Law, or Should They Bring Their Own Values to the Task?* [online]. Available from: https://www.michaelkirby.com.au/images/stories/speeches/2000s/2009%2B/2390.Transcript_Of_Form_With_Bernard_Schlink_Aug_2009.pdf [Accessed 17 January 2024].

URBANIAK, K., 2017. *The Division of Competence in the Areas of State Security and Foreign Affairs withn Executive branch in light of the 1997 Constitution of the Republic of Poland* [online]. Available from: https://doi.org/10.14746/ps.2017.1.11 [Accessed 17 January 2024].

US CONGRESS, 2022. *Recognizing Russian Actions in Ukraine as a Genocide* [online]. Available from: https://www.congress.gov/bill/117th-congress/house-resolution/1205/text [Accessed 28 November 2023].

UŚCIŃSKA G., 2022. Wsparcie prawne i społeczne państwa polskiego dla obywateli Ukrainy w obliczu konfliktu zbrojnego [Legal and Social Support of the Polish State for Ukrainian Citizens in the Face of Armed Conflict]. *Labour and Social Security Journal*, 18(3), 3–14.

USUN, 2021. Joint Statement on the Occasion of the Seventh Anniversary of the Adoption of UN General Assembly Resolution 68/262 "Territorial Integrity of Ukraine" [online]. Available from: https://usun.usmission.gov/joint-statement-on-the-occasion-of-the-seventh-anniversary-of-the-adoption-of-un-general-assembly-resolution-68-262-territorial-integrity-of-ukraine/ [Accessed 9 July 2022].

UVAROVA, O., 2022. *New Study: Responsible Business Conduct in Times of War: Implications for Essential Goods & Services Providers in Ukraine* [online]. Available from: https://www.business-humanrights.org/en/latest-news/new-study-responsible-business-conduct-in-time-of-war-implications-for-essential-goods-services-providers-in-ukraine/ [Accessed: 23 November 2023].

UVAROVA, O., 2023. *Sustainability in Transition: Corporate Respect for Solidarity* [online via SSRN]. Available from: https://ssrn.com/abstract=4365497 or http://dx.doi.org/10.2139/ssrn.4365497 [Accessed 17 January 2024].

UWN, 2023. *Cyberattacks on Ukraine: The Number of Attacks Almost Tripled last year, and 90% of Russian Hacker Groups Are Controlled by Security Forces* [online]. Available from: https://uworld.news/news/kiberataky-rosii-na-ukrainu-ie-1002005.html [Accessed on: 29 October 2023].

VAN DE RIET, J., 2022. *No, Russia Cannot Be Removed from the UN Security Council* [online]. Available from: https://leidenlawblog.nl/articles/no-russia-cannot-be-removed-from-the-un-security-council [Accessed 17 July 2022].

VON DER LEYEN, U., 2022. *Ukrainians Are Ready to Die for the European Perspective. We Want Them to Live With Us the European Dream* [online via Twitter]. Available from: https://twitter.com/vonderleyen/status/1537739940942991360 [Accessed 17 January 2024].

VAN ZEBEN, J., 2020. The European Green Deal: The Future of Apolycentric Europe? *European Law Journal* 26, 300–318.

VEDERNIKOVA, I., 2023. *War and Elections. Which Victory Is More Important?* [online]. Available from: https://zn.ua/eng/war-and-elections-which-victory-is-more-important.html [Accessed 23 November 2023].

VEITCH, S., CHRISTODOULIDIS, E. & FARMER, L., 2006. *Jurisprudence: Themes and Concepts* [online]. Available from: http://eprints.gla.ac.uk/61206/ [Accessed 28 November 2023].

VENICE COMMISSION, 2014. *Opinion on "Whether the Decision Taken by the Supreme Council of the Autonomous Republic of Crimea in Ukraine to Organise a Referendum on Becoming a Constituent Territory of the Russian Federation or Restoring Crimea's 1992 Constitution Is Compatible with Constitutional Principles* [online]. Available from: https://www.venice.coe.int/webforms/documents/?opinion=762&year=all [Accessed 28 November 2023].

VENICE COMMISSION, 2022. *Opinion on the Draft Law "On amending some legislative acts of Ukraine regarding improving the procedure for selecting candidate judges of the Constitutional Court of Ukraine on a competitive basis"* [online]. Available from: https://www.venice.coe.int/webforms/documents/default.aspx?pdffile=CDL-AD(2022)054-e [Accessed 28 November 2023].

VENICE COMMISSION, 2023a. *Follow-up Opinion to the Opinion "On the draft law"On Amendments to Certain Legislative Acts of Ukraine on Improving the Procedure for the Selection of Candidates for the Position of Judge of the Constitutional Court of Ukraine on a Competitive Basis"* [online]. Available from: https://www.venice.coe.int/webforms/documents/?pdf=CDL-AD(2023)022-e [Accessed 28 November 2023].

VENICE COMMISSION, 2023b. *Opinion on the Law "Preventing Threats to National Security Associated With Excessive Influence by Persons Who Wield Significant Economic and Political Weight in Public Life (oligarchs)"* [online]. Available from: https://www.venice.coe.int/webforms/documents/?pdf=CDL-AD(2023)018-e [Accessed 28 November 2023].

VENICE COMMISSION, 2023c. *Urgent Follow-UP Opinion to the Opinions on the Law "On Amendments to Certain Legislative Acts of Ukraine to Clarify the Provisions on the Competitive Selection of Candidates for the Position of Judge of the Constitutional Court of Ukraine"* [online]. Available from: https://www.venice.coe.int/webforms/documents/?pdf=CDL-AD(2023)042-e [Accessed 28 November 2023].

VENICE COMMISSION [no date]. *European Commission for Democracy Through Law* [online]. Available from: https://www.venice.coe.int/webforms/documents/default.aspx?pdffile=CDL-AD(2021)005-e [Accessed 17 January 2024].

VERDIRAME, G., 2000. The Genocide Definition in the Jurisprudence of the Ad Hoc Tribunals. *International and Comparative Law Quarterly* 49(3).

VERESHCHAK, V., 2021. International Practice of Criminal Proceedings in the form of *in absentia* [online]. *Entrepreneurship, Economy and Law*, 7, 85–90. Available from: https://doi.org/10.32849/2663-5313/2021.7.13 [Accessed 17 January 2024].

VERKHOVNA RADA OF UKRAINE (2014, October 14), Law "On Prevention of Corruption", No. 1700-VII, Retrieved from: https://zakon.rada.gov.ua/laws/show/1700–18#Text

VERKHOVNA RADA OF UKRAINE (2019, February 7), the Law of Ukraine "On amending the Constitution of Ukraine (regarding the State's Strategic Course towards Obtaining Full Membership of Ukraine in the European Union and the North Atlantic Treaty Organisation)" of 7 February 2017, No. 2680-VIII (in Ukrainian). Retrieved from: https://zakon.rada.gov.ua/laws/show/2680-19#Text

VERKHOVNA RADA OF UKRAINE (2021, November 5), the Law of Ukraine on Preventing Threats to National Security Associated With Excessive Influence by Persons Who Wield Significant Economic and Political Weight in Public Life, No. 1780-IX, 5 November 2021. Retrieved from: https://www.venice.coe.int/webforms/documents/default.aspx?pdffile=CDL-REF(2021)086-e

VERNON, R., 1998. *In the Hurricane's Eye: The Troubled Prospects of Multinational Enterprises* [online]. Available from: http://ci.nii.ac.jp/ncid/BA38330431 [Accessed 28 November 2023].

VIEIRA, A., 2020. The European Union's 'Potential We' between Acceptance and Contestation: Assessing the Positioning of Six Eastern Partnership Countries. *Journal of Common Market Studies*, 59(3), 1–19.

VILLA, V., 1997. Legal Theory and Value Judgments [online via JSTOR]. *Law and Philosophy* 16(4), 447–477. Available from: http://www.jstor.org/stable/3504984 [Accessed 17 January 2024].

VIŽULIS, J., 1985. *Nations under Duress: The Baltic States.* New York, NY: Associated Faculty Press.

VOLTERRA, R. G., MANDELLI, F., G. & NISTAL, A., 2018. The Characterisation of the Dispute Concerning Coastal State Rights in the Black Sea, Sea of Azov, and Kerch Strait. *The International Journal of Marine and Coastal Law*, 33(3), 614–22.

VON DER LEYEN, U. [@vonderleyen]. (2022, June 17). Ukrainians are ready to die for the European perspective. We want them to live with us the European dream. [Tweet]. Twitter. Retrieved from: https://twitter.com/vonderleyen/status/1537739940942991360

VYTVYTSKY, B., 2022a. At what point do Russian war crimes in Ukraine qualify as Genocide? [online]. Available from https://english.nv.ua/opinion/at-what-point-do-russian-war-crimes-in-ukraine-qualify-as-genocide-50233527.html [Accessed 28 November 2023].

VYTVYTSKY, B., 2022b. *At what point do Russian war crimes in Ukraine qualify as Genocide?* [online]. Available from https://www.atlanticcouncil.org/blogs/ukrainealert/at-what-point-do-russian-war-crimes-in-ukraine-qualify-as-genocide/ [Accessed 28 November 2023].

VYTVYTSKY, B., 2022. *At What Point Do Russian War Crimes in Ukraine Qualify as Genocide?* [online via the New Voice of Ukraine]. Available from https://english.nv.ua/opinion/at-what-point-do-russian-war-crimes-in-ukraine-qualify-as-genocide-50233527.html [Accessed 28 November 2023].

WALCZAK P., 2022. Świadczenie z tytułu zapewnienia na własny koszt zakwaterowania i wyżywienia obywatelom Ukrainy. In: LACHIEWICZ,W., KOZŁOWSKA, A. OLECH, M. PIETRZYKOWSKA, D. PROCHOPIEŃ, G. ROGOWSKI, Ł. & WALCZAK, P. eds., *Pomoc obywatelom Ukrainy. Zadania samorządu terytorialnego i ich finansowanie*. Warszawa: Wydawnictwo C.H. Beck, 25–36.

WALDRON, M., 2013. *Free to Believe: Rethinking Freedom of Conscience and Religion in Canada*. Toronto, Canada: University of Toronto Press.

WASILEWSKA, E., 2022. Commentary on Article 37. In: DREMBKOWSKI, P. ed., *Ustawa o pomocy obywatelom Ukrainy. Komentarz z wzorami dotyczącymi pobytu, dostępu do rynku pracy, świadczeń społecznych, edukacji i opieki zdrowotnej* [Law on Assistance to Citizens of Ukraine. Commentary with Models on Residence, Access to the Labour Market, Social Benefits, Education and Health Care]. Warszawa: Wydawnictwo CH. Beck, 237–243.

WEERAMANTRY, C., 2004. *Universalizing International Law*. Leiden: Martinus Nijhoff Publishers.

WEGEN, G. & SHEPEL, T. 2020. *The Functioning of the Commercial Lay Judges in Germany. The History and the Perspective of Resuming the Activity of Commercial Lay Judges in Ukraine with the Application of German Experience* [online]. Available from: https://drive.google.com/file/d/1WfSt8t-e6vUt_GJiIkE1l-Uz8-Hsgxkn/view?usp=sharing&usp=embed_facebook [Accessed 17 January 2024].

WEILL, R., 2022. *"We the Territorial People" and the Russia-Ukraine War* [online via Verfassungsblog]. Available from: https://verfassungsblog.de/we-the-territorial-people-and-the-russia-ukraine-war/ [Accessed 17 January 2024].

WETTSTEIN, F., 2020. The History of 'Business and Human Rights' and its Relationship with Corporate Social Responsibility. In: DEVA, S. & BIRCHALL, D. eds., *Research Handbook on Human Rights and Business* [online via Elgaronline]. Available from: https://doi.org/10.4337/9781786436405 [Accessed 28 November 2023].

WETTSTEIN, F., 2022. *Business and Human Rights: Ethical, Legal, and Managerial Perspectives*. Cambridge: Cambridge University Press.

WHATCOTT, E., 2022. *Compilation of Countries' Statements Calling Russian Actions in Ukraine "Genocide"* [online via Just Security]. Available from: https://www.justsecurity.org/81564/compilation-of-countries-statements-calling-russian-actions-in-ukraine-genocide/#_ftn1 [Accessed 28 November 2023].

WHITE, J. B., 2012. Justice in Tension: An Expression of Law and the Legal Mind. No Foundations [online]. *A Journal of Law and Justice*, 9, 1-19. Available from http://www.nofoundations.com/issues/NoFo9WHITE.pdf [Accessed 28 November 2023].

WHITE, J., 2020. *Holding an Election during the Civil War Set the Standard for Us Today* [online via Washington Post]. Available from: https://www.washingtonpost.com/outlook/2020/10/05/holding-an-election-during-civil-war-set-standard-us-today/ [Accessed 19 January 2024].

WILKEN, R. L., 2019. *Liberty in the Things of God: The Christian Origins of Religious Freedom*. New Haven: Yale University Press.

WILSON, P., 2011. *The Thirty Years War: Europe's Tragedy*. Cambridge, Massachusetts: Harvard University Press.

WOOD, A., 2020. *Kant and Religion*. Cambridge University Press.

WORLD BANK GROUP, 2015. *A Measured Approach to Ending Poverty and Boosting Shared Prosperity: Concepts, Data, and the Twin Goals* [online] Available from: https://openknowledge.worldbank.org/handle/10986/20384 [Accessed 28 November 2023].

WRIGHT, Q., 1963. Toward a Universal Law for Mankind. *Columbia Law Review*, 63(3).

WRIGHT, G., 2022. *Ukraine War: Is Russia Committing Genocide?* [online via BBC]. Available from https://www.bbc.com/news/world-europe-61017352 [Accessed 28 November 2023].

WRONKOWSKA, S. 2000. W sprawie postępowania legislacyjnego w przepisach regulaminu Sejmu Rzeczypospolitej Polskiej [On the Legislative Procedure in the Rules of Procedure of the Sejm of the Republic of Poland]. *Przegląd Sejmowy*, 2, 74–83.

WUETRH, J. O., 2021. Categorical Imperative. In: WUETRH, J. ed., *The Cambridge Kant Lexicon*. Cambridge University Press, 65–137.

ZAKERHOSSEIN, M. H. & DE BROUWER M. A., 2015. Diverse Approaches to Total and Partial in Absentia Trials by International Criminal Tribunals. *Criminal Law Forum*, 26(2), 181–224.

ZAKHARCHENKO, N., 2020. *Суд присяжних в Україні. Що треба зробити, аби реформувати українське правосуддя*' [Trial by Jury in Ukraine. What Needs to Be Done to Reform Ukrainian Justice] [online]. Available from: https://18000.com.ua/strichka-novin/sud-prisyazhnix-v-ukrayini-shho-treba-zrobiti-abi-reformuvati-ukrayinske-pravosuddya/.

ZAVHORODNYA, YU. V., 2022. *NATO's Role in the Fight Against Cyber Conflicts: Political and Legal Aspect*. Regional Studies.

ZDANOWICZ, M., 2021. Poland's Stance on the Refugee and Migration Crisis in the European Union. *Bialystok Legal Studies*, 26(1), 85–103.

ZELENSKY, V., 2022. *Звернення до громадян іноземних держав, які прагнуть допомогти Україні у її боротьбі проти російської агресії* [Appeal to Citizens of Foreign Countries Who Want to Help Ukraine in its Fight Against Russian Aggression] [online]. Available from: https://www.president.gov.ua/news/zvernennya-do-gromadyan-inozemnih-derzhav-yaki-pragnut-dopom-73213 [Accessed 15 December 2023].

ZIERLER, D., 2011. *The Invention of Ecocide: Agent Orange, Vietnam and the Scientists Who Changed the Way We Think about the Environment*. London: The University of Georgia Press.

ZMINA, 2023. *Google Discovered Five Hacker Groups Associated with the Russian Federation that Attack NATO Countries and Ukraine* [online]. Available from: https://zmina.info/news/google-vyyavyv-pyat-hakerskyh-ugrupovan-povyazanyh-zrf-yaki-atakuyut-krayiny-nato-ta-ukrayinu [Accessed on: 29 October 2023].

ŻOŁĘDOWSKI C., 2022. Nowi uchodźcy w Europie. Przemieszczenia zewnętrzne z Ukrainy między 24.02 i 24.03.2022 r [New refugees in Europe. External movements from Ukraine between 24.02 and 24.03.2022]. In: WORKING PAPER KATEDRY POLITYKI SPOŁECZNEJ ed., *Inwazja Rosji na Ukrainę. Społeczeństwo i polityka wobec kryzysu uchodźczego w pierwszym miesiącu wojny, Raport roboczy* [Russia's Invasion of Ukraine. Society and Politics in the Presence of the Refugee Crisis in the First Month of the War, Working Report]. Warszawa: Uniwersytet Warszawski, 4–9.

ZUBKOVA, D., 2023. *Ukraine Must Hold Free and Fair Elections, Even If They Are Not Ideal – PACE President* [online]. Available from: https://ukranews.com/en/news/933630-ukraine-must-hold-free-and-fair-elections-even-if-they-are-not-ideal-pace-president [Accessed 19 January 2024].

ZUCCA, L., 2012. *A Secular Europe: Law and Religion in the European Constitutional Landscape.* Oxford, England: Oxford University Press.

ZVIERIEV, I., 2018. Legal Interpretation in Post-Truth Society: Ukrainian Case [online]. *Kyiv-Mohyla Law and Politics Journal*, 4, 81-98. Available from: https://doi.org/10.18523/kmlpj153253.2018-4.81-98 [Accessed 28 November 2023].

ŽALIMAS, D., 2019. *The Consolidation of Western Geopolitical Orientation in the Constitution.* Ukraine: III Kharkiv International Legal Forum in Kharkiv.

СУДОВА ВЛАДА УКРАЇНИ, 2022. *Електронне декларування присяжними* [Electronic Declaration by Jurors] [online]. Available from: https://dg.hr.court.gov.ua/tu03/pres-centr/news/1258121/ [Accessed 20 February 2023].

ГРОМАДЯН ДО СУДОВОЇ ГІЛКИ ВЛАДИ, 2020. *Громадська думка про правотворення* [Public opinion on lawmaking] [online]. Available from: http://nbuviap.gov.ua/images/dumka/2020/18-19.pdf [Accessed 8 October 2020].

ЗАМЕТКИ, 2020. *На суде по делу об убийстве Павла Шеремета сменили присяжного* [Juror Changed at Pavel Sheremet Murder Trial] [online]. Available from: https://graty.me/news/na-sude-po-delu-ob-ubijstve-pavla-sheremeta-smenili-prisyazhnogo/ [Accessed 8 October 2020].

ГРОМАДСЬКЕ, 2018. *Суд по делу убийства Вороненкова отобрал присяжных* [Voronenkov Murder Trial Selects Jury] [online]. Available from: https://hromadske.ua/ru/posts/sud-po-delu-ubyistva-voronenkova-otobral-prysiazhnykh [Accessed 13 July 2020].

УКРАИНА, 2022. Судья по делу Бузины взял самоотвод [The Judge in the Buzina Case Has Recused Himself]. Available from: https://ukraina.ru/20180209/1019899391.html [Accessed 8 February 2024].

Legal Regulations

ACN, 2002. The European Charter of Patients' Rights [online]. Available from: https://ec.europa.eu/health/ph_overview/co_operation/mobility/docs/health_services_co108_en.pdf [Accessed 20 October 2024].

Act Amending the Homeland Defence Act and the Public Finance Act, Official Journal of Laws "Dziennik Ustaw" item 172, 5 August 2022.

Act Amending the Act on Export Insurance Guaranteed by the State Treasury and Certain Other Acts, Official Journal of Laws "Dziennik Ustaw", item 1859, 13 July 2023.

Act Amending the Law on Assistance to Citizens of Ukraine in Connection with the Armed Conflict on the Territory of Ukraine and Certain Other Laws, Official Journal of Laws "Dziennik Ustaw", item 185, 13 January 2023.

Act on Amending the Law on Assistance to Ukrainian Citizens in Connection with the Armed Conflict on the Territory of Ukraine, Official Journal of Laws "Dziennik Ustaw", item 683, 23 March 2022.

Act on Amending the Law on Assistance to Ukrainian Citizens in Connection with the Armed Conflict on the Territory of Ukraine, Official Journal of Laws "Dziennik Ustaw", item 930, 27 April 2022.

Act on Amending the Law on Assistance to Ukrainian Citizens in Connection with the Armed Conflict on the Territory of Ukraine and Certain Other Laws, Official Journal of Laws "Dziennik Ustaw", item 830, 8 April 2022.

Act on Amending the Law on Assistance to Ukrainian Citizens in Connection with the Armed Conflict on the Territory of Ukraine and the Law on Informatization of Activities of Entities Performing Public Tasks, Official Journal of Laws "Dziennik Ustaw", item 1087, 12 May 2022.

Act on Amending the Law on Assistance to Ukrainian Citizens in Connection with the Armed Conflict on the Territory of Ukraine and the Law on Higher Education and Science of, Official Journal of Laws "Dziennik Ustaw", item 682, 23 March 2022.

Act on Amending the Act on Special Solutions in the Field of Counteracting Support for Aggression to Ukraine and Serving to Protect National Security and the Act on National Fiscal Administration, Official Journal of Laws "Dziennik Ustaw", item 1713, 5 August 2022.

Act on Amending the Act on Professions of Nurse and Midwife and Some Other Laws, Official Journal of Laws "Dziennik Ustaw" 2022, item 1733, 5 August 2022.

Act on Assistance to Ukrainian Citizens in Connection with the Armed Conflict on the Territory of Ukraine, Official Journal of Laws "Dziennik Ustaw", item 583, with later amendments, 12 March 2022.

Act on the Defence of the Homeland, Official Journal of Laws, "Dziennik Ustaw", item 655, with later amendments, 11 March 2022.

Act On Ensuring Rights and Freedoms of Internally Displaced Persons: Law of Ukraine of 20 October 2014 No. 1706-VII. [Про забезпечення прав і свобод внутрішньо переміщених осіб: Закон України від 20 жовтня 2014 р. № 1706-VII] [online]. Available from: https://zakon.rada.gov.ua/laws/show/1706-18?find=1&text=%D0%BC%D0%B5%D0%B4#w1_1. [Accessed 20 October 2024].

Act on Foreigners, Official Journal of Laws, "Dziennik Ustaw" 2013, item 1650, with later amendments, 12 December 2013.

Act on Granting Protection to Foreigners on the Territory of the Republic of Poland, Official Journal of Laws "Dziennik Ustaw", No. 128, item 1176, with later amendments, 13 June 2003.

Act on Medical Devices, Official Journal of Laws "Dziennik Ustaw", item 974, 7 April 2022.

Act on Reconstruction and Technical Modernisation and Financing of the Armed Forces of the Republic of Poland, Official Journal of Laws "Dziennik Ustaw", No. 76, item 804, with later amendments, 25 May 2001.

Act on Special Solutions for Counteracting Support for Aggression against Ukraine and Serving to Protect National Security, Official Journal of Laws "Dziennik Ustaw", item 835, with later amendments, 13 April 2022.

Act on Special Solutions to Prevent Support for Aggression against Ukraine and to Protect National Security, Official Journal of Laws "Dziennik Ustaw", item 835, with later amendments, 13 April 2022.

Act on the Universal Duty to Defend the Republic of Poland, Official Journal of Laws "Dziennik Ustaw", No. 44, item 220, with later amendments, 21 November 1967.

Application of the Convention on the Prevention and Punishment of the Crime of Genocide (Bosnia and Herzegovina v. Serbia and Montenegro, 2007), Judgment: Case Reports 2007 p.43 (International Court of Justice).

Civil Code of France, No. 70–643, 17 July 1970.

Civil Code of Ukraine, No. 435-IV, 16 January 2003.

Civil Procedure Code of Ukraine, No. 1618-IV, 18 March 2004.

Commercial and Procedural Code of Ukraine, No. 1798-XII, 6 November 1991.

Commonwealth Parliamentary Association 2021

Concept on Administrative Reform in Ukraine approved by the Decree of the President of Ukraine, No. 810/98, 22 July 1998.

Constitution of the Republic of Estonia, 29 June 1992.

Constitution of Greece, 18 April 2001.

Constitution of Georgia, 24 August 1995.

Constitution of the Republic of Lithuania, 6 November 1992.

Constitution of the Republic of Macedonia, 6 January 1992

Constitution of the Republic of Poland, No. 78, 2 April 1997.

Constitution of Ukraine, No. 254к/96-ВР, 28 June 1996

CONTINENTAL CONGRESS, *Declaration of Independence. The Unanimous Declaration of the thirteen united States of America*, 4 July 1776.

CONSTITUTIONAL COURT (2018). Summary to the Opinion of the Grand Chamber of the Constitutional Court of Ukraine № 3-v/2018 dated November 22, 2018, in the case upon the constitutional petition of the Verkhovna Rada of Ukraine on providing opinion concerning the compliance of the draft law on introducing amendments to the Constitution of Ukraine (regarding the strategic course of the state for gaining full-fledged membership of Ukraine in the European Union and the North Atlantic Treaty Organization (Reg. No. 9037) with the requirements of Articles 157 and 158 of the Constitution. Constitutional Court, 2018. Retrieved from: https://ccu.gov.ua/en/docs/2260

COUNCIL OF EUROPE, *Convention for the Protection of Human Rights and Dignity of the Human Being with Regard to the Application of Biology and Medicine: Convention on Human Rights and Biomedicine*, No. 164, 1997 April 4.

COUNCIL OF EUROPE, *European Convention for the Protection of Human Rights and Fundamental Freedoms*, as amended by Protocols Nos. 11 and 14, ETS 5, 4 November 1950.

COUNCIL OF EUROPE, *Second Additional Protocol to the European Convention on Extradition*, No. 98, 17 March 1978.

COUNCIL OF EUROPE, *Committee of Ministers Resolution on the Criteria Governing Proceedings Held in the Absence of the Accused*, (75)11, 21 May 1975.

COUNCIL OF THE EUROPEAN UNION, *Council Directive on Minimum Standards for Giving Temporary Protection in the Event of a Mass Influx of Displaced Persons and on Measures Promoting a Balance of Efforts between Member States in Receiving such Persons and Bearing the Consequences Thereof*, 2001/55/EC July 2001.

COUNCIL OF THE EUROPEAN UNION, *Council Implementing Decision Establishing the Existence of a Mass Influx of Displaced Persons from Ukraine Within the Meaning of Article 5 of Directive 2001/55/EC, and Having the Effect of Introducing Temporary protection*, 2022/382, 4 March 2022.

COUNCIL OF THE EUROPEAN UNION, *Council Implementing Regulation Implementing Article 8a of Regulation (EC) No. 765/2006 Concerning Restrictive Measures in View of the Situation in Belarus*, 2022/300, 24 February 2022.

COUNCIL OF THE EUROPEAN UNION, *Council Framework Decision Amending Framework Decisions 2002/584/JHA, 2005/214/JHA, 2006/783/JHA, 2008/909/JHA and 2008/947/JHA, Thereby Enhancing the Procedural Rights of Persons and Fostering the Application of the Principle of Mutual Recognition to Decisions Rendered in the Absence of the Person Concerned at the Trial*, 2009/299/JHA, 26 February 2009.

COUNCIL OF THE EUROPEAN UNION, *European Convention on the International Validity of Criminal Judgments*, No. 70, 28 May 1970.

Criminal Code of Ukraine, No. 2341-III, 5 April 2001.

Criminal Procedural Code of Ukraine, No. 4651-VI13, April 2013.

Decree of the President of Ukraine On Military Service of Aliens and Persons Without Citizenship in the Military Forces of Ukraine [Про Положення про проходження військової служби у Збройних Силах України іноземцями та особами без громадянства] No. 248/2016, 10 June 2016.

Decree of the Cabinet of Ministers of Ukraine, No 299, 4 April 2023.

Decree of the President of Ukraine, No. 64/2022, 24 February 2022.

Decree of the President of Ukraine on the Regulations on the General Staff of the Armed Forces of Ukraine, No 23/2019, 30 January 2019.

Decree of the President of Ukraine on the Cybersecurity Strategy of Ukraine, No 447/2021, 26 August 2021.

Decree of the President of Ukraine on the Strategic Defence Bulletin of Ukraine, No 473/2021, 17 September 2021.

Decree of the President of Ukraine "On the Imposition of Martial Law in Ukraine" of 24.02.2022 No. 64/2022 [online]. Available from: https://www.president.gov.ua/documents/642022-41397 [Про введення воєнного стану в Україні: Указ Президента України від 24.02.2022 № 64/2022. URL: https://www.president.gov.ua/documents/642022-41397]

Directive of the European Parliament and of the Council of on Public Procurement and Repealing Directive 2004/18/EC, 2014/24/EU, 26 February 2014.

Directive of the European Parliament and of the Council on the Strengthening of Certain Aspects of the Presumption of Innocence and of the Right to Be Present at the Trial in Criminal Proceedings, 2016/343, 9 March 2016.

Draft Law on Amendments to Articles 48 and 109 of the Constitution of the Republic of Lithuania [Lietuvos Respublikos Konstitucijos 48 ir 109 straipsnių pakeitimo įstatymo projektas], No XIIIP-3273, 12 March 2019.

EUROPEAN COMMISSION, Proposal for Directive of the European Parliament and of the Council on the Protection of the Environment through Criminal Law and replacing Directive 2008/99/EC, 2021/0422(COD), 15 December 2021.

EUROPEAN COMMISSION, *Commission Opinion on Ukraine's application for membership of the European Union*. COM(2022) 407 final, 16 June 2022.

EUROPEAN COUNCIL, European Council Meeting – Conclusions. EUCO 24/22, 23-24 June 2022.

EUROPEAN PARLIAMENT, *Resolution on Russian aggression against Ukraine*, P9_TA(2022)0052, 1 March 2022.

EUROPEAN PARLIAMENT, *Report on the Proposal for a Directive of the European Parliament and of the Council on Corporate Sustainability Due Diligence and Amending Directive (EU) 2019/1937*, A9-0184/2023, 8 May 2023.

EUROPEAN UNION, *Charter of Fundamental Rights of the European Union*, No. 2012/C 326/02, 26 October 2012.

EUROPEAN UNION, Consolidated version of the Treaty on the Functioning of the European Union, Conference of the Representatives of the Governments of the Member States, OJ L. 326/47–326/390, 26 October 2012.

Explanations Relating to the Charter of Fundamental Rights, C303/02, 14 December 2007.

Explanatory Note to the Draft Law of Ukraine "On Administrative Procedure", No. 3475, 14 May 2000.

GA, *Draft Declaration on the Right to International Solidarity*, No. A/73/206, 20 July 2018.

HRC, *General Comment No. 32, Article 14, Right to Equality before Courts and Tribunals and to Fair Trial*, CCPR/C/GC/32, 23 August 2007.

HUMAN RIGHTS WATCH, *Human Rights in Supply Chains. A Call for a Binding Global Standard on Due Diligence*, 2016.

HRC, Report on the human rights situation in Ukraine (16 November 2019–15 February 2020), A/HRC/43/CRP.7, 18 March 2020.

ICRC, *Geneva Convention Relative to the Protection of Civilian Persons in Time of War (Fourth Geneva Convention)*, 75 UNTS 287, 12 August 1949.

ICRC, *Geneva Convention for the Amelioration of the Condition of the Wounded and Sick in Armed Forces in the Field (First Geneva Convention)*, 75 UNTS 31, 12 August 1949.

ICRC, *Geneva Convention for the Amelioration of the Condition of Wounded, Sick and Shipwrecked Members of Armed Forces at Sea (Second Geneva Convention)*, 75 UNTS 85, 12 August 1949.

ICRC, *Geneva Convention Relative to the Treatment of Prisoners of War (Third Geneva Convention)*, 75 UNTS 135, 12 August 1949.

ICRC, *Protocol Additional to the Geneva Conventions of 12 August 1949, and Relating to the Protection of Victims of Non-International Armed Conflicts (Protocol II)*, 1125 UNTS 609, 8 June 1977.

Law on the Nationwide target program "Portable water of Ukraine" for 2022-2026: draft law]. [online]. Available from: https://w1.c1.rada.gov.ua/pls/zweb2/webproc4_1?pf3511=72415. [Закон про Загальнодержавну цільову соціальну програму «Питна вода України» на 2022 - 2026 роки: проєкт. URL: https://w1.c1.rada.gov.ua/pls/zweb2/webproc4_1?pf3511=72415]

Law of Ukraine „On Amendments to the Constitution of Ukraine (on the Strategic Course of the State to Gain Full Membership of Ukraine in the European Union and in the North Atlantic Treaty Organization)", No. 2680-VIII, February 7, 2019.

Law of Ukraine of 19 November 1992 No. 2801-XII on Fundamentals of Legislation of Ukraine on Health Care. [online]. Available from: https://zakon.rada.gov.ua/laws/show/2801-12#Te [Accessed 20 October 2024].

Law on Military Duty and Military Service [Про військовий обов'язок і військову службу], No. 2233-XII, 25 March 1992.

Law on the Foundations of National Resistance [Про основи національного спротиву], No. 1702-IX, 16 July 2021.

Law of Ukraine "On the Legal Regime of Martial Law", No. 389-VIII, 12 May 2015.

Law of Ukraine "On Administrative Procedure", No 2073-IX, 17 February 2022.

Law of Ukraine "*On Approval of the Decree of the President of Ukraine "On the Imposition of Martial Law in Ukraine*" of 24.02.2022 No. 2102-IX. [online]. Available from: https://zakon.rada.gov.ua/laws/show/2102-20#Text. [Про затвердження Указу Президента України «Про введення воєнного стану в Україні»: Закон України від 24 лютого 2022 року № 2102-IX. URL: https://zakon.rada.gov.ua/laws/show/2102-20#Tex

Law of Ukraine About the Legal Regime of Martial Law, No. 766-VIII, 10 November 2015.

Law of Ukraine on Prevention of Corruption, No. 77-VIII, 28 December 2014.

Law of Ukraine On the Judiciary and the Status of Judges, No. 1774-VIII, 6 December 2016.

Law Approved by Order of the Ministry of Health of Ukraine of 19.03.2018 No. 503 on Procedure on the Selection of a Physician Who Provides Primary Medical Care [online]. Available from: https://zakon.rada.gov.ua/laws/show/z0347-18#n22 [Accessed 20 October 2024].

Law Approved by Order of the Ministry of Health of Ukraine of 19.03.2018 No. 504 on Procedure on the Provision of Primary Medical Care [online]. Available from: https://zakon.rada.gov.ua/laws/show/z0348-18#n19 [Accessed 20 October 2024].

Law of Ukraine public health system, Про систему громадського здоров'я: Закон України від 6 вересня 2022 року № 2573-IX *[On Public Health System: Law of Ukraine of* 6 September 2022 No. 2573-IX]. [online]. *Available from:* https://zakon.rada.gov.ua/laws/show/2573-20#Text.

Law of Ukraine public health system, Про систему громадського здоров'я: Закон України від 6 вересня 2022 року № 2573-IX *[On Public Health System: Law of Ukraine of* 6 September 2022 No. 2573-IX]. [online]. *Available from:* https://zakon.rada.gov.ua/laws/show/2573-20#Text.

Law of Ukraine "On amending the Constitution of Ukraine (Regarding the State's Strategic Course towards Obtaining Full Membership of Ukraine in the European Union and the North Atlantic Treaty Organisation)", No. 2680-VIII, 7 February 2019.

Law of Ukraine on Preventing Threats to National Security Associated With Excessive Influence by Persons Who Wield Significant Economic and Political Weight in Public Life, No. 1780-IX, 5 November 2021.

Law of Ukraine on the Defense of Ukraine, No 1932-XII, 6 December 1991.

Law of Ukraine of 29 July 2022 No. 2494-IX on Introducing Changes to Some Law of Ukraine Regarding the Increase of Accessibility of Medical and Rehabilitation Care During the Martial Law Period [online]. Available from: https://zakon.rada.gov.ua/laws/show/2494-20#Text. [Accessed 20 October 2024].

Law of Ukraine on the Main Principles of Ensuring Cybersecurity of Ukraine, No. 2163, 5 October 2017.

Law of Ukraine on the State Financial Guarantees of Healthcare Servicing of the Population of 19 October 2017 No. 2168-VIII. [online]. Available from: https://zakon.rada.gov.ua/laws/show/2168-19#Text [Accessed 20 October 2024].

LUBINETS, D., 2022. Report on the Observance and Protection of Human and Civil Rights and Freedoms in Ukraine in 2022. [online]. Available from: https://ombudsman.gov.ua/report-2022/sotsialna-derzhava. [Accessed 20 October 2024].

MOH, Law on Approval of Temporary Measures at Healthcare Institutions for Ensuring Their Preparedness to the Provision of Medical Services to the People Injured as a Result of the Military Aggression of the Russian Federation Against Ukraine: of 24 February 2022 No. 374] [online]. Available from: https://zakon.rada.gov.ua/rada/show/v0374282-22#Text. [Accessed 20 October 2024].

OAS, *American Convention on Human Rights, "Pact of San Jose"*, No. 36, 22 November 1969.

OHCHR, Business after conflict: respecting human rights to help sustain peace, 2019.

Order of the MOH of Ukraine of 27.02.2022 No. 385 on the Involvement of Intern Doctors and Some Other Persons in Taking the Measures Connected with the Provision of Medical Care to the Persons Injured During the Emergency Occurred Within the Period of Martial Law in Ukraine. [online]. Available from: https://dmu.edu.ua. [Accessed 20 October 2024].

Order of the MOH on Introducing Expanded Neonatal Screening in Ukraine of 04.08.2022 No. 1396. [online]. Available from: https://moz.gov.ua/article/ministry-mandates/nakaz-moz-ukraini-vid-04082022--1396-provprovadzhennja-rozshirenogo-neonatalnogo-skriningu-v-ukraini. [Accessed 20 October 2024].

PCA, *1899 Convention for the Pacific Settlement of International Disputes*, 1 Bevans 230, 1 AJIL 103, 18 October 1907.

Regulation of the European Parliament and of the Council of on the Protection of Natural Persons with Regard to the Processing of Personal Data and on the Free Movement of Such Data, and Repealing Directive 95/46/EC, 2016/679, 27 April 2016.

Regulation of the European Parliament and of the Council of on Sustainability-Related Disclosures in the Financial Services Sector, 2019/2088, 27 November 2019.

Resolution of the Cabinet of Ministers of Ukraine on Some Issues of Response by Cybersecurity Entities to Various Types of Events in Cyberspace, No. 299, 4 April 2023.

Resolution of Council of Europe Committee of Ministers on the Criteria Governing Proceedings Held in the Absence of the Accused, No. (75)11, 21 May 1975.

Regulation of the European Parliament and of the Council on the Making Available on the Union Market and the Export from the Union of Certain Commodities and Products Associated with Deforestation and Forest Degradation and Repealing Regulation (EU) No 995/2010, 2023/1115, 31 May 2023.

Regulation of the European Parliament and of the Council laying down the Obligations of Operators Who Place Timber and Timber Products on the Market, No 995/2010, 20 October 2010.

Regulation of the Cabinet of Ministers of Ukraine on the Voluntary Formation of Territorial Communities, No. 1449, 29 December 2021.

SECOND INTERNATIONAL PEACE CONFERENCE, *Hague Convention (IV) Respecting the Laws and Customs of War on Land and Its Annex: Regulations Concerning the Laws and Customs of War on Land*, 18 October 1907.

UN, *Charter of the United Nations*, 1 UNTS XVI, 24 October 1945.

UN, *Recommendation on Multilingualism and Universal Access to Cyberspace*,15 October, 2003.

UN, *Statute of the International Court of Justice*, –, 18 April 1946.

UNGA, *Convention on the Prevention and Punishment of the Crime of Genocide*, United Nations, Treaty Series, 78, 277, 9 December 1948.

UNGA, *International Covenant on Civil and Political Rights*, United Nations, Treaty Series, vol. 999, p. 171, 16 December 1966.

UNGA, *Resolution "On Territorial Integrity of Ukraine"*, No. 68/262, 27 March 2014.

UNGA, *Resolutions Calling on Withdrawal of Forces from Crimea, Establishing Epidemic Preparedness International Day among Texts*, GA/12295, 7 December 2020.

UNGA, *Resolution "Aggression against Ukraine" (A/ES-11/L.1): Resolution / adopted by the General Assembly.* UN. General Assembly (11th emergency special sess: 2022). 2022. [online]. Available from: https://digitallibrary.un.org/record/3965290

UNGA, *Rome Statute of the International Criminal Court*, ISBN No. 92-9227-227-6, 17 July 1998.

UNGA, *Universal Declaration of Human Rights*, 217 A (III), 10 December 1948.

VENICE COMMISSION, *Code of Good Practice in Electoral Matters Guidelines and Explanatory*, CDL-AD (2002) 23, 30 October 2002.

VENICE COMMISSION, 2005. *Draft Joint Opinion on the Law on Elections of People's Deputies of Ukraine*, CDL-EL(2005)055, 8 December 2005.

VENICE COMMISION, *On the Measures taken in the EU Member States as a Result of the Covid-19 Crisis*, No. 995/2020, 8 October 2020.

VENICE COMMISSION, 2022. *Opinion on the draft law „On amending some legislative acts of Ukraine regarding improving procedure for selecting candidate judges of the Constitutional Court of Ukraine on a competitive basis*, CDL-AD(2022)054. 19 December 2022.

VENICE COMMISSION, 2023. *Follow-up opinion to the opinion "On the draft law "On amendments to certain legislative acts of Ukraine on improving the procedure for the selection of candidates for the position of judge of the Constitutional Court of Ukraine on a competitive basis*, CDL-AD(2023)022, 10 June 2023.

VENICE COMMISSION, 2023a. *Opinion on the Law "Preventing Threats to National Security Associated With Excessive Influence by Persons Who Wield Significant Economic and Political Weight in Public Life* (oligarchs), CDL-AD(2023)018, 12 June 2023.

VENICE COMMISSION, 2023b. *Urgent follow-up opinion to the opinions on the Law "On Amendments to certain legislative acts of Ukraine to clarify the provisions on the competitive selection of candidates for the position of judge of the Constitutional Court of Ukraine*, CDL-AD(2023)042-e, 9 October 2023.

WHO. Human rights. WHO. 1 December 2023. [online]. Available from: https://www.who.int/news-room/fact-sheets/detail/human-rights-and-health#:~:text=Core%20components%20of%20the%20right%20to%20health&text=-Accessibility%20requires%20that%20health%20facilities,(affordability)%20and%20information%20accessibility.

WHO. Surveillance System for Attacks on Health care, 05.11.2023. [online]. Available from: https://extranet.who.int/ssa/Index.aspx.

WMA Declaration of Lisbon on the *Rights of the PatientDeclaration. Adopted by the 34th World Medical Assembly, Lisbon, Portugal*, September/October 1981. [online]. Available from: https://www.wma.net/policies-post/wma-declaration-of-lisbon-on-the-rights-of-the-patient.

Jurisprudence

CIVIL CODE OF UKRAINE, Цивільний кодекс України: Кодекс від 16.01.2003 № 435-IV [Civil Code of Ukraine: Code of 16.01.2003 No. 435-IV]. [online]. Available from: https://zakon.rada.gov.ua/laws/show/435-15#Text.

CJEU, *Openbaar Ministerie v Paweł Dworzecki*, Case No. C-108/16, 24 May 2016.

CJEU, *Pesti Központi Kerületi Bíróság v. IS*, Case No. C-564/19, 23 November 2021.

CJEU, *Relu Adrian Coman and Others* v. *Inspectoratul General pentru Imigrări and Ministerul Afacerilor Interne*, Case No. C-673/16, 5 June 2018.

CJEU, *Stefano Melloni v Ministerio Fiscal*, Case No. C-399/11, 26 February 2013.

CJEU, *Specialised Public Prosecutor's Office of Bulgaria v. IR*, Case No. 569/20, 19 May 2022.

CJEU, *Special Court for Criminal Cases of Bulgaria v. TX and UW*, Case No. C-688/18, 13 February 2020.

CONSTITUTIONAL COURT OF LITHUANIA, Decision No. 2/98, 9 December 1998.

CONSTITUTIONAL COURT OF LITHUANIA, Decision No. 22/2013, 24 January 2014.

CONSTITUTIONAL COURT OF LITHUANIA, Resolution of 24 December 2002.

CONSTITUTIONAL COURT OF LITHUANIA, Resolution of 9 October 2003.

CONSTITUTIONAL COURT OF LITHUANIA, Resolution of 20 March 2004.

CONSTITUTIONAL COURT OF LITHUANIA, Resolution of 5 November 2004.

CONSTITUTIONAL COURT OF LITHUANIA, Resolution of 20 March 2007.

CONSTITUTIONAL COURT OF LITHUANIA, Resolution of 9 November 2010.

CONSTITUTIONAL COURT OF LITHUANIA, Resolution of 11 May 2011.

CONSTITUTIONAL COURT OF UKRAINE, Case No. 3-v/2018, 22 November, 2018.

CONSTITUTIONAL COURT OF UKRAINE, Case No. 1-24/2020(393/20), 27 October, 2020.

CONSTITUTIONAL COURT OF UKRAINE, Case No. 7/2019, 25 June 2019.

DISTRICT COURT OF CHERNIVTSI, Case No. 727/1911/22, 18 March 2022.

DISTRICT COURT OF THE CHERNIVTSI, Case No. 713/1098/22, 20 July 2022.

DISTRICT COURT OF DNIPROPETROVSK, Case No. 206/11/17, 28 March 2022.

DISTRICT COURT OF DNIPROPETROVSK, Case No. 191/3557/21, 5 May 2022.

DISTRICT COURT OF DNIPROPETROVSK, Case No. 176/950/22, 10 May 2022.

DISTRICT COURT OF DNIPROPETROVSK, Case No. 178/425/22, 10 June 2022.

DISTRICT COURT OF KREMENCHUK, Case No. 536/1112/19, 7 June 2022.

DISTRICT COURT OF KHMELNYTSKYI, Case No. 686/7071/22, 15 April 2022.

DISTRICT COURT OF KHMELNYTSKYI, Case No. 676/1501/22, 16 May 2022.

DISTRICT COURT OF KYIV, Case No. 359/3962/20, 14 June 2022.

DISTRICT COURT OF KYIV, Case No. 367/6693/20, 14 June 2022.

DISTRICT COURT OF KYIV, Case No. 359/3962/20, 18 July 2022.

DISTRICT COURT OF KYIV, Case No. 362/1064/21, 18 July 2022.

DISTRICT COURT OF KYIV, Case No. 757/33903/21-k, 3 May 2022.

DISTRICT COURT OF KYIV, Case No. 759/4623/22 5 May 2022.

DISTRICT COURT OF KYIV, Case No. 761/7319/22, 12 May 2022.

DISTRICT COURT OF KYIV, Case No. 754/18888/21, 26 May 2022.

DISTRICT COURT OF LVIV, Case No. 454/2322/21, 1 April 2022.

DISTRICT COURT OF LVIV, Case No. 944/5877/19, 18 April 2022.

DISTRICT COURT OF LVIV, Case No. 466/7097/17 27 April 2022.

DISTRICT COURT OF LVIV, Case No. 441/1858/21, 18 July 2022.

DISTRICT COURT OF MOSCOW, Case No. 1-719/2022, 8 July, 2022.

DISTRICT COURT OF ODESA, Case No. 523/3984/22, 11 April, 2022.

DISTRICT COURT OF ODESA, Case No. 505/928/22, 19 May 2022.

DISTRICT COURT OF ODESA, Case No. 504/4242/19, 26 May 2022.

DISTRICT COURT OF POLTAVA, Case No. 532/308/15-k, 11 April 2022.

DISTRICT COURT OF POLTAVA, Case No. 553/3316/21, 26 May 2022.

DISTRICT COURT OF POLTAVA, Case No. 552/2173/22, 21 July 2022.

DISTRICT COURT OF POLTAVA, Case No. 583/2641/21, 1 June 2022.

DISTRICT COURT OF POLTAVA, Case No. 544/2074/21 3 June 2022.

DISTRICT COURT OF RIVNE, Case No. 572/879/22, 22 April 2022.

DISTRICT COURT OF RIVNE, Case No. 572/879/22, 17 May 2022.

DISTRICT COURT OF THE TRANSCARPATHIAN, Case No. 308/13185/17, 5 April 2022.

DISTRICT COURT OF THE TRANSCARPATHIAN, Case No. 308/4709/22, 10 June 2022.

DISTRICT COURT OF VINNYTSIA, Case No. 129/1573/20, 31 May 2022.

DISTRICT COURT OF THE VINNYTSIA, Case No. 145/207/22, 21 July 2022.

DISTRICT COURT OF ZAPOROZHYE, Case No. 337/1428/22, 30 June 2022.

DISTRICT COURT OF ZAPORIZHZHIA, Case No. 336/5497/20, 27 May 2022.

ECtHR, *A. O. Falun Dafa and others v. Moldova*, Application No. 29458/15, 29 June 2021.

ECtHR, *Alekseyev v. Russia*, Application No. 4916/07; 25924/08;14599/09, 21 October 2010.

ECtHR, *Atanasova v. Bulgarie*, Application No. 52009/07, 26 January 2017.

ECtHR, *Avotiņš v. Latvia*, Application No. 17502/07, 23 May 2016.

ECtHR, *Bosnia and Herzegovina v. Serbia and Montenegro*, Application No. 91, 26 February 2027.

ECtHR, *Arrowsmith v. the United Kingdom*, Application No. 7050/75, 5 December 1978.

ECtHR, *Aždajić v. Slovenia*, Application No. 71872/12, 8 October 2015.

ECtHR, *Bayatyan v. Armenia*, Application No. 23459/03, 7 July 2011.

ECtHR, *Boychev and others v. Bulgaria*, Application No. 77185/01, 27 January 2011.

ECtHR, *Buscarini and others v. San Marino*, Application No. 24645/94, 18 February 1999.

ECtHR, *C.R. v. The United Kingdom*, Application No. 20190/92, 22 November 1995.

ECtHR, *Catan and Others v. The Republic of Moldova and Russia*, Application No. 43370/04, 19 October 2012.

ECtHR, *Chong Coronado v. Andorre*, Application No. 37368/15, 23 July 2020.

ECtHR, *Colozza v. Italy*, Application No. 9024/80, 12 February 1985

ECtHR, *Dahlab v. Switzerland*, Application No. 42393/98, 5 February 2001.

ECtHR, *Dogru v. France*, Application No. 27058/05, 4 December 2008.

ECtHR, *Dragin v. Croatia*, Application No. 75068/12, 24 July 2014.

ECtHR, *Davydov and others v. Russia*, No. 75947/11, 30 May 2017.

ECtHR, *Drėlingas v. Lithuania*, Application No. 28859/16, 12 March 2019.

ECtHR, *Einhorn v. France (dec.)*, Application No. 71555/01, 2001.

ECtHR, *Eweida and Others v. the United Kingdom*, Application No. 48420/10; 59842/10; 51671/10; 36516/10, 15 January 2013.

ECtHR, *Goddi v Italy*, Application No. 8966/80, 9 April 1984.

ECtHR, *Haas v. Switzerland*, Application No. 31322/07, 20 January 2011.

ECtHR, *Hamidovic vs. Bosnia and Herzegovina*, Application No. 57792/15, 5 December 2017.

ECtHR, *Hermi v. Italy*, Application No. 18114/02, 18 October 2006.

ECtHR, *Ivanova and Cherkezov v. Bulgaria*, Application No. 46577/15, 21 April 2016.

ECtHR, *Jakobski v. Poland*, Application No. 18429/06, 7 December 2010.

ECtHR, *Jelcovas v. Lithuania*, Application No. 16913/04, 9 July 2011.

ECtHR, *Jones v. the United Kingdom (dec.)*, Application No. 30900/02, 9 September 2003.

ECtHR, *Károly Nagy v. Hungary*, Application No. 56665/09, 14 September 2017.

ECtHR, *Kjeldsen, Busk Madsen and Pedersen* v. *Denmark.* Application No. 5095/71; 5920/72; 5926/72, 7 December 1976.

ECtHR, *Khalfaoui v. France*, Application No. 34791/97, 14 December 1999.

ECtHR, *Knudsen v. Norway*, Application No. 11045/84, 8 March 1985.

ECtHR, *Kokkinakis vs. Greece*, Application No. 14307/88, 25 May 1993.

ECtHR, *Kolegovy v. Russia*, Application No. 15226/05, 1 March 2012.

ECtHR, *Kounov v. Bulgaria*, Application No. 24379/02, 23 May 2006.

ECtHR, *Korchagin v. Russia*, Application No. 12307/16, 28 August 2018.

ECtHR, *Krombach v. France*, Application No. 29731/96, 13 February 2001.

ECtHR, *Kudła v. Poland* [GC], Application No. 30210/96, 26 October 2000.

ECtHR, *Lala v Netherlands*, Application No. 14861/89, 22 September 1994.

ECtHR, *Lautsi and others vs. Italy*, Application No. 30814/06, 18 March 2011.

ECtHR, *Leyla Sahin v. Turkey*, Application No. 44774/98, 10 November 2005.

ECtHR, *Medenica v. Switzerland*, Application No. 20491/92, 14 June 2001.

ECtHR, *Mihelj v. Slovenia*, Application No. 14204/07, 15 January 2015.

ECtHR, *Mockute v. Lithuania*, Application No. 66490/09, 27 February 2018.

ECtHR, *Mozer v. The Republic of Moldova and Russia*, Application No. 11138/10, February 2016.

ECtHR, *Netherlands v. Russia*, Applications Nos. 8019/16, 43800/14 and 28525/20, 25 January 2023.

ECtHR, *Nyyssonen v. Finland*, Application No. 30406/96, 15 January 1998.

ECtHR, *Otto Preminger Institute v. Austria*, Application No. 13470/87, 14 January 1993.

ECtHR, *Perihan and Mezopotamya Basın Yayın A.Ş. v. Turkey*, Application No. 21377/03, 21 January 2014.

ECtHR, *Poitrimol v. France*, Application No. 14032/88, 23 November 1993.

ECtHR, *Pretty v. the United Kingdom*, Application No. 2346/02, 29 April 2002.

ECtHR, *Romuva v. Lithuania*, Application No. 48329/19, 48329/19, 8 June 2021.

ECtHR, *Russian Conservative Party of Entrepreneurs and Others v. Russia*, Application No. 55066/00, 11 January 2007.

ECtHR, *Sejdovic v Italy* [GC], Application No. 56581/00, 1 March 2006.

ECtHR, *Sekmadienis LTD v. Lithuania*, Application No. 69317/14, 30 January 2018.

ECtHR, *Skugar and Others v. Russia*, Application No. 40010/04, 3 December 2009.

ECtHR, *Somogyi v. Italy*, Application No. 67972/01, 18 May 2004.

ECtHR, *Soering* v. *The United Kingdom*, Application No. 14038/88, 7 July 1989.

ECtHR, *Sanader v. Croatia*, Application No. 66408/12, 12 February 2015.

ECtHR, *Stoichkov v. Bulgaria*, Application No. 9808/02, 24 March 2005.

ECtHR, *Stübing v. Germany*, Application No. 43547/08, 12 April 2012.

ECtHR, *Timke v. Germany*, Application No. 27311/95, 11 September 1995.

ECtHR, *Van Geyseghem v. Belgium*, Application No. 26103/95, 21 January 1999.

ECtHR, *Van Schijndel and Others v. Netherlands*, Application No. 30936/96, 20 May 1998.

ECtHR, *Van Den Dungen v. Netherlands*, Application No. 13535/88, 7 April 1992.

ECtHR, *Vasiliauskas v. Lithuania*, Application No. 35343/05, 20 September 2015.

ECtHR, *Vilches Coronado et autres c. Espagne*, Application No. 55517/14, 13 March 2018.

ECtHR, *Yeğer v. Turkey*, Application No. 4099/12, 7 June 2022.

ECtHR, *X v. the United Kingdom*, Application No. 8416/78, 13 May 1980.

ECtHR *W vs. the United Kingdom*, Application No. 9749/82, 9 June 1988.

HRC, *Maleki v. Italy*, UN Doc CCPR/C/66/D/699/1996, 13 September 1999.

ICC, *Prosecutor v. Omar Hassan Ahmad Al Bashir*, Case No. ICC-02/05–01/09, 12 May 2010.

ICJ, *Ethiopia v. South Africa*, Second Phase,18 July 1966.

ICJ, *Malaysia v. Singapore*, Case No 130, 23 May 2008.

ICJ, *Nicaragua v. United States of America*, Case No. 70, 26 November 1984.

ICTR, *Prosecutor v. Jean-Paul Akayesu*, Case No. ICTR-96-4-T, 2 September 1998.

ICTY, *Prosecutor v. Duško Tadič*, Case No. IT-94-1-AR72, 7 May 1997.

ICTY, *Prosecutor v. Jelisić*, Case No. IT-95-10-T, 14 December 1999.

ICTY, *Prosecutor v. Kupreškić et al.*, Case No. IT-95-16 14-T, January 2000.

ITLOS, *Mauritius* v. *Maldives*, Case No. 28, 28 January 2021.

PCA, *Mauritius v. United Kingdom*, Case No. 2011-03, 18 March 2015.

PCA, *Netherlands v. Russia*, Case No. 2014-02, 10 July 2017.

PCA, *Ukraine v. the Russian Federation*, Case No. 2017–06, [no date].

PCA, *The Republic of Philippines v. The People's Republic of China*, Case No. 2013–19, 12 July 2016.

SUPREME COURT OF U.S., *Hopt v. Utah*, Case No. 110 U.S. 574, 3 March 1884.

SUPREME COURT OF U.S., *Reno v. American Civil Liberties Union*, Case No. 96–511, 26 June 1997.

SUPREME COURT OF LITHUANIA, Case No. 2K-7-39-1073/2022, 30 June 2022.

List of Tables

List of Figures

Notes on Contributors

RIMA AŽUBALYTĖ is a doctor of social sciences (law), professor at the Department of Criminal Law and Procedure at the Law School of Mykolas Romeris University. Her research interests are criminal procedure, protection of human rights in criminal procedure, evidence, also the tendencies of development of criminal procedure – constitutionalization, internationalisation and differentiation of criminal procedure, remote criminal procedure, juvenile criminal procedure.

ASTA BENETYTĖ is a Ph.D. in Law candidate and a lecturer of the Institute of Public Law at the Law School, Mykolas Romeris University, in Vilnius, Lithuania. Her research focuses on the issues of legal reasoning, interpretation of law and legal theory. She is also a legal advisor in criminal law at the Supreme Court of Lithuania and a member of the Advisory Groups at the Research Council of Lithuania.

OLHA BODNAR-PETROVSKA graduated with honors from the Academy of Internal Affairs, Ukraine, Kyiv; politician, honored lawyer of Ukraine, doctor of philosophy, currently conducting scientific activity at Mykolas Romeris University, in Vilnius, Lithuania. Her principal research focuses on constitutional law, human rights, in particular.

SIMONA DEMENTAVIČIENĖ is a Ph.D. candidate at the Institute of Public Law at Mykolas Romeris University, and a judge at Kaunas Regional Court. Her research interests include constitutional law, Lithuanian comparative and European Union constitutional law, court systems of European Union member states, public representatives in court proceedings (lay participation), and the interaction between European Union law and national law.

IEVA DEVIATNIKOVAITĖ is a professor of administrative law at Mykolas Romeris University, Lithuania. Her research focuses on administrative law and legal history. She has published widely on these issues.

OLESIA GORBUN is a PhD candidate at the Institute of the International and European Union Law at Mykolas Romeris University in Vilnius, Lithuania. She is Member of the Scientific Expert Council of International Law at the Yaroslav Mudryi National Law University in Kharkiv, Ukraine. Her research interests include international law of the sea, humanitarian law, state responsibility, international dispute settlement.

RADMYLA YU. HREVTSOVA is associate professor of public administration and medical law of the Law School at the Taras Shevchenko National University of Kyiv and professor of public health at the Kyiv Medical University. She is also a practicing attorney-at-law. Dr. Hrevtsova focuses her research and practice on health law and governance, bioethics, and human rights. She is a Governor of the World Association for Medical Law.

ANDRZEJ JACKIEWICZ is associate professor of constitutional law at the University vof Bialystok, Poland. His research focuses on parliamentary law, electoral law and comparative constitutional law. He has published more than a hundred scientific works, including books and scientific articles.

SAULIUS KATUOKA is a professor of international law at Mykolas Romeris University School of Law in Vilnius, Lithuania, specializing in international maritime law and awarded the title of Honorary Professor for his contribution to the creation of the modern state of Lithuania and the development of international and EU studies and research at the University. Professor Katuoka has been actively involved in governmental and international initiatives, serving as a member of the State Delegation for Negotiations with Russia, the Chief Offial Commision, the Permanent Court of Arbitration, and the Central Electoral Commision of the Republic of Lithuania. Since 2002, Professor has served as Vice President of the Forum for the Future of the European Union in Lithuania, Chairman of the Council of the Lithuanian Centre for Human Rights, and as an Expert of the Republic of Lithuania to the Council of Europe on Electoral Issues.

LAURA MATJOŠAITYTĖ is a PhD candidate and lecturer at the Public Law Institute at Mykolas Romeris University in Vilnius, Lithuania. Her research interests include constitutional and comparative constitutional law, electoral law, and human rights. She is an election expert, a former Chairwoman of the Central Electoral Commission of the Republic of Lithuania, and an attorney at law.

JOLITA MILIUVIENĖ is a associate professor of constitutional law at the Institute of Public Law of Law School at Mykolas Romeris University in Vilnius, Lithuania. She is also a Parliamentary Ombudsperson of Lithuania and a member of International Society of Public Law. Previously she worked for more than fifteen years in the Constitutional Court of the Republic of Lithuania. Her research interests are constitutional and comparative constitutional law, constitutional adjudication, human rights protection, interaction between constitutional and international law, constitutional *soft law*.

INGA MOTUZIENĖ is a Ph.D. candidate at Law School of Mykolas Romeris University, in Vilnius, Lithuania. Her PhD focuses on the human right to property in international law. She works as a lecture at Mykolas Romeris University since 2011. Research interests: public international law, international dispute resolution, international human rights law, and legal philosophy.

PAULO PEREIRA is a professor of environmental sciences at Mykolas Romeris University, Vilnius, Lithuania. His research is focused on land degradation, ecosystem services and nature-based solutions. He has published articles on war impacts on the environment, agriculture intensification and urban areas.

ANNA RYTEL-WARZOCHA is an associate professor of constitutional law at the University of Gdansk, Poland. Her research focuses mainly on direct and participatory democracy, constitutional systems of foreign states, constitutional justice, current political changes, European aspects of constitutional law, citizenship, migration and protection of human rights. She is an author of more than 120 scientific publications of various types (books, articles, book chapters, entries in encyclopaedias) published in Poland and abroad.

DOVILĖ SAGATIENĖ is a postdoctoral researcher at Centre for Military Studies in University of Copenhagen (Denmark) and an Associated Professor at Mykolas Romeris University Law School in Vilnius, Lithuania. Her recent publications addressed Soviet genocide debate on legal level as well as the transformation of memory regarding Soviet crimes in Lithuania.

RŪTA SLIDŽIAUSKAITĖ-MASKOLIŪNĖ is a lecturer of Law and Global Security programme of the Law School at the Mykolas Romeris university in Vilnius, Lithuania. Her research interests include environmental law, energy law, human rights law. Her research focuses on the challenges to global security and development, the interplay between law, politics, international relations, and sustainability across the fields of human rights, peace, security and conflict.

OLENA UVAROVA leads the International business and human rights Lab at the Yaroslav Mudryi National Law University, Ukraine. She is currently a MSCA4UKRAINE postdoc in the Law Group, Wageningen University and Research, the Netherlands. Her research focuses on the impact of corporate actors on human rights and environment in different contexts (in different political regimes, in the strong and weak rule of law environment, in situation of war and other emergencies).

JUOZAS VALČIUKAS is associate professor of comparative law at the Mykolas Romeris University in Vilnius, Lithuania. His research interests include comparative constitutional law, legal theory, legal philosophy, and human rights law. His work has a particular focus on the right to freedom of conscience, the right to freedom of expression and related comparative aspects.

YULIIA VASHCHENKO is professor of administrative law at the Comenius University in Bratislava, Slovakia. Her research interests include European and comparative administrative law, energy law, and human rights law. Her work has a principal focus on the system of public administration, general administrative procedure, human rights aspects of the access to modern energy services.

MINDAUGAS VERBICKAS is a lecturer and researcher in Philosophy of Law and comparative constitutional law at Mykolas Romeris University. His research focuses on the new natural law theory.

JUSTINAS ŽILINSKAS is a professor of International Law at the International and EU Law Institute, Mykolas Romeris University, in Vilnius, Lithuania. He has been researching and publishing in international humanitarian law and international criminal law for over two decades. His field of interest includes contemporary armed conflicts, the role of private actors on the battlefield, as well as human rights and international crimes. Additionally, he served as a member of the International Humanitarian Fact-Finding Commission from 2012 to 2022.

Index

www.ingramcontent.com/pod-product-compliance
Lightning Source LLC
Chambersburg PA
CBHW050519240926
51846CB00003B/625
* 9 7 8 3 6 3 1 9 2 3 5 0 4 *